The Buffer State

THE HISTORICAL ROOTS OF
THE DEPARTMENT OF THE ENVIRONMENT

The Buffer State

THE HISTORICAL ROOTS OF
THE DEPARTMENT OF THE ENVIRONMENT

MARY E. DALY

IPA
INSTITUTE OF PUBLIC
ADMINISTRATION

DUBLIN

First published 1997
by the Institute of Public Administration
57-61 Lansdowne Road
Dublin 4

ISBN 1 872002 83 8

British Library Cataloguing in Publication Data
A catalogue record of this book is available from the British Library

Design by Butler Claffey Design
Origination by Phototype-Set Ltd., Dublin
Printed by Betaprint, Dublin

To Alice and Nicholas

CONTENTS

ACKNOWLEDGEMENTS

The idea for this book originated with Brendan O'Donoghue, Secretary of the Department of the Environment; he felt that the transfer of the Department's files to the National Archives, in accordance with the conditions of the National Archives Act, should be marked by a history of the Department, its origins and early years. He has proved to be the ideal patron: interested and supportive, but never intrusive. I wish to thank him for his encouragement and for his patience. The text has benefited considerably from his unrivalled knowledge of the Department's history; in particular, he brought some important information to my attention and saved me from several errors.

The Department's support for the project was approved by the Minister for the Environment, Padraig Flynn TD, by his successors, Rory O'Hanlon TD, Michael Smith TD, and the present Minister, Brendan Howlin TD. Although the Department's support has been of immense assistance in this project, this is not an official history. All decisions as to the structure, contents, terminal date and the weight given to different subjects were taken by me, and I alone am responsible for the opinions expressed in this book.

I am grateful to Tony Boland, Owen Ryan and Seamus O'Connor of the Department of the Environment for their assistance in the early stages of this research. The hard-pressed staff of the National Archives did everything possible to make my task easier; my thanks to the Director David Craig, to Ken Hannigan, Frances Magee and, above all, to Caitríona Crowe. Seamus Helferty in the UCD archives department and Tony Eklof and the staff in the UCD library's government publications section were extremely helpful, as ever. The trustees of the Mulcahy Collection in the UCD archives department kindly granted me permission to consult and to quote from the papers of Richard

Mulcahy. My colleague Ronan Fanning persuaded me to consider taking on this research. My thanks also to Maura Cronin, Colm Gallagher, Tom Garvin, Michael Laffan, Patrick Lynch and Joe Robins. Diarmaid Ferriter and Emer Purcell helped with xeroxing.

The final stages of this book were completed in an environment that was far removed from the ideals of leisurely scholarship. I have survived it, in large part thanks to the editorial assistance and good humour of Jonathan Williams. At the Institute of Public Administration Jim O'Donnell, Tony McNamara and Kathleen Harte have been extremely supportive.

To P.J., Paul, Elizabeth, Nicholas and Alice Daly, my gratitude as always.

Mary E. Daly.
1 March 1997

INTRODUCTION

The Tudor poet Sir Philip Sidney once accused the historian of 'authorising himself (for the most part) upon other histories'. If true, this book rests upon very slender foundations. In this instance Sidney's description of the historian 'loaden [*sic*] with old mouse-eaten records'[1] is more probably accurate. Most of the subjects covered in these pages have been ignored by historians of modern Ireland, in large part because the necessary sources have become available only in recent years. This has presented both an unrivalled opportunity and a major challenge. No obvious guidelines existed that indicated the major landmarks in the history of the Department of the Environment and its antecedents. The narrative that has emerged reflects the material found in the archives and, to a lesser extent, topics that have been in other histories of twentieth-century Ireland.

This is a history of the relationship between Irish central government and local authorities, including those various forms of assistance that central government provided for the major spending programmes, such as roads and housing, carried out by local authorities. It is not a history of Irish local government. The title, *The Buffer State,* has been chosen in order to emphasise this point. The phrase comes from a letter that John Garvin, secretary of the Department of Local Government, wrote to J.J.McElligott, secretary of the Department of Finance, on 16 July 1949. McElligott had demanded that Local Government take steps to slow down the pace of housing construction being carried out by local authorities, because the Department of Finance was experiencing difficulties in raising the necessary capital. In his reply, Garvin outlined the delicate nature of the Local Government's role: it had to see that the momentum of the housing programme was maintained, because ministers had repeatedly

1

emphasised its importance; at the same time the Department was required to keep the demand for capital from local authorities under control. John Garvin added:

> I trust you will appreciate that while we have the honour of being the buffer State between the central and local authorities, this honour is one for which we have to pay dearly — in unremitting surveillance of local demands and in conscientious sponsoring of that minimum proportion of them which we know are inescapable.[2]

This book explores the Department's 'buffer functions' (another phrase used by Garvin) in detail, from the foundation of the state until 1973. One of the recurrent themes is the Department's efforts both to protect its own interests and to preserve the separation of functions between central and local government. The story is written from the perspective of the Custom House and Government Buildings, rather than from the point of view of county council offices. Given the efforts that have recently been made to salvage and to catalogue the archives of Irish local authorities, it is to be hoped that somebody will write the other side of this story.

The responsibilities of the modern Department of the Environment and its antecedents range from elections to physical planning, to roads and housing, libraries and graveyards and, of course, environmental protection. Any book that attempted to provide a comprehensive history of such multifarious activities would almost certainly stand accused of being either a 'rag-bag' or an 'impenetrable jungle' — epithets levelled by Richard Mulcahy, a former Minister for Local Government and Public Health, at the enormous mass of local government legislation that was in existence by 1945.[3] Although Myles na gCopaleen once said that 'the function of the historian is to record completely, not selectively',[4] this is a selective history. The most conspicuous omission is the election process. Although the Department has responsibility for all elections from the Presidential down to urban district councils, and for the electoral register, and was also charged with determining constituency boundaries until 1983 when the task passed to an electoral commission, the franchise section of the Department seems to have functioned very much as a self-contained entity, which did not significantly affect other aspects of the

2

Department's work. The administrative history of Irish elections is probably best tackled in a separate study.

Before 1947, when the Departments of Health and Social Welfare were established, the Department of Local Government and Public Health was responsible for the country's health system and for most social welfare programmes, though unemployment insurance was handled by the Department of Industry and Commerce. It was decided to ignore the history of health and social welfare policy, during the years that these matters were under the control of the Department of Local Government and Public Health,[5] and to concentrate on the programmes that remained the responsibility of the Department of Local Government after 1947. Although this means that there is a certain imbalance in the analysis of the Department's work from 1922 until 1947, the options would have been either to examine health and social welfare programmes until 1947 but not beyond, or to undertake the impossible task of writing the history of three major government departments simultaneously.

On the whole, the degree of attention given to particular subjects reflects the importance that they were given, both in Dáil Éireann and within the cabinet, together with the volume and quality of surviving archival records. Many of the responsibilities once handled by the Department, such as cemeteries, exhumations, the regulation of markets and fairs and abattoirs have been ignored.

Although I have received considerable assistance from the Department of the Environment during the course of my research, the archives that have been consulted are all now accessible to the public in the National Archives. Consequently the files consulted are all at least thirty years old. The Department took the justifiable decision not to transfer its Establishment (i.e. personnel) files to the National Archives and, with the exception of two files relating to appointments made in the early 1920s, these have not been made available to me. For that reason, it did not prove possible to write a satisfactory account of the changes which took place in the personnel and organisation of the Department. The topic would probably be best approached as part of a study of civil service recruitment and organisation. Neither have I made any attempt to duplicate the biographical profiles or the discussion of personalities associated with the Department that Joe Robins provides in a recent book,[6] though I hope that this book will provide insights into the careers of well-known figures such as

W.T. Cosgrave, Kevin O'Higgins, Seán T. O'Kelly, Seán MacEntee, Neil Blaney and John Garvin and will stimulate interest in others who deserve greater recognition, such as Hugo Flinn, T.J. Murphy, the first Labour Minister for Local Government, Patrick O'Donnell, Minister for Local Government 1954-57, and Edward McCarron, the first secretary of the Department of Local Government and Public Health.

The wide-ranging nature of the Department's interests, and the extent to which they impinged on those of other government departments, also presented some difficulties. No department is an island; during the 1930s Local Government became deeply involved in the government's programme of unemployment relief works; during the Emergency years the Department devoted considerable efforts to organising and overseeing the production of turf by county councils. Yet this book does not provide a history of turf development in Ireland, nor of government policies towards unemployment, though it provides information on both topics. The Department of Local Government also had intermittent involvement with the building societies, as part of its concern with the availability of capital for housing, and this is covered. Until 1970, however, responsibility for overseeing the building societies rested with the Department of Industry and Commerce, with the result that much of the story remains untold. Although chapter ten discusses the process of regional planning, in so far as it related to the Department's activities, no effort is made to examine the different structures of regional administration that were created to co-ordinate the public health system or industrial development.

One of the most difficult decisions was how to determine the balance between chronology and a thematic approach in organising the material. The solution adopted can perhaps be described as an uneasy compromise. Chronology has been given precedence, in order to highlight the degree to which the matters that concerned the Department were the product of specific historical circumstances, such as the conflicting concerns of unemployment and government budgetary difficulties during the 1950s. The dates chosen for individual chapters were determined by electoral politics; each marks a change of government. Yet within each chronological chapter some themes are highlighted and occasionally the story is told up to a date beyond the chapter's chronological limits.

Chapter one, which provides a survey of local government policy under the Union, is primarily intended to set the scene and to enable

4

the reader to take account of the extent to which various attributes of central/local relations in independent Ireland predate the foundation of the state. Chapter two examines the little-known story of local government under the First and Second Dála: it highlights the political aspects of a story that is often told only from the military angle. The account of the financial difficulties facing local authorities from 1920 to 1922 and the tensions that existed between the Dáil Éireann Department of Local Government in Dublin and local authorities that had declared allegiance to Dáil Éireann, is an indication that, for many Irish people, the future of a local hospital or the possibility of employment as a county council labourer often assumed a greater importance than national independence. Chapter three, covering the years 1922-32, concentrates on two major themes: the problems that the foundation of a new state posed for the local government system, and the impact of depressed economic circumstances and of Cumann na nGaedheal's commitment to a conservative economic policy, on local authority revenue and expenditure. With the establishment of the Local Appointments Commission, the appointment of the first city managers and the abolition of rural district councils, Local Government emerges as one of the most active ministries in the first ten years of the Irish Free State.

The uncertainties associated with the transfer of power to Fianna Fáil following the 1932 general election, particularly the possibility that the power of the Local Appointments Commission might be diluted, form a major part of chapter four. This chapter also examines the imposition of Irish language tests in local appointments, a topic that has previously been ignored. During the years 1932-38, falling farm prices — a result of the combined effects of international depression and the economic war — meant that some local authorities were in financial difficulty because of rate arrears. With the option of emigration closed, the government gave considerable attention to devising a programme of unemployment relief works. At first sight, this might appear to have presented major opportunities for the Department of Local Government. In fact, the Department found many of its programmes being turned into little more than employment relief schemes.

Housing was a major responsibility for the Local Government Board before 1922, and in later years for the Department of Local Government and Public Health. Chapter five examines government housing programmes up to 1939. At the beginning these were concerned only with providing cottages for rural labourers and removing urban slums; by the late 1930s they included generous provisions to assist the construction and repair of houses for private owners. Many of the latter programmes proved more successful than the schemes designed to clear urban slums.

Chapter six deals with the Department's role during the Emergency; this ranged from drawing up contingency plans to evacuate most of the population of Dublin, to its role in overseeing the production of turf. Local Government was also heavily involved in planning a major programme of public works, to be carried out when the war ended, though at times this process gave rise to undoubted tensions with other government departments. Chapter seven should be seen very much as an appendix to chapter six, in that it explores two different strains of thinking about local government reorganisation: county management and parish councils, which were both under active discussion during the Emergency years. The appointment of county managers aroused considerable opposition from local authorities, and this chapter explores the moves by both inter-party governments to abolish the post, up to its reform in 1955.

The formation of the first inter-party government in 1948 brought the appointment of the first Labour Minister for Local Government. Chapter eight looks at the steps taken during the years 1948-51 to provide for uniform wages for local authority labourers and the introduction of a proper superannuation scheme. Most of the chapter is devoted to housing, because this was the major preoccupation of the Department from 1948 to 1957. The large sums required to fund both local authority housing and mortgages and grants for owner-occupiers meant that the Department was forced to do battle at regular intervals to secure the necessary funds. Given that housing accounted for 30 per cent of public capital expenditure during these years, the problems involved in financing housing expenditure, and the story of Local Government's relationship with the Department of Finance, proves extremely revealing about the nature of economic management in Ireland before the publication of *Economic Development*. On the whole it suggests, not that the Department of Finance was all-powerful, but that it was grappling to gain control of public expenditure; on several occasions, Finance's efforts were seriously weakened by ministerial pronouncements that lack of money would not prove a handicap.

Chapter nine looks at the history of roads. During two decades, the

1920s and again during the 1940s, the Department's engineers developed comprehensive plans for a national road network. On both occasions the plans were pushed aside: in the 1920s, this was due to a combination of a lack of capital and lack of political will. In the 1950s the planned road network, which included several bridges and by-passes that were constructed only in the 1980s and 1990s, was abandoned in large part because it failed to attract popular support. Spending money on local roads, often as a form of relief work, proved much more popular with voters and politicians alike.

The 1958 White Paper *Economic Development*, with its emphasis on 'productive' investment, as opposed to investment in housing or sanitary services, seemed to relegate Local Government to the margins of Irish political and economic life. As chapter ten shows, this was not the case. Once the pace of economic growth began to quicken, there was a major need for investment in housing, water and roads to meet the demands of a growing economy. The vogue for planning in the 1960s gave Local Government considerable scope to redefine its role, by using the powers given to the Department in the 1963 Planning Act and by playing a major part in the drawing up of regional plans. Several topics scrutinised in this chapter, such as the National Building Agency and the proposals for regional planning authorities, suggest that the historic structures of local government were ill-suited to coping with the demands being placed on them.

This chapter also includes a discussion of local government finances and taxation. Although the inadequacies of the rating system arose at various stages during earlier decades, it was only in the 1960s that the government began to make serious efforts to examine the possibility of reforming the system of local authority taxation and finance. That it failed to do so testifies to the difficulties involved. Although the story, as told from government files, ends about 1964, the chapter continues the story until 1973. Thus the events of the late 1960s and early 1970s are examined only from published sources. The terminal date has been chosen because it marked a change of government. It was also the year of Ireland's accession to the European Community; this opened up new sources of capital funding for services such as roads and water. The 1970s also saw a growing concern with environmental matters, which is reflected in the change of name in 1977 to the Department of the Environment.

CHAPTER ONE

ORIGINS: THE BRITISH ANTECEDENTS

The origins of the present Department of the Environment (1977-) and its predecessors, the Department of Local Government (1947-77), the Department of Local Government and Public Health (1924-47) and the Ministry of Local Government (1922-24), lie in nineteenth-century Irish administration, though there is also evidence of indirect eighteenth-century antecedents. Although local government, as the term suggests, was primarily a matter of local concern, during the later eighteenth century the Dublin parliament set up the Wide Streets Commission to redevelop the city of Dublin[1] and took steps to promote a national road network.[2] Central government involvement in local affairs increased substantially during the nineteenth century in both Britain and Ireland, though the process was more pronounced in Ireland.

In England the parish was the basic unit of local government, but in Ireland the ruling class were too few in number to support parish administration, so local government was based on the county.[3] Central government in each county was represented by the high sheriff, who was generally a prominent local landowner. Although he was formally appointed by the lord lieutenant, in practice each high sheriff selected his successor; he also selected the grand jury from the ranks of local landowners. As the name suggests, grand juries were originally responsible for criminal justice within each county. During the seventeenth century they also received authority to levy local taxes, which were then used to finance the construction and repair of roads, bridges and houses of correction. In 1727 the Irish parliament confirmed the status of grand juries as the key organ of local government and in later years made them responsible for providing hospitals, dispensaries, lunatic asylums, poor relief and police.[4] Representatives of the hundred highest cesspayers (local taxpayers) in

9

every barony were chosen by the grand jury to hold annual presentment sessions to draft proposals for local expenditure. These were approved by the grand jury, which also levied the county cess, a tax paid by occupiers of property.[5] Larger towns and cities were ruled by municipal corporations, which tended, like grand juries, to be self-selecting bodies, though the criteria for admission differed in each borough.

During the early decades of the nineteenth century, Irish local authorities were regularly accused of corruption, and their unrepresentative membership was challenged both by Daniel O'Connell's Catholic Association and by reforming liberals. Critics claimed that road improvements were carried out in members' interests: areas not represented on grand juries were neglected, while elsewhere there were double or treble presentments for the same piece of road, even for non-existent pieces of road. Virgina Crossman points out that catholic dissatisfaction

> . . . with the forms and the functionaries of local government could not be dismissed as a matter only of local concern. It was felt to taint government in general, with the result that people had little confidence in government or the law to protect their interests. The belief that by improving local administration and thereby winning the confidence of the people, lawlessness and turbulence would disappear from Ireland, and with them the clamour for separation from England, provided the impetus behind much local government reform in the nineteenth century.

By the 1830s Crossman notes that grand jury reform 'became part of the package of reforms advocated not only by O'Connellite radicals but also by British and Irish Whigs anxious to do "justice to Ireland".' Although the Whig administration of the 1830s tried to appoint as sheriffs and other office-holders men who would be acceptable to catholics, most reforms took the form of increased central control and the transfer of responsibility to paid officials, such as engineers or stipendiary magistrates.[6] Unelected grand juries continued to levy taxes until they were superseded by elected county councils in 1899, but they were given few extra responsibilities. Their procedure was subjected to tight central control, and expenditure was often mandated by central government.[7]

The need to strike a balance between demands from the catholic majority and the risk of antagonising the protestant ascendancy was not the only factor leading to central control. In Britain, central government was forced to intervene in local affairs because of increasing concern about the impact of urban growth and the Industrial Revolution on public health. The publication in 1843 of the Report of the Health of Towns Commission,[8] which explicitly linked high death-rates with inadequate water and sewerage services, is believed to have triggered this process. The Irish administration's concern with local services predated that report by almost thirty years and was prompted by poverty and lack of development, rather than by the consequences of industrialisation.

In 1815 the Richmond lunatic asylum opened under central government control; in 1817 the lord lieutenant was empowered to set up district asylums and to appoint boards of governors. During the same year he was given power to create fever hospitals and to take measures to prevent a raging epidemic from spreading,[9] while a threatened famine in the same years led Dublin Castle to provide loans for road improvements. Between 1817 and 1831 the Irish administration provided approximately £1m. for roads, bridges and similar projects. The investment was concentrated in remote western areas in the hope that the employment provided on public works would relieve the immediate distress, while better communications would make famine a thing of the past.[10] In 1831 most funds for public works were put under the control of the Irish Board of Works. Three Commissioners of Public Works set up office in the Custom House in Dublin where they remained until 1905,[11] establishing a direct physical link with the present Department. Between 1831 and 1845 the Board advanced over £1m. in loans, mostly to grand juries.[12] Although the Board of Works had no formal authority over grand juries, in practice it became the most important agent of central control. From 1831 almost all road and bridge construction was financed by loans provided by the Board of Works, which scrutinised applications from grand juries and demanded that schemes be supervised by qualified surveyors, who were appointed by the lord lieutenant but paid by the grand juries. A select committee which examined these procedures in 1857 concluded that they had resulted in better roads and considerable savings. In 1854, 36,703 miles of county roads were repaired, as against 13,191 in 1834; costs increased from £228,326 to £312,297.[13]

Urban government was also subjected to greater central control. In

1840, faced with demands from O'Connell and the Whigs for electoral reform, the House of Lords abolished all except the ten largest Irish municipal boroughs.[14] The new urban authorities created during the nineteenth century were given minimal autonomy. Under the 1828 Lighting of Towns Act, the town commissioners, elected to provide services such as lighting, cleansing, water and paving, were given little financial discretion. Although the 1854 Town Improvement Act permitted these commissioners to levy higher rates, their borrowing and spending power remained limited. In 1849, much to its chagrin, the reformed Dublin Corporation (which by then had a catholic majority) saw its improvement rate capped at 2 shillings (10p) in the pound, a limit which was more onerous because the city's valuation was sharply reduced in 1847.[15] However, within the limits set on borrowing powers, towns and cities had greater freedom to determine expenditure, though any extension of their powers required Dublin Castle's approval.

The Poor Law Commission is the most direct antecedent of the present Department. There is an unbroken line between the Irish Poor Law Board, established in the famine year of 1847, and its successor, the Irish Local Government Board, founded in 1872, whose former officials constituted most of the original staff of the Irish Free State Department of Local Government and Public Health. The Poor Law Commission introduced a new range of public services and administrative structures. Before 1838, Irish local authorities, unlike those in England and Wales, had no statutory responsibility for poor relief, although many made grants towards county infirmaries, and Dublin Corporation had made some provision for poor relief.[16] In the 1830s the Poor Inquiry Commission recommended that the government embark on an elaborate programme of public works and establish institutions to care for the non-able-bodied poor, but its recommendations were rejected on grounds of cost and because they were not in keeping with the new economic orthodoxy of *laissez-faire*. In 1838 Ireland adopted a variant of the new English poor law, with the workhouse as the all-purpose relief agency.

One writer has noted that the blueprint for the new English poor law 'reflects deep hostility to local government'.[17] Historic boundaries of counties, for instance, were disregarded in favour of poor law unions, which were based on the main market towns and their catchment areas. Unions were subdivided into district electoral divisions (DEDs), consisting of several townlands; each DED elected members of the board of guardians.[18] Funding came from a tax on property, the poor rate, which was based on a nationwide valuation, the poor law or Griffith's valuation. Efforts were made to equalise taxes in different unions, with the result that unions in poorer areas, such as the west of Ireland, were larger than the national average. Initially there were 130 unions, but in 1848 some were subdivided because of problems experienced during the Famine, resulting in 163 unions.[19]

The Irish poor law was originally placed under the control of the English poor law commissioners, without reference to Dublin Castle.[20] In practice, from the beginning the system was controlled by a Dublin-based commissioner and a separate staff, drawn from the English Poor Law Commission, which was based in the Custom House.[21] When a separate Irish Poor Law Commission was created in 1847, consisting of the Irish chief secretary, the under-secretary and the Irish poor law commissioner, the change was nominal. Twistleton, the resident Irish commissioner, became chief commissioner.[22]

Unlike grand juries, boards of guardians included both elected and *ex officio* members. The initial legislation provided for a maximum of one-quarter of guardians to be *ex officio* members; in 1847 this was increased to one-half, because an amendment in 1843 had made landlords responsible for paying the poor rates on properties valued at £4 or less. *Ex officio* guardians were chosen from the local magistracy, who were invariably landowners; they were obliged to serve. The electorate consisted of ratepayers with property valued in excess of £4, but a system of multiple votes gave greater weight to larger tenants and landowners, reflecting the nineteenth-century belief that representation should reflect property rather than democracy. Candidates had to occupy property valued in excess of a specified figure, generally £20.[23]

The Irish poor law originated from the new English poor law, which was dominated by the utilitarian canons of efficiency, centralisation, uniformity and accountability. Commissioners based in London and Dublin could dismiss local officials without consulting the board of guardians. Other essential weapons in the quest for efficiency and uniformity were the power to hold a regular audit and the use of inspectors, the quintessential Benthamite instrument to report on the standard of local administration.[24] Both the auditor and the inspector remained key agents of the twentieth-century Irish Department of Local Government during its early years.

Despite its English origins, operating procedures within the Irish poor law diverged from the outset from those in England. The Irish poor law was more centralised, as were the Irish police force and the education system. This reflects Ireland's colonial status.[25] Irish commissioners had power to alter the area of taxation covered by a DED to ensure that it would be solvent. Workhouses were built by the commissioners and vested in them; in England they were vested in the boards of guardians. Commissioners could replace a recalcitrant or insolvent board of guardians with salaried assistant guardians, and boards of guardians were required to secure the commissioners' permission before embarking on some forms of expenditure, such as assisted emigration. A report into the Poor Law Commission in the early 1850s described it as 'practically an intermediate court of appeal'; such close supervision was designed 'not so much for the purpose of enabling Commissioners to exercise their powers as of anticipating and preventing any occasion for its exercise'.

The full-time commissioners met daily; twice a week they consulted the chief secretary and the under-secretary about more difficult matters. Such centralisation resulted in an immense volume of correspondence. In 1853 — a normal year — the Commission received almost 86,000 papers. Minutes of boards of guardians were regarded as 'the principal medium of correspondence between boards of guardians and the commissioners', enabling the latter 'at once to interpose their authority when any irregular or unauthorised proceeding takes place or is contemplated'. All minutes were forwarded to the Commission, where they were first read by a correspondent — a clerk, 'who places against any part of statistics contained in the minutes which appear to require observations or explanations and against any of the resolutions which appear to require reply or comment from the Commissioners, a letter or figure'. He also attached a 'reference sheet (consisting of a half sheet of foolscap, ruled in half margin with a printed heading), which he marks with the corresponding letters or figures; he then writes on the reference sheet the name of the inspector to whom the minutes are to be referred, with date of reference, and obtains the initials of one of the Commissioners thereto.'

Even changes in the diet served in a particular workhouse had to be sanctioned by a sealed order from the commissioners. Centralist tendencies extended to the Custom House. All decisions, however trivial, were initialled by at least one commissioner; a report in 1854 concluded that, in an effort to ensure complete uniformity, 'not even the minutest direction takes effect without such authority'.[26] The procedures described above remained unchanged until the abolition of the Local Government Board. Indeed they were adopted — complete with the attached foolscap 'reference sheet' — by the Dáil Éireann Local Government Department in 1920/21. Either W.T. Cosgrave, Dáil Éireann Minister for Local Government, or Kevin O'Higgins, the Assistant Minister, scrutinised and initialled all minutes in a manner identical to previous poor law commissioners or Local Government Board members.[27]

The key agent in the commission's control was the inspector. In addition to inspecting workhouses, he regularly attended meetings of boards of guardians, showing particular interest in the poorer unions. The Commission consulted inspectors constantly about matters arising in the minutes, or about the innumerable allegations of inefficiency or dishonesty on the part of local officials. Sir Henry Robinson, who served as vice-president of the Local Government Board from 1898 until 1922,[28] described an inspector's duty as 'to act, in fact, as the eyes and ears of the Government'.[29] The inspectors' investigations ranged from the cost of constructing a new workhouse to the state of landlord-tenant relations. By 1860 each inspector had travelled an average of 22,613 miles during the preceding three years.[30] The ratio of inspectors to Poor Law Unions was much higher than in Britain, suggesting a greater distrust of local administration. However, inspectors often mediated between the commissioners and boards of guardian to ensure that irregularities were resolved without undue interference by Dublin.[31]

The other critical official was the auditor. An inquiry held in 1854 suggested that auditors placed undue trust in the bookkeeping of union clerks and recommended that accounts should be subject to a more detailed scrutiny. Although the report recommended recruiting additional auditors and appointing an inspector of audits, the recommendations appear to have been ignored.[32]

Boards of guardians seem to have resented the detailed scrutiny of their affairs by commission staff. They took particular exception to the commissioners' overriding powers of appointment and dissolution.[33] Until the 1880s boards of guardians were invariably under landlord control, and most inspectors shared a similar background, which suggests that the resentment owed little to religion or nationalism. The saga of Captain Wynne, a member of a Sligo landlord family and a temporary inspector during the Famine years, who became involved in highly acrimonious inquiries in the House of Lords, is a case in point.[34]

15

THE FAMINE AND IRISH LOCAL ADMINISTRATION

The Famine years imposed extraordinary pressures on Irish local government and on the central support agencies. Until the spring of 1847, public works constituted the major form of relief. Most schemes were initiated by grand juries and were vetted and supervised by the Board of Works from its headquarters in the Custom House. By March 1847 over 700,000 people were employed on schemes directly under the Board's control.[35] Its staff was increased to meet this challenge; by February 1847 over 14,000 supervisory staff were employed, including more than 76 inspecting officers (all military men) and 500 engineers. There was considerable conflict among Board of Works officials, local presentment sessions and the clergy over the scale of relief works and the numbers employed.[36] Local agencies appear to have been least competent in the poorest areas, such as the west of Ireland.[37] Although Edward Twistleton, the resident poor law commissioner, was a member of the government's famine relief commission from November 1845[38] and local poor law officials assisted relief efforts in their areas, the poor law was given no specific role in famine relief until 1847. George Nicholls, who had drafted the blueprint for the Irish poor law, had emphasised that workhouses, with a capacity for 100,000 inmates, were not designed to cope with a major famine and most had vacant places until the late autumn of 1846. During the autumn/winter of 1846, however, many began to operate soup kitchens in defiance of the commissioners' orders, and by April 1847 the majority of unions were providing outdoor relief.[39]

The control usually exercised by the poor law commissioners appears to have collapsed. R.B. McDowell describes the Dublin officials during these years as occupying a position 'analogous to that of the staff in the eyes of a fighting soldier. In their Dublin office, at a decent distance from the struggle for survival, they were able to enunciate general principles with cold lucidity. Theirs was the unpopular task of forcing the others into the fight.' On this occasion Dublin was forced to endorse the actions of the unions by authorising outdoor relief. By the autumn of 1847, the poor law, which had initially been given no official role, became the sole state agency responsible for famine relief.[40]

Rates poundages — the rate charged on electoral areas — soared, particularly in poorer western areas, though rates were often uncollectable because the local economy had collapsed. Rates constituted the largest single source of funds for famine relief, which meant that landlords, medium and large farmers and businessmen bore the cost of famine relief in their locality.[41] Poor law guardians were caught between the commissioners' exhortations to ensure a union's solvency, relentless demands for relief, and ratepayers' resistance to higher taxes. Many unions became insolvent. Thirty-nine boards of guardians were dismissed and were replaced by salaried vice-guardians, though the latter were not noticeably more successful in controlling expenditure. The numbers receiving outdoor relief peaked at 833,000 in July 1848, but the number of workhouse inmates did not fall significantly until 1850. Thereafter workhouse conditions became more humane, diet improved and the burden of poor rates fell steadily. Only two boards of guardians were dissolved between 1850 and 1879.

The Famine forced the poor law to provide medical facilities. A temporary central board of health was established in March 1846 under the authority of the lord lieutenant, with the power to require any union to provide a fever hospital, dispensaries and medicine, which could include food.[42] In 1851 the Medical Charities Act transformed these emergency measures into a permanent feature of the Irish poor law,[43] something which did not happen in England and Wales. Each union was required to provide free medical care for the poor through local dispensaries. The existing patchy network of dispensaries, which had been funded by a combination of private subscriptions and grants from grand juries, was transferred to poor law control, and dispensaries were established in areas where they were lacking. The commissioners could also appoint salaried medical officers, pharmacists and midwives, who would be paid by boards of guardians.[44] Two additional full-time commissioners were appointed to cope with the extra work, one an *ex officio* medical commissioner. Throughout the 1850s and '60s the Poor Law Commission was given a range of duties which were far removed from poor relief: supervising cemeteries, birth and death registration, smallpox vaccination and controlling cattle disease. In 1862 non-destitute patients were admitted to workhouse infirmaries. Under the 1866 Sanitary Act, boards of guardians assumed responsibility for public health in small towns, villages and in rural areas. Poor law expenditure, which had fallen from a record level of £2.1m. in 1849 to £513,000 by 1859, began to rise, reaching £1,045,555 by 1876. By contrast, grand jury presentments rose only from £1.018m. in 1856 to £1.13m. in 1876.[45] Their additional duties were limited to weights and measures and dog control.[46]

Many temporary clerks joined the Poor Law Commission during the

Famine years. By December 1850 three-quarters of the clerical staff held temporary positions, with little prospect of permanent appointments. There was also many temporary inspectors, though some ultimately joined the permanent ranks. Employment fell steadily during the early 1850s. In 1853 the commission proposed to dismiss a further forty clerks, though a cholera outbreak provided a temporary reprieve.[47] In 1873 Alfred Power, vice-president of the Local Government Board and formerly chief commissioner, claimed that 1858 represented the nadir of Poor Law Commission responsibilities: 'we were almost at our greatest ease since the Famine'. Since that date the workload had been increasing.[48]

THE ESTABLISHMENT OF THE LOCAL GOVERNMENT BOARD

In 1872 the Irish Poor Law Commission was transformed into the Irish Local Government Board. The change of title reflected the increasing range of duties and it followed British legislation.[49] However, while the English Local Government Board had a full-time cabinet minister as its president, the Irish chief secretary presided over the Irish Board. Although he was consulted on important matters and was responsible for introducing legislation concerning Irish local government in parliament, the chief secretary had many other responsibilities and spent much of his time outside Ireland.[50] According to O'Halpin, this meant that 'most Irish departments were left to fend for themselves, the inevitable result being that they became administrative backwaters cut off from either attention or scrutiny'.[51] Day-to-day power rested with the vice-president, the senior full-time official, and this was recognised by the 1898 Local Government Act, which required acts of the Board to be executed by the president, the under-secretary or the vice-president, or by a person appointed by one of these to act on their behalf.[52] The only apparent challenge to the vice-president's authority came during the years 1887-92 when the then under-secretary (the senior Irish civil servant), Sir West Ridgeway, allegedly 'dominated the Board' and determined which papers were seen by the chief secretary, a practice much resented by the vice-president of the Local Government Board.[53]

Most of the Board's energy during the 1870s was devoted to public health. The 1866 Act made the Poor Law Commission responsible for public health in non-urban areas, the 1872 Act gave the board authority over public health in urban and municipal areas. The 1874 and 1878 Public Health Acts, both Irish variants of landmark English legislation, imposed additional responsibilities on all Irish local authorities. The 1874 Act divided the country into sanitary districts, which were required to establish water and sewer authorities and given power to borrow money for public health purposes. In rural areas and towns with a population of less than 6,000, the board of guardians became the sanitary authority; in boroughs and larger towns, responsibility rested with the municipality.[54] Although the 1874 report of the Local Government Board claimed that 'our ordinary poor law union correspondence gives indication daily of increased attention to the supply of pure water in the digging of new wells, construction or repair of pumps effected at no considerable expense, sometimes with, and sometimes without, the aid of the landlord', many boards of guardians were reluctant to borrow money for improvements which would benefit only the minority of ratepayers who lived in a village. To meet these objections, the 1874 Act provided that the cost could be levied on the area which would benefit directly from the pump or well, rather than on the entire union or DED, a clause not found in the English legislation. By 1878 orders fixing contribution areas for public health schemes had been applied to 132 out of 163 unions, which indicates a considerable volume of public health improvements.[55]

The legislative changes of the 1870s proved most significant in urban areas. Before 1872, if a town or city wished to extend its borrowing powers or engage in a major investment, it was forced to ensure the passage of a private act of parliament. It could now petition the Local Government Board to hold a public inquiry. If this was favourable, the board would grant the necessary authorisation by means of a provisional order, which was rubber-stamped by parliament. These inquiries marked the beginning of the board's scrutiny of urban public health. The first annual report noted that the new authority 'entails a serious responsibility on the department concerning towns in Ireland, the governing bodies of which, as too frequently is the case, neglect the performance of their sanitary duties.' The Board reserved its strongest criticism for smaller towns, which 'from the constitution of their governing bodies are less disposed to act in a public spirit and to expend money for sanitary purposes . . . . Town or Township Commissioners, can, if so minded, evade any expenditure of this nature in the present state of the law.'[56]

Irish towns and boroughs deeply resented being subject to audit by the LGB, because this provision did not apply to English boroughs. In 1877 Mr Ellard, the town clerk of Limerick, claimed that 'there was a general objection to the [LGB] auditor, that he exercised too much control.' Unlike a local auditor, who would not act 'with such strictness', 'the LGB inspector reports on everything and whatever he recommends to the Board, the Board generally act on'. Ellard regarded LGB control in municipal areas as 'handing over the control indirectly to an individual'. Mr Nagle, a former lord mayor of Cork, expressed the view that this requirement undermined the concept of a corporation: 'I do not see how we can be municipal corporations with governments and centralisation over us'; it subjected Irish municipalities to 'an indignity that would not be endured by any English corporation'. The town clerk of Waterford regarded it 'as virtually saying that they are all mismanaging their affairs, or that they are rogues'.[57] Such antagonism stemmed from both financial and political factors. Irish towns and cities had not experienced the buoyant growth in rateable income of British cities, and funds for sanitary improvements were tight.[58] Demands by faceless bureaucrats for increased sanitary expenditure, coupled with sanctions against financial profligacy from the same bureaucrats, were calculated to arouse resentment. In addition, although municipal electorates were heavily weighted towards property-owners, they were more in tune with popular opinion than boards of guardians.

Some of the hostility shown by Limerick or Dublin Corporations reflected antagonism between Dublin Castle and Irish nationalists. Edward Dwyer Gray, a nationalist MP and member of Dublin Corporation, voiced the opinion that 'If the Local Government Board managed in a way to command more general confidence, that might do away with some of the hardships we complain of; . . . the corporation have very little confidence in the Local Government Board as at present constituted.'[59]

DISTRESS AND THE LAND WAR: THE LOCAL GOVERNMENT BOARD IN THE 1880s AND 1890s

The quarter-century or so after the Famine was a relatively calm period for the Irish poor law. The number of workhouse inmates remained low, unions were solvent, disputes with the Custom House were few.

Boards of guardians appear to have taken additional responsibilities in their stride. During the 1880s, however, the cost of outdoor relief rose sharply in Connacht and Munster and several boards of guardians were dissolved. This was the outcome of both economic distress and political agitation, though it is impossible to assess the relative weight of each factor; indeed, the land war and the home rule campaign were partly caused by economic distress. The Home Rule Party's takeover of Irish parliamentary politics during these years was mirrored by a similar process in the poor law unions. In 1877, 87.9 per cent of office-holders were landlords, their agents or family members. By 1886 this had fallen to 38.9 per cent. Feingold sees this as 'the local movement for self-government', a campaign which was directed against two enemies – 'the British government as represented by the Local Government Board, and the landlord sitting as ex-officio guardian'.[60]

Many new guardians were determined to assert their political views, so clashes with the LGB were inevitable. The fact that W.E. Forster, Irish chief secretary and president of the Irish LGB, allegedly instructed Board inspectors to attend evictions and report on them[61] placed the LGB directly in opposition to tenant interests. The board of guardians of the North Roscommon union was dissolved in 1887 because it gave special treatment to evicted tenants, in contravention of regulations. In 1888 a further four unions — Glin, Gortin, Killadysert and Tulla — were threatened with dissolution.[62] The last was among the most radical in Ireland and refused on several occasions to recognise the LGB, behaviour which foreshadows the years of the first Dáil. Feingold notes that until 1879 expenditure on outdoor relief was broadly similar in Ulster, Connacht and Munster; after that date it increased sharply in Connacht and Munster. Feingold observes a 'striking resemblance' between the timing of the increase and the capture of control of boards of guardians by tenant representatives.[63] However, this interpretation ignores the extent of economic distress in western areas during the 1880s.

The Irish administration tended to treat with scepticism claims of distress in the west of Ireland. According to Sir Henry Robinson, then a temporary inspector and subsequently vice-president of the LGB, the Board initially decided that demands for relief in the autumn of 1879 were politically motivated,[64] and information from inspectors about the extent of distress proved contradictory.[65] By the spring of 1880, however, reports from temporary inspectors assigned to western unions convinced the authorities that the distress was real. A relief programme was introduced under LGB control, consisting of public works, outdoor relief (the Gregory clause was suspended) and the provision of seed potatoes. The Board drew up a list of unions which were believed to be suffering exceptional distress. Low-interest loans for public works were offered to landlords, grand juries, drainage boards and boards of guardians in those areas. Applications poured in; landowners applied for a total of £1.2m.; local authorities sought almost £144,000. But LGB inspectors sanctioned only one-quarter of the amount applied for. In unions where the Board believed that the relief provided was inadequate, it could request the lord lieutenant to convene extraordinary presentments sessions to approve additional road works. According to Sir Henry Robinson, most of the money spent on relief in 1879/80 was wasted: 'Never was money more easily obtained, and never, I fancy, did it fail more lamentably in its object'. He claimed that little of the money lent to landowners or to sanitary authorities reached the most distressed areas, while the £271,000 spent on road works went to small contractors, who hired friends and neighbours, rather than the most necessitous poor.[66] The 1909 report of the Royal Commission on the Poor Laws reached a similar conclusion, claiming that charitable agencies had borne the brunt of the relief effort.[67]

This experience brought a hardening of official attitudes. When distress reappeared in 1882/83, following yet another failure of the potato crop, the Irish administration resisted demands for relief works on the grounds that they were 'not only extravagant and demoralising in their effects, but they often fail to aid the most necessitous'.[68] Temporary inspectors were recruited to ensure 'constant attention' to, and 'prompt information' on, distressed unions, and the Board made determined, if unsuccessful, efforts to prevent an upsurge in outdoor relief. The cost had jumped from £117,275 in 1879 to £153,586 in 1880; by 1886 it had reached £183,298.[69] Attitudes towards distress tended to reflect the governing party's policy towards Ireland. According to Sir Henry Robinson, who was unsympathetic to Irish nationalism, the Liberals proved more responsive than the Conservatives. When 'unusual distress' recurred in 1886, John Morley, chief secretary in Gladstone's fourth administration, relaxed the criteria for granting outdoor relief, against the Board's advice, and expenditure reached £235,500 in the following year. The government agreed to meet part of the cost of outdoor relief in the poorest unions in Counties Mayo and

Galway. As a result, Robinson claimed that 'Boards of guardians, believing it was a case of first come first served, gave outdoor relief broadcast and practically refused no one, never doubting that the friendly Government would increase the £60,000 to whatever sum was necessary to cover total expenditure'.[70] An investigation into outdoor relief in western unions, carried out by Robinson and a colleague, concluded that most unions administered relief 'in a very lax, extravagant and inefficient manner, and that very grave abuses were allowed to prevail'.[71]

Arthur Balfour, who became Irish chief secretary in 1887, apparently accepted this diagnosis and even claimed that some of the money allocated to boards of guardians had been used for electioneering.[72] When the potato crop again failed in 1890, Balfour determined that the 'scandalous fraud' of the previous years would not be repeated. Outdoor relief was not extended; where reports indicated that an area was suffering distress,[73] the government initiated a programme of relief works which was directly under its control. The Royal Irish Constabulary (RIC) acted as gangers, paymasters and timekeepers, and LGB inspectors organised relief works with the assistance of the Royal Engineers and the county surveyors, a group which Balfour termed 'unreliable'.[74] By June 1891 they employed over 16,000 persons.[75] Although the government adopted strict criteria in granting loans to buy seed potatoes,[76] expenditure under this heading reached £250,000,[77] which suggests that distress was not solely a figment of the nationalist imagination.

The Board's report for 1892 praised the measures adopted in 1890/91, noting that experience showed that it was 'inexpedient to entrust Boards of Guardians with extensive powers over public funds for relief of exceptional distress';[78] similar measures were repeated in 1895. However, in 1898 the Conservative government returned responsibility for relief works to boards of guardians, though the exchequer met 75 per cent of the cost. Timothy P. O'Neill sees this change 'as a means of forcing local contribution, of avoiding total reliance on central government' and of preventing 'the recurring prospect of central government works being relied upon by the distressed areas'. Gerald Balfour, chief secretary for Ireland, and Arthur's brother, justified the volte-face by citing the heavy supervision costs incurred in both 1891 and 1895. He feared that the policy had relieved local authorities of the cost of alleviating distress, while giving them an incentive to lobby for assistance.[79] Yet, despite the desire to promote local responsibility, four of the eleven unions assisted under this programme were wholly or partly relieved of their share of the cost.[80]

The Congested Districts Board, established in 1891, strove to replace crisis relief by long-term development aid. The new agency assumed responsibility for various public health and amenity schemes which had previously been carried out (if at all) by boards of guardians, under the supervision of the LGB.[81] Relations between both agencies appear to have been amicable; the LGB may have been relieved to lose some of its most intractable problems. Several of the founding staff of the Congested Districts Board were former officials of the LGB, notably W. L. Micks, its secretary, who served as a LGB commissioner from 1899 to 1909. Like the LGB, the Congested Districts Board was heavily dependent on a team of inspectors. It appears to have been more popular with local interests, perhaps because it made no demands on rate and cess-payers. All expenditure was centrally funded and, although its board made no provision for local representation, it appears to have been responsive to public opinion.

LOCAL GOVERNMENT REFORM

It was almost inevitable that the political ferment of the 1880s would focus attention on local government reform. Once the Irish Party had captured most parliamentary seats outside Ulster, and nationalists had gained control of many boards of guardians, the unelected grand juries became almost the last bastion of landlord political privilege. The Irish Party introduced legislation to reform Irish local government during every parliamentary session of the 1880s except 1889. The 1884 bill was typical in proposing to replace grand juries with elected county boards; ex officio poor law guardians would be abolished, and guardians would be elected by secret ballot, rather than by the existing system where ballot papers were collected from voters' residences by the RIC. By 1886 the issue had become inextricably linked with opposition to Home Rule. Joseph Chamberlain, the leading Liberal expert on local government, who left the party over Home Rule in 1886, proposed that, as an alternative to Home Rule, Irish domestic affairs would be administered by elected county councils headed by a supervisory central board.[82] As a result of their alliance with Joseph Chamberlain's Liberal Unionists, the Conservative Party became committed to reforming Irish local government, to the extent that in 1898 one unionist MP described all general elections fought after 1886 as 'a battle of local government against home rule'.[83] The case for reform in Ireland was strengthened when the 1888 Local Government Act introduced democratically elected county councils in England, Wales and Scotland. Irish legislation was delayed by Conservative government efforts to retain special representation for landlords: a bill introduced by Arthur Balfour in 1892[84] failed for this reason. These clauses were omitted in the successful 1898 Act, which won landlords' approval by reducing their tax liabilities.

The Act provided for the establishment of county, urban and rural district councils, elected triennially by an electorate comprising male and female ratepayers, together with non-ratepaying male occupiers and lodgers. All eligible voters could stand for election.[85] Landlords assented to this sweeping extension of democracy and their taxes were substantially reduced. In 1896 the government had introduced an agricultural rate grant which halved the rates paid on agricultural land in Britain, but Ireland was excluded from the measure because the country lacked a democratic system of local government. Irish landlords were also smarting from additional rent reductions imposed by the 1896 Land Act and threatened to retaliate by blocking legislation to establish the (British) Board of Agriculture unless the agricultural rate grant was extended to Ireland. Ireland's share would amount to £720,000; £170,000 of this was to be used to establish an Irish Department of Agriculture. Irish nationalists were particularly incensed at being deprived of this money because in 1896 the Childers Committee on the financial relations between Britain and Ireland had concluded that Ireland was overtaxed to the tune of £2.5m..[86] Thus the 1898 Act proved acceptable to both landlords and nationalists.[87]

The bill, assembled so hastily that Sir Henry Robinson was first informed of its existence while on a sailing holiday in Scotland only days before it was announced, was modelled directly on the 1888 Act.[88] Grand juries retained the power to administer justice and to determine malicious injury decrees, a matter of considerable importance in Ireland, but their local government duties passed to county councils. The 214 rural district councils assumed responsibility for initiating public works; their proposals were approved or rejected by county councils. Rural district councils were also made responsible for public health and for labourers' cottages. Urban district councils took charge of health and housing in urban areas.[89] Boards of guardians retained control over poor relief, workhouse hospitals and dispensaries, but their membership was now identical to that of rural district councils because the provision in the 1898 Local Government Act, which would have permitted rural district councils to co-opt non-elected members to the boards of guardians, was never exercised.

The financial clauses in the 1898 Act were designed to placate landlords and to curb spending sprees by the new councils. Landlords had previously paid the full cost of rates on properties valued at less than £4 and half the cost on larger holdings. The landlords' share was now met from the agricultural grant. As a concession to farmers, occupiers of agricultural land were relieved of half the burden of the county-cess. This provision was unique to Ireland and has been interpreted as partial compensation for previous overtaxation.[90] All rates were now paid by occupiers, i.e. farmers, farm labourers and businessmen, a change which was designed to encourage economy in the council chambers.[91] County councils became the sole and final rate-making authority, though urban councils and town commissioners retained the power to strike an urban or town rate.[92] All other local taxes — poor rates, drainage rates and county-cess — were consolidated into a single rate which was collected by the county council. The union became the area of charge for poor law purposes, rather than the smaller DED, or specially designated areas.[93]

The LGB responded nervously to the coming of local democracy. By February 1900, the Board had dispatched a total of 72,000 circular letters instructing the new councils of their duties in minute detail.[94] The Board's secretary suffered a nervous breakdown from overwork, and Richard Bagwell, a Tipperary landowner and author of a multi-volume history of Tudor Ireland, was appointed in 1899 as an additional commissioner to share the burden.[95] Councils were subjected to a battery of additional controls on their expenditure. When the Local Government bill was going through parliament in 1898, Sir Henry Robinson told the Irish chief secretary, Gerald Balfour, that the local government audit was 'the sheet anchor of your Local Government Bill on which you rely to prevent abuse'. However, the Irish Act also contained a clause, not found in the corresponding British Act, which limited spending on road works in any area to 125 per cent of the average spent by grand juries in their final three years, unless the LGB approved an increase.[96] Although grand juries and boards of guardians appear to have routinely run overdrafts,[97] the banks insisted that all overdrafts granted to the new councils should be sanctioned by the LGB. The board welcomed this 'shrinkage of credit' because it forced 'the new rating bodies to see that the only possible way to carry on their business is to strike rates fully adequate to meet all possible requirements'.[98]

The imposition of detailed regulations and restrictions reflected the board's fear that the new councils might escape their control. Although Feingold rightly emphasises that nationalists gained control of most boards of guardians in the 1880s, the 1899 local government elections marked the true beginning of local democracy in Ireland. Nationalists captured three-quarters of county council seats. Outside Ulster, unionists won just 39 out of a possible 495 seats and, even in the nine Ulster counties, nationalists won only six per cent fewer seats than the unionists. According to police files, 114, or ten per cent, of county councillors and five per cent of district councillors had links with the militant Irish Republican Brotherhood. Although many of the new councils introduced resolutions in support of the Boer army, then at war with Britain, or motions demanding immediate Home Rule,[99] such gestures appear not to have resulted in serious conflict with the Board.

Irish MPs complained about the Local Government Board's heavy-handed interference in the affairs of the new councils, but Sir Henry Robinson countered that the LGB exercised 'very little control over general administration'; its control was limited to sanctioning loan applications, auditing accounts, restricting expenditure on road works and arbitrating in the event of disputes between county councils and district councils, which usually related to their respective liability for road expenditure.[100] In December 1900 he informed the chief secretary that

> . . . things are going satisfactorily all around; the Councils are not so difficult to lead as you might think from the aggressive tone of their resolutions about us. We have half a dozen struggles going on, but we shall be able to make everything right, I hope.[101]

Superficially, Robinson was correct. If the Board's annual reports are accurate, there appears to have been less overt conflict with local authorities than in the 1880s. This may be because, as Shannon suggests, from 1902 the LGB intervened less in the councils' affairs,[102] or because it made some strategic concessions to councillors' wishes. Robinson's statement that 'the Councils are not so difficult to *lead* [italics added] as you might think' provides a clue to one contentious matter. Nationalist politicians did not see why elected councils should be led or supervised by 'Castle Boards', which lacked any mandate from the Irish people and whose senior officials were unlikely to be sympathetic to Irish nationalism.[103] That the formation in 1904 of the General Council of County Councils, which acted as a political umbrella for the overwhelming majority of councils outside Ulster,[104] led to a greater politicisation of local government is evident from the proliferation of deputations of local councillors to the Board seeking funding for road works, housing schemes and water supplies.

Most disputes between the Board and councillors largely centred on the councillors' desire to foster clientilism and to carry out the wishes of their electorate, even if this conflicted with official regulations. Until 1898 the electorate for boards of guardians had been dominated by property-holders, who were often unsympathetic to demands for labourers' housing. Once smallholders, tradesmen and labourers were added to the electoral register, councils came under pressure to provide more cottages. The Board's 1901 report regarded the 'general revival in Ireland of operations under the Labourers' Acts' as 'one of the most remarkable features of local administration' during the previous year. Plans had been submitted by 82 rural district councils for almost 6,000 cottages, and proposals for a further 7,691 cottages were being prepared.[105] Irish MPs at Westminster presumably echoed councillors' views when they criticised the excessive red tape and delays in the administration of labourers' cottage schemes. They were also critical of regulations which deemed that fishermen and rural tradesmen, who were often poorly housed, were ineligible for labourers' cottages.[106]

The allocation of cottages was a very contentious issue: in its 1901 report, the Board complained that councils tended to include in their housing lists persons 'already in occupation of good houses who could not be deemed to be labourers'. Nevertheless, a clause in the 1903 Wyndham Act — which provided over £100m. to enable Irish tenant farmers to buy their holdings from the landlords — made a significant concession to councillors' views by extending the definition of 'agricultural labourer' to include all persons, other than domestic servants, working for hire (even if only for a short period) who occupied a maximum of one-quarter acre of land and whose wages did not exceed 2/6 (12.5p) a week. This meant that some farmers' sons and migratory labourers became eligible for rehousing.

Road expenditure was another matter where the Board and local authorities did not always agree. The transfer of responsibility for roads from unelected grand juries to rural district councils brought the allocation of road contracts and the determining of expenditure priorities into the popular domain for the first time. Councillors preferred to give priority to repairing and improving local roads, a move which was popular with voters, whereas the Board was keen to develop a national road network which could cope with motor traffic. Many councils also preferred to have road works carried out under direct labour schemes, i.e. with the council employing the workers, rather than hiring contractors, as had been done in the past.[107] Other disputes centred on the awarding of contracts to supply food, fuel and equipment items to institutions such as workhouses or hospitals. The Board appears to have been less conciliatory on this issue than on roads or on labourers' cottages and in some instances initiated prosecutions against councillors who voted on the awarding of contracts in which they had a pecuniary interest.[108]

STAFF RECRUITMENT

In the case of roads and contracts, the key issue was access to employment. Government employment, whether in local authority offices and road contracts or in the civil service, was keenly sought by nationalists and unionists alike, and the merits of an appointment were frequently assessed on the basis of religion, politics or ethnicity. Thus, in the early 1870s when it was proposed to reduce the number of poor law commissioners from four to three or even two, the vice-president argued that four commissionerships provided the opportunity to appoint a catholic commissioner and to combine the 'two chief religions' in the office.[109] With the exception of the small number of staff transferred from England to establish the Poor Law Commission office in Dublin, most LGB staff appear to have been Irish.[110] Until 1870, when competitive examinations were introduced, clerks in the LGB were appointed on foot of a nomination by the lord lieutenant. Salaries in Ireland were lower than those paid for comparable employment in Britain, and promotion prospects in the immediate post-Famine decades were poor because employment had expanded rapidly during the Famine years. Despite repeated demands by the Irish Local Government Board for equal pay with England, Irish officials continued to receive lower salaries for the duration of the Union.[111] Junior staff in the LGB were overwhelmingly Irish and the majority were probably catholic. Irish candidates had a high rate of success in lower-grade civil service examinations, and there was a constant waiting list of candidates seeking transfer to Dublin from London. However, competitive examinations for positions requiring professional and technical qualifications tended to be filled by men from more privileged backgrounds, because of unequal educational opportunities.

From 1834 county surveyors employed by grand juries were appointed on the basis of a competitive examination, conducted by the Commissioners of Public Works — the first appointments made on this basis in the UK.[112] In 1869 the examinations came under the control of the Civil Service Commission, with posts awarded to the candidate obtaining the highest marks in a written examination. The Office of Public Works continued to be responsible for examining the qualifications of assistant county surveyors. These arrangements did not, however, extend to the boroughs; in 1877 a member of Cork Corporation complained to the Select Committee on Taxation of Towns that all the main posts in Cork city, such as engineers and surveyors, were held by protestants.[113]

After 1898 county councils appear to have made considerable efforts to ensure that appointments went to local candidates, who were presumably from the majority religion. Publications such as *The Leader*, edited by D.P. Moran, drew attention to the small numbers of catholics in white-collar positions in major businesses, such as railway companies or the public service.[114] There is little evidence that the LGB had shown interest in the recruitment methods used by local authorities before 1899, but after that date it began to emphasise the need for written examinations and to attempt to impose standard qualifications for posts such as county secretary. However, pressure from local authorities forced the Board to make concessions. Although the 1898 Act had expressed the intention that candidates for senior local authority posts would be examined by the Civil Service Commission, which would also set the minimum qualifications, the Board decided that this would not be 'expedient' and it permitted individual local authorities to set their own examinations, subject to the Board's scrutiny.

Yet, despite this concession, appointments remained a contentious issue. The Board's 1902 report referred to 'certain political differences which have been introduced by some of the smaller bodies into their ordinary business transactions with reference to the appointment of officers and the giving out of contracts',[115] though it added that such cases were exceptional. Nationalist councils were not alone in challenging the Board's involvement in appointments: a bitter dispute erupted between the Board and the Clogher (Co. Tyrone) board of guardians, over the latter's failure to dismiss a delinquent rate collector, whose cause was then adopted by maverick unionist MP William Johnston.[116]

Ultimately local authorities won major concessions, particularly in the appointment of county surveyors. Although candidates continued to sit an examination organised by the Civil Service Commission, this was reduced to the status of a qualifying test and all who passed were eligible for appointment, with the final decision resting with county councillors. Appointments were made after frenetic canvassing. In 1908 the *Irish Builder and Engineer* claimed that 'none but candidates possessing considerable local influence, political or personal, have the slightest chance of being appointed to a County Surveyorship under the existing system'.[117] This procedure was further eroded in 1906 when Cork County Council refused to fill a vacancy for an assistant surveyor from the national panel and applied for permission to hold a special examination, which was restricted to candidates nominated by councillors. Four of the five nominees came from Munster. Other councils introduced Irish-language tests as a means of determining the political ideology of new recruits. Despite this social engineering, changes were slow to be introduced at the top of the local government service. In 1920, fifteen of the forty county surveyors had been appointed prior to 1899.[118]

The LGB's decision to tolerate some manipulation of local appointments may have been an astute move, given that the Board's own recruitment procedures fell far short of the ideals of objective meritocratic hiring. No first division clerks, who were drawn from the elite of university graduates, were employed by the Board until after 1898 when they were recruited for explicitly political reasons. By this stage the examinations to recruit first-division clerks had been tailored to the age, education and abilities of Oxford and Cambridge graduates, and few Irishmen were successful.[119] Sir Henry Robinson, the head of the LGB, believed that there were advantages to the appointment of Englishmen and Scotsmen. As Robinson explained some years later:

> Politics and religion find their way into many matters of living in some parts of Ireland, and as things stood then our staff was nearly all Irishmen and knew almost too much of the political and religious aspect of affairs. I was therefore very anxious to leaven them if I could with a few Englishmen and Scotchmen. I thought they would be perhaps ignorant of these political questions and might look upon things in a new and fresh light and break fresh ground of thought in our brains. The reason we had nearly all Irishmen in the second division was because the salary is very small and if an Irishman is appointed to England it is hard to live on his salary, and his first idea is to get an exchange over here and live with his people.[120]

Robinson had a poor opinion of Irish clerks; he claimed that the Irish lower division men were 'the sons of small farmers & tradesmen & catholics with strong nationalist sympathies', men of a 'much lower class' than their English equivalents.[121] In turn, Irishmen occupying junior positions resented the fact that senior posts went to outsiders. T. P. Gill, secretary of the Department of Agriculture, told the Royal Commission on the Civil Service that he was opposed to the creation of a 'distinct caste system'. He would prefer if senior posts were filled by promoting junior clerks who had obtained further qualifications, such as university degrees, by night-study.[122]

Robinson's attitude was undoubtedly racist. In his memoirs he paints a picture of the Irish people as simple-minded, ignorant and emotional, prone to deceit and violence. He described western guardians as 'such friendly, delightful, simple people. They knew little or nothing of what was going on in the outside world. Few of them could read the newspapers, and had no interest outside their own locality.' His description of sacks of meal being allocated by a government relief ship to the winners of races for bachelors, married men, pregnant women and three-legged races, or of a candidate for local elections seeking contributions to replace his ragged trousers,[123] smack of considerable embroidery, although his evidence to the Royal Commission on the Civil Service was more circumspect: 'the Irishman is brilliant, resourceful and quick but he is rather impulsive and wants [for] the steadiness of the English and the Scots.' It is also laden with racial stereotypes. These were not the most helpful attitudes in a man whose job entailed constant contact with the new councils and whose members may have resembled the western guardians caricatured above.

How far Robinson's attitudes were common to other Board officials is a moot point. Most inspectors — the group who were in closest contact with councillors and local authority staff — were recruited from the younger sons of the Anglo-Irish gentry.[124] Names recurring among inspectors and auditors included those of several landowning families in the west of Ireland: Morris, O'Conor, Kirkwood[125] and Martin of Ross — the family of the writer Violet Martin, of Somerville and Ross fame. The 1873 inquiry into the Irish civil service argued successfully against recruiting inspectors by examination on the grounds that the 'qualities required to make good inspectors are peculiar and not ascertainable by competitive examination'; in addition to 'intellect and education', the position required 'firmness of character combined with mature age and experience'. Alfred Power, the Board's vice-president, believed that office training would spoil a man for such duties.[126] Most inspectors were hired initially on a temporary basis and subsequently were promoted to the permanent staff. Their background was similar to that of the inspectors recruited by the English LGB, which believed that 'above all, the inspector must be a gentleman'. In Ireland, however, such attitudes were more politically contentious. Ireland was also subject to much more detailed inspection. Between 1892 and 1914 the English LGB had an average of fourteen inspectors, plus from three to five assistants; in 1911 Ireland had twenty permanent and temporary inspectors.[127] Although a recommendation was made in the 1870s that auditors should be recruited by open competition, this was successfully resisted by the vice-president of the LGB[128] and they continued to be nominated by the viceroy until the end of British rule in Ireland.

By March 1911 the Board employed 182 established officials and 92 unestablished officials; 108 of these had annual salaries of £160 or more. Although competitive examinations for home civil service

33

appointments were introduced in 1870, 87 of the board's staff with salaries in excess of £100 (probably a majority of the senior staff) who were appointed during the period 1895-1905 did not sit a competitive examination. These included all twenty inspectors, all nineteen permanent or temporary auditors, the legal staff, and thirty-six clerks.[129] Their ranks included two 'temporary lady inspectors', Mrs Dickie and Miss Fitzgerald Kenny, who were appointed in 1902 to supervise the care of boarded-out children. Although they were not the first female civil servants in Ireland — the Department of Agriculture hired female typists in 1901[130] — they were the first to hold senior posts. Many of those who were hired without having to sit examinations held specialist legal, medical or engineering positions, but only patronage can account for the thirty-six clerks. Although the ranks of inspectors still included men such as E.A. Saunderson, a son of the Irish unionist leader Colonel Edward Saunderson of Castle Saunderson, Belturbet, Co. Cavan (previous activity 'travelling' — presumably not as a commercial traveller!), many held medical or engineering qualifications,[131] and had been hired for specialist duties, such as overseeing the construction of labourers' cottages.

Professional qualifications did not exclude patronage: Lady Aberdeen, the vicereine, who was extremely interested in maternity, child health and tuberculosis treatment, tried unsuccessfully to have her favourites appointed as medical inspectors.[132] Although auditors continued to be promoted from the ranks of clerks, from 1902 those appointed were required to obtain a certificate from the civil service commissioners stating that they were qualified to carry out the work: some had previously been employed in banking, stockbroking or insurance. In 1904, following a report by a committee on the audit service, three temporary auditors and additional clerks were hired to bring the audit up to date, and the number of permanent auditors was increased to seventeen, as against nine in the early 1880s. J.W.Drury, an established auditor, was appointed as inspector of audits, fulfilling a recommendation first made in the early 1850s. It was also decreed that future auditors would be required to hold qualifications in either law or accountancy, although men who had served for ten years or more in the accounts branch of a government department were exempt.[133]

Because of the destruction of LGB records in the Custom House fire of May 1921, much remains unknown about relations between Board officials and local councils. As O'Halpin notes: 'it suited the purposes both of advanced separatist groups like Sinn Féin and of committed unionists to denigrate the conduct of local affairs by the Nationalist Party, which until 1918 appeared set fair to become the party of government under home rule'.[134] There were instances of corruption and incompetence in Irish local government, but the LGB does not appear to have been able to confront them; perhaps it felt ill at ease criticising a democratically elected council. The Board's *modus operandi* meant that reports from auditors and inspectors concentrated on detail, rather than on policy, and the Board's powers over unsatisfactory local authorities were more reactive than proactive.[135]

There were also some inherent contradictions in its approach. For example, between 1900 and 1914 the Board carried out three major inquiries into public health and housing in Dublin. The 1900 inquiry revealed a picture of appalling housing conditions, inadequate cleansing, plus a proliferation of insanitary slaughterhouses within the city centre. In 1906 D. Edgar Flinn, the board's medical inspector, produced another critical report which suggested that little attention had been paid to the recommendations contained in the 1900 inquiry. The 1914 report on housing reiterated many points made on previous occasions.[136] It contained detailed evidence of the Corporation's failure to enforce existing sanitary legislation, for which the LGB was ultimately responsible, without addressing the question of whether the LGB had been negligent in failing to ensure the Corporation's compliance. The report was also tainted by its political subtext: an attempt to make the city's tenements and Dublin Corporation scapegoats for the 1913 Lock-out and to present the shortcomings of Dublin Corporation as evidence that Irish nationalists were incapable of self-government.[137]

LOCAL GOVERNMENT REFORM: FINANCE AND OTHER MATTERS

The difficulties which Dublin Corporation faced in attempting to provide a growing range of services without adequate income were common, to some extent, to all Irish local authorities. The LGB report for 1896 revealed that liabilities exceeded assets in 30 per cent of the country's poor law unions and, although the situation was worst in western areas, no part of Ireland was immune. The widening gap between expenditure and revenue was not unique to Ireland.[138] In 1888 the British government assigned half the income from probate duties to a new local taxation account, which transferred it to local authorities as a subsidy towards the cost of current expenditure. The move was prompted by growing resentment from ratepayers at rising poundage charges. Ireland received 9 per cent of the Local Taxation Account,[139] and its share remained constant when beer and spirit duties were subsequently diverted to this account. Asa Briggs has noted that by the 1890s English cities were no longer able to fund additional expenditure from rising valuations.[140] The position was worse in rural areas which were suffering the consequences of agricultural depression.

In Ireland, land provided the overwhelming majority of rateable income. The Royal Commission on Local Taxation was established in 1896 to explore possible solutions to this problem.[141] Like the British equivalent, the commission's Irish report emphasised the need to distinguish between local and national services and maintained that the latter should be funded by central taxation. Many Irish boards of guardians had been arguing this case for years. A majority of Commission members agreed that Ireland should receive a higher share of Imperial funds relative to population, to take account of the country's poverty and more centralised administration. They recommended that the Irish share of beer and spirit duties should be increased from 9 to 11 per cent. A more radical minority report focused on the inequitable incidence of local taxation between rich and poor areas and emphasised the need 'to equalise the burdens in all localities except where extravagance entails an exceptionally heavy charge; and, to discourage extravagance in wealthy districts so as to make possible the levelling up of administration in backward districts to a proper pitch of efficiency.' It recommended that the Irish local taxation account should be increased 'to a moderate extent' following the reorganisation of local taxation in the United Kingdom, and that the money should be allocated on the basis of need.[142]

By 1900 the highest levels of local taxation were found in the poorest areas. Annual average rate poundages ranged from 2/7 (13p) in Armagh and 2/9 (14p) in Newtownards, Co. Down, to 6/6 (32.5p) in Belmullet, Co. Mayo, 6/7 (33p) in Clifden, Co. Galway and 7/3 (36p) in Glenties, Co. Donegal.[143] Although the produce of 1d (.4p) in the pound varied from £584 in Killmallock, Co. Limerick to £45 in Belmullet, both were expected to provide identical services. Exchequer grants in aid of local taxation took no account of local per capita valuation, or expenditure commitments. The agricultural grant transferred a sum to each poor law union equal to half the amount levied in poor law and county cess on agricultural land. In 1906/07 Killmallock Union received £6,104 and Belmullet Union £765. Wealthy unions also benefited disproportionately from grants towards the salaries of workhouse medical officers and dispensary doctors or the salaries of workhouse school teachers. In 1902 the LGB froze each union's share on the basis of the previous year's expenditure, a step which did nothing to redress previous inequities.[144]

Sir Henry Robinson acknowledged that in order to introduce a system of exchequer grants which would equalise the rates burden throughout Ireland, it would first be necessary to ensure that all rateable property was valued on a uniform basis. It was widely believed that Griffith's valuation was no longer an 'efficient or fair basis on which to impose local taxation'.[145] A government inquiry, carried out in conjunction with the Royal Commission on Local Taxation, recommended that a general revaluation be conducted which would remedy inconsistencies such as the failure to take account of drainage and land reclamation and the undervaluing of Dublin property.[146] This recommendation was strongly opposed by both landlords and farmers because they feared that it would lead to higher taxes and to an increase in judicial rents, which were paid by three-quarters of all farmers.[147] Consequently the select committee concluded that it would be unwise to carry out a revaluation until most farmers owned their land.[148]

Local authority finances became a live political issue in the years immediately after 1898. Unionists and nationalists united in criticising the fact that local taxes rose in most counties in 1899 and 1900, despite the introduction of a sizeable agricultural rates grant.[149] The LGB argued that this was only a temporary phenomenon, resulting from the cost of establishing the new councils. However in 1902/03, rates poundages in most local authority areas remained above the 1899/1900 levels and they continued to rise steadily until the outbreak of World War I. By 1913/14 the local authority rates bill stood at £3.534m., compared with £2.889m. in 1899/1900.[150] Irish politicians of all political persuasions demanded that the exchequer should meet the cost of lunatic asylums, cattle disease eradication and workhouses.[151] Farmers protested that the agricultural grant had provided much less relief than had been anticipated because the growing complexity of local administration had resulted in higher administrative costs.[152]

Administrative costs were widely criticised. Councillors objected to the high salaries paid to county secretaries and surveyors and, when the LGB recommended that these be increased to take account of the additional work following on the 1898 Act, many councils refused to do so.[153] When Wexford County Council mounted a successful court challenge to the LGB's authority to determine the pay of its assistant county surveyor in 1901, the Board was widely condemned at Westminster as a 'tyrannical' and 'dictatorial' body. Some nationalist politicians harboured the suspicion that the Board was forcing councils to increase expenditure, in the expectation that the ensuing rate increases would make nationalist councillors unpopular. They also believed that the board had delayed some items of expenditure until landlords had been largely relieved of rates.[154] Yet despite recurrent protests, rate collection figures after 1898 remained satisfactory.

POOR LAW REFORM

Although workhouses accounted for a declining share of local expenditure,[155] they were a perennial target for those seeking to reduce costs. Many workhouses built or extended during the Famine years were now more than half empty. In 1883 boards of guardians from east Ulster unions demanded that the Board begin a programme of amalgamating unions. Similar resolutions proliferated from 1886 onwards. A small number of unions were amalgamated, but in 1896 the LGB announced that no further requests would be granted, pending a comprehensive reorganisation of the Irish poor law.[156] A bill dealing with these matters was introduced into parliament in 1897, though it was hastily abandoned until legislation reforming local government had been enacted.[157]

The report of the Royal Commission on Local Taxation, published in 1902, recommended that local authorities should be relieved of the cost of main roads and of poor relief, and in 1903 a Viceregal Commission was established to ascertain 'whether any changes are necessary or desirable, with the object of reducing or adjusting local taxation without impairing efficiency in administration'. It recommended replacing workhouses with specialist institutions catering for the elderly, the insane and unmarried mothers. Children would be boarded out in the community; destitute widows with one child would become eligible for outdoor relief, and the Gregory clause, prohibiting outdoor relief for landholders, would be repealed. The Commission also recommended the establishment of a state medical system, funded by the exchequer, and that all hospitals, regardless of their status, be placed under county or district control. All contact between hospitals and the poor law should be severed and public sanitoria should be established for the treatment of tuberculosis. Two of the Commission's three members, the chairman, W.L. Micks, secretary of the Congested Districts Board and LGB commissioner, and E. Coey Bigger, a medical inspector at the LGB, recommended that the county replace the union as the area of charge, with county councils being given greater control over the estimates furnished by district councils and committees. They also recommended that, with minor exceptions, union boundaries should no longer cross county lines.

The Commission opposed the introduction of a national rate because of the anomalies in valuation. If these anomalies were overcome, it proposed that a national rate should be struck by a small body of salaried officials, who would be selected by representatives of local councils. Micks and Bigger also endorsed the recommendation in the minority report of the Royal Commission that the local taxation fund should be allocated on the basis of need. However, they expressed the hope that this would be done by an 'elected body' representing local authorities. This proposal must be seen in the context of the abortive 1904 devolution scheme adopted by the Conservative chief secretary George Wyndham. The Commission proposed the establishment of a financial council, presided over by the lord lieutenant, with equal numbers of nominated and elected members to 'examine, supervise and control' all Irish expenditure. Similarly unsuccessful proposals for an Irish Council were developed by the Liberal chief secretary, James Bryce, and his under-secretary, Sir Anthony McDonnell, in 1907 in an effort to free the Liberal government from the albatross of Irish Home Rule.[158]

Since the majority report of the Viceregal Commission was drafted by an LGB commissioner and a medical inspector, it probably reflected the Board's views.[159] In contrast, the dissenting report of the Commission's third member, nationalist MP George Murnaghan, objected to the centralising tendency which, in his view, would result in the move to county rating and the 'curtailment of the control of local authorities'. Murnaghan claimed that the main supporters of county rating were medical practitioners who sought uniform standards of hospital management, whereas only ten of the country's 159 boards of guardians favoured such a move.[160] He suggested that the financial problems of impoverished western unions should be met by a grant-in-aid from the state, not by amalgamation. Many ratepayers undoubtedly objected to widening the area of charge, on the grounds that it forced them to pay for services from which they did not benefit. Before 1898, the cost of public water supplies was charged to the area which benefited directly, such as a village; the 1898 Act made the union the unit of charge. Although this change was designed to remove some long-standing tax inequities,[161] it created new anomalies. A witness to the Royal Commission on Local Taxation alleged that in the Inishowen peninsula of County Donegal it had resulted in rural councillors, mostly farmers, blocking water or sewerage schemes in small towns and villages.[162]

Both the majority and minority reports of the Viceregal Commission were overshadowed by the Liberal government's mammoth Royal Commission on the Poor Laws. The majority Irish report, published in 1909, concurred with the majority report of the Viceregal Commission in recommending county rating, the restructuring of poor relief on a county basis and the replacement of workhouses by specialist institutions, though it adopted a more stringent approach to outdoor relief. Unlike the Viceregal Commission, which had favoured detaching medical services from the poor law, the majority report of the Royal Commission recommended that the link be retained, with those who received medical treatment being required to prove need. Both reports favoured centralisation: the Royal Commission recommended abolishing boards of guardians, reducing the number of rural district councillors and their responsibilities and transferring most authority to county level. Poor relief would be administered by a new statutory authority — the Public Assistance authority — with members chosen by the county council, half of them council members and the remainder drawn from voluntary bodies. It would work closely with voluntary committees representing religious and other charitable institutions. This recommendation was also included in the English report.

The majority Irish report was a conservative document, reflecting the views of Dr Denis Kelly, bishop of Ross. Russell Wakefield, Francis Chandler, George Lansbury and Beatrice Webb, authors of the celebrated English minority report, produced a minority Irish report which advocated more generous treatment for the unemployed and a state medical service, on the lines recommended by the Viceregal Commission. This report was savagely attacked by both Dr Kelly and Sir Henry Robinson; they alleged that two of the quartet had failed to visit Ireland, while a third had made a visit even briefer than the notorious six-week visit of Sir George Nicholls, originator of the Irish poor law, in 1837.

HOME RULE FINANCE AND LOCAL GOVERNMENT

By the time the Royal Commission on the Poor Laws reported in 1909, the issue was increasingly overshadowed by the financial implications of Home Rule. Local government was among the departments earmarked for transfer, and it was envisaged that a ministry for local affairs would replace the Local Government Board.[163] By 1910, however, the financial basis of Home Rule was looking rather uncertain. In 1896, when the report of the Childers Committee was issued, Irish revenue exceeded expenditure by almost £2m.; by 1911, when the topic was investigated by the Primrose Committee, expenditure had increased by £5.4m., a rise of almost 50 per cent. It now exceeded revenue by more than £1m..[164] Half this increase, £2.4m. for old-age pensions and £850,000 as a grant in aid of local taxation, was controlled by the LGB.[165] Old-age pensions were awarded to those over seventy years of age, subject to a means test, and eligibility was determined by committees appointed by county councils which were supervised by the LGB. Because civil registration of births did not begin in Ireland until 1864, there was considerable scope for falsifying ages, with the result that Ireland had proportionately twice as many old-age pensioners as England, Scotland or Wales.[166]

Senior Home Rule politicians were dismayed at the growing gap between expenditure and revenue. Erskine Childers believed that it damaged the prospects of Home Rule; Tom Kettle, the Irish Parliamentary Party's acknowledged financial expert, regarded it as part of a unionist conspiracy to prevent Home Rule.[167] Both men emphasised the need for economies in order to restore balance to Irish finances, and Kettle also advocated tax increases. However the party offered few concrete suggestions for economies, other than Childers's proposal to halve old-age pensions, or his statement that an Irish parliament would find it necessary to revise the system of local taxation grants. There was a naive belief that the public service was

41

overmanned and overpaid, and that this offered considerable scope for economy.[168] Proposed economies took no account of the growing demand from local authorities for central government to assume a greater share of their costs. The 1914 Dublin Housing Inquiry revealed that it would need a capital investment of £3m. and a substantial exchequer subsidy if the city's housing crisis was to be resolved.[169] A report by the General Council of County Councils on the financial clauses in the 1912 Home Rule Bill was unable to suggest 'any effective economies'.[170] In January 1914, with Home Rule apparently only months away, a deputation of mayors met John Redmond and J.J. Clancy, the Irish Party's spokesman on housing, to seek assurance that housing grants would continue to be available from the Imperial exchequer after the introduction of Home Rule.[171]

By August 1914 when the outbreak of war led to Home Rule being postponed indefinitely, the Liberal government had already conceded that Ulster would receive separate treatment, including the provision of its own local government administration.[172] Despite the decision to postpone the introduction of Home Rule, Dublin Castle officials and leaders of the Irish Party held meetings to discuss the transition to Home Rule until September 1915.[173] The meetings, held in John Dillon's house in North Great George's Street, were attended by John Redmond, John Dillon and J.J.Clancy and various senior Dublin Castle officials. At the first meeting, Irish under-secretary Sir Mathew Nathan presented a document which envisaged replacing the existing 'Castle' boards with government departments, including a department of local affairs.[174] At a later meeting he informed the Irish politicians that he had requested the heads of the Irish departments to prepare confidential memoranda on the implications for their departments of the 1914 Home Rule Act,[175] though the only memorandum which survives concerns the Department of Agriculture.[176] The first meeting discussed the extent of the Irish Treasury's control over the new departments. A subsequent memo by Frank Greer, the parliamentary draftsman of Irish bills,[177] suggested that the Irish Treasury should be established without an order in council, thus obviating the need to define its powers and functions in a manner 'which might prove too narrow'.[178] The fact that the Irish Party leaders accepted this idea suggests that they envisaged tight controls on spending, which was unsurprising given the financial difficulties they faced.

Although few details survive concerning the proposed structure of the Ministry of Local Affairs, we know that it would have assumed responsibility for the duties of the Local Government Board, the Registrar General's office, the inspection of lunatic asylums, charitable donations and bequests, and the functions of the lord lieutenant concerning hospitals and charities. Dublin Castle later added to this list the Alkali Acts and the criminal lunatic asylum at Dundrum, though Irish politicians suggested that they should be controlled by the new Irish Department of Justice.[179] The proposed transfer posed few problems, since, unlike other departments, such as Justice or the Treasury, none of the LGB's functions would remain under Westminster control, though in March 1915 Dillon asked how new and existing local loans would be affected by Home Rule;[180] there is no evidence that he was given an answer.

Although the Irish leaders were anxious to have an executive in place before the new legislature came into being, they were unwilling to commit themselves in advance to major administrative reforms. At the second meeting, J.J.Clancy, MP for North County Dublin, proposed that only changes 'shown to be imperative' should be considered.[181] A memorandum drafted subsequently by Dublin Castle agreed:

> It is essential that the identity of the transferred department should
> not be lost if its work is to be carried on without intermission,
> because all transferred departments have functions and
> constitutions of their own and any radical alteration of these
> beyond what is absolutely required owing to the changes of
> Government would lead to very many difficulties and great
> confusion, without any compensating advantage.

This official argued that it would be disastrous to abolish an existing agency such as the LGB or the Congested Districts Board.[182] When these negotiations ended in September 1915, the titles and functions of the proposed ministries and the transfer orders had been agreed. All that remained was to name the ministers. No list appears to have survived, so the name of the putative Minister for Local Affairs is unknown.

CONCLUSIONS

The Irish Local Government Board and its antecedents played a major role in what has been termed the nineteenth-century revolution in government. Central government involvement in local government increased dramatically under the Act of Union. Part of this growth, such as the LGB's involvement in public health and housing, followed on English development, but other aspects, notably the extension of public access to workhouse hospitals and the provision of public dispensaries, were in response to specific Irish needs. Unlike its English counterpart, the Irish LGB cannot be seen as an agency that was concerned only with 'gas and water' or with housing and sewers.

The Board was one of the most prominent manifestations of Britain's presence in Ireland: workhouses, dispensaries, public works schemes, LGB inspectors and rate collectors touched all lives. The authority exercised by grand juries, local councils or boards of guardians was of much greater importance to most Irish men and women than distant doings in Westminster. This had multiple consequences: on the one hand, the Board was a source of finance for distressed communities, to be petitioned or hoodwinked as the need arose. During the nineteenth century, many impoverished areas along the western seaboard became heavily dependent on its assistance. Local communities often resented the Board's intrusion into their affairs and the supervision exercised by inspectors and auditors frequently created tensions between the centre and the periphery. Some disputes reflect cultural and political divisions: nationalist councils were incensed that what they regarded as a unionist board in Dublin should veto their appointments or surcharge them for spending money on bunting to welcome a prominent catholic churchman or a national hero. However the fact that landlord-dominated boards of guardians in the mid-nineteenth century also resented outside intrusion suggests that the issue transcends the question of nationalism versus unionism.

Throughout the nineteenth century it is notable that the preferred method of reforming local government invariably entailed an increase in central control. The only exception is the 1898 Act. Thus, instead of reforming the method of selecting grand juries and early nineteenth-century corporations, the Irish administration preferred to enact legislation such as the 1840 Municipal Corporations Ireland Act, which significantly reduced the autonomy of local authorities. It also transferred much of the grand jury's traditional responsibility for the administration of justice to stipendiary magistrates and established a centralised police force. Although this attitude reflected a reluctance to strip the Anglo-Irish ascendancy of its remaining powers, it also suggested that the Irish administration deeply distrusted the popular will. It furthermore implies an unwritten assumption that paid officials constituted a politically neutral caste, though the background and attitudes of some key LGB officials suggests that this was not so.

The system of local government which the independent Irish state inherited contained many flaws. There was an urgent need to reform the poor law, and both the Viceregal Commission and the Royal Commission favoured a county-based system. Although this matter appeared capable of resolution, the broader problems of local taxation and the demarcation between central and local expenditure were more intractable. By the end of the nineteenth century it was apparent that rates were incapable of providing adequate funding for local government expenditure. The problem was compounded when the British government introduced partial de-rating of agricultural land, both in response to agricultural depression and as a means of placating Irish landlord interests. The concession set a precedent for further demands.

In the case of Britain, where agriculture accounted for only a small proportion of income and wealth, meeting this demand was not impossible. However, in an agricultural country such as Ireland, the chronic pressure for further reductions in the amount of local taxes paid by agriculture threatened to undermine the basis of local authority finance. Despite the fragile nature of their tax base, Irish local authorities were under considerable pressure, from both the LGB and from voters, to provide higher standards of public service. The Board attempted to ensure that Irish towns and cities met standards in housing and public health which had been set in a more affluent England; rural labourers and small farmers demanded labourers' cottages and jobs on public works. With the exception of some Ulster ratepayers and those living in middle-class Dublin suburbs, there was little pressure for curbs on expenditure. Elsewhere, protests against high rates took the form of demands for greater assistance from central funds. Such a tendency was unwelcome to a prospective Home Rule administration, given the existing deficit of Irish expenditure over revenue. It also appears that the detailed scrutiny of local authority business conducted by auditors and inspectors failed to tackle strategic financial issues. Maurice Hayes, who served as town clerk in Downpatrick in the 1950s (at a time when he claims the powers and functions of local government had been unchanged for almost a century) noted that the audit 'was conducted as a legalistic scrutiny of correctness rather than as a review of efficiency or effectiveness'.[183]

Nevertheless, it is important not to be unduly critical. In the absence of LGB auditors, standards of probity and efficiency would have been lower. Inspectors raised public awareness of the relationship between dirt, poor housing and disease. This was particularly important in those rural communities which lacked a body of educated and committed lay men or women. The high degree of continuity in administrative procedures between the Local Government Board and independent Ireland cannot be entirely attributed to conservatism or inertia; some of it reflects the fact that parts of the old system functioned effectively.

CHAPTER TWO

LOCAL GOVERNMENT ADMINISTRATION AND THE IRISH REVOLUTION, 1919-22: A TALE OF TWO RIVAL ADMINISTRATIONS

DÁIL ÉIREANN AND LOCAL GOVERNMENT: THE STORY BEFORE JUNE 1920

The original blueprint of the early twentieth-century Sinn Féin party had assigned county councils and the General Council of County Councils a key role in any campaign of passive resistance against the British government. It also assumed that councils would give Irish manufacturers preference in awarding contracts in order to foster the revival of Irish industry. Although Sinn Féin failed to capture a parliamentary seat before 1917, it was more successful in local elections and by 1911 the party held 12 of the 80 seats on Dublin Corporation, where Sinn Féin councillors included two future Ministers for Local Government, W.T. Cosgrave and Seán T. O'Kelly.[1] In 1917, however, the party was taken over by veterans of the 1916 Rising and, although ten per cent of those elected to the first Dáil had served on local authorities,[2] local government was not mentioned directly in the statements issued by Dáil Éireann in January 1919, nor did the Dáil address a message to Irish local authorities, though it sent a communication to the free nations of the world. However, the Democratic Programme, drafted as a *quid pro quo* for Labour's abstention in the 1918 general election, committed the Dáil to substituting 'a sympathetic native scheme for the care of the nation's aged and infirm' as an alternative to the poor law and gave an undertaking 'that no child shall suffer hunger or cold from lack of food or clothing or shelter'.[3]

The rise of militant nationalism, which culminated in the founding of Dáil Éireann, was slow to affect local government. Although many local authorities passed resolutions condemning the 1916 executions or expressing opposition to partition, these were in the tradition of earlier

47

resolutions supporting the Boers or Home Rule and did not bring any significant change in relations with the Local Government Board. During 1916/17 the Board approved requests from Galway County Council and Enniscorthy, Carlow, Drogheda, Naas, Navan, Wexford and Tipperary Urban District Councils for permission to invest in the war loan. Although the threat of conscription in the spring of 1918 brought a flurry of protests from councils whose officials would have been responsible for its implementation,[4] the Board continued to receive the usual stream of deputations from nationalist councils. Two LGB officials were dismissed for political reasons: J. J. McElligott, a first-division clerk (and future secretary of the Department of Finance), was the most senior civil servant to take part in the 1916 Rising;[5] Thomas McArdle, a second division clerk, who later joined the staff of the Dáil Department of Local Government and who became first secretary of the Department of Health, was dismissed in December 1918 for refusing to take the oath of allegiance as required under the Defence of the Realm Regulations.[6] Any temptation which local authorities might have felt to join the Dáil Éireann bandwagon was probably offset by the lure of government money. With the coming of peace, the British government promised not only to restore the grants and loans which had disappeared during the war years, but to provide unprecedented subsidies for local authority housing. Indeed, one scholar has argued recently that the British government was prepared to offer substantial funds for housing in an effort to retain the support of Irish nationalists.[7]

Dáil Éireann made no immediate effort to win the loyalty of Irish local authorities. In February 1919 a committee of Sinn Féin was unable to decide whether local authorities should continue to co-operate with the LGB.[8] At its second session on 2 April 1919, the Dáil appointed W.T. Cosgrave as Secretary (Minister) for Local Government[9] and nominated a committee of ten Teachta Dála (TDs) to help him prepare a policy statement. Cosgrave reported to the fourth session of Dáil Éireann on 17 June. Although his statement is not reproduced in the minutes, the ensuing debate indicates that TDs were primarily concerned about housing and poor relief. Cosgrave proposed a motion, endorsing the 'laudable desires of the people towards ownership' and drawing the attention of Sinn Féin clubs or *cumainn* to the urgent necessity of dealing with the housing question 'in a manner satisfactory to the people'. Local committees should draw up an estimate of housing needs and exert pressure on local authorities to embark on housing schemes.[10] The motion was mere window-dressing; the LGB had already made similar recommendations to greater effect and was actively encouraging councils to build houses.

The Dáil also established a housing committee consisting of twelve TDs plus Mrs Jenny Wyse Power and Dublin Councillor J.V. Lawless. After three meetings they concluded that 'no better machinery' for the advancement of working-class housing existed than the 1919 Housing (Ireland) Bill and they urged all local authorities to proceed 'full steam ahead' to avail of its facilities. It was decided that the Dáil Ministry should issue a circular to all Sinn Féin *cumainn* summarising the provisions of the 'English' legislation and urging them to promote appropriate schemes; 2,000 copies were duly produced.[11] Unfortunately, the LGB's reaction to this unsolicited publicity is not known. When some TDs objected to the circular, Cosgrave replied that it was not designed to influence the course of legislation enacted by the 'English' [*sic*] parliament 'or in any way to assist or recognise that body'.[12]

Issuing the circular was probably an attempt to disguise the Dáil's impotence, which was entirely due to lack of capital. In March 1920 Clonakilty Rural District Council requested a loan of £1,300 from the Dáil-controlled National Land Bank, to help finance a housing scheme. When Cosgrave formally requested that the loan be granted, Diarmaid Ó hEigeartaigh, secretary to the Ministry (government), pointed out that the money would have to be provided by the Department of Finance. Although Michael Collins, Minister for Finance in the Dáil government, dismissed Cosgrave's intervention as 'nonsense', the Dáil Ministry approved the loan on 18 March. This appears to have been an isolated case: in July 1920 when the acting town clerk of Nenagh made a similar request, Collins initialled a memorandum to the effect that it already had been decided to refuse all applications for housing finance and suggesting that a general letter to this effect be kept on file.[13] In the autumn of 1919 the Dáil nominated Cosgrave, Seán T. O'Kelly and Robert Briscoe to attend a special meeting of the Association of Municipal Authorities which was demanding better financial assistance for housing from the Local Government Board.

The other matter concerning TDs was poor law reform. When Galway TD Frank Fahy drew the Dáil's attention to a resolution from Loughrea Board of Guardians, urging that state aid be substituted for the system of poor relief, he was informed that the matter would be dealt with 'as soon as the Irish Government is in a position to function'.[14] The committee responsible for local government circulated a report, prepared for propaganda purposes, highlighting the limitations which English poor law legislation imposed on Irish local authorities.[15] Otherwise, the Dáil's concern with local government was limited to urging TDs and *cumainn* to improve their constituency organisations and to exercising due attention in selecting candidates for the forthcoming local elections.[16]

THE 'CLEAN BREAK'?

Although in January 1920 Sinn Féin captured control of 72 out of the 127 urban councils and county boroughs, including a narrow majority on Dublin Corporation,[17] this brought no obvious extension in the Dáil's remit.[18] The Dáil requested that Sinn Féin-controlled councils pass a resolution of allegiance to Dáil Éireann and refuse to assist the British authorities in their efforts to replace information lost in raids on income tax offices. Urban and municipal authorities were reluctant to act independently of rural councils and county councils, but the Dáil gave no direction on the appropriate relationship between republican local authorities and the Local Government Board. Kevin O'Higgins, the substitute Minister for Local Government, who was appointed following Cosgrave's arrest on 25 March,[19] believed that any 'drastic instructions' would lead to the postponement of forthcoming rural and county council elections.

When O'Higgins took office, the Local Government Committee (established the previous year) was in disarray. In May 1920 he convened a conference of local authority officials and elected local representatives to examine the consequences of local authorities severing contact with the LGB. While this would entail the loss of exchequer grants, equal to a rate to 3/2 (16p) in the pound in Dublin County Borough and 2/6 (12.5p) in Cork, in areas which were active in the Anglo-Irish war, this was only a fraction of the cost of malicious injury awards. Claims lodged in Cork during the first half of 1920 amounted to a rate of 14/3 (71p) in the pound. O'Higgins suggested that if councils chose to break with the LGB, they should see that this occurred over the question of criminal and malicious injuries claims because it would 'bring many people on our side who would be against us if they considered we had ourselves invited or precipitated it'. O'Higgins emphasised the desirability of 'keeping the enemy in the wrong in the eyes of the people' and recommended that officials should send copies of local authority minutes to both the LGB and the Dáil. He was loath to adopt a 'self-denying ordinance' against accepting British government loans for housing or drainage and was equally reluctant to forego the 'very good value' afforded by LGB audits, though he believed that councils should be prepared to defend their right to appoint officials and to require them to take an oath of allegiance to Dáil Éireann.

O'Higgins's caution was governed by his belief that the banks, which acted as local authority treasurers, would meet any legal claim served on them to pay malicious injury awards. Although he suggested that 'a skilful and friendly accountant' could ensure that a local authority never ran a credit balance, he recognised that this would require that the banks approve councils operating on overdraft for most of the year. As an alternative to 'endeavour[ing] to function ourselves under hopelessly unfavourable conditions necessitating the invidious alternatives of drastic reductions of staff or drastic increase of rates', O'Higgins suggested that Sinn Féin should abandon local administration to the British or, as he termed them, 'the plunderers, adding to their other difficulties the problem of collecting rates from a hostile population with an unfriendly staff'.[20]

When the ministry (cabinet) considered this report, opinions were clearly divided. While some members favoured making a clean break with the LGB, O'Higgins refused to take responsibility for issuing such a recommendation. He believed that inexperienced councils might not survive in such circumstances; if they collapsed, it would 'cause a lamentable political reaction'. A decision was deferred. O'Higgins prepared a second report, which again argued that the Dáil should attempt to manoeuvre the 'enemy' into taking full responsibility for local government. He also expressed the view that councils which refused to strike a malicious injury rate were unlikely to suffer the loss of exchequer grants until April 1921 (the new financial year); by then the Dáil would have explored the feasibility of functioning without such aid and would have identified possible economies. In the event, the special meeting of the ministry was deferred, allegedly because of the arrival of an American visitor; this either suggests that local government was given a low priority, or more probably that the cabinet was divided on the issue.[21]

JUNE 1920: LOCAL ELECTIONS AND AFTERMATH

Sinn Féin gained control of 28 out of 33 county councils and 172 of the 206 rural councils in the local elections of June 1920.[22] As instructed, the majority passed resolutions of allegiance to 'the authority of Dáil Éireann as the duly elected Government of the Irish People' and transmitted a copy to the Dáil.[23] It was unclear what would happen next. Although O'Higgins claimed that 'it would be news to him that big issues were to be decided at Strokestown or Clonakilty, and not by the Dáil', the latter failed to give any guidance to the new councils. On 29 June, O'Higgins again argued in the Dáil against a break with the LGB and proposed the establishment of yet another commission of experts to examine whether local government could survive without British loans and grants. Local authorities were ordered to take no action without the minister's authority, pending this report. Although this motion was carried, opinion was clearly divided. Michael Collins, who apparently favoured a break, argued that forwarding minutes to the LGB was tantamount to recognising their authority. Cathal Brugha proposed undermining local government by a combination of rates' strikes and guerrilla warfare. Cork lord mayor Terence MacSwiney was one of the few to support O'Higgins.[24]

In the event, the big decisions were taken by Clare County Council and by the British Lord Privy Seal Andrew Bonar Law. On 24 July the former decided to cease lodging rates with the county treasurer or bank because it feared that the money would be sequestered to pay malicious injury awards. Rates would be lodged in future with three secret trustees. If the British government withheld the agricultural grant, the largest component of the local taxation grant, the council proposed that farmers should deduct an equivalent amount from their rent or land annuities and pay it to the council. Clare County Council would deem landlords to be liable for their gross rates, including the value of the withheld agricultural grant. The council urged rate collectors to resign their service with the LGB and guaranteed that they would be reappointed by the Republic without loss of pension rights.[25] On 29 July, before the Dáil could respond, the LGB issued a circular letter to local authorities announcing that all grants would be withheld unless they gave a formal undertaking in advance to submit accounts for audit by the Board and to obey all its rules. This pre-emptive strike was ordered by Bonar Law, apparently against the advice of Sir Henry Robinson.

On 22 July 1920 Robinson had supplied Sir Alfred Cope, a senior official in Dublin Castle, with a list of all local authorities which had formally expressed the intention of disregarding demands for the payment of malicious and criminal injuries, adding 'I think you may take it that every county and borough council outside those included in the area of the Northern parliament intends to disregard demands made for payment for compensation'.[26] Although only county and borough councils were liable for malicious injury claims, the circular acted as a pre-emptive strike against urban and rural district councils which had not yet declared any intention of illegal activity.

The LGB circular deprived the Dáil of the luxury of indecision. The first meeting of the Dáil Commission on Local Government, which consisted of TDs and councillors plus Tady Ó Cinnéide, accountant to Kerry County Council, and Denis Carolan Rushe, secretary to Monaghan County Council, adopted an interim report. This recommended that councils consider following the Clare strategy, though it also approved an alternative proposal by James MacNeill of Dublin County Council (a future governor general of the Irish Free State) that rates should be paid to parish-based ratepayers' protection associations which would assume responsibility for settling bills. On 10 August 1920, however, the Dáil Ministry of Local Government instructed all councils to adopt the Clare solution.[27]

The remainder of the interim report was largely rhetorical: local authorities were urged to safeguard rate books and to make provision for auditing local authority accounts; they should consider introducing economies such as the abolition of workhouses and the adoption of combined purchase schemes; labour leaders were entreated to curb demands for wage increases and to prevent the transport of goods seized in lieu of rates. Councils should urge all men between the ages of eighteen and forty to join the Irish Republican Army. When the report was debated in the Dáil on 6 August, the acting President, Arthur Griffith, objected to the final clause on the grounds that 'it would mean that they were conferring on the local bodies the power to determine National Policy'. The word 'advise' was substituted for 'urge'.[28] The brief exchange signalled the potential tensions between local initiative and national control.

By 28 September 1920 only Counties Antrim, Armagh and Londonderry had given the assurances sought by the LGB, though Down County Council was expected to follow suit. The majority responded with formal refusals, marking the circular as read, burning it or formally placing it in the wastepaper basket. Outside Ulster, only Navan and Midleton Urban Councils, Gorey and Tuam Rural District Councils and Gorey Board of Guardians gave the commitments sought. Loyal counties which contained rebel urban or rural districts had their grant payments reduced *pro rata*. At first the Board was unable to pay grants to loyal urban and rural councils or boards of guardians in rebel counties, but by January 1921 it had authorised payments to loyal areas in east Donegal and in County Cavan. Several boards of guardians — Athy, Boyle, Ardee, Kinlough and Athlone — almost received grants from the Board, though no money was actually paid.[29]

Although Dublin Castle files suggest that the break with the LGB was almost universal outside six Ulster counties, this appears to underestimate the ambiguous response of many nationalist councils. Kilkenny County Council does not seem to have contacted the Dáil ministry until the spring of 1921.[30] Even though O'Higgins had opposed the clean break, perhaps because he was aware of the potential pitfalls, once the decision had been taken, both he and Cosgrave were determined to end all contact with the Custom House. Dublin Corporation was severely reprimanded when a press notice in October 1920 announced that the LGB was to audit its accounts.[31] Clifden Board of Guardians and Rural District Council, whose members were described by the Dáil inspector as 'a shifty lot', continued to send copies of minutes to both the Dáil and the LGB until the Truce, which marked an end to the fighting in July 1921, despite his efforts to 'whip them to a sense of dignity'.[32] County councils appear to have condoned the fact that many county tuberculosis committees, which included unelected members who were often from landed families, continued to submit reports and accounts to the LGB, since the alternative was to abandon treatment because of lack of funds. When Cosgrave discovered that the South Tipperary TB committee was in contact with the LGB, he warned that the 'council cannot serve two masters and if they cannot make up their mind to break off communications with the English [*sic*] LGB they can have no further dealings with this Department.'[33] Dublin Castle continued to pay grants to county committees of agriculture, 'provided they abstained from passing objectionable resolutions and undertook to submit their accounts to audit'.[34] Cosgrave assented to this practice, although O'Higgins deplored his inconsistency.[35]

Even though many councils believed that breaking with the LGB did not preclude them from communicating with other British ministries, the unemployment grants committee rejected all grant applications from councils which had sworn allegiance to Dáil Éireann on the grounds that they were 'unwilling to comply with a Local Government Board audit'.[36] In contrast, in the autumn of 1920 the Ministry of Transport issued a circular to Irish local authorities offering grants for road improvements on condition that councils acknowledge the Ministry's power to sanction the appointment or dismissal of the surveyors who supervised the work. The Dáil ministry alleged that this conciliatory approach was prompted by a wish to improve roads in order to facilitate military traffic and by a desire to gain control over local authority engineers. It advised councils to reject the ministry's conditions. Councils applying for Ministry of Transport grants should indicate that they were legally entitled to this money.[37]

Ministry of Transport grants constituted a benign effort to suborn republican councils. Crown forces also raided council offices and seized documents in an effort to render local administration unworkable. Kerry County Council found it difficult to function after the burning of Tralee County Hall in the autumn of 1920.[38] The Royal Irish Constabulary seized minute books and other documents in raids on Carlow County Council offices on 16 and 22 November 1920.[39] Documents and minutes books were removed from the offices of Meath and Sligo County Councils in January 1921.[40] Cork City Hall was destroyed when crown forces set fire to a large area of the city centre on 11 December 1920.[41] During November and December 1920, Counties Cavan, Carlow and Monaghan were served with writs of mandamus, ordering them to hand over their books for audit by the LGB, and this forced council chairmen to go on the run. The Department instructed the councils to place the books with a safe person.[42] When Clifden Board of Guardians was about to declare its allegiance to Dáil Éireann, crown forces surrounded the workhouse where the meeting was to take place, causing it to be abandoned. Because of threatened raids, Clare County Council was forced to meet in secret, once in a cowhouse outside Ennis, on another occasion in Knappogue Castle, which they occupied in the absence of Lord Dunboyne.[43] One lord mayor of Cork, Thomas MacCurtain, was murdered, as were two lord mayors of Limerick, George Clancy and Michael O'Callaghan. Terence MacSwiney, lord mayor of Cork, was arrested in August 1920 and later died after a prolonged hunger-strike.[44] Cork County Council was unable to achieve a quorum during the first half of 1921 because councillors were either detained or threatened with arrest.[45] Others faced similar difficulties. In April 1921 Cosgrave noted that Counties Meath and Westmeath

> . . . have given us more trouble than half a dozen others . . . . The secretaries of both are not loyal to this Department and the County Councils are deprived of their best men, some in jail, some on the run. This action of removing pivot men from various counties and of pivot men being on the run, renders our difficulties almost insuperable, as in almost all cases the ablest administrators are prevented from carrying out their duties as public representatives.[46]

The offices of Wexford County Council were ransacked on several occasions and the county secretary, the acting chairman and other members were arrested; still, the council claimed that no important business 'had been undone'.[47] Yet, although the LGB had the legal power to dissolve rebel councils and to appoint paid commissioners, it was apparently reluctant to take such a step.[48]

Many local officials actively supported Dáil Éireann. The accountant to Waterford County Council and the Waterford borough treasurer and town clerk were detained during armed raids,[49] and both the Monaghan county secretary and the accountant to Kerry County Council served on the Dáil's Local Government Commission. Others, including the secretaries of Counties Meath, Westmeath, Carlow, Galway and Roscommon were regarded with suspicion. Galway County Council's problems were greatly increased because councillors felt unable to take the county secretary, W. G. Seymour, into their confidence. In 1921 Seymour made several unsuccessful attempts to have the council accounts audited by the LGB. Armed republicans raided the council offices in an effort to seize the account books in order to prevent him doing so, but Seymour managed to thwart their efforts.[50] Several councils wished to administer a loyalty pledge to their officials on the lines recommended by A. Mooney, a Leitrim representative on the General Council of County Councils, though Roscommon County Council was the only local authority to do so. All the officials complied except the county secretary, M.J. Heverin, who regarded the pledge as retaliation for the fact that he had placed his motor car at the disposal of the military during the 1916 Rising.[51] The Dáil ministry prevented Meath County Council from a similar step and informed the chairman that it was 'straining the instructions issued to public bodies by this Department to interpret any portion of them as authorising the proffering of any test or pledge to officials of public bodies.'[52]

A circular letter issued in November 1920 informed councils that any official who was unwilling to carry out orders originating with the Dáil Department of Local Government could resign on pension, but those who clung to office and attempted to thwart the council's wishes would be dismissed. No pensions would be paid to officials who were dismissed 'for endeavouring to thwart the will of the people of Ireland'. Although the letter was dispatched in Cosgrave's name, O'Higgins sent a covering letter to the secretary of the Dáil, pointing out that he had drafted the circular and that it contained his views. He added: 'Mr. Cosgrave will explain his personally to the Ministry'.[53] Unfortunately, they are not recorded.

O'Higgins showed an uncompromising hostility towards Richard Keogh, the Carlow county secretary, which was deeply resented by councillors:

> I do not know what your view as an individual may be as to the proper basis of just government, whether you recognise the will of the people as a factor to be considered or place all your faith and hope in the big battalions. What I do know is that you are a paid official of Carlow County Council, and that if a situation should arise in which you would feel from whatever motive you could not agree to carry out instructions of your council, you have a clear duty to resign. If you persist in clinging to your position and in using it to obstruct the will of the Council and the will of the people, we will set on foot proceedings against you.

Matters came to a head in December 1920 when Keogh was served with a writ of mandamus, ordering him to produce the council's books for audit by the Local Government Board. Keogh, like other county secretaries, was extremely conscious of his legal obligations and requested Carlow County Council to permit him to make a sworn affidavit stating his willingness to comply. Although the council refused his request, it appears to have condoned his subsequent absence from council meetings until after the Truce of July 1921 when he was again in attendance.[54]

The secretaries of Counties Meath and Roscommon were suspended for alleged disloyalty. Roscommon County Council suspended Heverin, the county secretary, in the autumn of 1920, pending instructions from Dublin. He resumed work in April 1921, having made 'certain promises' to the vice-chairman, but was again suspended in August. When Cosgrave inquired why 'more definite action' had not been taken and reminded the council that it had the power to remove the secretary with the Department's concurrence, the local inspector advised 'very cool consideration as in my opinion something between an out and out dismissal and a "resignation" will have to be arrived at'.

Heverin resigned in January 1922; Grennan, Meath county secretary, in September 1921.[55] In May 1921 the Dáil Ministry of Home Affairs decreed that any communication with the LGB by an official who was employed by a local authority that had declared allegiance to Dáil Éireann would be deemed a treasonable offence 'and dealt with accordingly'.[56]

RATES

Lack of money posed the greatest threat to the survival of rebel councils and many of the compromises which local authorities contemplated making with the British authorities were motivated by financial pressures, rather than a lack of patriotism, though the Dublin-based ministry, and particularly Kevin O'Higgins, often failed to understand this. Galway County Council delayed breaking with the LGB until it had collected money outstanding from the Ministry of Transport's road board. The council's solicitor informed the Department of Local Government that the finance committee had thought it 'wise to collar road board grants which are still coming in'. When Kevin O'Higgins wrote to the vice-chair, Miss Alice Cashel, who was national secretary to Cumann na mBan, to voice his alarm at a press report that the council had consented to have its books audited by the LGB and expressing the hope that the decision could be reversed, she asked for his advice on how to meet the council's financial difficulties. O'Higgins's reply was singularly unhelpful:

> Your council must keep fundamental facts well in mind. The
> country is in a state of revolution. The members of your council

were put forward as standard bearers in that revolution. No one, I suppose, contemplated that an enemy 700 years in occupation could be driven out without considerable hardships and dislocation. Vested interests have grown up about the English occupation of Ireland and we are fighting not alone the foreign enemy but also the enemy within our gates. It is for your Councils [sic] to see that no action of theirs gives hope or comfort to either of these enemies. I tell you and your council that it would be better a thousand times for the Irish Nation that there should be a financial breakdown here and there amongst the public bodies than that there should be the moral collapse of a surrender to enemy regulations.[57]

Few councillors shared O'Higgins's belief that 'financial breakdown' was a lesser evil than 'moral collapse'. Miss Cashel dismissed the tirade as 'an unnecessary homily rather than the departmental instructions asked for'.

Loss of government grants was not the only problem facing rebel councils. Councils that dismissed the official treasurer lost access to overdraft facilities and jeopardised the legal basis of rate collection. They also ran the risk that British authorities would identify the nominee accounts which were being used to collect rates and pay bills, as Alan Bell, a resident magistrate working with British intelligence, had attempted to do with the Dáil loan. Bell was killed by the IRA in March 1920.[58] Some bank managers went to considerable lengths to facilitate republican councils. The manager of the National Bank in Galway claimed that he could provide the county council with overdraft facilities which could not be traced and Laois County Council negotiated a new agreement in August 1920, no longer one between the local authority and its treasurer, but between a customer and its bank.[59] The Dáil ministry advised Carlow County Council to suspend the bank as treasurer, but to take it into its confidence, adding reassuringly that 'in cases where this has been done, the Bank realising the difficulties of the local authority have been perfectly willing to facilitate the Council in every way'. The council was instructed to inform the bank that, while it would honour its overdraft, it would not pay interest. The Dáil ministry also suggested that it emphasise that, since the appointment of nominees had the council's support, the 'closest co-operation should exist between the bank, the nominees and the council'.[60]

This letter smacks of wishful thinking; the experience of Mayo

County Council was more typical. Although the Bank of Ireland continued to act for the council immediately following its break with the LGB, it refused to co-operate with the council's use of private accounts, so the county secretary transferred business to the Munster and Leinster Bank's Westport branch. That bank's directors became suspicious at the volume of business passing through a personal account and ordered the local manager to suspend all dealings. When the secretary attempted to transfer council business to the National Bank, the branch manager informed him that the bank's directors would object if 'any considerable sums' passed through the account. His report to the Ministry concluded:

> The impression here is that all Banks are agreed to help the enemy to defeat us. It is no use seeing local managers. The Directors must be approached and the issue put to them. If argument will not induce them to issue instructions to local managers to facilitate local bodies in every way reasonable, then other weapons must be found to make them realise their treachery.[61]

O'Higgins lamented that the banks were 'amenable to enemy influence . . . drawn into the ring against the Irish people in their struggle'.[62] Given that they had proved less than accommodating to the legally constituted Irish Free State,[63] this is scarcely surprising. Dublin Corporation appears to have been the only local authority that was bailed out by the banks. The Corporation was on the verge of bankruptcy in August 1920 when the withdrawal of government grants left it with an overdraft of £100,000 and an urgent need to find £160,000 in order to fund three major contracts. Cosgrave believed that if Dublin Corporation declared bankruptcy, he would be forced to resign from public life, so he approached the banks to take Corporation stock at a 50 per cent discount. The Hibernian Bank and the Bank of Ireland agreed to participate on condition that the Munster and Leinster Bank, the Corporation's bank, did likewise. When the Munster and Leinster proved unenthusiastic, it was suggested that 'pressure would be brought to bear upon the Bank from a very influential source'. Michael Collins (presumably that source) arranged for Cosgrave to meet Mr Dawson, manager of the Munster and Leinster's Dame Street Dublin branch, but he excused his own absence 'from an interview at the gate of Dublin Castle', presumably because of the risk that he might be captured.[64]

However, there was nothing illegal or unprecedented in the banks' purchase of Corporation stock, and the transaction did not require LGB approval. Although there is no evidence that British authorities pressed the banks not to accommodate dissenting local authorities, when John J. Murphy, chairman of the South Dublin Union, proposed meeting the secretary of the Bank of Ireland in February 1921, to discuss the financial problems facing the Union, Cosgrave suggested that it 'would be well not to show the Banks that there was anything political in this matter, that it was confined to the Local Authority'.[65] Councils who dismissed their treasurers nullified the legal basis of rate collection. Collectors who paid rates to designated trustees, as instructed by the Dáil, risked forfeiting the bonds or sureties which they had lodged prior to appointment, while ratepayers whose collections were not lodged to the official treasurer could be regarded as not having paid their rates.

A minority report to the Commission on Local Government, written by Monaghan county secretary, Denis Carolan Rushe, in the summer of 1920, had predicted that 'the difficulty most to be dreaded is the conduct of the Rate Collector'. The majority had other sources of income and were in a 'very powerful' position, where they could 'seriously obstruct' republican councils.[66] In October 1920 the ministry ordered the arrest of a Roscommon rate collector who had lodged his collection in his personal bank account and then had written to the LGB asking for instructions as to its disposal.[67] When collectors in County Kildare asked if their sureties were safe from distraint, the Dáil ministry advised them to resign and seek reappointment, though it had not yet decided whether or not collectors would be required to post new bonds. If Kildare collectors were reassured by the comment that the 'law is only formidable when it has the consent and approval of those whose action it is intended to guide',[68] a circular letter from the LGB, dated 11 November 1920, reminded them that any instructions to deposit rates to trustee accounts, rather than to the treasurer appointed by the LGB, were 'unlawful and invalid'. Collectors were informed that they and their sureties remained liable for all rates not accounted for by the Board's auditor.

Those who disobeyed LGB instructions were threatened with dismissal by sealed order; loyal collectors were reassured that the Board would refuse to sanction their dismissal by a republican council and would pay a retirement allowance to those who had been forced to resign. Wexford collectors reacted to this circular by refusing to pay their rates to trustees, as directed by the council, forcing the council to suspend them.[69] Resignations were also reported in other counties.[70] Collectors in Clare were described as 'funky', refusing to collect rates unless LGB regulations were respected.[71] The North Tipperary county secretary informed the ministry that the county's 'rate collectors to a man have ratted'; he attributed their behaviour to the many 'bearer[s] of Cromwellian blood in North Tipperary'.[72] The Dáil Department of Local Government urged councils to try and retain their collectors because appointing substitutes compounded legal difficulties; collectors were formally appointed by the LGB. This recommendation was accompanied by a threat: 'if any rate collector in his dealings with public monies puts it within the power of the enemy government to seize these monies, he or his friends will have no cause to feel aggrieved if this Department takes steps to vindicate the authority of Dáil Éireann'.[73]

In County Monaghan, unionists, who paid the majority of rates, claimed that the collection was illegal because the treasurer had been suspended. On 29 November 1920 Monaghan County Council proposed restoring the Hibernian Bank as its treasurer in an effort to 'tide the council over some months'. Rushe, the county secretary, informed the Department that bankruptcy was imminent because collectors refused to lodge rates with designated trustees. He feared that creditors would obtain judgments against the council and that the LGB would appoint a receiver, to whom the largest collectors would transfer rates. Although the council deferred a decision on this occasion, it reinstated the treasurer on 14 December without waiting for a reply from Dublin.[74] Other councils did likewise. On 6 December Kildare County Council reinstated its treasurer, having first considered letters in support of this step from Longford County Council, Galway County Council and Dundalk Urban District Council.

Meanwhile a meeting of rate collectors in Dublin threatened to cease collection pending a settlement between the Dáil and the Local Government Board.[75] The introduction of martial law throughout most southern counties in December 1920 added to the crisis. When martial law was extended to Wexford on 30 December 1920,[76] the British authorities issued a proclamation stating that anybody who paid rates to a collector not in possession of a permit from the military governor was liable to prosecution.[77] The Department's response to the threatened breakdown in rate collection was confused and this appears to reflect a difference of opinion between Cosgrave and O'Higgins. When O'Higgins learned that Kildare County Council had reappointed its treasurer he informed the chairman, Donal Ó Buachalla, who later became Ireland's last governor general:

> If action is taken owing to financial difficulties and with a view of obtaining an overdraft, I have to state that if your council had realised the strength of their position as representatives of the people by whose goodwill the bank exists and flourishes, it would not have been necessary for them to renege on their allegiance to the Nationalist government and to flatly infringe the instructions of a department of that Government in order to obtain an advance from the bank.

Ó Buachalla denied that the council had repudiated Dáil Éireann; it had taken this step because council services were in danger of breaking down owing to a lack of money. The bank had agreed to provide overdraft facilities if it was reappointed as treasurer, and the council had worked out procedures to avert the risk of funds being seized.

Kevin O'Higgins reiterated that the council was in breach of the Department's instructions and claimed to have 'personal knowledge that Kildare, Galway and Longford County Councils are quoted as victories' in the Custom House. He no doubt feared that the Local Government Board could represent the fact that these counties had reappointed the treasurers whose original appointment had been sanctioned by the lord lieutenant as evidence that the Dáil's hold over local authorities was weakening . He suggested to Ó Buachalla that 'the proper step would have been to bring pressure on the Bank to advance money to nominees of the Council on the security of the rates, or failing this to endeavour to obtain collateral security on the personal guarantee of Republicans throughout the Constituency'. He continued:

> . . . the attitude of the Bank is directed by political considerations, and a desire to bring the public bodies of Ireland to heel. That attitude must be sternly fought. If pressure on the Bank had failed to give the desired results and the personal guarantees I speak of were not forthcoming, your Council should not have yielded to the pressure of the Bank to reappoint it treasurer but should have consulted the Department.

O'Higgins informed Ó Buachalla that, although 'it was not expedient to divulge at the moment, sooner than have a collapse on the Local Government front, a large sum would be expended by way of subsidy or loan, and such loan or subsidy would be immediately forthcoming, if it were clearly shown to be necessary rather than have an important body like a county council conform, or rather seem to conform, to English Local Government Board regulations.' He further warned that the bank, as official treasurer to the council, could 'be called before any Star Chamber Court' and compelled to disclose information about the council's finances. Unlike the Alan Bell inquiry, the banks could not take refuge in the confidentiality of banker/client relations, because the relationship was between a public body and a public official.[78]

While O'Higgins was penning such salvoes, the Department (presumably Cosgrave) was attempting to rescue the system of rate collection. A circular letter dated 7 December advised collectors to lodge rates in their own names (a practice also recommended by the LGB) and to give a crossed cheque for the full amount to the county secretary. However, Carlow County Council, whose secretary's loyalty was suspect, construed this letter as a plot by the LGB to gain control of the rates, and confusion was compounded when the council received a letter from O'Higgins condemning these instructions.[79] It was illegal under LGB regulations to pay rates to the county secretary, so many collectors sought assurances that the council would indemnify them against loss if they followed this instruction. The Department advised Wexford County Council to give this assurance, but offered contrary advice to Laois County Council. Sligo County Council agreed to the collectors' request without consulting the Department.[80] O'Higgins persisted in telling councils that they should be in a position to obtain overdraft facilities without giving an undertaking to restore the bank as treasurer.[81]

The reality was rather different. When Wexford County Council applied for an overdraft of £5,000, it was informed that the directors of the National Bank would require the usual security: the consent of the LGB and an undertaking to mortgage the rates to secure repayment.[82] Given the confused instructions emanating from Dublin, it is scarcely surprising that councils reappointed their treasurers without consulting the Department. Carlow County Council did so in order to cash a draft for £1,850 from the Ministry of Transport, which the bank had refused to honour.[83]

The revised instructions, issued on 10 January 1921, are yet another case where the Dáil gave retrospective sanction to the decisions of local authorities. County secretaries were instructed to issue receipts for rates paid in order to alleviate fears that ratepayers would be required to pay their rates twice; uncooperative collectors would be asked to resign, or failing that, dismissed, and an alternative team appointed; lists of defaulting ratepayers should be sent to the Department 'to be dealt with by the Defence Department where necessary'; a sum of £100,000 was voted for loans to county councils that were in financial difficulties and the Minister for Local Government was given discretionary power to sanction the reappointment of a bank as treasurer in cases where this was deemed necessary.[84] On 22 January W.T. Cosgrave informed the chairman of Louth County Council that, 'owing to the peculiar circumstances' of the council, which apparently had the worst financial position in Ireland, the Department recommended that the bank be reappointed as treasurer.[85] Three days later in Dáil Éireann he expressed the hope that 'money would come in' following the reappointment of treasurers. He attributed the financial difficulties facing local authorities to 'the disloyalty of some Rate Collectors'.[86] However, as Dublin County Council's finance committee noted, rate collectors had not been appointed to take risks.[87] In fact six County Wicklow rate collectors had been imprisoned by the spring of 1921 and collectors were arrested in Counties Meath, Limerick and Wexford.[88]

By May 1921, according to the Dáil Department, fifteen counties had reappointed their treasurers, twelve had not.[89] The Belfast-based Northern Bank refused to resume its position as treasurer to Leitrim County Council and both the county council and the Dáil inspector failed to find a replacement. Wexford and Sligo County Councils decided not to reappoint a treasurer because they were unable to obtain guarantees that the bank would refuse to pay over council funds if presented with criminal injury decrees. The manager of the local Hibernian Bank informed Sligo County Council that he had obtained legal advice that he would be bound to pay such decrees 'out of the first monies coming in for credit of the county council'.[90]

Councils who reappointed treasurers appear to have done so without obtaining such formal undertakings. Kildare County Council was satisfied that 'due arrangements' had been made to avoid council funds being seized to meet malicious injury decrees, but the bank refused the council's request for an increased overdraft in February

1921.[91] The situation was volatile: Dublin County Council again dismissed its treasurer in August 1921 when the bank was presented with a malicious injuries decree to compensate for the destruction of the Balbriggan Hosiery Factory by crown forces.[92]

Rate collection improved in the early months of 1921, presumably because the reinstatement of the banks had ended doubts about its legality. Monaghan County Council received substantial lodgments from unionists, but the collection remained heavily in default in both Carrickmacross and Castleblaney Rural District Councils, despite the fact that both areas had voted strongly for Sinn Féin. The most recalcitrant rate collector was 'a patriot who won't close [hand over] the rates which he had collected to the council] and does very much as he pleases'. One Monaghan collector absconded to Dublin with rates in his possession; unionist ratepayers refused to make payments to his successor because his appointment had not been authorised by the Local Government Board.[93] By May the Department noted that the rate collection for 1920/21, which was due to be collected on 31 March 1921 had been completed in all counties except Cork, Kerry, Leitrim, Longford, Louth, Roscommon and Sligo. In Cork £25,000 remained outstanding, in Kerry £20,000. Lack of co-operation between rate collectors in Louth and the Dáil administration meant that £25,000 was outstanding; in Sligo, where £30,000 was outstanding, no attempt had been made to collect the second moiety because all rate collectors except two had been dismissed. The second moiety of the 1920/21 collection in Leitrim remained in collectors' hands, but they refused to pay it to the council until a treasurer had been appointed. Leitrim's problems were attributed to poor management and lack of initiative by local councillors.

Councils such as Wexford, which had been seriously disrupted by the British authorities, were in a much healthier position. Most county councils had succeeded in paying monies due to poor law unions and rural district councils, though some subsidiary bodies in Cork, Sligo and Leitrim received no funds for several months. Outdoor relief was suspended in County Roscommon and officials in some councils had not been paid for several months.[94] Councils faced a new threat in the spring of 1921 when solicitors acting on behalf of clients who had been awarded malicious injury decrees attempted to garnishee rates owed by large ratepayers such as railway companies. Orders totalling £60,000 were lodged against Cork County Council.[95] When Kerry County Council was threatened with the loss of rates from the Great Southern and Western Railway Company, Cosgrave promised to discuss the problem with Tim Healy, the veteran Irish Party MP and GSWR director.[96] In March 1921 O'Higgins informed the Dáil that he approved of attacks being carried out on men who made payments on foot of garnishee orders, because he regarded these orders as constituting 'a trial of strength between two governments'. Austin Stack, Minister for Home Affairs, disagreed.[97] Dublin County Council appears to have been the only council to sustain significant losses through garnishee orders.[98]

THE DÁIL LOCAL GOVERNMENT DEPARTMENT INSPECTORS

Short tempers are much in evidence in communications between the Department and county councils during the second half of 1920. The débâcle over rates indicates that the Department's control of local authorities was extremely limited. O'Higgins emerges as both unrealistic and intolerant, with little understanding of the pressures facing local councils or officials. The Department was poorly informed of conditions in provincial Ireland and tended to reject councillors' claims as special pleading. Before August 1920, the Department appears to have existed only in name. The working model provided by the Dáil Local Government Commission in August/September 1920 suggests that it was starting from scratch. On 17 September, Cosgrave summarised its findings to Dáil Éireann: as 'Clean break: the Local Government Department to function on the lines of the Custom House'.

The new Department duly replicated all the Custom House rituals, down to the correct colour of ink used to annotate the minutes which were submitted by local authorities. The members of the Local Government Commission who were least enthusiastic about breaking with the LGB — Denis Carolan Rushe, and Dublin county councillor James Magee — emphasised that the new Department should minimise discontinuity. Respecting this point of view, the Department rejected the proposal by Dublin city councillor James Lawless that it should abolish boards of guardians and town commissioners. The Department would consist of a Secretary (Minister) and a senior official who would act for the Secretary on occasions — M.D. de Lacy.[99] Four divisions — housing and public health, loan, audit and general — were proposed, though there is no evidence that these were established. The Commission recommended hiring at least four inspectors, including a qualified medical officer and an engineer, plus nineteen auditors and ten clerks. Staff would be recruited from local authority offices.

Little progress was made in implementing these recommendations during 1920. Although the cabinet approved the recruitment of four auditors for a trial period in November 1920, the first two appointees refused to take up their posts[100] and the colourful language in many letters sent to local authorities suggests that they were written by Kevin O'Higgins. Most councils do not appear to have sent copies of minutes to the Dáil Department on a regular basis until 1921. Although councils were provided with covering addresses of private citizens, some persisted in addressing letters openly to the Dáil ministry. Cosgrave commented on one letter from Kilrush UDC, which had been addressed to the Mansion House, that 'one would imagine that the fact that a war was on would be obvious even in Kilrush'; O'Higgins attributed a similar error by Listowel UDC either to 'crass stupidity or malice'.[101]

The foundation of an effective Department can be dated to 10 January 1921, when the cabinet approved the appointment of fourteen inspectors. By June at least twenty were employed, including three women. The resort to inspectors, the key supervisory grade within the LGB, is further evidence of the Department's respect for precedent. The appointments were a response to growing concern at the state of local government. Addressing the Dáil in January 1921, O'Higgins referred to the 'hollowness of the Declaration of Allegiance made by some local authorities' and the Department's need for 'some means to deal with people who did not know the meaning of public morality and decency'.[102] Inspectors were responsible for one or more counties. They moved from one hotel to another; expenses were reimbursed only after considerable delay and the Department often complained that claims were too high. The Department resisted pleas from one inspector that a car would increase his efficiency. Inspectors were instructed to report to Dublin at least twice weekly; failure to do so could result in blunt reminders. One inspector who was informed that his recent report had been 'a serious disappointment' humbly replied that he would 'be grateful for a few words of criticism'.[103]

The work entailed personal risk. An inspector based in Leitrim wrote that he was being followed by crown forces. Two inspectors were arrested in Wexford; the second complained that he had been sent there without adequate warning 'of the state of affairs', in particular the 'treacherous' attitude of some local officials, who had reported his presence to the military. The Department was unsympathetic, rejecting his request to have his salary paid for the period he had spent in prison, though the Dublin office informed him that he would still be of use despite his arrest.[104]

Most inspectors were not natives of their area. Since they were responsible for implementing national policies, which often ran contrary to local wishes, they frequently clashed with local personalities. Tensions between the Department and local authorities do not appear to have eased with their appointment. In his splendid account of nineteenth-century politics, Theo Hoppen claimed that 'the parish pump has long been the true symbol of the "hidden Ireland" and its deep and constant importance is best revealed in those periods when it was able to emerge from the closet of national mobilisation and nationalist rhetoric into the full light of demotic day.'[105] Hoppen underestimates the resilience of the 'parish pump' at a time of heightened national tension such as the Anglo-Irish war. Far from subduing local interests, the breakdown of law and order and of central government gave them greater scope. Many councils and boards of guardians were under the illusion that they were supreme. Louth Sinn Féin TD Peter Hughes objected to the Dáil inspector intervening in council discussions and pointed out that 'on one occasion he nearly threw the inspector of the English Local Government Board out of the council chamber for attempting to interfere in this way with the council's business.'[106] O'Higgins accused the commissioners who were running the Cork Poor Law Union of acting as 'absolutely Czars of Cork Union responsible to no one and with their acts subject to supervision or veto by no one'; he urged Cosgrave of the need to 'have it finally established that the authority of your Department holds good in Cork Unions as well as in every other part of Ireland'.

The failings were not all on the side of local authorities. One inspector told the Department that relations with local authorities could be improved by responding more promptly to queries and by showing less arrogance: 'The people here will not take anything lying down even from a Dáil Department.'[107] The Department transferred at least one inspector in an effort to improve relations with local authorities. One inspector based in Mayo reported that the local LGB inspector was spreading a story to the effect that the Dáil Department had been forced to withdraw inspectors from some counties because of their dictatorial attitude towards public bodies. O'Higgins advised one inspector that he 'should aim at maintaining a strictly official tone in your letters on the Department's business, and guard against allowing your personal feelings towards officials to become too obvious in your communications' and later instructed him 'not to get mixed up in politics, labour or White Cross work'.[108] (The White Cross was a nationalist organisation which provided aid for victims of the Anglo-Irish war, particularly those made homeless following attacks and reprisals by the Crown forces.)

Local appointments proved particularly contentious. Many republicans believed that they had a right to replace existing local authority staff with their supporters. However, Cosgrave argued that 'persons appointed to public positions on definite terms must have some security of tenure': he rejected the American precedent where the election of a new president led to the appointment of a new set of officials.[109] Many disputes over appointments are remarkably similar to earlier confrontations between local authorities and the LGB. Laois County Council wished to restrict all appointments to natives of the county and tried to have a favourite candidate appointed as secretary of the home and hospital committee, despite the fact that he had failed the qualifying examination. The council was also accused of having engineered the appointment of the lady superintendent of boarded-out children.[110] Waterford County Council restricted the number of candidates sitting the examination to one 'popular local candidate'. Although such practices ran contrary to Sinn Féin's commitment to appointments on merit, one inspector, J. Gleeson, told the Department 'that local bodies cannot be deprived absolutely of their power to elect a local favourite who is qualified for the post'.[111] Kildare County Council wished to restrict the recruitment of clerks to those with republican sympathies, with preference being given to members of the Irish Volunteers, though this blatantly defied a Department regulation that no religious or political tests could be imposed on current or prospective employees.[112] The officer commanding the Mid-Limerick Brigade of the IRA was strongly condemned by the Minister for Defence when he attempted to have one of his officers appointed as visiting medical officer in Croom hospital.[113]

The most extreme case of interference occurred in November 1921 when Inspector Éamon Coogan was holding an examination to recruit the secretary to the county home in Killarney. Three armed and masked men entered the examination room, ordered Coogan and the candidates into an inner room and confiscated the examination answers and copies of the forthcoming paper in accountancy, warning 'that it was unfair to allow shirkers and slackers to secure positions whilst men were suffering in jail, and warning all present that anyone who spoke about the affair would pay the penalty.' Coogan stayed up that night to set alternative papers and the examination resumed the following day. The successful candidate was later approached by a member of the home committee — the committee appointed by the Kerry County Council to run the county home — and asked to withdraw in favour of an ex-internee who had been awarded second place; he did so and the ex-internee was appointed.[114]

Inspectors' reports reveal a high level of absenteeism and petty corruption within local government, though it is unclear whether this was due to the unsettled conditions or was a chronic problem. Many normal tasks carried out by local authorities, such as repairing roads, were in disarray. The staff of one county was described as 'largely incompetent and grossly careless and lazy'.[115] The Offaly county surveyor carried out few road inspections and visited his office only twice a week, arriving on the 11 am train and leaving at 4 o'clock in the afternoon.[116] The secretary of Cork County Council attended daily mass before reaching his office around noon. The inspector proposed that the Department suggest that he attend mass outside official hours and urged that the letter include a quotation from St Francis, 'a great favourite of the secretary's: to work is to pray'.[117] The secretary in Tipperary South Riding County Council regularly arrived at work by train at 11 am and left before 2.30 pm.[118] The Department threatened a surveyor in County Cavan with dismissal for failing to live in his allotted district and for submitting inaccurate reports of schemes which he had never visited.[119]

Several workhouse officials were suspended on suspicion of corruption and were later dismissed following sworn inquiries. An inquiry into alleged irregularities in the county surveyor's office in Mayo concluded that one assistant surveyor was guilty of repeated insubordination and of gross irregularities in awarding employment and in handling money and official correspondence. He was also alleged to have written a series of scurrilous letters to local newspapers signed FUR (Fed-up Ratepayer). Two clerks in Cork who were asked to resign for refusing to sign time-sheets were reported to be leading lights in

Sinn Féin. One particularly incompetent clerk in another county was described as 'a spy pure and simple', a man 'who always carried an automatic and when drunk demonstrates how he will fell his assailants when they come for him'. The inspector and the local committee were reluctant to confront him, for fear of reprisal.[120]

Many elected representatives were also found wanting. One inspector described Kilrush as holding the 'distinction of having one of the worst urban councils in Ireland' – 'six chronic maladministrators and five new members who were partially if not wholly ignorant of the business governing such bodies'. Rates were unpaid, tolls uncollected, streets were filthy and lacked public lighting, the gas works had been shut for the previous two years and the council had evaded all responsibility by proroguing itself.[121] In October 1920 the chairman of Baltinglass No 2. Rural District Council resigned to take up a paid appointment as temporary clerk to the council. Although O'Higgins reminded the rural district council that the Dáil had adopted LGB regulations, which precluded any councillor from taking up such a post within six months of holding office, it promoted its former chairman to a permanent position some months later, though it eventually capitulated when the Department threatened to surcharge all councillors on audit.

Inspector Éamon Coogan contrasted the management of Killarney Union, the best he had visited in Ireland, with Listowel RDC and Board of Guardians — 'both as poor as I have met anywhere'; they were chaired by a man who did not have 'remotest conception of how to conduct a chair'. Coogan claimed that 'meetings were more like a Conference in Bedlam than a meeting of "public" men: The Clerk rules the roost. He is a man of forceful character, who insists on his being heard and who is always heard.'[122]

The 1920 elections had returned many councillors who were inexperienced and who perhaps lacked interest in local administration. Local administrative competence was also eroded by raids on local authority offices and by the fact that many councillors were interned or on the run. In February 1921, An Seabhac, chairman of Kerry County Council, told Austin Stack, Minister for Home Affairs, that 'Down here only three or four of the council bother their heads. The same three or four with our chief officials do all the work and shoulder all the responsibility . . . . I wish that the three or four of us had got Dictator power over the other bodies also.'[123]

LOCAL GOVERNMENT REFORM

The critical state of local government finances forced the Dáil to consider potential savings arising from a reform of local administration. Even if all outstanding rates were collected, local authorities had lost an average of 19 per cent of total revenue as a result of the withdrawal of LGB and Road Fund grants. The Dáil Commission on Local Government ruled out the option of striking an additional rate, but suggested that the Dáil try to collect land annuities and income tax and consider the possibility of tapping revenue from dog licences, publicans' licences, motor taxes and estate duties. However, Denis Carolan Rushe, secretary of Monaghan County Council, argued that any effort by Dáil Éireann to collect land annuities in County Monaghan 'would be fraught with great danger both to the community and to the Republic'. Farms occupied by men who paid annuities to Dáil Éireann might be sold by the Land Commission and bought by 'greedy neighbours', as had happened during the Land War. James McGee of Dublin County Council agreed that farmers would regard efforts by Dáil Éireann to collect land annuities as jeopardising the security of their holdings; he also opposed giving local authorities the power to collect or use 'any monies regarded as national or to control any organisation rightly regarded as national',[124] a view shared by the Ministry of Finance. The difficulties which the Dáil experienced in collecting rates suggest that efforts to collect land annuities would have proved disastrous. Many farmers defaulted on land annuities during these years. By June 1921 arrears in County Meath stood at over £31,000, though this was probably due to economic depression.[125]

In the absence of new sources of revenue, it was essential to cut local authority spending. The Commission on Local Government identified a number of economies, which it estimated would reduce the half-yearly deficit to £202,500: withholding repayments due on local loans and sheriffs' fees, reducing road works, abolishing venereal disease clinics and child welfare clinics, amalgamating workhouses and reducing the number of inmates in lunatic asylums and tuberculosis hospitals. They anticipated further savings from the operation of combined purchase schemes, the closure of agricultural and technical instruction committees and the sale of labourers' cottages where repairs exceeded rental income. Proposed cuts in child welfare services were dropped at the Dáil's behest; Michael Collins, Minister for Finance,

73

opposed the recommendation to withhold local loan repayments and suggested that they should be paid to Dáil Éireann pending a settlement with Britain. Although the Dáil adopted the Commission's report, it largely ignored the financial implications. There is little evidence of any efforts to cut expenditure until inspectors were appointed early in 1921.

The core of the proposed economies was a proposal to organise all local services on a county basis. The Local Government Department's report of May 1921 emphasised that county councils were 'the dominant body in local administration, having an interest in the national principle as well as in the efficient and economic administration of each subsidiary body'.[126] Subordinate local authorities were regarded as both uneconomic and disloyal. In January 1921 O'Higgins suggested that county councils should act as 'watch-dogs over local administration' and subject subordinate authorities under their control to a series of questions designed to test their loyalty. He predicted that many boards of guardians would fail this scrutiny.[127] Some county councils apparently undertook such an exercise as a form of 'examination of conscience',[128] though the results are unknown. Continuing this moralising theme, the Department hoped that the 'financial stringency' which had been forced on the counties would 'prove a blessing — if rather heavily disguised — if it results in awakening public interest in local affairs and ensures the moral support of the community for those who are eager to put an end to inefficiency, waste and corruption in local administration.'[129]

When local authorities were asked to propose economies, they tended to favour scrapping schemes which intruded into ratepayers' lives: abandoning sheep-dipping, dispensing with school attendance officers, ending the analysis of food and drink samples and the inspection of dairies and cowsheds by public health inspectors, and abolishing tuberculosis schemes. The Dáil Ministries deprecated such proposals, often to little avail. Donegal County Council informed the Department of Agriculture that it had dispensed with sheep-dipping inspectors and sold its equipment; it was now up to the department to supervise dipping.[130] Several councils found time to adopt a resolution calling for the introduction of a film censorship board,[131] though they were unable to complete proposals for reforming poor relief. The Department of Local Government sought economies in expenditure on roads and poor relief by introducing combined purchasing for all local institutions. All these proposals involved a significant loss in local employment and local influence. One inspector warned of the strong feelings in Cork among 'certain public representatives against too much centralisation and favouring the widest local authority under the mild supervision of the central authority'. Local officials and councillors bridled when they were given unduly detailed instructions from Dublin: 'they resent being told how they may insure their ambulances'. Councillors approved of combined purchase and would avail of it where it offered good value, but 'they believe in spending money locally and in not sending it away'.[132]

THE END OF THE WORKHOUSE

Poor law reform appeared to offer the greatest scope for savings. The reports of the Viceregal Commission and the Royal Commission on the Poor Law provided a ready-made blueprint. These entailed closing workhouses, transferring as many inmates as possible (orphans and single mothers) to the community, and providing a county hospital and county home for the infirm and elderly. Although the proposals had been discussed at length and appeared popular, once they came to be implemented, they were widely opposed because they meant the loss of local institutions and local employment. In County Mayo the inspector alleged that:

> Every influence, clerical, medical, official, lay contractors is at work to defeat the scheme. Ballina, Westport and Swinford Unions are very hostile. Chaplains, doctors, nuns and contractors are ruling the roost in these places. All are jealous of Castlebar and say that already having County Council offices, the County court, asylum and other appurtenances of a county town it now wants to grab all amalgamation. The scheme may, in these jealous minds, be described as made in Castlebar, for Castlebar and by Castlebar.[133]

Amalgamation plans were drafted by a subcommittee of the county council, assisted by the Dáil inspector and local officials. The committee's proposals were ratified by the county council and were subject to the Department's approval. Where the chairman of the county council and the inspector agreed, amalgamation was generally completed without difficulty: Counties Cork and Cavan appear to have achieved a smooth transition and the Cavan-Monaghan Asylum had made substantial savings by May 1921. The Cork scheme seems to have been a triumph for the inspector's diplomacy. As he told the Department:

> I had to move very delicately as these people here are convinced that they have nothing to learn from Dublin and that they are quite capable of amalgamating their County without our intervention. I must say the Local Government Department is quite small in the eyes of a number of people here. I was complimented at yesterday's meeting on having given the first evidence of sanity or commonsense as coming from this department. I assure you I did not feel very much on this score, but rather I felt sorry that the Department should have fallen so low in the estimation of these Cork men who rightly or wrongly credit themselves with 'brains'. I should say they err in giving themselves a little too much credit in this respect.[134]

In Kerry progress was much slower, perhaps because of the presence of a more abrasive inspector, or because of the complexity of local politics. An unofficial amalgamation committee was established in opposition to the official committee; this was dominated by Albinia Broderick, sister of Irish unionist leader Lord Midleton, and a militant republican. In January 1922 inspector Éamon Coogan reported that 'some hidden forces' were blocking his efforts to implement reforms:

> I had to report before the apathy of public bodies towards reforms and their reluctance to cooperate with me in effecting tangible reforms. For aiming at the latter, I have been accused of being too materialistic. Incidentally I must say, therefore, that to such people as my accusers the constructive policy of this Department is too materialistic and lacks the fine qualities and ideals of those more progressive reformers in Kerry who have spent their time since 22 June last building castles in the air from the County Council offices.

Coogan reported that he was 'thoroughly sick and disgusted with Kerry'.[135]

The IRA occasionally featured among the opponents of reform: the East Mayo Brigade protested at the proposed closure of Swinford hospital on the grounds that it was the Brigade hospital.[136] Opposition was particularly vociferous in County Leitrim where Carrick-on-Shannon, Mohill and Manorhamilton each asserted its claim to secure the county hospital or county home. The board of guardians of Manorhamilton Union disputed the county council's power to draw up an amalgamation scheme and proposed that the question be deferred 'until the National Question is finally settled'. This provoked a stern rebuke from W.T. Cosgrave. When Carrick-on-Shannon was not chosen as the location for either the county hospital or the county home, the Sinn Féin club passed a resolution condemning the decision, the parish priest wrote a letter of protest and a visiting priest preached a sermon against amalgamation.[137] Several counties opted to retain district hospitals, allegedly for a short period, in order to diffuse opposition.

Although all schemes had to be approved by the Department, some councils dispensed with this detail. In County Offaly, a former workhouse clerk and other dissidents formed 'a Self-Appointed Visiting Committee' to organise home assistance.[138] Members of the Dáil were often prominent opponents of reform. When Wexford County Council rejected an amalgamation scheme, Kevin O'Higgins informed the secretary of the Dáil that Deputies Etchingham, Ryan and Corish had been active in the opposition camp. This, he claimed, was 'not an isolated instance of interference and obstruction by individual T.D.s in the work of the Department'; such intervention meant that 'it was becoming daily more difficult to carry any agreed scheme of reform or economy'. O'Higgins argued that there was a need to define the relationship between TDs and the Dáil ministry. He claimed that most deputies showed no understanding of a need for 'drastic economies in local administration' if the deficit resulting from the loss of British grants was to be met. When one Mayo TD disputed the Department's authority to veto the county council's decision to retain a district hospital, O'Higgins claimed that his intervention had swayed ordinary councillors, who were inclined to accept as *ex cathedra* the judgment of councillors who were Dáil deputies and to give it much greater weight than the words of the inspector.[139]

Lay nurses and religious sisters battled for control of new county hospitals and homes. In Leitrim a laywoman became matron of the county home, a nun of the county hospital. The inspector overseeing amalgamation in County Mayo favoured placing the county home in the hands of nuns because it would 'cut out a lot of the wirepulling that is going on and would make for decided improvement in the whole management'.[140] However, when the Limerick amalgamation committee voted to appoint a lay matron and lay nurses to the county hospital and to assign nuns to the county home, the parish priest of Kilfinane, Rev. Lee, wrote to Cosgrave, questioning the *bona fides* of the Department's inspector and reminding him that the decision — which, he alleged, was opposed by the people of the district — was 'a test of your faith and of the religion of Sinn Féin'. He begged Cosgrave 'to act the part of a Catholic administrator', not to allow 'the scandal of expelling the nuns from the care of the sick and dying poor and replacing them with lay people'. The letter bears a hand-written note initialed KOH — 'this is a personal letter — no one here is inclined to deal with it. It is *your* orthodoxy that is challenged.' Although the Department's medical adviser, Dr Boyd Barrett, visited Fr Lee at Cosgrave's behest, the staunchly republican priest persisted in his opposition and a further visit by Dr Boyd Barrett to the bishop of Limerick proved equally unsuccessful.

There was considerable opposition in County Limerick to a county scheme; one correspondent objected that relatives of sick people would now face long journeys to visit them in hospital: 'the relatives of the patients are not riders on motor cars: the jolly donkey cart or even Shanks mare are far more likely to be their mode of progression'.[141] In Callan, Co. Kilkenny, according to the inspector, 'arguments good and bad, lame, blind, relevant and irrelevant, were all availed of to boost the case for retention of the local hospital. "Where", one protester asked, "does self-determination come in, if the people of Callan are to be ignored when they call for the preservation of the Hospital?" ' The curate contacted Cosgrave, TD for Kilkenny City, seeking his support, but Cosgrave replied that he had received similar representations from practically every county in Ireland. He rejected Callan's case on the grounds that the decision had been approved by the county council.[142]

Church and state also came into conflict when the Department vetoed the generous salary increases approved by local councils to priests in their capacity as chaplains to hospitals or the county home.[143]

ROADS, EMPLOYMENT FOR LABOURERS AND THE ROLE OF TRADE UNIONS

Local authority employees constituted another active lobby against amalgamation. In Longford the campaign was orchestrated by the medical officer and nursing staff. The Union and Rural District Clerks Association was active in the anti-amalgamation cause in County Clare.[144] The number of trade unionists affiliated to the Irish TUC increased from under 100,000 in 1916 to 225,000 four years later. Much of the recruitment took place in provincial towns or rural areas where new members tended to be agricultural and general labourers or local authority employees. New recruits resented the fact that wages had not kept pace with wartime inflation.

Rising unemployment during 1919 as a result of post-war demobilisation was a further source of grievance.[145] In 1920 clerical staff employed by local authorities, including workhouse staff, formed the Local Government Officials (Ireland) Trade Union. Most manual workers employed by local authorities joined the Irish Transport and General Workers' Union, whose membership increased from 12,000 in 32 branches in mid-1917 to 102,419 members in 433 branches by late 1919. This growth was achieved by recruiting new members and by taking over and radicalising existing local labourers' groups.[146] Rapid expansion led, in the words of one writer, 'to a diverse and untidy structure', which was often beyond the control of union headquarters.[147] Local branches become prominent in a variety of disputes, sometimes in response to a genuine grievance, in other instances as a form of attempted tyranny. In Ballinrobe, Co. Mayo, the ITGWU branch secretary — 'a disreputable type', according to the clerk of works — demanded to be appointed as supervisor of the town's cleansing squad and brought street cleaning to a halt when this was refused.[148] In turn, the growth in trade union representation brought significant labour gains in local elections. In 1920 the Labour Party won 324 seats in urban and municipal elections, against Sinn Féin's 422 seats.[149]

Dáil Éireann's attitude towards labour is often summarised in de Valera's phrase 'labour must wait'. It is frequently suggested that labour was marginalised during the Anglo-Irish war, an argument which appears to underestimate its achievements, such as persuading the Dáil to approve the Democratic Programme and to establish a Ministry of Labour and a Dáil Conciliation Service to arbitrate on wage and employment disputes. For its part, the labour movement refused to handle imports of war materials.[150] In August 1920 Cosgrave expressed the hope that labour would assist in preventing property being seized in lieu of rates.[151] However, labour's support came at a price that was hardly conducive to achieving economies in local expenditure. Trade unionists demanded that wage increases compensate fully for price inflation since 1914 and opposed the imposition of pay cuts when prices fell. They also demanded shorter working hours, a closed shop in local authority employment, the use of direct labour, rather than contractors, in road maintenance, and the creation of additional labouring jobs to compensate for the decline in agricultural employment after 1919. Trade unions opposed hospital and workhouse closures, though they were more concerned with employment and wages on road works where their demands were directly at variance with the Department's economy programme.

The Dáil Local Government Commission had anticipated savings of only £50,000 (5 per cent of total expenditure) from roads.[152] However, it rapidly became apparent that closing workhouses offered few immediate savings because of the need to compensate redundant officials and to provide modern county hospitals and county homes. Since road workers were hired by the week, and maintenance and improvement programmes were organised on an annual basis, roads offered much more scope for immediate savings. Cuts could be further justified on the grounds that road repairs helped the crown forces: a Dáil Éireann Local Government circular, dated 30 September 1920, advised councils that preference should be given to repairing by-roads, rather than the main roads which were used for British military traffic.[153] By the autumn of 1920 most counties had cut expenditure, following the withdrawal of Ministry of Transport grants and the collapse of income from rates. One rural district council in County Galway, however, was forced to abandon plans to dismiss all road workers when labourers threatened retaliatory action against 'responsible members of the rural council in their capacities as individual employers'. Labourers in nearby County Roscommon successfully resisted being laid off following their protest that it was unfair to make the working class responsible for economies in local spending at a time when there was little alternative employment.[154] In January 1921 a member of Tipperary North Riding Council informed the Department that 'there is no use lecturing us on economies, we have cut everything we can; but damn it don't expect us if we can help it to throw labourers at this time of year out of employment, I have had several severe lessons in unemployment myself and can sympathise with others.'[155] In County Mayo, by contrast, where most road work was carried out by contractors who were small farmers, the inspector alleged that he had been informed 'on all sides' that stopping road works 'entails no hardship'.

Trade union leaders argued that cuts in local authority expenditure should involve 'equality of sacrifice'. They criticised the practice of dismissing labourers while salaried officials, such as the county surveyor, remained on full pay, though when Mayo County Council stopped payments to assistant surveyors because road works had been suspended, they refused to stop work.[156] In counties where it appeared necessary to stop road maintenance for military reasons, trade unions demanded that alternative employment should be provided: crushing stones, which would be used for future road repairs. If employment was limited, preference should be given to labourers, at the expense of farmers and their families, and to workers on direct labour schemes, rather than contractors. When Limerick County Council cut road expenditure, priority was given to men who supported a family, and a limit was set of one man and one animal per household.[157] In response to pressure from the unions, Kildare County Council decided to exclude from employment on road schemes farmers with more than 30 acres and boys aged less than sixteen; it also determined that no family would have a second horse employed on public works while another horse could be obtained.[158]

The Department vacillated between placating trade union interests and attempting to reduce expenditure. It did not oppose the imposition of a closed shop, if a local authority voted in favour. When Meath County Council took this step, Rev. P. Farrell, parish priest of Ballivor, protested to W.T. Cosgrave that it was discriminatory: 'We had hoped that we were emerging from foreign oppression, is it going to be replaced by domestic tyranny?' Cosgrave argued that the council was within its rights and refused to intervene.[159] In January 1921 the Department issued a circular letter supporting trade union demands that wage cuts and unemployment should be spread among all local officials and employees, though it pointed out that many senior officials, such as assistant surveyors, had already been suspended or faced reductions in pay. However, the Department rejected calls for county secretaries and county surveyors to be suspended, arguing that such action would 'bring local government to a standstill'.

Local authority finances, 1921-22

Many Dáil deputies believed that the financial year beginning in April 1921 would bring about the collapse of local government. Seán MacEntee suggested that after 31 March county councils 'would have to accept the inevitable and refuse to carry on', adopting the position of a country at war. An equally pessimistic de Valera urged each county to 'hold out to the last' in order to vindicate claims that Irish nationalists were able to 'govern their own country'.[160] Rate demands for the 1920/21 financial year had been based on the assumption that councils would receive the usual grants from the Local Government Board. The Department insisted that estimates for the 1921/22 financial year should compensate for this loss. Circular letter number 35 informed local authorities that it was 'essential that steps should be taken to inaugurate every possible economy'.[161] Kerry County Council approved an estimate of £243,866, an increase of 22.6 per cent on the 1920/21 figure. This was actually a triumph for economy: the county had lost grants of approximately £100,000. The estimate for poor relief increased from £85,558 to £112,666; provision for roads declined by one-third from £48,848 to £32,129.[162]

The prospect of a collapse in local authority finances was made greater by the deteriorating economic conditions. Agricultural prices peaked in the second half of 1920, with the exception of fat cattle prices which peaked in the first quarter of 1921,[163] and many farmers were unable to meet their rates demands. Larger farmers insisted that local authorities reduce the wages of council labourers and the number of jobs on offer, in the belief that this would enable them to cut agricultural wages. Tipperary South Riding placed its hourly paid road workers on reduced hours in January 1921, claiming that they had recently been awarded wage increases which could no longer be met. Labourers were dismissed in February, re-employed in early April and dismissed again on 29 June, when they were owed 8-10 weeks' wages. The council chairman claimed that labourers were urgently required for agricultural work, though this was denied by trade unionists, who alleged that there was considerable local unemployment.[164] When several councils dismissed road workers in the spring of 1921, ITGWU general secretary Thomas Foran wrote to Cosgrave demanding that they be paid a dole, but Cosgrave informed the Dáil that he disapproved of paying dole to the unemployed.[165] In a private letter to Foran in April

1921, Cosgrave emphasised that there was a link between rate collection and expenditure on roads and he appealed to the ITGWU secretary to recruit council workers to a campaign to encourage the payment of rates, particularly in Counties Meath and Westmeath.

> . . . we quite appreciated that you cannot influence rate collection in any county, but we had hoped that the road-workers themselves would have been able to exercise some influence upon the rate payers and collectors with a view to prompt payment.[166]

Cosgrave assured Foran that the Department was doing 'everything possible to assuage the hardship of your members'; he also claimed that most of the Department's expenditure was occasioned by efforts to ensure that road-workers were kept at work and paid for their labour. There is no evidence to support this assertion; although the Dáil voted a sum of £100,000 in January 1921 to assist local authorities, only £10,000 had been spent by August.[167] In May, Local Government attempted to shift responsibility to the Department of Agriculture by suggesting that it devise a tillage scheme to employ idle road-workers.[168]

Although the Truce of July 1921 brought peace, it provided no relief from the problems facing local government. The Local Government Board attempted to regain control of local authorities: in August 1921, the LGB inspector visited the offices of Carlow County Council and announced that all outstanding grants would be paid and the appointment of any irregular rate collectors would be sanctioned if the council submitted its accounts for audit.[169] Rumours persisted that the withheld British government grants would be restored, so labourers were not prepared to accept economies, while ratepayers were equally unwilling to pay the high poundages levied. Kerry County Council had cut its estimate for road expenditure by one-third over the previous year; on 15 August 1921 council labourers demanded the restoration of expenditure and working conditions to 1920 levels. They were in no mood to accept the economies proposed by the inspector, including an end to the practice of having 116 road stewards supervise an average of two men apiece. Thomas Meany, chairman of the Murroe branch of the ITGWU, implored the Dáil to reverse Limerick County Council's decision to cut expenditure on road works to the minimum: 'the peace outlook is bright, so for God's sake do not let us follow the example of

Russia and let penury be the first fruits of the victory that seems to be at hand'.[170]

In an effort to respond to the post-Truce euphoria, Cosgrave announced that the Dáil would make £100,000 available to provide loans to county councils, a sum which would compensate them for approximately 10 per cent of the amount lost by the withdrawal of British grants.[171] This was a token sum: Wexford County Council received only £4,000.[172] The Department urged local authorities to provide more employment for road labourers if finances permitted and, after 'many stormy meetings, unions persuaded Laois County Council to initiate a programme of road works by direct labour which dispensed with overseers as an economy measure, though the Dáil inspector insisted on their reinstatement. This was an isolated labour victory. When Cavan County Council handed over road contracts to ITGWU branches, it faced angry protests from farmers who had previously carried out the work. The Dáil inspector claimed that Cavan had the worst roads in Ireland.[173] (Some things never change.) In October 1921 the Department circulated all inspectors with a copy of a letter from Foran which alleged that the Department's circular of January 1921, seeking 'Equality of Sacrifice' among local authority employees and officials, had been 'almost totally disregarded'. Foran claimed that only 400 road-workers were at work in March 1921, many on short-time, compared with an average of 8,500 in previous years, and that Laois was the only county to register higher employment since that date. Local Government did not rebut the charges. In October one inspector reported that not a single road was under repair in County Mayo.[174]

The report of the Dáil Éireann Department of Local Government in July 1921 had lamented the fact that with the 'almost complete disappearance of the Sinn Féin Organisation . . . there is no local authority or organisation to control the action or censure the inaction of those who were put forward as public representatives'.[175] By mid-1921 individual branches or members of Sinn Féin and the IRA were often doing more to hinder than to assist the effective working of local government. In County Longford, Foran alleged that the IRA was attempting to exercise a closed shop, allocating jobs to farmers and their relatives and leaving labourers unemployed. Although the inspector discounted these allegations, several disputes occurred between farmers and labourers concerning employment on roads in Longford, and the county council passed resolutions urging that priority

84

be given to ex-internees who had previously worked on direct labour schemes.[176]

In County Leitrim, where trade union activity appears to have been minimal, Sinn Féin clubs took control, appointing foremen, initiating road schemes, setting work quotas and allocating employment as they saw fit. Kinlough Sinn Féin club directed the local rural district council (which had attempted to retain links with the Local Government Board for some considerable time) to end direct labour and to advertise for contract tenders. One club confirmed Battie Cooney, a foreman, in his post, but gave him 'strict warnings about time and for to get a certain amount of work done each day' [sic]. Another foreman, Peter Maguire, wrote as follows to the county surveyor: 'I put my clame [sic] before Kiltyclogher Club today. I am the man that is appointed there is no change in my section. You will have a letter today from the secretary of the Club. There is part of my section very bad can I fill the ruts . . .'. In Tarmon, local people demanded a voice in the appointment of foremen. The Department ordered the county surveyor not to comply with Sinn Féin demands, but the inspector reported that the surveyor was powerless and concluded that 'every Sinn Féin Club in County Leitrim is a County Council'.[177]

When military action ceased following the Truce, some members of the IRA became involved in the burgeoning anti-rates campaign. In the Gorey area of north County Wexford, where rate collection had collapsed by August 1921, several delinquent collectors were active Volunteers.[178] In County Offaly, a protestant rate collector, working on behalf of Dáil Éireann, was threatened when he attempted to collect rates owed by a republican policeman.[179] In County Galway, where public notices had been posted urging the non-payment of rates, the campaign was led by the IRA.[180] Rate collection broke down in the Swinford area of County Mayo when the (republican) chairman of the Board of Guardians, 'a gombeen bully who has held sway for years', a man feared by the country people who obeyed him without question, alleged that rates had been struck 'on a false basis' and demanded that the collection be postponed.[181]

Other factions that engaged in anti-rates campaigns were motivated by opposition to Sinn Féin. Joseph Campbell, vice-chairman of Wicklow County Council, resigned in June 1921, charging the council with 'nepotism, graft and inefficiency'. A Department inquiry concluded that his claims were unfounded and noted that he had been a leader of the anti-rates campaign in County Wicklow. Campbell extended his campaign into north County Wexford, where he made speeches about the corruption and extravagance of Sinn Féin-controlled local authorities.[182] The anti-rates campaign flourished in the deepening agricultural recession, against a climate of rumours that the announcements of a Truce meant that ratepayers would become liable for malicious injury claims.[183] In July 1921 the Queen's (Laois) County Farmers' Association established a ratepayers' protection association to protest at council spending and institute defence measures against malicious injury claims. The meeting was held, despite Cosgrave's objections to such action 'in the present condition of the country'.[184] In an effort to diffuse this issue, in August 1921 the Dáil ministry warned decree-holders (those holding decrees awarding them compensation for malicious injuries) and solicitors acting on their behalf that the government would resist and punish any attempts to secure payment.[185]

This problem subsided, unlike the anti-rates campaigns, which developed into an anti-labourer movement. Tarbert Farmers' Union (Co. Kerry) refused to pay a rate of more than 10 shillings (50p) in the pound because of deteriorating economic conditions, and this demand was subsequently endorsed by farmers in other parts of the county; by the spring of 1922 collectors in north Kerry were being openly intimidated by members of the Farmers' Union.[186] When Patrick Belton, chairman of Dublin Ratepayers Association, who was in the process of challenging the legality of a flat rate levied by Dublin County Council, addressed a public meeting in Wexford in November 1921, O'Higgins urged Home Affairs Minister Austin Stack to have him charged with contempt of court. Stack refused.[187] By the autumn of 1921 many farmers' groups were justifying their refusal to pay rates with the argument that the growth of trade unions had forced local authorities to undertake extravagant public spending programmes. In County Kildare the Farmers' Union demanded a reduction of 3/4 (17p) in the pound on the 1921/22 estimates, to be achieved by wage cuts and reduced expenditure on roads. Unemployment gave rise to particular concern in Kildare because of the pending withdrawal of British troops from the Curragh Camp. Athy Board of Guardians, which came under labour control as a result of farmer abstentions, demanded that Kildare County Council introduce a programme of relief works, which would be financed by overdraft. Pending this, the board of guardians, which was chaired by a local ITGWU official, authorised illegal payments of outdoor relief to the unemployed, in direct contravention of the Department's orders. Farmers who had dismissed their labourers, because they allegedly could not afford to pay the higher agricultural wages authorised by Dáil Éireann, refused to pay rates and accused the labourers of 'trying to make farmers pay them by means of outdoor relief when they cannot get it any other way'.[188]

In September one prominent Tipperary farmer wrote to Cosgrave justifying his refusal to pay rates because the Truce would release large sums in withheld grants which, 'knowing the present composition of local bodies . . . would be forthwith squandered'. The writer, who asked Cosgrave if 'Dáil Éireann is a part of or allied with the Irish Transport Union', claimed that 'strikers threaten to use the power of its armed forces if their demands are not at once agreed to'. In his mind, there was little choice 'between government by the Black and Tans and government by this anti-Christian organisation'.[189] A Sinn Féin councillor in Wexford also remarked on the similarities between the Black and Tans and the Transport Workers' Union;[190] his comments might have reassured the Tipperary farmer that the Dáil and the ITGWU were not in alliance.

The Department considered various mechanisms for improving rate collection. In March 1921 Kevin O'Higgins informed the Dáil that he favoured handing over collection to either the IRA or the republican police — a police force established by Dáil Éireann whose members were mainly drawn from the Volunteers — though the latter did not offer a sufficiently strong instrument.[191] The collection in County Clare had been in the hands of the republican police for some time. However, Clare had the highest arrears in Ireland; Michael Brennan, the local IRA commander, alleged that the Truce prevented the IRA from enforcing collection.[192] The Department issued a circular letter to Clare ratepayers which blamed the higher rates poundage on the British government's decision to withhold grants; it promised substantial reductions in the following year. Clare County Council reproduced this letter in poster form, and displayed it widely in the hope of improving collection;[193] other councils followed suit. John Kelly, chairman of Offaly County Council, wrote to all defaulting ratepayers outlining the consequences of their actions.[194] When Wexford and Wicklow County Councils decided to publish lists of defaulters, the local papers refused to accept their notices, arguing that they could be liable to legal action. Wexford County Council printed the lists in poster form, though it feared that these would probably be destroyed.[195] When Kildare County Council published lists of defaulters in the *Leinster Leader*, one Church of Ireland clergyman, who had refused to pay rates to a collector whose appointment had not been sanctioned by the LGB, appealed to Dublin Castle for protection. His letter somehow made its way into the Dáil archives.[196]

Tipperary County Council persuaded Cosgrave to write personal letters to some of the largest defaulters. Perhaps the most original initiative came from the pen of a ratepayer 'who has already cheerfully faced the music':

In the trial of the Nation, when the Mother's ringing call
Speeds to men of every nation, 'your assistance children all.'
When the Tyrant is retreating, fleeing from his usurped gates,
Lend a hand in that great beating — Men of Mayo pay the Rates.

Weak your shout of 'up the rebels' — well-intentioned though you be
Might as well to try with pebbles, to dry up the mighty sea.
For your National Destruction Bull, like Satan lurking waits,
Miss the meshes of that Monster — Men of Mayo pay the Rates.

This continues for a further three verses, ending 'County finances demand it — Men of Mayo pay the rates'.[197]

Others favoured more physical methods. One collector in County Offaly felt that it would help if prominent defaulters 'got a quiet shaking up'.[198] When Wexford County Council requested the assistance of the republican police, Austin Stack pointed out that 'the police cannot be employed in the ordinary sense in the collection of rates', but assistance could be sought from the brigade police officer in specific cases.[199] In County Leitrim, where only £1,000 of almost £50,000 due in September 1921 had been collected by the following October and large arrears remained from 1920/21, the inspector attended one anti-rates meeting in an effort to explain the reasons for the high poundage. As he reported, the crowd was unreceptive; 'but for the fact that I went prepared to defend myself, I was liable to have a rough time.' He escaped by firing bullets over the heads of the crowd. The only solution to non-payment was, he suggested, to draft at least forty young men into the county with power to collect outstanding and current rates 'by any means which they may deem necessary'. His report was forwarded to cabinet, with a covering note from Cosgrave emphasising that the task could not be given to the local IRA because many of its members were identified with the anti-rates campaign. Although Cosgrave assured the cabinet that this step was necessary to avert a collapse of local administration in Leitrim, his colleagues were reluctant to acquiesce lest it might constitute a breach of the Truce.[200] If the Dáil resorted to force, it ran the risk of alienating sections of the populace.

In December 1921, James Gilven of Ardara, Co. Donegal complained to the Department that rate collectors were intimidating the people by collecting rates accompanied by members of the IRA, who threatened to seize cattle and goods in lieu. He also claimed that members of the IRA had been threatened with being sent to an unknown destination if they failed to serve civil bill processes on neighbours and relations. Gilven protested that, unless something was done, 'a state of things may arise that would be just as bad as the Black and Tan persecution that we have gone through'. The local inspector told the Department that:

> This communication gives an idea of the difficulties the rate
> collectors are up against in some of the areas of Donegal.
> Members of the IRA did go round with some collectors advising the
> people to pay and warning them of the consequences of refusal.
> I understand some of the police forces refused to service Civil Bill
> processes for rates and in one case two of the presiding justices
> were the men in the areas responsible for the anti-rates campaign.

The inspector suggested that, in its reply, the Department should emphasise that the Dáil supported all efforts to collect rates. This letter was duly sent.[201] There was a real risk that local democracy would be further damaged if the IRA became involved in tax collection. Mayo IRA attempted to impose a liquor tax in Charlestown and Westport; in early 1922 it succeeded in imposing a county rate to finance a republican police force. In County Sligo, where military assistance was used to force rate collectors to hand over money which they were refusing to lodge because the council had dismissed the bank as treasurer, the IRA demanded and illegally received £1,000 as a collection fee.[202]

Such issues occasionally led to tense relations between Local Government and the military authorities. Supple, the inspector responsible for County Galway, obtained a note from the local commandant asking certain IRA officers to assist in rate collection; five collectors were provided with two men each. After three days they had achieved a 'marked success' in collecting outstanding rates; at that stage the commanding officer withdrew the men, claiming that the instructions 'did not come from proper quarters'.[203] When an inspector requested, or instructed (there was some dispute as to which), the East Mayo brigade of the IRA to assist in suppressing the anti-rates campaign led by the Swinford IRA leader, the adjutant-general, Gearóid O' Sullivan, wrote to Cosgrave, pointing out that

> . . . the position from the army point of view is sufficiently awkward in East Mayo at the moment and if somebody from a Government Department can go around and issue instructions, specially ones which are so irregular as that alleged in this letter, a time will soon come when the Volunteers in East Mayo will not exist even on paper.

Relations between the Department of Local Government and the adjutant-general were strained. In July 1921 he forwarded reports from the Mayo inspector to the Department, but emphasised that he objected to his lines of communication being encroached on by 'documents of this nature'.[204]

The autumn of 1921 saw a strange proposal to establish administrative committees in every county. They would operate as a local cabinet; Dáil departments would delegate responsibility for local government, home affairs, education, agriculture, labour and trade and commerce. The proposal appears to have been the brainchild of either Éamon de Valera or Austin Stack. On 1 September de Valera instructed Stack to work with P. O'Keeffe, a Sinn Féin administrator,[205] and the Minister for Local Government to list committee members, 'county by county', choosing the 'very best men in the county, those who will stick through thick and thin'. It was envisaged that each committee would consist of six to nine members, including TDs, who would be appointed by the Dáil. Other members would be nominated by the local council, or by the ministry or the council chairman if the council failed to make nominations.

It was subsequently decided that all members would be chosen by the government and Cosgrave forwarded to de Valera lists of names provided by local inspectors. Each committee would have a salaried organising secretary, appointed by the ministry, with special responsibility for home affairs (e.g. police, law and order), though all committees would report to Dublin via the Department of Local Government.[206] They may have been envisaged as emergency bodies to be activated if the Truce broke down. It is unclear whether they would have supplanted local councils or acted as a further administrative layer. The proposal must be read as a vote of no confidence in existing councils.

Conclusions

The traditional nationalist account of the years 1918-22 told the story of Irish republicanism's war against the British forces. Revisionist accounts, such as that by Charles Townshend, played down both the heroism and significance of the Irish Volunteers, emphasising the limited scale of military action and the fact that Britain largely lost the conflict by default. Townshend also tended to underplay the significance of Dáil Éireann, emphasising that it held infrequent sessions which were poorly attended.[207] The history of the Dáil Department of Local Government does not fit easily into either genre. It suggests that the Dáil administration had an impact much wider than the small number of Volunteers or limited incidence of military engagements suggest. Men and women, such as local authority officials, rate collectors, bank managers and some ratepayers became involved in the struggle, willingly or otherwise, not as fighters, but in efforts to sustain a rebel administration. Much of the story is unheroic, showing people more concerned to protect property or employment than to make personal sacrifices for Irish nationalism. The Dáil's control over local government was both belated and uncertain; leadership on issues such as rates, often came from below, not from above.

The leadership's caution was motivated by a strong sense of reality. During the first half of 1920, O'Higgins was reluctant to recommend a formal break with the Local Government Board because he feared that the system would collapse without British funds. Subsequent events suggest that his fears were largely justified. Although the system of local government survived until the signing of the Anglo-Irish Treaty, by mid-1921 it appears to have been on the verge of collapse in counties such

91

as Kerry, Sligo and Leitrim. While the Department was uncertain in its handling of some matters, such as what to do about local authority labourers, or rate collection in the autumn/winter of 1920/21, it was unequivocal in its determination to prevent the emergence of a spoils system for contracts and appointments.

The real heroes are the department's inspectors: men and women working in hostile environments, their enemies not simply the British, but, as O'Higgins termed them, 'the enemy within': unhelpful banks, incompetent local officials, recalcitrant republican leaders. Like Kevin O'Higgins, the inspectors were young men and women in a hurry, who were deeply committed to the cause of Dáil Éireann, but who often lacked sympathy for local concerns and for the more mundane interests of people who did not share their commitment. Both O'Higgins and Cosgrave seem to have developed a poor opinion of the calibre of local administration during these years, though Cosgrave appears to have been more tolerant of human failings. These experiences undoubtedly influenced the Free State administration's attitude to local government in the 1920s.

Conflicts over the closure of district hospitals, or the repeated harangues which the Department delivered to hapless councils and council officials, did little to improve relations between central government and local authorities. The chairman of Louth County Council, who was determined to exclude the Dáil inspector from council meetings because he had taken similar action against a Local Government Board inspector, suggests a sobering continuity of attitudes towards supervision by Dublin, whether undertaken by a native government or by an occupying power. There is a tendency to suggest that the years after 1922 were marked by deflated expectations, as the Irish people confronted the harsh reality of independence. Reality was all too evident in local government before 1922: years when councils were faced with the need to close workhouses, to save money, and to satisfy the conflicting aspirations of labourers and large ratepayers. The following decade brought few surprises.

CHAPTER THREE

CONTINUITY OR CHANGE? THE NEW STATE, 1922-32

The final months of the Local Government Board were dominated by preparations for partition, battles against Treasury cuts and efforts to secure the future of its officials. Life was considerably disrupted by the Custom House fire of May 1921 which destroyed Board records and left it without a home. Work resumed the following day[1] in Jurys Hotel on College Green, which the Board of Works commandeered under the Defence of the Realm Act, despite protests from Dublin hotel workers.[2] The old age pensions branch moved to 198 Great Brunswick Street (now Pearse Street)[3] and the secretariat settled in Lower Fitzwilliam Street pending completion of new offices in Upper Merrion Street (now Government Buildings), which had been assigned to the LGB when the building was first planned. In January 1922, however, these premises were occupied by the provisional government, and when the Board tried to secure space in Dublin Castle, it was pre-empted by the Revenue Commissioners, and the LGB ended its days in temporary accommodation.

THE IMPACT OF PARTITION

By 1921, three-quarters of the Board's business concerned Northern Ireland.[4] The Government of Ireland Act, passed in December 1920, provided for the establishment of two subordinate parliaments. No legal basis was determined on how exchequer money for local government should be allocated between the two parliaments, so the Board provisionally assigned to Northern Ireland one-quarter of the sum available for urban housing in 1921/22.[5]

The date for transferring responsibility for local government and transport to the Government of Northern Ireland was 1 December 1921.[6] By November, seven of the Board's staff of 194 were on loan to Belfast; a further 31 either wished to transfer to Northern Ireland or were indifferent about the move; seven of these were temporary staff, who may have believed that this offered the prospect of permanent employment.[7] The Board assumed that one-quarter of staff should transfer to Belfast, but it refused to deploy anybody who was unwilling to work there, even for temporary duty. Many officials feared that service in Belfast would prejudice their chances of a post in Dublin, despite commitments to the contrary. The accounts of the future Northern Ireland Department were organised by D.L. Clarke, a LGB auditor, who attempted to replicate the Board's procedures. Arthur Scott Quekett, the LGB legal assistant, also transferred to the Northern Ireland service.

Auditors, general inspectors, medical, housing and engineering inspectors, and architects whose territory straddled the border,[8] were divided between both jurisdictions. Sir Henry Robinson tried to take advantage of the transitional arrangements to appoint his son, who had served as an LGB inspector, as an extra inspector in Northern Ireland. The overwhelming majority of LGB staff opted to remain in Dublin. They included future secretaries of the Department of Local Government and Public Health, E.P.McCarron, then an auditor class I; J. Hurson, an auditor class II who was serving as private secretary to the president of the LGB, and John Collins, second division clerk in the Lunatic Asylum office; P. A. Kennedy, a second division clerk, who was a future secretary of the Department of Health; O.J. Redmond, a lower executive officer in the poor law division, who was to become secretary of the Department of Finance in 1953, and Arthur Codling, principal clerk in the housing division and a future assistant secretary in Finance, also elected to remain in Dublin.[9] None of the Irish staff of the Ministry of Transport moved to Belfast.[10]

The Northern Ireland Department had originally been planned as a combined ministry of health and local government, the model adopted by the Irish Free State. In May 1921, however, this was altered to a Ministry for Home Affairs, which included responsibility for law and order. Samuel Watt, its first permanent secretary, was a former official of the Irish LGB and had served as Sir Henry Robinson's private secretary before his appointment in 1918 as private secretary to Edward

Shortt, then Irish chief secretary. Only 42 of the 187 officials employed in the Northern Ireland Department by 1924 had previously worked for the Board.[11]

Despite the fact that the LGB's days were numbered, its administrative structures were subjected to an overhaul in November-December 1921 which was carried out by 'some of the best brains in the British civil service'.[12] Staff were organised into grades which remain recognisable today: heads of sections, higher executives, junior executives and clerical staff, and the number of separate sections was reduced, as recommended by the Whitley Report.[13] The Treasury (Ireland) office scrutinised the Board's operations in search of economies: housing was a particular target.[14] On 30 November 1921, A.P. Waterfield, head of Treasury (Ireland), informed the Board that no new housing schemes were to be sanctioned, existing schemes were to be cut as far as practicable and the number of engineering inspectors and housing inspectors would be reduced.

This memorandum was forwarded to the Board by Joseph Brennan, a senior official at the chief secretary's office, who subsequently became secretary of the Department of Finance. This would not be Brennan's last attempt to impose economies on local government expenditure. The Board contested the proposed economies in a memorandum dated 14 December 1921, arguing that, while existing staff numbers were excessive for the present workload, they would be inadequate if conditions returned to normal.[15] One week after the Treaty had been signed, did the Board really believe that 'normal' conditions would be resumed?

THE PROVISIONAL GOVERNMENT

The Dáil ratified the Anglo-Irish Treaty on 7 January 1922, paving the way for a transfer of power. On 12 January a provisional government was established; some time later W.T.Cosgrave was allocated the Local Government portfolio, which he held until he became President on 31 August, following the death of Michael Collins. He was succeeded by Ernest Blythe.[16] Ministers of the provisional government went to Dublin Castle on 16 January for the formal hand-over of power. Sir Henry Robinson arrived for the ceremony, to find 'all the heads of departments sitting on one side of the under-secretary's room and the Sinn Féin leaders sitting opposite, glowering at each other'. Robinson remarked on the 'extreme youth' of most of the ministers; to his eyes, they seemed 'scarcely out of their teens, and all looked pale and anxious'.[17]

The provisional government had extremely limited powers. It had no authority to levy taxes and could legislate only on administrative matters.[18] This resulted in the rather unreal situation where the 1922/23 Local Government estimates were drafted by LGB officials in early January, scrutinised by the British Treasury and approved by Westminster.[19] Although the estimates assumed that the Free State government was about to take office, they took no account of its views. The estimates noted that the new government was 'sure to embark on certain new schemes, e.g. housing,' but it was decided to 'disregard this possibility'. No provision was made for a resumption of grant payments to rebel local authorities. A.R.Barlas, the LGB secretary, 'made it perfectly clear that the existing LGB would never resume relations with many of those local authorities'.

On 28 February 1922 Herbert Gattiff, a senior official in Dublin Castle, suggested that the Board discuss the estimates with Mr O'Brien[20] and Mr Brennan. He assumed that the Dáil would draw up a separate estimate providing for grants to republican local authorities and for a 'large housing policy' and that both estimates would 'need fitting together'. On 21 January the provisional government had announced an allocation of £1m. for housing from 1922/23 revenue.[21] Dublin Castle officials expressed concern at the implications of launching a housing programme 'in a great hurry' and proposed to pass on the benefits of their experience to the new administration. They also suggested that the 'Southern Treasury' press for the LGB to be replaced by 'an informal committee of heads'.[22]

'Fitting together' two sets of estimates was a relatively easy task in comparison with the problems posed by the existence of two competing departments. A proclamation issued on 16 January instructed all British civil servants in Ireland to continue with their normal duties unless instructed otherwise by the provisional government. No transfers, dismissals, promotions or appointments were to take place without the latter's authority.[23] The public was informed that all departments would continue to perform their duties unless changes were ordered in the public interest.[24] In January 1922 one LGB official noted that there were many of his colleagues 'who don't want to serve the Provisional Government but won't volunteer for Ulster'.[25] Senior officials, particularly those with over forty years' service, were encouraged to retire; eleven did so between August 1921 and 31 March 1922.[26]

All heads of sections either transferred to Northern Ireland or retired, with the exception of Arthur Codling, who tried to secure a transfer to London, both for domestic reasons and because he saw few prospects of promotion in Local Government. He soon moved to Finance.[27] The Board lost both its chief architect, L.E.H. Deane, and its legal adviser, Sir George Vanston. P.C. Cowan, the chief engineering inspector, was dismissed by Ernest Blythe in 1923. One of the Board's inspectors, E.A. Saunderson, son of the former Ulster Unionist leader who had been given a permanent post through the patronage of Irish chief secretary Sir Walter Long, and had subsequently served as secretary to the lord lieutenant Viscount French,[28] wrote from 35 Belgrave Square, London seeking a transfer to London. Richard Eckersley, a higher executive officer, wished to transfer to Edinburgh, or any other provincial centre, because he was an English national. R.P. Beresford, a general inspector, requested a transfer to London if the new ministry intended to retire him because he was entitled to only a modest pension, though he would prefer to remain in employment in Ireland. A. Tennyson, another inspector, wrote from Eaton Square, London in September 1922 seeking transfer to London, because if he stayed in Dublin he would be required to take an oath of allegiance to the Irish Free State. Tennyson claimed on his return from military service that he had taken an 'oath of allegiance to the King, to which allegiance I have never ceased to adhere'. He requested a copy of the Irish oath. Although numerous London-based officials with Irish names requested transfer to Dublin, they tended to be junior clerks, and transfers were possible only between officials of similar grade;[29] only two transfers took place in the Department of Local Government.[30]

The story of the former staff of the Dáil Éireann Department of Local Government is complicated. On 21 January 1922 ministers were given the authority to make necessary staff appointments and six days later the provisional government approved Cosgrave's proposal for the administration of the Local Government Board 'by associating in its control certain members of his department', presumably former officials of the Dáil Éireann Department of Local Government.[31] Relations between the rival administrations were not improved by the LGB's efforts to press ahead with the Soldiers and Sailors scheme, which provided land and housing for British army veterans, or by its decision to establish two new rural district councils in unionist areas of east Donegal.

Early in 1922 officials of the Dáil Department drafted a memorandum for submission to cabinet (though there is no evidence that it was actually sent), protesting that there was 'no unity of ideas, or co-relation of work between the staffs, and the old staff are doing official acts, which, in the eyes of the outside public, we are responsible for, as the people presume we are in effective control.' They demanded that all LGB officials be placed on indefinite leave, with the exception of those in the old age pensions section, and that a new Board whose members would be drawn from the heads of Dáil departments be appointed, with Mr McArdle as secretary. The memorandum insisted that members of the Dáil staff be promoted to section heads in the Local Government Department. The memorial also demanded that the Department 'continue to function as a Dáil Department'; this presumably meant that it would be controlled by the Dáil, rather than by the provisional government. Although officials requested a move to larger premises (from the City Hall), they were unwilling to join the LGB in Jurys Hotel since 'it might be thought that they were taking our Staff over and we do not want to create that impression'. The Dáil officials conceded that the existing staff of 60 was incapable of handling all the Department's work and decided that they needed LGB expertise in formulating a housing programme.

Although Cosgrave allegedly agreed with 'the facts as stated,' he refused to hand over control to Dáil officials. As a compromise, he suggested that the assistant minister (presumably O'Higgins) pay a daily visit to the LGB offices to oversee correspondence and to ensure that all instructions received his sanction. The latter was unwilling to take on the additional duties; he claimed that it would leave him with an excessive workload. Because he feared that 'the old staff' (i.e. LGB) would question his authority; he favoured giving overall control to the Dáil staff.[32]

On 22 February, however, the Dáil staff came under the control of a former LGB official. A handwritten note signed by Cosgrave stated:

The Minister of Local Government desires that Mr E.P. McCarron
B.L. be facilitated freely in all respects as regards any information
he requires in all matters affecting Local Government. Officials in
charge of papers shall submit them for decision at the City Hall and

take any necessary directions from Mr McCarron, who is authorised by the Minister to receive them.[33]

A copy of this letter was formally initialed by Barlas, the Board secretary. It is unknown how McCarron was selected for this role. An auditor class I, he had been on loan from the LGB from November 1921 to February 1922, but his actual role during these months is not recorded. The provisional government appointed Joseph Brennan, another Irishman, who held a senior post in the British administration in Ireland after Michael Collins had asked Sir Alfred Cope, then in charge of the British administration in Dublin, for the names of suitable Irishmen working in Dublin Castle who might help in founding an Irish exchequer.[34]

In contrast to Brennan, McCarron proved a controversial appointment. On 1 March 1922, Joseph McDonagh, an anti-Treaty TD, asked Cosgrave in the Dáil whether he had taken McCarron into his service. Cosgrave denied doing so and claimed that McCarron remained on the payroll of the LGB, though he was 'acting under my direction, with my authority in all matters affecting all functions of the Local Government Board in such activities as were not dealt with by the Local Government Department in the pre-Truce period.' McDonagh claimed that McCarron had attempted to enlist in the British army during the war but had been refused permission because Sir Henry Robinson thought him indispensable; he also alleged that McCarron had offered his services to the British military in Drogheda during Easter Week 1916 and that, as LGB auditor, he had surcharged the Balrothery Board of Guardians because it had paid the salary of its medical officer of health, Sinn Féin TD Dr Richard Hayes, while he was interned. Cosgrave pleaded ignorance of the first two charges and pointed out that McCarron would have failed in his duty if he had not imposed a surcharge on the Balrothery Board of Guardians. It also emerged that Cosgrave had consulted Dr Hayes and the lord mayor of Dublin before making the appointment; Hayes had not objected.[35]

On 10 March 1922 Cosgrave informed the provisional government that he was taking control of the housing board of the LGB. On 1 April 1922 all remaining British government functions passed into provisional government control. A draft public notice to this effect was published on 4 April.[36] On 4 October 1922 the provisional government transferred responsibility for 'roads, bridges, ferries and traffic thereon' from the

Ministry of Economic Affairs to the Ministry of Local Government.[37] The 1924 Ministers and Secretaries Act brought a change of title, to the Department of Local Government and Public Health,[38] but no change in remit.

Both administrations appear to have continued to operate separately for some time. M. de Lacy, who had acted as secretary of the Dáil Department of Local Government, contacted Cosgrave directly on matters concerning inspectors,[39] though many inspectors transferred to other duties. Éamon Coogan became Garda Commissioner, Seamus Murphy was appointed special commissioner in charge of the South Dublin Union; one inspector joined the civil service as an executive officer, others were deployed to deal with refugees from Belfast. An attendance book from 1922 suggests the cultural chasm in the ministry: former members of the Dáil Department signed the register in Irish, ex-LGB members in English. G. Gumbrille, R.J. Baker, J. Bridgeman and others signed side by side with Caitlin Ui Bebhinn, Seamus Ua Caomhánaigh and their colleagues. McCarron's ascendancy was clear. By April (and possibly earlier; file survival is poor) he was in regular contact with Finance about the allocation of funds for housing, local taxation grants and the Department's budget and was being described as the accounting officer, equivalent to a department secretary.[40]

Meanwhile the Department of Finance, which was dominated by former Dublin Castle officials, was exerting its authority over personnel and expenditure. On 7 April 1922 Finance circulated a memorandum requiring that all proposals for expenditure be submitted for its approval; in normal circumstances its decision would be final.[41] On 4 May the provisional government approved Collins's announcement that the Minister for Finance was responsible for the transfer of staff necessitated by the establishment or reorganisation of departments; the decision of the secretary of the Treasury would be regarded as final.[42] In June W. O'Brien, of the Ministry of Finance, drew ministers' attention to the necessity for obtaining Finance sanction 'for new or increased charges on public funds and particularly for any appointments, promotions or alterations of status or remuneration of any offices'. Accounting officers of the individual departments were responsible for ensuring compliance.[43]

On 20 July 1922 Local Government submitted a memorandum to Cornelius Gregg in Finance, outlining proposals for reorganising the staff in Local Government. It claimed that 'under the recent duality of control and consequent disorganisation we have found it quite impossible to carry on the duties of the Local Government Section on an efficient and ordered basis, and have necessarily had recourse to temporary expedients of various kinds. One effect has been that some of our officers have been engaged continually for some months past on multifarious duties for ten or twelve hours daily.'[44] A further memorandum submitted in September 1922 claimed that the former Board's junior officials had been 'largely dispersed on loan to other departments', whether by accident or design we do not know. Local Government proposed to appoint six acting section heads and to appoint deputies and sub-deputies of sections within six weeks, although nine vacancies in the accounts branch had not been filled by September 1923.

Most vacancies were filled by former LGB officials, the majority of them Irish and probably catholic. Their triumph at the expense of the former officials of the Dáil Department was probably inevitable, given the number of former LGB officials in key posts and the power exercised by the Department of Finance, which was determined to uphold the procedures of the British civil service. Arthur Codling, still in Local Government, bombarded McCarron with lists of recommended names. A memorandum to Finance, dated 29 September 1922, claimed that

> The accession of Dáil staff did not solve the resulting practical
> difficulties because the extent and methods of government
> involved in the Dáil system required only a very small intern staff.
> In examining the qualifications of this intern staff it has been found
> that only three or four members possess qualifications superior to
> the standard of lower clericals in the ordinary Civil Service.

Cosgrave, now President, contacted Gregg to argue the case for paying higher salaries to some former Department of Local Government officials, though he agreed that the majority were of low calibre and that the proposed appointments 'provide a very good method of dealing with an unusual and rather difficult situation'. Although the new Department was dominated by ex-LGB officials, its composition differed dramatically from the Local Government Board of 1920/21. By 1927 only eleven senior officials of the Irish LGB survived, whose former status entitled them to first-class travel and generous subsistence allowances: E.P. McCarron, now secretary; J.F. Miley, chief legal adviser and former auditor; J. T. Keily, registrar and inspector of old age pension appeals; Dr E. F. Stephenson, chief medical adviser; R.J. Baker, inspector of audits; plus two auditors and four medical inspectors.[45]

Despite the fact that most senior LGB officials had retired or been transferred, relations between both factions of the merged Department remained uneasy. The former staff of the Dáil Department were not formally absorbed into the new Department until July 1922. McCarron's status was uncertain for some months. A surviving draft of a letter from Cosgrave to Gregg in August 1922 contains a sentence, which is crossed out, stating that 'Mr. McCarron desires that any proposals affecting his position should be deferred for the present'.[46] He was appointed secretary on 12 September 1922. Blythe's minute to Finance, recommending the appointment, hints at McCarron's triumph in a departmental schism. It states that McCarron 'will act as chief administrative officer and will exercise authority generally over the work of the General Local Administration Branch (to include all services heretofore conducted by the Local Government Board and Local Government Department, the General Register Office, the Office of Reformatories and Office of Inspector of Lunatics). Mr de Lacy will act as Principal of General Local Administrative Branch'. de Lacy served as assistant secretary until he retired on 11 November 1943, his sixty-fifth birthday.[47]

In an unpublished memoir, written many years later, Blythe claimed that McCarron's appointment, made on Cosgrave's advice, resulted in a crisis of authority within the Department, 'corresponding to that which had arisen in the Civic Guards when certain Ex-RIC men had been employed as officers and instructors': the LGB was viewed 'with some of the hatred with which Volunteers looked upon the headquarters staff of the RIC'. Following the announcement of McCarron's appointment, rumours (subsequently confirmed) reached Blythe that former officials of the Dáil Department were threatening to resign *en masse* and hoping to carry all county councils over to the anti-Treaty side. Blythe rejected McCarron's offer to resign and succeeded in splitting the dissident ranks. According to his uncorroborated account, Cosgrave and McCarron had fixed the salaries for all ex-DELG officials at approximately £500, though these had not yet been announced. Blythe took the list and, without any knowledge of the individuals concerned, increased and reduced salaries at random, while maintaining the total bill. When the differences in salary became public, it led to a 'deep and lasting split' and the threat of mutiny receded.[48]

The administrative transition took place against a background of incipient and actual civil war. Discontent over local government matters merged with the anti-Treaty campaign. In May 1922 Tubbercurry Union, Co. Sligo, which had opposed the reform of the poor law, passed a resolution calling for the resignation of the provisional government.[49] The Dáil Department's final report in April 1922 noted that raiders had seized explosives designed for quarrying, and money belonging to local authorities, including proceeds of dog licences, an important source of local revenue, had been taken in post-office raids.[50] The Department was also concerned about the illegal practice of voting a rate in aid of the Volunteers.[51] Michael Hopkinson has emphasised that the disruption of these years

> . . . should not be seen purely in the context of political and military divisions over the Treaty. Much of the lawlessness of the whole Civil War period should be put down to the weakness of central and local government.[52]

Anti-treaty elements made no attempt to establish an alternative local government administration, though some councils, notably Kerry County Council, passed into 'republican' control. Despite the problems which the civil war posed for local authorities, the threat of bankruptcy was removed because the banks provided councils with temporary overdrafts, on the Department's authorisation.[53] In July 1922, the provisional government suggested that it enlist the help of 'influential persons such as clergy doctors and bankers' in deterring the irregulars (those who opposed the Anglo-Irish Treaty) from obstructing roads. Cosgrave issued a circular, pointing out that the disruption of transport would lead to unemployment.[54] The destruction continued. Waterford city was effectively cut off when its rail link was broken and roads were blocked.

Although the Department of Industry and Commerce was primarily responsible for employment policy, Local Government's report in April

1922 noted that, 'Unemployment is always revealed at once in the pulse of Local Government'. Reports suggested that conditions in parts of the western seaboard were 'clearly bordering on famine'. The abolition of the Congested Districts Board, which had been responsible for western affairs for the previous thirty years, left the Department to tackle problems that were reminiscent of the 1880s. When Cosgrave requested a sum of £5,000 in March 1922 to provide loans for seed potatoes in Clifden and Oughterard, LGB veterans must have felt a sense of *déjà vu*.[55] Deputations to the provisional government complained of severe unemployment; foundries in Wexford town were at a virtual standstill. Many groups requested the government to inaugurate relief works.[56]

Cosgrave reacted cautiously to such pleas. On 13 February O'Higgins complained to the provisional government that Cosgrave had objected to spending £250,000, which had become available from withheld local taxation grants, on housing and road schemes; he would prefer to use the money to reduce rates. The government decided that Collins and O'Higgins should meet Cosgrave to 'explain the position' and on 10 March the money was made available to county councils for unemployment schemes.[57] The promise of grants helped to ensure the continuing loyalty of local authorities; in May the provisional government approved Cosgrave's decision to refuse a grant to Mayo County Council which had 'adopted a defiant attitude towards the Local Government Authority . . . until he is satisfied that business was transacted according to generally accepted regulations.'[58]

By 7 April the Department had allocated £66,000. Only £75,000 was actually spent on public works during 1922/23. Finance appropriated the remainder of the £250,000, which came from withheld local taxation grants, for other purposes.[59] This was by no means the only occasion when Finance plundered money belonging to Local Government. In March 1922 the House of Commons approved the release of £1.13m. in withheld local taxation grants. By September 1922 Finance had plundered almost £200,000, which it refused to repay, despite repeated pressure from W.T. Cosgrave and expressions of despair on the part of local authorities.

Although Finance's actions are intelligible, given the precarious state of government finances, they tested the loyalty of local authorities at a sensitive time. When the Department informed An Seabhac, chairman of Kerry County Council, on 1 May 1922 that the council would receive £10,000 from deferred local taxation grants, he told the minister that 'it will carry us on for a fortnight or so — no more. £10,000 is precious little help to us who owe c. £65,000 and have weekly expenditure of £3,700 to £4,000.' He warned that it was futile to collect rates until after the election in June: 'collectors are only laughed at — though we have three armies in Kerry'. The county urgently needed funds to pay 'the army of unpaid officials and public employees', whose pay was often nine months in arrears. Finance was unsympathetic and proposed withholding all grants from counties where land purchase annuities were heavily in arrears and dog licence receipts had been seized, or where councils were defying the orders of the provisional government. Cosgrave argued that, for greater discretion, the Department's policy 'would be regulated by consideration of all the local conditions and by information available from local inspectors'.[60]

UNFINISHED BUSINESS: REGULARISING THE DECISIONS OF THE DÁIL MINISTRY

Among the first tasks facing the government of the Irish Free State when it took office in December 1922 was the need to give legal sanction to decisions taken by the Dáil administration. The 1923 Local Authorities Indemnity Act did so in respect of the acts of local authorities between 31 March 1920 and 6 December 1922,[61] including local appointments and poor law reform. It also made provision for compensating rate collectors who had forfeited their bonds as a result of obeying orders issued by Dáil Éireann[62] and gave the minister greater control over expenditure on poor relief by local authorities.[63] This was merely a holding operation; the Department was determined to impose a greater degree of uniformity on county health and welfare schemes and did so in the 1925 Local Government Act.

FINANCIAL SETTLEMENTS

The government of the Irish Free State and local councils both expected to receive substantial sums from the British Exchequer in the form of withheld grants from the Road Fund or from the local taxation account, and many councils disregarded all pleas for economy for that reason. Such an attitude failed to recognise that the Department of Finance, which was responsible for negotiating these settlements, was primarily concerned with the health of the national exchequer, and was prepared to appropriate any windfall sums for its own needs, even if this threatened the survival of county councils. For perhaps the first, but not for the last time, Local Government found itself in an invidious intermediary role.

The Road Fund appeared to offer one of the largest pots of gold. Proceeds from road licences and motor excise taxes throughout the British Isles were divided among the four countries of the UK on the basis of their respective populations, initially by the Road Board and later by the Ministry of Transport, which was based in London.[64] During World War I this money was commandeered for general purposes. When the war ended, the Westminster parliament voted a special grant of £8.25m. for road expenditure. Although Ireland believed that by March 1919 it was entitled to £833,000, both from this special vote and from the proceeds of excise and motor vehicle duties, the country was allocated less than £300,000.[65] Ireland received little money from the Road Fund after 1919. Motor registration nearly collapsed when the RIC retreated to the major towns and many vehicle-licensing records were destroyed during the Anglo-Irish war.[66]

In February 1922 the provisional government began the lengthy process of reclaiming the money owed to Ireland from the Road Fund. Dublin-based officials of the Ministry of Transport, the only people who understood the complex financial arrangements, gave their full support to the provisional government's efforts. On 8 March 1922 O'Higgins wrote to J. J. Blake in the Dublin office reminding him of 'the necessity of keeping close on the tail of monies, which in your opinion may properly be regarded as Irish monies'. Officials in the London office of the Ministry of Transport were reluctant even to pay grants which had been approved in 1920. They also disputed Ireland's claim to 7 per cent of the £8.25m. post-war restoration fund, arguing that this was not a *quid pro quo* for money diverted from the Road Fund, though they left open the possibility of making an *ex gratia* lump sum payment in view of the poor state of Irish roads and the fact that Southern Ireland had received little by way of grants during 1920/21.[67] Dublin-based officials were confident that their claim would be upheld if it was submitted to arbitration and they produced a detailed memorandum in support. By the summer of 1922 they estimated that Ireland was owed approximately £300,000 in untransferred licence and fuel duties. More than half this sum had been promised to local authorities for work that had already been completed. However the Irish authorities did not pursue their claim to an unspecified share of the Road Fund surplus of £13.3m..

The Department of Local Government found itself in an invidious position: caught between angry councils that were demanding grant payments which had been due since 1920, yet dependent on Finance to extract the money from Britain and to pass it on to local authorities. Damage to roads and bridges arising from the Anglo-Irish war and the civil war totalled £553,642. Over £310,000 of this damage occurred after the Truce.[68] According to J. Quigley, who subsequently became the Department's chief roads engineer, bridge-wrecking became 'a kind of national pastime', the resort of a 'small and turbulent minority' who were often disgruntled unemployed road workers.[69] When McCarron asked Finance in June 1923 to put pressure on the British authorities to pay outstanding Road Fund grants, Brennan minuted that he did not believe that 'these alleged past commitments of the Road Fund should be accepted automatically against our own Fund even when we have taken over our apportioned share from the British'. Although Brennan agreed some months later that all proper claims by local authorities should be met from the Irish Road Fund, with the matter of British commitments being left to international negotiations, this was of dubious benefit to the councils, since the claims were to be met from a sum of £100,000 which had been earmarked for improving trunk roads. Irish claims on the Road Fund were gradually whittled down; by 1926 over £38,000 was outstanding; by March 1927 this had fallen to £7,000.[70] Most of the cost of repairing damaged roads and bridges was met by the Irish Exchequer via the 1923 Damage to Property (Compensation) Act. Britain provided £70,000 towards the repair of roads and bridges damaged by Crown forces, and the Road Fund provided £1.7m. for general repairs and reconstruction.[71]

The outstanding financial arrangements concerning the Local Loans Fund were settled without controversy. This fund was established in 1887 to consolidate all Exchequer loans for local purposes; special Local Loans Stock was issued to fund loans authorised by the Treasury, the Public Works Commissioners, the Irish Board of Works and the Irish Land Commission. By 1920/21 a total of £15m. was outstanding in Ireland.[72] Irish liabilities were not finally resolved until the so-called 'ultimate financial settlement' of March 1926, when Ireland agreed to pay an annuity of £450,000 for twenty years to wipe out all loans.[73] Outstanding repayments under the Local Fund were treated as revenue of the Irish Free State.[74]

Claims for compensation were an entirely different matter. According to Ronan Fanning, 'the question of liability for compensation for property damaged and injuries suffered during the Anglo-Irish War of 1919-21' was 'undeniably the most complex and sensitive of the post-Treaty problems to be resolved in Anglo-Irish financial relations'.[75] By December 1921 malicious and criminal injury awards against local authorities totalled £1.486m.. Britain proposed to settle these claims from withheld local taxation grants. According to their calculations, this would leave them owing only £250,000 to local authorities.[76] Most claims had arisen during the course of the Anglo-Irish war and had not been contested by local authorities. In January 1922 a three-man commission (one Irish and two British nominees) was appointed to adjudicate on all claims involving property which had arisen during the period 21 January 1919 to 11 July 1921.[77]

Under the 1923 Damage to Property (Compensation) Act, the Irish Exchequer assumed liability for claims arising from political disturbances between 11 July 1921 and 20 March 1923, the end of the civil war, though local authorities were expected to assist the state solicitor in contesting them. Local authorities remained liable for awards resulting from incidents before January 1919, but since most of these decrees had not been contested, councils were unwilling to honour them, on the grounds that many awards were excessive. The majority had already been paid by the British government and they suggested that Finance recover the money by withholding it from grants paid to councils from the Local Taxation Account. However Finance sought advice from Local Government about the legality of doing this. The response was unequivocal. McCarron told Brennan that the Minister 'feels that the position of this Department has been already somewhat prejudiced by efforts made to induce local bodies to meet claims arising from their refusal to recognise British authorities after the Local Government Elections in 1920'. Enforcing such payments was not strictly within the Department's jurisdiction; he suggested that the parties concerned should avail of the 'ordinary processes of the law'.[78]

Local authorities also resented being lumbered with the cost of compensating officials who were either dismissed or had resigned during the Anglo-Irish war because they were unwilling to co-operate with the Dáil Department. Thirty-five people were affected, half of them rate collectors — twelve from County Wexford — together with the former county secretaries of Roscommon, Meath and Offaly; Sir H. Campbell, former town clerk to Dublin Corporation, and his assistant; several clerks of unions or clerks to rural district councils, a former midwife from Killadysert Union, Co. Clare, and seven members of the staff of Limerick Technical Institute: the principal, the assistant secretary, four teachers and the charwoman. The majority were awarded pensions or gratuities by the Local Government Board under the 1919 Local Government Act and these were confirmed by sealed order, though Irish civil servants believed most settlements to be excessive.

In other cases no award had been determined. In February 1922 the House of Commons insisted that the provisional government agree to honour those awards as a precondition for handing over outstanding local taxation grants. All awards were submitted to arbitration by Mr Justice Wylie, and the Irish government agreed to honour his decision; if the Wylie award was less than the original, the British government would pay the difference.

When the Irish government attempted to make the local authorities which had formerly employed these officials responsible for paying the awards, the councils dug in their heels and threatened to resist any legal action by the aggrieved pensioners on the grounds that the dismissals were valid. Local Government put pressure on the exchequer to bear the cost because officials feared that they would be forced to suspend the defiant councils.[79] The agreed compromise provided for the cost of the awards to be deducted from the Local Taxation Fund, before it was divided between individual counties. This saved face all round: the cost was borne by local funds, but no individual county was liable. It also proved necessary to make provision for compensating some categories of officials who had lost their jobs as a result of the closure of workhouses but were not entitled to pensions under existing regulations, such as assistant clerks, who had been employed directly by county secretaries or by clerks of boards of guardians, rather than by the local authority.[80]

Awards of local authority pensions were undoubtedly coloured by clientilism and by politics: while councillors refused to pay pensions to former unionist sympathisers, the Department uncovered numerous instances where men were hired for pensionable positions without medical examination and then were pensioned off on grounds of ill-health within a short period of time, often with pensions amounting to two-thirds of salary. In 1923 the Department introduced temporary powers to subject all local authority pensions to ministerial sanction.[81] Regulations were clarified and made permanent in the 1925 Local Government Act.[82]

The Reconstruction of Dublin

By 1923 O'Connell Street, the main street of the new state's capital city, was in ruins. Lower O'Connell Street was a casualty of the 1916 Rising, Upper O'Connell Street was wrecked during the civil war. Town planning enthusiasts had responded to the destruction of 1916 by drafting ambitious plans for a city centre, which would be worthy of a capital city. The Dublin Reconstruction (Emergency Provisions) Act 1916, which was drafted following negotiations between the LGB, city business interests, Corporation representatives and Raymond Unwin, a leading British town planner, gave the city architect a virtual veto over redevelopment plans, though there was provision for arbitration in the event of a dispute. The LGB would provide loan capital for redevelopment, and Dublin Corporation was empowered to acquire derelict sites in order to widen streets.[83] However, most of Lower O'Connell Street was still derelict when civil war broke out in 1922. The 1924 Dublin Reconstruction (Emergency Provisions) Act strengthened Dublin Corporation's power to acquire derelict sites and extended the Corporation's power to include the redevelopment of Upper O'Connell Street.[84]

Reconstruction was further delayed by the diverging wishes of the city commissioners (Dublin Corporation had been suspended), who were primarily concerned with the streetscape and the desire of O'Connell Street businessmen to rebuild their premises as cheaply as possible. On 9 September 1924 McCarron told the secretary of the Royal Institute of the Architects of Ireland that the major cause of delay was the question of 'the coordinated treatment of frontages with reference specifically to the costs of simple cut stone fronts as compared with fronts of brick and stone'. Although McCarron consulted architects and the building trades employers' association, the views of W.T. Cosgrave and Ernest Blythe proved more influential. J.J. McElligott of the Department of Finance informed McCarron that both the President and the Minister for Finance had agreed that

. . . Corporation requirements from the aesthetic and town-planning point of view should be reduced to a minimum in order to expedite rebuilding. They consider that insisting on the proper alignment and fenestration is of course essential and as to materials they think that brick and stone fronts, if not plain brick fronts, should be sufficient.

Cosgrave cited his personal experience of using cut-stone. Although the specifications for the Cosgrave family home required cut-stone only on the four corners, the porch and chimney top, this had cost £800, or nearly one-sixth of the total bill of £4,900. In the light of Cosgrave's experience, McElligott emphasised that, while they should endeavour to have brick and stone fronts as 'the maximum requirement', it was essential to 'take a bold line of action' to ensure speedy rebuilding.[85]

Reconstruction continued to be postponed because the Department of Finance refused to provide the Dublin Commissioners with the necessary capital. In 1923, 1924, 1925 and 1926 they rejected requests from Local Government to sanction loans for this purpose from the Local Loans Fund and denied that their parsimony was delaying reconstruction. In September 1926 John Leydon, then in Finance, told James Hurson, a senior official in the Department, that his (Hurson's) 'representations leave me unmoved'. Finance adopted a hard-line because the Dublin Commissioners had not involved them in determining the amounts awarded to owners of damaged property, which Finance believed had been made on 'a wholly fictitious basis'. The fact that the rebuilt properties would represent a permanent asset to the city (in the form of rates income) was also cited as an argument against any Exchequer contribution.[86]

Rebuilding was eventually made possible as a result of legislation passed in 1925. Local Government made a major contribution to the city of Dublin, handing over Charlemont House, formerly the Registrar General's office, for use as a Municipal Gallery of Modern Art, ending the saga associated with this project and providing partial compensation for the destruction of the Hibernian Gallery in 1916.[87]

PARTITION

There was little contact between the Dáil Department of Local

Government and nationalist councils within the six counties of Northern Ireland during the years 1920-22, though some lesser councils swore allegiance to Dáil Éireann in 1920.[88] The Irish Parliamentary Party continued to dominate nationalist politics in northern counties while the Dáil failed to formulate a clear policy on Ulster. During the summer and autumn of 1921, with the establishment of a separate Northern Ireland state imminent, many nationalist councils, particularly those in west Ulster, contacted Dáil Éireann to seek support for their campaign to be excluded from the Northern state. The Dáil ministers decided that these local authorities should pledge allegiance to Dáil Éireann and repudiate the authority of the Northern state in an effort to exert some leverage at the Anglo-Irish talks then underway in London.

By early December 1921 Tyrone County Council and eight smaller local authorities had followed this course of action and the Dáil Department of Local Government moved its inspector Seán MacCraith to Omagh. However when Dawson Bates, Northern Ireland Minister of Home Affairs, introduced legislation empowering him to replace any refractory local authority by paid commissioners, Tyrone County Council acknowledged the *de facto* jurisdiction of the Northern Ireland parliament. Fermanagh County Council declared its allegiance to Dáil Éireann and was dissolved on 21 December.[89] MacCraith's report from Omagh, dated 1 December 1921, indicates the uncertain attitudes of both Northern nationalists and the Dáil administration.

> Here at the present moment supporters cannot make up their minds on the best course to adopt: they appear to think (perhaps rightly) that local tactics should be changed with the changed proposals. Personally I think that, as the great principle cannot and will not change, the work should go on irrespective and in the teeth of shouts from the North East Corner. I am persuaded that much capital could be made out of the majorities in our favour in Carsonia.* But I cannot venture on any lines unless I have authority to do so and I hope guidance also. Seeing that I have neither and that local supporters think that they are not yet in a position to give

---

*'Carsonia' was a term which was widely used both by politicians and officials associated with the first and second Dála to describe the Ulster counties that were included in the Northern Ireland state. The term also occurs in files relating to Northern Ireland during the early 1920s but seems to have died out after the Boundary Commission collapsed in 1925.

any useful information or to take any definite steps, then I have no alternative but to move to some place where there is work to be done.[90]

On 1 February 1922 Collins and Griffith received a memorial, which had been signed by chairmen of three rural district councils, three boards of guardians, one urban district council and one body of town commissioners in County Down. It claimed that every local governing body but one, in an area stretching from Strangford Lough to Carlingford Lough — territory 'not incomparable in area with some of the smaller counties' with a valuation greater than nineteen counties and a population greater than fourteen, had an anti-partition majority.[91] Yet there is no evidence that the provisional government's irredentist approach to Northern Ireland, which was most evident in Dublin's commitment to pay the salaries of Northern teachers and to arrange for pupils to sit the intermediate certificate examinations,[92] ever extended to local government. In April 1922 Griffith, Cosgrave and O'Higgins, who, unlike Collins, were cautious on this issue, urged a delegation of Northern nationalist councillors to recognise the Stormont government on the grounds that, otherwise, they would be deprived of representation at the Boundary Commission. In support of his case, Cosgrave referred to the difficulties that the Dáil had faced in preserving local government during the Anglo-Irish war.[93] When anti-Treaty deputies pressed him for a statement of government policy, Cosgrave pointed out that few Northern counties had pledged allegiance to Dáil Éireann before the Truce. He claimed that future policy was being considered by a 'Board of Directors of Local Government'.[94]

The provisional government lost interest in Northern Ireland following the outbreak of civil war. In the summer of 1925, with the report of the Boundary Commission imminent, the Department of the President instructed Local Government to make preparations for taking control of local authorities in areas which would be transferred to the Irish Free State. They were to ensure that there should be no interruption in vital services, minimal inconvenience to residents, and if possible to avoid the need for special legislation. Transferred areas were to be placed under the control of adjoining Saorstát counties, though if a full rural district council was transferred it would remain an autonomous unit, despite the fact that these councils had been abolished in the Irish Free State.

The President's Department apparently assumed that a substantial part of south Down would be transferred. The Department of Local Government obtained maps of district electoral divisions in the Newry area and gathered data on unemployment in the Newry and Kilkeel Unions. No maps were provided for Tyrone and Fermanagh; there may have been an assumption that both counties would be transferred *in toto*. Local Government proposed to allocate a sum of £10,000 to replace unemployment relief works being funded by the Northern government. This was sanctioned by Finance, and McCarron was advised to collect as much advance information as possible about distress and relief works in Newry and other areas 'likely to be affected by the decision'. Brennan recommended that Local Government establish temporary offices in border areas, which would act as the 'main channel of information and instructions for settling problems' in transferred areas; he stated that 'it would be quite unsatisfactory for us to place our sole reliance in such matters upon more or less casual help from friendly individuals across the border, who may or may not be transferred'. The decision to suppress the report of the Boundary Commission brought an end to these plans.

The major point of contact between both ministries related to the transfer of documents. In 1922 the Northern Ireland Ministry of Home Affairs sought to acquire the title deeds of workhouses, maps and plans of sewerage schemes and the civil registers of births, marriages and deaths relating to the territory of Northern Ireland. McCarron recommended that no transfers take place pending the report of the Boundary Commission. On 20 January 1922 Sir William Thompson, the Registrar General, wrote to the under-secretary in Dublin Castle proposing that civil registration records remain in Dublin because it would be impractical to split them. He suggested that an agency arrangement to facilitate access and provide copies should be negotiated with the Northern Ireland authorities. Some time later the assistant registrar suggested that there might be legal obstacles to the transfer of documents relating to the period before 1 July 1922 when a Northern Ireland Registrar General's Office had come into existence.

At this point the file goes cold, save for a note dated 14 August 1923, stating that all papers in connection with this topic had been destroyed in a fire at the Rotunda Skating Rink in November 1922.[95] By the summer of 1926 both governments had reached agreement on a number of minor claims concerning local authorities in border areas and Dublin had approved the transfer of plans, maps and deeds, together with personnel records of former LGB officials then working in Northern Ireland. However the Department refused to contemplate segregating Northern Ireland birth, marriage and death registration records because it would entail the destruction of more than 2,000 bound volumes and would reduce the Registrar General's Office to chaos. T. Ó Muirgheasa, assistant registrar general, subsequently admitted that these difficulties could have been surmounted. Dublin's intransigence was politically motivated, as was Stormont's determination to obtain these documents. When Stormont requested the transfer of wills and other documents controlled by Irish Departments, Henry O'Friel, secretary of the Department of Justice, responded:

> If it were clear that the retention of these documents in Dublin was imposing an unfair burden on the administration of Government Departments in Northern Ireland that would, no doubt, be a good reason for considering favourably the question of a transfer. So far as the knowledge of this Department extends however the object of the Government of Northern Ireland, in seeking the removal of North of Ireland records generally to Belfast, is not administrative convenience, but the desire to emphasise the separate existence of the government of the North of Ireland and to enhance the importance of the Departments concerned. In the case of original Wills for example, it is most improbable that a Government looking solely to administrative convenience, and not influenced by a desire to add to its own *status and importance would propose to undertake the labour and cost of identifying and removing these documents not one in a thousand of which is ever consulted after being deposited with the Probate Registry.* [The italics indicate underlining in the original.]
>
> If the Government of the Free State decide to comply with the request of Northern Ireland, and if statutory authority is obtained for the transfer (or if the Government is advised that such authority is not necessary) there will be no insuperable administrative difficulty in carrying out the Government's instructions.

In October 1927, G.C. Duggan, formerly a senior Dublin Castle official, contacted McCarron in an attempt to break the deadlock. He had previously asked a former colleague 'what was the real reason for the hold up' and was informed that the matter had been discussed at the Executive Council. Duggan admitted to McCarron that 'there is no doubt legally we here are in an untenable position because we have no control over your Registrar General while he in turn has no legal existence in Northern Ireland'. In reply, McCarron professed himself favourably disposed to the suggestion that Stormont make copies of the relevant entries from the original registers, though he added that the Department's legal experts had advised him that the Registrar General lacked authority to alter original registers or to make copies on the authority of the Registrar General of Northern Ireland, and Richard Mulcahy,[96] the Minister for Local Government, refused to bring the matter before the Executive Council. This ended Stormont's representations. A memorandum dated 1941 noted that the Northern Ireland authorities had obtained the necessary documents from local registers within their jurisdiction.[97]

THE DEPARTMENT OF LOCAL GOVERNMENT AND PUBLIC HEALTH OF THE IRISH FREE STATE

Many accounts of the Cumann na nGaedheal government of 1922-32 place considerable emphasis on the continuity of policy and personnel between Ireland before and after independence. The Department of Local Government is an exception.[98] Few senior officials of the Department of Local Government and Public Health (DLGPH) had served at senior level in the Local Government Board, and the policies followed show greater continuity with the Dáil Department, perhaps because its commitment to efficiency, economy, meritocracy and the rationalisation and centralisation of old structures was in keeping with Cumann na nGaedheal's efforts to control public spending.[99] Whereas Cumann na nGaedheal's economic policy discarded the Sinn Féin blueprint, much of its policy on local government respected that party's belief in the need to stamp out waste and corruption in local authorities. However, the combination of these ideals and the government's parsimonious approach towards public expenditure lent a certain imbalance to the Local Government programme. It was dynamic in matters which did not entail major expenditure, such as administrative or personnel reform, conservative on costly items such as housing.

The DLGPH was more centralised than the former Board. The offices of Inspectors of Lunatics, Reformatories and Industrial Schools and the General Registrar's Office, which had previously been separate bodies, were incorporated into the Department by the Ministers and Secretaries Act 1924,[100] though many former LGB officials, including McCarron, continued for some time to use former titles such as vice-president, lay commissioner and medical commissioner. In April 1922 the combined staff of the Dáil Éireann Local Government Department and transferred LGB staff totalled 288; approximately 70 had previously worked for the Dáil Department. By 1926 this total had fallen to 253.[101] In July 1931 there were 174 men (129 established and 45 unestablished) and 74 women (48 established and 26 unestablished) on the Department's payroll.[102]

McCarron was conscious that the need to recruit experienced professional and technical staff posed particular difficulties. In October 1924, in a memorandum on the Local Government Bill, he informed Finance that, while he accepted that clerical staff could be recruited through 'the usual Civil Service methods', he questioned the ability of the Civil Service Commissioners to hire technical personnel such as medical inspectors or the head of the roads section. The Minister wished to recruit officers from local authorities 'who possess both expert technical knowledge of his [sic] subject and wide practical experience . . . cases infrequently but not likely to be obtained by the Civil Service Commissioners'. To facilitate this, the 1925 Local Government Act enabled superannuation entitlement to be transferred between local authorities and the civil service.[103] Among the recruited local authority officials was James Quigley, Meath county surveyor, who became chief engineer of the roads department in September 1923 and subsequently chief engineering inspector.[104]

W.T. Cosgrave maintained an active interest in local government; he frequently contacted McCarron on policy, especially relating to housing, and on several occasions he, rather than the minister, James Burke (Séamus de Burca), who was an extern minister (not a member of the Dáil or Seanad), introduced legislation in the Dáil. Cosgrave believed that the foundation of the Irish Free State meant that local authorities need no longer concern themselves with wider political issues and he tried to promote a technocratic and de-politicised local government:

The meeting of the local authority is not the place for discussion of political issues. In the past these questions were indeed obtruded — to the disadvantages of local administration, but there was an excuse in the absence of a national assembly where they could properly be dealt with. The Oireachtas, the sovereign assembly of the nation, is now available to settle such matters. It is the only place they can be effectively considered. Henceforth they have no place in the local councils. These councils are elected to carry out specific functions. To carry them out effectively will require all their ability and attention . . . it is our duty to see that it will be entrusted only to persons who are willing to attend the multifarious activities. . . . The whole energies of our comhairle ceanntair [local councils] should be applied to the matter.[105]

The determination to divorce local government from national issues was an appropriate, if idealistic, ambition for a country divided by civil war. Some local authorities were controlled by Irregulars, who had been defeated in the civil war. A technocratic de-politicised local administration would reduce any possible threat from this quarter.

LOCAL AUTHORITY STRUCTURES: CENTRALISATION AND PROFESSIONALISATION

Under the 1898 Local Government Act, many services, such as labourers' cottages, road works, water and the control of infectious diseases, passed into the control of rural district councils. It is unclear whether or not the councils were capable of carrying out these duties efficiently; many Dáil inspectors appear to have doubted their competence.[106] The Irish Free State continued to reorganise local authority services on a county basis. In June 1923 a series of ministerial orders gave permanent status to county-based health and poor relief schemes.[107] In May 1924 the Minister announced that responsibility for road works would be transferred to county councils in order 'to get away from this parochial attitude'.[108]

Ernest Blythe, Minister for Local Government, had proposed to abolish RDCs before the 1923 local elections. In a memorandum to the Executive Council he claimed: 'It is thoroughly realised that Rural District Councils are not required any longer — there is no objection to their extinction except that proceeding from a few interested Clerks.'

Blythe feared that there would be a shortage of 'bona fide candidates' in the forthcoming elections, with the result that 'every crank and impossibilist in the country will get a platform'. However, in view of the 'controversial nature' of the proposal, the government decided to wait until after the general election.[109] Provisions for abolishing RDCs were included in the 1924 Local Government Bill. Burke, who became Minister for Local Government and Public Health in October 1923, told the Dáil that 'if you are going to reform local government you will have to do away with rural district councils'. He described them as 'obsolete, uneconomic', 'inefficient in managing rural housing', 'an anomaly and a foreign imposition', with 'roots neither in Irish history nor in Irish tradition nor in Irish character'. Rural district councils had been introduced by Gerald Balfour 'as a bribe to defeat the Home Rule Policy of the Liberal Party'. No hurling club, football club or pipers' band was organised on the basis of a rural district council, unlike county councils, which 'conform to an area which is historic and which is everywhere rooted in the whole history of the country'. The Labour Party leader, Tom Johnson, attacked the proposal as evidence of a tendency towards centralisation, greater bureaucracy and the loss of local responsibility. He suggested that parish councils might offer an alternative structure for local government; this appears to have been the first reference to these bodies.[110] The decision was also condemned by most county councils.[111]

Between 1923 and 1925 the government dissolved a total of nineteen local authorities. By 1931 this had risen to thirty-six, including Kerry, Leitrim, Mayo and Offaly County Councils, Dublin and Cork Corporations, fourteen boards of health including all in the Cork area, two rural district councils, Dublin Board of Guardians, three town commissioners and ten urban district councils.[112]

The 1923 Local Government (Temporary Provisions) Act gave the Minister power to hold an inquiry into the performance of any local authority where he was satisfied that its duties were not being 'duly and effectually discharged', or in cases where the local authorities failed to comply with ministerial orders and directions.[113] If the inquiry confirmed his assessment, the local authority could be dissolved. These powers were made permanent in the 1925 Local Government Act, which also gave councils power to delegate duties to a manager or commissioner. Although the LGB had possessed similar authority, it exercised it sparingly and never against a body as powerful as Dublin

Corporation. Augustine Birrell, a former chief secretary for Ireland, noted in his memoirs:

> Mr Cosgrave has abolished the Corporation of Dublin by a stroke of his pen. Any English Chief Secretary who had attempted to do the same piece of good work would have been compelled to resign by a combination of Unionists and Nationalists in the House of Commons. I had to be content with the abolition of the Corporation of Sligo.[114]

Most local authorities were dissolved because of political dissent or financial difficulties. Rate arrears mounted because of the collapse of law and order during the civil war and as a result of agricultural depression, which was particularly marked in the disastrous year 1924/25.[115]

By September 1922 rate collection in County Kerry was in a shambles: books had been seized by Irregulars and it was impossible to estimate the amounts outstanding. Twenty-nine collectors were suspended from duty and efforts were made to devise an alternative method of collection. Rates were collected through branches of the National Bank; temporary staff were employed to draw up lists of ratepayers, and the Special Infantry Corps and civic guards were employed to track defaulters. However these measures failed to avert the dissolution of Kerry County Council in May 1923 and its replacement by a commissioner, who also took control of Kerry Board of Health.[116] The suspension of Leitrim County Council in 1923 further reflected cumulative political and financial difficulties.

By January 1924 rate arrears in County Offaly totalled £59,000. The council had exceeded its £20,000 overdraft by £9,000 and the bank had stopped all payments; the county hospital, county home, and the tuberculosis hospital were all without funds, and home helps were unpaid. The county council pressed the Department to release payments due from local taxation grants, adding that 'we cannot understand why these grants are still being withheld, in view of the fact of success of the National Loan'. The Minister authorised an increased overdraft pending a departmental inquiry, but in September 1924 the council was dissolved; a commissioner was appointed and 'drastic measures' were threatened against defaulting ratepayers.[117] By March 1926 the value of uncollected rates had fallen from £44,000 to £16,000 and by 1927 the overdraft had been reduced to £12,000.[118]

Minor local authorities were generally dissolved because of dishonesty or incompetence, problems which probably predated the revolutionary period. An inquiry into the affairs of Roscommon Town Commissioners, which was sparked by a number of complaints to the Department from local inhabitants, discovered that the chairman, town secretary, assistant secretary and two commissioners were all employed by a local newspaper, the *Roscommon Messenger*. The tenants of artisans' dwellings which had been constructed by the commissioners included the contractors, several town commissioners and other *Messenger* employees; the rents charged were so low that loan repayments were in arrears. The gas company refused to provide public lighting because payments were in arrears; the commissioners did not strike a lighting rate, preferring to rely on voluntary contributions to cover bills; rate arrears were high and sewerage provisions inadequate. Following the abolition of Roscommon Town Commissioners in February 1924, Roscommon County Council delegated authority to a nominated committee, chaired by the parish priest, which included three county councillors and nine local businessmen.[119] The Town Commissioners were reconstituted in the 1930s. Rathkeale Town Commissioners, who were suspended in 1925, appear to have been even more impotent. They were incapable of carrying out their sole task — to provide public lighting — and had somehow managed to accumulate debts. The town clerk had been appointed in 1869; the rate collector, who was unavailable for interview by the inspector, because he was at the seaside (in April), was deemed 'totally unsuitable . . . not making the slightest effort to collect', but was immune from dismissal because both his father and his uncle were commissioners.[120]

Faced with such evidence of maladministration, the Department had little option but to dissolve the offending local authorities. However, the case of Dublin Corporation is less clear-cut and seems to give some credence to the belief that the Cosgrave government was determined to reduce the autonomy of local authorities. Although the departmental inquiry revealed a less than perfect administration, the Corporation's record would not have justified its suspension in the era of the Local Government Board. The inquiry criticised the Corporation's wages policy and its failure 'to suit their administration to prevailing economic conditions'. Corporation employees had been awarded generous wage increases in 1920 in line with the prevailing inflation,

121

but these were not reduced when prices subsequently fell. The inquiry also concluded that the cost of waterworks maintenance and improvements was excessive, as was the cost of items manufactured at the municipal workshop, where wages averaged 1/7 (8p) per hour, against a trade union norm of 1/4 (6.5p). Dublin Corporation wage rates set a benchmark for other urban workers. Lord Mayor Laurence O'Neill's assertion that Dublin Corporation should be 'if not the best employer, one of the best in the city' brought the Corporation into direct conflict with the government's economic policy, which was predicated on the need to reduce costs, particularly wages, as a precondition for agricultural and industrial prosperity and for initiating a workable public housing programme.

Other matters also contributed to the decision to suspend Dublin Corporation: the decision to award half-pay to the dependants of employees who had been interned after the civil war (following the precedent of payments to dependants of soldiers during the Great War), though this was reversed when Blythe threatened to withhold housing subsidies;[121] government dissatisfaction at the lack of progress of the Corporation's housing programme, the fact that the Dublin Board of Assistance had been dissolved in November 1923 because of malpractices,[122] and, what an editorial in the *Freeman's Journal* condemned as the Corporation's practice of 'treating the Government elected by the Irish people as a foreign Government'.[123]

Offaly, Leitrim and Kerry County Councils were guaranteed reinstatement once the threat of insolvency, which had led to their suspension, was removed. However there was no intention of restoring the *status quo ante* in the case of Dublin Corporation; in fact, the suspension may have been contrived in order to facilitate a major reorganisation of local government in the Dublin area. The government's interest in Dublin reflected the city's restored status as a capital. In January 1923 when it emerged that Dublin Corporation's law agent was in the process of drafting a bill which would extend the city's boundaries to include all urban districts in the county from Howth to Killiney, plus Bray, Co. Wicklow and a large tract of the adjoining countryside, Ernest Blythe informed the Executive Council that since Dublin was now the seat of government, its boundaries were 'no longer merely a matter for the corporation'.

Blythe commissioned Charles O'Connor, a former LGB inspector, to prepare a memorandum on future boundaries.[124] O'Connor rejected

Dublin Corporation's proposals; he preferred a more modest enlargement of the city boundaries to include the adjoining suburbs of Rathmines and Pembroke plus some undeveloped land, though he recommended that large parts of the county should pay a rate in aid towards city expenses, following the precedent of payments made by Rathmines and Pembroke under the Equalisation of Rates Act 1901.[125] O'Connor also proposed that Local Government should draft legislation providing for a reduction in the number of local authority representatives throughout Ireland.

Responding to O'Connor's report, the Department proposed to establish a departmental committee of inquiry to examine the future administration of the Greater Dublin area, but the cabinet subcommittee replaced this with a commission of inquiry. The distinction is important and may be seen as a partial defeat for Local Government: the terms of reference for the committee suggested by the Department made specific reference to securing 'more economical and efficient local administration' in the city and environs. Local Government further proposed that special attention be given to town planning and that the committee confer with the Dublin Reconstruction Movement and other groups that were interested in that topic.[126] The Greater Dublin Commission of Inquiry was given a more neutral brief:

> To examine the several laws and the practice affecting the
> administration of local and public utility services, including local
> representation and taxation throughout the Capital City of Dublin,
> and the County of Dublin and to recommend such changes as may
> be desirable.

The comission's report, which appears to have been largely written by the chairman, William Magennis, TD and Professor of Metaphysics at UCD,[127] combined a disregard for existing institutions with a distrust of local democracy. Greater Dublin would absorb Rathmines, Pembroke and the adjoining rural areas, plus Dun Laoghaire, Blackrock, Dalkey, Killiney and some undeveloped land adjoining these areas. The lord mayoralty of Dublin and other historic offices would be swept away, and the question of a company franchise for local government elections was considered. Town planning received sympathetic attention.

CITY MANAGEMENT

The Commission's most radical contribution was a proposal to transfer most executive functions from an elected council to a salaried city manager, who initially would be appointed by the Minister for Local Government for a three-year term; the council would decide whether or not to renew the appointment. The manager would be responsible for preparing the budget and for all appointments, subject to the Minister's sanction and to statutory regulations laid down by the Department. Although councillors would consider and approve the budget, they would play no role in the appointment, promotion or dismissal of officials. The manager could appeal to the minister against the council, whereas the only redress open to councillors was to hold a referendum, though this could take place only if councillors voted to do so by a two-thirds' majority. Councillors would be precluded from interfering with the manager's decisions, unless the Minister empowered the council and the manager to hold an investigation into civic affairs.[128] According to O'Halpin, this report marks 'the first quasi-official endorsement of the suggestion that a distinction in law should be made between the functions of elected politicians and of permanent officials in local government'.[129]

The office of city manager originated in the United States of America. Cork solicitor John J. Horgan claims to have been the first to propose the appointment of a city manager in Ireland,[130] though in 1924, immediately following the dissolution of Dublin Corporation and before Horgan had publicised his ideas, McCarron informed the Dublin town clerk that the government proposed 'to have the problem of the City government examined adequately and without avoidable delay in the light of the results achieved elsewhere in modern experiments in city management'.[131]

In a letter to McCarron, marked 'Private and Confidential', dated 19 March 1926, Horgan outlined his blueprint for the future government of Cork city, which was then controlled by a commissioner appointed by the Minister for Local Government. Horgan did so at the behest of the Cork Progressive Association, a body representing business and large ratepayers' interests. The Association was considering promoting a private member's bill and wished to appoint Philip Monahan,[132] the Cork commissioner, as city manager. In his reply, McCarron welcomed Horgan's proposal as evidence of 'valuable constructive thought'.

However, he indicated that the department was unwilling to support this proposal pending the report of the Greater Dublin Commission. If this was so, the Department changed its mind, and the first draft of a bill providing for city management in Cork emerged in Local Government about November 1926, *before* the publication of the report of the Greater Dublin Commission; copies were sent to both Horgan and Monahan.[133]

The draft Bill was similar in many respects to the recommendations of the Greater Dublin Inquiry, which may indicate a common origin. All executive functions, including drafting estimates and control of council officers, would be carried out by the city manager, whom the council would appoint. The elected eleven-person city council would appoint members of subsidiary bodies and amend the estimates; in the event of a disagreement over the estimates, the manager could appeal to the minister, who could order an official inquiry. Although O'Halpin has described Monahan as a man who 'had no time at all for elected councillors and did not attempt to conceal this from them',[134] Monahan made considerable efforts in private to persuade McCarron to give greater power to elected councillors. He objected particularly to granting the manager power to appeal to the Minister against council-imposed amendments to the estimates, because it 'does not make for amicable working between the Manager and Council, and if unsuccessful, it takes a good deal from the Manager's prestige, a commodity of which he will have little to spare'. Monahan added: 'the council is well within its rights in deciding what it shall devote to its housekeeping, and neither an idealistic manager nor a Minister has any right to impose his view on them', though he remained adamant that councillors should not have power to sell or lease lands because he feared that it would be abused. Despite Monahan's comments, a Department official recommended that the manager's power of appeal to the Minister be retained; this suggests that much of the 'autocracy' associated with the measure originated in Local Government, though the Department made surreptitious efforts to present its proposals as a private bill.

On 8 January 1927, Cork TD and Minister for Posts and Telegraphs J.J. Walsh submitted a copy of the Bill to the Ceann Comhairle, Michael Hayes, for his informal opinion. Hayes told Walsh that he objected to the piecemeal reform of borough local government because it could result in a variety of administrative structures; if the objective was to test Dáil opinion on the merits of city management, this could be achieved under 'ordinary rules of procedure'. In order to protect 'the machinery of the Oireachtas', Hayes suggested to Cosgrave that the government invite the House (the Dáil) 'as a non-party matter, and without regard to the Government's views of policy on the subject matter of the Bill', to refuse leave to introduce the Cork Bill.

Following this rebuff, Horgan and Walsh explored other options. Horgan was disconsolate, writing to McCarron, 'I suppose it all means my poor legislative child is dead. Perhaps its ghost may arise in some other shape in the future'. McCarron was more sanguine: 'I have great hopes that the "legislative child" will not appear in Statistics of Infant Mortality'.[135]

At this stage Local Government appears to have taken responsibility for the measure and on 1 February 1927 the Department informed the President's office that it proposed to introduce the Bill.[136] Nothing happened for a further year until Richard Mulcahy, Minister for Local Government, met members of the Cork Chamber of Commerce while on a visit to the city and gave a commitment to introduce a bill providing for city management, if Cork interests agreed on the general outlines.[137] Some Cork businessmen, including Sir John Scott, wished to use the bill to reduce democratic control by re-establishing a strong business presence through carefully drawn ward boundaries and the restoration of a business vote (giving owners of business premises additional votes proportionate to the rateable value of their property). Scott urged the Department to retain ultimate control over all aspects of city government in the light of the 'publicly announced policy of the Republican Party to "get control of all the Public Boards in the Free State".'

By March 1928 Monahan was having second thoughts about city management. He argued that reserving special powers to the manager was likely to create

. . . a disposition to jealousy and antagonism on the part of members of the council. If it did create such feelings, only a superman as Manager could carry on without continuous discord and conflict. Putting the matter more broadly, the Manager would be in the position of the detestable friend who continually tells us about our minor faults, the existence of which we are conscious, and which perhaps are the only things which make life worth living. He would be constantly preaching the perfection which no

126

human being is anxious to achieve and which in those who do achieve it is always a little annoying. Putting it another way, the man would possibly be regarded by the Council as school-children regard the Master's pet. They would always want to kick him.

Monahan suggested to McCarron that executive powers should be in the hands of a triumvirate consisting of the lord mayor, the ex-lord mayor and the city manager. His views lacked support.

Although Mulcahy wished to defer the Cork legislation until the Dublin reforms had been clarified, Cork business interests kept up the pressure. A bill providing for a 15-person council, against the previous membership of 56, reached the department by the end of April.[138] In the Dáil Mulcahy emphasised that the proposals were a response to Irish local needs and had not been dictated by practices in any other country. He justified ceding executive power to a city manager with the argument that it would give the Corporation the opportunity 'to pay the fullest possible attention to the really big questions of policy and control in the city'. Éamon de Valera welcomed the restoration of local government in Cork, but deprecated the fact that it was being done 'so grudgingly'. Both he and Seán Lemass saw merit in the new structure, though Lemass questioned whether executive power should rest with a single person appointed by the Local Appointments Commission, which was outside the council's control.[139] Despite some opposition from Fianna Fáil and Labour ranks, and privately from some government supporters, the Bill became law in February 1929. The Dáil increased the number of city councillors to twenty-one.

Following on the Cork blueprint, the 1930 Local Government (Dublin) Bill provided for the appointment of city managers in both Dublin and Dun Laoghaire boroughs.[140] The area of the city more than doubled with the inclusion of Rathmines and Pembroke, plus large swathes of land to the north and south of the city. Dun Laoghaire borough expanded to include Blackrock, Dalkey, Killiney and Ballybrack UDCs. The Department believed that the new city area was the minimum required 'to meet the needs of a reasonable homogeneous area for uniform municipal services'. The boundaries marked a compromise between the reluctance of county ratepayers at being included in the city and the 'progressive ideals of persons interested in city planning and development'. No provisions relating to town planning were included; the government claimed that this was a matter for general legislation.[141] The bill had a contentious passage through the Dáil. The Fianna Fáil TD Seán T. O' Kelly criticised the fact that all but four of the ninety-five recommendations of the Greater Dublin Commission of Inquiry had been disregarded. He highlighted the failure to expand city boundaries to include the south coastal zone, which he appears to have regarded as a bastion of Anglo-Irish influence, and also criticised the 'autocratic powers' granted to the city manager and the introduction of a commercial franchise.[142] This franchise remained a contentious matter until its repeal by Fianna Fáil in 1935, but opposition to the city manager eased considerably with the appointment in 1930 of Gerald Sherlock, who had served as both assistant town clerk and town clerk to Dublin Corporation. O'Kelly and other critics had feared that the manager would be one of the government's 'pets' — the three commissioners who had run the city from 1924.

RECRUITMENT: THE LOCAL APPOINTMENTS COMMISSION

Appointments to public service positions were among the most contentious issues during the 1920s. Many government supporters underestimated its commitment to a non-partisan recruitment process. In October 1924 a statement from the Coiste Gnótha, the organising committee of Cumann na nGaedheal, protested that 'the Organisation's influence on Government policy and its power to affect patronage has been negligible, if not, nil'. State appointments were described as 'perhaps the sorest question of all'; 'those who won the fight have not done well out of the victory, whereas the pro-British ascendancy who lost the fight have done disproportionately well and got a new lease of life from the Free State'.[143] Neither the Civil Service Commission nor the Local Appointments Commission gave formal recognition to military service, though many IRA veterans were hired as temporary clerks in 1922 and 1923. In 1924, after the establishment of the Civil Service Commission and the introduction of a requirement that all permanent civil service appointees be recruited by competitive examination, 276 clerical posts were filled by an examination open only to ex-servicemen. In 1925 a further examination was held 'of a particularly easy standard', suited to persons who had long left school, and the process was repeated in 1927, with the result that the lower ranks of the civil service were filled by 'material of much poorer quality than that normally obtainable by open competition'. In addition, all boy messengers were dismissed and replaced by ex-servicemen.[144]

IRA veterans were not alone in expecting preference. If the Mulcahy papers are typical, every minister was bombarded with requests from friends and acquaintances, parish priests, reverend mothers or Christian Brothers seeking employment for relatives, neighbours or former pupils. One man seeking a post as a dispensary doctor complained that a rival candidate 'gave his service to the Dev. government in the Four Courts' and asked that Mulcahy (Minister for Local Government and Public Health) or Patrick McGilligan (Minister for Industry and Commerce and for External Affairs) should take steps to 'prevent, as I say, the indirect murderers of poor Kevin O'Higgins' from being appointed. One of Mulcahy's regular correspondents, Jim Kennedy, town clerk of Nenagh, referred to the 'widespread belief that you can always "pull the strings" in Ireland'.[145] Competition for posts as dispensary doctor was particularly acute and in 1924 two members of a local authority were convicted of attempted bribery, though such practices long predated the foundation of the state.[146]

Government reform of the local appointments process was sparked both by a desire to stamp out jobbery and by a wish to exclude those who had opposed the Anglo-Irish Treaty from public appointments. Local authorities had traditionally possessed considerable power over recruitment, pensions and pay. When the Executive Council wished to block the appointment as engineer to Athy Rural District Council of a former internee who had been removed by sealed order from his post as assistant county surveyor in Kildare, James Burke pointed out that his only statutory function was to ensure that the appointee had sufficient knowledge or experience to hold the post. In February 1924 the Department of Defence received a letter protesting at the reinstatement of an 'active Irregular' recently released from internment as a local authority ambulance driver in County Cork, although there were many unemployed demobilised soldiers in the area. When the Executive Council considered this and the Athy case, it recommended that former internees should be reinstated only on the approval of the Ministers for Defence and Home Affairs.

Such a directive was at variance with the first Dáil's clear commitment to filling all public appointments without reference to religion or politics. When James Burke, in compliance with the wishes of the Ministers of Defence and Home Affairs, refused to sanction the Athy appointment (probably illegally), Athy RDC passed a resolution that 'penalising individuals for their political or religious opinions is very detrimental to the Nation's welfare, and what Nationalist Ireland always condemned in the Northern Government should not now be practised by the Government of Southern Ireland.' The Executive Council eventually approved the appointment temporarily, because there was an urgent need to repair labourers' cottages in that area,[147] but they became determined to secure greater control over future appointments. The 1924 Local Government (Temporary Provisions) Amendment Act required local authorities to obtain ministerial sanction before vacancies were advertised, appointments made or officials suspended or dismissed; the minister could control the remuneration of local authority surveyors, their clerks and local tax officers. The accompanying file noted that there had been substantial irregularities in advertising vacancies, filling appointments and establishing minimum qualifications.[148]

The calibre of local tax officers was a particular cause of concern; it was believed that 'some indifferent officials have been selected'; one was 'practically illiterate', several were incapable of keeping accounts. Competence was not the sole desideratum. A clause in the 1925 Local Government Act required all persons appointed or promoted to local authority posts to make a formal declaration of allegiance to the state in the presence of a peace commissioner.[149] This remained in force from March 1925 until it was removed in the 1933 Local Government Act,[150] though the number who refused to make the declaration fell sharply after 1927 when Fianna Fáil entered the Dáil. In 1928 two former Dáil inspectors, D.J. O'Donovan and Simon Moynihan, who had been dismissed for 'irregular activities', were reinstated, as was Annie Browner, a former auditor to the Dáil Department of Local Government.[151] When Fianna Fáil took office in 1932, thirty-two local officials applied for reinstatement or compensation, or to have additional years counted for pension rights. They included eleven technical instruction teachers, rent and rate collectors, relieving officers, engineers, doctors, and a man who had acted as an interpreter in Galway County Council for twenty-three years.[152]

The introduction of *ad hoc* controls over local appointments threatened to create as many problems as it solved. The establishment of a commission, similar to the Civil Service Commission, to handle local appointments was first proposed by Farmers' Party TD Michael Heffernan in June 1924, in the course of a debate on the Local Government Bill.[153] The government initially considered giving the Civil Service Commission responsibility for local appointments, but the chairman protested that the workload would prove excessive. H.P. Boland, head of establishment in the Department of Finance, favoured setting up a separate commission which would maximise the use of the Civil Service Commission resources, while keeping the two bodies 'as far as possible distinct in the public eye'. With considerable foresight, Boland argued that any body responsible for local authority appointments 'will have to operate in an atmosphere and deal with problems quite different from those of the Civil Service Commission'.[154]

In contrast to the Civil Service Commission, no precedent existed for the Local Appointment Commission. There was no uniform grading system for local authority staff, and Boland was apprehensive about the cost of holding separate examinations for every local authority. In 1926 only candidates for the post of county surveyor and assistant county surveyor were required to sit an examination. The establishment of the Local Appointments Commission meant a significant loss of power for local authorities. To soften the blow, the Department hoped to fill most vacant posts by internal promotion *'before the Bill now suggested becomes law'*, (underlined in the original). Local Government also succeeded in excluding all clerical posts from the Commission's remit, and Finance's proposal to introduce uniform grades for all local authority staff was ignored.[155] Only posts requiring professional qualifications and appointments of chief executive officers would be filled by the Local Appointments Commission.

For two months following the enactment of the Local Authorities Officers and Employees Act in 1926, local authorities remained free to promote existing officers and make appointments under the old system. Burke claimed that the Act went 'a long way' to implement 'the ideal cherished by the founder of the Sinn Féin movement . . . the establishment of a national service which should be carried on the principle of merit alone'. Patrick Baxter, TD for Cavan, condemned the Commission as 'a vote of no confidence in Counties and Boards of Health that have been recently. elected'. In a characteristically blunt retort, Kevin O'Higgins rejected such opposition as 'the hanging on to vested interests, the sturdy struggle for the right to appoint the fifth best man for personal reasons'.[156] For ministers, the Commission offered welcome relief from begging letters: Richard Mulcahy sent a *pro forma* reply to all requests for employment, pointing out that posts were filled by the Local Appointments Commission, which was outside his control.[157]

Local authorities mounted several challenges to the Commission during its early years. When Monaghan Board of Health was informed in 1927 that the Commission had selected an English-based Irish doctor as medical officer for Scotstown, it referred the appointment back to the Local Appointments Commission with a request that it supply 'in order of merit a selection from the names of applicants who belong to this County — so that the Board may make the appointment from names submitted.'[158]. Waterford Corporation passed a resolution protesting against the practice of submitting only one name to the appointing authority and expressed the opinion that the Commission's duty should be confined to providing a list of all 'qualified and suitable' candidates and that the final choice should rest with the appointing authority.[159]

Fianna Fáil was not slow to exploit such grievances for political ends. In 1928 de Valera attempted to move an amending Bill on the lines of the Waterford resolution. The government rejected this amendment, but accepted a proposal from Labour Party leader, T.J. O'Connell, for the establishment of a select committee to examine the working of the Commission.[160] In fact the select committee's report, which was published in 1930, proposed a substantial increase in the powers of the Commission. It recommended that all posts be filled by competitive examination, except for technical or professional positions; that the Commission be made responsible for all promotions; and that the Civil Service and Local Appointments Commissions be amalgamated.

Although the recommendations were welcomed by the Irish Medical Committee, Local Government objected to proposals to extend central control on the grounds that an 'intimate personal knowledge of the merits and demands of applicants' was often valuable in assessing fitness for promotion, while the minister already had power to block the promotion of unsuitable candidates. The Department also rejected proposals to establish national panels because this would eliminate the possibility of taking local factors into consideration. The Department opposed any extension of competitive examinations and of the Commission's powers over the recruitment to 'minor clerical posts' and ultimately 'ward maids, labourers and like employments' on grounds of expense; it would lead to standardised pay and conditions of service on unnecessarily favourable terms. The latter had long been demanded by trade unions, which may explain O'Connell's support for this recommendation.

On 20 April 1931 the Executive Council decided not to act on the select committee's recommendations.[161] This may have been owing to the fact that the committee's proposals for greater central control were out of step with burgeoning demands that greater account should be taken of local wishes. There is some evidence that the government, or at least Cosgrave, may have favoured a move in that direction. When a County Limerick curate complained in 1930 about the candidate appointed as medical officer, Mulcahy issued the standard reply that he had no influence over the Commission's decisions, but Cosgrave demanded that the Commission give him access to their records of the marks and placings awarded in interviews and examinations. Boland contacted the Commission informally to test the waters and was told 'that they should not be asked for this information; that if they are asked they will feel they have not the option to decline'. As a compromise, Boland suggested that the government request the commissioners' observations on the representations which had been made. He was supported by the cabinet secretary Diarmaid O'Hegarty. In fact there is no evidence that this was done. On 30 December 1930 the Attorney General, John Costello, gave his opinion that the Commission was neither independent of Parliament nor of the Executive Council; while the Executive Council was not entitled to control the manner in which the commissioners carried out their duties, it was bound to see that those duties were properly performed and was consequently entitled to obtain any information from the commissioners which it thought proper.[162]

By this stage, attention had shifted from the Limerick appointment to that of Miss Laetitia Dunbar-Harrison, a member of the Church of Ireland and a graduate of Trinity College Dublin, as county librarian in Mayo. To date, this has been the sole appointment made by the Local Appointments Commission which has engaged the attention of historians and there is an impression that it was an isolated event, and that the issue was one of catholic triumphalism. In truth it was merely the most prominent in a series of appointments where local interests, lay and religious, championed a local candidate against an unknown applicant, foisted on them by Dublin. The central issue was thus one of the parish pump versus national control. In Mayo the favoured daughter was a Miss Burke; Joseph Lee notes that 'there must have been a hard clerical push for her in Tuam'. On this occasion local interests were able to employ the catholic/Gaelic card in defence of their candidate; Fianna Fáil, long alert to the potential of the local appointments issue, saw the Mayo case as a vote-winner, given the imminence of a general election. Éamon de Valera attacked the loss of local autonomy resulting from the Local Appointments Commission and made adroit if indirect use of the sectarian issue.[163] Fianna Fáil's opposition to the Local Appointments Commission may actually have strengthened the government's resolve to uphold the appointments system.

Mayo County Council was dissolved on 1 January 1931; it was replaced by a commissioner, following a sworn inquiry by a Local Government inspector. McCarron informed the Mayo county secretary that almost 1,000 appointments had been made by the Commission since its foundation and all had been honoured by local authorities. However, other councils applauded Mayo County Council's defiance. Leitrim County Council also rejected a non-local candidate as county librarian. Among the many messages of support which Mayo County Council received from other local authorities was one from Carlow County Council, praising the council for standing up to the government: 'They had got things driven down their necks by the Government. There was over-lapping all round.' Miss Dunbar-Harrison was appointed to a position in Dublin; her successor, an outsider but presumably a catholic, received a cool welcome. The *Mayo People* asked if there had been any local applicants and 'were they overlooked?'[164]

In the light of the Attorney General's ruling, the Commission opened its files to cabinet scrutiny, a decision which permitted W.T. Cosgrave to reveal the low standard reached by the local favourite. The breach of confidentiality may have been necessary to defend the Commission's reputation and its existence.

COMBINED PURCHASING

Combined purchasing is yet another example of a reform which brought greater efficiency and probity to local government at the cost of further loss of local autonomy. Sinn Féin had been committed to the policy from its foundation, though Arthur Griffith's interest was primarily motivated by a desire to boost Irish industry. The programme was begun in December 1921 by the Dáil Department of Local Government's trade department.[165] In contrast to other divisions in the Free State Department, it appears to have remained under the control of former Dáil officials after 1922. Its first head, D. Meagher, a former official of the Dáil ministry, held the appointment until 1933 when he was transferred to the Department of Defence in circumstances which remain obscure; he was replaced by Professor Timothy Smiddy, who doubled as de Valera's economic adviser.[166]

At the beginning, some local authorities refused to participate.[167] offering the excuse that they required products with specifications which differed from those set by the Department. To overcome such objections, the Department involved representatives of county homes, mental hospitals, county councils and other public bodies in drawing up specifications and selecting suitable products. Despite the apparent savings, local authorities objected to the loss of local patronage and many argued that ratepayers' money should be spent among ratepayers. Legislation formally establishing the combined purchasing service was passed in 1925 in the teeth of considerable opposition. In order to diffuse local hostility, the Department introduced an additional clause providing for the establishment of a local supplies advisory council, though Finance opposed this concession since 'if there is to be a centralised system, the central executive machinery should be able to do its own work and should be organised from that standpoint. The fewer and the more efficient the people concerned with business transactions where public funds are concerned, the better.'[168]

REFORMING LOCAL GOVERNMENT, GAINS AND LOSSES?

Cumann na nGaedheal's reform of local administration was motivated by a concern for efficiency and economy together with the belief that independence left little scope for party politics in local government. Reducing the number of local authorities and local representatives, removing their discretion in awarding contracts or employment, and transferring executive power to professional managers were all steps which de-politicised the system while promising greater efficiency. The Department of Local Government apparently believed, or at least claimed to believe, that the reforms ultimately would result in less central control. A memorandum submitted to the Executive Council in connection with the Local Government (Dublin) Bill claimed that 'since the executive side of local administration was vested in him [the Cork city manager] he has shown an independence of thought and initiative that did not require the intervention of the Department on phases of local administration that formerly had often required a great degree of careful supervision on the part of the central Department.'[169] Dáil deputies saw matters in a different light. The rationalisation of health and welfare services had proved unpopular in many communities, where, as Labour Party leader Tom Johnson pointed out, 'The Union was regarded as a kind of local industry'.[170] During the course of the debate on the 1925 Local Government Bill, which gave ministers power to dissolve local authorities, Johnson criticised the 'tendency to deprive citizens of a sense of responsibility' and 'the substitution of bureaucracy for democracy'. Johnson succeeded in having an amendment inserted limiting the term of office of commissioners to three years; he claimed that holding such an office without time limit would be 'autocratic and undemocratic'.

Although Kerry and Leitrim County Councils were restored in 1926 after three years, Offaly was controlled by a commissioner until the local elections in June 1928, and Dublin city was without local representation from 1924 to 1930. Efficiency was increasingly seen as synonymous with bureaucracy. In 1931 Kerry TD F. H. Crowley complained that 'You may talk about bribery and everything else, but if you wipe out the county councils and remove the human touch, the connecting link between the administration and the poor, it will be a bad day for the country.'[171] In 1931 Richard Mulcahy claimed that commissioners had proved extremely popular in the areas under their control and that the Department had received representations favouring their retention.[172]

Yet the involvement of Cork businessmen in the campaign for a city manager indicates that some aspects of local government reform had a decidedly undemocratic aspect. Although Ernest Blythe claimed that proposals for the abolition of local authorities 'would command a good deal of support through the country', both from those who protested at the level of local authority rates and from others who 'take the view that, with the ease and speed of modern communications, a small State like ours, with a small population, does not need local elected bodies at all', he was opposed to an extension of the commissioners' roles. He argued that, as long as their appointments were temporary, the 'Government need accept no responsibility for their actions'; if the number increased, the government would be obliged to assume responsibility for their acts, making the commission 'merely the agent of a Department of the Government'.[173] The curbs imposed on local democracy might have proved more popular if they had resulted in lower rates, or if they were counterbalanced by generous expenditure on roads, housing or sanitary services. However, the 1920s appeared to bring the worst of all possible worlds: less autonomy and patronage for local politicians and little largesse from Dublin.

LOCAL AUTHORITY RATES

Rate collection is one instance where the Department of Local Government capitulated to local wishes and abandoned efforts to introduce a more stream-lined collection system. In November 1923, nationwide rate arrears were estimated at £2.9m., or 90 per cent of the 1923/24 assessment of £3.2m.,[174] and they continued to mount despite the end of the civil war. The Department believed that this was because the 'old type of rate collector' had been replaced by 'a class which showed neither the same energy nor desire to carry out their duties properly' and it determined to transfer rate collection to post offices. The original draft of the Collection of Rates Bill gave the Minister for Local Government power to transfer 'all or any of the powers of rate collectors' to the post office, but the Executive Council authorised the temporary transfer of collection only in areas where the system had broken down.[175] Counties Kerry, Sligo and Galway were singled out for special treatment. The post office would receive commission of three pence in the pound.[176] By 1926 the experiment was deemed a success and Local Government appears to have envisaged the post office becoming the normal method of rate collection, though H.P. Boland (Finance) told McCarron that, in the light of discussions with Posts and Telegraphs, Finance considered it desirable to extend the experimental period.

Legislation passed in July 1926 provided for rate collection through the post office to become a permanent measure, if a county council approved.[177] Yet by the end of 1926 Galway and Sligo County Councils had both reappointed rate collectors, though the county commissioner in Kerry continued to use the post office. Sligo County Council claimed that it had proved difficult and expensive to deal with defaulters via the post office.[178] Although councils argued that the Department of Posts and Telegraphs was charging too high a commission, their main, if unstated, objection was the erosion of local control and employment.

Although the calibre of rate collectors and the erosion of civil authority partly account for the rising level of rate arrears, the depressed state of agriculture was of greater long-term significance. In 1923 the British Agricultural Rates Act relieved farmers in Britain and Northern Ireland of approximately 75 per cent of their rates bill. Agricultural land in the UK was derated in 1928; the loss in income was met by the exchequer. Since agricultural land accounted for 72 per cent of county valuations in Ireland — ranging from 25 per cent in County Dublin to 87 per cent in County Meath — the introduction of British-style derating (including concessions to industry and freight transport) would have meant that up to 95 per cent of local authority revenue was drawn from non-local sources.[179]

Yet derating was not simply a matter of Irish farmers envying their counterparts in Britain or Northern Ireland. The economic policy of the Cumann na nGaedheal government was based on maintaining free trade and promoting exports. Agriculture was rightly regarded as the main export sector, Britain as the major market, so the fact that Irish farmers were subject to a higher level of taxation than their competitors gave cause for concern. Agriculture Minister Patrick Hogan, the most coherent economic thinker in the 1922-32 government, repeatedly emphasised the relationship between high rates and the profitability of agriculture. In two separate memoranda to government in February/March 1924, he began by noting that the high level of unpaid rates constituted a serious burden on agriculture, given the current agricultural depression, and then proceeded to condemn the impact on the industry of extravagant local government expenditure, particularly high local authority wages. Hogan claimed that the 1896 Agricultural Rates Act had aimed to provide farmers with 50 per cent relief; existing relief amounted to only 25 per cent because the agricultural rates grant constituted a fixed sum and local authority spending had increased substantially since 1896.

In order to clear the high level of arrears, Hogan proposed a once-off reduction in rates demands on agriculture from an estimated £2.8m. to £200,000 by doubling the agricultural grant of £600,000 and enabling local authorities to borrow £2m., which would be repaid from future rates. The cabinet referred Hogan's proposal to a subcommittee consisting of the secretaries of Finance, Agriculture and Local Government. Agriculture, not surprisingly, supported the request, as did Local Government. Finance attacked the proposal on multiple fronts: lack of revenue to fund a doubling of the agricultural grant; the fact that the burden of rates and income tax on agriculture was lower than in other sectors of the economy. They also included the well-worn argument that borrowing for non-capital purposes, such as rates relief, was inflationary. On 15 March 1924 Brennan informed the secretary of the Executive Council that the committee was unable to present an agreed report. This forced the politicians to confront the issue. A committee consisting of Cosgrave and the Ministers for Finance, Agriculture and Local Government[180] abandoned Hogan's proposal to double the agricultural grant but decided to introduce legislation which would permit county councils to borrow money in order to provide for up to two-thirds temporary rates remission on agricultural land,[181] though only twelve counties availed of the provision.[182] The 1925 Rates on Agricultural Land Act provided for an additional grant, equal to the existing grant of almost £600,000, and this was renewed annually in subsequent years.

Despite the virtual doubling of agricultural rate relief, the campaign for further concessions was revived after 1928 in reaction to the British government's introduction of agricultural derating. Some resolutions demanded that central government take responsibility for the cost of items such as main roads and lunatic asylums; others sought the derating of agricultural land. In January 1929 a special meeting of Wicklow County Council passed a resolution demanding that agricultural land be given exceptional treatment by rates relief 'if that [agriculture], our only remaining industry, is to survive', and that the government pay the full cost of repairing and maintaining main roads. The council also deferred adopting a rate for the coming year. The resolution passed by the General Council of County Councils demanded British-style agricultural derating; Dublin County Council urged that the second moiety of the 1928/29 rates on agricultural land be relieved by a government grant.[183] A committee set up by Cumann na nGaedheal to consider the matter concluded that 'the Farmers in the Free State should be kept as far as possible on an equality with their competitors' and passed a resolution demanding that the state assume full responsibility for the cost of mental hospitals and the maintenance of trunk and main roads.[184] Similar resolutions proliferated in the following months; many came from government supporters.

An interdepartmental committee, which examined the financial implications of derating in the summer of 1928,[185] no doubt in response to the British concession, concluded that a similar concession in Ireland would cost £2.23m. — 9.5 per cent of state expenditure — and could be met only by increasing other forms of taxation. It would cost in excess of £2m. to derate agriculture, against less than £100,000 for concessions to industry and freight transport. The committee believed that derating agriculture was more likely to result in higher living standards for farmers than in higher output. If the Exchequer assumed responsibility for mental hospitals and roads, there would be a levelling up in standards of service and an increase in expenditure 'chiefly because of pressure from the Local Authorities themselves'.[186] The cabinet endorsed the committee's conclusion that it was not feasible to abolish rates on agricultural land. Ernest Blythe explored the subject in some detail in the course of his 1929 Budget speech. He believed that derating agricultural land, while leaving local authorities with their existing power, would lead to 'an orgy of expenditure'.[187] His speech did nothing to stem demands for further concessions and in July 1929 the government approved terms of reference for a commission of inquiry into derating, including an examination of the potential effect on local government.[188]

The commission held public sessions from January to July 1930 and produced one majority and two minority reports, which were published in May 1931. The majority report, signed by all representatives of government departments plus the chairman Judge C. Davitt, A.R.S. Nutting, a director of the Bank of Ireland, E. McArdle, chairman of the Associated Chambers of Commerce, R.J. Mortished, the assistant secretary of the Labour Party, and Professor George O'Brien, endorsed the main conclusions of the 1929 interdepartmental committee. Members of local authorities and farming representatives signed a minority report. The majority report concluded that if the government conceded derating, or assumed responsibility for the cost of roads or other services, there would inevitably be a sharp rise in expenditure as 'national standards' and national wage levels emerged for all services. This, in turn, would lead to 'complete [central] control over all local expenditure', a loss of interest in local administration which would make it difficult to attract 'the right type of representative for local politics' and 'the termination of local government as it is at present known'. Central control of local expenditure would become 'repressive and restrictive', with 'local power of initiative and local control of policy . . . reduced to a minimum in the interests of the public purse'.

The majority report concluded that if the government decided to assist agriculture, it should grant partial rates remission, rather than assume responsibility for specific items such as roads; most of the benefit in the latter case would go to sectors other than agriculture.[189] Its diagnosis — that reduced local initiative, increased central intrusion in the affairs of local authorities and pressure for increased expenditure inevitably would follow if the exchequer took responsibility for a greater share of local expenditure — was to prove highly prophetic.

On 13 October 1930, McElligott, secretary of the Department of Finance, reported to the Executive Council that the Commission was unanimous in rejecting calls for total derating, but was divided on the merits of partial derating, though all departmental representatives were opposed.[190] Events did not stand still while the Commission deliberated. The continuing deterioration in agricultural markets brought renewed demands for rates relief and the government came under pressure in a number of by-elections.[191] In March 1931 de Valera initiated a Dáil motion calling for the additional rates relief of £600,000, which had been granted annually since 1925, to be increased to £1m.. The government raised it to £750,000.[192]

It is difficult to decide whether the demands for rates remission during these years were a true reflection of agricultural depression or merely an opportunistic effort to achieve concessions which had been granted in Britain. Although farmers constituted the largest single category of ratepayer, arrears fell sharply from £2.9m. in November 1923 to £468,384 by March 1932. The scale of relief that was granted appears to have been sufficient to shore up the system. The proportion of rates collected rose from 76 per cent in 1927/28 to 80 per cent in 1928/29 and 85.5 per cent in 1930/31, though national averages conceal local problems. Only 23 per cent of rates were collected in Leitrim in 1927/28. Donegal was little better, but by 1928/29 the collection had reached 48 per cent in Leitrim and an impressive 70 per cent in

Donegal.[193] By March 1931 County Leitrim reported an amazing 99 per cent collection — testimony to the successful, if unnoticed, restoration of tax collection after years of unrest.

LOCAL GOVERNMENT AND PUBLIC EXPENDITURE

In contrast to the impressive range of legislation reforming the system of local administration, legislation dealing with housing and sanitary services was sparse during the years 1922-32. If the Department of Local Government's administrative reforms were broadly compatible with the government's desire for economy, more generous provisions for housing and public health were in direct conflict with this ethos. The anti-rates agitation imposed severe constraints on local authority spending and meant that any significant improvement in services was dependent on Exchequer subsidies. Yet the debt burden left by the civil war gave little scope for largesse. The powerful Department of Finance subscribed to what has been referred to in Britain as the Treasury view: that public expenditure on unprofitable items such as water, roads or subsidised housing was inherently wasteful and should be kept to a minimum.[194] The commitment to free trade, and the Irish economy's dependence on the British market meant that policy had to conform to that in Britain, which was dominated by a determination to restore and maintain the gold standard at pre-war parity; so both the British and Irish governments tried, without success, to reduce wages and costs to something approaching 1914 levels. Such attitudes made life difficult for a spending department such as Local Government and Public Health, which faced innumerable deputations and representations from TDs and local authorities all seeking additional funds, while remaining conscious of the fact that most requests would be rejected. This may explain why so much of the Department's energy was devoted to administrative reforms.

Civil war left the Irish Free State with a substantial burden of public debt which had to be serviced and reduced. The Department of Finance curbed local authority access to capital, because the available money was needed for other purposes, and because officials objected to housing or water schemes being financed by public borrowing. Consequently Irish local authorities found it more difficult to fund capital investment during the 1920s than at any stage since the establishment of the LGB. While Dublin Corporation was sufficiently large to raise capital via stock issues, most Irish local authorities depended on local banks or on the Local Loans Fund.

On 31 March 1922 Irish access to the British government-funded Local Loans Fund came to an abrupt end. The obvious solution was to establish what Joseph Brennan termed 'a Local Loans Fund of our own'. When Local Government asked if this was a possibility, Brennan at first suggested that the state would be prepared to give 'reasonable facilities' on terms similar to the British Local Loans Fund, though Local Government should not advertise that fact. However, in a letter to the Board of Works, dated 12 May 1922, he announced that no loans would be made to local authorities, 'pending further consideration', though loans could be issued to other eligible borrowers. The Board of Works replied that there was little demand for loans except from local authorities.[195] During 1922 several councils applied to Local Government for loan sanction. In the past if the LGB gave approval, the application was forwarded to the Board of Works, the body responsible for granting LLF loans.

In November 1922, in response to an application from Loughrea RDC for permission to borrow £2,000, McCarron again asked Finance 'whether it is proposed to obtain the sanction of Parliament [sic] to the establishment of an Irish Loans Fund'. Brennan replied that a Free State LLF was already in existence, though only limited funds were available, and applications would be considered if they were forwarded to Finance. Although Local Government sent several urgent applications in December 1922, they appear to have been ignored. The 1923/24 Budget voted a sum of £705,000 for local loans, but this was an accounting device: £680,000 would be used to make repayments to the British fund and this would be collected from the borrowers. Only £25,000 was available for new loans[196] and Finance ruled that local authorities were ineligible. In practice, Finance controlled the £25,000 so tightly that only £7,000 was actually spent. When Cosgrave tried to secure a loan of £500 for Fr. Byrne, the catholic curate at Monasterevin, to complete the building of a presbytery at Nurney (LLF loans had traditionally been granted for this purpose), Brennan convinced him that the loan should not be sanctioned in view of a general ban on 'more deserving' cases.[197] The 1924 budget provided only £7,000 for LLF advances, which restored the sum available to a princely £25,000.[198] Local authorities continued to be denied access to the LLF until 1926 and were forced to finance capital expenditure by bank loans, which often proved unobtainable. When Finance restored local authority access to LLF loans in 1926, it excluded loans for housing, which accounted for the overwhelming majority of local authorities' capital requirements.

Housing policy during the 1920s was a casualty both of Finance's determination to restrict borrowings and public expenditure and of the government's desire to reduce costs in order to restore Irish competitiveness. Wages of building labourers and craftsmen were particular targets because they were regarded as barometers of general wage levels. The government believed that a comprehensive housing programme should be deferred until construction costs had returned to something approaching pre-war levels. Because costs remained stubbornly high, the housing programme throughout the 1920s was viewed as a temporary measure. This rather naive attitude ignored the fact that in the supposedly golden age before 1914, rural labourers' cottages had been heavily subsidised with the Exchequer and ratepayers between them bearing up to two-thirds of the cost, while most urban housing schemes incurred losses, despite charging rents which were beyond the reach of most labouring families. (Housing policy is discussed in detail in chapter five.) By the 1920s the acceptable minimum standards for working-class housing assumed separate toilet facilities, perhaps even a bathroom and a minimum of three bedrooms: separate bedrooms for parents and for children of either sex. This put decent housing even further beyond the reach of the average labourer.

During the latter stages of World War I and its immediate aftermath, the British state began to assume greater responsibility for working-class housing. Both the British and Irish governments reversed this trend during the 1920s as part of their efforts to curb public expenditure. Irish housing policy tended to follow Westminster; an Act of 1924, which provided lump-sum grants for all new houses, was virtually identical to legislation passed in Westminster in 1923. A survey of local authorities (all Ireland) carried out in 1919 had estimated that there was an urgent need for almost 62,000 dwellings,[199] yet between 1922 and 1931 the number of houses built in the Irish Free State with Exchequer assistance was in excess of 20,000: 13,675 were built by private individuals or public utility companies and 6,644 by local authorities. Local authorities found it difficult to borrow capital for

144

housing schemes: the banks proved unaccommodating and the Local Loans Fund would not consider applications for housing finance until 1929.

Investment in roads should have been immune from the financial stringencies of the 1920s. The Road Fund constituted an independent and reasonably buoyant source of income. Unlike Britain, where Winston Churchill, while Chancellor of the Exchequer, began the practice of 'raiding the Road Fund', the Irish Road Fund survived the 1920s intact. Motorised road transport grew rapidly during the decade: in 1919 there were only 7,286 registered motor vehicles; by 1927 the number had reached 45,757.[200] Road development promised to be one of the Department's success stories. By 1925 it had identified a national road network of 3,000 miles, which would be given priority in the allocation of Road Fund grants. However the plan suffered a number of setbacks. The 1919 Ministry of Transport Act had envisaged a centralised road unit. The Irish Free State made county councils and borough councils responsible for all road construction.

Technical problems, such as the county councils' lack of equipment and expertise, could have been surmounted,[201] but the political difficulties were formidable. Most councillors regarded improving national roads as a waste of money and preferred to 'invest' in lanes and by-roads, because they regarded them as giving greater benefit to local ratepayers. The second problem was financial. Although income from the Road Fund rose steadily, it never matched the Department's plans. In 1924 Local Government succeeded in borrowing money for roads against future Road Fund income. In 1925 it proposed to begin an accelerated trunk road improvement programme which would be financed by an Exchequer grant. The Minister for Finance announced a £2m. trunk road investment programme in his 1926 Budget speech, which would be financed by borrowings against the Road Fund.[202] Despite this apparent victory by Local Government, the outcome was disappointing. Local Government assumed that the £2m. was in addition to existing Road Fund revenue of £804,000 in 1926. Finance saw £2m. as the ceiling on expenditure.

In the long run, the £2m. appears to have been a mirage: although £1.875m. was spent on the national scheme by March 1929, only £750,000 came from borrowings; the balance was from normal Road Fund income. Instead of giving priority to major national roads, the Department came under increasing pressure to share out the money between all counties, so progress on major routes was slow. Before 1927, all money distributed by the Road Fund was spent on improvements; after that date an increasing share was diverted to maintenance, so that by 1931/32 barely more than 50 per cent of income went on improvements. This was primarily a concession to the anti-rates campaign, but it failed to placate local authorities, which demanded that the Road Fund should contribute to the cost of maintaining local roads.

This capsule history of roads policy raises several issues. Although Finance's normal parsimony undoubtedly reduced the money available for improving trunk roads, the failure to complete the proposed development programme was due to political factors. The Department's roads plan lacked popular support; many local authorities and ratepayers preferred money to be spent on maintaining local roads.

Politics, together with lack of finance, also explain the lack of improvements in water supplies and sanitary services, though Local Government tended to blame the latter.[203] When LLF loans became available for sanitary services in 1926/27, the value of loans sanctioned under this heading actually fell. W. Sterling Berry, the Department's medical inspector, believed that sanitary conditions in many small towns were deteriorating. In 1927 he reported that in Tubbercurry, Co. Sligo,

> New houses with modern sanitary conveniences are being built and the better class of older houses are having conveniences put in; connections are being made to stone sewers which were only meant to deal with storm water and are almost useless for dealing with house drainage. The situation is further complicated by an inadequate water supply which as a rule is not sufficient to keep these large sewers properly flushed. This means that the ground on which these towns are built is rapidly becoming heavily polluted, a very undesirable state of affairs.

A departmental inquiry in 1928 concluded that there were two options: to provide an adequate water supply or 'to evacuate the town'. Despite this unequivocal message, ratepayers objected to a new water scheme on grounds of cost. Tubbercurry's rateable valuation could not bear the borrowing charges, residents of the surrounding rural area objected to

146

paying for a scheme from which they would not benefit, and Sligo County Council was reluctant to meet the bill.[204] Ratepayers in Kilmacthomas, Co. Waterford also opposed a proposed water scheme, despite the fact that the local medical officer of health believed that inadequate water and sewerage services were responsible for an outbreak of diphtheria which had claimed several lives.[205]

Although ratepayers expressed considerable opposition to any expenditure which would lead to higher rates, no lobby campaigned for Exchequer grants to be provided for improvements to sanitary services. Clean water was not high on the list of priorities for Irish voters in the 1920s. Housing had been an important issue in Irish politics in the years 1914-22. The topic was debated on several occasions in the first Dáil and in 1922 the provisional government provided £1m. for housing grants. For the remainder of the 1920s, however, the government does not seem to have been under pressure to promote a major housing programme, despite the fact that conditions were deteriorating in Dublin and probably in other towns. The suspension of Dublin Corporation silenced one key interest group; when the Corporation was restored in the autumn of 1930, it immediately established a housing committee with a view to formulating a housing programme. In response, the government announced that it was in the process of considering new housing legislation, though there is no evidence to support this assertion. However this exchange sparked renewed interest in the Dublin slums; the Civics Institute organised a public meeting to lobby for government action, and newspapers gave extensive coverage to what they termed 'Dublin's shame'.[206] The 1931 Housing (Miscellaneous Provisions) Act, which passed the Dáil on 17 December 1931 — the date it adjourned for the Christmas recess — marked the beginning of a new effort to clear urban slums and to rehouse the poorest sections of the community. The Act was modelled on the British 1930 Housing Act (the so-called Greenwood Act).

Since the publication of Fanning's *The Irish Department of Finance* in 1978, it has become almost mandatory to blame the conservative practices of the Department of Finance for most sins of omission by Irish governments. Yet what is interesting is the consensus on housing policy between officials in Finance and in Local Government in 1931. Both agreed that state funds should be spent on rehousing the poorest families. Both resented the fact that for most of the 1920s state aid for housing had largely gone to 'owner occupied farms and speculative builders', with 'nothing' being done for those in the worst housing conditions. Although the two Departments had disagreed over allowing local authorities to borrow money for housing from the LLF, there is no evidence that Local Government had developed a comprehensive housing programme before 1931, or that its failure to do so can be explained by opposition from the Department of Finance.

Local Government did, however, have an ambitious national road plan. Why no national housing plan, given that the Local Government Board had devoted considerable attention to housing during its final years? The explanation may lie with people. The senior staff in the Ministry of Transport's Dublin office transferred *en bloc* to the Department of Local Government and Public Health, bringing with them the skeleton of a roads programme. Quigley, who became chief engineer in the DLGPH, had been a member of the Ministry's Road Board. By contrast, most of the LGB's housing experts appear to have been dispersed, other than housing inspector Thomas Strahan.[207] Ideology was also a factor. Successive Ministers for Local Government and senior officials appear to have wholly subscribed to the central tenets of government policy during these years; if the Department failed to obtain large sums of money for housing, this was largely because it never asked for it. Although the appointment of James Burke, an extern minister to the Local Government and Public Health portfolio, is unlikely to have strengthened the Department's negotiating hand, there is no evidence that it proved a significant handicap. Richard Mulcahy, who served as Minister from 1927 to 1932, was a much more formidable politician, but he too subscribed to existing orthodoxies. In 1929 he told the Dáil that housing was primarily the responsibility of local government: 'the state cannot bear on its shoulders the burden of solving this particular problem, particularly where there does exist or is supposed to exist, as far as central Government is concerned, machinery in local authorities which could be adapted for the purpose'.[208]

Local Government's failure to press for higher Exchequer funding for services such as housing or water reflects the central dilemma facing that Department. It had to protect the financial integrity of the local government system, by ensuring a high level of rate collection; to do this, it was desirable to prevent local authority borrowings from getting out of hand. It was also desirable that the bulk of local expenditure would be financed from local sources. A significant programme of investment in sanitary services or housing would jeopardise the financial and political equilibrium of local government. Consequently, a Department that was eager to centralise local appointments and local administration was determined not to demand uniform standards of sanitary services or housing, because this would invariably mean increased expenditure.

LIBRARIES

Libraries were one of the few local authority services to be improved during the years 1922-32. A clause in the 1925 Local Government Act opened the way for the introduction of a county library service. Until that time, the authority to levy a rate of up to 3d (1.5p) in the pound rested with boroughs, urban districts or rural district councils. Both the 1925 clause and the earlier Library Acts were permissive: councils could levy a rate in aid of a local library, but they were not compelled to do so, and many rural district councils made no provision for a public library.[209] In 1925 county councils assumed responsibility for library services outside urban areas, and urban district councils were permitted to transfer their library functions to the county council. This resulted in the appointment of county librarians. The Department's official role in this process was passive: county councils were not required to implement a county library service. Nevertheless, by 1933 every county with the exception of Westmeath and Longford had done so and it appears that the Department made efforts to improve library services. The public libraries in all the major towns of County Kerry were destroyed during the course of the Anglo-Irish war and the civil war and the Department expressed concern about the delay in rebuilding them. Such concern did not extend to providing funds for either current or capital expenditure.[210] The cost of building, or rebuilding, libraries was met by the UK-based Carnegie Trust (named after Scottish-born steel millionaire Andrew Carnegie); the additional costs were met by the library rate. Carnegie Trust grants for libraries were ended after World War II.[211]

RELIEF WORKS

Despite an apparent consensus on the direction of government policy, relations between Local Government and Finance were often fraught during these years, because Finance's determination to have a veto over all expenditure proposals threatened to turn Local Government into little more than a forwarding agency for requests from local authorities. As we shall see below, this was particularly true of water and sewage schemes, which were funded under the guise of employment relief schemes. Reforms introduced by the British administration in the dying months of the Union had resulted in substantially greater Treasury control. In 1922 Joseph Brennan insisted that all applications by local authorities to the Local Loans Fund should be forwarded to Finance for consideration, a change from previous practice where applications were approved by the LGB and forwarded for payment to the Board of Works.[212] Finance's attempt to control LLF allocations was largely symbolic because there were no funds available, but it sought to apply similar procedures to all applications from local authorities for grants towards the cost of relief works. Throughout the 1920s reports of distress or unemployment tended to trigger modest allocations of money from the Exchequer.

In March 1922 the provisional government voted a sum of £375,000 for relief works; £100,000 of this was earmarked for emergency relief measures along the west and south coasts.[213] An additional £250,000 was allocated in 1924. Most of this money was doled out in modest grants for minor works: £1,000 to Ennis UDC for footpaths; £2,000 to Dundalk UDC for foreshore reclamation; £750 to Tullamore UDC and £500 for Offaly County Council for road works — this constituted the entire allocation to Offaly County Council in 1924. Although Local Government was required to certify that the scheme was 'of distinct public utility' and perhaps that the area was suffering from acute distress and/or unemployment (this might also be done by another government agency), all schemes had to be approved by the Department of Finance. Local Government acted as sub-accountant: supervising the work, verifying that the expenditure had been incurred, and claiming funds from Finance.[214]

Although Local Government had an unrivalled knowledge of local conditions and was the destination of most deputations from local authorities who were seeking grants — one senior official claimed that deputations were a major cause of delays in carrying out relief works[215] — its control over relief works was largely negative. Schemes which Local Government rejected were unlikely to receive assistance, but

Finance tended to prune and often reject those which Local Government had approved. In December 1930, during the course of a conference to review government relief works, attended by officials from Local Government, Finance, the Board of Works and the Irish Land Commission, Local Government asked to be allocated a specific sum and be given a free hand in its allocation. No decision was taken on this proposal; an alternative proposal to establish an interdepartmental committee which would examine all applications for grants — this was opposed by Local Government — can be taken as an implicit rejection of the idea. Further evidence of tension between Finance and Local Government is evident in a letter from McElligott to McCarron some days later. Although this was dated 24 December and ended by wishing him the compliments of the season, the letter is not noteworthy for its Christmas spirit. McElligott commented that files received from Local Government concerning unemployment relief schemes indicated

> . . . that you appear invariably to have entered into a commitment
> before submitting your proposals for our approval. We do not wish
> to hamper you in any avoidable way in the early stages because
> I appreciate the difficulties that have to be faced by your
> Department. At the same time we find it a little difficult to see
> exactly what principles are being followed regarding the approval of
> schemes or the proportion which should be contributed by local
> authorities. As the Vote must be accounted for by this Department
> and as I shall have to answer questions before the Public Accounts
> Committee concerning the administration of this Grant, I hope that
> after the end of the current month you will submit your proposals to
> us before you enter into any arrangement with local authorities.[216]

McCarron's response does not survive and Finance continued to carry out a detailed scrutiny of minor relief schemes. Although Finance criticised the apparent lack of principles behind Local Government's approach to relief works, their actions show little awareness of local needs or political pressures. Finance insisted on fixing wage rates on minor relief works, despite being advised by Local Government that similar action had simply embroiled their minister in disputes with local authorities, delaying the start of public works. In the winter of 1930/31 such intervention occasioned several disputes and led to innumerable representations from Dáil deputies.[217]

CONCLUSIONS

The Cumann na nGaedheal government is often regarded as having achieved little in domestic affairs other than the restoration of law and order. This is belied by the achievements of the Department of Local Government and Public Health, which pursued a coherent and sustained policy line in all matters under its concern. Its goals were efficiency, economy, accountability, uniformity and professionalism: a list which encompasses measures ranging from the city management system, stricter scrutiny of applications for old age and blind pensions and the establishment of the Local Appointments Commission. The Department implemented several aspects of Arthur Griffith's Sinn Féin policy, such as the introduction of combined purchasing, with preference for Irish-made goods and the use of meritocracy, rather than favouritism, in awarding contracts and filling jobs.

It is perhaps surprising that while law and order, foreign policy or agriculture are strongly identified with the personalities of the respective Ministers — Kevin O'Higgins, Patrick McGilligan and Patrick Hogan — this is not true of Local Government. James Burke, the Minster for much of this period, remains something of a mystery figure. Despite Richard Mulcahy's high profile, he tends to be remembered for his time in Defence rather than in Local Government. Mulcahy would not have been surprised at the absence of plaudits for his achievements or those of any other Minister of Local Government. In July 1927 Jim Kennedy, a regular correspondent of Mulcahy's and town clerk of Nenagh, wrote to the Minister:

> There are so many people affected by Local Government matters that inevitably there is bound to be criticism of whatever it is that one is doing as you can't please everybody and the Minister is a cockshot for all the disappointed and disgruntled. You'll have deputations asking for grants (everyone wants a grant, this Council for drainage, that for this and that and so on) to have so and so appointed to this, to have salaries reduced, to have them increased, to have this fellow not sacked and so on. It's a tough thing to deal with all those people and it's utterly impossible to please everybody, so expect criticism but don't mind. A lot of criticism is gallery play.

Many of the reforms carried out between the years 1922 and 1932

152

interfered with various vested interests. Although the abolition of the RDCs in 1925, the suspension of local authorities and the introduction of city managers probably raised the quality of local government, they did not necessarily win votes. While Jim Kennedy recognised the benefits of reforming local administration, he suggested that it would be a 'thorny field'. Kennedy, who had considerable practical knowledge of local government, believed that there was much to be said for replacing county councils with appointed commissioners, though he warned that it would prove to be an unpopular move:

> The enforcing of sanitary laws will never be done by Councils, here's where a Commissioner can do the work better. Popularly elected men will not do the necessary things that may antagonise their supporters. The good of the general community is not welcomed for it is inconvenient for an individual to refrain from keeping pigs up against the dwelling house, or a manure heap or some other nuisance. Hence sanitary laws are not administered and it is false to think they will be unless an independent outsider has the ordering of things.[218]

This epitomised the dilemma facing the Department of Local Government. Much of what it did, though conducive to the national good, proved politically unpopular, not least with government supporters, and the reforms gave the Fianna Fáil opposition ample opportunity to adopt a more sympathetic stance. It might have been possible to overcome such drawbacks if the Department had also been more generous in funding housing and other expenditure, but this was not possible. Yet it would be foolish to place undue blame on the Cumann na nGaedheal government's austere attitude towards public spending. The Department's imaginative road programme probably lost it more friends than it made; more money for sanitary services would have been welcome only if the cost had been wholly borne by the Exchequer.

Amid all the details of legislation and expenditure, one issue looms large: local authority finances. The fragility of rates as a financial base for local government underpins all other matters.

CHAPTER FOUR

FIANNA FÁIL IN THE CUSTOM HOUSE,
1932-39

The Fianna Fáil government, which took office in February 1932, had promised the electorate a programme of more intense nationalism, economic self-sufficiency and more intervention in the economy. The depressed state of the international economy had removed Ireland's traditional safety valve of emigration, forcing the government to tackle the issue of unemployment. Both the change of government and the altered economic circumstances had major implications for the Department of Local Government. Expenditure on roads, housing and sanitary services came to be assessed for their potential to provide jobs, rather than as desirable for their own sake. While superficially this appeared to strengthen Local Government's case for obtaining a greater share of government expenditure, in practice it meant that the Department suffered considerable interference from other agencies, such as the Office of Public Works, which had different priorities. Tariff protection and the drive for self-sufficiency brought higher costs and some supply problems for housing and water schemes, while the combined effects of international agricultural depression and the Economic War with Britain led to anti-government protests which often took the form of refusing to pay rates. In 1932 Seán T. O'Kelly was appointed Minister for Local Government and Public Health.[1] A former Sinn Féin member of Dublin Corporation, O'Kelly carried the title of vice-president, which gave Local Government more seniority in cabinet.

LOCAL APPOINTMENTS

Irish civil servants were concerned that the change of government would usher in a spoils system, with senior officials who had served the previous government being replaced by men, and perhaps even a small number of women, who were regarded as more politically compatible. Although Fanning claims that such fears proved groundless,[2] he may have overstated the case. Éamon de Valera's commitment to protect the existing system was not necessarily shared by O'Kelly. The dismissal of McCarron, secretary of the Department, in 1936 suggests that the fears which senior civil servants expressed in 1932 were not altogether groundless and, although the Local Appointments Commission survived in its original form, at times it was a close-run thing. When, in the spring of 1932, Fianna Fáil lifted the ban on representations from TDs concerning disallowed old age pensions, it appeared to herald a shift towards a more politicised public service.[3]

In opposition, Fianna Fáil had championed local interests against the Local Appointments Commission, most notoriously in the case of the Mayo county librarian. With Fianna Fáil in government, local authorities anticipated that the powers of the Local Appointments Commission would be curbed and some had begun to challenge the Commission's authority in the courts. The joint management committee of the Cork District Mental Hospital queried the minister's authority to refuse it permission to promote an internal candidate to the post of resident medical superintendent as an alternative to filling the post via the Local Appointments Commission.[4] A legal challenge concerning the appointment of the Cork county secretary also appeared likely. In March 1932, the new Attorney General, Conor Maguire, produced a paper for the Executive Council which examined the possibility of incorporating some form of local preference within the existing legislation.

Maguire informed the government that, although the High Court had recently held (in the case taken by the management committee of the Cork District Mental Hospital) that ministerial sanction was necessary not only to the appointment but to the method of appointment by the local authority, the decision to recommend one or more names to local authorities rested with the commissioners 'without reference to the Minister'. Under Section 7 (1) of the Act, however, the Minister must consent to the qualifications prescribed by the Commissioners for every appointment, and Maguire expressed the opinion that 'it would be open to the Minister to require that candidates should have training and experience gained in contact with conditions similar to those which exist in the locality to which an appointment is about to be made.' He also believed that it would be 'open to the Minister' to ask the Commission to recommend more than one person for appointment. Having considered Maguire's paper, the cabinet decided that the President should consult the chairman of the Local Appointments Commission about any amendments 'which might appear to be desirable' in the Commission's procedures.

Before the consultation could take place, O'Kelly informed de Valera that Section 5(1) of the 1926 Act enabled a local authority, *'subject to the Minister's sanction'* [the words in italics were underlined in the original], to fill an appointment without recourse to the Local Appointments Commission, providing the person appointed already held a pensionable post with a local authority. He had decided *as a matter of general policy* [underlined in pencil] not to withhold sanction since he was of the opinion that the powers already vested in him were adequate to prevent local authorities from making unsuitable appointments. He told de Valera that this was 'regarded as a radical change in policy'; Mulcahy, his predecessor, had refused to sanction this method of appointment where the office was 'one of any importance'. O'Kelly believed that this concession would result in 'more harmonious relations between the Department and local bodies, and restore to a considerable extent the reasonable powers of which local authorities have heretofore been deprived'; it would also pre-empt several pending legal challenges. This would restore the power of appointment to local authorities where posts were filled by incumbents; in other cases, O'Kelly proposed that the Local Appointments commissioners should recommend two or more names 'if they so think proper'. Although the decision to do so rested with the commissioners, the minister suggested that the Executive Council 'should intimate' to them that a panel of qualified names should be submitted if either the Minister or the local authority so requested. Until the revised policy was introduced, O'Kelly suggested that the Commission should proceed only with urgent appointments. He also questioned 'whether it would not be expedient' to change the membership of the Commission 'at an early date'.

When de Valera met the commissioners to discuss giving local authorities the names of more than one qualified candidate 'in furtherance of the principle of decentralisation', they expressed the fear that 'possibly frequent requests would be made for more than three names' and the Commission would be forced to supply the names of all qualified candidates, which would give rise to the possibility that poorly qualified candidates would be appointed. They were also concerned that the proposed procedures would deter applications from Irish doctors working in Britain. Nevertheless the Commission reluctantly agreed to supply three names, adding the proviso 'that if this concession is made, and friction with Local Authorities is to be avoided', 'a clear and definite statement' should be attached 'that in no case will the figure of three be exceeded'. de Valera asked if it would be possible to hold interviews outside Dublin, but the Commission foresaw difficulties in finding qualified personnel, with 'no embarrassing local relationship on whose reports the Commissioners could with confidence rely'.

On 24 April 1932 de Valera informed the commissioners that he 'would be glad' if in future they would submit three names for each appointment, except in cases where the appointment was made in competitive examination or where a local authority requested only one name.[5] This concession created more problems than it solved: it failed to placate local authorities and it proved unpopular with job applicants. The Irish Medical Association demanded that only one candidate be recommended. Carrickmacross Urban District Council passed a resolution demanding the abolition of the Local Appointments Commission and several local authorities rejected the three names submitted. On 30 June, following discussion in cabinet, the President informed the Commission that where a local authority rejected the panel of qualified names, the Executive Council would offer no objection to the Commission substituting the name of one qualified candidate; in the case of appointments which were pending, the Commission should provide three names to local authorities that had already requested this, but in all other cases they should revert to the practice of naming one candidate.[6]

This climb-down by the government was not the only occasion where this administration and the Commission came into conflict. While de Valera appears to have accepted the Commission's remit at all times, O'Kelly continued to yearn for a greater political say in the matter of appointments. This is evident in the case of local authority officials who were either dismissed or were forced to resign because the previous government had required those newly appointed or promoted to take an oath of loyalty. O'Kelly wished to introduce legislation in April 1932 to repeal this requirement, but the cabinet decided to wait until an omnibus local government bill was ready. The oath was eventually repealed in the 1933 Local Government Act. In the meantime, public servants who objected to the oath continued to be threatened with losing promotion or appointment. By April 1932 one such case had already arisen and others were imminent.[7] It is not clear how this problem was met. Those who had lost office or promotion in the past sought reinstatement or compensation.

In July 1932, O'Kelly wrote to cabinet expressing frustration at his inability to speed the reinstatement process because all appointments were made either by the Local Appointments Commission or by local authorities. He proposed to issue a circular requiring local authorities to give preference in appointments to dismissed officials and suggested that the President should make a similar request of the Local Appointments Commission. The Commission stood firm, perhaps emboldened by the government's retreat over appointments some weeks previously. Frank Fahy, the Ceann Comhairle, who was chairman of the Commission, replied that the Commission had 'always regarded itself as agents of Local Authorities and, recognising how members of public boards divided on political questions, have [sic] never suggested that preference should be given to any section'. He recalled that a memorandum drafted in 1925 had specifically excluded the Commission from seeking information about 'service in the national forces' on application forms and from taking such service into consideration in making appointments. Any departure from these procedures would present serious difficulties. de Valera concurred with the Commission's views.[8]

The 1933 Local Government Act provided for a commission of inquiry to be established to consider cases of resignation or dismissal from local authority service for political reasons. Senior officials in the Department objected that several applications had no political basis but appeared to have arisen 'out of personal dissatisfaction with Departmental decisions'. They feared that the commission of inquiry would 'entice a mass of miscellaneous applications from all sorts of people whether they were or were not connected with political divisions'.[9] Officials who had refused promotion would be compensated for loss of salary; political prisoners or internees would be eligible for back pay, and those who had resigned or been dismissed for political reasons could count their period of dismissal as years of pensionable service. The provisions also applied to officials who had been dismissed from local government service in Northern Ireland for political reasons. O'Kelly failed to have dismissed officials reinstated. He was also unsuccessful in securing the appointment of officials, whose appointment had not been sanctioned in the past because of their failure to take the oath, though local authorities were given ministerial sanction to regard these officials as qualified to hold either their former post or a similar position.[10] The cost of compensation fell on local authorities, and councils with an anti-government majority were slow to honour their obligations. Labourers and caretakers were not compensated until 1936.[11]

Although the saga of the Sligo town clerkship has not yet featured in any history of independent Ireland, it is at least as important an example of parish-pump politics and clerical interference as the case of the Mayo county librarian. When the post was advertised in 1932, many members of Sligo Corporation supported the candidacy of R.G. Bradshaw, the acting town clerk, although he had held that position for only some weeks. At forty-seven, he was above the usual maximum age of forty-five which had been specified in the Commission's advertisement.

Sligo Corporation protested against his exclusion on grounds of age, and, at O'Kelly's request, the Commissioners, 'with much hesitation and with a feeling of uneasiness that such an alteration would raise suspicion and create an impression unfavourable to the Commissioners', agreed to readvertise the post with a higher age limit, though they informed the minister that it was undesirable to change the conditions of appointment after an advertisement had appeared. When Bradshaw's name was not among the three submitted to Sligo Corporation, it demanded a public inquiry on the grounds that the commissioners had discriminated against Bradshaw, the man best qualified for the post. The Corporation also alleged that another candidate had falsified his qualifications, that bribery had been employed, and that the Knights of Columbanus and the catholic clergy had combined to oppose Bradshaw's appointment on the grounds that he was a protestant, an atheist and a republican. (He had been interned between 1922 and 1924.) The mayor of Sligo subsequently alleged that Bradshaw's republicanism, not his religion, was the key issue, adding that Sligo priests had never objected to the fact that all the officers of the mental hospital and the harbour commissioners were protestants; the priests in question also socialised extensively with protestants.

In response to these allegations, O'Kelly admitted privately that local TD Frank Carty had arranged for him to meet Canon O'Beirne (the administrator in Sligo, a rank equivalent to parish priest in a town which has a resident bishop), though he claimed to have been unaware of the purpose of the meeting. Canon O' Beirne gave O'Kelly a letter 'for delivery to the Chairman of the Local Appointments Commission' which O'Kelly claimed to have forwarded unopened. When the chairman of the commissioners opened the letter and discovered its contents (they were not specified, but apparently objected to Bradshaw's appointment), he claimed to have destroyed it without noting the name of the correspondent and without informing his fellow commissioners. De Valera asked the Attorney General, Conor Maguire, to investigate these claims. Maguire concluded that Bradshaw's qualifications were inferior to those of several other candidates; the allegedly falsified *curriculum vitae* was the result of a minor transcription error in the Commission, and, according to the Commission, it had not influenced the assessment (how this was known to Sligo Corporation is unclear). On the question of undue influence being brought to bear, the Attorney General concluded that 'while they [the facts] point to reprehensible conduct on the part of certain persons it is difficult to say that they reflect in any way upon the Commissioners'. He continued:

> I think Mr. Carty's experience should not have allowed him to put the Minister in the awkward position he was placed in connection with this interview. Arising out of the interview is the still more unfortunate action of the Minister in accepting from Canon O'Beirne a letter directed to the Chairman of the Appointments Commission. The sending of this letter undoubtedly was a deliberate attempt to bring influence to bear on the Commission against Mr. Bradshaw.

Maguire told de Valera that all the evidence that would be available to a commission of inquiry was already in his possession, but it was important that the 'Commissioners and the Selection Board should be above suspicion'. A commission of inquiry 'might clear the air'.[12] Although the Executive Council apparently decided to hold an inquiry, de Valera informed Sligo Corporation some weeks later that he had found no case to support its allegations. McCarron wrote to the mayor of Sligo that 'no person ever attempted to approach [the members of the selection board], either directly or indirectly' and neither the board nor the other commissioners had any knowledge of Canon O'Beirne's letter.

When Sligo Corporation refused to appoint any of the three names submitted, the Commission nominated Seán Higgins for the post. The Corporation again refused to make the appointment; the government issued an absolute order directing them to do so. Sligo Corporation appealed the order to the Supreme Court, which dismissed the case in July 1934. The Corporation then appointed Higgins, but demanded that he start work at once. When he failed to do so (he had to give one month's notice to Cavan County Council), they dismissed him for failing to carry out orders, and Bradshaw again served as temporary town clerk; the appointment was sanctioned by Seán T. O'Kelly. Higgins's dismissal was duly quashed by the Minister and, following several bouts of hospitalisation, possibly as a consequence of the controversy, he took up his post. The Corporation then attempted to appoint Bradshaw to the new, and in the Department's eyes, unnecessary post of housing manager. Higgins appealed to the Department for help: 'I have nothing against the man personally but from my position here as Town Clerk I know the feelings of the people — the bigger ratepayers — towards his attitude in the past.'

Although Bradshaw's appointment was quashed, Higgins's purgatory continued. In 1937 members of Sligo Corporation demanded access during office hours to all incoming and outgoing correspondence and to all papers concerning council business. Higgins informed the Department that the proposer was 'a gentleman of leisure' who 'practically lives in the Town Hall; calls daily on every conceivable excuse and occupies time of the Staff to a very considerable extent'. He added: 'should this resolution be adopted, I will refuse to have the members, many of whom are unemployed, making this office a club where they can foregather and prevent the work being done'.[13] Higgins died shortly afterwards, and Bradshaw again became acting town clerk; he held this post into the 1940s. Appointments at acting or temporary status remained under local control; O'Kelly appears to have seen long temporary appointments as a means of placating local interests.

O'Kelly's continuing hostility towards the Local Appointments Commission may reflect his belief that the process was not as impartial as it seemed, or rather, given that interview panels were drawn from people holding senior positions, they were more likely to favour pro-Treaty candidates or those closely associated with the former British administration. In March 1934, O'Kelly launched a savage personal attack in the Dáil on Dr T.F. O'Higgins, a Fine Gael TD. He alleged, incorrectly, that O'Higgins was serving as medical officer of health while in receipt of a state pension. O'Kelly also claimed that O'Higgins's appointment as MOH by the Local Appointments Commission had been politically motivated, but withdrew this statement when O'Higgins challenged him. Referring to O'Higgins's claim to have been appointed by a board consisting of two professors in the National University and a distinguished medical officer of health, O'Kelly asked if O'Higgins was suggesting 'that there is no such thing in the National University as men with a political outlook?'[14] Both McCarron and Boland, who was head of establishment in Finance, were extremely concerned by this exchange. In a note marked 'confidential', Boland informed McCarron:

> . . . the political aspect of this discussion, or anything that the Minister may have intended to effect politically by his statement, is no concern of ours. But the harm the statement is likely to bring about in a possible increase in expenditure and otherwise is a matter of much official importance especially to our Department.
>   . . . As you know we have till now secured the service gratuitously of outsiders in addition to Civil Servants to act on Selection Boards . . . . These gratuitous services, sometimes of very important people, would represent a high annual bill if they had to be paid for. During the first five years of the Local Appointments Commission's life, as I am aware from personal experience, the rectitude both of the Commission and of the Boards it appointed was constantly assailed, not merely by persons who did not support the Government but also by persons who sympathised with that Government. . . .
>   The effect of the Dáil statement on personnel of the Commission and unpaid personnel . . . on persons invited to give their gratuitous services on Boards, if their motives in arriving at the recommendations are to be assailed later on by the highest authorities of Government in the most public manner, its effect will certainly not be favourable and the likelihood of these persons being willing to undertake without payment a troublesome and thankless task which carried with it always the unfavourable regard

of unsuccessful candidates must at least become doubtful. It
might conceivably lead to the breakdown of the Act which
the Government is desirous of maintaining.[15]

McCARRON'S DISMISSAL

O'Kelly's troubled relationship with local appointments culminated in
the cabinet's dismissal of Edward McCarron in November 1936. The
immediate issue concerned a medical appointment in the Dublin
mental hospitals. Both Grangegorman and Portrane psychiatric
hospitals were regarded as one hospital for administrative purposes,
under the control of the chief medical superintendent, though the
deputy resident medical superintendent was responsible for routine
administration at Portrane. When the chief medical superintendent
retired aged sixty-five, the committee of management decided to
abolish the post of deputy resident medical superintendent at Portrane
and replace it with a post of resident medical superintendent. They
envisaged appointing a second resident medical superintendent when a
new, and as yet unbuilt, hospital came on stream. The minister formally
approved this proposal in August 1936, together with salary scales for
the posts of chief medical superintendent (based at Grangegorman) and
resident medical superintendent. On 18 September the committee of
management asked for ministerial sanction to fill the vacant post of
chief medical superintendent by internal promotion, instead of via the
Local Appointments Commission; this was refused. In October the
management committee approved the abolition of the post of deputy
resident medical superintendent at Portrane on condition that Dr Blake,
its current holder, was appointed to the new post of resident medical
superintendent. The Department issued a minute, dated 18 November
1936, giving ministerial approval, though Seán T. O' Kelly subsequently
claimed to have no knowledge of this until he read about it in the
newspapers on 20 November.[16]

Shortly before this event, O'Kelly had come under pressure from
party members to sanction the promotion of Dr Ada English, one of the
six women TDs who had voted against the Treaty and a long-standing
member of the staff of Ballinasloe Mental Hospital, to the post of
resident medical superintendent there. His apparent volte-face over the
Portrane appointment gave rise to considerable embarrassment. In the

Dáil John A. Costello, a Fine Gael TD and future Taoiseach, claimed that a letter agreeing to the Grangegorman committee's request to appoint Dr Blake was 'on file ready for signature and ready to be sent out', but on reading this letter McCarron came to the conclusion that if it were sent, the Minister 'would be caused serious political embarrassment'. McCarron consequently made a number of 'unimportant' changes to the letter 'which were intended to ease the Minister's political past concerning the Ballinasloe appointment' and left a note on the file giving reasons for the alteration. Costello claimed that the original draft letter approved Dr Blake's appointment 'owing to peculiar circumstances', provided that the post attached to the yet-to-be-built hospital was filled through the Local Appointments Commission.[17] This letter does not appear to have survived.

On 24 November 1936 O'Kelly informed the Executive Council that an incident had occurred 'which, considered in conjunction with previous incidents, caused him to feel he could no longer have that complete confidence in McCarron's discretion and general appreciation of government policy'. He had first learned of the letter sanctioning Blake's appointment in a press report dated 20 November. Since this was a new position, he argued that filling it by internal promotion was contrary to the Department's policy. Given that O'Kelly had been widely criticised for insisting on using the Local Appointments Commission in similar cases in the past, he felt that McCarron ought to have consulted him before sending the letter sanctioning the appointment.

The Executive Council asked O' Kelly to consult with the Minister for Finance on the steps necessary to remove McCarron from his post. McCarron refused to accept a position as Commissioner for Public Works at his existing salary and the cabinet made an order removing him from his position with effect from 1 December 1936.

In a letter seeking a meeting with de Valera, McCarron claimed that the circumstances in Portrane were 'peculiar', involving 'not an ordinary promotion but an upgrading of a post'. The Attorney General disagreed, though he noted a number of legal inconsistencies in the appointments made to the Dublin mental hospitals. On 24 December, Seán Moynihan (secretary to the Executive Council) wrote to McCarron expressing the Executive Council's 'great regret', but emphasising that

. . . the relations between the secretary of a Department and his

Minister are of peculiar importance. In the interests of efficient administration, it is necessary that the Minister, in addition to trusting in the secretary's integrity and efficiency, should also have complete confidence in his discretion and general appreciation of Government policy. Certain incidents of which you are aware, culminating in your action concerning the Portrane appointment, made the Minister for Local Government feel that he could no longer have such confidence in you.[18]

In response, McCarron claimed that the Executive Council had been misinformed by the Minister, by the Ballinasloe Mental Home committee and by other parties. He claimed that there had been only one previous disagreement between himself and O'Kelly, concerning a promotion within the Department in 1935, and that this had been ended 'by my full acceptance of the Minister's decision, and with expressions of mutual regret that anything had arisen to disturb the harmonious relations which had existed'.

McCarron subsequently fuelled the controversy by releasing copies to the press of his correspondence with de Valera and Seán Moynihan. *The Irish Times* claimed that the government had deliberately delayed the dismissal until the Dáil had adjourned for the Christmas recess. On 26 January 1937 John A. Costello tabled a motion demanding that a select committee be established to inquire into the circumstances surrounding McCarron's dismissal. When Costello's motion was debated in the Dáil, O'Kelly was conspicuously silent. The government's case was put by de Valera and Seán MacEntee, who as Minister for Finance appointed each departmental accounting officer — i.e. the departmental secretary — though the actual appointment as secretary was made by the cabinet. Before the debate, MacEntee informed de Valera that he was 'trying to think out a statement which, while making it clear that it was necessary to remove McCarron from his post in the Department . . . will make it clear also that his removal was not to be ascribed to disgraceful or dishonest conduct.' He was concerned that the incident had left higher civil servants 'unduly apprehensive as to the security of their positions' and he urged de Valera to make a statement clarifying the position of ministers.

MacEntee's speech in the Dáil emphasised that the relationship between minister and secretary was 'a peculiarly personal one, dependent on the Minister's confidence'; the secretary was the 'recognised channel' through which the Minister communicated with his Department. Confidence became a central theme in the government's case, as did the fact that ultimate responsibility rested with a minister. Seán Moynihan, secretary to the Executive Council, urged ministers not to refer to specific incidents in their speeches; if they did so, the Government's discretion would be 'impaired'.[19] de Valera, who regarded Costello's motion as a 'motion of censure', quoted the statement made by a former Minister for Justice, James Geoghegan, following the dismissal of General Eoin O' Duffy in February 1933:

> The law however does envisage the possibility of circumstances arising which without reflecting any discredit on the individual concerned might render it undesirable in the interests of the state that he should be any longer permitted to retain his appointment.[20]

Almost sixty years after these events, there is a sense that the matter had gone out of control. In some respects both parties were right: although the Portrane appointment upgraded an existing post, it meant abolishing a post held by a serving doctor: filling the post by internal promotion might have been perceived as evidence of a weakening of ministerial resolve to support the Local Appointments Commission. Some compromise would presumably have been possible if there had been better understanding between minister and secretary; McCarron's reference to differences over a previous appointment suggests that all was not well. The case also carried an unspoken political dimension: a deputy had openly opposed McCarron's appointment in 1922. In the debate concerning McCarron's dismissal, John A. Costello quoted a Mr Tracey from Cork: 'We are not going to be bossed by any Castle Clique. Sack the whole damn lot of them and it would be a better job.' In an effort to challenge this image, Costello noted that McCarron had been educated by the Christian Brothers in North Richmond Street, Dublin, and had been a member of the Gaelic League.

Edward McCarron was undoubtedly a man of outstanding ability. His evidence to the Brennan Commission on the Civil Service suggests an extremely active and reforming secretary. He claimed that the Department was engaged in a 'continuous overhauling of duties'; all 'superfluous checking of work' had been weeded out; he was personally committed to seeing that staff were given 'early responsibility'. He also emphasised the specialist nature of the

Department's work, the low proportion of routine work, and his wish to promote officials within the Department. McCarron was particularly angry at losing staff on promotion to other departments.[21]

McCarron was succeeded by James Hurson, an assistant secretary and former official of the LGB, who served until 1946 when he retired because of ill-health.

THE IRISH LANGUAGE AND APPOINTMENTS

Criticism of the Local Appointments Commission gradually receded from the mid-1930s, though some councillors were still lamenting their loss of control over appointments twenty years later (see chapter six). Many councillors also resented the fact that candidates for an increasing number of local authority posts were required to pass a test in Irish because this could mean that local favourites were disqualified. Yet opposition to compulsory Irish, though deeply felt, remained muted, either because local politicians were afraid to confront a national icon, or because the Department mitigated the impact of the regulations by failing to enforce them to the full.

In June 1928 the Cumann na nGaedheal government issued an Order that all future appointees to local government positions in Gaeltacht areas — which included parts of Clare, Cork, Donegal, Galway, Kerry, Mayo, Sligo, Tipperary South Riding and Waterford — would be required to demonstrate sufficient knowledge of Irish to enable them to conduct business in that language. Only labourers and tradesmen would be exempt. Those who were appointed without reaching the necessary standard were required to obtain a certificate of competence within three years; failing this, the post would be readvertised. The Order implemented a key recommendation in the report of the 1926 Gaeltacht Commission, which was chaired by Richard Mulcahy.[22] An amending Order introduced in 1931 extended the exemption from an Irish language test to porters, ward maids, mental hospital attendants and those with an annual remuneration of less than £40.

In retrospect, it is obvious that the 1928 Order was utterly unrealistic; its introduction may reflect the fact that Mulcahy, the then Minister for Local Government, felt compelled to implement the Commission's recommendations. In 1931 the Department extended the time-limit for achieving competence in Irish by several months in order to delay the day of reckoning. In May 1932, the qualifying period was extended to four years from the date of appointment and further extensions could be granted in certain circumstances.

In 1939 Thomas Derrig, the minister responsible for Gaeltacht matters, noted that Fianna Fáil had the task of deciding which of the numerous unqualified candidates appointed by the previous government should be dismissed.[23] By 1935 the qualifying period had expired in 65 cases and 28 had either resigned or been removed from office, though only eight had been dismissed because they lacked a knowledge of Irish. A further 350 local authority employees were liable for dismissal, including dispensary doctors, nurses, midwives, rent and rate collectors and home assistance officers. Many doctors and nurses had worked for long periods in England which militated against their studying Irish, while most midwives had only primary schooling.

The Department suggested that the Order should be relaxed on the grounds that it was unfair to require a knowledge of Irish from people who had been educated at a time when opportunities for learning the language were not readily available. Officials feared the 'serious and unfavourable repercussions' which would follow mass dismissals. The secretary of the Department of Lands, which was also responsible for the Gaeltacht, noted that Gaeltacht Orders 'have functioned only to a slight extent in the direction intended, but to a very great extent in the direction of making trouble for the Government, for Local Authorities and for the unfortunate officials who are suspended between heaven and earth.'[24] Several local authorities demanded that the Order be waived, particularly for older employees. Clare County Council claimed that requiring officials aged fifty years and over to meet qualifications in Irish 'brings the language into ridicule and retards its revival'. The Department of Local Government suggested that all candidates aged thirty years or over should be exempt from the language test, but that all younger appointees should be required to show competence in Irish. Most nurses and clerks, who were normally recruited in their twenties or younger, had a knowledge of Irish. In 1936 O'Kelly brought a proposal to this effect before the Executive Council, though for reasons that are not apparent he subsequently withdrew it in favour of strengthening the preference given to candidates with a knowledge of Irish.

The modified requirements would give the Minister for Local Government the authority to require competence in Irish as an essential qualification for appointment to individual posts or categories of posts. An absolute preference in appointments would be given to candidates with a competent knowledge of Irish. If no candidate was competent in Irish, preference would be given to candidates with a good knowledge of Irish. The Executive Council was divided on these proposals and so they were referred to the Gaeltacht subcommittee of the cabinet where they hung fire. In 1937 O'Kelly expressed his concern to the Local Appointments Commission at the fact that persons without a knowledge of Irish were being recommended for appointment within the Gaeltacht. In response, the Commission began to advertise certain positions only in Irish and to list a knowledge of Irish as an essential qualification.

On 3 May 1938 the cabinet approved the second set of proposals which O'Kelly had presented to government in 1936. When James Hurson voiced his concern, Maurice Moynihan, secretary to the government, pointed out that they were designed to bring regulations concerning local appointments into line with those in the civil service. The cabinet minuted that the Department of Local Government should give 'special consideration . . . to the case of minor posts with a view to preventing a situation in which, as a result of the arrangements now to be adopted, only candidates who are native speakers of Irish would have a reasonable prospect of obtaining such posts.'

Local Government was primarily concerned about the impact of the new order on professional and technical appointments. The Local Appointments Commission showed that there were an insufficient number of qualified Irish-speaking candidates to fill all these positions in Gaeltacht areas. Between 1938 and 1940 inclusive, 59 per cent, 54 per cent and 68 per cent respectively of the candidates recommended for appointment in Gaeltacht areas lacked a knowledge of Irish. Of 195 nurses, 166 doctors and 21 midwives competing for non-Gaeltacht posts in 1940, only three doctors, one nurse and one midwife were competent in Irish. A review carried out some years later revealed many instances where poorly qualified candidates were appointed because of an absolute preference for candidates with competence in Irish, such as the doctor placed last of twenty-four candidates who was appointed to a dispensary post.

Officials regarded such appointments as 'detrimental to the best interests of the local government service' and sought to prevent them recurring by setting higher qualifying standards. By 1943 they were particularly concerned that the numerous vacancies at county secretary level, which had been created when many county secretaries were appointed to the new posts of county managers, would be filled by candidates who were competent in Irish, at the expense of better applicants, and suggested that the absolute preference for Irish-speakers should be abolished in the case of senior appointments and professional and technical posts. The Department also recommended that county councils in non-Gaeltacht areas should be free to decide whether or not rate collectors should be required to have a knowledge of Irish. Their views were disregarded. The Local Officers (Irish Language) Regulations 1943 extended an absolute preference for candidates who were competent in Irish to posts that were not filled by the Local Appointments Commission, such as home assistance officers, even in cases where Irish was *not* an essential qualification. If no applicant for a post was deemed to be competent in the Irish language, the absolute preference for candidates with a knowledge of Ireland was retained, though a lower standard of Irish was accepted. Thus, if even one candidate for a post was judged to possess a 'good knowledge' of Irish, only candidates who also displayed an equally 'good knowledge' of the language could be considered for appointment.[25]

The government's decision in 1938 and again in 1943 to extend the scope of the preference given to candidates who were competent in Irish took no account of reality. An increasing number of officials who had been appointed to posts on condition that they passed a language test within four years, were failing to meet this requirement. The problem was averted during the Emergency because language tests were suspended. Of 635 men and 807 women appointed to posts covered by Gaeltacht Orders between 1928 and 1945, only 130 were competent in Irish at the time of their appointment. Fewer than half had passed the Irish language test within five years of their appointment. Although 88 candidates were facing their 'last chance' examination in 1945, only 38 sat the test and just eight passed. Many regarded the language test as a chronic affliction. By 1945 one County Clare rate collector who had succeeded her father in a temporary capacity in 1932, and was appointed to a permanent post the following year, had failed the test on ten occasions. She was then 47 years old and, because of her lack of Irish, was not entitled to a pension, despite the fact that she was regarded as 'generally the best collector in the county'.

In order to resolve this and a further 43 problem cases, including rate and rent collectors, nurses, midwives, a veterinary surgeon, a waterworks inspector and an ophthalmic surgeon, the Department proposed that officials with a minimum of ten years' service should be exempt from future examinations. They also wished to exempt posts which proved difficult to fill such as dispensary doctors, nurses and midwives. In 1946 the government gave the minister discretion to exempt nurses. Doctors and midwives aged 45 or over were given further time to qualify, with dire warnings of the consequences if they failed to do so. The government was caught between local authorities, TDs, parish priests and civil servants, who all urged concessions, and the insistence of Comhdháil Náisiunta na Gaeilge (the national council for the Irish language) that it maintain a tough stance.

The first inter-party government removed the Irish language requirement for local appointments in non-Gaeltacht areas, except for a limited number of posts, such as county librarian. Irish became an optional subject carrying up to 6 per cent in additional marks. Recruiting professional and technical staff for Gaeltacht areas continued to present problems. In September 1955 John Garvin, secretary of the Department of Local Government, noted that 'efforts to recruit local officers with a competent knowledge of Irish for Gaeltacht areas and to require local authorities to have Irish used in those areas have not been successful but it is most difficult in the current climate of public opinion to devise methods that will be practicable and effective'.[26] This contribution to the government's policy of restoring the language must be deemed a failure.

PAY AND EMPLOYMENT CONDITIONS FOR LOCAL AUTHORITY PERSONNEL

During the 1930s Local Government failed to advance its ambition to develop a national local government service with standard pay, grades and pension rights which could be transferred between local authorities.[27] The limited powers which the Department exercised over pay, and the wide variation in pay and conditions, were highlighted in 1933 when the government attempted to introduce cuts in the salaries of local authority officers, similar to those applying in other branches of the public service. Although the Department had been trying since 1923 to ensure that most officers were paid an inclusive salary, the wide variety of methods of payment continued, including salary plus a variable cost-of-living bonus, salary plus a fee or fees, and salaries which included an element of expenses. This made it difficult to calculate salary reductions. The fact that salaries were paid by local authorities, rather than the Exchequer, was a further complication. The Executive Council wanted to introduce legislation permitting local authorities to reduce remuneration, but Local Government insisted on mandatory cuts: a council which refused to implement them would have its Exchequer grant reduced *pro rata*. However, the Department was unwilling to permit councils to reduce salaries by more than a national minimum; officials argued that this would be in conflict with the Minister's responsibility to supervise local authority salaries, and would damage relations between the Department and local officials.

The 1934 Local Services (Temporary Economies) Act required that a local authority which introduced salary reductions in excess of the minimum figure should obtain ministerial sanction.[28] The Department was in an invidious position. Representatives of local authority officials were demanding the introduction of standard rates of pay and conditions,[29] which would result in salaries and wages rising to the levels paid by the most generous local authorities. On the other hand, many councils wished to cut salaries by more than the national figure in order to placate disgruntled ratepayers. When trade unionists protested at the mandatory cuts enforced in 1934, the Department retorted that they were but a 'fraction of the reductions which Local Bodies generally desire to effect' and that they represented 'a reasonable compromise, which local officials would be most unwise to oppose, as it is designed to inflict minimum hardship on local staff'. The Department also informed trade unionists who were demanding the introduction of uniform salary scales that standardised scales would lead to reduced pay scales for many positions.[30]

Despite the pressures to cut salaries, many professional and technical staff employed by local authorities succeeded in negotiating additional fee income, despite the Department's efforts to stamp out such payments. In 1933 the Dublin Board of Health agreed to pay its supervising engineer a fee of £2 for every labourers' cottage that was constructed. Although the Department tried to have the agreement rescinded, it was forced to approve a fee of 25 shillings (£1.25) for each of the 351 cottages completed under the 1933 scheme, though it ruled out further payments. If housing schemes gave rise to additional work, the Department argued that local authorities should recruit extra staff. Despite this directive, engineers employed by Dublin County Council continued to demand fees in addition to their salaries. One engineer claimed a total of £2,346, another £2,898. In 1938, 'as an exceptional measure', the Minister agreed to their being paid a 'small gratuity' as compensation for unpaid overtime, plus a fee of £1 for each house inspected and certified as eligible for a Small Dwellings Acquisition Act loan. This was backdated to 1932.[31]

Ministers and officials chafed at such obvious evidence of the limits to their authority. There was considerable disquiet in 1933 when the Supreme Court overruled a ministerial order issued in 1930 appointing the Kerry county secretary (who was a qualified solicitor) to act as county solicitor on the grounds that the Minister did not have jurisdiction to specify the duties of the secretary to the county council.[32] In a memorandum to the secretary of the Executive Council in September 1934, McCarron emphasised that the minister had consistently acted on the assumption that his powers to sanction or refuse sanction to the appointment or mode of remuneration of local officials was beyond question. After the Supreme Court decision, the Department set out to draft legislation giving it power to regulate leave of absence and sick leave among local authority workers. Previous efforts to apply civil service regulations had failed owing to lack of authority.[33]

LOCAL AUTHORITY RATES: THE IMPACT OF AGRICULTURAL DEPRESSION

Rate collection during the 1930s was strongly influenced by the state of Irish agriculture. By 1935 the value of agricultural output was 40 per cent below its 1929 level.[34] Most Irish farmers blamed all their difficulties on the so-called Economic War, when Britain imposed duties on Irish cattle exports in retaliation for the Irish government's dismantling of the Anglo-Irish Treaty and the refusal to pay land annuities, ignoring the fact that agriculture was depressed in most countries at this time. County councils suffered a loss of income when land annuity arrears rose, despite the fact that payments were halved in 1932. Annuities were secured by the local taxation grant, so the Department of Finance reduced each county's grant to compensate for annuity arrears, forcing them in turn to run higher overdrafts. Arrears were highest in Counties Kildare, Meath, Wicklow, Waterford, Kerry and in both parts of Tipperary. Local Government pointed out to Finance that most farmers postponed paying their rates until the harvest was complete, and councils relied on the agricultural grant to tide them over. Although Finance wished to retain the unissued balance of the grant, £1.1m., to meet arrears in annuity payments due in November 1932, the cabinet decided to release a further £250,000.[35] This concession kept local authorities afloat during 1932/33.

By January 1934 Finance had withheld almost £400,000 from that year's local taxation grant, to meet annuity arrears. In Counties Kerry, Kildare, Meath, both parts of Tipperary, Waterford and Westmeath arrears exceeded the grant and counties which were in net credit (i.e. arrears were less than the local taxation grant) had their grants further reduced to meet the deficit on the fund. Local Government feared that county councils could not survive this loss of income on top of the poor level of rate collection. In April 1934 it persuaded the Executive Council to authorise payment of grants withheld during 1932/33, advancing the argument that the annuities unpaid during those years were now being funded under the terms of the 1933 Land Act.[36] This probably averted a collapse of local government in several counties.

By 1931/32, concessions to agricultural interests meant that the Exchequer was carrying almost two-thirds of the cost of rates on agricultural land. This rose further in 1932/33 when an additional £250,000 was provided to relieve the first £10 in valuation, in an apparent stopgap measure. The initial draft of a letter to the General Council of County Councils, written by Seán Moynihan, suggested that a concession of agricultural derating was dependent on a resolution of the annuities dispute with Britain. McElligott condemned this statement as 'rather dangerous', because it contained an unconditional commitment by the government to increase the cost of agricultural rates relief by a further £1.4m.. On de Valera's direction, the letter was altered to rule out the full derating of agricultural land in the 'present circumstances'.[37]

From 1933 Fianna Fáil came to see the agricultural grant as a means of encouraging labour-intensive farming and of favouring smaller holdings. Minister for Agriculture James Ryan proposed that relief on holdings with a valuation of £15 or more should be contingent on the farmer providing full-time employment for one adult male, who could be a relation, for every £10 valuation. He expressed the hope that

. . . if this system of derating is adopted and if there is also a tendency in the same direction when we come to deal with reductions in annuities, many of the big grazing ranches will become uneconomic and it will be easy to take them over and have them divided.

Local Government prevented this proposal being implemented in 1933/34 by claiming that it was administratively impossible. However, the Executive Council requested that the Department formulate a scheme on these lines for the following year.[38] Although the 1935 Rates on Agricultural Land (Relief) Act was originally drafted as a temporary solution, it remained the basis for allocating agricultural rates relief for several decades. The additional allowance granted on the first £10 of agricultural valuation in 1932/33 (the primary allowance) was now extended to the first £20. On higher valuations, relief was dependent on the number of men employed full-time during the previous nine months (employment relief), though a small supplementary allowance applied to land which received no relief under the primary allowance or the employment allowance.[39] A total of £250,000 in agricultural rates relief was switched to smaller farms from holdings valued in excess of £20.[40] This tinkering concealed the fact that Fianna Fáil provided relatively less generous relief on agricultural land than Cumann na nGaedheal. Total expenditure on agricultural rates relief fell by £250,000 in 1933/34 and Finance tried to set a ceiling of £1.5m., a figure which the government had declared to be its 'normal' level in 1933.

When the Economic War ended in 1938, Finance argued that the anticipated improvement in agricultural prices provided scope for a 'substantial reduction in the agricultural grant without appreciable hardship'. Local Government countered that the increase in the level of agricultural rates support since 1931 had failed to compensate farmers for the increase in rates poundage. It believed that the agricultural grant should amount to 'at least half the levy for general charges'. Finance concluded that there was little prospect of persuading either Local Government or the cabinet to agree to a reduction in the level of agricultural rates support and contented itself with holding the grant at its existing level.[41] The 1939 Rates on Agricultural Land (Relief) Act put the 1935 formula for distributing the agricultural grant on a permanent basis. If the sum available was increased, it would be divided in proportions similar to 1935, with nearly two-thirds allocated to the primary allowance and the balance divided almost equally between employment relief and supplementary relief, though if the sum available increased by more than £370,000, the basis of distribution could be changed by government Order.[42] By 1939 the Exchequer was bearing less than half of all charges on agricultural land.

TABLE 4.1

Agricultural grants as a percentage of the general charges on agricultural land (per cent)

1929/30	38.0
1930/31	37.9
1931/32	64.0
1932/33	68.1
1933/34	49.5
1934/35	57.2
1935/36	51.4
1936/37	51.5
1937/38	49.8
1938/39	47.5

The percentage of rates collected fell from 72 per cent in 1932/33 to a low of 64 per cent in 1933/34 and then rose to 69 per cent in 1934/35, 72 per cent in 1935/36 and 77 per cent by 1938/39. Counties in the west and north-west recorded the highest collection rates; the heaviest arrears occurred in Tipperary South Riding, Waterford, Kilkenny, Limerick and Clare.

This pattern of rate collection may owe more to differences in political allegiance than to economics. Fianna Fáil's electoral support was strongest in western counties. Dairy farmers appear to have suffered more severely than graziers from the fall in cattle prices.[43] In 1934 County Waterford rate collectors blamed their rate arrears on low cattle prices and a lack of dividends from the creamery. Most denied that there was a conspiracy against paying rates, though there was some evidence to the contrary.[44] Given the depressed state of agriculture and the limited concessions made by the Exchequer, the fact that arrears were much lower than in the early 1920s suggests that administrative standards were high. Local Government bombarded councils with circular letters urging them to use all legal means to ensure collection, including distraint, and it threatened to suspend councils which failed to enforce satisfactory rate collection or which refused to strike an adequate rate. The high number of councillors who were in arrears was a particular cause of concern. The report of the Banking Commission recommended that the government enact legislation disqualifying from membership of a local authority those in arrears with land annuity payments.[45] Rate collection featured prominently on the agendas of the annual meetings which Seán T. O'Kelly began holding with county secretaries.

Local Government worked closely with the Department of Justice to ensure that decrees were enforced against defaulting ratepayers. In 1937 Roche, secretary of the Department of Justice, told Hurson that sheriffs were no longer capable of dealing with the large volume of arrears and in some areas it had proved necessary to use a 'small army of police and Court Messengers'.[46] When rate collectors attempted to sell cattle which they had distrained, they were often bid sums as low as one shilling (5p). To overcome this, Local Government arranged for cattle distrained by Limerick County Council to be bought by a government representative, who travelled to the county from Dublin. One sale was cancelled at short notice when the farmer paid more than half his arrears; by this stage the buyer was already *en route* and rate collectors were ordered to telegram Dublin if this occurred in future.[47]

TRENDS IN LOCAL AUTHORITY BORROWINGS AND EXPENDITURE

Public expenditure and public sector borrowing both rose sharply between 1932 and 1934. Agricultural subsidies were the largest component in higher current government expenditure. On the capital side, expenditure on housing rose from £.5m. in 1931 to £2.8m. by 1934 and hovered around that figure for the remainder of the decade. Housing accounted for an increase of 1-1.5 per cent in the public sector's share of GNP in 1933/34.[48]

Capital expenditure by local authorities, mostly on housing, averaged £4.15m. a year during the years 1932-39, compared with

£1.23m. in the years 1926-31.[49] Local authority housing debt more than doubled between 1926 and 1936, rising from £7.8m. to £18.7m. as councils responded to the assistance available under the 1931 and 1932 Housing Acts. Total local authority debt increased from £14m. to £24.5m. during the same period. Dublin and Cork municipal authorities raised almost £4.5m. on the stockmarket from 1932 to 1935; smaller councils relied almost entirely on borrowings from the Local Loans Fund.[50]

TABLE 4.2

Loans sanctioned to local authorities

	Housing	Total
1931/32	£693,526	£1,346,166
1932/33	£1,705,622	£2,100,139
1933/34	£3,006,663	£3,551,977
1934/35	£3,945,225	£4,479,885
1935/36	£2,931,709	£3,649,646
1936/37	£2,004,671	£2,665,133
1937/38	£2,718,378	£3,577,961
1938/39	£4,156,027	£4,607,302
1939/40	£1,379,154	£1,892,913

Source: Annual Reports Department of Local Government and Public Health

(Fluctuations in the totals are heavily affected by the borrowing practices of large municipalities, especially Dublin Corporation.)

RELIEVING UNEMPLOYMENT BY MEANS OF PUBLIC WORKS

The majority report of the Commission on Banking Currency and Credit, which is generally believed to reflect the views of the Department of Finance, was highly critical of the increase in 'dead-weight debt' accumulated by both central and local government, much of it relating to housing.[51] During the years 1932-39 there was constant tension between Finance's desire to control public expenditure and efforts to sustain the government's housing programme and to create additional employment on public works. Although the Banking Commission claimed that the government's housing schemes constituted a veritable public works programme, housing was regarded as desirable in its own right and was not viewed as part of a job-creation programme. This contrasts with expenditure on roads, water and sewerage where improvements in services appear to have been given a low priority relative to efforts to provide employment.

Given that responsibility for employment and unemployment rested with the Department of Industry and Commerce and the Office of Public Works, Local Government was often in danger of losing control of sanitary services and roads. Housing and roads are discussed at length in later chapters. This section examines the problems which the programme of relief works posed for Local Government, particularly in regard to sanitary services.

There is a long tradition in Ireland of resorting to public works as a means of relieving distress and unemployment. As we saw in chapter one, the Local Government Board was involved in organising relief works throughout the west of Ireland during the depressed years of the 1880s. Whether the innumerable politicians, both British and Irish, who sanctioned schemes of public works believed that they were an effective method of relieving distress, or simply saw them as the easiest way to placate supplicants, is a moot point. Although Patrick McGilligan, Minister for Industry and Commerce 1924-32, was highly sceptical about their effectiveness, and officials in the Department of Finance regarded them as damaging to the economy,[52] the Cumann na nGaedheal governments provided modest sums for public works in most years up to 1932. The amount allocated made little impact on employment; Finance officials calculated that the £250,000 provided in 1924 would create 2,000 man-years of employment if *none* of the money was spent on materials.[53] However, they were popular with party supporters. In 1922 the provisional government gave a committee of TDs responsibility for allocating £100,000 for emergency relief works.[54] Applications for minor drainage works or road repairs often carried the endorsement of the local TD or party *cumann*.[55] The government established relief works in Adrigole in west Cork in response to the outcry following the deaths from influenza of four members of an impoverished family in 1927,[56] though only five of the twenty-five neediest people contacted reported for work; the others were apparently sowing potatoes or claimed that the work was too distant from their homes.[57]

Such knee-jerk reactions favoured schemes which could be implemented at short notice, using the maximum number of unskilled labourers and minimal equipment or materials; they were unlikely to bring many long-term benefits. When James Hurson queried the decision to award a grant towards the cost of constructing a sewer in Dungarvan in 1927, he was told that 'it is the only item which could be sanctioned immediately'.[58] Allegations of distress in Clifden RDC in 1924 resulted in the initiation of basic drainage schemes which used a minimum of machinery and materials.[59] In order to find work for labourers in Erris, Co. Mayo, the government broke a long-established prohibition on providing public funds to repair private lanes leading to turf banks or farmhouses. Seán MacCraith, the Local Government inspector, justified this decision, with a claim that it was necessary 'to wean them of the habit of receiving money for nothing'.[60]

The report of the Committee on the Relief of Unemployment, published in 1927, recommended a more coherent approach to relief works, substituting long-term investment programmes, such as improving coastal roads, slum clearance and improvements in water supplies or minor drainage schemes.[61] In December 1930 officials from Finance, Local Government, the Office of Public Works and the Irish Land Commission recommended that road works and all projects which qualified for state assistance under another heading should be ineligible for relief works grants, and that the wages paid on relief works should 'reflect the fact that assistance from public funds is being given as a measure of relief in the strictest sense'. However, road works were often the only projects to hand,[62] while the insistence on lower wages led to numerous disputes and representations.[63]

Public works assumed greater significance when Fianna Fáil came to power in 1932. Because emigration had almost ceased, it became essential to provide work or maintenance within Ireland on a more extensive scale than in the past. Moreover the government depended on Labour TDs for its survival until after the 1933 general election. While Seán MacEntee, as Minister for Finance, shared his predecessor's scepticism about public works, other ministers appear to have been more receptive. In April 1932 two Labour deputies proposed a motion in the Dáil demanding work or maintenance for all the unemployed. On 29 March, possibly in an effort to prepare for the forthcoming debate, each minister was asked to advance proposals which were calculated to give 'immediate' employment. Local Government responded with a ten-page document listing public health works and road and housing schemes, though it emphasised that all were dependent on the Exchequer providing a higher proportion of the total cost: many water and sewerage schemes, which had been approved for grants under the 1930/31 relief scheme had been abandoned because ratepayers were unwilling to contribute towards the cost.

Local Government argued that road improvements offered the highest employment relative to expenditure, though substantial sums would be needed: £2-£4m., in addition to the money provided by the Road Fund because Road Fund improvement grants had come to provide 'a normal means of employment'.[64] At the suggestion of the Minister for Finance, this and other proposals for public expenditure were forwarded to the parliamentary secretary of the Minister for Finance, Hugo Flinn, the minister responsible for both the Commissioners of Public Works and government relief works. Four days later, on 18 April, Flinn requested officials from Local Government to submit a statement of possible works 'on the assumption that there was no limit to Government money'. The roads department responded with proposals to create an estimated 6,745 jobs within six weeks by improving 'important county roads' at a cost of £400,000. An additional 10,700 men could be employed over a longer period in improving main roads, at a cost of £1.5m..[65] The 1932 Budget provided £1.55m. in grants and loans for relief works and a further £550,000 for the Local Loans Fund. This would be financed by borrowing £1m. on the security of the Road Fund, to be used for 'immediate relief works'. The remainder, provided from current expenditure, would be allocated to local authorities in the form of grants for minor public health and road works; £150,000 was 'to be used in work which will absorb the greatest possible amount of labour', i.e. clearing derelict sites.[66]

On 16 May, five days after the Budget, the first meeting of the economic committee of the Executive Council considered how to allocate the additional £1m. which had been earmarked for roads. The committee, consisting of Éamon de Valera, Seán Lemass and Senator Joseph Connolly, Minister for Posts and Telegraphs (Seán MacEntee, Minister for Finance was conspicuously excluded), was set up to 'examine and report on the economic conditions of the Saorstát'. H.S. Moylan, head of the Department's road's department, also attended.

During the years 1922-32 Local Government had contested Finance's efforts to oversee all public works expenditure (see chapter three). The Department again argued against being required to provide Finance with details of each scheme before obtaining sanction for expenditure. Moylan mentioned that deputations from the country frequently visited the Custom House, and the Department needed 'a substantial amount of freedom' in order to respond to these representations. The committee decided that all workers would be recruited through employment exchanges; Lemass and Connolly would devise a scheme to use post offices as employment exchanges in outlying areas. A sum of £250,000 was provisionally set aside for urban districts and county boroughs, a further £250,000 was earmarked for immediate work on county roads and by-roads. Local Government was asked to consider bringing forward work on concreting roads out of the £1m. grant and deferring work on main roads (funded from the Road Fund) if necessary until the winter. Local Government's demand that grants should not be conditional on local contributions was accepted.

Finance does not appear to have objected to the decision to pay for £1m. in road improvements by borrowing, because it believed that the money could be recouped from sums allegedly still owed to Ireland from the UK Road Fund. As these expectations faded, Finance became less sympathetic to the proposal. On 3 June 1932 Arthur Codling, an assistant secretary in the Department of Finance, wrote to Local Government to point out that, since the £1m. was being made available, 'the Minister considers that it may not unreasonably be assumed . . . that normal calls on the Road Fund should be appreciably lightened'. As the Anglo-Irish financial dispute intensified during the summer of 1932, Finance's objections became more strident and the department protested against the 'wholly indefensible position' of borrowing for unemployment relief; Finance claimed that the expenditure was not essential to the country's transport system, would never have been undertaken except for unemployment relief, and was therefore 'not a proper charge on the Road Fund'.

This accusation was accurate. Hugo Flinn, who was responsible for the Office of Public Works, took control of the £1m., dividing the money between counties on the basis of numbers on the Live Register, except in Mayo and Donegal where the figures were so high that he treated them 'with caution'. Although a separate sum of £350,000 had been allocated for improvements to bog roads and culs de sac, the government came under pressure to divert most of the £1m. to similar work. Dáil deputies lobbied Local Government, and Mayo County Council passed a resolution to this effect. The Department retorted that 350 miles of main roads in Mayo had yet to be steamrolled and 453 miles of main roads needed reconstruction. If the council improved bog roads and culs de sac, they would become liable for all future maintenance and this in turn would lead to demands for a higher Exchequer contribution towards road repairs. However Flinn believed that too much money had been allocated to 'roads of orthodox type' and suggested that a further £150,000 be spent on bog roads.[67]

Most of the £550,000 allocated in the 1932 Budget for minor relief works, such as clearing drains, building ditches and improving bog roads, came under the control of the Office of Public Works (OPW) or the Land Commission. Since neither body had sufficient professional staff to supervise these schemes, they were forced to rely on county surveyors, who were employed by local authorities. Local Government had consistently opposed demands from county councils that they be reimbursed for the cost of supervising road improvements financed by the Road Fund, but on this occasion the Department conceded that the surveyors deserved extra payment. However, an extensive programme of minor public works, supervised by county surveyors who reported to the Commissioner of Public Works, threatened to undermine existing lines of authority. Local Government insisted that no scheme should be permitted which was not 'properly covered' by official correspondence between their Department and local authorities. Finance supported this demand, and Flinn eventually agreed.[68]

Most councils traditionally paid lower wages to workers employed on relief schemes than to regular road labourers. In 1932, however, the numbers employed on relief works were much greater than in the past and the distinction between relief road works and works funded by the Road Fund was becoming blurred; in some cases men on relief works were 'apparently . . . working side by side with men employed out of normal Grants from the Road Fund'.[69] By June 1932 labourers employed on relief road works in Nenagh were demanding the same wages as permanent crews in North Tipperary, 35 shillings (£1.75), compared with 30 shillings (£1.50) per week. The local trade union organiser told Seán MacEntee that most of the temporary workers were Fianna Fáil supporters and 'a good number members of the local club, so if you could see your way to level up wages at 35 shillings which is the standard rate here, it would greatly strengthen the Fianna Fáil organisation here.' Labour TDs and union representatives argued that low wages made the work attractive only to small farmers and their sons, i.e. men who already had some income. The government was eventually forced to pay workers on minor relief schemes the going rate for local authority labour; by 1939 the Office of Public Works actually claimed that this had been government policy since 1932.[70]

Disagreements over such matters go some way to explaining the delays in putting men to work. Few jobs had been created by September 1932. Local Government protested that most schemes required a minimum of 1 to 3 months between approval and commencement and the cabinet permitted the Department to give provisional sanction in order to reduce delays.[71] However Seán Lemass was not convinced that the existing system was capable of creating sufficient jobs. On 1 November 1932, as the Economic War was beginning to bite, he tabled proposals for a major expansion of the public works programme, which would be carried out under direct government control, rather than using local authorities. Lemass's proposal was designed to provide work for all the unemployed until they could find work in the new protected industries.

It can be argued that Lemass never intended his 'drastic proposals' to be implemented; the document may have been an attempt to shock de Valera into abandoning the Economic War. Whatever his motive, the proposal sparked an unequivocal riposte from Finance, an Irish version of the Treasury view. It argued that Lemass's proposal would do little to reduce unemployment, but would lead to a sharp rise in debt and the creation of 'either useless or objectionable public works of all types', which would make Finance's task of controlling expenditure more difficult and encourage other departments to adopt misleading standards of value for public money.[72] However, Finance conceded that the state had an obligation to maintain those in need. This concession shifted cabinet attention from public works to the possibility of introducing a means-tested benefit, which would be available to all unemployed or underemployed males who were ineligible for unemployment insurance. Under the 1933 Unemployment Assistance Act, central government assumed responsibility for maintaining able-bodied uninsured workers and their dependants. This brought a significant reduction in the cost of home assistance to local authorities.[73]

The failure to embrace a Lemass-style 'dictatorial' public works programme left many issues unresolved, such as who should control public works and how expenditure priorities were determined. As a result, the Executive Council and individual ministers began to divert money to favoured projects, partly in an effort to put men to work. In December 1932 Local Government discovered that money earmarked for water and sewerage had all been exhausted when £72,000 was allocated to Dublin Corporation for relief works. This sum included a special grant of £50,000 awarded by the Executive Council without reference to Local Government, which had provisionally allocated the money for other purposes. Expenditure was beginning to outstrip the sum provided in the Estimates. In January 1933 MacEntee wrote to O'Kelly offering him the choice between spending £72,000 in Dublin and 'starving the Public Health side of your proposals' or cutting the grant to Dublin to fund other schemes. O'Kelly refused to cut the grant to Dublin, because he claimed that the city had taken on 'an adequate proportion of liability' for unemployment relief in the form of poor relief and public works schemes.[74]

After an apparently shaky start, Flinn tightened his control. By June 1933 he was demanding that Local Government supply details of the labour content of sewerage and water schemes. When the Department submitted a figure for relief works grants in July 1933, the Office of Public Works demanded details of location, cost, the nature of the work, labour content and a time-schedule for each scheme. Flinn queried data provided by Hurson, which showed that labour accounted for 40-60 per cent of the cost of public health works, and demanded a detailed justification of the Department's estimate for indirect labour costs.[75] Flinn was determined that relief works should be spread throughout each county on a basis which reflected poverty and unemployment, rather than sanitary or public health needs. In September 1933 his office complained that all schemes approved for grant assistance in Kerry were located in the north-east of the county, which was not the poorest area, and Local Government was instructed to find a project in Kenmare. The OPW complained that all schemes in County Limerick were in the 'rich portion of the county' and rejected the schedule of relief works for North Tipperary because all the money had been allocated to Roscrea.

In order to persuade impoverished areas to embark on public works, the Exchequer was forced to bear an increasing share of the costs. By May 1933 most local authorities sought a minimum grant of

50 per cent.[76] Some minor schemes administered by the Land Commission or the OPW were wholly funded by the Exchequer.[77] Finance became increasingly concerned at this trend and in August 1933 succeeded in obtaining a decision from the Executive Council that the Ministers for Finance and Local Government would reconsider the basis on which grants were awarded. In practice this meant that all public health schemes, irrespective of size, were subjected to detailed scrutiny by Finance, with grants allocated on the basis of employment, rather than public health needs. In October 1933 officials from Local Government were informed that MacEntee and Flinn both agreed that 'expenditure must be related as closely as possible to the purpose for which it as primarily intended — the relief of unemployment'.[78]

Other departments also interfered. Industry and Commerce insisted on maximising the amount of employment provided and protested when a mechanical excavator was used on a sewerage scheme in Lisdoonvarna, Co. Clare.[79] In 1934 responsibility for hiring workers on relief schemes passed from Industry and Commerce to Local Government, though Industry and Commerce reserved the right to investigate complaints from those who had been refused employment. Local Government saw this as tantamount to having its work reviewed by yet another department and protested that such interference diverted inspectors from essential duties. Local authority engineers grumbled at being forced to recruit workers from the UA (Unemployment Assistance) register. When the engineer responsible for the Kilkee water scheme was asked to justify the fact that only nine out of seventeen workers had been recruited from the register, he protested that three men on the register had refused work. He also pointed out that it was impossible to adhere to the official regulation that 75 per cent of workers recruited from the register should be married.[80]

These conditions were eventually eased. In 1937 the OPW gave Local Government permission to hire outside labour in order to meet a deadline, if it was satisfied that UA workers or others registered at the employment office were not available.[81] In 1939 Fianna Fáil TD Frank Carty and the Coolooney, Co. Sligo *cumann* complained that local men on Unemployment Assistance had not been employed on the town sewerage scheme. When the Department reprimanded the contractor, he claimed that the work required a high proportion of skilled men and that he was under pressure from the Board of Health to complete the work on time.[82]

THE INTERDEPARTMENTAL COMMITTEE ON PUBLIC WORKS

Finance succeeded in containing expenditure on relief works during 1933/34. Seán MacEntee's Budget speech in May 1933 provided a further £2,806,000 for so-called employment schemes. The minister claimed that, despite the introduction of unemployment assistance, 'the Government has not lost sight of the fact that the only satisfactory solution of the unemployment problem is to be found in the provision of useful work'. However, most of the money allocated in May 1933 was devoted to housing; only £550,000 was earmarked for other purposes.[83] In his 1934 Budget speech, MacEntee announced the government's long-term commitment 'to replace as large a portion as possible of present expenditure on unemployment maintenance by expenditure on socially remunerative work', though this would require planning and effective organisation. MacEntee expressed the hope that in the future a proportion of tax revenue would be allocated to funding the Local Loans Fund. He spoke of 'heaps of litter and rubbish, mountain roads often impassable, flowers along the roadside . . . towns without design and almost without ornament . . . few agreeable buildings, few public gardens, few spacious streets or delightful squares' and expressed his regret that local authorities appeared reluctant to provide such amenities.[84] On a more prosaic note, he announced the appointment of the interdepartmental committee on public works:

> . . . to consider the extent to which it is practicable to devise a scheme of useful and desirable public works to be carried out within a period of four years with a view to reducing expenditure on Unemployment Assistance to a minimum and to report upon the nature and extent of such works, the steps to be taken to initiate them, the best method of financing them and the organisation to be set up to carry them out.

Whether or not this speech marks MacEntee's conversion to a Swedish-style public works programme is unclear. The interdepartmental committee, which was chaired by Hugo Flinn and included John Collins[85] and H.S. Moylan from Local Government plus John Garvin as its secretary, examined proposals for public works, concentrating on those with a high unskilled labour content which

187

could be carried out in areas of high unemployment. An interim report in January 1936 presented a programme of works costing £3.24m. which could be implemented by government departments in the coming financial year, in addition to their normal work. The committee assumed that the Exchequer would contribute a minimum of £2.9m..

All proposals were rated under three criteria: the number of labourers employed per £100, total employment-years and social utility. Minor relief schemes, drainage and bog road construction in connection with bog development provided the most employment: 61 man-weeks on per £100, against 34 man-weeks on roads or 18.5 man-weeks on water and sewerage schemes. If all criteria carried equal weight, minor relief schemes topped the list, followed by bog development. Roads and public health works ranked third and fourth, ahead of mineral exploration, arterial drainage, providing telephones, and minor building works.

Local Government submitted proposals for road works costing £1.85m. and water and sewerage schemes costing £650,000. Although public health works were ranked first on the basis of social utility, the committee noted that these schemes did not necessarily provide employment where it was most needed. It also construed the unwillingness of local authorities to spend money on public health works in the absence of grants as evidence that they were not a priority. Finance recommended maintaining expenditure on public health works at the current level of £104,000, but demanded that all proposals be subject to detailed scrutiny to ensure that the money went to areas of high unemployment.[86] Garvin pleaded in vain that these schemes were essential on 'hygienic and social grounds' and should be undertaken even in the absence of an extensive public works programme.[87]

The committee approved Local Government's proposal to allocate £350,000 for road works in urban areas, presumably because urban workers could not be employed on bog roads or minor drainage schemes, but it was unenthusiastic about plans to spend an additional £1.5m. on improving main roads and county roads, because such work would provide employment for regular road labourers, rather than 'the agricultural labourer, the smallholder and the poverty-stricken'. The committee believed that there was 'no public demand for improving the roads', present conditions were 'generally satisfactory', and it feared that such expenditure would encourage a trend to transfer the cost of road maintenance from local authorities to the state.[88] The Department of Finance condemned public works as offering bad value for money. To reduce the cost of Unemployment Assistance by £1, it was necessary to spend £4-£5 on relief works. However the OPW argued that public works would be cost-effective if material and equipment costs were kept to a minimum and if workers on the UA register were employed in rotation. In July 1935 it proposed establishing two pilot schemes in Counties Limerick and Kildare and the cabinet approved a trial scheme in County Limerick. Workers would be given sufficient work during each four-week period to ensure that they earned approximately 40 per cent more than their UA benefits. If the scheme proved feasible, the OPW envisaged that most jobs would be provided on road works, minor relief schemes and arterial drainage, with the emphasis on low-skilled activities, such as 'quarrying and breaking of stones by hand' (eerily reminiscent of the stone-breaking carried out in Victorian workhouses). OPW officials were confident that such schemes could absorb the entire UA register, though they recognised that women and skilled workers would be excluded (there were no women and almost no skilled workers in receipt of Unemployment Assistance). If 80 per cent of UA recipients transferred to relief schemes, the OPW calculated that relief works would cost 13 per cent more than the combined current cost of UA and relief works.[89] However, Finance expressed the fear that the proposed scheme could 'degenerate to the level of the return which was formerly given by vagrants etc. engaged in public workhouses on stone breaking and other tasks'.[90]

Although the Limerick pilot scheme went ahead, the cabinet acceded to Finance's request that the interdepartmental committee should examine whether or not it was feasible to rotate labourers on relief works. In the course of the review, Local Government criticised the fact that priorities for road and public health expenditure would be determined by the level of unemployment in an area and whether or not a scheme would employ sufficient unskilled labour. The OPW proposal to set a ceiling of 15 per cent for non-labour costs meant that all conventional road works and public health schemes would be ineligible for government grants. Local Government also claimed that rotating the labourers employed on regular road works would displace or reduce the earnings of existing labourers and result in 'grave discontent in sections of organised labour'.

The Department was even more reluctant to include public health works in any special employment programme, because it regarded them as matters of 'social urgency'. Most water and sewerage schemes were carried out by contractors who paid market wages; experience suggested that using direct labour or rotating workers were both unsatisfactory. Most local authority engineers had no experience of supervising major public health schemes. This was a thinly disguised attack on the OPW's pilot sewerage scheme in Kilfinane, Co. Limerick, supervised by a local authority engineer who was using rotated workers drawn from the UA register.

E. MacLaughlin of the OPW responded to this critique by warning the secretary of Local Government that this scheme might soon become the sole source of Exchequer funds for public health works. Hugo Flinn was extremely anxious to secure 'every co-operation' from Local Government in order to ensure that the Department would receive larger sums under the new scheme.[91] Despite this threat, Local Government persisted in its opposition, in part because the Department believed that the OPW's scheme would undermine the whole basis of local authority administration. John Garvin emphasised the distinction between the need 'to obtain the concurrence and good will of the local authorities' and the OPW's practice of carrying out works directly. County surveyors were already devoting substantial time to supervising unemployment relief works. If the OPW plan was introduced and a rotating workforce employed, their commitments would increase. Since the engineers received additional fees for this work, they had a vested interest in its expansion. In October 1936, H.S.Moylan told officials from the OPW that the position had become 'objectionable'. Engineers were demanding fees amounting to 4 or 5 per cent of the contracts. The county surveyor for Limerick was co-operating with the OPW in the Kilfinane water scheme, for which he and another engineer were demanding fees amounting to 11.5 per cent of costs.

Some local authority engineers shared the Department's concern. The engineer responsible for another experimental rotational work scheme, the Kiladysert water project in County Clare, told the Department that 'the whole question bristles with difficulties of a serious nature'. The council did not have the necessary equipment; it also lacked experience in obtaining competitive tenders for materials. Many of the workers, such as unemployed tailors and shoemakers, were unsuitable, and no account was taken of the fact that skilled workers were required. While this engineer accepted that 'Every right-thinking Irishman will agree that the issue of Employment Assistance on works of improvement is a step in the right direction', he believed that a qualified engineer should be appointed to supervise each scheme because he was already fully occupied with his regular duties.[92]

The report of the interdepartmental committee on rotational employment, completed on 31 January 1936, emphasised that no workers should be deprived of regular work as a result of the new scheme and that local authorities should keep their expenditure at normal levels. However these principles were in direct conflict with the committee's decision that rotational employment should apply to 'normal works of a sporadic nature' — such as telephone development and work financed by the Road Fund. The committee suggested that both these funds should be compensated for any loss of efficiency as a result of rotating workers. 'Abnormal' work was defined as any scheme which 'would not be likely to be carried out for some time to come . . . owing to lack of funds from normal sources'. The report took into account the reservations expressed by the Department of Local Government. The 15 per cent ceiling on non-labour costs disappeared without trace; rotational work would be phased in gradually; public health works would be excluded until a number of pilot projects had demonstrated that they could be carried out satisfactorily. The committee calculated that it would cost an additional £623,500 a year to provide rotational employment for UA recipients, more than double the cost estimated by the OPW. The introduction of rotational employment, together with the operation of employment period orders (periods when UA was suspended in rural areas because recipients were expected to be engaged on agricultural work), were expected to mean the end of UA for rural workers, though it would continue in urban areas because the decision to exclude public health works from the employment schemes meant that there would not be sufficient jobs available.

We should not read these proposals as evidence that Keynes had invaded the Irish public service by the mid-1930s. This was not a programme of deficit spending designed to lift the economy out of recession, more an effort to replace a means-tested dole with a less demeaning way of supporting the able-bodied poor and unemployed.[93] The money would be provided from revenue, not from borrowing. When the committee first met, it asked the Minister for Finance to indicate his reaction to several statements:

That the proposed scheme of public works provided no permanent solution to the unemployment problem and made little contribution towards improving the skill level of the young.

No scheme of public works could be devised which did not include a high percentage of works of little or no economic value. Reducing unemployment assistance, by instituting a public works programme, would entail increasing government spending and therefore taxation, which would have adverse consequences for industrial and agricultural employment, and would lead to increased unemployment in the long-run.

The committee interpreted the Minister's reply, which is not quoted and does not appear to survive, as a directive to leave such issues aside. This is consistent with a note which MacEntee sent to Seán T. O'Kelly, enclosing a copy of the committee's second interim report; MacEntee wrote that the need for finding solutions to the unemployment problem 'is pressing'. However the representative of the Department of Industry and Commerce refused to sign the report because it failed to determine the principles involved in providing a relief works programme.

Local Government representatives signed the report with caveats. The Department wished to retain the power to determine if schemes proposed by a local authority constituted normal or abnormal expenditure. They were concerned that the wages on offer — 40 per cent more than UA, plus entitlement to free beef — would cause dissatisfaction among workers, and they criticised attempts to apply rotation to regular road maintenance and improvement.

It is puzzling that the third interim report of the interdepartmental committee, dated April 1936, which set out a four-year programme of relief works, made no reference to employing rotated labour. This report appears to have deliberately played down the administrative difficulties involved in implementing its proposals. It concluded that it would be feasible to achieve a substantial reduction in expenditure on unemployment assistance by 'an intensification of expenditure on standard departmental services, together with some grants for services outside the ambit of Government departments', such as clearing derelict sites. No special measures were needed other than simple enabling legislation and some additional staff. The OPW would co-ordinate the programme.

However, the report concluded that since the scheme could not be wholly funded by taxation, 'competent advice' should be sought on the possibility of funding a considerable portion by loan.[94] This statement challenged the core of the economic philosophy to which the Department of Finance subscribed. Finance responded predictably: declaring that public works were objectionable, whether financed by borrowing or by taxation; taxation reduced the amount available for normal expenditure; borrowings absorbed capital which would otherwise have been available for productive purposes and created a long-term burden of debt that would have to be met by higher taxes. However the objections had a half-hearted tone, especially the parting shot that 'as far as possible works without a definite economic value should be excluded'.[95]

On 1 May 1936 the Executive Council decided to allocate £2.5m. for unemployment relief works during the 1936/37 financial year; £825,000 of this would be contributed by local authorities. A total of £250,000 would be funded by borrowings, with the balance coming from a combination of sources, such as the Road Fund and higher taxes. The sum provided by the Exchequer was less than in 1932/33. It would employ 15,000 people for a year without rotation, double that number on a limited rotation programme and three or four times that number with intensive rotation.

This was a singularly cautious outcome. No national organisation was given responsibility for public works and the Exchequer did not assume 100 per cent liability; indeed the Exchequer's share of the bill for public works fell from over 75 per cent in 1935/36 to under 50 per cent three years later. The pattern of subsidising projects that were initiated by local authorities was continued, though there was a greater emphasis on recruiting workers from the UA register, and some efforts were made to rotate workers.

The outcome marked a defeat for Hugo Flinn at the hands of the Department of Local Government. In January 1937 Flinn exclaimed to MacEntee that 'even the patience of Job can be exhausted . . . answering every case however nebulous that has been put up against Rotation on Relief Schemes'. MacEntee complained to de Valera that other departments were not co-operating with Flinn's efforts to promote rotational schemes. According to MacEntee, the decline in the numbers on the unemployment register testified to the success of this concept, though the rise in emigration seems a more probable explanation. Flinn appeared to concede defeat some months later, though he may have been angling for a cabinet post, when he demanded that a definite policy should be initiated, 'openly backed and helped' by the Executive Council, 'instead of the present position in which we carry on a miniature revolution with, at most, passive support, inadequate staff and without the necessary legislation to enable this work to be properly done'. He suggested that the existing arrangements, where responsibility for public works was shared between Local Government, Industry and Commerce and the Office of Public Works, should be ended. Full authority should be given to one member of the Executive Council, preferably the Minister for Local Government, because practically all the work was done through that department. According to Tod Andrews, Flinn 'should, by any standards, have held a ministerial post'. Andrews believed that he did not achieve one, 'because de Valera thought he would not fit into the cabinet team'.[96] The Executive Council adjourned without deciding on who should be given overall responsibility for public works.[97]

Local Government retained its ambivalence towards relief works. Ted Courtney,[98] the Department's chief engineer, reported favourably on the quality of work performed by rotated labour on the Kilfinane sewerage scheme, though he did not believe that this provided a reliable precedent because he had discovered that most labourers were fully employed on other jobs during periods when they were released from the scheme; some had requested time off to complete other work. Courtney was uncertain if unemployed workers would be equally efficient and would accept the pay and conditions on offer.

Any expansion of relief works threatened unrest among the county surveyors. In 1937 the Limerick county surveyor persuaded the county council to reject all relief works grants because he was dissatisfied with his scale of fees. Several surveyors complained that the additional work left them unable to attend to normal duties: the Kerry assistant surveyor was coping with 2,500 men on relief works, in addition to his regular duties. Others protested at the volume of paperwork, the quality of workers, that the relief works had demoralised regular council workers, and that county surveyors were being transformed into relieving officers. One county surveyor protested that the OPW had taken control of the assistant surveyors and was interfering with his work. Only the Mayo county surveyor expressed satisfaction: the money enabled him to complete road improvements that he had never envisaged being able to carry out.[99]

Opposition to relief works and to rotated workers was greatest in the cities of Dublin and Cork. Dublin Corporation passed several resolutions condemning the use of rotated workers, and Corporation officials were unwilling to recruit road workers from the employment exchange. Engineers estimated that using rotated workers increased costs by at least one-third and cancelled the benefit of an Exchequer grant. Rotated labour was inefficient and needed greater supervision.[100] Dublin Corporation also complained that many unemployed men in their area were incapable of carrying out navvying work and they found it difficult to devise projects which met government criteria other than site preparation for housing schemes. By 1939 this was running at least two years ahead of actual need.[101] In February 1937 the Cork city engineer told John Garvin that the Cork main drainage scheme involved work of a highly technical nature 'and not of a type which I would care to carry out by direct labour on any system'. He claimed that direct labour, and particularly rotational labour, was suitable only for 'straight ahead jobs which do not require much plant and do not involve any risks'.

Cork Corporation came under considerable pressure to carry out its main drainage scheme by using direct labour and rotational employment. Hugo Flinn believed that this 'would solve the unemployment problem in Cork for several years' and the OPW offered Cork Corporation a substantially higher subsidy, plus a commitment to meet the cost of additional staff. The Cork city engineer replied that he was concerned with 'securing good and accurate work at minimum cost rather than providing an ideal unemployment relief scheme'.[102] For a similar reason the Poulaphouca reservoir in County Wicklow, the largest public works project of the decade, received no grant from the Exchequer. Yet it gave employment to hundreds of labourers and was urgently needed to relieve a chronic shortage of water in Dublin city and county. When the reservoir was being planned, one official claimed that the absence of a public water scheme in the north Dublin village of Finglas meant that sanitary conditions were similar to those found in an African kraal.[103]

The absence of Exchequer assistance for water and sewerage schemes, other than in the guise of a grant to relieve unemployment, meant that the Department was in no position to force local authorities to improve the standard of sanitary services. Local Government vetoed a proposal by Dún Laoghaire Corporation to construct a new sewer which would dump untreated sewerage into Bullock Harbour, and the Department informed Dun Laoghaire Corporation of its concern at the increased pollution in Scotsman's Bay and the polluted state of the foreshore at Blackrock. Yet although all parties recognised the need for a main drainage scheme,[104] an adequate system was beyond Dun Laoghaire's resources. Since no grants were available, foreshore pollution continued for many decades to come.

Public opinion appears to have been singularly unconcerned about the inadequate standard of water and sanitary services. Although the Offaly medical officer of health reported that the Clara water supply was contaminated, and that a new supply would be essential before a proper sewerage system could be installed, the cost was beyond the capacity of local rates and the Department was forced to take the unpopular step of making it the responsibility of the county at large.[105] The housing boom of the 1930s placed an additional strain on water and sewerage schemes, but although Local Government was conscious of this fact, it was unable to provide local authorities with the funds to meet this need, and the modern façade of many new houses hid primitive water and sewerage services. The Housing Board — a body established by Seán T. O'Kelly to ensure that the targets which had been set for house construction were achieved — applauded the decision of the Limerick city manager to refuse small dwellings acquisition loans for 'undesirable' houses, which were built with cesspits in unsuitable areas,[106] but his decision was exceptional. Exchequer grants went instead to less essential projects, which employed workers on the UA register and needed little material or capital equipment. Many of the carparks, seaside promenades, bathing areas, sea walls, access steps to beaches and shelters found along the Irish coast were constructed under such programmes, including rather ugly concrete structures along the seashore at Dun Laoghaire, Seapoint, Clontarf and Skerries.[107]

Exchequer expenditure on employment schemes totalled £4,698,000 during the years 1932-39, most of it on programmes associated with the Department of Local Government: £901,000 on public health, £1,494,000 on roads, £147,000 on housing site development and £482,000 on miscellaneous works, including parks. Grants for minor employment schemes, which were generally supervised by local authority engineers under the control of the OPW, totalled £1,450,000. In 1934/35 government grants for relief works accounted for £353,316, or 28 per cent of expenditure on unemployment (excluding unemployment insurance). By 1938/39 this had increased to £1,327,857, or 49.8 per cent of the total.[108]

CONCLUSIONS

The first seven years of Fianna Fáil government posed major challenges for the Department of Local Government. The Local Appointments Commission, one of the major achievements of the previous administration, came under sustained attack, largely because of the actions of Seán T. O'Kelly, Minister for Local Government. The Commission survived, owing to the more moderate attitude of de Valera and other cabinet ministers, but the process was not painless, as the dismissal of Edward McCarron testifies.

The economic conditions of the 1930s also placed considerable strain on the local government system. Rate collection suffered, local finances were tight, and some local authority staff became heavily involved in running unemployment relief schemes. Department officials were forced to handle the additional work created by a major housing programme and an expanded programme of relief works. Unfortunately, surviving records reveal little of this human story. When we recall that the Department was simultaneously involved in a programme of hospital construction (financed by the Hospital Sweepstakes), in providing public assistance, old-age and widows pensions — to mention but a few of its other concerns — the enormity of the burden placed on one department and on the minister and secretary becomes apparent.

The increasing involvement of the Exchequer in housing and unemployment relief programmes raised serious questions about the role of the Department of Local Government. No department is an island: all must operate within a wider cabinet structure. Most have responsibilities which overlap with other departments and these occasionally result in interdepartmental conflicts, sparked by differing priorities. Few departments faced this problem to the same extent as the Department of Local Government in the years after 1932. The overlap of responsibility for relief works among Finance, the Office of Public Works, Industry and Commerce and Local Government involved senior officials in complex interdepartmental negotiations. Since Local Government also had to confront the needs of local authorities, John Garvin's later description of the Department as a 'buffer state'[109] is fully justified.

By the late 1930s the volume of capital needed for housing meant that the Department of Finance was an almost constant presence in the life of the Department of Local Government — a presence which continued through subsequent decades. Local Government was forced to tread a narrow path between the extremes of the create-jobs-at-all-costs-almost-regardless-of-the-utility-of-the-public-works-project mentality of the OPW and the stolid pressure for economy emanating from the Department of Finance, while endeavouring to recall the Department's original purpose: improving local services and maintaining the financial stability of local authorities. The 1930s put a considerable strain on the structure of local government. Many urban councils were too poor and too small to meet their financial commitments, while the ability of Dublin Corporation and many smaller councils to manage a major housing programme was called into question. Such issues emphasised the need for a more professional system of local administration, if only to bridge the gap between directives issued by the Custom House and their implementation by local authorities.

Seán T. O'Kelly, Minister from 1932, emerges as a powerful and controversial figure, determined to pursue his personal agenda, often one suspects despite the reservations expressed by senior officials. O'Kelly's political acuity is not in doubt. He placed considerable emphasis on being informed about local conditions: a programme of regular meetings with county secretaries proved to be particularly valuable, as were the reports from the Housing Board. After 1932, both the Minister and the Department appear to have been more in tune with local public opinion than during the 1920s. O'Kelly also showed considerable skill in pushing the Department's programmes through cabinet and in obtaining finance. Much of this was achieved by dubious methods which were in breach of cabinet procedure: the files contain many letters from the Minister's secretary, Brian Ó Nuallain (better known as the writer Flann O'Brien and the columnist Myles na Gopaleen)[110] apologising for breaches of cabinet procedure, though the breaches are so frequent that they are unlikely to have been accidental. There is no obvious instance during the years 1932-39 of Local Government being denied funds for a scheme for which it had fought. On many occasions Finance failed to impose its will. There is equally little evidence that Industry and Commerce was blocked in its projects during these years.[111] By 1939, however, Finance was attempting to tighten its control over capital expenditure for housing.

O'Kelly's attention to the details of the Department's programmes appears cursory. As a Dubliner, he took the city's interests very much to heart, yet by the mid-1930s Dublin's slum-clearance programme was well behind target. There is no evidence that O'Kelly intervened.

The history of the Department of Local Government during the 1930s provides an insight into various domestic policies, such as relief works, which have been largely forgotten. While it is easy to condemn the confused objectives of proposals for rotational work schemes, we should perhaps also note the considerable efforts which were being made to solve major social problems; efforts which belie naïve images that independent Ireland was characterised by stagnation and inactivity.

CHAPTER FIVE

HOMES FIT FOR IRISH CITIZENS? THE EVOLUTION OF HOUSING POLICY UNTIL 1939

Although most Irish families on the eve of the Famine had adequate food and fuel, housing conditions were appalling.[1] Only a minority of landlords provided housing for tenant farmers, while many farmers were equally negligent, leaving cottiers to build their own cabins. The hundred years following the Famine saw a dramatic improvement in Irish housing standards. In 1841, over 40 per cent of Irish families lived in fourth-class accommodation (one room units) and only 7 per cent in houses of more than three rooms. By 1946 only 3 per cent of the population lived in one-roomed units. Although the Famine and the population decline of post-Famine decades played a major role in reducing the proportion of families living in rural squalor, the Local Government Board and subsequently the Department of Local Government and Public Health were also important agents of change.

The first housing programmes that the Local Government Board introduced in the 1880s concentrated on rehousing rural labourers and urban slum-dwellers. By the 1930s the government was providing a subsidy for most new houses catering for the middle classes and was providing funds for the repair and improvement of farmhouses. The years between 1920 and 1939 were an important stage in the evolution of the housing market; the policies which then evolved are a major reason why Irish home-ownership is one of the highest in Europe and a major proportion of all houses have been constructed since independence with state assistance.

URBAN HOUSING PROGRAMMES UNDER THE LOCAL GOVERNMENT BOARD

On the eve of World War I, Dublin labouring households devoted a lower proportion of income to housing than similar households in London.[2] Although many squalid, overcrowded cottages could still be found in rural Ireland at the end of the nineteenth century, the standard of housing had improved considerably. Housing conditions in Dublin and in towns and cities outside Ulster were among the worst in the British Isles, despite the fact that the population had stagnated or even fallen.[3] Poor housing was primarily a reflection of economic circumstances: families in Belfast had higher incomes, and rents for modern houses were low, whereas the poorly paid casual labourers who predominated in Dublin or Cork crowded into old buildings.

The Local Government Board's involvement in housing began as a result of its responsibility for public health. Early legislation, such as the 1866 Sanitary Act, concentrated on cleaning and ultimately closing insanitary houses, which were believed to harbour disease. Responsibility for enforcing these regulations rested with local authorities. Dublin Corporation was extremely lax in this regard, largely because of the political power of tenement landlords; there is no evidence that other cities were different. The LGB was slow to intervene. This was probably fortuitous: closing insanitary houses without building replacement dwellings only increased the level of overcrowding in slum areas. There is no evidence that the Board or any other contemporary agency asked why labouring families were living in such squalor; the high rent charged for decent housing was ignored.

State involvement in housing moved to a second stage with the passing of the 1875 Artisans and Labourers' Dwellings Improvement Act, the Cross Act, which permitted a local authority to clear an unhealthy area if an LGB inquiry confirmed that this should be done. The cost of clearance was met by a loan from the Commissioners of Public Works, and the local authority was required either to build working-class housing on the site or to sell it to a philanthropic body for a similar purpose.[4] At first the Act applied only to the five boroughs of Dublin, Cork, Belfast, Limerick and Waterford, but in 1884 the provisions were extended to all urban areas with more than 12,000 inhabitants. Dublin Corporation's clearance of the Coombe marked the first use of the Act in Ireland. Shortly after this, Cork Corporation cleared the Blackpool Market area and erected 76 cottages on the site.[5] The 1890 Housing of the Working Classes Act gave local authorities additional power to condemn premises which were 'unfit for habitation' and to compel their removal; it also permitted them to construct housing on virgin sites, in the hope that lower site costs would mean cheaper housing.[6]

Local authorities made little impact before 1914. Dublin Corporation had built almost 1,400 houses, accommodating 2.5 per cent of the city's population, which may have been the highest proportion in the British Isles; Cork Corporation was another front-runner.[7] In 1914 it was estimated the 14,000 houses were needed in Dublin, ten times the number erected in the previous thirty years, in order to close tenements unfit for habitation and to relieve overcrowding. There was no provision for subsidising local authority houses, with the result that rents were far beyond the means of the poorest families. Tenancies appear to have been allocated to those who could afford the rent, rather than on the basis of need, and most families in council houses had incomes above the working-class average.

The LGB could do little other than investigate housing conditions. An inquiry, which the Board carried out in 1900, into the causes of Dublin's high death-rate revealed appalling housing conditions, inadequate cleansing and numerous slaughterhouses in centre city areas. However, the Board could not compel a local authority to clear insanitary areas, or build additional houses. A report in 1906 by D. Edgar Flinn, the board's medical inspector, suggested that Dublin Corporation had largely ignored the recommendations of the 1900 inquiry.

The Board's 1914 inquiry into Dublin housing provided a further damning indictment of local administration, which also highlighted the scale of the problem. The 14,000 houses that were urgently needed would cost £3.5m., a sum which was far beyond the city's borrowing capacity. Financial orthodoxy, as dictated by the Treasury, assumed that local authority housing should break even, and the rents that would be charged on the 14,000 new houses were higher than those paid by 93 per cent of tenement families. Solving the Dublin housing problems would either require a magical reduction in construction costs, or a substantial subsidy from the Exchequer. In 1914, the total Exchequer subsidy for Irish urban housing amounted to £6,000 which was provided by the 1908 Clancy Act, a private member's measure introduced by a nationalist MP. Urban Ireland had gained nothing from the British policy of 'killing Home Rule by kindness', partly because there was no effective lobby campaigning for aid for urban housing, but also because as Irish Chief Secretary Augustine Birrell pointed out in 1914, any concession would involve 'opening the flood-gate of public grants to the other cities of the Kingdom'.[8]

THE LOCAL GOVERNMENT BOARD AND AGRICULTURAL LABOURERS

Rural labourers fared better than their city cousins under the Local Government Board, because they were seen as an interest group to be placated as part of the solution to the land question and because it was possible to detach assistance for Irish agricultural labourers from the wider United Kingdom problem. Although the number of one-room cabins fell sharply after the Famine, 40,000 were still inhabited in 1881.[9] LGB inspectors had documented the very inadequate housing occupied by many married rural labourers, and several had emphasised the need to provide them with allotments and decent housing.[10] Donnelly claims that poor housing was 'probably the most contentious issue between labourers and farmers in the 1880s'[11] and most protest meetings organised by labourers demanded immediate improvement.[12] Both the 1881 Gladstone Land Act and the 1882 Labourers' Cottages and Allotments Act included clauses which were designed to improve labourers' housing, though they appear to have been ineffectual.

The 1882 Act gave the Land Commission power to order farmers who had obtained judicial rents to repair their labourers' cottages or to provide new houses. However the clause was rarely enforced, except against landlords, because responsibility for enforcement rested with boards of guardians, which were dominated by prosperous farmers and their shop-keeping friends and relations.[13] Farmers also could evade the law by evicting labourers, because labourers, unlike farmers, did not have security of tenure. The 1883 Labourers Act, a private member's bill introduced by nationalist MPs, gave boards of guardians power to erect cottages on half-acre sites for rent to rural labourers, using low interest Exchequer loans. This Act is a landmark in Irish housing legislation because it provided for rents to be subsidised by the rates. The initiative for building cottages rested with boards of guardians; applications had to be supported by the signatures of twelve local ratepayers — a category which did not include agricultural labourers.[14]

The LGB held an inquiry to determine whether or not the cottages were needed; it then approved or amended the proposed scheme, determined the amount to be paid in compensation if land was compulsorily acquired, adjudicated on objections, supervised the arrangements for loans which were granted by the OPW[15] and specified the size and number of rooms and standards of construction.[16] Cottages were constructed from stone and mortar, with slate roofs in place of the traditional thatch. The first cottages contained a kitchen and two bedrooms, but several priests argued that three bedrooms should be provided, one for the parents and one each for male and female children. Cottages constructed in later years tended to be larger and in 1892 the plots were extended to one acre.[17] In 1884 the Board estimated that a cottage and site cost an average of £100.[18] Rents, averaging one shilling (5p) a week, were heavily subsidised; the rental income from 164 cottages erected by Naas Board of Guardians covered only one-third of the total costs.[19]

Until 1898 it was quite common for landlords and farmers to unite to prevent cottages being built in a locality. If three ratepayers objected, a scheme could be postponed. Few cottages would have been erected in County Tipperary without the persuasive, almost coercive, powers of the catholic clergy, who pressed farmers into providing sites and lobbied boards of guardians. An active local labourers' organisation could also act as a persuasive force.[20] In 1891 the LGB was given power to hold inquiries in unions where no cottages had been constructed, in order to determine whether cottages were needed, and to take action against negligent local authorities. It did not obtain similar powers in urban areas until 1918. In 1895, when boards of guardians in Strabane, Stranorlar and Cootehill had refused to respond to local demands for the construction of labourers' cottages, the Board gave its inspectors power to enforce the labourers' acts. Other unions were threatened with similar action.[21]

By 1900 approximately 16,000 labourers' cottages had been built or authorised: 9,000 in Munster, 6,500 in Leinster, but only 300 and 160 in Ulster and Connacht respectively.[22] The imbalance between the provinces reflected the fact that most labourers in Connacht and Ulster were smallholders who took seasonal jobs and did not qualify under the labourers' acts, though the Congested Districts Board rehoused smallholders in its area.

Labourers became entitled to vote in local elections as a result of the 1898 Act and this forced many rural district councils to initiate labourers' cottage schemes. By 1901, 82 rural district councils had submitted plans for almost 6,000 cottages, and the Board recruited additional inspectors to deal with the growing volume of applications; plans for a further 7,691 cottages were being prepared.[23]

Irish MPs criticised the Board for tying rural district councils in red tape and for excluding fishermen and rural tradesmen from rehousing lists.[24] However the Board's 1901 report complained that councils tended to include in lists of designated tenants persons 'already in occupation of good houses' who could not be deemed to be labourers'. A clause in the 1903 Wyndham Land Act widened the categories who were eligible for labourers' cottages by extending the definition of 'agricultural labourer' to include all persons, other than domestic servants, working for hire, even if only temporarily, who occupied a maximum of one-quarter acre of land and whose wages did not exceed 2/6 (12.5p) a week. The 1903 Act also gave the LGB power to compel rural district councils to provide houses for labourers living in their district.[25]

Amending legislation passed in 1906 simplified the procedures for drawing up schemes, extended the period for repaying loans, and provided additional funds. The LGB established a special labourers' acts branch and recruited architects and housing inspectors to cope with the ever-growing volume of work. By 1910 the Board had drawn up revised specifications for labourers' cottages; they were based on those used by the Land Commission, the OPW, the Congested Districts Board and the labourers' cottages on the Earl of Carrington's Cambridge estate.[26] Construction of labourers' cottages continued at a steady pace until 1915 when the stringent borrowing restrictions imposed on local authorities brought activity to a standstill. Until then money does not appear to have been a problem: the Treasury provided £1m. in 1911 and a further £1m. in 1914.

'HOMES FIT FOR HEROES'?

By 1914 there was a growing consensus that the housing needs of rural labourers had been largely met; attention shifted to the cities and towns. Labour unrest in Dublin in 1913 and the publication of the report of the 1914 Housing Inquiry had awakened public interest. Town-planning enthusiasts associated with the vicereine, Lady Aberdeen, drafted proposals for garden-city-style workers' housing in their blueprint for the capital city of a Home Rule Ireland.[27] While rural Ireland prospered during World War I, Dublin did not. The war brought publicly funded housing programmes to a halt, but the British government later gave a commitment to provide 'homes fit for heroes' for returning troops, in the belief that this would reduce the threat of a British 'Bolshevik' revolution.[28]

The Irish LGB reflected this shift in priorities by establishing a separate housing department, which was controlled by a four-man committee, chaired by P.C. Cowan. It also abandoned its traditional passive attitude towards urban housing, establishing an internal housing committee to assist local authorities in drafting proposals for housing schemes. Perhaps the best indication of the importance now attached to urban housing reform is the fact that Lloyd George, the British prime minister, gave a commitment to consider including 'a substantial provision' for housing in any settlement of the Irish question which was agreed by the Irish Convention, the all-party body (though Sinn Féin refused to attend), which was attempting to arrive at an agreed political settlement for Ireland in 1917/18. The Convention's housing committee estimated that a total of 67,500 urban houses were needed, at a cost of £27m..[29] These proposals lapsed when the Convention split early in 1918, but the aborted Home Rule Bills, drafted in that year, provided for an annual housing subsidy of £2m..

The 1919 Housing (Ireland) Act, passed by a Westminster parliament that included no sitting Irish nationalist MPs, extended the provisions of British post-war housing legislation to Ireland. Subsidies, amounting to 25 shillings or 27/6 (£1.25 or £1.37.5) for every £1 charged in rent, were offered to local authorities, to persuade them to construct houses for the working classes at a time when high labour and material costs made such investment unattractive. The subsidies would lapse within two years, by which time it was expected that costs would have returned to normal. If the LGB believed a local authority was failing to provide 'adequate' housing, it had the power to carry out the task directly. While the bill was going through parliament, the LGB instructed local authorities to survey their housing needs, and temporary staff were hired to help prepare plans, so that by August 1919, when the bill became law, almost half the local authorities had submitted schemes for 42,000 urban houses. In December 1919, Exchequer grants were extended to private builders who undertook to build houses similar in standard to those erected by local authorities. However, Balbriggan and Dalkey UDCs were the only local authorities in what became the Irish Free State, to complete housing schemes under the 1919 Act, a total of only 30 houses.[30] By the summer of 1920, most local authorities outside Ulster were unable to benefit from the 1919 Act because they were required to give an undertaking to submit their accounts for audit to the LGB.

The subsidies offered in the 1919 Act were designed as a temporary measure to offset the high costs applying in the immediate post-war years. However, local authorities appear to have regarded them as a benchmark for future Exchequer assistance. Dáil Éireann managed to fend off demands to provide funds for housing, with the excuse that the country was at war, but this argument lost currency once the Treaty had been signed. On 2 February 1922, less than a month after the Treaty vote, a deputation from the Association of Municipal Authorities in Ireland visited the Department of Local Government to demand that the provisional government provide assistance for housing on more generous terms than the 1919 Act. On 16 March, before the provisional government had formally taken control, local authorities were informed that £1m. was being allocated for housing.

Cosgrave rejected the method of awarding subsidies used in the 1919 Act. He claimed that calculating the subsidy on the basis of rent 'often had the most undesirable result of affording State aid where it was least needed', with the largest subsidies going to the most expensive houses. A revised scheme produced by 'housing experts of the Local Government Board' under Cosgrave's direction, provided a subsidy from the Exchequer equal to two-thirds of the capital cost, councils would borrow one-quarter of the amount on the open market, and the balance (one-twelfth) would come from a special housing rate. The subsidy was designed to compensate councils for higher housing costs. Officials hoped that it would lead to the construction of over 2,000 houses within six months — at an average cost of £750 and an average weekly rent of 10/6 (52.5p). Cosgrave appears to have circulated details of the measure to local authorities without consulting the fledgling Department of Finance. In a letter justifying his actions to the 'Treasury' of the provisional government, he mentioned that he had been subjected to 'the most insistent pressure' from local authorities to formulate 'a satisfactory Housing Scheme'. He also persuaded the Irish Banks Standing Committee to provide loans for housing to local authorities at 4.5 per cent, one per cent below the commercial rate. The committee informed him that its attitude was 'entirely sympathetic' and that it realised that 'the making of these loans is intimately connected with the welfare of the body politic'. McCarron warned the Department of Finance against adopting an unduly restrictive approach in paying the subsidy: 'the manner of disbursement of the grant of £1m. should not bear any greater semblance of distrust of local authorities than the system to which they are accustomed'.[31] On 15 May local authorities were informed that at least half the grant would be advanced when a scheme was approved and contracts signed.

Housing never commanded the same degree of urgency or high-level attention during the remainder of Cumann na nGaedheal's term in office and, although the subsidies proved less generous than the 1919 Act, they were more effective than anything available until the 1931 Act. A circular that was issued to announce the terms indicated that it was a short-term measure because the provisional government 'cannot adopt any policy of financial assistance which may involve the future government of the Saorstát in financial commitments extending over a long period of years'.[32] By 1924 almost 2,000 houses had been constructed by twenty local authorities under this scheme.[33] Councils were forced to charge high rents on these and many preferred to sell them in order to avoid incurring long-term losses.[34]

ASSISTING THE PRIVATE SECTOR: THE 1924 ACT

After this burst of energy, housing policy marked time. The government was unwilling to embark on a long-term housing programme until wages and other costs had fallen sufficiently to make decent housing affordable to the working class. This was pure fantasy: although the cost of housing had been much lower before 1914, it had not proved economically possible to rehouse tenement families. By the 1920s the triumph of Unwinian notions of garden suburbs and the growing demand for higher standards of amenities meant that the gap between affordable rents and decent housing had widened considerably.[35] In addition, during the 1920s, the Irish government followed the British example in attempting to place the onus for housing reform on the local authorities. This was most clearly stated by the Minister for Local Government, Richard Mulcahy, in 1929 when he told the Dáil that the financial aspect of the question was so great that, 'apart from other reasons, the State cannot bear on its shoulders the burden of solving this particular problem, particularly where there does exist or is supposed to exist, as far as central Government is concerned, machinery in local authorities which could be adapted for the purpose'. A promise of 'considerable' state aid for housing would serve to maintain high housing costs, saddling the community with considerable debt and would 'create an interference that would react in future years of provision of houses to meet ordinary wear and tear.'[36] We should also bear in mind that the argument that the government was waiting for costs to fall provided a convenient excuse for postponing costly expenditure which would have proved difficult to finance and for which the government showed little enthusiasm.

The 1924 Housing (Building Facilities) Act, which was almost identical to British legislation passed in 1923,[37] provided subsidies of £60, £80 and £100 to new houses containing 3-5 rooms, with a floor area of between 520 and 1,000 square feet, though houses to be occupied by civil servants could have a floor area of up to 1,500 square feet! Private builders and local authorities were eligible for grants on equal terms. Grants were provided to all qualifying new houses, whether they were owner-occupied or for rent. The Act, which appears to have been the brainchild of T.J Byrne,[38] a former housing inspector with the LGB who had become principal architect with the Board of Works, was primarily designed to create employment. Early drafts included clauses requiring a reduction in building industry wages and material costs as a condition for obtaining a grant. Local Government objected to this proposal and was equally opposed to the clause enabling local authorities to grant rates remission on new houses, since this would erode the local tax base.[39] These objections proved to be effective: the draconian wage and cost clauses disappeared, as did the provision for rates remission, though this resurfaced in 1925.[40]

The 1924 Act proved to be the beginning of a long tradition of state assistance for private-sector housing; it was also the first occasion when rates remission was proposed as an incentive to the housing industry. The sum provided, £250,000, was modest. If the 1924 Act was expected to reinvigorate the private rental market, it proved an utter failure. The decision in 1923 to extend the provisions of the 1915 Rent Restrictions Act, which froze rents at 30 per cent above pre-war levels and was introduced as a temporary wartime measure,[41] marked the beginning of a revolution in Irish urban housing. Before 1914 most middle-class Dublin families rented their homes. Many business and professional men erected or bought houses which they rented out; they saw such investment as a form of life insurance or pension fund which would provide an income for their widows and children. Rent control made such investment unattractive, as did the demands of the Town Tenants Association that tenant rights, similar to the 1881 Land Act, be extended to urban tenants.[42] Most houses grant-aided by the 1924 Act were owner-occupied. Farmers who could build their own homes during slack periods in the agricultural year were major beneficiaries.[43] The majority opted for four- or five-room houses; by November 1924 only 50 three-room houses had been grant-aided, compared with 399 four-room and 977 five-room houses (the number of civil servants who benefited is unknown).[44] The 1925 Housing Act continued to offer grants similar to those introduced in 1924, though houses built by local authorities and public utility companies would receive larger grants than those constructed by private builders; rates remission was introduced for new houses. These measures were renewed annually for the remainder of the decade, though the level of grants was reduced in 1929.[45] The 1930 Housing Act retained grants at 1929 levels,[46] though the government announced that grants for private houses or houses erected by public utility societies would end on 31 March 1931.[47]

Local Government had initially been unenthusiastic about the 1924 Act; by 1925, however, it was arguing that the state should continue to make small sums available on a year-to-year basis 'pending the obtention [sic] of more stabilised conditions' which would permit a long-term solution to housing needs. This change of mind reflects a realisation that there was no immediate prospect of obtaining the level of state spending needed to tackle slum clearance. In October 1924 W.T. Cosgrave acknowledged that it would cost the Exchequer an estimated £14m. to provide 70,000 new houses at rents which working families could afford and that it was impossible 'to foresee any immediate likelihood of such a scheme being adopted as would eventually solve the housing problem.'[48] The £100 grant, provided for each local authority house from 1925, would cover only an estimated 25 per cent of construction costs, against 50 per cent under the 1922 scheme.

Local authorities were further deterred from embarking on housing schemes because they were unable to borrow the necessary capital. Although Finance admitted that this might 'impede' the local authority housing programme and might even bring it to a halt, officials saw little hope of persuading the banks to advance loans to local authorities for housing. In 1926, following 'repeated representations by the Minister [for Local Government]' the banks provided a limited amount of capital for small developments in Clonmel, New Ross, Enniscorthy and Tipperary, and there was a trickle of similar loans in subsequent years. During the years 1924-28, 80 per cent of local authority houses were erected in Dublin and Cork county boroughs — the only two local authorities that were sufficiently large to raise money independently on the stock exchange. Local Government pressed Finance to permit the Local Loans Fund (LLF) to issue loans for housing. Although Finance conceded that it was 'somewhat illogical' to provide loans for water and sewers, but not for local authority housing, they were determined to offset this concession by reducing or abolishing housing grants; otherwise, one official minuted, 'we would be introducing a new principle into the history of Housing of the Working Class if both loan and grant were provided'. However, McElligott pointed out that grants were popular with the Oireachtas and removing them would 'evoke the strongest opposition'. Brennan seized on this argument and advised the minister not to provide housing loans from the LLF.[49]

Finance and Local Government continued to dispute this issue until June 1929 when Ernest Blythe announced that the LLF would consider applications from local authorities for housing loans.[50] The concession appears to have been in response to pressure from Dáil deputies who, in late March, had objected to the terms in the 1929 Housing Bill which had cut the subsidies provided for local authority housing in line with the alleged reduction in costs that had taken place since 1924. Mulcahy's statement on this occasion was the most laissez-faire made by any Minister for Local Government on this issue between 1922 and 1932. He placed responsibility for working-class housing squarely on the shoulders of local authorities and argued that in normal conditions the 'public purse should not provide assistance for private housing'. Fianna Fáil and Labour TDs objected so strongly to this speech that Cosgrave was forced to concede a higher grant per house to local authorities, which levied a special housing rate of at least one shilling (5p) in the pound, in response to a proposal from Fianna Fáil TD Bill Rice.[51]

Although few records survive of the discussions between officials from Finance and Local Government which followed this debate, it seems probable that it was decided to permit all local authorities other than Dublin and Cork county boroughs to apply for LLF loans for housing.[52] Loans would normally be provided only for the construction of 4-roomed houses 'of modified standard' and there would be a ceiling on the cost per house; local authorities were required to contribute a sum equal to the value of Exchequer grants, and councils that failed to levy one shilling in the pound housing rate would have their advances limited to five-sevenths of total cost.[53] In retaliation for this concession, which was achieved without the abolition of housing grants, Finance proceeded to subject all applications for grants to more detailed scrutiny. It devoted special attention to the 'bogus building societies' which had been established by farmers in Monaghan and Mayo in order to qualify for higher grants available to houses built by public utility societies.

Local authorities derived little immediate benefit from being permitted to borrow housing capital from the LLF. In mid-October 1929, after the Wall Street crash, Finance attempted to increase the rate of interest charged by 2 per cent, to 7.75 per cent; Finance claimed that it could no longer raise long-term finance, given the uncertainty in international money markets. Local Government argued that the rate should be set at 6.75 per cent; otherwise, the concession of LLF loans would prove worthless.[54]

THE BACKGROUND TO THE 1931 HOUSING ACT

By the late 1920s it was proving increasingly difficult to argue in favour of postponing the drafting of a long-term housing policy. Wages and other costs had fallen since the early 1920s: housing costs in Cork allegedly fell by 25 per cent between 1925 and 1928,[55] though the prospect of a return to pre-war prices appeared slim. Fianna Fáil's entry into the Dáil in 1927 and the party's commitment to a comprehensive housing programme had put the government under pressure, as did a recommendation in the final report of the Committee on the Relief of Unemployment that the government summon a housing conference to draw up a long-term housing programme.[56] Cosgrave responded by calling a conference of Dublin builders and trade unionists.[57] By 1928 Local Government was attempting to cut housing costs by means other than wage reductions:

In a memorandum on future housing policy, the Department noted that:

212

In order to bring down costs, every reasonable economy in planning and construction must be availed of and a decision on desirable standards must be made in the light of what standards are possible of attainment. Idealism may prove a dangerous foe to solutions of the housing problem and in facing facts it will almost be necessary to come down so low as to admit that it will be preferable to have the poorer classes of the community housed in dwellings of the 'shanty' types than not housed at all. If slums are to be cleared we must not aim at providing dwelling houses with hall, back entrances, hot water circulating systems, parlours and such 'luxuries' for all present slum dwellers. There is a medium between the misery of slums and the advanced type of a five room house with hot water etc. . . . . If this medium can be attained authorities concerned might well congratulate themselves on an equitable achievement.[58]

This reference to providing 'dwellings of the "shanty" types' suggests that Local Government was attempting to reach agreement with Finance on a major housing programme. Arthur Codling, a principal officer in Finance who had served as secretary of the LGB housing committee from 1916 to 1922, believed that LLF loans should be used only to finance housing for the very poor; he also thought that it was possible to achieve a further reduction in building costs by drawing up a 10-12-year programme which would guarantee long-term employment.[59]

Such a programme was predicated on further cost reductions; to Finance, this was synonymous with low wages and the department was unwilling to announce a long-term housing programme while negotiations were continuing between building industry employers and workers. By 1929 McElligott was suggesting that a new survey of housing needs should be conducted; he believed that the 1919 housing census was 'evidently framed on liberal lines and not a very useful guide to present housing requirements'. Mulcahy voiced similar sentiments in the Dáil during the debate on the 1929 Housing Act. This may have been another stalling device, or a genuine effort to limit the cost of a housing programme; perhaps Finance had both aims in mind. McCarron was concerned at the implied threat to apply a strict definition of need. However he informed Finance that Local Government would have an accurate indication of housing requirements within two or three months.[60]

Dublin's requirements were already known: evidence given to the

Committee on the Relief of Unemployment revealed that the number of houses that were unfit for habitation and incapable of renovation had risen by 15 per cent since 1914.[61] Construction of local authority housing had stopped shortly after the outbreak of war, and the destruction of property during both the 1916 Rising and the civil war brought increased overcrowding. In 1922 the Dublin town clerk asked Michael Collins to make vacant British military barracks available to rehouse families living in tenements which had been condemned as unfit for habitation, and some military accommodation was allocated to Dublin Corporation in March 1924.[62] In 1924 the report of the Local Government inquiry, which led to the dissolution of Dublin Corporation, concluded that the Corporation's building programme had failed to keep pace with the deterioration in housing conditions, though it absolved the Corporation of responsibility. The inquiry accepted that any other committee 'working under similar conditions' would have also been unable to 'stop the growth of the Dublin housing difficulty'.[63]

High post-war building costs presented a particularly severe problem because Labour members of Dublin Corporation had persuaded the Corporation to construct its housing schemes under direct labour, and productivity on such schemes was extremely low.[64] Most of the 4,000 houses erected during the years 1922-32 were expensive; they were constructed 'in the belief that people would filter upwards and so gradually vacate the slums'[65] — a long-standing Victorian myth. The suspension of Dublin Corporation in 1924 and the appointment of commissioners who were primarily concerned to restore the city to financial health may have contributed to the neglect of slum clearance.

Most of the data needed to estimate national housing needs were available from the 1926 Census. This indicated that most farmers living in overcrowded conditions resided in western counties where special Gaeltacht housing subsidies were available. On the basis of Census data, Local Government recommended that grants to private persons who were building houses for personal occupancy should be discontinued on the grounds that the beneficiaries were rarely in need of rehousing. In a twenty-six page memorandum produced in 1930 as a response to the report of the government's economy committee,[66] Local Government argued that all Exchequer grants should be used to subsidise houses built for rent, with the aim of reducing rents to a level which was 50 per cent higher than in 1914. Sufficient funds should be provided for a long-term programme, which would satisfy all housing needs at these rent levels; in the case of Dublin, this would take an estimated ten years. The Department also recommended easing the Rent Restrictions Act and replacing annual subsidies for once-off grants, as in Britain. However the memorandum did not include any estimate of the number of houses needed or the cost of building them.

In 1931 McCarron publicly signalled the change of direction in housing policy in a speech to a public health conference, where he argued that public expenditure on housing should be targeted at the 'direct eradication of worn-out insanitary or over-crowded habitations'; and specifically at rehousing of the lowest paid.[67]

Public opinion began to show a much greater interest in Dublin's housing problems after the restoration of Dublin Corporation in the autumn of 1930. By 1931 the intense publicity campaign to highlight conditions in the city's slums[68] had even penetrated the offices of the Department of Finance. On 17 July 1931 Herlihy (Finance) noted that 'a public outcry seems to be gathering on the slum question in Dublin'. He feared that the Department would soon come under pressure from ministers to do something 'at short notice'; to forestall this, he suggested that Finance begin negotiations with Local Government.

In response, McCarron indicated that Local Government would prefer to see future subsidies being based on a percentage of loan charges, with centre-city flats receiving a higher subsidy than houses. The high cost of inner-city flats had been a contentious issue between Local Government and Finance for some time. Finance had previously refused to approve the maximum grant for a scheme of two-roomed flats in the Dublin suburb of Rathmines on the grounds that only four-roomed dwellings were eligible. Local Government argued for a maximum grant, because the scheme, like all Dublin flat developments, would bear a substantial loss. Finance official Frank Duff, better known as the founder of the Legion of Mary, recommended rejecting the application; he claimed that the proposed rent of five shillings (25p) a week was inadequate and would entail a weekly subsidy of six shillings (30p), while construction costs were 'fantastic'.[69] Other Finance officials were also 'staggered' at the high cost of erecting flats, though they ultimately accepted that the figures were *bona fide*.

In an effort to cut costs, Local Government proposed to omit baths and hot water from flat developments, though it acknowledged that Dublin Corporation 'in their present humour, were not disposed to eliminate baths and hot water'. Finance, however, rejected this suggestion, while expressing concern at the high cost of housing; it was also determined that state aid would not be granted for houses which failed to meet minimum standards.[70] McDunphy of the cabinet office argued in favour of moving displaced slum families to the suburbs on grounds of economy. However, Cosgrave, who took an active role in all aspects of the legislation (he received an advance copy of the Bill and made extensive marginal notes), argued

> . . . that we have churches, schools and work in the city convenient
> to present habitations. Cost of transport to outskirts no matter how
> arranged is an additional charge to rent and no extra cost is
> possible in many circumstances. Open spaces — baths, drawing
> rooms — are most desirable when we can afford them. But when
> we can't it's a waste of time talking of them. People want decent
> habitations at rents they can pay. We can't supply them without
> adding a big burden to city and national exchequer.[71]

Cosgrave's intervention may have proved decisive: a special subsidy for flat construction was conceded, though McCarron promised Finance officials that steps would be taken to ensure that flats would not be occupied by men earning good wages,[72] a commitment which threatened to replicate the social composition of traditional tenements in the new flats.

The 1931 Housing (Miscellaneous Provisions) Act sought to distinguish between 'the better paid artisan class' and 'the casual unskilled worker'.[73] Officials in Finance and Local Government agreed on the need to target Exchequer assistance towards the poorest families. McCarron argued that the lowest paid workers were the main victims of tuberculosis and the major recipients of public assistance. Better housing would mean long-term savings in welfare expenditure. Herlihy in Finance urged the need 'to square up to our duty' by providing housing for the poorest section of the community. Both Herlihy and McCarron expressed their resentment that state funds for housing had been misallocated during the preceding years to 'owner-occupied farms and speculative builders', expenditure which did 'nothing' to relieve housing need. However, while Finance wished to abolish all aid for private housing and to defer state grants for 'luxury' working-class dwellings until the slums had been tackled, Local Government wished to retain grants for non-clearance local authority houses.

216

Reflecting these priorities, the 1931 Act followed the example of the 1930 British Housing Act (the Greenwood Act) by doubling the level of grant paid on schemes which rehoused families who had previously lived in slum dwellings. The initial memorandum presented to cabinet by Local Government in September 1931, which Finance had approved 'without qualification', provided for fixed subsidies for different categories. Finance favoured this approach because it was the practice followed by 'the British who are wise guys, and probably thought the whole thing out carefully'; Finance believed it would be easier to monitor costs. Four-room dwellings catering for 'normal workers', i.e. not slum-clearance families, would attract a subsidy of £45; the subsidy on three-roomed dwellings for slum-clearance families would be £85, while a subsidy of £163 would be paid for each three-room flat provided for a slum-clearance family.

In the event, the Act provided for subsidies covering a percentage of loan charges, subject to a specified maximum cost: 40 per cent for the initial fifteen years and 33.3 per cent for a further fifteen years in the case of flats; 30 per cent and 20 per cent for houses built to accommodate displaced families and 15 per cent over twenty years for other local authority housing.[74]

Subsidies based on a percentage of interest charges allowed the Exchequer to spread the cost over a longer period. It was estimated that the subsidies provided by the 1931 Act would cost £810,000 in total over the years 1933-40, significantly less than the £2.58m. which was paid between 1922 and 1932. The main cost to the Exchequer would be in the form of capital loans, rather than grants — an estimated £9m., though this figure was reduced considerably by the proviso that Dublin and Cork Corporations would raise the necessary capital 'for the first two years' by issuing stock.[75] The act also streamlined the procedures for compulsory purchase, clearing unhealthy areas and closing unfit houses —following precedents in British and Northern Irish legislation. Dublin Corporation succeeded in having a clause included in the bill, providing for a maximum Exchequer grant of £200 towards the acquisition and repair of tenement houses, despite McCarron's fears that it would result in 'terrible jobbery'.

Although officials in Finance and Local Government had initially wished to abolish all grants for private housing, the 1931 Act provided a reduced grant of £20 and raised the maximum cost of houses eligible for mortgages under the Small Dwellings Acquisition Acts from £800 to

£1,000, subject to a maximum of 90 per cent of the market value. This was a response to Mulcahy's concern that the 'absence of financial provisions for rural housing would be received very unfavourably'.[76]

The 1931 Act, which was passed by the Dáil on 17 December 1931, the date set for the Christmas recess, was one of the last pieces of legislation enacted by the Cumann na nGaedheal government. Fianna Fáil, which came into office early in 1932, proved the main beneficiary. By giving priority to local authority housing, and more specifically to slum clearance, the Act reversed the thrust of government housing policy in the years from 1924. During the years 1923-32, two-thirds of all houses constructed with state assistance were privately owned. Of the £2.58m. which the Exchequer provided to subsidise house construction between 1922 and 1932, £1.077m. went to private individuals and public utilities societies (the latter obtained only a negligible amount), £33,790 was spent under the Labourers Act, and the balance went to local authorities — £1m. under the 1922 scheme and a further £468,000 from 1924. After the £1m. provided in 1922 had been exhausted, over two-thirds of state funds went to the private sector.

It would be naive to assume that all local authority housing catered for needy families or that all grants for the private housing sector benefited more prosperous families. The overwhelming majority of houses constructed with state aid between 1922 and 1932 — whether publicly or privately owned — catered for families who were in relatively comfortable circumstances. Over 15,000 of the 25,500 houses subsidised contained five rooms and more than 8,000 had four rooms. Until the 1931 Housing Act, no effort was made to target local authority housing towards those in greatest need, or to structure a scheme of housing grants specifically towards slum-clearance. In this respect, Irish housing policy was similar to Britain.[77]

A comparison between the estimated cost of subsidies under the 1931 Act — £810,000 for the years 1933-40 — and the actual cost incurred between 1922 and 1932 — £2.58m. — suggests that the 1931 Act appeared to offer better value for money, while catering for those in greatest need. Unfortunately, by 1931 groups other than slum-dwellers had come to expect state assistance for housing as a right; as Mulcahy noted, such schemes were politically popular. Despite the intent of the 1931 Act, it would prove difficult to shift expenditure towards those in greatest need and to redress the balance between public and private sector housing.

Table 5.1

Houses built under state-aided schemes, 1922-32 (including £1m. scheme)

	Private/ Public Utility	Local Authority
1922/23	-	18
1923/24	-	446
1924/25	512	955
1925/26	2,304	1,077
1926/27	2,468	1,243
1927/28	1,739	385
1928/29	2,037	696
1929/30	2,359	1,065
1930/31	2,256	759
1931/32	3,489	1,732
Total	17,164	8,376

Source: *Reports of the Department of Local Government and Public Health.*

The 'fiery cross':[78] the Fianna Fáil housing programme 1932-39

Housing is generally regarded as one of the most successful programmes pursued by Fianna Fáil in the period 1932-39.[79] During its years in opposition, the party had been highly critical of the government's failure to implement a comprehensive housing programme. Increased investment in housing was in keeping with Fianna Fáil's desire to create employment; it would also provide a market for many of the proposed new industries — furniture plants, joinery, bricks and cement.

From 1932 Local Government managed, on the whole, to retain control of housing policy, despite the threat posed by O'Kelly's decision to set up a housing board. By the late 1930s, however, the Department of Finance was becoming more involved in housing, largely because of the rising cost of the housing programme, and particularly the impact of stock issues by Dublin and Cork Corporations on Exchequer borrowings. For most of the decade, though, Local Government appears to have succeeded in keeping Finance at bay. This was often achieved by (deliberate?) breaches of cabinet procedure, specifically the requirement that all proposals involving expenditure should first be submitted for evaluation to the Department of Finance. Finance complained repeatedly that legislative proposals were presented to the Executive Council without their prior scrutiny; on one occasion a Housing Bill was circulated in the Dáil without being seen by either the Executive Council or the Department of Finance.

The 1931 Housing (Miscellaneous Provisions) Act provided the administrative framework for the Fianna Fáil housing programme. However Fianna Fáil increased housing subsidies from 40 to 66.6 per cent for slum clearance housing and from 15 to 33.3 per cent for other local authority housing. The scale of the proposed housing programme also increased dramatically, from the 1931 target of almost 25,000 houses over ten years[80] to a projected construction of 43,600 urban houses and flats and 10,000 cottages for rural labourers. One-quarter of the houses would be completed within three years, as would detailed preparatory planning for the remainder. Local authorities would be encouraged to renovate tenements, and a scheme would be devised to attract public utility companies to provide houses for letting. Rates remission and grants for new privately owned houses would be available for a further three years.

The total cost to the Exchequer during the first three years was estimated at £5m.: £4.33m. in loans and £750,000 in grants. The cabinet approved these proposals at a marathon meeting on 23-24 May, with two crucial provisos: that the level of grants to local authorities that constructed labourers' cottages in rural areas should be increased, and that the Minister for Local Government should report on the advisability of providing grants to small farmers for erecting or reconstructing their homes and to individuals or public utility societies who erected cottages for rent to rural labourers.[81] These amendments must be seen as dictated by political pressures: all Local Government memoranda had emphasised the need to give priority to urban slum-clearance projects. In the event, the 1932 Housing (Financial and Miscellaneous Provisions) Act provided grants to cover 60 per cent of the loan charges on rural labourers' cottages.

Housing legislation for the remainder of the 1930s followed the model established during 1931/32. The amount of money available for housing loans or grants was increased, subsidies to private housing were extended, conditions were amended and subsidy levels reduced, but the framework remained unchanged. During the ten years 1932-42, local authorities built 29,000 urban houses and flats plus 20,000 labourers' cottages, while private individuals and public utility societies constructed 22,000 rural and 11,000 urban houses — a total of approximately 82,000 houses.[82] A substantial number of rural houses were also renovated and reconstructed and demolition orders were passed on 10,855 houses occupied by 13,933 families.

The housing debt of local authorities increased from £7.8m. to £18.6m. between 1926 and 1936; non-housing debt fell by £250,000.[83] Local authorities, other than Dublin and Cork Corporations, were almost wholly dependent on the Local Loans Fund for this capital. Between April 1922 and April 1934 the LLF provided loan advances totalling £6.5m., £3.7m. for housing. By April 1937 the sum outstanding had reached £10.3m., £6.7m. of which was spent on housing.[84] Until 1935 the LLF was financed by Exchequer advances in the form of voted grants-in-aid; a separate fund was then established, with a capital value of £11.9m., which had increased to £16m. by March 1937.[85] The annual cost of housing subsidies also increased from over £301,000 in 1933/34 to a peak of almost £813,000 by 1938.

While the construction of 82,000 houses in ten years was an impressive achievement, it is questionable whether the original intention of the 1931 Act was respected: that government assistance should go to those in greatest need. Double the planned number of rural labourers' cottages was built, against two-thirds of the targeted number of urban houses, and expenditure on loans and grants for private housing was much higher than originally intended. The gap between outcome and intent was greatest in Dublin city, which had the most acute housing problems. By 1939 Dublin Corporation had completed only half the planned number of flats and houses, whereas the 20,000 completed labourers' cottages were double the target figure, though local authorities later estimated that 22,000 rural cottages were needed. The Exchequer spent over £3m. in grants for new and reconstructed private houses, against an estimate of £700,000 in 1932. Local authorities suffered a substantial, if unquantifiable, loss of income as a result of continuing to award rates remission to new private homes.

Table 5.2

Houses Erected or Reconstructed: 1932-39

I New Local Authority Housing :
(a) Urban
Estimate 1932   Outcome December 1939

Numbers	Cost	Numbers	Total Cost	Cost to Exchequer
43,600	£17.6m.	23,142	£9.358m.	£4.158m.
[Slum clearance]				
[22,839	n.a.	12,858	£4.700m.]	n.a.

(b) Rural

10,000	n.a.	16,087	£4.820m.	£2.800m.

II Grants to New Private and Public Utility Houses, 1932-39

(a) Urban	Numbers	Cost to Exchequer
Private Houses	8,668	£446,294
Public Utility		
Societies	3,097	£165,978

(b) Rural
Houses Erected by Private Individuals

Agricultural			
Labourers		622	£43,258
Farmers with			
valuation less			
than £14		1,123	£77,861
Farmers £15-£25	351		£20,984
Others		5,882	£261,613

Houses erected by Public Utility Societies

(a) Agricultural			
Labourers	2,349		£186,861
(b) Farmers			
under £15		8,208	£654,427
(c) Farmers			
£15-£25		1,609	£111,558
Total New			
Houses		31,909	£1.969m.

III Reconstructed Houses

Estimate 1932		Outcome December 1939
Numbers	Numbers	Cost to Exchequer
Reconstructed by agricultural labourers	2,505	n.a.
Reconstructed by farmers with less than £25 valuation	26,838.	n.a.
Total reconstructed houses	29,343	£1.115m.
Total for Private New and Reconstructed Houses	61,252	£3.084m.
Total for Local Authority Houses	39,229	£6.958m.

Source: D/F S32/1/39. State aid for housing, urban and rural.

The high level of expenditure on grants for private housing was a direct consequence of the cabinet's decision to provide additional assistance for this sector, contrary to the advice given by officials in Local Government. By 1939 the amount provided by the Exchequer in subsidies for private housing had reached £3m., almost 75 per cent of the amount spent subsidising local authority housing in urban areas. Two-thirds of expenditure on new housing grants went to rural areas, mainly to farmers, as did most of the money spent on reconstruction grants. In 1934 there were 1,200 applications awaiting inspectors' reports in County Louth alone.[86]

WOOING THE ELECTORATE: GOVERNMENT ASSISTANCE FOR PRIVATE HOUSING

The Department of Finance conducted a sustained campaign to have Exchequer grants for private housing withdrawn or at least reduced. Although Local Government had shared Finance's views on this subject in 1931, the official Department view altered after 1932. This probably reflects the differing views of Ministers Mulcahy and O'Kelly. Local Government foiled repeated efforts by Finance to curb the level of grant assistance for private houses by providing minimal information and by deliberately delaying requests to the Executive Council for additional funds until the money available was practically exhausted and the Department had entered into commitments, allegedly 'on the Minister for Local Government's personal direction', for expenditure considerably in excess of the sum available.

In 1935 Local Government approved grant payments of £200,000 without having the necessary funds. Legislation to provide additional funds was rushed through the Dáil in order to prevent Finance adding amendments which would have restricted eligibility. Finance wrote a letter of protest to McCarron, though Finance admitted that 'it may not be the officials who are at fault'. One senior official in Local Government had phoned a colleague in Finance to inform him that the Minister for Local Government's submission to the Executive Council about this Bill had been made against the wishes of his officials, who had advised him that they should first approach the Department of Finance.[87] Although the cabinet suggested that the Minister for Local Government 'should indicate his intention to consider the advisability of concentrating increasingly on the provision of houses for the working classes and reducing or withdrawing State grants and remission of rates on middle class houses',[88] this was little more than posturing.

Grants for private housing proved extremely popular with the public and they presumably brought major political dividends. As one Finance official noted in March 1934, 'judging by the unqualified approval which our Minister recently gave to the provision of enormous sums to be issued out of the Local Loans Fund for housing, it must be taken that it is Government policy to press ahead as rapidly as possible — provision of money is only a secondary consideration.' Finance argued that the demand for new middle-class houses in urban areas was rapidly being met and tried to reduce grant levels when the interest charges on Small Dwellings Acquisition Act (SDAA) loans fell.[89] Officials in Finance also claimed that grants for urban housing resulted only in higher prices and higher profits for speculative builders. Their arguments eventually bore fruit: in 1936 grants for private houses in urban areas were reduced, though grants for rural houses were unchanged and the maximum floor space of eligible urban houses was reduced from 1,250 to 800 square feet.[90] Grants were again lowered in 1937 and it was announced that grants in urban areas would end in 1938.[91] However, building contractors successfully lobbied the government to defer the ending of urban housing grants since they had been unable to complete houses because of bad weather, strikes and a shortage of skilled craftsmen.[92]

Although Local Government was conscious that priority should be given to slum-clearance schemes, the Department objected to Finance's efforts to impose a ceiling on the cost of subsidies to private housing. Hurson, secretary of Local Government, told Finance in August 1937 that 'it is quite impracticable [sic] to measure the need for State assistance to encourage the erection of new houses by private persons and public utility societies or for the reconstruction of houses by small farmers and agricultural labourers. As long as there is an apparent demand for such assistance, the Minister intends to press it.'[93]

Grants accounted for only part of the Exchequer's assistance provided for private housing. The 1899 Small Dwellings Acquisition Act permitted local authorities to provide up to 80 per cent mortgages to individuals purchasing houses costing up to £400, with repayments spread over 30 years. The maximum price of qualifying houses was increased in 1919 and 1931. By 1932 mortgages covering up to 90 per cent of the purchase price were available for houses costing up to £1,000, with repayments spread over 50 years. There appears to have been little demand for SDAA loans before 1932. Between 1922 and 31 March 1933, only 1,090 loans were advanced at a cost of £477,678, almost 92 per cent of them in municipal areas. Dublin and Cork Corporations could fund SDAA loans from stock issues, whereas smaller councils found it extremely difficult to raise the necessary capital. By 1936/37, the number of SDAA loans had risen to 5,309, costing over £2.3m..[94] Almost one-quarter had been issued in county council areas — i.e. in the countryside or in small villages — with a further 16 per cent in urban districts. Many applicants sought loans in order to take advantage of grants for new housing.

Owners of new houses also benefited from rates remission. This had been introduced under the 1924 Housing Act in order to boost the construction industry, which was then in recession. It had been due to lapse in October 1930, but was extended, first until 1933 and then to 1938. Finance opposed the measure because it provided a subsidy for housing 'well-to-do people' at a time when the government was allegedly committed to improving working-class housing. Finance also contended that rates remission reduced the income of local authorities, making it more difficult for them to repay loans. When the idea was first mooted in the 1920s, Local Government had opposed the erosion of the local tax base. By the mid-1930s, however, the Department argued that rates remission gave 'a needed stimulus to building enterprise', involved no cash outlay and brought a long-term increase in taxable capacity. Until 1938, when the cabinet ended rates remission for all buildings except houses, it applied to all new buildings and to all houses irrespective of cost or size.[95]

LOCAL AUTHORITY HOUSING: LABOURERS' COTTAGES

Labourers' cottages also absorbed substantially more Exchequer funds during the 1930s than had been originally intended. Few labourers' cottages were built during the 1920s because county councils thought that costs were too high and many councils had reached the borrowing limits of twice the rateable valuation set by the 1878 Public Health (Ireland) Act. This constraint was lifted in 1930 when borrowings for labourers' cottages were excluded from calculations of the borrowing limit, bringing them into line with urban housing.[96] Fianna Fáil was committed to retaining the maximum numbers on the land and the government depended on the support of Labour TDs, many of them representing rural labourers, so it was probably inevitable that some concessions would be granted towards labourers' housing in 1932. As already noted, the cabinet altered the 1932 Housing Act to provide a subsidy amounting to 60 per cent of loan charges for all new labourers' cottages.

Until 1923, labourers' cottages were constructed by rural district councils. However, the schemes constructed after 1932 were drawn up on a county basis. The definition of 'labourer' expanded to include almost all wage-earners living outside boroughs and urban districts and this inevitably resulted in soaring demand. Some counties deemed

226

creamery managers, who were allegedly a well-organised and 'vocalised' [*sic*] group, eligible for tenancies.[97] In theory, preference was given to families with at least one member suffering from tuberculosis, to families containing at least one person, other than parents, who was aged sixteen or over, and to those living in houses which were unfit for habitation.

Plans to build additional cottages polarised rural communities. Opposition from local farmers whose land was requisitioned was often as vocal as present-day protests against halting sites for travellers. Offaly County Council received 778 hostile representations against plans to acquire derelict cottages compulsorily and to erect 300 cottages. Farmers whose land was to be compulsorily acquired objected bitterly that local authorities invariably selected their best fields.[98] Each scheme was preceded by a departmental inquiry which determined whether or not the cottages were needed and adjudicated on objections. The medical officer of health who examined 278 dwellings in Balrothery Union in north County Dublin, found 123 to be totally unfit for habitation and a further 38 to be grossly overcrowded; in Rathdown Union in south County Dublin, 81 of the 181 cottages visited were unfit for habitation and 16 were grossly overcrowded.[99]

Labourers' cottages were also erected in villages and small towns which lacked urban councils. In County Limerick the county MOH and the local MOH disagreed publicly over the number of cottages needed in Bruff, so the county council sought outside arbitration. Communities and individuals bombarded ministers, TDs and the Department of Local Government with deputations and petitions demanding priority.[100]

County councils did not always build cottages where they were most needed. The Department complained that Sligo Board of Health had neglected small towns and villages such as Ballymote where housing conditions were described as 'absolutely deplorable and insanitary'. The Department believed that 75 houses with 224 inhabitants in the town of Ballymote should be demolished immediately. Houses in Humbert Street, Tubbercurry had 'water and sewerage coming up through kitchen floors from back yards and flowing out front doors'. Landlords had refused to fit yard gullies to connect the houses to the main sewer, or indeed to carry out any repairs, so the houses were 'most insanitary' and 'in a state of collapse'.[101] Other councils were reluctant to build cottages because of the cost to local rates. In November 1935 the North Cork Board of

Health passed a resolution expressing anxiety about the poor state of local housing, but emphasising that it would not undertake to build cottages 'until the farmer is in a better position and the labourers can afford to pay rent'.[102]

By 1939 the government had given county councils authority to sell cottages to sitting tenants. Local authorities had been demanding this concession for some time, primarily because they believed that it would relieve ratepayers of the cost of maintenance. For many years the tenants occupying labourers' cottages had been arguing that they should be given the right to buy their house and the adjoining plot of land; a right which all farmers had achieved under the Land Acts. By now many tenants were children of the original occupants, who were often theoretically ineligible for tenancy.[103] Although a commission reported on the matter in 1927, no action was taken until 1936 when the Department instructed every board of health to draw up purchase schemes covering a total of 51,492 cottages, 41,375 of them built before 1922. Tenants whose rents were in arrears were initially ineligible, though this was eased in 1937. Tenant purchase proceeded slowly. Local authorities were required to put cottages into good repair before vesting them in the tenants, and some councils had misplaced the title deeds, but a long-term process of transferring ownership had begun.

LOCAL AUTHORITY HOUSING IN TOWNS AND CITIES

The Fianna Fáil housing programme was much less successful in towns and cities, with the greatest shortcomings in the larger urban areas. This is ironic, because the 1931 legislation had been specifically designed to deal with such problems. Although most descriptions of slum housing refer to Dublin, conditions in provincial cities were equally bad. In September 1932 the Waterford MOH reported on a scarlatina epidemic in the city's slums:

> I understand the Minister for Local Government is making special offers of assistance regarding housing schemes and is pressing for such action as will abolish 'slums' and 'slum residences'. I suggest a special effort on a large scale to give effect to his appeal, provided the Sanitary Authority is satisfied there is no obstacle from a financial point of view. The clamours of tenants suffering from

serious dilapidations, insanitary conditions, or acute congestion in their quarters are growing daily louder and more frequent. The percentage of the old tenement and cottage residences of the poorer workers, which would, if alternative accommodation were available, come under condemnation as unfit for human habitation, is daily increasing. The owners of these dwellings need not be expected to make any effort to put them into a reasonably habitable condition. The only hope that I can see for these tenants lies in the erection without delay of several hundred more of the cheaper type of new Corporation cottages, and also one or two large blocks of modern tenements for these workers to whom it is a great advantage to be close to their work.[104]

Exchequer grants covered two-thirds of the cost of demolishing such property and rehousing the displaced families. However, some local authorities treated these requirements in a very cavalier manner. Although Sligo Corporation removed tenants from 92 condemned houses in its clearance scheme, only 40 houses were demolished and many of the replacement houses were allocated to other families. Forty-two of the 134 houses in Barrack Street and the Abbey quarter, which attracted slum clearance grants of 66.6 per cent, housed families who had not previously lived in condemned houses, including members of Sligo Corporation and their relatives.[105]

Sligo Corporation may have been a particularly difficult local authority, though other councils posed equally intractable problems for the Department. In 1934 Tralee Urban District Council earned the dubious distinction of building the most expensive houses subsidised, to that date, by the Department of Local Government. At a cost of £340 per house, they exceeded the original estimates and the ceiling for grant-aided housing by £40. Local Government blamed the high cost on collusion by 'a ring of builders determined to get rich quick by taking advantage of Government eagerness to provide slum dwellers with decent houses'. Several contractors which had offered lower tenders subsequently withdrew. Although the Department deferred a decision on whether to sanction grants for the scheme and delayed approval of a LLF loan, Tralee UDC instructed the contractor to begin work, presumably in order to put pressure on the Department. The contractor then complained to Local Government that he was unable to obtain payment from the UDC. He proposed downing tools and initiating legal action against the urban council. When Éamon de Valera visited Tralee, he came under considerable pressure from local politicians to sanction the housing scheme. However Finance was determined to take a definite stand against 'exorbitant building costs'. One official minuted that

> . . . the position in Local Government appears to be that houses must be built at all costs. Apparently no scheme can be definitely rejected on grounds of cost. But if schemes of this nature continue to be sanctioned loans from the LLF must continue to be made on a princely scale for some years to come regardless of the value of security or the ability of local authorities to repay.

As Finance suspected, Local Government was prepared to sanction the estimate of £340 per house, though it reduced the number of houses to be built by one-third and determined that grants and loan payments would be based on an estimated cost of £300 per house, which would force the local authority to absorb the excess. Finance rejected this compromise as offering 'only a partial solution'; although it saved 'a subhead of the LG vote from being robbed', it left the local authority 'as sheep to wolves'.[106] Although Finance sanctioned the loan to Tralee UDC 'after considerable hesitation', McElligott announced that no future loans would be granted to the council until the Minister for Finance was satisfied that the cost per house in Tralee approximated more closely to the average in similar urban district councils. To prevent a recurrence of this problem, Frank Duff proposed that Local Government should be required to obtain separate sanction from Finance for each housing scheme, though Codling felt that this should be required only in cases where the cost per house exceeded a specified figure. Local Government argued that this additional scrutiny inevitably would mean delays in sanctioning housing schemes. In April 1935, as a compromise, Finance proposed that all applications from local authorities should be examined by the Board of Works and by Finance before being sanctioned. If this took more than two weeks to complete, Local Government would be free to sanction housing tenders without waiting for Finance's approval.

Local Government countered that Finance would be duplicating work carried out by Local Government, though Finance claimed that the intention was 'to exercise some control' only in cases of excessive cost.

McCarron argued that the maximum cost per house admissible for subsidy had been fixed in order to induce local authorities to control costs, but it was never intended that sanction should be denied to all schemes costing more than that figure. Because costs had increased since 1932 when the £300 limit had been set, he proposed that all schemes costing more than £330 per house should be scrutinised by Finance, though Local Government reserved the right to justify the high cost.

This dispute was part of Finance's effort to limit the cost of housing grants to the Exchequer. Local Government was determined not to permit its detailed decisions to be scrutinised by Finance. Finance official Owen Redmond noted that up to then, July 1936, Finance had sanctioned all applications for housing loans from local authorities and would 'undoubtedly in future if we get briefly reasons which the LGD are so loath to give'.

> That Department's communications regarding housing matters generally are, more often than not, models of brevity and inadequate information; particulars frequently have to be extracted almost forcibly from them; up to a week ago they left the OPW in a fog as to what maxima [the maximum cost for local authority flats or houses which the Department of Local Government would sanction] really were. In general the LGD do not give us more than a whit of information. I am not inclined to give them an inch in the matter now under consideration.

Construction costs continued to rise and in 1937 Finance grudgingly agreed to give provisional sanction without scrutiny to all schemes costing up to £330 per house, with a higher ceiling applying for county boroughs. Since subsidies continued to be based on a maximum figure of £300 per house, this meant that local authorities were bearing a higher percentage of housing costs. The Association of Municipal Authorities lobbied for the £300 ceiling to be raised. Finance countered that such a concession would mean higher tender prices and pointed out that the Exchequer contributed four times as much as local authorities to housing expenditure, 'as much if not more than [the Exchequer] should equitably be called upon to carry'.[107] Although the £300 ceiling was not raised, except in Bray, Co. Wicklow — which was brought into line with Dublin and Dun Laoghaire — there is no evidence that the restriction had any adverse effect on house completions.

Finance also tried to ration demand for LLF loans for housing by keeping interest charges relatively high. During 1933/34, the Department rejected demands to reduce the rate of interest from 5.5 per cent to 4.5 or 4.75 per cent because it believed that a reduction would lead to a 'big efflux of capital' from the LLF and would bring forward the day when a new national loan would be needed. The department also attempted to keep the cost of repayments due from each local authority to the LLF below their subsidy from the local taxation grant. LLF repayments were deducted from local taxation grants, if repayments exceeded grants, Finance feared that councils would incur bad debts. Local authorities repeatedly demanded a reduction in interest rates, an extension in the loan repayment period from 35 to 50 or even 90 years, plus permission to refinance earlier loans which had been issued at higher rates of interest.

Officials in the Department of Local Government favoured a conservative approach to local authority debt. At a conference in March 1934, held to discuss the introduction of lower interest rates for LLF loans, McCarron emphasised that his Department had never encouraged local authorities or their officials, neither directly nor indirectly to complain of existing rates of interest and that, given the high rates of housing subsidy, 'there was no substantial argument that could be made' against the rates of interest charged. He expressed his opposition to any decision to reduce interest rates 'as the result of clamour, as to do so would only produce another variety of the theory that the State should issue all loans free of interest.' However McCarron's attitude was in direct conflict with what he termed the 'fiery cross', which Seán T. O'Kelly carried 'through the country' as he urged local authorities to expand their housing programmes and kept repeating that money would be found to solve the housing problem.[108]

THE HOUSING BOARD

As the above quotation indicates, officials of the Department of Local Government tempered their enthusiasm for the housing programme with a caution, which was somewhat at variance with O'Kelly's 'fiery cross' attitude. Although Local Government actively promoted the government's housing programme, it remained conscious of the dividing line between the responsibilities of central and local government. Much of its work involved monitoring local authorities to prevent fraud and ensuring that minimum standards were met.

While government departments drew up targets for housing and provided loans and grants, the onus for clearing slums and building new houses rested on the competence and political will of local authorities. Seán T. O'Kelly appears to have believed that a more interventionist, more pro-active agency was needed to bring about a substantial improvement in housing standards. In June 1932 he presented the Executive Council with proposals to establish a Housing Board, consisting of a full-time chairman and two part-time members. The Board would be vested with all the powers of the Minister for Local Government in relation to housing, and would assume responsibility for all aspects of housing policy, though it would be subject to a ministerial veto. Staff of Local Government's housing section would transfer to the new agency. O'Kelly's proposals would have entailed a substantial increase in central government intervention in the housing market. In addition to the powers possessed by the Department, it would have the authority to requisition land compulsorily and to encourage other agencies to supply housing. If it believed that a local authority was failing in its duty, the Board could assume its responsibility for housing. It could engage in the manufacture, sale and purchase of building materials and establish co-operatives for this purpose, subject to the consent of the Minister for Industry and Commerce.

We can get some sense of Local Government's hesitancy over the radical nature of these proposals and the potentially hostile reaction of local authorities from a note originating in the Department (there is no indication as to its author) which emphasised that it would be desirable to ensure that the Board's power to provide houses or acquire land corresponded exactly with the powers vested in local authorities in order to prevent incompetent local authorities from alleging that their failure to tackle housing problems was the result of a lack of such powers. Officials in Local Government were also wary of the proposal that the Board should manufacture building materials, though it looked more favourably on the proposal to establish co-operative societies.

When O'Kelly presented his proposals for a Housing Board to the Executive Council on 3 June 1932, he was asked to have them redrafted, though the minutes do not indicate what form the revision should take. The proposal was ultimately withdrawn,[109] which suggests that it was met with hostility. The Housing Board, established in

November 1932, was a mere shadow of the original proposal, its duties 'to examine housing conditions thoroughly, and to advise and assist the Minister in the solution of the present housing shortage'. It was chaired by Michael Colivet, a former Sinn Féin TD and an expert on rural housing, and its other members were Michael Buckley, a former Dublin Corporation engineer, and Labour senator Thomas Johnson.[110]

The few surviving records of the Housing Board[111] give some impression of its wide-ranging role. It attempted to persuade lackadaisical local authorities to embark on housing schemes,[112] examined the implications of changes in housing finance, moved to avert threatened rent strikes, and to diffuse labour relations difficulties or shortages of skilled labour and raw materials. It was inevitable that the sudden increase in housing activity would lead to bottlenecks and higher prices for both labour and materials. The requirement that Irish materials should be used in all grant-aided houses compounded such difficulties because it restricted competition. Irish-made ranges installed in most local authority houses left much to be desired and the Board received innumerable complaints about smoke-filled kitchens. Killaloe housing slates were in continuously short supply from the passage of the 1932 Housing Act. A report prepared by Senator Thomas Johnson claimed that the price of Dolphin's Barn bricks was excessive and expressed considerable concern at the cost of cast-iron goods, where the market had been cornered by the Dublin firm of Hammond Lane.[113] The Department of Industry and Commerce, which was responsible for price control, was reluctant to take action against domestic firms.[114] Housing costs rose further in 1937 when cheap cement imports ended because of the impending opening of a domestic cement plant. Local Government had steadfastly opposed the establishment of an Irish cement factory because it feared that this would mean a substantial increase in construction costs, but the urge for self-sufficiency proved triumphant.[115]

The Housing Board was the major conduit for public complaints and appears to have been an effective device for diffusing criticism while keeping O'Kelly *au fait* with potentially controversial matters. In April 1936 the Board warned O'Kelly that his correspondents from Letterkenny who had accused the Department of delaying a housing scheme 'do not appear in very good light in newspaper reports of the Council's discussion. One at least is a slum owner and his protests have a strong savour of hypocrisy.' The Board often enlisted the assistance of

Fianna Fáil deputies to put pressure on dilatory councils. In 1936 they asked the Minister for Posts and Telegraphs, Gerry Boland, to use his influence to persuade Boyle Town Commissioners to proceed with a housing programme. When the Town Commissioners in Passage West, Co. Cork refused to begin a housing scheme until they had received guarantees that the government would help establish an industry in the town which would 'enable occupants to pay the rent', the Board asked O'Kelly to enlist the support of the local Fianna Fáil *cumann*, though without effect.

Some of the Board's views were in direct conflict with the Department's, and relations between the Board and McCarron appear to have been cool. The Department sympathised with the financial problems facing Passage West Town Commissioners and refused to sanction a housing loan. The Board retorted that employment and economic conditions in the town were 'outside our province' and warned O'Kelly that failure to sanction a loan would result in 'indignant protests . . . against the alleged callousness of the Minister'. The Board appears to have been less tolerant of the failings of local authorities than the Department. Michael Colivet, the chairman, argued that claims by local authorities that there was a limit to the number of houses which they could construct at any one time 'should not lightly be admitted as a reason for accepting slow progress'; he believed that they used this 'as a cloak to cover other and less admissible objections'.

O'Kelly had been informed that Sligo Board of Health was taking no steps to build houses in towns such as Ballisodare and Ballymote. When Senator Johnson visited the area to investigate, he confirmed that the Board of Health was refusing to build additional houses until it had completed those in hand. Although contracts for an additional 70-80 cottages had been approved four years earlier, they had yet to be placed. Wrenne, the Department's housing inspector, argued that Sligo Board of Health was doing its best in the face of problems which were common to all counties along the western seaboard: lack of competent contractors, an absence of competitive tenders, a shortage of skilled tradesmen, cartels among local contractors, heavy financial burdens on the county council, and delays in arbitration awards and site acquisition. McCarron added that the problems which Wrenne had identified were insoluble and that 'flogging the horse' would only impede progress.

There was some truth in this argument. Experienced contractors were few in number along the western seaboard, and many cottages built in Kerry and Clare were seriously defective.[116] By 1936 only 100 out of a proposed 431 cottages had been completed in County Donegal because of a shortage of contractors. Although Donegal Board of Health and local authority engineers attempted to persuade contractors to tender to local authority schemes, experienced contractors preferred to tackle 'more attractive work'. The Donegal Board of Health was loath to take action against one dilatory contractor because it was not confident that it could secure a replacement. This problem was not exclusive to western areas: lack of progress in County Laois was also blamed on inefficient contractors, but local authority engineers were reluctant to enforce penalties 'for fear of frightening off contractors, believing they cannot get better'.

Colivet rejected claims by the Department and by various Boards of Health that a shortage of skilled tradesmen was delaying the housing programme. When Sligo Board of Health put this argument, Colivet cited statistics showing the numbers of unemployed carpenters and masons registered at the local employment exchange, though since his data referred to January, the trough of the housing year, his argument may be open to question.

The Board appears to have underestimated the ability of craftsmen to protect its interests and to exploit the increased bargaining power which it had acquired as a result of political pressure to build the maximum number of houses. The high cost of labour in Tralee was a major factor pushing up the cost of houses. In Newcastle West, Co. Limerick, the Woodworkers Union threatened to strike if wages were not increased. The Housing Board complained that many local authorities included 'vexatious and ambiguous clauses' in contracts, requiring all joinery to be manufactured locally. These often resulted in considerable delays. Cashel UDC, Co. Tipperary, refused a contractor permission to have joinery executed in the nearby town of Clonmel, although it was impossible to recruit sufficient local carpenters.

Colivet argued that if there were proven local shortages of labour or materials, housing should take priority over the construction of schools, cinemas or barracks, and that the Department should initiate a national building programme. He also favoured using direct labour, though he believed that the direct labour housing schemes, which were already underway in Clare and Donegal, 'should not be left to the uncoordinated efforts of individual counties'. In 1936 the Board concluded that progress in housing 'could have been far better if the

Organisation had been amended as previously suggested by us'. The Board complained of 'a kind of "drift" which allowed out of date methods to continue in an entirely new atmosphere'.

Criticism of local authorities, requests for a national building policy and recommendations for a radical reform of administration threatened to undermine the existing relationship between the Department and local authorities. In November 1935 Colivet informed McCarron that much of the Board's work had little practical value. He wished to alter the remit of the Department's inspectors so that they would make regular visits to all housing schemes in order to monitor progress and 'to check the tendency to local delays'. The Board had received numerous complaints from aggrieved customers about delays in sanctioning grants for new houses, because of a shortage of engineering staff. It recommended that the Department reorganise the engineering section in order to speed up inspections. McCarron informed Colivet that the engineering services were being reorganised, but the Department secretary appears to have ignored the Board's recommendations.

McCarron jealously guarded the Department's authority against encroachment by the Housing Board. He objected when the Board wrote to Sligo Board of Health to reprimand its members about delays in the housing programme. The Board protested to O'Kelly that the Department's objections contradicted instructions given to the Board. Colivet told O'Kelly that the Board was unhappy at proceeding 'on lines seriously at variance with what the Secretary considered essential for good conduct of the Department for which he is responsible . . . while the present system *could* cause trouble and could not be regarded as a normal course of procedure, it is necessitated by the unusual circumstances which brought about our establishment.' Colivet claimed that an examination of the Board's correspondence with the Sligo and Kerry Boards of Health would confirm that they had not interfered 'in matters of administration that should be exclusively left to the Housing Section'; in numerous instances they had steered such cases 'into the official channel'. This did not placate McCarron. At a meeting between the Board and the Department on 20 May 1936, called to discuss the Sligo affair, McCarron said that he considered it 'unfair' that the Minister should be 'burthened with a report . . . which gave an utterly wrong impression of the state of affairs and implied there was something seriously wrong with the machinery'. If the Board communicated directly with local authorities, McCarron feared that there was serious danger that such 'overlapping would undermine the authority of the Department'; all communications should go through the Department's official channel.

DUBLIN HOUSING

Because of the poor survival of files, the history of relations between the Board and the Department must remain incomplete. This dispute between two rival government agencies actually raised issues of considerable importance. Among them, how far could any national agency ensure that a particular housing programme was being carried out, given that the initiative rested with the local authorities? The problem was most conspicuous in Dublin city. Surviving government files reveal little about the city's housing programme until 1938/39. Although both the Board and the Department were aware that Dublin Corporation's housing programme was well behind target, they appear to have been reluctant to intervene. In January 1936, Senator Tom Johnson chaired a meeting on behalf of the Housing Board, which was attended by O'Kelly, McCarron, senior officials of the DLG and the Dublin city manager. When Department officials remarked on the poor rate of completion for local authority houses, the 'deficient use of the Small Dwellings Acquisition Acts and the abnormal provision of small-capacity houses', Gerald Sherlock, the city manager, attributed it to difficulties in securing finance and a shortage of building labour, though the Board rejected the latter excuse. The meeting ended inconclusively; Sherlock promised to examine the possibility of increasing the rate of construction of local authority houses, while Ted Courtney of the Department of Local Government offered his assistance in procuring skilled engineers.[117]

The meeting was not entirely fruitless. O'Kelly had expressed the opinion that the Corporation's practice of building three-roomed dwellings (73 per cent of dwellings completed between 1932 and 1937) would create a new generation of slums. In 1937 Dublin Corporation announced that in future 70 per cent of dwellings constructed would contain four rooms.[118] This was merely a detail. A six-month strike of building workers in 1937 left the Corporation housing programme further behind, while the substantial wage increases which were conceded to end the strike added to the problem.

Dublin and Cork cities financed all capital expenditure by means of stock issues because they were denied the right to borrow from the Local Loans Fund. Although all borrowings required sanction from the Department of Local Government, Dublin and Cork housing programmes appear to have been subject to less scrutiny than those of other local authorities. Despite the slow pace of construction, the housing programme placed an enormous burden on Dublin Corporation. By 31 March 1939 the Corporation's debt totalled £10.9m., 80.5 per cent of it attributable to housing. Dublin Corporation had borrowed £7.59m. to finance expenditure under the Housing Acts (i.e. slum-clearance and working-class housing) plus a further £1.23m. to finance SDAA loans. In 1934/35 the amount which Dublin Corporation provided for SDAA loans appears to have equalled the amount provided by insurance companies, the Irish Civil Service Building Society and the Property Loan and Investment Company — a mortgage agency owned by the Irish banks.[119]

These sums were being drawn from an Irish capital market which was simultaneously funding higher Exchequer borrowing, much of it also for housing, plus the stock issues floated by new protected industries.[120] When Dublin Corporation issued £650,000 in stock in September 1932, it was oversubscribed; a proposed issue of £1.35m. in February 1935 proved more difficult. On this occasion the banks underwrote the issue 'with some hesitation' because they recognised that the Corporation had already entered into 'irrevocable commitments' which would absorb most of the money. However, they warned that they were reluctant 'to undertake commitments' which might force them 'to take up substantial blocks of Stock of a virtually unmarketable nature'. The banking spokesmen added that if the issue failed to attract public support, the banks could not be expected to associate themselves with future flotations. In December 1935 Dublin Corporation raised a further £250,000 by borrowing on mortgage from the Royal Liver Friendly Society, and simultaneously arranged for the Irish Banks Standing Committee to underwrite a £1m. stock issue.[121]

By January 1938 Dublin Corporation had belatedly responded to criticism of its poor performance by announcing an ambitious five-year plan to construct an average of 2,000-2,500 dwellings per annum, mainly in the new suburbs of Crumlin and Cabra, at a cost of £10m. In 1936 and again in 1937 Dublin Corporation was forced to curtail the issue of SDAA loans because of a shortage of capital and in 1938 it took a policy decision to devote all its resources to providing working-class housing.[122] When contracts for the houses in Crumlin and Cabra had been signed, Dublin Corporation approached the banks with a request that they underwrite a £2m. public issue. The Irish Banks Standing Committee protested against 'the Corporation's policy of entering upon contractual obligations running into millions of pounds on the assumption that the Banks would provide the money', but 'in order to relieve the embarrassing situation in which the Corporation had placed itself' the Irish Banks Standing Committee had 'reluctantly agreed' to consider a short-dated stock issue of £1.5m.. This issue was deferred, at the government's request, because it clashed with the £10m. national loan which had been issued to meet the cost of the 1938 Anglo-Irish financial settlement. It was again deferred when the Munich crisis destabilised the capital markets.

In June 1938 the banks agreed to take up a direct issue of £500,000 to avert the threatened layoff of workers employed on Corporation housing schemes,[123] but Dublin Corporation rejected the terms on offer and attempted instead to launch a stock issue in both London and Dublin, despite the well-publicised objections in the *Report of the Banking Commission* to foreign borrowings. Seán T. O'Kelly refused to grant Dublin Corporation permission to borrow on the London market and cited the success of the £10m. National Loan, which was oversubscribed, as evidence that 'credit-worthy borrowers could have their requirements fulfilled in the local market'. Seán MacEntee, the Minister for Finance, refused to meet Dublin Corporation, pleading pressure of parliamentary business.[124] The banks eventually took £750,000 of Corporation stock, and a further £750,000 was placed with insurance companies. By January 1939, however, Dublin Corporation needed a further £2m., mainly to finance housing contracts which had already been signed, and an additional £840,000 for the Poulaphouca Water scheme and other non-housing projects. When the banks refused to underwrite yet another issue, Local Government brought the Corporation's capital needs before cabinet, apparently for the first time.[125] The Department delayed circulating the memorandum, which supported the Corporation's case, until the last possible moment, in 'flagrant breach of Cabinet instructions', presumably in an effort to pre-empt criticism from the Department of Finance.

If this was the intention, it proved an utter failure. The cabinet deferred a decision pending observations from Finance. It eventually decided that Local Government and Finance should consider whether it was advisable to bring pressure on the banks to provide the necessary capital. If this option was excluded, they should consider advancing money from the Local Loans Fund. This would have marked a major break with precedent, and the file contains the puzzling note that 'No record need be made in the minutes at this stage'. In February 1939, perhaps with a view to exerting pressure on the government, Dublin Corporation passed a resolution requesting the Minister for Local Government to institute an inquiry into the housing shortage in the state 'with prior and special application to all aspects of the matter in the City of Dublin'. O'Kelly readily approved this request. In the meantime it was decided that the Minister for Finance would underwrite the proposed Corporation loan of £1.5m. jointly with the banks.

When Dublin Corporation was notified of this decision, it requested that the issue be increased to £2.5m.. Local Government recommended a limit of £1.75m., pending the report of the housing inquiry — expected by August 1939.[126] The banks agreed to underwrite the issue of £1.5m., on the understanding that the Corporation would not enter into any further commitments without making prior financial arrangements. Meanwhile, to prevent the Corporation's housing programme being halted, the government reluctantly agreed to lend it £250,000 from the Local Loans Fund — the first such loan.[127] Despite having a government guarantee and offering favourable subscription terms, the 1939 issue flopped because of the unstable international situation; the public subscribed only £500,000.

The report of the Dublin Housing Inquiry, which was chaired by Michael Colivet, provided a comprehensive assessment of Corporation housing output during the years 1932-39. Although it built an average of 1,273 houses and flats a year from 1933 to 1939, more than three times the rate for the years 1922-33, this was only half the annual target of 2,500. Between 1932 and 1938 private contractors and public utility societies built an additional 7,051 houses, and all but 872 of these received state grants. Superficially, housing standards within the city appear to have improved. In 1936, 10.6 per cent of Dublin families of four or more persons occupied one-room tenements, compared with 12 per cent in 1911 and 13.2 per cent in 1926, but this is largely a statistical mirage because the city boundaries had been extended in

1930 to include middle-class suburbs such as Rathmines and Pembroke. By March 1939, the inquiry found that 21,000 dwellings were needed.[128]

The report conceded that while statistics suggested that the Corporation had succeeded only in preventing a 'further deterioration', housing standards had risen, as had the state of public health and hygiene. The pace of house construction rose considerably in 1938 and 1939. Between January 1938 and April 1939, 3,854 Corporation houses had been completed or were under construction.

Although the 1931 and 1932 Housing Acts specifically targeted slum dwellers, Corporation tenants continued to be drawn from families with relatively high incomes. The Dublin Housing Inquiry concluded that ability to pay rent appeared to have remained 'a primary consideration governing allocation', despite statutory obligations to rehouse families made homeless as a result of slum-clearance.

TABLE 5.3

A comparison between the weekly income of Dublin Corporation tenants and that of a sample of working-class families

	Survey Group	Corporation Tenants
under £1	20.0%	5.2%
£1-£2	25.5%	9.3%
£2-£3	21.4%	22.7%
£3-£4	17.6%	34.2%
£5 +	6.7%	11.4%

Source: Dublin Housing Inquiry

Many new flats and houses were allocated to larger families, as had been the case before 1914;[129] some probably had multiple incomes. Demand for Corporation housing far outstripped supply and the requirement to accommodate tenants displaced by slum-clearance may have deterred Dublin Corporation from demolishing tenement properties. Schemes completed between 1932 and 1939 attracted an average subsidy of 38.5 per cent, at a time when slum-clearance schemes were eligible for 66.6 per cent. This reflected the fact that most Dublin houses and flats cost more than the maximum price on which subsidies were calculated: £400 per unit for slum-clearance, £450 for other houses and £500 for flats, but also that many Corporation houses were not built under slum-clearance schemes.

A newspaper advertisement in 1933 inviting applications for 500 houses in Cabra brought 8,659 replies. Of these, 758 came from tubercular families living in one room; in 1,290 cases three or more adults lived in one room; 6,783 applicant families lived in one room or in a basement. The majority of applicants could not afford to pay weekly rents of six or seven shillings (30-35p).[130] The report of the Dublin Housing Inquiry concluded that for a 'very large percentage' of the Dublin working classes 'it is impossible under the present renting system for the Corporation to house them, and that the financial consequences to the Corporation of an attempt to house only the remainder was such as to render the task impracticable'. In 1939 over 2,000 families living in Corporation housing were receiving out-door relief or home assistance; many had accumulated heavy rent arrears.[131] The inquiry suggested that Dublin Corporation should give priority to introducing differential rents. However a deputation of city councillors, which had studied the differential rents scheme in Leeds, had rejected it as inapplicable to Dublin, despite the fact that Cork had operated differential rents since 1935.

Cork Corporation appears to have been much more successful at rehousing its poor than Dublin: 22.2 per cent of Cork tenants had incomes under £1; 57.5 per cent under £2. The Dublin inquiry cited approvingly the comment of Philip Monahan, Cork city manager, that municipal authorities showed a tendency to select tenants on the same principles as if they were private property-owners — ability to pay. Monahan believed that a family's claim to free or cheap housing equalled its claim to free medical care.[132]

Because the inquiry was prompted by Dublin Corporation's inability to finance its housing programme, it devoted considerable attention to the cost of housing. In 1938 it cost £800 to erect a three-room flat in the city centre, compared with £616 for a four-room cottage in the suburbs.[133] Cottages appear to have offered better value. Construction costs in Dublin were much higher than in British cities as a result of high wages, low output, temporary shortages of skilled tradesmen (especially plasterers) and the apparent rigging of contracts.

On several occasions in 1937 and 1938, Dublin Corporation received only two tenders for large contracts. One firm had built 38.5 per cent of Corporation houses, three accounted for 82.7 per cent. W.C. Dwyer, a former city commissioner, suggested that costs had fallen when non-local contractors were employed. In 1939, Dublin skilled building workers earned 1/11 (9.5p) per hour, compared with 1/7 to 1/9 (8-9p) in Britain, while unskilled workers earned 1/5 (7p) per hour against 1/2 to 1/3 (6-6.5p). Productivity of craftsmen was low, and labour costs *for the work described* were estimated to be 41.7 per cent to 91.6 per cent above London figures and 32.8 per cent to 96.3 per cent higher than in Belfast, though the productivity of unskilled workers equalled or exceeded that in Britain. Irish social legislation, notably the 1936 Conditions of Employment Act, was estimated to have added 7 per cent to labour costs.

There appears to have been little scope for saving money by reducing specifications for Corporation housing. The high standards introduced at Marino, a Dublin suburb, which included a low density per acre, imaginative layout of the site and attention to housing design,[134] had been subjected to 'a ruthless reduction of the specifications' by the Department of Local Government. W.C. Dwyer dismissed most of the houses built during the 1930s 'somewhat scornfully' as 'Box Houses'. While further savings were possible by changing specifications, Dwyer believed that it would be 'quite unfair to ask the Corporation or Local Government Architects to risk their personal reputations by recommending such experiments'.[135]

Dublin Corporation and the Department both believed that the solution lay in negotiating competitive building tenders, long-term wage agreements and the removal of restrictive practices in return for guaranteed employment. In April 1939 de Valera contacted the Dublin Trades Council to arrange a meeting with representatives of the Building Trades Unions. He informed them that Dublin Corporation's housing programme was in danger of collapse as a result of high building costs and that government assistance for a five-year programme was dependent on securing a reduction. When asked by Leo Crawford of the Dublin Operative Plasterers' Trade Society if 'anything tangible' should be considered, de Valera indicated no, though he reassured Thomas Dunne, who represented the city's carpenters, that labour would not be only group required to make sacrifices.[136]

If higher productivity remained an important issue, attention increasingly focused on how to provide Dublin Corporation with the estimated £13-£14m. it would need for housing alone in the coming five years. Cork Corporation needed smaller, though still sizeable, amounts.[137] Local Government recommended that both Corporations should be given access to the Local Loans Fund, as did evidence given to the 1939 inquiry by the Irish Banks' Standing Committee in private session. By the late 1930s, the cost of providing capital for housing had become a major headache for the Exchequer. The *Report of the Commission on Banking, Currency and Credit*, published in 1938, laid considerable emphasis on the dangers resulting from the rapid expansion of dead-weight debt, much of it contracted by local authorities. While the report strikes an unduly shrill tone and can be read as an attack by the Department of Finance on a government which had manifestly failed to heed its strictures, it would be foolish to disregard the report's conclusion that the capital cost of housing and other social investment was putting considerable pressure on the Irish capital market. It recommended that steps be taken to reduce the current level of dead-weight debt by establishing a Debt Investment Council, with responsibility for monitoring public debt. The Council, which would include a representative of the Department of Local Government, would be responsible for controlling and scrutinising all public capital expenditure, including expenditure financed by the Road Fund and the operations of the Local Loans Fund. The Commission sought to replace existing subsidies for local authority housing, which were based on a percentage of loan charges, by a flat rate subsidy financed from the current budget. The subsidy would vary, depending on the fiscal position. This would have meant a significant reduction in the level of housing subsidy provided by the Exchequer; instead of the open-ended guaranteed subsidy, there would be a finite sum available, which would vary annually.

The majority report of the Banking Commission was of the opinion that the Department of Finance should play a more active role in sanctioning all borrowings by local authorities because the current scale of borrowings made it necessary to take account of the overall monetary and financial situation. It also recommended that Local Government prepare a detailed estimate of the annual borrowing requirements of all local authorities. These proposals embodied the views of current and past senior officials of the Department of Finance, notably the Commission's chairman, Joseph Brennan, and the secretary of the Department of Finance, J.J. McElligott. Finance's determination to gain greater control of government spending had major implications for a high-spending department such as Local Government.

In a reservation to the majority report, James Hurson, secretary of the Department of Local Government and a member of the Banking Commission, condemned as 'too drastic' the proposal to replace loan subsidies with finite lump-sum support funded out of the current Budget. He estimated that an annual sum of £1.5m. would have to be provided in the Budget if the housing crisis was to be met. He pleaded that the proposed restrictions on incurring future dead-weight debt be deferred until March 1943 when the housing programme was expected to be completed.[138]

Although Finance and the majority report of the Banking Commission were attempting to reduce public-sector borrowings for non-productive purposes such as housing, the government was under pressure to provide funds for both local authority and private housing on more generous terms. In evidence to the Banking Commission given in 1935, the Association of Municipal Authorities of Ireland and the General Council of County Councils demanded that housing loans be provided at an interest rate of 3 per cent by some new agency, such as a central bank or a statutory corporation which would handle local authority stock issues, in a manner similar to the Industrial Credit Company.

The Dublin and District House-Builders Association asked the government to assist in establishing a building society or some other mortgage institution to finance house purchase.[139] The Association had been impressed by the expansion of building societies in England and had commissioned George Boys, secretary of the Institute of Building Societies in England, to report on whether or not it was feasible to encourage similar developments in Ireland. The Association wished the government either to provide seed capital to promote the formation of an Irish building society or establish a subsidiary of the state-owned Agricultural Credit Corporation to provide capital for housing. Either scheme could, the Association suggested, provide an alternative to SDAA loans.[140]

When the Dublin and District House-Builders Association sent another memorandum to the government in 1938, the situation had deteriorated sharply. Dublin Corporation had ceased to provide SDAA loans, the Royal Liver Friendly Society had temporarily closed its house purchase facilities, and there was a long waiting list at the Irish Civil Service Building Society. The Association proposed the establishment of an Irish National Building Society; the building industry would provide the initial share capital of £15,000 and would be represented on its board. It requested a government guarantee of up to £500,000 plus income tax concessions, to encourage depositors; if these were provided, it was envisaged that the new society would provide an additional £250,000 a year for housing finance. The Association also wished to encourage British building societies to invest in Ireland; it had established contact with one large society, which had expressed interest, though it might be precluded from doing business in Ireland under current British legislation. If this difficulty could be surmounted, the Association sought an assurance that British societies could avail of any tax concessions provided for Saorstát societies and that restrictions imposed on foreign companies by the Control of Manufactures Acts would not apply.[141] Whether or not there was any prospect of British building societies operating in Ireland is unclear. Irish society was extremely hostile towards foreign investment. By 1938/39 the uncertain political conditions would have militated against such developments. The Association may have raised the possibility in an effort to persuade the government to establish an Irish, or state-controlled, agency.

Local Government was unenthusiastic about proposals for greater government involvement in financing private housing. The Department preferred to improve the supply of capital from existing institutions such as building societies, and to persuade agencies such as banks or insurance companies to play a more active role in providing finance for housing. Between 1939 and 1941 lengthy negotiations took place among Local Government, building societies, insurance companies and the Irish Banks Standing Committee on the possibility of providing more capital for private housing. In the event, the 1942 legislation dealing with building societies, which was handled by Industry and Commerce, envisaged only modest changes. Banks would be permitted to make loans to building societies 'in approved cases', on foot of guarantees of repayment given by local authorities in Dublin and Dun Laoghaire; building societies would be permitted to increase borrowing from the existing two-thirds of the amount secured to the society by members' mortgages, to a maximum of three-quarters, and societies would be permitted to accept collateral security on houses that it was proposed to mortgage.[142] The Act reflected the more conservative views expressed by the Irish Civil Service Building Society and the Irish Banks Standing Committee, rather than more ambitious demands of the Dublin House-Builders Association or the Educational Building Society. By 1941, however, most of Europe was at war, supplies of building materials were virtually unobtainable and the availability of house mortgages must have seemed of purely academic interest.

CONCLUSIONS

There are several features of note in the evolution of housing policy up to 1939. Although it began with a concern to improve housing standards for rural labourers and the urban working class, from 1924 a substantial proportion of government funds went to property-owners, such as farmers and the urban middle class, and this trend became more pronounced during the 1930s, despite the expressed intentions of the 1931 and 1932 Acts to give priority to clearing urban slums. Dublin city, the housing black-spot, showed the least improvement. While some responsibility rested with Dublin Corporation and with Dublin contractors and building craftsmen, the government and DLG officials appear to have ignored the city's lack of progress until the late 1930s when Dublin Corporation was experiencing serious difficulties in raising capital.

By 1939 the sums needed to fund house construction threatened to pose long-term difficulties for the Exchequer: if the war briefly removed them, by bringing house-building to a halt, they re-emerged in the post-Emergency years. The shift of expenditure on housing from tenants to owner-occupiers and from cities to rural areas is yet another instance where a particular policy was manipulated to meet national social and political ends. Industrial policy is a further example.[143] In both instances, the resulting compromises were politically popular, at the cost of disadvantaging specific groups — in this case urban slum-dwellers.

CHAPTER SIX

'PLATO'S CAVE'? THE EMERGENCY YEARS

Most accounts of life in Ireland during the years of World War II have presented a picture of a stagnant, rather complacent, country, largely unaffected by the historic changes taking place elsewhere.[1] While neutrality enabled Ireland to avoid many difficult decisions, it is untrue to assume that the country was insulated from changes which were taking place elsewhere. Social and economic issues came to occupy a much more prominent place in Irish political life, though the hardship resulting from wet turf or dark bread appears trivial when contrasted with the injuries or loss of life and home experienced by civilians in states at war.

Nevertheless, the incidence of tuberculosis in Ireland rose and the health, or ill-health, of children, gave cause for concern. High levels of emigration during the Emergency years meant that rural Ireland seemed to lack sufficient workers to harvest crops and to save the turf. Based on the precedent of World War I, there was widespread fear that peace would herald an economic recession in Britain which would lead to many Irish emigrants returning home, so the government tried to plan a major public investment programme, which would provide them with jobs. Contact with Britain meant that politicians and the public were aware of the Beveridge proposals for a welfare state and this in turn brought pressure for better services in Ireland. One outcome was the decision to establish separate Departments of Health and Social Welfare. This happened in January 1947, leaving the Department of Local Government and Public Health to continue as the Department of Local Government.

The Emergency years take their name from the 1939 Emergency Powers Act which enabled the government to act swiftly, by making an emergency order without the need for specific legislation or for detailed scrutiny by the Dáil. Although the 1940 County Management Act was not a response to special wartime conditions, it also resulted in a significant transfer of authority from elected councillors to the executive. The prospective appointment of county managers, combined with the specific socio-economic problems of rural Ireland, sparked a major debate into the need to restore, or more correctly to create, some new form of community organisation which would redress the growth of centralised bureaucracy and preserve the fragile fabric of rural society.

When the Emergency was declared, the Minister for Industry and Commerce, Seán Lemass, moved to the new Department of Supplies and the Co-ordination of Defensive Measures; Seán MacEntee became Minister for Industry and Commerce and was succeeded as Minister for Finance by Seán T. O'Kelly. P.J. Ruttledge became Minister for Local Government. Ruttledge appears to have made little impression on the Custom House. In August 1941 he resigned from the government because of ill-health and was succeeded by Seán MacEntee, who was a much more forceful personality. The flavour of MacEntee's temperament and ministerial style is evident from a letter he wrote to James Hurson, the Department secretary, on 18 May 1942. MacEntee had just discovered that officials in his Department had replied to a memorandum from Seán Lemass concerning proposed restrictions on emigration to Britain, without first consulting him. He insisted that the observations be immediately withdrawn and, in order to avoid a similar situation in the future, demanded that:

1. All proposals to be immediately referred to my private office and as a matter of urgency brought to my personal attention, so that I may be aware at the earliest possible moment of proposals touching on my responsibility as a member of the Government or affecting the work of this Department.
2. After I have seen them, the documents are to be issued to the general secretariat of the department for written observations and advice.
3. When fully examined by all sections affected, written observations and recommendations to be submitted for my consideration.
4. Where proposals affecting those sections of the Department under the immediate control of a Parliamentary Secretary, the originating Department should be asked for a second copy — to be

sent to the private office of the Parliamentary Secretary for observations and attention. The observations of officers of sections in question may then be submitted to me, either through the Parliamentary Secretary's private office, or through my office as the Parliamentary Secretary may find convenient.

5. Only when the procedure here outlined has been followed and views of the Department formulated to my approval and satisfaction may any observations be offered on a proposal which another Minister intends to submit for consideration by Government.[2]

EMERGENCY MEASURES

In November 1945, shortly after the end of the Emergency, the Department of the Taoiseach suggested that a book should be prepared setting out the steps to be taken in the event of any future emergency, 'with a view to securing the public safety'. In response, Tom Barrington, who was to become first director of the Institute of Public Administration and one of the country's leading authorities on local government,[3] listed the major issues which had concerned the Department of Local Government during the Emergency years: turf production by local authorities and the acquisition and supply of timber for fuel, plus the distribution of cheap fuel; organising air raid precautions in co-operation with the Department of Defence; providing cooked meals at emergency centres; supplying children's footwear and providing special assistance to various categories of welfare recipients; controlling public transport and the driving licences and petrol supplies of private citizens; controlling the wages of local authority employees; and assuming the authority to fix a new rate where a council had set too low a figure.[4] This list is radically different from any which might have been made during peacetime and it gives some indication of the scale of change in the Department's interests.

Despite the passing of the Emergency Powers Act on 3 September 1939, the government appears to have been complacent about the threat to national security. The interdepartmental committee on emergency measures, which included a representative of Local Government, concentrated on cutting public spending and, until a German invasion of Britain and/or Ireland appeared imminent in the summer of 1940, there seems to have been little planning for possible invasion or a state of war. On 9 July 1940 the interdepartmental committee for emergency measures drafted proposals for the appointment of regional and county commissioners, who would assume control in the event of invasion or a break-down in civil administration.

The country was divided into eight regions which would be governed by regional commissioners, all senior civil servants. The Dublin, Meath, Wicklow and Kildare region — arguably the most important from a national point of view — would come under the authority of John Collins, then a principal officer in the Department and a future secretary. The majority of county commissioners, who were expected to 'meet any contingencies that may arise', subject to the direction of the regional commissioner, were county secretaries, who were chosen because they were familiar with the area; the remainder were secretaries of boards of health, county commissioners (where a local authority had been abolished), a county registrar and an inspector of taxes. If contact was lost with the regional commissioner, the county commissioner was authorised to assume full control of the gardaí unless the area was under military control. He would also exercise 'all the powers of all Departments of the central Government and of every local authority'. Commissioners had power to purchase and commandeer food, fuel, transport and accommodation as part of the remit to maintain essential services and to prevent distress.[5]

In October 1940 Local Government asked the cabinet to draw up guidelines on how local authorities and their staff should act in the event of a successful invasion. Should they carry out their normal duties subject to the direction of the invader, or should they adopt a policy of non-co-operation? The Cabinet Committee on Emergency Problems deferred making a decision on this occasion and again in January 1941.[6] Seán T. O'Kelly expressed the view that public servants in occupied territory should discharge their normal duties as far as possible and should play an active role in rehousing displaced inhabitants and organising communal feeding, but they should be expressly prohibited from co-operating in any activities that would be of military value to the enemy: such as acquiring supplies for troops. The government asked External Affairs for information on the international law and practice applying in such circumstances and, in June 1941, a modified version of the O'Kelly approach was drafted which would be issued to local authorities in the event of such an emergency.[7]

Despite these deliberations, there appears to have been a relaxed attitude towards the threat of war. In the Custom House, W. McGowan, the chief air raid prevention officer, was perturbed 'by the failure of the staff generally to appreciate to the proper extent the danger to their lives'. McGowan pointed out that, in the event of hostilities, the Custom House would present 'an attractive target area': on Dublin port beside a very important rail link and between two rail termini. Staff needed thorough training in air-raid precautions. Although McGowan had 'endeavoured to push arrangements whereby the building might be made as safe as possible, except for partial blacking out nothing has been done.' He believed that 'the fact that junior staffs comprise a high proportion of women' made it more difficult to apprise them of the danger.[8] The interdepartmental committee on emergency matters showed a similar lack of urgency, despite the fact that they were all men. In late October 1940 it made a decision in principle that the government should leave Dublin in the event of an invasion. Since Dublin was the sole area where a county commissioner had not been appointed, this raised the question of who would assume control. It was decided that Ruttledge would nominate a commissioner 'without public announcement' — no doubt lest it precipitate panic.[9] Responsibility for the city was eventually assigned to John Collins, the regional commissioner.[10]

On 30 September 1940, Hurson informed the committee that Local Government had instructed all local authorities to draw up contingency plans to shut off gas supplies and provide alternative water supplies in the event of air raids or invasion. If damaged water mains had to be shut down, communities would have to rely on water carts and disused wells, though most of these were contaminated. The committee asked Industry and Commerce to report on the availability of water carts. Dublin would be supplied with Liffey water in the event of damage to the Stillorgan reservoir, Cork with water pumped from the river Lee. There were plans to chlorinate the emergency Dublin supply, but no such luxury appears to have been proposed for the citizens of Cork. If the water system had suffered major damage, it would have been difficult to restore supplies because of shortages of pipes, valves and other equipment; only Bray and Cobh UDCs had adequate stocks of spares.

The Department of Defence proposed to establish a reserve unit of engineers, which would be called up for service in the event of an emergency. They would wear uniform and take responsibility for electricity and other essential services. A file in the Taoiseach's Department reported that both the Department of Local Government and local authorities 'had accepted the arrangements as reasonable',[11] a bland comment which conceals the tensions which existed between the defence forces and the local government service.

In July 1940, Ian Bloomer, the Department's assistant chief engineering adviser, reported on a meeting he had held with county surveyors from Louth and Monaghan to discuss co-operation with the defence forces. Both men and their staffs had been approached by army personnel (apparently without prior contact with the Department) with a view to their joining the Second Line Volunteers. The army sought to incorporate the technical and road staff of local authorities into the proposed volunteer force, while local authority clerks would act as headquarters staff. Volunteers would come under military discipline and be liable to transfer to any part of the country. The army officer had requested the county surveyors to persuade county council foremen, gangers and workmen to enlist in the new service. A similar approach had been made to the county surveyor in Wicklow. Both the Monaghan and Cavan county surveyors sought direction from the Department on how to respond.

Although the county councils had resolved 'not to stand in the way' of staff who wished to volunteer, the Cavan county surveyor was less enthusiastic. He returned from holidays to discover that the military had commandeered his only compressor set, forcing him to abandon all road works because he could no longer supply broken stone. The army had also recruited two assistant surveyors into the engineering corps and had removed all road signs, including danger signs, without authority. Bloomer argued that local services and normal staff discipline would be severely disrupted if surveyors and other key staff joined the Volunteers. Active co-operation with the defence forces could be achieved 'without going to such extremes'. He was particularly anxious to ensure that local authority staff would be required to work only in their own districts.

Local Government was also determined to curb the army's enthusiasm for mining bridges which carried water and sewerage pipes or gas and electricity cables. Blowing up the main road bridge at Dundalk would leave the town without water. By July 1940, however, the army had yet to discuss its mining and demolition plans with Local Government.[12] Defence and Local Government did not reach an agreement on their respective responsibilities for repairing roads damaged by bombing or exceptional wartime traffic until July 1942, by which time the threat of invasion had receded. In the event of invasion, local authorities would assist in repairing and reopening damaged roads and restoring them 'to trafficable conditions' only as requested by military authorities. A request from the Department of Defence for authority to requisition the services of local authority staff and equipment to prepare bridges for demolition, in the event of a major emergency, was rejected[13] — a victory for Local Government.

Plans to evacuate 70,000 children from Dublin and Dun Laoghaire were first drafted in the summer of 1940. By 1942 there were contingency plans to evacuate up to 160,000 people, almost half the area's population, in the event of air attack.[14] Some evacuees would be moved as far away as County Leitrim. Local Government designated the evacuation routes; other roads would be closed to public access by gardaí and the military reserve. In February 1941 county surveyors were ordered to remove overhanging branches from roadside trees to ensure the safe passage of double-decker buses. Some weeks later the county surveyor in Longford drew the Department's attention to the existence of low railway bridges on several designated roads and suggested alternative routes. Low bridges in other areas also forced changes.[15]

Local Government came under pressure to make provision for communal feeding in Dublin city in order to alleviate the hardship resulting from fuel shortages. Industry and Commerce supported these proposals because the department believed that they might avert demands for an increase in Unemployment Assistance; the Irish Housewives Association campaigned for the communal feeding of schoolchildren. Although the Dublin and Cork city managers were not enthusiastic, plans were drawn up for the establishment of field kitchens and the Department investigated the possibility of using canteen facilities in large firms such as Guinness. In February 1942, however, Hurson told the Department of Finance that present conditions did not warrant introducing communal kitchens, though the position might change. He believed that

> . . . there are strong moral and social reasons for refraining as far as possible from interfering even in very difficult circumstances with

the normal family regime of the people. These reasons appear to be lost sight of [sic] by certain persons who are prepared to take any advantage of any conditions, emergency or otherwise, to advance their own political and social conceptions. While Government is fully alive to distress which may exist and has taken such steps as are in its power to relieve it, its policy has been based on the principle that there will be as little interference as possible with family life and custom and accordingly it will only be under the compulsion of very exceptional circumstances such as a more drastic curtailment of fuel supplies . . . that it will sanction communal supply of food. Should the necessity arise meals should be supplied for consumption by the family in the home so as to preserve so far as possible family responsibilities as they obtain at present. No encouragement therefore should be given to a proposal by which any of the children's ordinary meals in the family home should be replaced by meals provided in the school or elsewhere.[16]

The Emergency Committee decided that plans for communal feeding would be activated only if significant numbers were 'rendered homeless by enemy action', or 'in the event of hostilities breaking out'.[17]

DUBLIN BOMBINGS

The most acute test of the emergency services came in 1941 when bombs were dropped on Dublin's South Circular Road and on the North Strand. Thirty-four people were killed and ninety wounded in the bombing of the North Strand area in May 1941 and 300 houses were damaged or destroyed.[18] Following the bombing of the South Circular Road in January 1941, in other words *before* the bombing of the North Strand, Local Government drew up guidelines, though by the time they were issued, Dublin Corporation had already settled claims with most owners. Owners and local authorities were permitted to spend a maximum of £130 on damaged property without seeking detailed prior approval from the Department. This was less than the cost of repairing many houses on the South Circular Road, and Dublin Corporation feared that if this figure was rigidly enforced in the North Strand, 'there would be complaints from North Strand people that they were not being treated as well as others'.

The Department gave Dublin Corporation authority to exceed this limit, provided that the average cost per house was not greater than £130. Despite this concession, rebuilding proceeded slowly. Slaters were in short supply because most of them were working in England and by September 1941 local property-owners were protesting at the delay. Many damaged buildings were old and had been in poor condition before the bombs fell. Dublin Corporation was reluctant to assume sole responsibility for renovating the most decrepit houses and many owners were unable to make any contribution towards the cost.

Some were unwilling to reach a settlement until the 1941 Neutrality (War Damage to Property) Act had been enacted. This gave local authorities power to purchase and demolish war-damaged buildings and to enter such buildings to carry out essential repairs before purchase had been completed. Officials hoped that the Act would 'tend to lessen the need for action by a local authority in the direction of carrying out any repairs to injured buildings' and that it would help Dublin Corporation to reject demands from people who insisted that the Corporation paint or repaper their premises. One year after the bombs were dropped, many claims had not been settled. Yet when Local Government and Finance reassessed their experiences, they concluded that existing procedures were adequate and that the government should continue to limit the power of local authorities to carry out permanent repairs and should maintain a limit on expenditure per house, despite the ensuing delays.[19] Some of these problems are reminiscent of the delays in rebuilding O'Connell Street after the 1916 Rising and the civil war; there is no evidence that the civil service had learned from that experience.

FIRE SERVICES

Before 1939 fire services attracted little attention within the Department of Local Government, perhaps because, as one 1939 file admitted, they were 'not at present dealt with by any particular section in the Department'. Applications from urban areas for powers to appoint fire officers were considered by the local administration section; the public health section dealt with applications from rural areas.[20] Local authorities were not required to provide fire services, and nobody was responsible for promoting training or for extending the service. A departmental tribunal, established following a fire in Dublin's Pearse Street in 1936, in which three firemen died, merely emphasised the need for better training and recommended that the government institute regular inspections of fire brigades.[21]

The 1940 Fire Brigades Act, which was passed because of the threat of air raids, required local authorities for the first time either to establish a fire brigade or, subject to ministerial approval, to contract with another body to provide this service. Local authorities were also required to provide fire hydrants and to ensure that adequate supplies of water were available at sufficient pressure. By December 1940 courses on fire-fighting had been organised under the 1939 Air Raid Precautions Act; it was intended that trainees would instruct other members of their unit. The Department decided to concentrate on improving fire services in towns with over 4,000 inhabitants, but when Britain curtailed exports to Ireland early in 1941, it proved difficult to acquire necessary equipment. In March 1942 the Department pointed out that many local authorities had failed to meet the requirements of the 1940 Act, though in most cases the shortage of trained fire-fighters, for instance, this could not be blamed on wartime difficulties.[22]

The inadequacy of the fire service was highlighted in a tragic manner by the death of thirty-five girls and one adult in a fire at St Joseph's Orphanage in Cavan Town in February 1943. The fire broke out at night when the children were in bed; all lights had been turned off and fire escape routes were locked. The premises had been *re*certified by the Department of Education in 1933, which required the orphanage to comply with various rules and regulations, including compulsory fire drill, at least once every three months.

A tribunal appointed to investigate the Cavan fire made various recommendations relating to emergency exits, staff training and the provision of fire-fighting equipment in all institutions which were in receipt of public funds, but its recommendations went much further. Having concluded that it was impossible 'owing to financial and other reasons, for a small centre . . . to provide an efficient service', it recommended that small fire services be merged and that mobile fire appliances, staffed by full-time officers, should be sited in larger centres of population. These would tackle all fires within a fifteen-mile radius. Smaller centres would have a service capable of operating within a ten-mile radius. Although the 1940 Act had permitted local authorities to group together to provide joint fire services, few had availed of these powers. The tribunal deduced that the 'conflicting interests of the various authorities probably need a more specific type of legislation to reconcile them'.[23]

These recommendations seem to have been ignored. In November 1945 when wartime air raid precautions were under review, the government decided that existing arrangements for protecting the civilian population should be maintained and the Department of Defence should determine whether ARP fire-fighting equipment should be retained or sold. However, the government subsequently referred the matter to an interdepartmental committee, with the 'very strong opinion' that both departments should develop plans for the establishment of 'proper fire-fighting services throughout the country', as a precaution against any future emergency and for peacetime purposes. They also impressed on the Minister for Local Government that the necessary staff to carry this out should be added to his Department, which suggests that Local Government was seen as responsible for the failure to develop an adequate fire service.[24]

The Cavan fire raised the question of cross-border co-operation. The assistance provided by Dublin fire crews and teams from other parts of the Irish Free State to bomb-damaged Belfast in April 1941 is regularly cited as a warm-hearted, if isolated, incident in cross-border co-operation during the Emergency years, though Robert Fisk notes that there is no reference to this event in the archives of either government.[25] After the Cavan fire, the Stormont government suggested that Local Government call on the services of Northern Ireland fire-fighters if a similar disaster occurred along the border. Local Government proposed that the Garda Síochána be given authority to summon Northern Ireland units and on 26 May 1943 representatives from the Departments of Defence and Local Government met to consider the offer. As a result of objections voiced by the Department of Defence, it was decided that:

> As circumstances might arise which would make it undesirable to summon assistance from outside the state, any arrangements made arising out of the Northern offer should provide for centralised control by some Government Department, preferably the Department of Defence.

Although the Department of Defence claimed that it would be on 24-hour standby to authorise such a request, the probable delay in obtaining approval would have seriously reduced the value of summoning fire crews from Northern Ireland. National sensibilities and territorial possessiveness appear to have been given precedence over the need to save life and property.[26]

LOCAL AUTHORITY FINANCES

The Emergency was an unhappy time for Irish local authorities. Their autonomy appeared to be threatened by various government programmes and they faced considerable financial difficulties. Although by 1944 the cost-of-living index had risen by 70 per cent above its 1938 level, rateable valuations were static: 104.5 in 1939 (1933=100) and 104.4 in 1944, having dipped slightly during the intervening years. Rateable income increased by 27 per cent between 1938 and 1944, with all the increase coming from higher rates poundages. Exchequer grants also rose by much less than the rate of inflation — by a mere 7 per cent — with the result that local authority income fell from 3.7 per cent of national income in 1938 to 3.0 per cent in 1944. Local authority borrowings also showed little growth, because shortages of supplies halted most capital expenditure.[27] One possible benefit from the relatively small rise in rates bills was the improvement in collection relative to the 1930s. In 1941, the worst wartime year, 71 per cent of rates were collected and this had risen to 87 and 89 per cent by 1943 and 1944.

Councils cut back on existing services in order to balance their books. Although in 1940 Local Government piously exhorted local authorities to pay attention to 'the conservation of existing resources and the elimination of waste', the Department became concerned at the 'drastic retrenchments' introduced in social services and in public health and the treatment of tuberculosis.[28] In 1944 Roscommon County Council reduced the estimate that the county manager submitted for repairing main roads by almost 50 per cent, in protest against high rates. In a break with precedent, the Department did not dissolve the council, but it did introduce an Emergency Powers Order permitting councillors to vote an additional estimate.[29]

Higher prices meant that local authorities came under considerable pressure to grant wage and salary increases or special cost-of-living allowances to employees. Although the government had previously

260

been reluctant to interfere unduly in this matter, lest it would be forced to concede national pay scales for local authority posts, it now feared that any concessions might constitute a precedent for other workers. In November 1939, while introducing a supplementary budget, Seán T. O'Kelly, now Minister for Finance, announced that the government would oppose any wage increases which compensated for the increased cost of living.[30]

This issue came to a head in January 1940, when Dublin Corporation workers demanded a weekly wage increase of 8 shillings (40p) to compensate for higher prices. The Dublin city manager regarded the request as 'justified'. Local Government was initially prepared to approve the manager's decision to introduce a cost of living bonus, but when the matter was referred to cabinet, the government decided to make this a test of its tough policy on wages. The city manager was informed that no increase should be granted 'without full regard to prevailing rates in comparable employment outside the Corporation' and the consequences for general wage rates. The cabinet decided to take steps to maintain essential services in the event of a strike, though the city manager was not informed of this. A minute, penned by Maurice Moynihan (secretary to the government), dated 26 January, noted that 'at the close of the discussion I spoke to the Minister for Local Government who agreed that no formal record of the discussion need be made in the Government minutes. I gathered from him that he would deal with the matter himself, bearing in mind the views he had heard expressed in the course of the discussion.'[31]

Dublin Corporation offered an increase of 2 shillings (10p) a week, based on the rise in the cost of living index, with a promise of further increases or decreases of sixpence (2.5p) for every ten-point change in the index.[32] When Corporation workers went on strike on 1 March, Industry and Commerce Minister Seán MacEntee responded by drawing up stringent provisions, based on the British 1920 Emergency Powers Act and the 1927 Trades Disputes and Trades Union Act,[33] restricting the trade-union rights of civil servants and local authority workers. Workers engaged in essential services who failed to return to work would suffer loss of employment and pension benefits and their jobs would be given to others. Although the cabinet rejected the proposals as excessive, Patrick Ruttledge, Minister for Local Government and Public Health, was asked to do everything in his power to encourage the Dublin city manager to adopt 'an unyielding attitude' towards the strikers.[34] The

261

men returned to work on 20 March without obtaining further concessions.[35]

Despite the government's victory in this case, it did not mean an end to labour disputes. Workers employed on special employment schemes in County Mayo went on strike, demanding higher pay, early in 1940. This campaign was allegedly sparked by men who had returned from well-paid jobs in England and who now refused to work on local schemes unless they were employed as gangers. They were denied Unemployment Assistance.[36] This dispute revealed the limits of the authority of the Minister for Local Government. He could sanction or withhold grants for various schemes, and this gave him some indirect control over wages paid on grant-aided schemes, but he could not determine the wages paid by local authorities. When the Minister issued a circular letter to all local authorities on 8 August 1940, ordering that wages be frozen at the figure paid on 1 September 1939, the Labour Party attacked the circular as a departure from precedent. Ministers for Local Government had previously argued that wages were determined by the local authority and had invoked this argument to oppose demands for uniform rates of pay for all local authority workers. Several local authorities voted wage increases in defiance of the Department's circular.[37] Some counties paid different wage rates for similar work, depending on whether or not the scheme was grant-aided from central funds. Thus in April 1941 road workers in County Carlow received 32/6 (£1.625) per week if paid out of the council's ordinary account and 30 shillings (£1.50) if the work was funded by a government grant; similar discrepancies occurred in Counties Cork, Tipperary and Waterford.[38]

When the salaries of civil servants were frozen in May 1940, by fixing the cost of living bonus, Finance was determined to include the staff of local authorities; it claimed that 'the whole intention underlying the Government's decision regarding bonus stabilisation would be nullified' if local authority employees were exempt. This was done in the 1940 Cost of Living Act.[39] Local authority workers whose pay remained beyond ministerial control were caught by Emergency Powers Order (No. 56) of 12 November 1940, which required local authorities to obtain ministerial consent before granting increases of remuneration to officers and employees whose pay was not already subject to ministerial restrictions. Staff numbers could not be increased without ministerial authority.[40] The only increases permitted were in the wages of road labourers and turf workers. These were also subject to Departmental sanction.[41]

TURF PRODUCTION

The role played by the Department of Local Government and by county councils in ensuring an adequate supply of turf during the Emergency has not been recognised. While complaints about wet and poor quality turf were often justified, living conditions would have been much more miserable if it had not been available. Between the years 1941 and 1946, local authorities produced 2.75m. tons of turf for sale, and were indirectly involved in the production of a further 1m. tons from bogs leased to private producers.[42]

Despite Ireland's high dependence on imported fuel — coal imports averaged 2.5m. tons in the years before 1939, and over 40m. gallons of petrol were imported annually — the government did not take steps to boost turf output until June 1940, when the Minister for Local Government issued a circular letter warning local authorities of prospective shortages in supplies of imported fuel and urging them to make every effort to promote the use of turf.

County councils were asked to investigate local turf supplies, to encourage turf production and to lay in stocks for their own needs. Since this circular arrived too late to influence the 1940 turf harvest, it is unlikely to have had an impact. However the matter became urgent when the British government cut Irish fuel imports in the early months of 1941, in an effort to induce Ireland to abandon its neutrality.[43] On 25 March 1941 the government decided that every county should increase its turf production to the maximum extent 'as an act of state policy'. The state would undertake to buy all turf of marketable quality, whether produced by private individuals or by local authorities. An Emergency Powers Order gave councils power to acquire bogs and to produce turf for sale. Alternatively, they could assist private producers by improving bog roads and by draining and developing bogs. The government established an interdepartmental turf executive and Hugo Flinn, parliamentary secretary to the Minister for Finance, assumed the title of turf controller. County surveyors would act as his 'executive organisation'. Tod Andrews, who had been recruited by Seán Lemass in 1932 to develop Irish bogs, claims that the idea of using the local authorities and their officials in the national turf campaign originated with Hugo Flinn and with John Collins.[44] Most county councils responded readily to the call to boost turf output; in County Monaghan, an area not usually associated with turf, the council employed 500 turf-cutters during the summer of 1941. County council workers produced approximately 40 per cent of the estimated 1m. tons of turf which were cut in 1941.

It was originally intended that turf-producing counties would become self-sufficient in fuel, while other areas would be supplied by imports; this would reduce the need to transport turf over long distances. By May 1941, when coal stocks proved to be smaller than anticipated, it became apparent that Dublin and other parts of Leinster would have to be supplied with turf, if a fuel famine was to be avoided. However, the logistical problems proved daunting. Much of the turf cut in 1941 was still in producers' hands by the spring of 1942 and county councils faced substantial losses. Local Government recommended that the government assume responsibility for any part of a county council overdraft which was attributable to unsold turf, most of it unusable, which councils had produced in good faith.[45]

Emergency turf production was supervised by the turf executive, which operated from the Office of Public Works under the control of Hugo Flinn. At the beginning of every year, each county surveyor was ordered to produce a specific quantity of turf. Although the turf executive was theoretically based in the Office of Public Works, the fact that Ted Courtney, chief engineering adviser of the Department of Local Government, was its chairman, meant that Local Government was involved in all aspects of turf production. This is confirmed by the existence of files containing bog by bog reports, which were compiled by the Department's engineering inspectors.[46] In April 1942 the turf executive asked for Local Government's assistance in controlling costs. In August, Courtney detailed the steps which were being taken to ensure high quality turf, though he insisted that county councils must be paid for all turf produced in good faith, irrespective of quality, to which both the Departments of Finance and Supplies assented.

Hugo Flinn's death early in 1943 prompted Local Government to attempt to limit the OPW's involvement in turf production. In February the Department proposed that the turf executive should continue to set targets for individual counties, but that responsibility for overseeing production and transport arrangements should rest with Local

Government. The Department also wanted to have responsibility for allocating bog development grants and grants for improving and constructing bog roads, subject to Finance approval. Although Seán Moylan, the new turf controller, objected to these proposals, Local Government was supported by John Leydon, secretary of the Department of Supplies.[47]

This did not mark the end of interdepartmental disputes over turf. The national turf quota, which was set first by the Department of Supplies and after 1943 by Industry and Commerce, tended to be unrealistically high and both departments ignored demands from Local Government that more realistic, i.e. lower, targets be established. Although local authorities supplied Fuel Importers Ltd — the company which controlled the distribution of turf in non-turf areas — with 360,000 tons during the 1941 season, much of the turf was of poor quality. Supplies to Fuel Importers Ltd fell to 279,000 in 1942/43 and 237,000 tons in 1943/44.

Responsibility for turf production involved Local Government in issues — rural labour supply, controls on migration and setting wage rates — which went far beyond the Department's traditional concerns. Local authority surveyors, overseers, gangers and labourers were taken off road work and reassigned to turf production and, although some workers would have been otherwise unemployed because of a shortage of materials for road-making, the new duties brought increased responsibility. It proved difficult to supervise bog workers scattered over a wide area. In County Clare in 1941, 105 bogs were being worked and the assistant surveyors were committed to visiting each bog on every second day. In 1942 the county reduced the number of bogs worked to a manageable 45, partly to reduce the administrative workload, but also because some bogs proved too inaccessible and others produced poor-quality turf. Checking pay sheets and costings involved assistant surveyors in lengthy office work, in addition to time spent on the bogs. One assistant surveyor in the Castlerea area of County Roscommon was responsible for supervising 80 gangs, each employing an average of 26 workers. In County Sligo the 73-year-old county surveyor tendered his resignation because of the pressure of extra work.

The numbers employed on turf production were substantially greater than the regular complement of road workers. At the peak of the 1941 turf harvest, Roscommon County Council employed 1,780 men. By 1942, several counties were reporting shortages of labourers, owing to heavy emigration to England and the competing demands of compulsory tillage and private turf contractors. Many Monaghan turf workers emigrated to Northern Ireland. The Roscommon county surveyor expected to have 300 fewer men available than in the previous year. Sligo County Council employed a maximum of 962 workers in June 1942, compared with 1,344 in 1941. By June 1942 Kilkenny County Council could muster only 75 per cent of its labour requirements, and the surveyor was forced to hire women and boys for spreading and footing turf. Women were also employed in County Clare at 4 shillings (20p) a day, against 6/4 (32p) for men, 3 shillings (15p) for boys and 6 shillings (30p) for an ass and cart, or 5 shillings (25p) for an ass and basket.

Labour shortages persisted in some counties, despite a regulation in May 1942 that men living in rural areas who had previously worked in agriculture, turf or road construction were prohibited from emigrating until after 30 September. The order did not apply to traditional migrant labourers. According to the Mayo county surveyor, the restrictions were being 'evaded wholesale' in his area as gardaí issued passports without referring to the Labour Exchange; in some areas whole families had migrated, leaving him with 'any amount of banks available which were cut on two occasions and no men to cut'. A survey carried out in 1943 of 260 men who had worked on bogs in the Maam Cross area of Connemara in the summer of 1941 revealed that 85 had gone to Britain, 80 were working in Ireland on tillage or for private turf contractors, 40 had worked for the council earlier in the season, 20 were working as farm labourers, 20 had migrated to Turf Development Board labour camps in the midlands, and 15 were idle because they could not get bicycle tyres. Hundreds of other idle workers could not be hired because of transport problems.

Labour supplies were heavily dependent on wage rates. Wages were determined by county managers, who were in an invidious position. Labourers and some councillors pressed for higher wages, but a wage increase threatened 'unsettlement in the agricultural labour market' and led to accusations from larger farmers that workers were being attracted away from agricultural work. Bog workers in north Cork went on strike in 1942 when a wage increase granted by the county council was rescinded. A three-week strike in County Offaly in 1942 was blamed on the 'disturbing influence of town workers' and the high wages available in England. Workers in County Roscommon objected to working overtime unless tea, which was in scarce supply, was provided.[48] In 1943 the minimum wage paid to turf workers was increased from 33 to 38 shillings (£1.65 to £1.90) per week or 2 shillings (10p) per week above the minimum agricultural wage. When the minimum agricultural wage rose to £2 in December 1943, the Department voiced concern that any further increase in turf workers' wages would mean a permanent increase in the cost of local authority services because road workers and turf workers received equal pay. Officials proposed that wages on council turf schemes should be kept one shilling (5p) below agricultural wages, with their 48-hour week deemed to be equivalent to a 54-hour week in agriculture, though county managers were free to make individual decisions.[49]

Officials in Local Government and Industry and Commerce hoped to solve the labour shortage instead by imposing more effective restrictions on emigration from turf-producing areas. In County Donegal, from where many labourers had migrated to Scotland or Northern Ireland, the county surveyor suggested that all applicants for travel permits should be required to work on the bogs for a specified period. He conceded that it would prove difficult to select the 300-400 turf workers needed from thousands of applicants. People could emigrate to Northern Ireland without obtaining an exit permit, although they could be penalised on their return by being refused Unemployment Assistance. However, Seán MacEntee, now Minister for Local Government, announced that he was opposed to 'further restrictions being placed on the natural right of persons to sell their labour where it will give maximum return'.[50] He believed that it was possible to produce more turf without imposing stringent restrictions on emigrants. MacEntee suggested that the restrictions on emigration, which applied to all labourers who had worked on turf, actually reduced the supply of workers. Of 442 men employed in the summer of 1941 on the Attymon bog (Co. Galway), only 184 were available for work in 1943, though just 10 had emigrated to Britain; 24 had died or were otherwise employed. The majority remained in the area but were unwilling to work on bogs. MacEntee interpreted this as evidence of 'conscious or sub-conscious opposition to attempts to compel them to work there' (by the Labour Exchange) and the

> . . . knowledge that if they have the mischance ever to take a job
> on the bog they will be debarred from any prospect of doing better

for themselves and their families by seeking employment in Great Britain.

The Minister proposed that the Department concentrate on increasing turf production in the counties with the greatest potential — Mayo, Galway, Roscommon, Donegal and Kerry — and that efforts be made to reduce waste and increase productivity. Average output per man in Mayo was considerably higher than in Galway because Mayo workers were employed either on a contract basis, with teams committed to delivering a specified quantity to the council, or on piece work. MacEntee urged that higher wages, preferably incorporating piece-rates, should be offered and that the Turf Development Board turf camps in midland counties should be closed. Most of the workers came from western counties and should return there unless it was proven that midland bogs were more productive. MacEntee also discovered that hundreds of suitable workers were unemployed because of lack of transport. Their bicycle tyres were worn out and replacements were unobtainable. He proposed to supply new tyres to workers who gave a commitment to work a full season on the bogs.

MacEntee's attempt to reorganise the turf programme appears to have been only partially effective. There is no evidence that workers were supplied with bicycle tyres. However, in March 1944 a circular letter encouraged local authorities to introduce piece rates or bonus schemes for turf workers.[51] Piece rates eventually became the norm in Counties Galway, Mayo and Donegal; they were also introduced in parts of Wicklow and Tipperary, which had a tradition of turf-cutting, and workers were capable of high earnings.[52]

Labour shortages eased in 1944 because British authorities restricted movement between Britain and Ireland in order to reduce the danger of security leaks in the run up to the D-Day landings. In May 1944 Local Government reported that labour supplies had 'improved considerably' since February, though there were still insufficient turf workers in Cavan, Clare, north Cork, Kildare, Kilkenny, Laois, Leitrim, Meath, Sligo, Tipperary North and Westmeath. Officials feared that the improvement would be short-lived.[53]

Production was cut back considerably in 1945, since peace appeared imminent. Although Local Government had supervised turf production without complaint, it regarded the task as peripheral to the Department's main interests. In December 1945, when the British authorities announced that supplies of tar and bitumen would soon be available, local authority engineers became keen to transfer labourers to repairing neglected roads. However Industry and Commerce was determined to maintain a high level of turf output, much to the chagrin of Local Government and county council engineering staff. In January 1946 Local Government pressed Industry and Commerce to reduce the 1946 target for local authority turf from 400,000 to 300,000 tons. The Department pointed out that turf production was an exceptional duty which had caused county councils to neglect their statutory obligation of road maintenance. The peak season for tar-spraying coincided with the turf harvest, and the main turf-producing counties had insufficient labour to carry out both operations. County councils were eager to take advantage of the restoration of Road Fund grants. Although Local Government officials privately believed that they were 'up against a brick wall so far as the turf target is concerned', and Industry and Commerce initially claimed that there was sufficient labour to cut turf and repair roads, they eventually agreed to reduce the 1946 target from 400,000 to 350,000 tons.[54] In fact over 430,000 tons was cut.

Fuel was extremely scarce during the winter of 1946/47 because bad weather made it difficult to save sufficient turf, and rural labourers and hard-pressed council officials were diverted from the bogs into emergency efforts to save the grain harvest. With post-war Britain facing acute fuel shortages, there was no immediate prospect of increased imports of coal, and in the spring of 1947 Industry and Commerce demanded that the local authority turf target be set at 600,000 tons, an increase of 175 per cent over 1946. As evidence of the crisis, county engineers were summoned to Dublin to be addressed by the Taoiseach, Éamon de Valera, who emphasised that the current fuel emergency could be met only by increased production from county councils and he ordered them to abandon road improvements. Despite the Taoiseach's exhortations and his emotional reference to a potential fuel famine and the ringing refrain that 'famine is not a nice word to Irish ears', most county engineers were pessimistic about achieving the target.

Morale among council workers was low; many had been lured away by private producers with offers of bread and sugar rations.[55] In early May turf-cutting was running at one-third of its May 1946 rate and officials argued that it was necessary to offer higher wages. Wages of turf workers had remained above those of agricultural labourers until 1946 when agricultural wages were increased. The wartime differential in favour of turf was restored in the summer of 1947, despite considerable opposition from the Departments of Agriculture, Lands, Finance and Industry and Commerce. The last was concerned about the impact on fuel prices, apparently oblivious of the fact that without a wage increase there was no hope of producing a fraction of the necessary turf.[56]

By July 1947 Local Government believed that, 'even with the best endeavours', councils were unlikely to produce more than 330,000 tons, little more than half the target. Private producers offered the only hope and Local Government suggested that a special propaganda slogan, 'Ten Tons More or anything suitable', should be publicised on Radio Éireann.[57] Disastrous weather meant a slow start to the 1947 turf campaign and, despite considerable efforts in the summer and early autumn, local authorities produced only 420,000 tons.

The wartime experience left the Department of Local Government profoundly sceptical about the nation's ability to become more reliant on turf. In December 1945, when the government proposed to introduce various incentives to encourage turf production in post-war years — including a requirement that all new local authority houses or houses built with state grants in turf-producing areas should be equipped with a turf-burning range — Erskine Childers, parliamentary secretary in the Department,[58] responded wearily: 'I trust moreover that it is not too optimistically stated, in view of our past experiences with turf'.[59] Great was the enthusiasm in the Custom House and in county council offices when responsibility for turf passed to the new state body, Bord na Móna, in 1948.

Public expenditure and the Emergency

The Department of Finance reacted to the outbreak of war in 1939 by submitting a memorandum to government, dated 9 September, which emphasised the urgent need to decide 'what services are to be dispensed with or cut down'. It proposed that the cabinet establish an interdepartmental committee, chaired by Hugo Flinn, to review existing services and report on what economies would prove feasible. Accepting this proposal, the cabinet laid particular emphasis on a phrase in the Finance memorandum that

. . . so far as rural areas may be affected, the interests of the

Exchequer must be of primary concern, in view of the special measures which will be taken to stimulate agricultural production, but that in urban areas those State services which provide in one way or another for the unemployed should not be unduly restricted.

Committee members, nominated by Finance, included representatives of Local Government (John Garvin), the Office of Public Works, Industry and Commerce, Lands, Agriculture and Finance.[60] Pending the committee's report, Finance emphasised that it was 'most desirable that no undertaking should be given as to the extent to which it will be possible to continue expenditure by the State on public works, buildings, maintenance and so on'. No new loans were sanctioned from the Local Loans Fund.[61] The committee published three reports, the first dealing with lands, and the third with miscellaneous items, such as telephone development.

Local Government was primarily affected by the second report, which reviewed expenditure on unemployment assistance, employment schemes, housing and the Local Loans Fund. It recommended reducing the duration of unemployment assistance in rural areas from seven to four months a year; cutting the sum available for employment schemes; ending housing grants for private persons and Small Dwellings Acquisition Acts loans, reducing the level of Exchequer subsidy for local authority housing, and imposing a ceiling of £1.2m. a year on housing loans from the Local Loans Fund for the years 1940-42. If no restriction was imposed, the committee estimated that demand would run at an annual rate of £2.5m.. Since existing commitments plus loans, which were in the process of being sanctioned, came to £2.75m., this effectively meant a freeze on all new housing loans. A similar freeze applied to new loans for public health works and hospitals. Although the proposals were endorsed by all members of the committee, John Garvin dissented from the recommendation to reduce the Exchequer subsidy for local authority housing.[62]

This report appeared to signal a new era of austerity. In fact, as Fanning notes, there turned out to be a substantial 'gap between what Finance and the Economy Committee deemed economically necessary and what the government deemed politically unacceptable'.[63] The cabinet rejected the proposal to reduce the duration of unemployment assistance and urged the committee to give special consideration to the 'black areas', former congested districts where most recipients of Unemployment Assistance lived, on the grounds that the committee had concluded that these areas would gain little from a wartime agricultural boom. Most of the other proposed economies were also ignored; unemployment had begun to rise after the outbreak of war and the government feared that expenditure cuts would make things worse. de Valera's reluctance to cut public expenditure may have been strengthened by a memorandum, dated 25 September 1939, from his economic adviser, Professor Timothy Smiddy, which argued that building activity should be maintained at normal levels, even if it proved necessary to devise substitutes for imported products. Smiddy argued:

> There is an alternative of maintaining as far as possible our present economic activities . . . and alternatives of cutting down all schemes of public works, use of motor cars etc. The latter alternative will lead to considerable unemployment, with increase of doles on a colossal scale. Such doles lead to demoralisation while the idleness they involve will beget social and political trouble.

Smiddy claimed that the cuts in public investment which had been introduced in Britain were designed to release labour for the army and for munitions plants. Ireland, in contrast, was faced with the need to find employment 'for an abnormal reserve of labour'. He suggested that it was 'better economics and more prudent statesmanship to maintain as far as possible our present economic activities, even at the cost of unbalancing the budget. Otherwise it might be much more seriously unbalanced at a later stage.'[64]

Yet, despite repeated commitments by various ministers to maintaining or boosting public expenditure, it fell as a proportion of the Gross National Product between 1939 and 1945, though expenditure in monetary terms rose from £48m. to £64m.. Lee regards this as 'a truly remarkable record' — which is not meant as a compliment.[65] Revenue from rates fell from 3.7 per cent of national income in 1938 to 3.0 per cent by 1944, and Exchequer payments to local authorities rose by only 7 per cent in current prices, which was much below the rate of inflation.[66] This decline can largely be explained by materials shortages which halted housing and other programmes. Road expenditure also fell as a result of reduced income from motor taxation.

272

HOUSE CONSTRUCTION AND THE EMERGENCY

By 1939 many county councils and urban councils had almost completed the ten-year housing programmes which had been drawn up in 1932. The main exception was Dublin city, though even that black-spot was being tackled. The nervous state of financial markets following the outbreak of war made it much more difficult for Dublin Corporation to finance its housing programme. In December 1939 only 58 per cent of the government's National Loan was subscribed.[67] On 5 October the newly established temporary Dublin area joint council for the building industry requested a meeting with de Valera to discuss the problems posed by the outbreak of war. Employment in construction had declined sharply and the council suggested that the government initiate an elaborate programme of investment in housing, hospitals and roads.

In the meantime the council sought reassurances that capital would continue to be available and that supplies of imported raw materials would be maintained at existing prices. The delegation also suggested that a representative advisory body should be established to help formulate government policy for the building industry. Local Government firmly rejected this proposal. The Department did not foresee any immediate difficulty in obtaining supplies of building materials and urged that the Dublin housing programme should continue at the planned construction rate, with funds being diverted from the Irish Hospitals' Trust (the Sweepstake) and the Corporation being given access to the Local Loans Fund. Rural housing activity should be 'drastically curtailed' because most targets had been achieved and the Department saw little prospect of providing government funds for private housing. Nor did it envisage any increase in government investment on roads and similar schemes.

Seán Lemass, now Minister for Supplies, argued that government expenditure on construction should be increased in order to maintain employment. According to Lemass, 'the proper course is to determine on a programme and then proceed to carry it out in full if the supply of materials permits'. He believed that pressure on supplies would be eased because of an inevitable decline in private construction during the war. The cabinet appointed a committee consisting of Seán T. O'Kelly (now Minister for Finance), Seán MacEntee (Industry and Commerce), Seán Lemass and Patrick Ruttledge (Local Government) to consider the position of the building industry in the light of the

Emergency and 'to make recommendations to the government as to measures best calculated to ensure the continuance of building activities, with special reference to reducing building costs and to the desirability of affording the maximum employment practicable in the circumstances.' John Leydon, secretary of the Department of Supplies, gave the committee an extremely optimistic assessment about future supplies. He pointed out that many essential items were manufactured in Ireland and 'practically all' the raw materials were available from domestic sources. The most important import was timber, though the country also depended on imports of pig iron, pig lead, iron rods, asbestos, heavy copper shells for drawing into tubes or pipes, some semi-finished parts for electrical equipment and baths, sanitary fittings and locks. Despite this lengthy list, Leydon claimed that there was 'no serious danger of an immediate shortage of building materials'. Ireland's timber supplies from the Baltic countries had traditionally been purchased in Britain. Timber was not strictly controlled in Britain and the possibility of a 'serious curtailment of supplies' could not be ruled out, but the Department was attempting to arrange for direct imports and bulk purchase. Most other imports originated in Britain and no immediate shortages were envisaged.

Local Government does not appear to have been represented at a meeting of the government and employer and worker representatives of the Dublin building industry, which took place on 20 December 1939. Although the government promised to issue a 'public statement with a view to the restoration of confidence', no statement followed, probably because Lemass and MacEntee were at loggerheads over the appropriate policy. Lemass proposed extending government housing subsidies in both the public and private sectors in order to maintain employment. MacEntee wished to cut government support 'so as to put the industry on a more realistic economic basis'.

Although MacEntee's position gained credibility when the housing tenders submitted to Dublin Corporation in the winter of 1939 turned out to be surprisingly low, Lemass triumphed. On 19 January 1940 the government decided that the Department of Finance, in consultation with Local Government, should examine proposals to finance private sector housing and that consideration should be given to reducing the rate of interest charged on LLF loans for housing to the lowest figure which did not entail a loss to the Exchequer.[68] Irish newspapers gave considerable publicity to a speech by Lemass some days later in which he emphasised that 'unemployment must end' and that the government might take special action to sustain activity in the building industry. Lemass also criticised the Irish banks for adopting an unduly conservative attitude towards investment, and during the winter of 1939/40 de Valera and senior cabinet ministers met the Irish Banks Standing Committee on a number of occasions in an effort to persuade it to provide additional capital for housing, particularly in Dublin.[69]

At a further meeting between the Taoiseach and the National Council of the Building Industry, early in 1940, the government gave a commitment to maintain the current level of state expenditure on construction and to reduce the rate of interest charged on LLF loans. de Valera also promised to consider extending grants for new private houses beyond the April 1940 deadline and to provide additional facilities for house purchase. Building industry representatives were warned, however, that these proposals were dependent on the industry's 'co-operation' and on their making 'reciprocal efforts' to reduce costs and increase output. For its part, the industry suggested that government departments such as Local Government, Education and the OPW should prepare a shelf of construction schemes which would be ranked on merit and carried out or deferred 'according as the graph of building incidence fluctuates'. The similarities between this proposal and a 1937 proposal from the International Labour Organisation rang alarm bells in the Department of Finance, which claimed that it had only one purpose, 'in effect to throw all responsibility for the continued employment of all building operatives on the Government and to ensure the profits and dividends to the employing contractors, irrespective of the resources of the Government'.[70]

It was becoming increasingly unlikely that it would be possible to boost output in the construction industry, even if the political will to do so existed. By February 1940 supplies of some building materials were becoming scarce and Local Government proposed to extend the deadline for completing houses which had applied for grants.[71] On 17 June 1940 de Valera expressed fears that young men aged 19-22 who were drawing dole and who 'might be given money from other sources' (presumably the republican movement) 'were an element of danger' and reiterated his commitment to maintaining Dublin Corporation's building operations as far as supplies permitted.[72] Despite this statement, there is no evidence that Dublin Corporation was given priority in the allocation of supplies.

House construction gradually came to a halt during the first half of 1941 as the restrictions imposed by Britain on its exports to Ireland began to take effect. In March 1941 Dublin Corporation's architect drafted a grim contingency plan in the event of a cessation of imports. Shortages of coal and petrol would bring cement and brick manufacture to a halt and would make it difficult to move supplies to building sites. Costs would rise as productivity fell since mechanical concrete mixers would have to be abandoned because of lack of fuel. De Valera believed that sufficient supplies were available to complete all houses under construction, though shortages of copper sheeting and tubing meant that new houses would be without a hot water supply until the Emergency ended. If houses could not be completed, Dublin Corporation proposed that as many as possible be made 'occupiable', i.e. with doors, windows, fireplaces and ironmongery. Steel windows would be used so that scarce timber could be conserved for door frames; consideration would be given to substituting lead for copper piping and to using concrete staircases and pre-cast concrete products in place of wood. Carpenters would be unemployed. Acute petrol shortages might make it impossible to hold even to these arrangements.[73]

Dublin Corporation continued to acquire land and to process compulsory purchase orders in anticipation of the end of the Emergency. By 1943 it had drawn up plans for 4,771 houses and 669 flats and had confirmed compulsory purchase orders which would provide sites for a further 4,654 dwellings. By this stage the list of unavailable supplies included fabricated steel, copper tubing (though lead piping was being substituted), galvanised tiles, slating nails, weather bars, cisterns, manhole covers, hot water tanks, curtain rails, roofing felt. Supplies of other items, including nails, iron railings and gates and clear glass, were doubtful. Supplies of doors and metal windows were heavily restricted, as were pitch, tar and electrical wiring, while the only baths available were of inferior quality.[74]

Most water and sewerage schemes were also halted because of lack of supplies, and local authority borrowings fell sharply, though the actual figures seriously understate the fall in capital expenditure since they take no account of wartime inflation. In February 1943 the Department of Local Government estimated that building costs had risen by 43 per cent in rural areas, by 36 per cent in urban areas and by 26 per cent in Dublin city.[75]

Table 6.1

Loans to local authorities from all sources, including LLF

	Housing	Other*
1938/39	£4.156m.	£451,275
1939/40	£1.379m.	£513,739
1940/41	£1.720m.	£430,330
1941/42	£1.375m.	£602,009
1942/43	£1,059m.	£448,461
1943/44	£1.606m.	£156,187
1944/45	£0.767m.	£254,002
1945/46	£1.693m.	£261,188
1946/47	£0.115m.	£424,293

* including loans for vocational education, county homes and asylums, as well as sanitary services.

Source: Annual Reports of the Department of Local Government and Public Health.

TABLE 6.2

Number of houses erected and reconstructed with state aid, 1939/47

	Local Authority	Private	Total
1939/40	5,383	6,845	12,228
1940/41	3,432	4,992	8,424
1941/42	3,447	2,895	6,342
1942/43	1,771	1,894	3,665
1943/44	1,686	794	2,480
1944/45	1,084	567	1,651
1945/46	697	616	1,313
1946/47	619	1,146	1,765

Source: Annual Reports of the Department of Local Government and Public Health.

BACK TO THE BICYCLE AND THE HORSE

Expenditure on roads suffered both from lack of supplies and a shortage of funds, as income accruing to the Road Fund fell sharply. In August 1939 there were 73,813 licensed motor vehicles; by 1943 this had fallen to 26,188. Private motoring became almost a memory: in 1945 there were only 7,845 licensed private cars. Petrol for private motoring disappeared at the beginning of 1941 and on 31 January 1941 the cabinet agreed in principle to refund all road taxes paid by private motorists for that year[76] and to make monthly vehicle licenses available. Road Fund income fell until 1942/43, when it was less than half of its pre-war level. Revenue disbursed to local authorities fell from £792,659 in 1939/40 to £398,462 in 1940/41 and £236,015 in 1942/43. Improvement grants were suspended in 1940/41.[77]

Some money was provided for improving access roads to bogs, or via employment schemes, though expenditure and employment under the latter heading fell from £641,000 in 1939/40 to £355,000 by 1942/43. In 1939 local authority road works carried out by direct labour employed a monthly average of 16,000 men, with additional labourers employed on contract works and relief schemes. From 1942 to 1944 monthly employment averaged 12,600, though many labourers appear to have been engaged in activities which were little more than job-creation schemes.

Road Traffic Acts were amended to take account of emergency conditions. An Emergency Powers Order in March 1942 raised the legal maximum number of passengers which could be carried on large public service vehicles. Another Emergency Powers Order in November 1943 made it easier to obtain a conviction for the theft of bicycles — an essential means of wartime transport.[78] In order to prolong the life of rubber tyres, the maximum speed limit was reduced to 20 mph for double-decker buses, 25 mph for single-deck buses and 30 mph for other vehicles.[79] The shortage of motor fuel brought a revival of horse-drawn traffic, whose drivers demanded that road surfaces and gradients should cater to the needs of horses, rather than motor traffic.[80]

Most road materials were unavailable, despite the fact that the majority were produced in Ireland.[81] Bitumen, used to seal road surfaces, became unobtainable on the outbreak of war when the British government cut off supplies. Domestic output of tar provided for only 20 per cent of normal needs; the remainder had to be imported from

Britain. Even if tar and bitumen were available, there was a shortage of steel drums available to transport them, though it was hoped that these could be supplied by the Hawlbowline steel works.[82] Engineers were keen to use concrete, which was available as a road surface, though shortages of explosives, cement, petrol and rubber limited almost all road improvement work.[83]

PLANNING FOR EMPLOYMENT AND THE EMERGENCY

Wartime unemployment was very much an urban problem. Although cuts in public expenditure on roads and housing meant a loss of jobs in rural areas, the expansion in tillage farming and in turf-cutting more than filled the gap. Unemployment and short-time working rose sharply in Dublin and other industrial centres during 1941 as restrictions on British exports to Ireland left factories without raw materials and spare parts, adding to the problems posed by the decline in construction. The government initially feared that unemployment could reach 400,000 and that six out of seven of the new Dublin unemployed would be industrial workers. The outcome was less acute than had been feared, in large part because of emigration, but this was not apparent in 1941. The special employment schemes which were developed during the 1930s had little impact in Dublin or other large urban centres. The conventional wisdom suggested that it was difficult to find projects in Dublin which did not require either machinery or large quantities of materials, except site clearance for housing. Local Government hoped that the 1940 Derelict Sites Act, giving local authorities power to acquire derelict urban sites compulsorily with a view to clearing them, would provide urban authorities with a shelf of suitable projects.[84]

The organisation of wartime relief works raised some difficult questions. How to adapt schemes suited to seasonal rural unemployment to the needs of unemployed urban workers? Should work be organised and initiated locally or by central government? What projects should qualify? Which Department should assume responsibility? And finally, how to run a public works programme, given the acute shortages of fuel and materials?

Amid the welter of detail, explored below, the core of the Department's views can be discerned. A public works programme should concentrate on long-term improvements to roads, housing and sanitary services, if necessary at the expense of short-term job creation; an effective programme for Dublin could be carried out only if the three local authorities — Dublin city, Dun Laoghaire and County Dublin — were unified, or central government assumed overriding authority; the precarious finances of local authorities should not be burdened with costs arising from cosmetic schemes such as the Derelict Sites Act. Most of the unemployed lived in the city, but the most suitable public works were often located in the county or they straddled the three local authorities.

Local Government's preference was for a single local authority controlling the greater Dublin area, but this did not materialise, and the northward expansion of the County Borough to include Howth UDC did not relieve this difficulty. The Unemployment (Relief Works) Bill, which Local Government introduced in the summer of 1940, was an attempt to overcome this problem and to switch the emphasis of employment relief works towards larger and more permanent projects. The accompanying memorandum noted that it might prove necessary during the Emergency to supplement existing employment schemes by large-scale works undertaken by local authorities; 'in such circumstances', it might prove impossible 'to await the outcome of lengthy negotiations between several local authorities or go through the complicated procedure which normally governs compulsory acquisition of lands'. The Department hoped that the legislation would facilitate major road works in Dublin, Cork and Limerick. They proposed constructing two inner ring roads in Dublin: one running from Nutley Lane to Drimnagh via Dundrum and Rathfarnham and another from Drumcondra to Cabra; mention was also made of water and sewerage schemes, all funded by the employment schemes vote.

The Bill may be seen as Local Government's attempt to wrest control of relief works from the OPW and to channel expenditure towards long-term improvements rather than minor schemes. In a break with tradition, the Department would have power to initiate relief works in an area if the Minister for Local Government was convinced of the need. Any council which refused to carry out the Minister's orders could be dissolved without holding a public inquiry. If a road scheme straddled two local authorities, the Minister could direct one to carry out work in another's territory and the second local authority would be required to pay its share of costs.

The measure was an explicit response to emergency conditions.

Local Government initially proposed that the powers should cease one year after the expiration of the Emergency Powers Act, though the Department subsequently suggested extending this to two years, 'in the belief that the difficulties arising from unemployment may continue for a longer period after the end of the emergency'. The original draft included powers for compulsory acquisition of property similar to those embodied in the 1939 Air Raid Precautions Act,[85] though these were diluted and the clauses actually enacted were similar to those contained in the 1940 Acquisition of Land (Derelict Sites) Act.[86]

While this Bill was making its way through the Oireachtas, the cabinet committee on emergency problems explored the possibility of providing immediate employment in Dublin by using the employment schemes vote to subsidise the construction of children's playgrounds or additional work on Dublin Corporation's housing programme. It proved impossible to incorporate housing construction within the terms of the employment schemes grant, which required that all workers should be hired from the Unemployment Assistance register and that, where possible, work should be rotated among teams of UA recipients. The contractors who were building local authority houses insisted on having 'an absolutely free hand' in recruiting labour, to the dismay of the OPW, which vetoed the use of special employment schemes money for Dublin housing on the grounds that if special employment schemes were no longer required to employ UA recipients, 'the effect would be not to give employment to the most necessitous class of the unemployed but rather to those who had for some years past been most favoured regarding employment'. By 24 January 1941, only 667 workers were employed on emergency relief works in Dublin.[87]

Government officials were becoming increasingly concerned that local authorities were unwilling to initiate relief works. Maurice Moynihan, secretary to the government, noted that few councils had taken advantage of the Derelict Sites Act:

> Progress in this matter appears to be slow and I doubt if anything much will be done unless pressure is brought to bear on the local authorities concerned. Unfortunately the Derelict Sites Act leaves the initiative in the hands of sanitary authorities and unless something is done to urge them to utilise the powers conferred on them, they are not likely to see any spectacular results.

James Hurson explained that local authorities were unwilling to spend money on inessentials at a time when they were finding it difficult to provide funds for basic services. The commissioner, acting on behalf of the Kilkenny Board of Health, informed the Department of Local Government that 'with so many demands on the rates, the ratepayers should not be called on at present to spend money on clearing sites for appearance sake, even though same would give employment.' The Taoiseach's Department concluded that Local Government 'seem to be doing their best' to induce local authorities to avail of the Act, but decided that the Minister should be given power to compel local authorities to take action. Local Government was reluctant to compel councils to implement the Derelict Sites Act; the Department preferred to encourage expenditure on roads, housing and water. In February 1941, despite the emerging squeeze on imports from Britain, the Department produced an extremely sanguine report which suggested that up to 2,500 men could be employed for one year on sewerage and major road improvements in Dublin County Borough, at an estimated cost of £400,000.[88]

This proposal is a classic instance of Local Government's preference for spending money on long-term improvements, rather than on *ad hoc* job creation, which appears to have been the sole concern of the cabinet emergency committee. In October 1941, Local Government informed the committee that 'the designing of such schemes takes considerable time as they require to be very carefully planned. It is somewhat difficult to fit them into an employment schemes programme.'[89] It remained difficult to devise relief works which could be carried out in the Dublin area, within the existing legal and administrative constraints. Despite the growing shortage of building supplies, employment on local authority housing construction continued to outstrip employment on relief works in Dublin throughout the summer and autumn of 1941; in June 1941, 1,431 were employed on housing schemes, against 1,041 on public works.

Since it seemed impossible to put unemployed Dubliners to work within the city, consideration was given to moving them to labour camps in rural areas where jobs could be more readily created. Initial efforts had proved disastrous. Unemployed Dubliners recruited to work on Clonsast bog in County Offaly absconded *en masse*. de Valera interpreted this as evidence of a 'general disinclination for work on the part of young unemployed men in the city';[90] more charitable accounts emphasise the culture shock of life in the rural midlands and inadequate living conditions. In 1941 the government responded by establishing the Construction Corps — a quasi military corps of young single unemployed males, who would be employed on national projects.

All that remained was to find the projects. In the autumn of 1941 Local Government came under pressure to devise 'a road scheme which would not interfere with local labour' but would employ a sufficiently high percentage of unskilled workers. The Department emphasised that if the Construction Corps carried out road works, it should be taken for granted that local authorities would refuse to contribute to the cost. Officials also emphasised that experienced gangers would be needed, though they were unlikely to be found in the Construction Corps. In response to further pressure from the cabinet, the Department suggested that the Corps be assigned to the Wicklow Gap road — which was sufficiently isolated to preclude being carried out with local labour — and to improving bog access roads in County Kildare.[91]

The establishment of the Construction Corps and the difficulties encountered in devising a relief works programme for Dublin highlighted the need for a more coherent approach towards planning for employment. During the Emergency years, the government's concern with planning for employment related to two issues, which could occasionally come into conflict: the immediate need to provide work for the unemployed, particularly in areas such as Dublin, and the desire to have a programme of work available which could be initiated in the months and years immediately following the ending of war. Confusion between both objectives permeates most of the files.

It was widely believed that the coming of peace would lead to mass unemployment on a scale similar to the aftermath of World War I. The government feared that unemployment would soar as demobilised soldiers and unemployed farm workers were joined by returning emigrants. Although Hugo Flinn expressed such fears as early as July 1940,[92] the government does not appear to have considered the issue until 1942.

Joseph Lee suggests that initial interest was prompted by a memorandum by External Affairs official F.H. Boland on the implications for Anglo-Irish relations if the Irish government imposed restrictions on Irish emigration to Britain because the labourers were needed in Ireland for tillage or turf-cutting. According to Lee, the fears which Boland expressed — that 'whatever the danger of social revolution may be, it is certain to be at its maximum during the final year of the war and during the next year or two after it' — prompted Lemass to propose establishing a Ministry of Labour as a planning agency which would assume responsibility for introducing a programme of construction works and other development schemes.[93]

Lemass's proposals were nearly identical to measures in operation in wartime Britain; they gave the state almost total control over labour: no worker who was registered as a pool employee attached to a particular industry would be permitted to emigrate, or to change to another occupation without official permission. While such restrictions might have been justified in wartime, Lemass envisaged retaining them after the Emergency as a key feature of national planning. For this reason it is scarcely surprising that the cabinet rejected the plan, contenting itself with the anodyne comment that there was a need for 'systematic planning not merely to meet the pressing problems of the moment but also to provide for the situation which will face us when the emergency comes to an end'.

Shortly afterwards, on 8 July 1942, de Valera requested that government ministers re-examine 'major projects of national development' which had been under consideration when the war broke out, with a view to being in a position to press ahead with their 'immediate execution . . . the moment the emergency had ended'. The letter emphasised that de Valera would be responsible for scrutinising all proposals, with Maurice Moynihan playing a key role. The original draft, which (unusually) was hand-written by de Valera, contains the statement that 'financial considerations will need to be subordinated to the imperative necessity of getting the work under way'. This was omitted from the final version,[94] apparently as a result of intervention by the Department of Finance.

A programme of long-term planning appears to have been eminently compatible with the interests of Local Government. The Department had been involved for some time in planning national road and housing programmes and was the intermediary between central government and local authorities. The long list of queries which Moynihan referred to Local Government on 14 August 1942 testifies to the Department's key role in any state planning process. Moynihan sought information on the current state of hospital planning; the extent to which sewerage works were handicapped by a shortage of cement; whether or not planning of water and sewerage schemes was underway so that 'rapid progress' could be made when supplies became available; whether or not the Department intended to urge county managers to survey their areas with a view to drawing up a programme of works lasting several years; the current state of progress on town planning in Dublin and the measures being taken to secure the more general adoption of the Town Planning and Regional Planning Acts; the current status of proposals for developing the Dollymount marine lake, on Dublin's north-side, known as the 'Blue Lagoon', and the improvement of tourist roads in County Wicklow.

Physical planning was an essential part of any national plan. Local Government had been responsible for both the 1934 Town and Regional Planning Act, a permissive act which enabled local authorities to prepare planning schemes,[95] and its successor, the 1939 Town and Regional Planning (Amendment) Act. The 1934 Planning Act was effectively ignored. By 1939 only 15 local authorities had passed planning resolutions, a necessary step *before* drafting a physical plan.[96] Local Government did not appoint its first planning officer until 1940 and at that date had not yet established a planning section; the work was being done by the housing section, which suggests a lack of commitment.[97] Both the 1934 and the 1939 Acts contained clauses enabling Dublin and Cork Corporations to take into consideration developments outside their respective areas if they would affect the future of the cities.

The sketch development plan for Dublin, prepared by Abercrombie, Kelly and Robertson, provided a framework for post-Emergency planning in the greater Dublin area. It proposed removing most of the city's tenement population to the suburbs and limiting the future population of the city to 765,300. Expansion would be blocked by a green belt four to six miles wide. A chain of satellite towns, based on existing towns and villages such as Malahide, Tallaght and Clondalkin, would accommodate the overflow. The report emphasised that there was a need to prevent 'a further influx of families from the country'.[98]

Most of these proposals were broadly compatible with Fianna Fáil's socio-economic and cultural ethos and were also in keeping with the Taoiseach Department's interest in post-Emergency planning. On 15 August 1942 Moynihan asked the Department 'what further steps remain to be taken with a view to final approval of the town plan for Dublin'.

285

Although Local Government indicated that the Dublin plan was only in the 'initial stages', there is no evidence that steps were taken to accelerate the process. Local Government appears to have been uncomfortable with the government's interest in planning; was it seen as a threat to the Department's authority, or does this attitude reflect MacEntee's hostility? In December 1942, when responsibility for post-war planning was entrusted to a cabinet committee consisting of de Valera, Lemass and O'Kelly, MacEntee was excluded.

This may be due to his earlier opposition to Lemass's proposals to restrict labour mobility. O'Kelly had already expressed his opposition to any major programme of public investment; he had suggested that priority should be given to formulating a long-term agricultural policy designed to increase exports, as opposed to 'taking the easy line of having recourse to state aid'.[99] Lemass and de Valera may have regarded one opponent on the committee as enough. Yet MacEntee should not be regarded as an outright opponent of planning, though he and Lemass differed on how it should be effected.

THE PLANNING BOARD

In October 1942 MacEntee drafted proposals for the establishment of a planning board 'to consider and make recommendations regarding the technical and other problems involved in providing housing accommodation for the people in Dublin City and County'. It would draw up statistical projections for the number and size of houses required; oversee technical, architectural and physical planning; allocate responsibility for housing development among the various local authorities and recommend the best machinery for planning and executing the work. MacEntee emphasised that he did not contemplate the establishment of 'another Commission of Inquiry'. His board would have a maximum of three full-time members, 'men of outstanding ability and administrative capacity as well as of enterprise and vision'; 'practical business executives', rather than architects or engineers, who would hire the appropriate technical staff. It would operate for approximately three years. Members would be paid a fee and an incentive bonus to complete the work as rapidly as possible.

On 30 November MacEntee sent a slightly revised version of this proposal to de Valera. In the accompanying letter he expressed his impatience at the delay in completing the report of the Dublin Housing Inquiry and the 'dilemma' which he faced of either accepting an incomplete report or waiting for a more satisfactory document. He had already concluded 'that there was no hope that a radical attack on our housing problem could be made through the medium of our existing machinery or organisation'. MacEntee expressed frustration at the government's dependence on local authorities, 'or more properly the officers of our local authorities', to initiate housing schemes. He was particularly scathing about the work carried out by the architects and engineers attached to Dublin Corporation and their housing plans which were

> . . . generally on stereotyped lines. On the one hand they represent the architectural evolution of the residential mansion in old Dublin through its various stages of decay as a hotel, lodging house, tenement, until it has emerged as a new type Corporation flat; or on the other hand they represent the development of the artisan's dwelling from the early hovels around industrial centres up to the suburban working-class housing colonies with which Dublin is studded [crossed out and 'being surrounded' inserted]. The common thing, however, about them all is that they belong to the pre-war age, and the men who have been engaged in planning them have been thinking, and are still thinking upon, pre-war lines.

In a passage which belies Fianna Fáil's image as a backward-looking, rurally oriented party, but may reflect MacEntee's training as an electrical engineer, he mused that 'the advent of air power as a military factor will have as revolutionary effects on the evolution of our social and civic habits and organisations as the development of heat, engines and electricity have had'. He foresaw the need for 'a rational and well-considered housing program' [sic] which, taking account of this fact, might involve 'a radical departure from the principles upon which we have hitherto proceeded'. No existing agency was capable of planning for the future: both the Department of Local Government and Dublin Corporation were 'overwhelmed' with work. A planning board, with a similar structure to the ESB, would provide 'the driving force and directive ability necessary'. The Housing Board would be retained to provide statistical data. MacEntee's proposals were discussed at the first meeting of the cabinet committee on economic planning on 2

December 1942, though no conclusion was minuted. On 18 February 1943 the committee considered another memorandum on housing which was submitted by the Department of Local Government. The contrast between both documents is so dramatic that they appear to come from different agencies. Whereas MacEntee envisaged a radical transformation of existing structures, the Local Government paper was complacent and suggested that no administrative changes were needed. All problems were attributed to high building costs and shortages of supplies, and the paper expressed satisfaction with the advance planning being carried out by Dublin Corporation.[100]

MacEntee had submitted the first draft of his proposal for a planning board to Hurson in October 1942, but no record of the latter's response survives; the February 1943 memorandum suggests that officials were unenthusiastic, possibly because a planning board would weaken the Department's authority. If this surmise is correct, it echoes the Department's earlier hostility to O'Kelly's efforts to establish a powerful housing board.

A memorandum from the Taoiseach's Department dismissed the Local Government report, complaining that 'the picture is very incomplete and does not provide sufficient data for the working out of any sort of a plan or programme of post-war building'. The memo emphasised that post-war planning for housing should be related 'to other employment-giving post-war schemes, such as road making, which compete with building for certain types of labour and materials'; the final programme should be adjusted in the light of the government's commitments. In keeping with this approach, the memo demanded that Local Government supply projections for private sector housing, factory construction and other forms of public construction, such as Garda barracks. They were also asked to assess whether or not there would be sufficient labour to enable all projects to proceed.

These questions could have pointed the way for Local Government to assume overall control of the post-war planning process. The Department had responsibility for physical planning; stronger planning controls could have been used to direct scarce resources towards slum-clearance, as happened in Britain following the recommendations of the Barlow Commission.[101] Local Government failed to grasp the opportunity and the initiative passed to Lemass and Industry and Commerce. During the summer of 1943 de Valera and Lemass met a deputation from the National Council of the Building

Industry of Ireland to discuss the post-war industry. In the autumn of 1943 the cabinet committee on post-war planning decided to assign responsibility for detailed planning of post-war construction to a newly established division or branch of an existing (unspecified) Department.

Although Local Government reacted with disquiet to these proposals, it made little effort to seize the initiative. On 20 October 1943 the cabinet committee decided that efforts should be made to co-ordinate plans for new housing on the outskirts of Dublin, in accordance with the draft development plan prepared by Abercrombie, Kelly and Robertson, pending the adoption of a definite development plan for the city. In December the committee asked Local Government if legislation should be introduced to make it mandatory for local authorities to adopt the Town and Regional Planning Acts. Local Government saw no need for such legislation, though de Valera undertook to discuss possible measures to expedite action on town and regional planning. The ensuing discussions between de Valera and MacEntee concentrated on Local Government's need to appoint specialist planners. A memorandum from Local Government to the Taoiseach's Department in April 1944 blamed the delays in adopting regional and urban plans on the Emergency and reiterated the view that there was no need for stronger legislative powers. A separate planning section was not established until 1946.[102]

Responsibility for the post-war building industry was assigned to a new division of Industry and Commerce, not to MacEntee's proposed three-man board. The outcome was consistent with Lemass's wish to keep control within the civil service, an attitude he most obviously expressed when he opposed the establishment of the Industrial Development Authority in 1949. The division would determine priorities for the building industry, in consultation with other Departments, and it would remain in existence as long as shortages of labour and raw materials persisted. In February 1945 Industry and Commerce published a White Paper, *The Post-War Building Programme*. MacEntee's absence and Lemass's presence on the committee influenced the decision to give control to Industry and Commerce, as did the fact that a shortage of materials appeared to be the major problem in the immediate post-war period. Local Government had consistently refused to show interest in any section of the building industry, other than housing; and the Department had

289

failed to realise the potential which comprehensive physical planning legislation offered.[103] It was a missed opportunity.

PLANNING FOR WARTIME AND POST-WAR EMPLOYMENT: THE ROLE OF RELIEF WORKS

Although the cabinet committee was theoretically concerned with planning post-war investment, in practice much of its attention was directed towards providing more immediate employment. Joseph Lee has derided its preoccupation with trivia such as resurfacing the railway embankment at Dollymount, the South Wall Reclamation Scheme and the possibility of converting the Dun Laoghire refuse dump at Salthill into a public park.[104] His scorn ignores the constant tension which existed between long-term planning and the immediate need for employment, however risible the projects.

Throughout the second half of 1942 Local Government came under repeated pressure from the Taoiseach's Department to increase the volume of relief works. When it was discovered that employment on relief schemes had fallen sharply in November 1942, Local Government was instructed to advance the status of works 'approved in principle' to the 'fully approved' stage without delay and to give renewed attention to proposals to clear derelict sites, because these required few materials.[105] The Department adopted a relatively relaxed attitude to such demands; it consistently argued that delays in carrying out projects were due to 'conditions arising from the present emergency'.[106] This assessment may have been correct, but the response was unwelcome in the Taoiseach's Department.

There was also an underlying tension between Local Government's desire to give priority to investments in roads, sewerage and housing, which would improve essential services, and the committee's concern to relieve unemployment. This is evident in Local Government's reply to de Valera's memorandum in July 1942 asking each Department to submit proposals for major development work to be carried out once the Emergency had ended. Local Government wished to give priority to road development, adding rather acidly that the road schemes already prepared to meet any abnormal increase in unemployment 'cannot properly be regarded as post-war planning as such planning is regarded as planning new forms of development rather than planning works for provision of employment'.

The Department provided an equally unsympathetic response to the committee's request in October 1943 that it draw up plans to provide employment for 10,000 unskilled workers in Dublin for two to three years after the Emergency. MacEntee informed the committee that proposals were already in existence to employ unskilled workers for a total of 14,000 man-years — a considerable shortfall on the 20-30,000 man-years sought. He added that it was difficult to find 'useful' employment schemes which were outside the scope of the normal public health and housing programmes and would not compete with these for plant, materials and skilled workers.

On 13 December 1943 de Valera proposed to interview MacEntee and the Dublin city manager.[107] Although the committee's minutes are uninformative, the recurring meetings between de Valera and MacEntee indicate substantial disagreement. MacEntee claimed that the committee overestimated the number of labouring jobs which were needed in Dublin. He pointed out that the number of registered male unemployed in Dublin had fallen by 36 per cent since the outbreak of war (due to emigration), whereas unemployment among women had risen by 100 per cent. Many unemployed men were of the 'cuff and collar' class not suited to employment on public works.[108]

This encounter appears to have resulted in a stand-off between MacEntee and the committee, which seems to have made no further reference to the number of jobs needed in Dublin after the Emergency. In January 1944, eschewing employment targets, the committee decided that 'a large sum should be made available from borrowed moneys, e.g. £10m., for the purpose of financing activities of Local Authorities in improving conditions in urban areas'. The money would be allocated in proportion to the number of registered unemployed in an area and would be used to provide 100 per cent grants for approved works carried out within three years of the end of the Emergency. Preference would be given to projects that used a minimum of imported materials. No returned emigrants would be employed unless they had lived in the area before emigration.

Local Government responded to this proposal by emphasising the Department's practice 'throughout the emergency to urge local authorities to proceed with all classes of work likely to provide employment and which could be undertaken with available supplies' and by reiterating its belief that the main bottleneck to carrying out relief works was a lack of supplies.[109] Behind this statement lurked a chronic suspicion of short-term employment schemes and rotational employment and a fear that wash-houses and park development would be given preference, in the allocation of funds, over roads and major sewerage works.

The most enthusiastic response to the prospect of post-war planning came from the Department's roads section. By May 1943 it had prepared proposals for road works costing almost £6.5m.. In May 1944 it presented the cabinet committee with a detailed five-year plan for an annual expenditure of £4.5m.. The roads section was determined to ensure that post-war expenditure on roads would bring a significant improvement in standards, even if this meant giving less attention to providing work for the unemployed. This was in direct conflict with the intentions of the cabinet committee. The dilemma is best summed up by the case of the Dublin-Bray road, one of the country's busiest routes and the Department's top priority. The cost of improving a 3.75 mile stretch was estimated at £181,000 if carried out by a contractor who was free to hire the workers of his choice; £214,000, if he was required to recruit UA recipients from Dublin City; and £312,000, if carried out by direct labour and rotating the workforce which would be recruited from the UA register. Local Government pointed out that it would be impossible to provide funding on this scale from the Road Fund, since its income would be wholly committed to improving main roads throughout the country. If the work was carried out efficiently by a contractor, it would attract a maximum grant of only £1,200 from the special employment scheme. A memorandum from the Department's road section argued that

> . . . it will be difficult to justify the procedure of planning if the State and Local Authorities will only be in a position to give effect to recommendations on a piecemeal basis. Expedition, economy and efficiency in the carrying out of public works cannot be achieved if they are carried out in accordance with the procedure obtaining in regard to works undertaken for the provision of employment.

If the Bray Road scheme received government grants in proportion to the small number of UA recipients living in the immediate area, and was carried out by rotated labour, using as little machinery as possible, many years would elapse before it was completed. The Department argued that the road should be reconstructed as efficiently and as speedily as possible using contractors who would be free to choose their workers.

However, this would require radical changes in the criteria for allocating either Road Fund grants or State Employment Scheme funds.[110]

The matter was examined in detail by a group in Local Government chaired by the parliamentary secretary, Erskine Childers.[111] The Department's new road plan would involve a break with precedent, 'in that the state will be initiating planning', rather than leaving local authorities to take the initiative. The group was insistent that no national roads were to be constructed by workers recruited under unemployment schemes and that all concrete roads should be constructed by contractors because one experimental stretch, which had been laid using UA workers, had proved disastrous.

Although MacEntee endorsed these decisions, he was wary of the group's insistence on using contractors rather than direct labour.[112] MacEntee's reservations proved all too prescient: there is no evidence that Childers's proposals were ever examined by the cabinet committee. Had they been, it is unlikely that they would have agreed to give priority to providing modern highways at the expense of job creation. It was originally intended that the post-war roads programme would form the subject of a White Paper. The fact that it never materialised was not due to lack of planning, but probably to major disagreement over the control and direction of post-war roads expenditure.

On the whole, Local Government adopted an ambivalent approach to the deliberations of the cabinet committee. It was sceptical about the merits of yet more *ad hoc* job creation schemes, and was equally unsympathetic to proposals to use Exchequer funds for the erection of parish or village halls, which would provide premises for Muintir na Tíre (a national association for community development) and the Local Defence Forces and serve as the local library and health clinic. Providing community halls was seen as a means of regenerating rural Ireland.[113] Local Government was determined that priority should be given to roads and housing. However, the Department was either incapable or unwilling to integrate its proposals into a planning framework. Whether the lack of a wider perspective reflects the realities of hard-pressed officials concerned with their individual sections, the absence of a planning section within the Department, MacEntee's abhorrence of excessive *dirigisme*, or perhaps his pique at being excluded from the committee, we do not know. MacEntee's opposition to imposing further restrictions on the emigration of turf workers indicates that he was unsympathetic to the more authoritarian aspects of planning, though his unsuccessful proposal for a planning board might suggest otherwise. He was also heavily engaged in plans for reforming health and social welfare.

Despite such ambivalence, in January 1944, the only occasion when the cabinet committee calculated the cost of all proposals on its books, Local Government had tabled proposals for expenditure totalling over £43m., fractionally more than half the total of £86m.. Slum-clearance was projected to cost £23.45m. — the largest single item.[114]

TABLE 6.3

Proposals for capital expenditure in the post-war years presented by the Department of Local Government and Public Health in May 1944

	Urban Areas	Rural Areas	Total
Hospitals	£2,846,000	£330,000	£3,176,000
Housing	£19,174,601	£4,196,867	£23,371,468
	(28,199 houses)	(8,646 houses)	(36,845 houses)
Water	£226,005	£573,300	£799,305
Sewerage	£1,933,980	£766,000	£2,699,980
Swimming Pools	£682,015	£164,700	£846,715
Other Amenities			
e.g. Parks	£318,670	£164,700	£483,370
Roads	£5,000,000	£17,600,360	£23,600,360
Total	£30,181,271	£23,677,227	£53,848,498

After January 1944, responsibility for supervising post-war planning tended to pass to Industry and Commerce, because that department controlled supplies. By May 1944, Local Government had tabled proposals for capital expenditure of almost £54m., to be carried out in the first five years after the ending of war. If supplies of raw materials were available, the Department planned to spend £18m. in urban areas during the first three post-war years. The £22.6m. allocated for roads covered only repairs and minor improvements such as tarring; it omitted 'works of major importance'. The Department remained unenthusiastic about a proposal to allocate £10m. for tree planting, parks and public lavatories, arguing that, although these would be 'of considerable amenity value', they 'can scarcely be regarded as having a prior claim on available resources (financial, material and labour) to that of housing, hospitals, waterworks, sewerage schemes, road improvements, public lighting and such works.'[115] Although Local Government's reservations were shared by Finance, it appears that what Lee has called 'the primacy of the political'[116] — and the desire to scatter crumbs of relief as widely as possible — triumphed over the logic of its case.

CONCLUSIONS

The Emergency years provided a major challenge for both the Department of Local Government and the local authorities. Many normal activities, such as house construction and road maintenance and improvements, were curtailed, and the additional functions which emerged, such as producing turf, appeared to require a more centralised administrative system. Centralisation and greater intrusion occurred at two levels: local authorities found themselves producing turf at the behest of the government; they also lost their power to determine the wages paid to their employees. Meanwhile, the Department of Local Government found its proposals for capital expenditure being subjected to the dictates of other government departments, whose interests lay in providing short-term employment rather than in improving road or water services. Local Government seems to have been uneasy in that environment, in part because of the attitude adopted by the Minister, Seán MacEntee. Given the wide range of responsibilities handled by the Department, and the potential offered by planning legislation, the Emergency years may be seen as something of a missed opportunity for the Department, a time when they failed to assume a more central role in shaping the economy of post-war Ireland. If Seán Lemass had been Minister for Local Government during these years, there seems little doubt that the Department would have assumed a more central role. Both the Minister for Local Government and Public Health and his senior officials appear to have been primarily concerned with planning for the major expansion of post-war medical and social welfare services, which culminated in the establishment of the Departments of Health and Social Welfare in 1947; the Department's elaborate plans for major road improvements were not seriously promoted at cabinet (see chapter nine).

MacEntee was not alone in having reservations about the government's plans for post-war capital expenditure. Many of the problems which unemployment relief works had raised throughout the 1930s, such as the concern to hire workers from the Unemployment Assistance register and the tendency to give priority to schemes which hired large quantities of labour at the expense of other criteria, also applied in this instance. There was also the question of the relative responsibilities of central and local government. MacEntee's proposal to devolve post-war planning to a three-man planning board suggests that he was aware of the difficulties involved in achieving national goals by working through local authorities. Although the planning board was never established, the introduction of county managers, together with the developments described above, brought about a considerable reduction in the autonomy of local authorities during the Emergency years.

CHAPTER SEVEN

THE REORGANISATION OF LOCAL GOVERNMENT:
COUNTY MANAGERS AND PARISH COUNCILS?

The Emergency years show a consistent pattern of increased intrusion by central government into the affairs of local authorities, whether in the form of wage controls, the high-handed actions of the defence forces or in turf production. However, councillors saw the 1940 County Management Act as the most extreme example. It was undoubtedly the most important piece of legislation relating to local government administration in the history of the state. Although the proposal predated the Emergency, many aspects of its implementation carry the authoritarian flavour of these years.

Centralisation and professionalisation had been the primary impulse in Irish local government reform for most of the preceding two hundred years. The eighteenth-century Dublin Wide Streets Commissioners are only the most prominent instance of the Irish parliament assuming responsibility for an aspect of local administration. During the nineteenth century, the number of boroughs was radically pruned and many powers originally exercised by bodies such as grand juries were transferred to salaried professionals. As we have already seen, similar tendencies persisted in the Irish Free State. The first decade of the new state saw the abolition of rural district councils and the appointment of city managers in Cork in 1929 and in Dublin in 1930.

Until 1948 there appears to be a striking similarity between the attitudes of Cumann na nGaedheal or Fine Gael and Fianna Fáil towards local democracy. In opposition they championed the cause of local authorities; in office they displayed centralist tendencies. Between 1922 and 1932, Cumann na nGaedheal suspended four county councils — Kerry (twice), Leitrim, Offaly and Mayo — and Cork and Dublin

Corporations. By 1942, after ten years in office, Fianna Fáil had suspended six county councils — Tipperary South Riding, Kilkenny, Laois, Waterford, Westmeath and Dublin.[7]

During the first twenty years of the Irish Free State, local elections, which were scheduled to take place at three-yearly intervals, were postponed in 1923, 1931, 1937 and 1940. Elections were held in 1925, 1928, 1934 and (reluctantly) in 1942. Some suspended local authorities even missed out on these rare elections. In June 1942, Richard Mulcahy, a former Cumann na nGaedheal Minister for Local Government, pointed out that the last county council elections in Counties Laois, Kilkenny, Tipperary South and Waterford had taken place in 1928.[2]

Both W.T. Cosgrave and Seán T. O'Kelly, leading figures in Cumann na nGaedheal and Fianna Fáil governments respectively, shared a common belief that the establishment of the Irish Free State had made democratic local government largely redundant. In 1925 Cosgrave told a Cumann na nGaedheal convention that 'the meeting of the local authority is not the place for discussion of political issues'.[3] In a similar vein, Seán T. O'Kelly presented a memorandum to cabinet in 1934, which described county councils as 'a relic of British administration when the people sought for the control of popular bodies for the furtherance of national agitations, rather than by reason of any intrinsic administrative merits possessed by such bodies.'[4] Such attitudes undoubtedly help to explain the frequent postponement of local elections. For both Cumann na nGaedheal and Fianna Fáil governments, there appeared to be a strong case for transferring power in local government from elected representatives to professional managers.

The first steps in this direction, the appointment of city managers in Cork and Dublin, have been described in chapter three. There is some evidence to suggest that Cumann na nGaedheal had considered introducing a county management system before it left office in 1932.[5] A memorandum, written in the Department of Local Government, on a proposed local government bill in 1931, anticipated 'a local government reorganisation on the managerial side being put into legislative form'.[6] Although Fianna Fáil had been critical of the city managers while in opposition, the views of the party's leaders at least altered radically in government. In October 1933 the Executive Council decided that the Minister for Local Government should submit proposals for the amendment of the Local Government acts to provide for the adoption of a managerial system and that local elections should be postponed to allow time for legislation incorporating the new system to be enacted. The original draft presented to the Executive Council by Seán T. O'Kelly signalled the 'frankly expressed intention of effecting further reforms at a later date with a view to acquiring central control and administration of all local affairs'.

O'Kelly proposed that county councils would be retained as an interim measure, but their powers would be drastically curtailed and the number of councillors reduced. The accompanying memorandum claimed that county councils had become 'an expensive anachronism' in the light of national independence and modern advances in transport and communications. Health, unemployment relief and housing were increasingly viewed as national concerns, and the state was assuming a growing share of the cost of services which had previously been financed by local taxes. Many local authorities had been proved guilty of maladministration and failed to comply with various laws; some had opposed the Local Appointments Commission and the combined purchasing system, while council meetings showed a tendency for 'the intrusion of worthless and irrelevant political discussions in respect of which the local body has no direct functions'. Elected representatives found it difficult to master the growing complexities of local administration.

O'Kelly suggested postponing the local government elections scheduled for June 1934 until the future shape of local administration could be determined: Cumann na nGaedheal had postponed the local elections due in 1931 for the identical reason. Councillors would remain in office in an advisory capacity, but they would be deprived of all administrative and executive functions and meetings would be restricted to four a year. Temporary county managers, appointed by the Minister, would administer one or more counties and assume the duties previously carried out by boards of health, mental hospital committees, vocational education committees, library committees, agricultural committees and old-age pension committees. Temporary managers would be seconded from the ranks of Local Government inspectors, pending the recruitment, through the Local Appointments Commission of 'young men [sic] of high educational qualifications between the ages of say, 22 to 27 years', who would serve as cadets in local administration and, 'on giving proof of their administrative capacity', would become permanent county managers. The proposal envisaged a French-style prefecture with a new elite grade of local officials, akin to the administrative officer grade in the civil service. Local Government would be directly responsible for selection, promotion, setting salary scales and for transferring personnel. County councils would remain 'to act as checks on the administration of the Managers until such time as the State can definitely claim control over them as State officials'.

Although these proposals were on the agenda for the Executive Council meeting of 23 March 1934, O'Kelly withdrew them and they did not resurface.[7] The reasons for their withdrawal are unknown, but it is probable, given the previous sympathy Fianna Fáil had shown for local interests, that some cabinet members may have regarded them as unacceptable. The proposal to emasculate local democracy may have been prompted by the intemperate state of local politics during these years, particularly the anti-rates campaigns associated with the Blueshirts. Edward McCarron, then secretary of Local Government, does not appear to have supported this plan. In the course of discussions between senior officials in Finance and Local Government on 1 March 1934 (almost the exact date when O'Kelly's memorandum was submitted to the Executive Council), McCarron expressed the opinion that, while there was 'a general feeling throughout the country in the different political parties in favour of the managerial system, his fear was that it might be forced on them too rapidly'. He would prefer to continue the experiments (of city managers) in Dublin, Cork and Dun Laoghaire for some time before deciding whether or not to extend the system. McCarron feared that there would be a shortage of suitable candidates for the post of manager. He dismissed McElligott's proposal to increase the power of county secretaries on the grounds that 'for the greater part [they] had too many local interests. Others of them were weak and dependent on local men.'[8] However city managers were appointed in Limerick County Borough in 1934 and in Waterford County Borough in 1939.[9]

THE 1940 COUNTY MANAGEMENT ACT

The question of appointing county managers was not raised again until May 1938 when Local Government submitted a 'preliminary outline of proposals' to the Department of the Taoiseach. This proved much less radical than its predecessor and included the suggestion that county secretaries might become the first county managers — a far cry from

O'Kelly's wish to appoint Local Government inspectors to the post. The cabinet deferred discussion until November 1938 when it gave approval for the preparation of heads of a Bill. In February 1939 Local Government was given permission to proceed with the preparation of a Bill, which was submitted in July and approved by the cabinet in November.

This provided for the appointment of managers in all counties except Dublin, where the future structure of local government was under consideration. Managers would assume responsibility for the executive functions of county councils, borough councils, urban district councils, and bodies such as boards of public assistance and mental hospital committees. Councillors would determine policy and exercise ultimate financial control; they would retain the power to levy rates, borrow money, make by-laws, bring enactments into operation, promote legislation, alter urban boundaries, nominate members to other local bodies and conduct parliamentary and local elections. All other powers, especially those relating to staff, rested with the manager, though the council could require him to carry out certain actions 'which can lawfully be done by them [the council] or the manager', provided that these did not relate to staffing or the payment of public assistance. Six pairs of counties — Carlow and Kildare, Kilkenny and Waterford, Laois and Offaly, Sligo and Leitrim, Longford and Westmeath and the North and South Ridings of Tipperary — would each share a manager. This appears to have been seen as a first step towards a further reorganisation of local administration; assistant managers would be appointed in these counties if the work proved excessive.

Although several months elapsed between the proposals being tabled at cabinet and their eventual approval, there is no evidence (if the surviving files are complete) that the delay was due to any concern over the implications of such reforms. Cabinet attention focused almost exclusively on who would be appointed as county managers. The government appears to have believed that appointing county secretaries *en masse* to the new posts would reassure local councillors. When the bill was withdrawn from the cabinet agenda in July 1939, a handwritten note on the file stated: 'In the meantime he [the Minister for Local Government] will give further consideration to the position of County Secretaries under the Managerial System and in that connection to the question whether the first appointments as County Managers should be made by the legislation itself.'

On 15 August 1939, the cabinet agreed to appoint county secretaries as county managers, unless they were either too old or inefficient, in which case the position would go to the secretary of the board of health. The minister agreed to consider scheduling the names of appointees in the bill. In October the cabinet decided that if both the county secretary and the secretary to the board of health were deemed unsuitable, the position would be filled by the Local Appointments Commission, 'subject to an over-riding preference to [sic] suitable and qualified persons who are County Secretaries or Secretaries to the County Boards of Health'. By the time the bill received its final approval in November 1939, Local Government had determined that six county secretaries were unsuitable for appointment because they were over sixty-five years of age; in only one of these cases could the secretary of the board of health be substituted. Five posts would be filled by the Local Appointments Commission.[10]

Were county secretaries, who had formerly been the most powerful officials in local administration, engaged in a lobbying campaign? At their annual meeting with the minister on 23 November 1939, they proposed that he should nominate the first county managers and that their names should be included in the bill. They also expressed dissatisfaction at the proposal to group counties because it would reduce the number of posts. Town clerks and secretaries of boards of health, whose posts had been abolished under the 1939 Public Assistance Act, objected to the favouritism shown to county secretaries. The auditor of the Cork Harbour Board claimed that many county secretaries were 'hampered by too limited vision on the one hand or too grooved experience [i.e. being set in their ways] or positive incapacity on the other'; he believed that secretaries to the boards of health were more intelligent and better suited to the post.[11]

In 1941 Hugo Flinn put forward the claims of county surveyors, arguing that 'if it was a question of the handling of any money in the efficient expenditure of which I was interested, I should certainly prefer the Engineer to the Secretary.' Although Flinn made efforts to secure de Valera's support and some opposition TDs spoke in their favour, the surveyors remained excluded from the initial appointments.[12] One Department of Local Government auditor felt it was inadvisable to recruit either county secretaries or secretaries to boards of health because, having acted as 'adviser' to the council or the board of health for many years, it would not prove easy for him to adopt the role of manager. He was particularly opposed to appointing any county secretary who was a native of the county in which he served, because he believed that such a man 'will find it particularly difficult to act impartially, owing to the pressure of friends and relatives when positions and patronage of various kinds are being dispersed.' Fianna Fáil senator Thomas Honan proposed that a county secretary should be qualified for every county except that in which he had already served.[13]

Only nine of the original county managers had served as secretaries in the counties in which they had been appointed. When the first appointments were made in 1942, six county councils were controlled by commissioners, who were given priority of appointment after the county secretaries,[14] and five former officials of the Department of Local Government who had served as commissioners in dissolved local authorities were appointed as county managers. Two of the original county managers had been secretaries to boards of health in that county; four former county secretaries or secretaries to boards of health became managers in other counties; the Dublin city manager became manager of County Dublin in addition to his existing duties.[15]

The only other aspect of the legislation to engage the cabinet's attention was whether or not the county manager should be required to attend all meetings of local authorities, and who should appoint rate collectors. Originally the bill provided for rate collectors to be appointed by the county manager, but the cabinet restored the power of appointment to county councils, subject to ministerial sanction, though councils would have to take the manager's views into consideration.[16] Local government auditors thoroughly disapproved of this decision. One auditor, J.P. Moran, claimed that the supervision of collectors would prove to be the most difficult task facing a county manager and that efficiency would suffer if he was unable to select the best collectors, while the fact that collectors were appointed by the council would give them a measure of independence from the manager. Alloting the county manager power to suspend unsatisfactory collectors would not provide a solution, because the council would probably fill the vacancy with somebody of similar calibre. Officials in the Local Government Department roads section claimed that county surveyors would prefer if road schemes were approved by the council rather than by the manager. It was claimed that all county surveyors submitted unduly optimistic estimates, which needed to be reduced; if this was done by the manager, it might lead to differences between the

303

two senior officials. Councillors would 'take sides in the matter', and the county manager would be criticised for the inadequate repair of roads, despite the fact that he was forced to work with an estimate that was beyond his control.[17] This advice went unheeded.

Local opposition to the management system began to surface even before the bill had been published. In November 1939 Clare County Council voted its disapproval by 26 votes to 3 and Fr Gaynor, parish priest of Kilnamona, Ennis, addressed a detailed critique to de Valera, justifying his intervention with the claim that the Taoiseach's interest in parish councils suggested that he was concerned 'at the gradual exclusion of the people from any effective share in local administration'. Gaynor viewed the 'inherent viciousness of the County Managers' Bill', and what he termed the replacement of independent local councils by 'sham councils for democratic camouflage', as a further step by bureaucrats to dismantle local government — a practice which had been continuing since the civil war years. He was in favour of what he termed 'the volunteer principles of local organisation': local authorities based around larger market towns in a model similar to that allegedly followed by the Volunteers during the Anglo-Irish war,[18] or, though the Rev. Gaynor might not have appreciated the analogy, the nineteenth-century Poor Law Unions.

When the County Management Bill was given its second reading in the Dáil in December 1939, opposition deputies denounced the 'craze for centralisation'; Fine Gael TD Dr T.F. O'Higgins claimed that 'we are . . . perhaps witnessing the passing of local government in this country in the popularly accepted sense'. Besides O'Higgins, Fine Gael's comments were muted, perhaps because they, or their political ancestors, had invented city management. Labour deputies were more outspoken. They criticised the grouping of counties, which appears to have been generally unpopular, and voiced fears that councils would be powerless to prevent managers from increasing expenditure in response to pressure from the Custom House. A proposal to reduce the number of county councillors was widely criticised.[19]

It was initially announced that county managers would not be appointed until local elections had been held. In February 1942, the government decided to postpone local elections, ostensibly because of the Emergency, but to press ahead with introducing the county management system. In justification for this action, it claimed that wartime travel restrictions made it difficult for councillors to attend meetings. Because county managers would assume all executive duties, fewer council meetings would be needed. As a token gesture towards democracy, managers would not be appointed in Counties Kilkenny, Laois, Tipperary South, Waterford and Westmeath until councils had been restored. (The remaining dissolved council was Dublin County Council.)[20]

However the decision to postpone local elections aroused considerable opposition and the government was forced to capitulate. Elections were scheduled for 19 August 1942; the 1940 County Management Act and the 1939 Public Assistance Act came into effect one week later.

Both Acts should be seen as the culmination of a reform process which had started with the First Dáil. The 1939 Public Assistance Act abolished county boards of health and transferred their functions to county councils. For the first time since 1921 there was a permanent code for the administration of public assistance and Dublin was brought into line with the rest of Ireland.[21] The 1941 Local Government Act, which began life as the 1939 Local Government Bill and which also came into effect in August 1942, consolidated and extended the minister's power over local officers and went a considerable distance towards introducing uniform conditions for retirement age, salaries and qualifications. The minister was given authority to remove individual councillors from office without dissolving the council as a whole. It was initially intended that the Bill would deal with superannuation, but these clauses were dropped in order to ensure its speedy passage.[22]

As a result of the 1941 Local Government Act and the appointment of county managers, councillors lost most of their remaining powers relating to staff. In 1943 the Department divested itself of responsibility for appointments and promotions in a wide range of minor local government posts, but control passed to the county manager, not to councillors.

PARISH COUNCILS

Amidst a plethora of clauses providing for greater central control, the 1941 Local Government Act made some minor gestures towards supporters of parish councils. Although the proposal to establish parish councils first emerged in the late 1930s, it gained additional momentum from the specific problems of the Emergency years. The idea seems to have originated with Fr Devane, a Jesuit priest, who had direct access to both de Valera and Seán T. O'Kelly.[23] In a letter to de Valera in 1938, urging him to establish parish councils as a new tier of local government, Fr Devane wrote of the need to 'create a central rallying ground for national unity through a full statement of our national Christian philosophy as crystallised in the constitution'. de Valera asked the Ordnance Survey to provide three maps of the 32 counties of Ireland; one with protestant and catholic dioceses superimposed, the others with catholics and protestant dioceses and parishes separately marked. Local Government produced a lengthy memorandum under the name of James Hurson, secretary of the Department, analysing the evolution of the parish as a unit of English local government.

Meanwhile the historian and librarian F.X. Carty produced a long essay on the history of Irish dioceses and counties. However, Major MacNeill, assistant director of the Ordnance Survey, informed de Valera that parish boundaries were not recorded on Ordnance Survey maps and 'from enquiries I have made it would seem that complete information is not even in the possession of ecclesiastical authorities'. In March 1939 Fr Devane informed de Valera that he had recently 'sent up a "ballon d'essai" by way of a broadcast lecture on Parish Councils in England', with results that 'surpassed anything I expected'. Three daily newspapers wrote leading articles supporting his proposal and published detailed accounts of his lecture.

Further documents on parish government emerged in subsequent months, including one dated 10 July 1939 from Limerick senator Martin O' Dwyer which appears to have been inspired by Fr Hayes, founder of Muintir na Tíre. Both Hayes and Devane saw parish-based organisations having a pivotal role in reviving rural Ireland — a key element in Fianna Fáil's philosophy, though one which was coming unstuck by 1939. The 1936 Census had revealed that the population of rural Ireland was continuing to decline. Hayes saw the role of parish councils as being limited to voluntary services. Devane was more ambitious and suggested that they be given responsibility for preserving the peace, determining eligibility for unemployment assistance and providing an employment exchange, administering school meals, overseeing town planning and the division of land-holdings, and providing security for loans taken out by farmers. He also suggested that they be used to boost agricultural output during the Emergency.[24]

Local Government was utterly opposed to parish councils. In a memorandum forwarded to the Taoiseach's office during the summer of 1939, officials argued that there was no Irish precedent for using the parish as a local government unit; the historic unit was the townland, 'an area defined by tradition, recorded on maps' which had formed the basis for boundaries of poor law unions, district electoral divisions and rural district councils. Unlike the parish, for which no agreed boundaries existed (boundaries of catholic and protestant parishes often differed), the townland could form the basis for local taxation. The Department argued that the creation of parish councils would be directly opposed to the trend of creating larger units of local administration, though it conceded that county councils and boards of health could be encouraged to appoint local committees. They subsequently produced evidence which suggested that most English parish councils were moribund.

Such views were out of step with the spirit of the times. On 4 October 1939 de Valera made a favourable reference to parish committees in the course of a speech in the Seanad.[25] Fears of invasion and the fact that parish councils were compatible with the ideas emanating from the Commission on Vocational Organisation — which was then sitting — gave the concept added momentum. Local politicians, letter-writers to the newspapers and interest groups such as the Gaelic League and the Catholic Young Men's Society (CYMS) jumped on the bandwagon. The historian and feminist Mary Hayden urged that each parish council should be required to include women. However Fr Devane's blueprint was based on Salazar's Portugal where parish councils were elected by heads of families (presumably male).[26]

The 1939 Local Government Bill provided for the establishment of voluntary local committees which would develop facilities, such as sports fields and local halls, or liaise with county committees of agriculture. On 11 July 1940 the cabinet committee on emergency problems agreed that the Minister for Local Government should take responsibility for urging the formation of parish councils, 'with particular reference to functions which such councils might discharge in time of general dislocation'. Four days later the committee requested the Department to issue instructions to all county secretaries to organise parish councils; Local Government should also prepare guidelines specifying their functions, both in present conditions and in the event of hostilities. County secretaries were summoned to attend a special meeting in Dublin to discuss this proposal, which suggests that it was seen as an urgent matter.

Before this meeting took place, an interdepartmental conference attended by representatives of nearly all government departments other than External Affairs and Post and Telegraphs, attempted to determine the duties of these new councils. Suggestions ranged widely, from 'carrying out duties somewhat similar to those performed by the village constable in England' in times of emergency, including the exercise of summary justice, to persuading local shopkeepers to lay in emergency stocks of food, finding billets for evacuees, organising the co-operative harvesting of crops 'in particularly disturbed areas', and helping employment exchanges to administer unemployment relief in the event of 'a great emergency'. There was general agreement that councils should be 'hand picked or selected', rather than elected; county secretaries should approach parish priests and 'other prominent personages' such as clergy, school teachers and the president of the local conference of St Vincent de Paul — a catholic charitable organisation. Although councils would be 'absolutely non-sectarian', they would be organised around catholic parishes.

The letter, from the Department of Local Government, summoning county secretaries to Dublin was eloquent on the need to prepare for the threatened emergency, though the inclusion of a detailed account of the case *against* parish councils suggests that Local Government's views were unchanged. In an apparent rebuke to Fr Devane and Muintir na Tíre zealots, it emphasised that if parish councils were to be established, 'they should have a definite purpose. It would not be sufficient to set up Parish Councils to improve conditions in rural areas', though 'in their present state of tension and anxiety about the future', people 'would probably come together to concert measures for their safety'. The circular also suggested that the Emergency might provide scope for rural regeneration.

> In the widescale tensions created by recent announcements, the apathy which has settled on the countryside owing to a falling population, depressed agricultural conditions and the attractions of urban life might be temporarily lifted. The farmers and the farm labourers have now become more important to the nation than the middle class and they may perhaps be aroused to collective action in some form for their own and the country's protection. The conservation of the Food Supply, preservation of order, defence of the civil population against the worst effects of invasion and the

establishment of some responsible organ which can deal with local authorities of which the parish forms a part and also if necessary with Government Departments and their representatives; for the moment all such aims as are usually compressed in social, cultural and recreational activities should be put aside in favour of the more immediate problem.

When Patrick Ruttledge, Minister for Local Government, briefed the county secretaries, he emphasised that, for the present, parish councils should be seen as having a role only during the Emergency: distributing emergency supplies of food and fuel or assisting the Local Security Forces and the Red Cross. Councils would be voluntary bodies. Elections should be avoided and party and religious divisions ignored, though the parish priest might be asked to act as chairman. While the forthcoming Local Government Act would enable county councils to delegate powers to parish councils, he was afraid that

> . . . if we do delegate these powers at the outset they might
> develop into bodies who were demanding certain conditions from
> County Councils rather than acting on their own and trying to see
> how best they could help themselves. That was not the intention
> and if they ever develop along these lines it should be in such a
> way that if they do demand things, then they must pay for them.

If parish councils proved effective in dealing with the Emergency, Ruttledge believed that 'they will likely find a permanent place in the management of local government'.[27]

A spontaneous movement to establish parish councils was already underway. On 7 July (before the idea had been adopted by the cabinet committee) a meeting to establish parish councils was held in Carlow, which was attended by the bishop of Kildare and Leighlin, Fr Hayes, Rev. Chancellor Ridgeway, the county medical officer of health, the chairman of Carlow County Council, and TDs James Hughes and Patrick Cogan. On 22 July 1940 de Valera endeavoured to ensure that the press would publicise stories about parish councils 'where these were of such a nature as to be a useful headline to others'. He had little hope that *The Irish Times* or the *Irish Independent* would co-operate, but was more optimistic about *The Irish Press*. Most county councils asked parish priests to take the lead in establishing parish councils, though in Counties Donegal and Monaghan clergy of 'both denominations' were involved. Committees in the diocese of Ossory were to be established on strictly vocational lines.

After an initial burst of enthusiasm, problems emerged. On 21 August Local Government reported that the respective duties of the new councils, the air raid prevention (ARP) service and the Red Cross had given rise to numerous misunderstandings.[28] On 29 August, four senators, Martin O' Dwyer, Michael Tierney, Liam Ó Cuimín and John J. Counihan, gave notice of a motion requesting that the government introduce legislation establishing parish councils on a permanent basis as an integral part of the local government system, with members elected by heads of families.[29] In response, Maurice Moynihan, secretary to the government, told Hurson that de Valera was convinced that the 'precise status and functions' of the councils should be more clearly defined; the public was unclear whether the councils were purely emergency bodies or were intended to continue in peacetime. Local Government replied that the establishment of parish councils had been accelerated because of the Emergency.

The Department issued a circular pointing out that parish councils were subordinate to other voluntary services. Suggested duties included helping the Red Cross, or, where no local Red Cross unit existed, helping in its establishment. Parish councils should encourage local people to join the Local Security Forces (LSF) and co-operate with the Garda Síochána and LSF in maintaining essential services if an area became isolated as a result of invasion.[30] In the light of reports from 'one or two responsible friends in other localities', MacEntee informed de Valera that the councils were in the process of becoming 'top heavy because "we can't leave old Mike out".' He believed that including shopkeepers as council members would create 'a young Tammaney' [sic] and would prove difficult if the councils were forced to handle emergency food distribution; he urged that they be excluded. Doctors should be relegated to the role of outside experts; MacEntee feared that, as members, they could be outvoted, despite making 'an unassailable case', and this would threaten their status in the community.

Many parish councils became moribund within months. Those that survived concentrated on providing allotments, securing access to turf, supporting the campaign for increased tillage and promoting the work of the Red Cross and ARP, though few tackled all these tasks. Some councils rented land which they divided into allotments; branches of Muintir na Tíre in County Tipperary paid farmers to grow produce for urban families. Although the momentum faded, the idea did not die. Éamon de Valera remained interested in the possibility of mapping catholic parish boundaries, and the catholic bishops responded to the publication of the report of the Commission on Vocational Organisation by issuing a circular letter calling for the introduction of parish-based local government.[31]

At first glance the establishment of parish councils appears to have been totally at variance with the trend towards county management. Yet by encouraging the creation of an unelected tier of local government, the government could be accused of hammering yet another nail into the coffin of county and urban councils. A Department of Local Government memorandum in 1940, concerning the establishment of parish councils, warned:

> County councils are still too much under the influence of the representative system working on party lines and would visualise the parish committee working on the customary party lines, having some little power and less money and carrying on a half life with the aid of paid officials. What is wanted is not a unit of self-government or local government but a unit of obligation, a body which will be called on to undertake duties and responsibilities and give their time and perhaps money for the common good without any reward by way of remuneration.

'OFFICE BOYS OF THE MINISTER'? : THE EARLY YEARS OF COUNTY MANAGEMENT

The Department of Local Government came in for increasing criticism during the Emergency years, in part because of the introduction of county managers, but also because the specific problems posed by the Emergency forced the Department to intervene widely in matters previously determined by local authorities, by issuing Emergency orders.[33] Labour TD Richard Corish argued that a gulf existed between Local Government officials and the people of provincial Ireland: 'People in the Custom House have not the same grasp of matters in the South or West of Ireland as the people there have.' He urged the Department to show greater deference to local democracy; 'where a local authority makes a proposal which is within the law, and to which there cannot be an serious objection, the Minister ought to see that proposal should be allowed to follow its course.'[34] Other Dáil deputies alleged that there was 'a sort of paralysis in the Department which prevents decisions being taken',[35] and there were suggestions that the Department should be split into two or more departments. The length of the estimates debate in 1942 and the range of speakers indicates that local government was a live political issue during the Emergency.[336]

The appointment of county managers marked the beginning of a contentious new relationship between councillors and the administration, which reverberated for at least a decade. The first warning signs came in the estimates debate in October 1943. William Davin, TD for Laois-Offaly, protested that some county managers refused to attend council meetings. Councillors in his area regarded county managers as 'nothing more or less than the office boys of the Minister'.

In his speech, MacEntee criticised Kerry County Council for refusing to provide the county manager with sufficient funds in the estimate and emphasised his determination to 'stand behind the managers in the proper exercise of their statutory functions'. He continued: 'I will not condone, nor expect members of an elected body to tolerate, any incivility, lack of respect or act of usurpation on the part of the manager' and suggested that councils would be more likely to prove co-operative if county managers confined themselves strictly to their job. He claimed to 'have noticed a tendency on the part of one or two individuals to seek the limelight in this or that organisation in a way which, to my mind, does not become a public servant, and which I have reason to believe, does not meet with general acceptance'. MacEntee reminded councils that they had the power to suspend a manager, to refuse supplies, and to ask for a sworn inquiry into any aspect of a manager's administration; the manager was required to act by signed order and to keep a register of every order to be produced at every meeting of an elected body.[37]

A circular letter issued by the Minister for Local Government in 1944 to each local authority can be read both as a reprimand to managers and an attempt to fend off proposals from local councils that the manager's orders should be implemented only if the council approved. It contained a sermon on the need for co-operation between elected members and the manager.

A loyal acceptance by the manager of the predominant position of the elected body will do much to elicit from them the support to which he is entitled in the discharge of his duties. The law gives the manager the right to take part in the discussions of local bodies. When he does intervene he should do so with tact and discretion. The manager must be prepared to give advice readily to members who are unacquainted with official routine and be obliging and courteous in his dealings with members of the local body and the public.

The circular emphasised that the manager had a statutory obligation to keep councillors fully informed about all the business of the local authority, including 'projects in contemplation' and the basis on which decisions were made on the estimates. A manager must inform councillors about all Orders which he had signed. (County and city managers exercised their executive authority by means of signed Orders.[38] These would cover functions such as the hiring of staff or the awarding of contracts.) The manager should 'not confine himself to the minimum that the law requires if the council wish him to go beyond that'; rather, councillors should be provided with the 'fullest information' available. The circular pointed out that councils could establish committees to supervise the managers's performance or consider the estimates; they could also appoint a public assistance committee, to which executive functions could be delegated.

Seán MacEntee appears to have followed this circular by requesting the Association of Municipal Authorities (and possibly other groups representing local authorities) to prepare a statement showing the practices of different managers on matters such as attending meetings, selecting relief works, accepting tenders, informing councillors about important letters from the Department, and contact between the manager and the chairman of the local authority.[39]

MacEntee's efforts appear to have done little to improve relations between councillors and managers. Many speeches at successive Fianna Fáil *árd fheiseanna* contained long lists of complaints against county management. Laois County Council attempted to dismiss its manager shortly after his appointment. In September 1944 Fine Gael TD J.M. O'Sullivan introduced a motion in the Dáil requesting the government to amend the County Management Acts 'in such a manner as will restore to the elected representatives of the people effective authority to direct the administration of local government'. Speakers supporting the motion described the county manager as a 'dictator', or as 'extending still further the strangle-grip of bureaucracy upon the people'. Oliver J. Flanagan TD alleged that the county manager responsible for Laois and Offaly absented himself on holidays on the occasion of practically every quarterly meeting of the county council. Both Seán MacEntee and Erskine Childers, parliamentary secretary to the Minister for Local Government, suggested in their speeches that the government would consider amending the legislation after a trial period. However, Childers ruled out any question of restoring councillors' control over local appointments, while MacEntee emphasised that there was no question of returning to the previous arrangements. He noted that there was no evidence that the electorate was dissatisfied with the new system.[40]

In April 1945, with local elections pending, MacEntee published a White Paper listing the powers of local elected authorities,[41] presumably in an effort to diffuse criticism. Most opponents of the county management system complained about the manager having control over appointments, an issue which echoed earlier grievances over the Local Appointments Commission. In 1946 Aodh de Blacam, presenting himself as a friend of Fianna Fáil and its supporters, wrote to MacEntee demanding that he produce 'some timely definition of the Managerial position, and an exhortation to councillors to exercise their power'. De Blacam, who subsequently joined the new political party Clann na Poblachta, saw the management system 'as doing so much harm both to the social well-being and to the Government's interests'. He believed that 'the withholding from Councils of control of appointments is bad for democracy, and that centralised appointments is [sic] bad for democracy, and that centralised appointments of doctors is a cause of district and local dissatisfaction'.

MacEntee countered by asserting that county managers were essential if local democracy was to be saved. Before 1942 local government was often guilty of 'waste and extravagance', and of failing to respond to people's needs.[42] In February 1946 the Minister instructed county managers not to receive deputations from local voluntary bodies without prior authorisation from the council and warned them 'not to follow any line which would prejudice the council in its line of action' during such meetings.

In March MacEntee provided his cabinet colleagues with a copy of the minimal background information on the estimates which the Mayo county manager had circulated to councillors. It was, he claimed, 'a fairly typical example'.[43] Speaking in the Local Government estimates debate some months later, MacEntee pointed out that the manager was not on a footing of equality with the elected body. He also emphasised that the chairman of the county council should be the main link between council and manager.[44]

RESTORING DEMOCRATIC RIGHTS? THE INTER-PARTY GOVERNMENT AND COUNTY MANAGEMENT

Although the Fianna Fail cabinet approved a proposal from Seán MacEntee in 1946 to introduce limited amendments to the 1940 and 1942 Acts, including an end to the unpopular practice of having one manager administering two counties,[45] no bill was drafted before the change of government in 1948. In January 1949, however, the first inter-party government granted the Minister for Local Government authority to draft a bill providing for the abolition of county managers, though city managers would be retained. Many of the functions carried out by county managers — planning and awarding contracts for sanitary and housing schemes, or deciding who was eligible for home assistance — would be carried out by executive committees composed of elected councillors.

Managers would be retitled county officers. They would retain responsibility for staffing and for allocating tenancies in local authority housing, though these functions would be closely scrutinised by councillors. In the longer term, the inter-party government proposed to amalgamate the posts of county manager (or county officer) and county secretary, despite the Department's opinion that the proposed legislation would actually increase the amount of administrative work because of the need for councils to provide detailed accounts to the executive committees.[46] The County Administration Bill was introduced in Dáil Éireann in June 1950 and had reached the committee stage when the Dáil was dissolved in May 1951, whereupon it lapsed. Its passage had been delayed by a series of disputes between the Departments of Local Government and Health over the organisation of local administration.

The Fianna Fáil government, which came into office in 1951,

delayed taking any decision on amending the County Management Acts until 1954 when the cabinet approved a limited bill providing for the degrouping of counties and for changes in the management structure in Dublin, plus a more controversial provision requiring the manager to obtain council approval before submitting a proposal to the Minister to create any new office. This was included, despite strong opposition from the Minister for Health, Dr James Ryan, 'because of the concern repeatedly expressed by the elected members [at the continuing expansion] of local staffs and the absence of any power enabling the elected body to control such increases'. The bill also attempted to give councillors greater control over the manager by simplifying the powers in section 29 of the 1940 Act, which enabled them to require the county manager to perform a specified function.

These concessions failed to placate the Fianna Fáil national executive. It demanded that local councillors be given a much larger role in allocating local authority houses, though the Department reported that some councils, notably Limerick Corporation, had formally decided to leave responsibility for this task with the county manager.[47] Numerous amendments were tabled in both the Dáil and the Seanad, all designed to increase the power of local representatives. The Minister for Local Government, Patrick Smith,[48] fended off critics by arguing that they had failed to appreciate the extent to which the bill increased the power of elected representatives.

When the Dáil was dissolved in May 1954, this bill also lapsed. The joint statement of policy objectives issued by Fine Gael and Labour on 31 May 1954, during the general election campaign, included a commitment

> To restore democratic rights in respect of Local Government by amending the County Management Acts and giving to Local Authorities greater autonomy and effective power in local affairs.[49]

During the 1954/55 estimates debate, Patrick O' Donnell, Minister for Local Government in the second inter-party government, announced his intention of visiting every county and county borough to obtain first-hand information on the relations between managers and elected members and to discover 'any defects thought to be inherent in the management system or that have developed in practice'.[50] In July 1954 O'Donnell also agreed to meet the chairmen of urban district councils and town commissioners.

These consultations revealed that there was much wider support for county management than many critics had suggested. Some county councils expressed outright opposition: Sligo County Council reaffirmed a resolution it had passed in April 1948 calling for a repeal of the County Management Acts; Cavan County Council also voted in favour of repeal; Waterford County Council passed a resolution to the effect that the present system was unsatisfactory, but that it wished to see the legislation amended, not repealed. Many councils expressed support for the local county manager. Clare County Council described their county manager as 'not a Czar'; Donegal County Council agreed unanimously that the Donegal county manager 'was completely overloaded with work' and recommended that steps be taken to ease this burden. Several members of Sligo County Council coupled criticism of the system with fulsome praise for the Sligo county manager.

Proposals for reform were confused. There was strong support for having the county manager appointed by the council, following the recommendation of the Local Appointments Commission, instead of the then current practice where the manager was appointed by the minister. Most councils wished to limit the increase in staff numbers and sought a more flexible system of amending estimates, but few wished to take responsibility for allocating tenancies of local authority houses, though councillors wanted to be kept informed and given an opportunity to advise on the 'character' of applicants. Most were divided on the merits of degrouping, except in the case of Dublin, where there was a strong demand for the appointment of a separate manager for County Dublin. One councillor claimed that most opposition to county management came from older councillors, who remembered the previous system and regretted their loss of authority. Many recognised this could not be restored. A Mayo councillor claimed that if there was no county manager, 'the Council would have to sit at least four times a week'.

The consultations revealed that harmonious relations between councillors and managers depended on managers keeping councillors informed. Several councils claimed that their power to control the managers was largely ineffective because they had no prior information of the manager's intentions. A memorandum submitted to the Department by Wicklow county manager Michael Flannery, emphasised the importance of consulting council members 'on certain executive matters in which they may have a special interest or intimate local knowledge' in order to avoid 'the possibility of members feeling embarrassed or suffering from a feeling of frustration when persons approach them for information on matters of public interest and concern'. Michael Flannery outlined the consultation procedures which were used in County Wicklow concerning roads, tenancies of local authority houses, home assistance, town planning and other matters, though he stressed that this involved senior officials in much additional work and extensive travel to attend meetings at night.

The grievances most commonly aired by councillors, such as the undue proportion of money spent on national as opposed to county roads (see chapter nine), their inability to give preference in appointments to local candidates, and the restrictions on their claims for expenses, had little, if any bearing on the County Management Acts. Similarly, the concerns expressed over rising staff numbers reflected councillors' unease at the increased burden of rates, another matter on which county management had little direct bearing, though it provided a convenient scapegoat. In a note dated October 1954, a senior official in the Department of Local Government wrote to John Garvin, the secretary:

> I have felt for a long time that individual members are sheltering behind the Manager and the Minister in these matters [salaries]; in fact I have a 'hunch' that in all matters of expenditure there is that feeling that the blame can always be put on somebody else's shoulders, with the result that the same detailed consideration is not being given to expenditure that we had in pre-managerial days when there could be no scapegoat except Councillors.[51]

The amending legislation, which was drafted following O'Donnell's tour, was a far cry from the inter-party government's original commitment, though it did transfer some executive power from the manager to councillors. Elected members of a local authority could require the manager to give prior notification of his proposals in all matters except personnel or individual health cases. It became mandatory for managers to provide councils with prior information on all capital expenditure projects. Section 4, the Act's most famous clause, gave councillors power to override managerial action by summoning a special meeting, if necessary. Any decision could be overturned by an absolute majority of all councillors, or by more than two-thirds of the voting members present. Councils were also empowered to elect an estimates committee which would be responsible for preparing the annual estimate, on the advice of the county manager and they were given additional powers to amend estimates.

The cabinet approved the proposals in December 1954, subject to a provision that members of a local authority could not direct a manager not to proceed with a proposed scheme which was a statutory requirement; further amendments were introduced to meet the wishes of the Departments of Health and Social Welfare.[52] The bill became law on 21 June 1955.

<h2 style="text-align:center">CONCLUSION</h2>

Although the genesis of the county management system can be traced back to the first decade of the new state, in other respects it was very much in character with the general tone of public administration during the Emergency, which was primarily concerned with efficiency, often at the expense of consultation and democracy. Given the pressure on government during the Emergency, fears of possible invasion, the need to generate sufficient supplies of turf and to maintain an administrative system despite serious shortages, little attention appears to have been paid to the culture and style of the new system. Shortages of petrol and cuts in public transport meant that meetings and consultative procedures were reduced to a minimum.

While, superficially, the proposal to establish parish councils could be presented as an attempt to restore power to local communities, in practice it was yet another attack on local democracy: most proponents wanted members to be either nominated, or, if elected, chosen by a restricted electorate. Criticisms directed against county management and the flirtation with parish councils both echo the concern expressed in the report of the Commission on Vocational Organisation about the progressive expansion of bureaucracy.[53] There was a widespread perception that government was intervening to an increasing extent in all aspects of Irish life. It could perhaps be argued that the administrative demands of running a modern state, particularly during wartime, were not fully understood by the Irish public. It is noticeable that when the second inter-party government contemplated abolishing the county management system, most local authorities realised that this office had become essential. The inhabitants of Plato's Cave may have been blind, or short-sighted, but they were not able to escape entirely from the changes taking place in a wider world, though they did not fully grasp their implications.

CHAPTER EIGHT

'IRELAND IS BUILDING' 1945-56

The Royal Irish Academy of the Post War World will have associated
with it countless subsidiary planning organisations. The Highways
Planning Board will arrange for vast concrete arterial roads to radiate
from every centre of population, each road having special lanes for
fast traffic, slow traffic, tramways, cycles, pedestrians, invalids,
readers of *The Standard*, school-children and Irish speakers. At
intervals of two miles there will be rest centres, health clinics, a
'People's Unit' embracing swimming pools, restaurant, cinema,
writing and reading rooms, gramophone recital apartments, a home
for the aged, a vitamin bureau and two aerodromes.

Meanwhile the National Housing Planning Board will be engaged
in erecting ten million vast arterial houses for the Planned People of
Ireland, each house complete with steriliser and small operating
theatre, a miniature pharmacy for a new planned science of
autotherapy, built-in wife, and hot-water on draught from the
system already provided by An Colucht Náisiunta um Uisce Galach,
or the National Hot Water Corporation. The Board of Transportation
and Communications will lay out and build vast arterial railroads
and canals, the railroads traversing only worthless mountain land
and being enabled to overcome the unthinkable grades by means of
locks. Vast arterial hydro-electric, sewerage, waterwork and mining
enterprises will be carried out by direct labour under the auspices
and aegis of the National Development Board.

Flann O'Brien, Myles Na Gopaleen, *The Best of Myles* (London,
    1968), pp. 364-65.
[This is an insider's view. Brian O'Nolan, alias Flann O'Brien served on
the staff of the Department of Local Government from 1935 to 1954.]

The immediate post-war years brought significant changes to the Department of Local Government and to Irish political life. In 1948, after sixteen years in office, Fianna Fáil was succeeded by Ireland's first inter-party, or coalition, government. From then until 1957, the government alternated every three years between Fianna Fáil and multi-party coalitions.

In 1948 T.J. Murphy became the first member of the Labour Party to serve as Minister for Local Government. He held the position for little more than a year, dying suddenly in 1949. Labour leader William Norton took over the portfolio briefly pending the appointment of Michael Keyes, yet another Labour Party minister. Cavan TD Patrick Smith served as Minister for Local Government in the Fianna Fáil government of 1951-54 and also held the post briefly in 1957. In the second inter-party government of 1954-57, Patrick O'Donnell, a Fine Gael TD from Donegal, became Minister for Local Government.

James Hurson retired as secretary of the Department of Local Government and Public Health in 1946 because of ill-health. He was succeeded for two months by Thomas McArdle, a veteran of the First Dáil's Department of Local Government. In January 1947 McArdle became the first secretary of the Department of Health; John Collins, who as a teenager had officiated at the 1899 local elections, became secretary. Collins retired after less than two years in November 1948, when John Garvin, the first secretary of the Department not to have worked for the British administration, was appointed to the post. Garvin had been among the first group of administrative officers recruited in 1925. A distinguished Joycean scholar in his spare time, he served until 1966, providing valuable continuity throughout a period of significant change.[1]

On 24 December 1946 the Ministers and Secretaries (Amendment) Act provided for the creation of separate Departments of Health and Social Welfare, which came into existence in January 1947. The Department of Local Government and Public Health was renamed the Department of Local Government. The formal transfer of services took almost a year to complete. Relations between the parent department and its offspring appear to have been amicable; most disputes concerned the division of responsibilities between Health and Social Welfare,[2] though a disagreement subsequently emerged between Local Government and Health over the mechanism for controlling the borrowing powers of local authorities. This was resolved when the

1953 Health Act set limits for local authority borrowings for health and provided a mechanism for both departments to consult on the matter.[3]

PUBLIC EXPENDITURE

The rise in public expenditure under Fianna Fáil during the years 1945-48 is probably best seen as a recovery from a depressed wartime level. Under the first inter-party government, however, the rate of growth accelerated. Public-sector expenditure (e.g. central and local government) accounted for 33.5 per cent of GNP (Gross National Product) in 1949/50 and 41.3 per cent in 1951/52; this share was maintained until the early 1960s. Public capital expenditure rose from an artificially low level of 0.5 per cent of GNP in 1945 to 10.4 per cent by 1951.[4] In 1938 central government expenditure accounted for only 11.6 per cent of Irish GDP (Gross Domestic Product), a figure which was lower than in most western European states and little more than half the UK level. By 1955 central government expenditure accounted for 35 per cent of GDP, the highest of eleven countries for which data are presented, and far outstripping the UK figure of 28 per cent.[5] The ratio of central government expenditure to GDP is partly a reflection of the weakness of local taxation, but it also indicates a substantial change in the place of government in the overall economy.

The significance of this post-war investment programme for Local Government is readily apparent. Housing constituted the largest item in the public capital programme, falling during the years 1948-56 only once below 30 per cent (in 1953/54). In 1949 housing accounted for a record 18.7 per cent of GNP.[6] Once released from wartime privation, the building and construction sectors proved the most buoyant components of both public and private investment. Building investment rose four-fold over the years 1947 to 1951 when it accounted for over 65 per cent of total investment. Although investment in building was almost static between 1951 and 1956,[7] it constituted a constant or slightly increasing share of total investment, as investment in machinery and other items stagnated or declined.

TABLE 8.1

State capital programme 1947/48-1957/58

	Housing	Total*
1947/48	£0.91	£7.93
1948/49	£3.20	£12.47
1949/50	£8.98	£24.34
1950/51	£11.06	£24.61
1951/52	£12.67	£32.73
1952/53	£11.91	£32.27
1953/54	£9.85	£34.59
1954/55	£10.49	£32.86
1955/56	£10.01	£26.71
1956/57	£10.72	£37.46
1957/58	£10.39	£32.10

* Other constituents included hospitals, electricity and turf development, agricultural development afforestation, fisheries, school, university and other state buildings, tourism, insurance, broadcasting and the national development fund, telephones, transport, industrial credit, state companies.

Source: *Capital Investment Advisory Committee: Third Report*

By the late 1940s capital expenditure on housing, roads and other Local Government programmes was no longer being driven by perceived social need or by departmental agendas: the spread, however hesitant, of Keynesian concepts of demand management, and the publication of data on national income caused public expenditure to be viewed in terms of its impact on the economy as a whole, rather than in a purely sectional or departmental manner. In the late 1940s, in Patrick Lynch's immortal words, 'Keynes came to Kinnegad',[8] often in the guise of a council housing programme. The heavy demands on capital resources meant that Local Government's activities were subject to increasing scrutiny by the Department of Finance. In turn, high expenditure on housing and related services placed considerable pressure on the rating system and on the balance between central and local government.

THE TRANSITION TO PEACE 1945-48

Fianna Fáil's final three years in government give an impression of inactivity, which contrasts with the frenzied energy of the inter-party government of 1948-51. This may be unfair. Shortages of materials and capital equipment persisted and even worsened in the years 1945-47 and costs remained high. Expenditure on construction stagnated. It is unlikely that this could have been averted by a more active government. J.J. Lee regards the decision to merge the cabinet committee on economic planning into a committee of the whole cabinet in April 1945 as evidence of a lack of commitment to investment and planning,[9] but it can be argued that the plans had already been drafted and it was now time to execute them. The White Paper, *The Post-War Building Programme*, published by Industry and Commerce in 1945, anticipated spending £99.5m. in the first five post-war years, a figure at least two-thirds above the pre-1939 level. Housing would account for £41.2m., roads for £13.7m., water and sewerage for £3.36m.. Over 56 per cent of the £73m. earmarked for building and 46 per cent of proposed expenditure on building and construction would be carried out in the Dublin area.[10]

In the course of the 1945 estimates debate, Local Government Minister Seán MacEntee gave a commitment that local authorities which started to construct houses immediately would be given an extra subsidy to cover the higher costs incurred,[11] and in 1946 the Transitional Development Fund (TDF) was established, with a sum of £5m., to provide additional, retrospective grants for all public investments carried out in the 1945/46 financial year.[12] In a further effort to encourage local authorities to carry out capital investment schemes, the rate of interest on LLF loans was reduced from 4.25 to 2.5 per cent in June 1946,[13] the lowest figure in the history of the state; the repayment period was extended from 35 to 50 years.[14] Although this was a popular move, local authorities remained reluctant to embark on major capital projects, owing to high costs and lack of supplies. By 31 March 1948, TDF grants for housing totalled only £460,000; £333,000 of this went to Dublin Corporation. Subsidies averaged £250 per house, or 25 per cent of costs, an inadequate amount because average costs had risen by 250 per cent between 1938 and 1947, from £394 to £990.[15] Nevertheless, a majority of the small number of houses completed between 1945 and 1947 were built by local authorities, probably because the Transitional Development Fund provided top-up grants. No additional incentives were provided for the private sector.[16]

The White Paper had envisaged local authorities constructing 3,200 houses in the first year after the war, with private builders erecting a further 1,200-1,500 houses. Yet there was only sufficient timber in stock to construct 2,360 houses. If some timber was allocated for other essential purposes, only 1,900 houses could be completed. Shortages of iron goods, copper and lead piping rapidly made even this target unrealistic. Road maintenance could not be carried out because of shortages of tar, bitumen and petrol, and plans to substitute concrete roads had to be abandoned owing to a shortage of steel, which was needed to reinforce concrete slabs. In late 1945 a promised shipment of tar from Britain was diverted to France.[17] Industry and Commerce attempted to use building licences to allocate supplies, but the 1945 White Paper had refused to establish clear priorities.

Even if there were something to quarrel with in the proposals which have been submitted, it is difficult to say by what criterion the merits of individual proposals should be judged. When one comes to distinguish between a house for a person to live in and a factory in which he can earn his living, a school for his child and a hospital for a sick relative, one wonders what is to be accepted as a standard of building merit.

The above quotation is symptomatic of the White Paper, in that it shows a determination to keep the role of the state to a minimum. The White Paper further proposed to give priority in allocating scarce building materials to the private sector. It recommended that preference should be given to buildings which needed little timber and that efforts should be made (despite the urgent need for houses in Dublin) to spread work throughout the country.[18]

Such attitudes meant that, although housing was expected to account for over 50 per cent of the first post-war year's expenditure on building, Local Government was unable to guarantee that the housing sector would obtain its 1939 share of national cement output.[19] Shortages of timber, cement, ironmongery, lead, copper, skilled labour and fuel persisted until May 1947. Public sector investment remained low until shortages eased. It began to rise significantly during 1947/48, though this was not yet evident at the time of the 1948 election.

TABLE 8.2

Local authority loans sanctioned
(£000s)

	Housing	Water and Sewerage	Other*	Total
1946/47	£115	£139	£285	£539
1947/48	£2,324	£216	£317	£2,857
1948/49	£8,361	£497	£374	£9,232
1949/50	£11,835	£603	£581	£13,019
1950/51	£8,946	£718	£1,570	£11,234
1951/52	£18,490	£1,189	£1,486	£21,165
1952/53	£13,778	£1,163	£1,452	£16,393
1953/54	£8,607	£1,571	£1,575	£11,753
1954/55	£6,321	£1,198	£1,639	£9,158
1955/56	£8,079	£2,094	£1,041	£11,214
1956/57	£11,664	£2,059	£929	£14,652
1957/58	£7,456	£2,142	£429	£10,027

*This includes loans for expenditure relating to burials, markets, roads, bridges and road machinery, county and district hospitals, sanatoria and mental hospitals, vocational education, fire brigades and miscellaneous items.

Source: Annual Reports of the Department of Local Government and Public Health and the Department of Local Government

All opposition campaigns during the 1948 general election were dominated by images of Fianna Fáil's failure: emigration, housing shortages, inadequate health services, alleged corruption associated with Locke's Distillery,[20] and the arrogance and lack of democracy associated with the county management system. A new political party, Clann na Poblachta, introduced a fresh dimension to Irish political campaigns with its documentary film *Our Country*, complete with images of urban tenements and barefoot children.[21] Nevertheless the Labour Party was given the Local Government portfolio.

THE IMPACT OF LABOUR: PAY AND CONDITIONS

Between 1945 and 1957 the post of Minister for Local Government was held by members of the Labour, the Fine Gael and the Fianna Fáil parties. Although there was substantial continuity in many policies, there is evidence that Labour Party views prevailed on matters such as constructing roads and houses by using direct labour, and on the reforms in pay and industrial relations procedures for local authority workers. Industrial relations was a subject of growing importance. The number of local officers under the control of the Minister for Local Government rose from 3,300 in December 1939 to approximately 5,000 by the end of 1951 and to 5,250 by 1954, despite the establishment of Departments of Health and Social Welfare. In 1954 the total number of local officers and employees stood at 57,000. Before 1939 the government had favoured a decentralised approach to local authority wages and salaries, but during the Emergency wages and salaries paid by local authorities were controlled by the government under the Emergency Powers Orders. There was no going back when peace returned. In 1946 the Industrial Relations Act provided for the establishment of a Labour Court to adjudicate on wage claims and other disputes. Representatives of the Trade Union Congresses (there were two at this stage) and the Federated Union of Employers met under the Labour Court's auspices to bargain over wage increases, resulting in what came to be regarded as the first national pay round.[22] Inevitably the process of wage bargaining became more centralised, with wage increases in one sector following those in another.

Although the Fianna Fáil government excluded local authority employees from the scope of the 1946 Industrial Relations Bill on the grounds that local authorities were already among the best employers, the establishment of the Labour Court and the emergence of national wage rounds had an inevitable impact on local authority pay scales. Seán MacEntee believed that the Minister for Local Government should protect local authorities from any additional pressures to concede higher wages or improved conditions[23] and the 1946 Local Government Act made the Minister responsible for approving changes in wage rates paid to local authority employees.[24] At this stage the Department appeared to favour a two-tier labour market: it believed that the pay of salaried officials who were recruited through the Local Appointments Commission should be determined nationally, whereas the wages of manual workers would vary in accordance with other local wage rates. In 1947 a national salary scale was introduced for local authority officers.

This policy changed under the first inter-party government. Road workers proved to be major beneficiaries of the Labour Party's tenancy of the Custom House. Although the wages of these workers had been linked to those of agricultural labourers since the 1920s, the Department's annual report for 1950/51 stated that there was no comparable class to which they could logically be linked.[25] In September 1950 Michael Keyes informed the government that he proposed to approve substantial wage increases for road-workers in all counties where these had been requested by the county councils and county managers. The increases were designed to compensate not only for the higher cost of living, but for 'the underpayment, absolute and relative, of these workers'. Increases ranged from 5 shillings (25p) to 18 shillings (90p) per week. This brought about a substantial narrowing of the gap between the wages paid to roadworkers in different counties. Wages rose in all counties except Dublin, the county that previously had paid the highest wages. The largest increases were awarded in western counties, where wages had traditionally been below the national average; wages of road workers in County Mayo rose by 30 per cent. Finance objected that these concessions had implications for the pay of other public service employees and their fears were realised in February 1951 when the government decided to tie the pay of certain categories of state employees to that of road-workers.

During the term of the first inter-party government, Local Government succeeded in securing a substantial increase in the cost-of-living allowance paid to local authority officers, which not only compensated them for price inflation during the Korean War, but removed a long-standing grievance. The 1946 wage settlement, on which all subsequent post-war increases were calculated, had not fully compensated local authority officers for wartime inflation, unlike the position in the civil service. On 4 May 1951, in the dying weeks of the inter-party government, the Department issued a circular announcing salary increases, which had allegedly been approved at cabinet on the previous day. Costello subsequently pointed out that 'no record should be taken indicating that the Government had taken a decision on the remuneration of local officials',[26] but the increase was conceded.

While civil servants had access to formal arbitration and conciliation procedures, pay and conditions of local authority staff continued to be governed by what the Department termed 'informal and perhaps haphazard arrangements'. Individual officers had a statutory right to appeal to the Minister on matters of pay, duties and conditions, though it is unclear how often this was exercised. It is scarcely surprising that trade unions, such as the ITGWU, lobbied Labour Ministers for Local Government to have council road-workers brought within the scope of the 1946 Industrial Relations Act. However, Keyes deferred a decision on the grounds that local authorities were not represented on the Conciliation Council. The inter-party government was committed to a more decentralised local administration and this may have made it reluctant to introduce a central conciliation system, despite pressure from trade unions.

The abortive 1950 Local Government (County Administration) Bill, whose primary purpose was the abolition of county management, included clauses giving local authority servants power to appeal to elected members against decisions concerning their remuneration and conditions. It was anticipated that each county council and county borough council would establish an advisory conciliation committee.[27] The Fianna Fáil government of 1951-54 proved much more reluctant to concede wage and salary increases than its predecessor. This was in keeping with the views of Seán MacEntee as Minister for Finance. Decisions on wage or salary demands were made on the basis of comparability with similar grades in the civil service, a policy that was in keeping with Fianna Fáil's more centralist tendencies. By 1952 claims for general pay increases made by local authority staff were automatically deferred by the Minister for Local Government until claims by civil servants had been resolved. Local authority staff were then offered identical terms.[28]

Although the second inter-party government of 1954-57 did not include a Labour Minister for Local Government, local authority officials appear to have regarded that administration as more amenable to granting pay increases than the previous Fianna Fáil government, and ministers were swamped with demands from county secretaries and county engineers. To press their case, the engineers organised a boycott of some Local Appointments Commission posts. However, the Minister, Patrick O'Donnell, decided that any decision to approve nationwide salary increases could be construed as contradicting the underlying policy of the County and City Management (Amendment)

Bill 1955 and he rejected proposals for a nationwide conciliation system. Local authority employees gained access to the Labour Court under the 1955 Industrial Relations (Amendment) Act.[29] This provided a conciliation system which avoided any formal commitment to centralised pay scales. The 1955 City and County Management (Amendment) Act provided that salaries of local authority officers would continue to be fixed by the Minister, though in 1956 councils were given greater discretion to determine the level of marriage and retirement gratuities.

The first inter-party government was determined to reduce the extent of central control. As part of that process, local authorities were again given power to recruit a total of 54 general grades of offices, which had previously been filled by the Local Appointments Commission, though the qualifications and other details were determined by the Minister. Local Government also attempted to devolve to local authorities, responsibility for recruiting consultant engineers, architects, clerks of works and rate collectors, though the Department specified general qualifications and the appropriate rates of pay. The duties of those who supervised road-workers were made uniform throughout all local authorities and a uniform premium over road-workers' wages was specified. This process continued under Fianna Fáil and in 1952 a circular letter was issued which left local authorities free, 'within wide limits', to appoint and remunerate temporary staff, though boundaries were set on the duration of temporary posts in order to avoid abuse. It was not unknown for councils to continue a 'temporary' post for up to ten years, in order to prevent it being filled by the Local Appointments Commission.

Curbing this practice proved difficult. From 1949 a succession of temporary officers and employees of local authorities, who either had lost their positions or were replaced by a permanent appointee, took successful court cases against their former employers, claiming that the local authority was imposing 'arbitrary' limits on temporary status. According to the Department, the lawsuits all carried the 'implication that when a person acquires, by one means or another, temporary employment under a local authority, he has a tenure of the job until he chooses to relinquish it'; these legal challenges once again called into question the role of the Local Appointments Commission. In June 1954 the Fianna Fáil government, which was less sensitive to the wishes of local authorities than the inter-party government, imposed a three-year limit on all temporary appointments to professional posts, though this could be overridden in exceptional cases.[30]

The Local Government (Superannuation) Act 1948 was a major landmark in the evolution of a national local government service. Local Government believed that introducing a proper pension scheme was an essential precondition for enforcing mandatory retirement on grounds of age or in cases of disability; otherwise, local authorities were unwilling to terminate employment. Edward McCarron, the first secretary of the Department of Local Government and Public Health, had dreamed of introducing such a pension scheme during the 1920s. The first serious attempt to do so collapsed in 1939 because the Department of Finance feared that local authorities would be unable to bear the cost. Finance also feared that the proposal to include women officials within the superannuation scheme would lead to demands for similar treatment from women civil servants, who were denied the benefits of the 1909 Act.[31]

The 1948 Act extended the terms of the 1909 Civil Service Pensions Act to local authorities, though local authority pensions were on a contributory basis, unlike those in the civil service. Pension rights were transferable from one local authority to another and between the civil service and local authority service. Before 1948, superannuation was provided only for officers (i.e. professional or white collar staff) and conditions varied considerably from one local authority to another. Although pensions for manual workers or employees remained optional, by 1950/51 three-quarters of local authorities were providing them with superannuation schemes. It proved difficult to define permanent employment. Labourers engaged on state-aided works schemes were excluded, unless they were employed as supervisors. However those employed on schemes financed by the Road Fund, or from the rates, were deemed to be permanent employees if they had been employed for three consecutive years with breaks of less than 60 days a year. In September 1950, the Department instructed local authorities to pay pensions in such cases in advance of amending legislation. Another point of contention was whether or not pensions should be increased in line with salary increases: the code provided for fixed pensions.[32] The 1951-54 Fianna Fáil government proved unsympathetic to this demand, but the Local Authorities Retired Officers and Servants Association obtained a commitment from the Labour Party to implement this change before the 1954 election.

HOUSING AND THE FIRST INTER-PARTY GOVERNMENT

Housing was the main preoccupation of the Department of Local Government during the first inter-party government and remained the most important issue facing it until 1957. This would also have been true if Fianna Fáil had been returned to office in 1948. Seán MacEntee's 1947 estimates speech identified housing as the service for which there was the 'most acute and widespread need'. As it was, the new Minister, T.J. Murphy, transformed Local Government into a virtual Department of Housing. In an effort to accelerate the housing drive, he met local representatives, negotiated with employers and building industry trade unions and pressed for increased use of direct labour in constructing local authority houses.[33] This commitment helped to forestall demands in Dáil Éireann, notably from Dublin lord mayor Alfie Byrne, for the appointment of a separate Minister for Housing.[34] In the 1948/49 Local Government estimates, 88 per cent of expenditure was allocated for housing[35] and, although Finance Minister Patrick McGilligan gave a commitment in his 1948 Budget speech 'to ensure retrenchment over as wide a field as possible' and emphasised the need 'to examine critically proposals for capital expenditure which add to the burden of tax and reduce savings', he conceded that there was a 'general agreement, that housing, though not productive of adequate direct return in the financial sense, is entitled to special consideration on social grounds'.[36]

This sense of a new era is best captured by the pamphlet *Ireland is Building*, published by the Departments of Local Government and Health in 1949. This glossy publication, replete with photographs, was designed for mass readership. It marks a new era for government publications. Seán MacEntee would have been unlikely to sponsor such a document. *Ireland is Building* became a sort of memorial to the late Minister, T.J. Murphy. His words are cited on the first page, beside his photograph, taken at the opening of a housing scheme. Taoiseach John A. Costello's vote of sympathy on T.J. Murphy's death in April 1949 is also quoted. The brochure, the brainchild of the cabinet subcommittee on employment, was designed to encourage emigrants, particularly building craftsmen, to return to Ireland. Free copies were distributed in Britain through Irish emigrant organisations; the brochure was advertised in posters displayed in halls used by Irish societies, and on a Sunday-night radio programme for emigrants broadcast on Radio

Éireann.[37] The campaign reflected the widespread fear that the post-war construction programme might be delayed because of a shortage of skilled workers; it also indicated a new concern with emigration.

Although *Ireland is Building* covered all aspects of the public capital programme — including hospitals, factories, hydroelectric and turf-powered stations — pride of place went to the commitment to build 100,000 houses within ten years. No mention is made of roads, water or sanitation services, which suggests that they were given a low priority. The brochure presented an image of modernity and national pride, combined with historical references. Turf-burning power stations became 'the new Round Towers of Ireland'; the airmail stamp, carrying letters to those who had emigrated, depicts the Angel Victor flying to St. Patrick (in exile) 'with many letters' calling him back to Ireland. Dublin tenements were juxtaposed with gleaming new houses in Sallynoggin, Co. Dublin. Photographs of house construction in Inchicore and Crumlin carried the heading 'Dublin "splendid among cities"'.

The text recalled the era of Grattan's parliament when Dublin was 'one of the finest Capital cities of Europe', and expressed the hope that under a native administration 'the Capital of the Republic of Ireland soon will be worthy of Pearse's words: "Splendid among cities!"'. Returning emigrants were assured of continued employment, even when the housing programme was complete, because 'higher standards of life will call for extensive works of reconstruction everywhere in order to better the entire built-up area of the country'. In addition to promises of higher wages and lower tax rates than in Britain, returning emigrants were given assurances about the quality of life. Food and drink were 'pure and wholesome'; in modern Ireland 'the amenities of life' were 'more attractive than anywhere else', 'especially to the home-coming Irishman', who was described as 'ill-fed and ill-housed in uncongenial places'.

This pamphlet captures the optimistic mood of the first inter-party government. Public capital expenditure rose sharply, as Fine Gael (hitherto the party of parsimony) and its coalition allies sought to outspend Fianna Fáil. The 1948 election campaign had highlighted major shortcomings in economic and social policy. Both Clann na Poblachta and Labour saw the solution in a programme of public investment which would create employment, stem emigration and develop Irish resources. A combination of Keynesian economics, then in vogue in Britain, and the O'Loughlen Minority Report of the Banking Commission,[38] which formed the basis of Clann na Poblachta's economic programme, provided intellectual justification for this approach. The increase in external assets during the war years[39] appeared to provide one source of funds. Taoiseach John A. Costello was among those who believed that it was justifiable to deplete external assets, i.e. run a balance of payments deficit, in order to stimulate the economy. The division of government expenditure into current and capital spending in the McGilligan budget of 1950, which is generally regarded as the first 'Keynesian' budget in Ireland, helped to facilitate this process, while the American government's Marshall Aid programme provided short-term relief from the dollar shortage.

Without Marshall Aid, investment would have been delayed because of lack of supplies. The United States was the sole supplier of many materials, and a European-wide dollar shortage, coupled with the suspension of sterling's convertibility in 1947, virtually ruled out Irish purchases from the dollar area other than via Marshall Aid. Loan counterpart funds generated by Marshall Aid[40] permitted a much higher level of investment than would otherwise have proved possible.

Current expenditure by local authorities rose from £12.3m in 1938/39 to £28.4m. by 1948/49, and the value of loans granted to local authorities from the Local Loans Fund totalled £9.75m. in 1948/49, as against £450,000 ten years earlier. The net debt of local authorities more than doubled by 1948/49.[41] The estimate for the Department of Local Government for 1950/51, £4.3m., was over £1m. higher than in 1950.[42]

THE FIANNA FÁIL GOVERNMENT 1951-54 AND THE SECOND INTER-PARTY GOVERNMENT 1951-57

The outbreak of the Korean War in the summer of 1950 brought fears of a return to wartime stringency, which were accentuated by the sudden termination of Marshall Aid the following spring. Plans for regional administration, which had been drawn up during the Emergency, were reactivated and in September 1950 Local Government secretary John Garvin proposed contacting county managers confidentially to advise them to build up reserve stocks of materials. Although the sense of urgency had eased by January 1951, and there is no evidence that local authorities stocked up on supplies,[43] panic buying on international markets led to higher inflation, an acute balance of payments deficit and considerable pressure from both the Department of Finance and the Central Bank for curbs on government spending.[44]

Nemesis came with the return of Fianna Fáil in 1951. Seán MacEntee, back in Finance, determined to re-establish financial orthodoxy. His 1952 Budget speech contained the warning that 'the fever spending of the Marshall Aid period is over' and a threat to adopt a more stringent definition of capital expenditure than his predecessor, which would in turn mean a less tolerant attitude to borrowing, to finance public expenditure.[45] However, MacEntee found it easier to increase taxes and reduce private spending than to restrain public capital spending, particularly on housing. In 1953 he pointed out that 'in recent years new dwellings in this country have accounted for a much higher proportion of domestic capital outlay than in most European countries, even those which have suffered devastation from war' and he reiterated his determination to concentrate resources on 'directly productive projects'.[46] Although the incoming second inter-party government gave a commitment in its 1954 'Principal Objects of Policy' to establish a Capital Investment Board in order to ensure that the 'State Capital Development Programme will be supplemental to and not in substitution for private investment', the axe did not fall on public investment until 1957 with the publication of reports of the Capital Investment Advisory Committee.

Government economic policy in this post-war period relied on boosting public capital expenditure on infrastructure as an alternative to restructuring agriculture or industry. In addition, the public capital programme was strongly influenced by wider socio-economic objectives. All governments channelled considerable sums to rural areas, particularly the underdeveloped western counties, in an effort to redress emigration and rural population decline. Many Fianna Fáil deputies, including Minister for Local Government Paddy Smith, believed that Dublin was 'too big' and saw the decentralisation of industry as a means of easing pressure on the city's housing.[47] Fears that the Korean War might herald the beginning of World War III and the threat of aerial bombardment reinforced this urge towards decentralisation, though no action was taken to relocate government offices. Both the incoming 1951 Fianna Fáil government and second inter-party government committed themselves to tackling the cultural and economic problems of Gaeltacht areas.[48] This resulted in additional resources for housing, roads and other Local Government services being directed to western areas, though this was in conflict with the demonstrable needs of Dublin.

HOUSING

The White Paper on Housing, published in 1948, estimated that a total of 100,000 houses were needed, at a minimum cost of £90m.. A survey carried out by local authorities indicated that 43,000 houses should be constructed in urban and municipal areas and a further 16,000 in rural areas to meet 'the existing housing needs of the working classes'. Dublin, Cork, Limerick and Waterford County Boroughs and Dun Laoghaire were estimated to account for 70 per cent of the total. The Housing Amendment Act, passed in January 1948, provided the legal and financial framework for the post-war housing drive. The Act was passed in the dying days of the Fianna Fáil government; the inter-party government was the main beneficiary, due recompense for the fact that the Fianna Fáil housing drive of the 1930s was launched on the back of legislation enacted by Cumann na nGaedheal.

Despite the widely held belief that housing should be a priority in the immediate post-war years, the Fianna Fáil government had been slow to draft a new housing programme. There is no obvious single explanation for this delay: the Department of Local Government may have been preoccupied with restructuring, or it may not have regarded the matter as an urgent one, given the shortages of materials. However, this delay created an impression that Fianna Fáil had lost interest in social problems.

The 1948 Act introduced substantially higher subsidies for both local authority and private housing. Although the repayment period for housing loans taken out by local authorities from the Local Loans Fund had been extended to fifty years in 1947, Exchequer subsidies ceased after 35 years; they were now extended to fifty years. Eligibility conditions for the 66.6 per cent slum rehousing subsidy were eased, and additional grants remained available from the Transitional Development Fund.

TABLE 8.3

New and reconstructed houses in receipt of Exchequer grants 1946-57

	Local Authority	Private Sector Housing*		Total
	New	New	Reconstructed	
1946/47	619	456	690	1,765
1947/48	729	773	577	2,079
1948/49	1,871	1,425	732	4,028
1949/50	5,299	2,667	1,249	9,215
1950/51	7.787	4,331	2,045	14,163
1951/52	7,185	5,221	2,173	14,579
1952/53	7,486	5,815	2,432	15,733
1953/54	5,643	5,107	4,068	14,818
1954/55	5,267	4,858	4,657	14,782
1955/56	4,011	5,368	6,160	15,539
1956/57	4,784	5,561	7,745	18,090

* Erected and reconstructed by private persons and public utility societies.

Source: Annual Reports of the Department of Local Government, 1947/48 to 1956/57.

The 1948 Act went further than the 1931 Act in focusing local authority housing programmes on slum clearance. Houses built as part of a slum-clearance scheme would continue to receive an annual subsidy as before; the subsidies provided for other local authority housing were reduced. Modest council houses, charging rents which could be afforded by labourers' families, were eligible for a once-off capital grant. More expensive houses, suitable for tradesmen, would receive no Exchequer support, though councils could provide a subsidy from the rates.

The White Paper seems to have assumed that many working-class families would be housed in rented accommodation provided by public utility societies, trade unions or large employers, which were offered incentives in the form of subsidies amounting to a maximum of £285 per house plus rates remission. This was an optimistic gesture, since only 379 houses had been grant-aided under similar provisions between 1932 and 1947. There was little alteration in Exchequer support for labourers' cottages, though agricultural labourers and farmers' sons working on the land were now given priority over other rural families living in substandard accommodation. The ceiling for Small Dwellings Acquisition Acts loans was raised to £2,000 in the summer of 1948, double its 1931 limit; given the increase in building costs, this amounted to a reduction in real terms.

In the first draft of the Housing Bill, this was the only incentive provided for owner-occupiers. In August 1947, however the Fianna Fáil cabinet approved the bill, subject to grants being provided for new and reconstructed private homes. Grants were set at a maximum of £275, four to six times pre-war levels. In an accompanying memorandum, Local Government pointed out that five-room houses which had cost £800 before 1939 were selling for up to £2,000. The grants were designed to enable more families to afford such houses and to encourage building contractors to construct smaller houses. Finance argued that raising the ceiling for Small Dwellings Acquisition Act (SDAA) loans would attract contractors away from slum clearance and would mean that prospective home-owners were more likely to borrow from the public sector, as opposed to relying on banks and building societies. Subsidies would merely inflate builders' profits, though grants for farmers' housing were exempt from this stricture. Nevertheless the proposals proved popular and went some way towards countering a press campaign that focused on the housing needs of the 'black-coated worker'.[49]

LOCAL AUTHORITY HOUSING

The 1948 White Paper provided the statistical basis for a comprehensive programme of local authority housing. Each local authority provided data on estimated housing needs, the number of sites available, and tenders approved, plus the number of houses under construction in November 1947. Local Government officials were aware that plans to construct 100,000 houses would place considerable pressure on labour and materials and they sought ways of overcoming bottlenecks. British housing authorities were making extensive use of prefabrication and other experimental building methods to reduce costs and speed up completion. However, the White Paper on housing reported that a committee appointed by the Royal Institute of the Architects of Ireland had rejected as unproven the case for the total prefabrication of houses. In May 1949 Michael Colivet, chairman of the Housing Board dismissed, on the grounds of poor design, the possibility of using system building schemes; he also pointed out that they were economical only for large urban developments and would be unsuitable in smaller urban or rural areas.[50] An attempt to import 500 aluminium houses from England was dropped because of opposition from trade unions,[51] and prefabrication played little part in the post-war housing programme. A shortage of bricklayers and masons led Local Government to promote the attractions of concrete houses which needed few skilled workers except carpenters, though it was necessary to reinforce walls with steel and to provide internal insulation in order to avoid condensation. Turf slabs appeared to offer the most promising insulating material and Bord na Móna, the state agency responsible for turf, was duly consulted.[52]

Despite pressure to complete a record number of houses, Local Government made efforts to improve standards of construction and design. In 1945 one housing inspector in the Department lamented the 'monotonous pattern of existing housing schemes', mostly based on plans provided by his Department. He deplored the fact that local authorities repeated them 'over and over again' and criticised the unimaginative layouts devised by local authority engineers, who had no training in this specialism. Most council houses were narrow-fronted because this economised on roads and services. The inspector suggested that the existing plans should be withdrawn and that local authorities should be presented with a set of construction and design standards and encouraged to hire expert technical advisers to draw up housing schemes. This plea for higher standards echoed the words of James Deeny, medical officer of the Department of Local Government and Public Health, in 1946 that piped water and the 'further refinement' of a domestic hot water system should be regarded as basic features of all new housing developments. Deeny hoped that modern technology would improve the quality of women's lives.

> Men, all over the world, are singularly lacking in thought for the welfare of their womenfolk. While any drudgery or inconvenience in man's work will soon be lightened by invention or improvisation, for women little or no effort is made to ease the

340

burden of their monotonous household tasks. All over this country hundreds of thousands of women depend for every drop of water on half-filled cans — drawn laboriously from surface wells sometimes hundreds of yards away. Therefore for the plain and simple reason that of all the people in this country the mother or housewife deserves most from the community, the provision of piped water and better still a domestic hot water system, should be our first consideration in household planning.

Deeny suggested that living rooms and kitchens 'should be oriented generally in a southerly direction', though east and west alignment was permissible. Urban housing schemes should be within half a mile of a playground, and most houses should be built on dead-end streets.[53]

The White Paper on Housing[54] recommended that all new rural cottages should be 'grouped' in order to make it easier to provide piped water, sewerage and electricity; it also included a commitment to increase the average size of new local authority houses from 700 to 750 square feet 'as soon as building costs show a reasonable reduction'. In 1949, however, the Department abandoned a plan to produce a manual of improved housing designs,[55] mainly because of the apathy shown by local authorities. Their demands were more basic: Westmeath County Council wished to provide cow parks attached to labourers' cottages.[56] Council tenants in Nenagh, Co. Tipperary wished to keep pigs in back gardens. Dublin Corporation tenants in Cabra West wanted small workshops where they could carry out businesses which had previously been conducted in tenement basements; although Corporation officials were sympathetic, the idea posed problems for planning regulations.[57]

Local authorities were more interested in economy than in raising standards. In 1947 the Dublin city engineer proposed that each new Corporation house be provided with one light socket in each room, plus one plug per house which would be suitable for a wireless. Electricity charges would be included in the rent and the maximum current available per house would be 150 watts, sufficient to power two or three (dim) lights, though if the radio was running, all lights except one would have to be switched off. Local Government objected that this proposal 'contains no suggestion for further amenities in the way of a point for an electric iron, electric kettle or anything of this nature' and instructed the Dublin city manager to provide a more extensive supply and to install individual coin meters.[58]

A memorandum, drafted in 1947, provides a fascinating insight into a civil servant's perceptions of the appropriate living standards for labourers and tradesmen. Houses catering for tradesmen would be fitted 'on as up to date lines as possible', with modern kitchen units, a small refrigerator, an electric or gas cooker, a boiler for washing clothes, and built-in cupboards. Bedrooms would contain built-in presses and the house would have 'a somewhat larger bathroom than usual in working-class houses'. Labourers' houses would be less elaborate, 'perhaps' with built-in presses in kitchen and bedrooms, but with no boiler or refrigerator.[59]

Despite lack of interest from local authorities, Local Government continued to press for higher standards. The Department resisted efforts on the part of Bord na Móna to have turf-burning ranges fitted in all local authority houses and tried unsuccessfully during the Korean War to persuade councils to install more fuel-efficient ranges. However the Department was fighting an uphill battle, in the face of 'the complete ignorance' of many officials employed by local authorities and the opposition of native manufacturers who produced outdated ranges, though Allied Ironfounders in Waterford eventually responded by designing Rayburn ranges. One official reminded a colleague who was depressed at the hostility of councils on this issue: 'We had exactly the same difficulty when we began our campaign to improve insulation and now we can say that all areas — with the outstanding exception of West Cork — have adopted our recommendations'.[60]

Local authority houses erected after World War II were larger than those built in the inter-war years. Only 1.8 per cent of local authority houses erected between 1932 and 1940 contained five rooms; 16.9 per cent had three rooms and 79.3 per cent contained four rooms; by contrast, 15.8 per cent of houses built between 1947 and 1957 contained five rooms.[61]

Although slum clearance was the priority for local authority housing programmes between 1948 and 1957, other criteria emerged once the worst of the slums had been cleared. The traditional statutory priority was given to families living in one room; and families suffering from tuberculosis were also added to this list.[62] The 1950 Housing (Amendment) Act gave urban authorities power to provide 'reserved' housing for categories such as newly-weds and the elderly. The idea was first mooted in 1944 when Dublin Corporation proposed to reserve a number of houses for newly-weds. The annual draw for Corporation houses soon attracted considerable interest; in 1946 there were 597 applicants. The idea captured the imagination of Seán MacEntee and in 1947 he oversaw the drafting of complex proposals for 'reserved' housing for newly-weds and for other categories, such as labourers and tradesmen with young families, which were to be included in the 1948 Act. Houses for newly-weds would have two bedrooms and would be allocated to couples who had been married for less than three months; MacEntee feared that assigning houses to unwed couples might pose difficulties. Applicants would be required to produce marriage certificates, and husbands would have to show evidence of 'reasonable continuity of employment' over the previous two years and provide a statement of their previous year's income.

Although MacEntee accepted that these requirements were open to criticism, he argued that there was 'no social wisdom in encouraging improvident marriages by the allocation of houses to couples unable to meet lawful obligations'. Other reserved houses would be allocated to families with young children whose fathers had secure incomes, with preference given to the largest families. Tradesmen would not receive a rent subsidy, though local authorities could grant abatements of 10 per cent for every dependent child, to a maximum of 30 per cent. Occupants of labourers' houses would be eligible for both a rent subsidy and rent remission for up to four children. For families with less than three children, tenancy would expire after five years and all families would be required to vacate these houses when the eldest child was twelve. This pro-natalist policy was discussed with Corporation officials, who raised questions about rehousing former newly-weds when the family had outgrown a two-bedroomed house.[63] Although councils avoided the complexities of MacEntee's scheme, they tended to give priority to the largest families when allocating non-slum clearance houses. The first special housing schemes for the elderly were not completed until the late 1950s.

T.J. Murphy, Minister for Local Government in the first inter-party government, did his utmost to ensure that targets set in the Housing White Paper were attained. Dublin was crucial, because of the scale of the problem, and because the city had been the slowest to respond to the 1930s' housing drive. Murphy was instrumental in having T.C. O'Mahony, Dublin assistant city and county manager, appointed as full-time director of housing. He also decreed that the city and county and Dun Laoghaire be treated on a co-ordinated basis for housing purposes, and was responsible for the establishment of a Dublin Housing Consultative Council, chaired by O'Mahony, which included councillors, building employers, trade union representatives and architects.[64] The hand of a Labour minister is evident in the emphasis which was placed on co-operative building programmes and the use of direct labour. Officials investigated co-operative housing in Sweden, hoping to transfer the model to Ireland.[65] They were more sceptical of proposals from the Waterford city manager to introduce the 'guild system of building'.[66]

CONSTRUCTING LOCAL-AUTHORITY HOUSES USING DIRECT LABOUR

In October 1948 Local Government issued a circular outlining procedures for using direct labour. Labour and trade union interests obviously favoured this approach, but direct labour gained wider support at this time because some housing contracts had attracted no bids, fuelling suspicions of a cartel among contractors. The White Paper noted that only 245 of the 1,300 labourers' cottages offered for tender in the previous twelve months had attracted bids. The Builders' Federation argued that direct labour was inefficient because it was difficult to supervise and spread skilled labour more thinly; they also claimed that it discriminated against private contractors. Local Government replied that it was essential to use direct labour, given contractors' unwillingness to tender for local authority schemes.[67] When Brendan Corish, parliamentary secretary to the Department of Local Government, made a speech in October 1949, claiming that direct labour meant cheaper houses, the Builders' Federation responded by issuing a publication entitled *The Truth about Direct Labour*, which argued that Corish's figures excluded the cost of site acquisition and servicing.[68] At a subsequent meeting with the Taoiseach, the Federation expressed fears that direct labour would be extended and alleged that workers on some schemes were being paid on the lump system, a process that enabled workers to avoid paying social welfare contributions or income tax.

The Builders' Federation was not the only critic. County managers complained that workers employed under direct labour had an incentive to delay completing a project and recommended that bonus schemes similar to those used by private contractors be introduced.

344

Murphy approved this suggestion.[69] John Garvin, secretary of Local Government, countered fears expressed by McElligott in Finance that direct labour would 'tend to the creation of vested interests' and might lead to a major increase in the numbers eligible for the local government superannuation scheme, by pointing out that houses had been constructed in County Wicklow under direct labour for twelve years, with 'excellent results'. He also emphasised that the Department was 'aiming at a position in which a fairly small and efficient organisation in each county will have before them a continuous programme of new building and maintenance'.[70] In 1949 Local Government set up a committee to determine how direct labour schemes could best be organised and how they should be costed, particularly how plant and overheads were charged. Six-monthly reviews of direct labour contracts were set in train.[71] By 1950/51 direct labour accounted for 20 per cent of local authority housing contracts, compared with less than 2 per cent in 1947/48. Local Government concluded that it was suitable for most urban housing schemes, but that high overheads and problems of supervision made it unsuitable for rural cottages.

Given the strong ideological commitment to direct labour shown by Murphy and Keyes, who served as Ministers for Local Government during the term of the first inter-party government, it is not surprising that the Builders' Federation renewed its attack when Fianna Fáil returned to office. Its representations resulted in a new circular which required all plans and costings for schemes using direct labour to be submitted to the Department of Local Government. Councils were also required to ensure that the cost of using direct labour compared favourably with the cost of contractors. If in doubt, they were to seek tenders. In 1953 a threatened reduction in the use of direct labour provoked Dublin Corporation to send a deputation to the Department. It claimed that the requirement to compare those estimates using direct labour with those submitted by contractors would delay the city's housing programme and result in more contracts being awarded to contractors because Corporation estimates were drafted on a conservative basis, whereas private contractors cut tenders to the bone. Although the Minister, Patrick Smith, acknowledged that Dublin Corporation's direct labour unit provided 'a useful check on builders' prices', he refused to give the Corporation 'what amounted to a blank cheque' to sanction direct labour schemes. Nevertheless, 18-19 per cent of all local authority houses continued to be built by direct labour.

When the second inter-party government was returned in 1954, the Builders' Federation launched a protest at being forced to pay heavy rates and taxes 'to maintain a system which is robbing them of their legitimate market'. This provoked yet another circular, urging local authorities to choose the most economical method of construction, though this appears to have had little impact on the allocation of housing contracts.[72] By the mid-1950s, the cost per square foot of houses built by direct labour in Cork, Dublin and Waterford cities was less than the cost of houses built by contractors, though houses built by direct labour in Limerick city cost marginally more than those put up by contractors.[73]

The post-war housing programme was subject to much more detailed monitoring than was the case in the 1930s. By 31 March 1951, 18 per cent of Dublin's local authority housing target had been constructed; a further 11 per cent was in progress; 1 per cent was out to tender and sites had been prepared for a further 19 per cent, though Dublin lagged behind other areas. This was to be expected, since the Dublin housing target amounted to eighteen times the average annual output for the years 1933-40, compared with ten times for other urban areas and seven times in rural areas.

TABLE 8.4

A progress report on 1947/48 housing targets, 31 March 1952

	Complete	Underway
Rural areas	46%	41%
Urban outside Dublin	33%	31%
Dublin	25%	29%

Source: Annual Report of the Department of Local Government 1951/52

FINANCIAL PROBLEMS: DUBLIN AND CORK CORPORATIONS

Although house construction to the north and north-west of Dublin was

346

handicapped by lack of sewerage facilities pending the completion of the Howth drainage outfall, the greatest difficulty facing Dublin Corporation continued to be a lack of capital. Dublin and Cork Corporations were still denied access to the LLF because the Department of Finance claimed that they were capable of raising funds from the money market. At the same time, their stock issues were subject to growing government interference, because of fears that they might jeopardise the success of a national loan.

In 1945 the Department of Finance successfully resisted a proposed private stock issue by Dublin Corporation to the Bank of Ireland at a price of 101 and an interest rate of 3.25 per cent because it believed that the terms were too generous. Although LLF loans then fell to 2.5 per cent, Dublin Corporation found it difficult to borrow money at 3 per cent. Local Government officials entertained hopes that Cork Corporation would be granted access to the LLF, but conceded that, 'short of a Government decision', there was 'clearly no hope of moving Finance' to open the LLF to Dublin Corporation. As supplies of raw materials eased and Dublin Corporation's investment programme gathered pace, the financial difficulties increased. By 1948 the Corporation was committed to spending an estimated £3.9m. a year on housing over the next ten years. Local Government informed Finance that if Dublin Corporation was not provided with capital from the LLF, it would be forced to have a stock issue, which might jeopardise the success of the government loan.

Money borrowed on the commercial market by Dublin and Cork Corporations was more expensive and had to be repaid in a shorter period than under the LLF, so both local authorities lost the benefit of 50-year subsidies provided under the 1948 Act.[74] Although Finance claimed that Dublin Corporation's capital needs would place an undue strain on an overburdened Exchequer, the Department promised to give partial support to Corporation stock issues. Dublin Corporation issued £2.5m. in stock in 1948; twelve months later Finance held approximately 10 per cent.

When Dublin Corporation attempted to raise a further £6m. in mid-1949, market conditions had deteriorated sharply because of the weakness of sterling. Following a special meeting attended by the Taoiseach and the Ministers for Finance and Local Government, the last agreed to discuss the matter with the city manager and the chairman of the Corporation's finance committee. On 29 June Hubert Briscoe, the

347

Corporation's stockbroker, informed Dublin Corporation that the Irish Assurance Company and the Representative Church Body of the Church of Ireland were no longer willing to provide capital for Dublin Corporation because interest rates were rising.[75] When no other source was forthcoming, Garvin approached McElligott, who dismissed Dublin Corporation's request for £6m. to fund its housing programme until the end of 1950 as 'staggering'. McElligott believed that Briscoe was unduly pessimistic about market conditions and he suggested that efforts be made to persuade the commercial banks to underwrite the loan. He also expressed the hope that a loan drive would prove successful 'on the basis of an appeal to the patriotism and civic spirit of the people of Dublin and the country generally'.

Dublin Corporation rejected an offer from the banks to support an issue of £2.5m., alleging that the sum was inadequate and the terms unduly onerous. When the Dublin city manager protested that the construction programme which the Corporation had undertaken at the government's behest was in jeopardy, Michael Keyes, the Minister for Local Government, contacted Labour and Clann na Poblachta ministers William Norton, Noel Browne and Seán MacBride in an apparent attempt to outflank the Department of Finance. MacBride appears to have given a commitment to make funds available from the Economic Co-operation and Administration Act (ECA or Marshall Aid) loan counterpart funds. Local Government, which had become, in Garvin's elegant phrase, 'the buffer State between the central and local authorities' — an 'honour' for 'which we have to pay dearly' — asked Finance to grant Dublin Corporation temporary access to the LLF or assistance from the ECA or the Transitional Development Fund. Garvin also employed the argument that the Corporation was 'pursuing a Governmentally encouraged programme'.[76] This case was incontestable. In February 1949, the Taoiseach, John A. Costello, told the Dublin Master Builders:

> The best way we can insure [sic] that each person is a good citizen is to give everyone a stake in the country and the way in which we can do that is to give him his own home. No matter what it costs, that is good business nationally and socially.
>
> The problem of housing can only be solved by enthusiasm amounting to fanaticism and by complete co-operation between every section of the industry.

In a speech to the Chartered Institute of Secretaries in October 1949, James Dillon, Minister for Agriculture, claimed:

> I know enough of the mind of the Minister for Finance to assure you that no citizen however humble will know the misery of wanting a home because it is too expensive to provide.
>
> The mind of the Minister for Finance and the Government can be stated for bankers, economists, politicians and simple men and that is that money will not stand in the way of providing a decent home for every citizen.[77]

McElligott replied to Garvin's request with a long lamentation: 'expenditure is increasing on all fronts'; the banks were 'apprehensive' at the scale of the Corporation's needs. He suggested that the Corporation slow down its housing programme and negotiate with the banks to secure a £2m. loan jointly underwritten by the banks and the Exchequer, with provision for a further £2m. at a later stage.[78] However, the Dublin Housing Consultative Council reiterated that the Corporation had been given a commitment that the state would assist it if the Corporation was incapable of raising capital on terms comparable to those charged by the state. Keyes submitted a memorandum to Finance which emphasised that public opinion would not accept any slowing down in the housing programme. Dublin Corporation had not yet rehoused all families of seven living in one room. If construction was delayed, the labour force, 'built up with so much difficulty', would disperse, and efforts to introduce new construction methods would meet increased resistance from workers. Partial or complete failure of a Corporation issue would damage the government's credit standing.

Keyes demanded that Dublin and Cork Corporations be permitted to borrow capital for housing from the LLF and that the cabinet confirm his interpretation of government policy: 'that the housing drive must proceed at the maximum rate'. Although Finance persisted in refusing access to the LLF, it conceded that Dublin Corporation might undertake a £5m. stock issue to be jointly underwritten by the banks and the Exchequer, with the latter's share coming from ECA loan counterpart funds. This offer was conditional on Dublin Corporation agreeing to introduce a differential rents scheme and on a review being conducted of the national housing programme which would take account of the availability of capital.

Keyes's memo was dated 21 October 1949; Finance's one week later. Costello directed that both be withheld from circulation until he had considered them. Some days later, he instructed that they be withdrawn and that the matter be settled by a meeting attended by himself and the Ministers for Finance, Local Government and Agriculture. The matter was obviously contentious: the ministers met on 2 November and resumed the following day. No record survives. On 18 November the Taoiseach, together with the Ministers for Finance and Education (Mulcahy) and Patrick Lynch, economic adviser to the Taoiseach's Department, met representatives from the Irish banks to discuss 'the immediate financial requirements of Dublin Corporation for housing purposes'. The absence of Keyes and any minister who was not a member of Fine Gael is significant.

Costello opened the discussions by demanding that the banks take up the proposed Corporation issue of £5m.. He emphasised that 'the Government had decided that no consideration of any kind would obstruct the carrying out of their housing programme' and referred at length to the social problems caused by inadequate housing, such as husbands being compelled to live apart from their wives: 'general social stability would be a direct result of decent housing conditions'. Costello informed the assembled bankers that 'the social and economic benefits would justify the adoption of financial measures which might even be regarded as unorthodox' and referred to the widespread criticism directed at the banks for investing such a high proportion of their deposits outside Ireland. Details of the ensuing argument would bring us into arcane matters of bank liquidity and the lack of a Dublin capital market, which are not directly relevant to this book. Costello made a scarcely veiled threat that if the Irish banks proved uncooperative, 'some Irish Government would be compelled by pressure of public opinion to adopt methods such as the Treasury Deposit Receipt system so as to ensure that Irish banks worked in the national interest'. He told Lord Glenavy, Governor of the Bank of Ireland, that his arguments, 'logical as they were . . . would not satisfy the demands of public opinion' and he reminded the banks that by investing in Dublin Corporation stock, they would be supporting government policy in regard to the repatriation of the sterling assets.

Although Patrick McGilligan, Minister for Finance, claimed that Costello had concentrated on 'social and economic aspects', whereas *he* was interested only in the 'purely finance side of the question', he proved no more sympathetic to the bankers' case.

The meeting adjourned for one week without reaching agreement. Before it resumed, the government announced its intention of realising sterling assets, much to the annoyance of the banks. This threat appears to have been effective; on 25 November, three days before the meeting was due to resume, the banks offered to take up £5m. in Dublin Corporation stock, though they insisted that this would not constitute a precedent.[79]

Although this confrontation provided Dublin Corporation with £5m. (£2m. for SDAA loans and £3m. for housing issues) on favourable terms, it brought only short-term relief because a further £5m. was needed by the end of 1950. The wrangling over the 1949/50 issue had politicised the matter. Public meetings were organised and trade unions demanded assurances from the Taoiseach that the housing programme would continue. Although Costello gave a commitment in March 1950 that continued employment in the building industry would not be jeopardised by lack of finance, newspaper headlines alleged that there was a crisis in the Dublin building industry.

Each capital issue by Dublin Corporation provoked another emergency, a renewed appeal to Finance via Local Government and a further ad hoc solution. When Dublin Corporation broached the possibility of making a stock issue in May 1950, stockbroker Hubert Briscoe pointed out that the Minister for Finance had already announced a public loan 'of considerable magnitude'. Both issues could not be made simultaneously; if they were made at different times, the later loan would suffer. On this occasion the Minister for Finance underwrote the Corporation's issue of £5m. and ended up holding most of that amount; only £247,190 was subscribed by the public. The Exchequer was also left holding substantial quantities of Cork Corporation stock. Since the Exchequer was providing an increasing share of capital for Dublin and Cork Corporations, their continued exclusion from the LLF appears illogical. We can only speculate that Finance believed that such periodic crises acted as a brake on expenditure. Finance persisted in arguing (e.g. on 13 March 1952) that the capital difficulties facing both cities were short-term and that the Exchequer would be in a position to sell its stock holdings when conditions improved, though by 1952 these had a nominal value of £7.25m..

During the term of the first inter-party government, Dublin-area building trade unions successfully exploited the government's public commitment to the housing programme to secure capital. Unions threatened that building craftsmen would return to Britain if the pace of construction slackened. Trade union leaders, particularly Councillor Jim Larkin, were quick to seize on any references to a shortage of capital. On 19 April 1950 Costello told a deputation from Dublin Corporation that in the presence of the Minister for Finance, 'who was in complete agreement with him, he had informed the Irish Banks Standing Committee that the Government was prepared to see the country face national bankruptcy, rather than have the housing programme held up for lack of finance'.[80] Such statements can hardly have helped Finance's efforts to control public capital expenditure. Dublin Corporation tended to raise approximately £5m. and then forget about the future until its capital was on the point of exhaustion. In December 1950, T.K. Whitaker, a principal officer in the Department of Finance and its future secretary, contacted Garvin in an effort to establish what the Corporation intended to do with the £5m. it was then seeking. Whitaker argued that since capital and materials were in scarce supply because of the Korean War, it was necessary to establish priorities. Dublin Corporation resented such inquiries, despite its growing dependence on government funding. It was equally unwilling to plan capital requirements on anything longer than a year-to-year basis.[81]

Between 1950 and February 1953 Dublin Corporation raised £15m. for housing in three £5m. issues. Banks and underwriters provided £5.92m.; the state £5.24m. and the public subscribed £3.62m., most of it in February 1953. Local Government continued to press for access to the LLF. In March 1952, Patrick Smith, Minister for Local Government, pointed out that Cork Corporation's housing programme was being financed by an overdraft of £500,000, which had been granted by their bankers following an assurance by the Minister for Local Government 'that irrespective of the source and method of borrowing, the necessary funds would be forthcoming'. Smith argued that although Cork Corporation's housing programme was behind target, the Department could not press for a higher output, given the uncertainties of the Corporation's capital funding. When the matter came before cabinet in early March, it was repeatedly postponed until 9 April when it was decided that the Minister for Finance should consider 'sympathetically' the question of admitting Cork Corporation to the LLF, though his decision would be final. Added to this record is a note in pencil to the effect that 'From discussion it seemed clear that the Minister for Local Government would not press his proposal that Dublin Corporation be admitted'. Smith disputed this version of events. On 13 May 1952 he informed Maurice Moynihan,

> . . . this decision, the wording of which has escaped my attention until now, is so completely at variance with my recollections that I would ask you to have the matter raised at a Government meeting on Friday for the purposes of accuracy and the more important matter, as far as I am concerned as Minister for Local Government, the effect of the recorded decision on the two municipalities concerned.

Moynihan responded with a note to Smith's private secretary, also dated 13 May, stating that the letter would be submitted to the Taoiseach 'as soon as possible' and noting that Smith had mooted the possibility of raising the matter at cabinet. The files contain a further handwritten note dated 14 May to the effect that the Minister had already raised the matter with the Taoiseach, who 'had made it clear to the Minister that he did not agree with the Minister's recollections'. Moynihan also minuted Garvin's version of Smith's recollections: that the Minister for Finance was to consider the admission to the LLF of both Dublin and Cork Corporations, 'giving specially sympathetic consideration to Cork'. In the event of a refusal, the Minister for Finance would underwrite a loan for each Corporation; the decision of the Minister for Finance would be subject to review by government in the event of a disagreement between ministers.

Éamon de Valera appears to have made some concessions towards Smith. Although the file records that the Taoiseach's recollections remained as stated, in the second paragraph of the minute of 9 April it adds:

> He recalls however that in the course of discussion he felt himself that underwriting would be necessary if admission to the Local Loans Fund not approved; he thinks it likely that his own remarks at the meeting were influenced by this feeling. Further, he takes the view that notwithstanding the statement that the decision of the Minister of Finance is final, a further appeal to the Government in

the event of disagreement between the two ministers, would not in practice be ruled out.

This olive branch prompted Smith to mend his fences with de Valera, and the Taoiseach agreed to allow Smith to raise the matter informally at cabinet. However, for reasons which remain unclear, Smith did not attend the next cabinet meeting. At the following meeting, discussion was deferred owing to lack of time. When Smith eventually raised the matter on 23 May, he referred to a note he had circulated — at this point Moynihan said that he had no prior knowledge of its existence (there is no copy on file) — and asserted that the cabinet minute was inaccurate. Smith concentrated his criticism on 'the attitude expressed in a minute which his department received from Finance'. The subsequent sentence, 'Remarks by the Taoiseach and Minister for Finance appeared to confirm the accuracy of our minute', suggests that de Valera and MacEntee were in agreement. At this point the record becomes cryptic in the extreme:

> An arrangement as to further action was made as a result of the discussion. I inquired whether I should make any record of the arrangement and the Taoiseach said that no record was necessary.[82]

In May shortly after this unspecified 'arrangement', the Cork city manager was asked to approach the Corporation's bankers to explore the possibility of a stock issue, 'on the suggestion of the Minister for Finance', and was instructed to inform Finance of the outcome. He duly informed that department, though not apparently Local Government, that the bank was unenthusiastic. Cork Corporation's overdraft sanction was increased to £750,000 to provide short-term relief. On 13 September 1952 McElligott informed Garvin that, 'following protracted negotiations' concerning a national loan and financial assistance to both Corporations, the banks had agreed to underwrite a £20m. public issue jointly with the government. McElligott was at pains to stress that £20m. 'will not suffice to cover even direct Exchequer commitments'; the banks had also intimated that they were 'prepared, but with the greatest reluctance and only at the Minister's urgent request', to provide £2.5m. to meet the capital requirements of Dublin Corporation: 'Beyond this figure they are not in any circumstances prepared to go.' They also wished to emphasise that they did so

. . . on the understanding that every effort will be made to impress upon the Corporation the necessity of regulating its capital expenditure programme in accordance with its ability to raise the necessary finance direct from the public, and that the Banks will not be called upon by the Government to finance any further capital expenditure by the Dublin Corporation.

Cork's request for £1m. was rejected.[83] Capital markets appear to have eased during the autumn of 1952 and in October Finance informed the lord mayor of Cork confidentially that negotiations were in progress to secure 'much if not all of the Corporation's capital commitments' from the banks. On 6 January 1953 the Irish Banks' Standing Committee intimated that it would be prepared to participate with the government in underwriting a public issue of £750,000 of Cork Corporation stock, when the response to Dublin Corporation's £5m. issue was known. Dublin Corporation raised £5m. in February 1953, its most successful issue since 1948. The public subscribed £3.25m., leaving the underwriters holding £.92m. and the banks with £.73m..

Following Dublin's success, the Cork city manager informed the Department that Cork Corporation was seeking £900,000 to pay for the construction of 600 houses. When Local Government pointed out that there was 'not an unlimited supply of capital available', Cork Corporation replied 'Ask the Minister'. This was interpreted as an effort 'to remind the Minister of statements by previous ministers that the solution of the housing problem would not be held up by shortage of money'. Refused a meeting with the Minister for Local Government, Cork Corporation demanded to meet the Taoiseach. Local Government minuted that this would be undesirable since confidential talks were continuing with the Irish Banks' Standing Committee in an effort to obtain finance for Cork Corporation on the best possible terms.[84] Cork's problems were eased temporarily by a stock issue of £740,000, which was fully subscribed by June 1953.

The difficulties involved in feeding Dublin and Cork Corporations' cravings for capital are merely a specific instance of the problem of financing the post-war housing programme. Between 1949/50 and 1953/54, the Exchequer and local authorities provided a total of £71.15m. for housing. By comparison, building societies provided only £6.86m. over the four years prior to 1953. Irish insurance companies provided an estimated £600-£700,000 per annum, some of it for commercial buildings.

TABLE 8.4

State and local authority finance for housing

	Repayable Capital*	Stock Issues#	Grants	Total
49/50	£6.05	£0.58	£2.95	£9.58
50/51	£6.17	£5.25	£4.92	£16.34
51/52	£9.33	£5.10	£3.68	£18.11
52/53	£8.93	£2.81	£2.60	£14.34
53/54	£7.25	£3.14	£2.39	£12.78

* Local Loans Fund, plus advances from Central Fund to Bord na Móna for turf workers' housing: £.34m. in 1951/52; £.14m. in 1952/53.
#Dublin and Cork Corporations.

Source: D/E Housing, box 34. H205/8/1 Interdepartmental committee on state capital programme

THE LOCAL LOANS FUND

All local authorities, other than Dublin and Cork Corporations, relied on the Local Loans Fund for capital. Between 1935 and 31 January 1949 issues totalled £16.8m., of which £12m. was for housing. In the post-war years, the Fund's limit was increased in almost geometric progression: from £25m. in 1949 to £35m. in 1950 and £50m. in 1951. Despite this, commitments regularly outstripped the Fund's limit; by 31 March 1950 they totalled almost £33.5m, against a limit of £25m..[85] The Department of Finance appears to have been powerless to control this expansion. In 1948 it argued that, as a temporary measure, LLF loans should not be used to provide mortgages for home-owners under the Small Dwellings Act. The inter-party government not only disagreed, in July 1948 it increased the maximum market value of eligible houses from £1,750 to £2,000.[86] In 1953 Finance agreed to extend the LLF limit to £70m., with the rider that 'this provision in no way implies that he [the Minister] will find it possible to finance the Fund from the Exchequer on this scale'; 'in future, commitments will not be allowed to exceed the legislative provisions for issues from the Fund'. Despite this threat, the limit was raised to £90m. in 1954.

Five years before, housing had accounted for 71.4 per cent of LLF loans; by September 1953 its share had risen to 84 per cent and it remained above 80 per cent for many years. From 1953 onwards, as councils other than Dublin and Cork completed their housing programmes, an increased share of LLF borrowings was used to provide SDAA loans; these accounted for £8m. in 1953, as against £16.6m. by March 1956.

EXCHEQUER SUBSIDIES FOR LOCAL AUTHORITY HOUSING

Despite the passage of the 1948 Housing (Amendment) Act, Exchequer subsidies for local authority housing remained in disarray for some years. Loan repayments for local authority housing or labourers' cottages continued to be subsidised under the 1932 Act at rates of 33.3 per cent and 66.6 per cent for working-class houses and 60 per cent for labourers' cottages. Subsidy payments continued to be based on a maximum cost of £300-£500 per house — figures set in the 1930s which had become utterly unrealistic. New houses built by local authorities were also eligible for lump sum grants of £300 to £600 from the Transitional Development Fund and, from 1948, local authority housing loans from the LLF received an additional subsidy in order to hold the effective rate of interest at 2.5 per cent. These complex subsidies meant that the Exchequer met almost 50 per cent of the cost of the average local authority house.

The TDF subsidy was originally introduced as a temporary measure to offset high construction costs in the immediate post-war years. By 1949/50 it was costing the Exchequer £1.2m. a year. The subsidy was withdrawn from all housing schemes sanctioned after 31 October 1950, other than those carried out by Dublin and Cork County Boroughs. It cost the Exchequer £9.6m. — £5.9m from the original fund and the balance from departmental votes.[87] In place of TDF subsidies, Local Government proposed that the Exchequer should bear two-thirds of the annual deficit incurred by a local authority on its housing programme, with the balance being financed by ratepayers. This would entail a significant increase in the proportion of housing costs borne by the Exchequer. Local Government conceded that such a 'radical revision' could be introduced only when uniform capital costs had been achieved for housing schemes throughout the country (an unrealistic objective) and when all local authority rents were calculated on a similar basis, involving differential rents. In the meantime, since the Minister was unwilling to press for the imposition of differential rents, Local Government proposed that the capital ceiling applying to interest subsidies be raised to a maximum of £1,000 in county boroughs, with *pro rata* increases applying to the interest subsidy available for houses built by urban district councils. These ceilings were below the actual cost of the houses. Local Government also demanded that Finance drop the proposal to end the special interest subsidy on housing loans from the Local Loans Fund.

The revised Exchequer subsidies were not announced until September 1951, almost one year after the ending of TDF subsidies. The delay may have been a deliberate attempt to curb expenditure; councils were unlikely to embark on new projects without foreknowledge of the level of Exchequer subvention. Government's finances had deteriorated, and Finance issued a succession of dirges, emphasising the dangers of excessive government expenditure on non-productive items such as housing.[88] The revised subsidies proved unpopular. Although the effective rate of subsidy on slum-clearance schemes remained unchanged, there was a 50 per cent reduction in Exchequer support for non-slum clearance housing and subsidies for slum-clearance schemes averaged 47-50 per cent of total costs, a far cry from the 66 per cent envisaged in the 1932 Act.

The years 1951-56 saw a never-ending succession of disputes over Exchequer subsidies for housing between Finance and Local Government, with the former battling to end or reduce subsidies and the latter campaigning for their maintenance or increase. In 1952 the conflict focused on the merits of continuing the interest subsidy on LLF housing loans. By October 1952 the government was borrowing money at 5 per cent, while providing housing loans to local authorities at half that price. The item was withdrawn from cabinet on 29 November, to give both departments time to submit a joint memorandum embodying agreed proposals. This proved impossible. In late March 1953 Finance certified that 'consultation was carried on as long as possible in an effort to reach agreement with the Department of Local Government' and asked the cabinet for a decision. The matter was referred to the Ministers for Finance and Local Government. Agreement was eventually reached on 29 April.

The outcome was an unqualified victory for Local Government.

The maximum cost of houses on which subsidies were calculated would be increased to the limits previously proposed by the Department of Local Government, which had been rejected by the Department of Finance. Loans already sanctioned but unissued, and supplementary loans needed to complete a housing scheme, plus all loans for 'normal' — i.e. non-slum clearance houses, for which contracts had been placed — would be funded at an interest rate of 2.5 per cent. Local Government won the battle by holding firm during the autumn/winter of 1952. By April 1953, concern over inflation and the balance of payments had eased and attention had shifted to unemployment, circumstances which strengthened Local Government's case.

By the summer of 1953, 27 local authorities had completed their housing programmes and completion was in sight for a further 23 authorities. The only substantial backlogs were in Dublin and Cork Corporations.[89] Dublin Corporation expected to have an average of 2,500 houses under construction in each of the succeeding three years.[90] Otherwise there was little scope for expanding the local authority housing programme.

OWNER-OCCUPIED HOUSING: THE EXPLOSION OF ASSISTANCE

Matters were different in the private sector. As council housing targets were met, private housing became more important. Local authority housing output peaked in 1950/51, fell in the following year, recovered in 1952/53 and then declined sharply. In contrast, the number of private houses constructed or repaired rose until 1954/55 when they accounted for two-thirds of new houses, compared with just over 50 per cent in 1950/51.

The original version of the 1948 Housing Bill had provided no subsidies for private housing, but the Fianna Fáil cabinet had insisted on including a clause providing Exchequer grants for building and reconstructing private homes. At a maximum of £275 per house, four to six times the pre-war level, the grants showed a substantial increase in real terms at a time when the value of subsidies for local authority housing had fallen. This concession was a response to pressure from both the public and local authorities. In May 1947 the General Council of County Councils demanded that farmers be given access to low-interest housing loans with long repayment periods. Some months later Wicklow County Council demanded the introduction of housing subsidies for small farmers who could not afford to build their own homes and were ineligible for labourers' cottages.

Urban middle-class families also pressed for more generous state assistance. Letters forwarded to Local Government in 1949 by the inimitable Alfie Byrne, independent TD and Dublin lord mayor, contain accounts of ostensibly prosperous middle-class families of engineers, architects and civil servants living in overcrowded rented flats because they could not afford to buy a suitable home.[91] The burgeoning demand for home ownership in urban areas reflects the continuing decline in the supply of privately rented housing. The Rent Restriction Acts were extended in 1939 and again in 1946, by which time they applied to all premises built before 7 May 1941 (practically all premises in Ireland) with a rateable valuation of less than £40 (£60 in Dublin and Dun Laoghaire). In 1949, following the report of a commission of inquiry into the Rent Restrictions Acts, rents of commercial premises were de-controlled, but controls were extended to all houses built after 1941.[92] With fewer private houses available for rent, families that were ineligible for council tenancies had little alternative to buying their own homes. It is also probable that the growing number of 'new Dubliners'[93] who came from rural farming backgrounds transferred their commitment towards owner-occupancy from country to city.

Once the details of the 1948 Housing Bill were made known, the government came under pressure to make grants for private housing retrospective. MacEntee was sympathetic. He argued that 'an impression [to this effect] may have been created by certain announcements made in May 1945', though Finance objected that it would be tantamount to making 'cash gifts'. On 2 December 1947 the cabinet appears to have agreed to pay grants on all houses built for owner-occupation after 1 November 1945, if they were still unoccupied two years later. A note to this effect from the Taoiseach's Department is struck out on the file and a further note adds that the decision had been cancelled. On 10 December all copies were recalled.[94]

The incoming inter-party government also came under pressure to raise both the size and price of owner-occupied houses which qualified for grants. In 1949 Agriculture Minister James Dillon suggested suspending the limit on house size; he believed that this would encourage 'trading up' and stimulate building activity — which by this point was over-heated. T.J. Murphy, Minister for Local Government, suggested that the limit should be increased to 1,500 square feet when supplies of materials and skilled labour had improved.[95] Dáil deputies repeatedly complained that existing conditions were too restrictive: to qualify, a private purchaser had to sign a contract with the builder before construction began. Deputies suggested that grants should be paid to the contractor rather than to the purchaser, though Local Government feared that this would stimulate a speculative housing boom which would attract skilled workers away from local authority housing schemes. It would also prove difficult to restrict grants to first-time buyers.

Grants for new private houses were due to expire in 1950, but they were extended for a further two years — beginning a process which continued for many years to come. The 1950 Housing (Amendment) Act also eased eligibility conditions. It was no longer necessary for applicants to have signed a contract prior to construction; first-time buyers of new houses were now free to shop around. It was hoped that competition would mean lower prices. The size of houses eligible for grants was raised to 1,400 square feet. New grant-aided houses also became eligible for rates remission and a clause exempting them from stamp duty was added at the cabinet's behest. Local Government argued that the concessions would reduce demand for local authority housing; according to the Dublin City housing director, 90 per cent of potential SDAA borrowers in the city would otherwise have to be housed by Dublin Corporation.

The 1950 Act provided further incentives for the private housing sector. Local authorities could acquire by compulsory purchase land which could be used to provide sites for private houses. Rural houses became eligible for a second reconstruction grant fifteen years after receiving the first. Finance opposed these concessions, but a conference, attended by officials from Dublin Corporation, the Tánaiste and the Ministers for Local Government, Posts and Telegraphs, and Defence, though not by either the Minister for Finance or his officials, endorsed Local Government's stand.[96] When Finance objected to a further extension of private-housing grants in 1952, Local Government countered with a quasi Keynesian argument that £1.5m. spent on housing grants generated £10m. in private capital expenditure and additional sales of Irish goods.[97]

In 1954 new private houses built for rent became eligible for grants and rural houses could now apply for a second reconstruction grant seven years after the first, provided that the second grant was used to replace a thatched roof with either slate or tiles.[98] On this occasion the Department's housing section gave some consideration to substituting a price ceiling of £3,000 per house for the existing grant limit of 1,400 square feet, but decided not to do so. One official pointed out that, although 'considerable architectural ingenuity is being misapplied towards trying to beat the 1,400 square feet maximum', a price limit would merely lead to collusion between solicitors, builders and owners. 'If a limit is to be preserved, better one which can be measured with an inch tape than one which involves keeping an eye on financial and legal juggling', though grants should be dependent on houses offering 'reasonable market value'.[99]

The cost to the Exchequer of grants for owner-occupied housing rose from £119,000 in 1948/49 to over £1m. in 1949/50 and to £1.8m in 1953/54. This excludes the cost of supplementary grants paid by local authorities, which Local Government estimated to account for local authority borrowings of at least £500,000 by 1953/54.[100] Most supplementary grants appear to have gone to farmers.[101] In 1956, as a gesture towards decentralisation, the second inter-party government proposed to devolve responsibility for administering all grants for private housing to local authorities. Local Government objected that this would result in lower standards of construction, would increase the risk of dishonesty and would lead to a weakening in state control over expenditure. The Department also argued that it would mean greater delays in processing claims, which would in turn generate considerable correspondence to the Department. John Garvin also claimed that it would be unpopular in Leinster House:

> Members of the Dáil and Seanad regard grants for housing, Old Age Pensions etc. as being peculiarly their sphere of influence. They have the edge on Councillors in these matters and will not relish a change which would put the Chairman of the Council and individual Councillors on an equal or possibly a stronger footing. The least the Deputies and Senators will expect is that the Minister will remain actively responsible and announce his willingness to entertain representations concerning delays or other matters.

The proposal was dropped.[102]

New houses also had two-thirds of their rates remitted for a seven-year period, though Local Government was less enthusiastic about this concession, because it reduced the taxable capacity of local authorities. Although it pressed the government in 1949 to announce that the concession would not apply to houses constructed after 31 March 1950, rates remission was extended for a further two years, and grant-aided houses, which had hitherto been ineligible, could now benefit. In 1953 the cabinet committee on unemployment recommended extending rates remission to new commercial buildings. The concession proved popular. In 1956 ACRA, the Association of Combined Residents Associations, demanded that rates remission should be extended to fourteen years, with one-third remission until the twenty-first year, claiming that its loss after seven years was a major hardship to families with children of school-going age.[103]

SMALL DWELLINGS ACQUISITION ACTS

Although the combined cost of rates remission and housing grants was not trivial, it pales in comparison with the cost to the Exchequer of financing Small Dwellings Acquisition Act loans. During the inter-war years, purchasers availing of an SDAA loan and a government housing grant had to provide a substantial deposit from personal savings. By 1948/49, however, the combination of 90 per cent mortgages in Dublin, plus grants of up to £275, meant in theory that some purchasers were providing only £50 from their own resources. The Department of Finance feared that this would lead to 'negative equity' (though the term had not yet been coined) if house prices fell. However John Garvin noted that, while his minister agreed that it was desirable that a person have a personal stake in his house, 'in the present abnormal circumstances when so many people are blamelessly not in that position he would not be prepared to transfer them to the already overburdened waiting lists' for council housing.

Local Government contended that the typical purchaser of a Dublin house costing £2,000 received a mortgage of £1,600 plus a grant of £275, leaving a deposit of £125. In practice, SDAA loans were calculated on a house's 'market value' — allegedly what it would fetch at auction, which was generally below its actual price — and prospective purchasers were often forced to fund a considerably larger deposit. Local Government had originally assumed that basing mortgages on 'market value' would force prospective purchasers to exert pressure for lower house prices; its only effect appears to have been to generate grievances against the government.[104] In May 1950 the Dublin city manager told government ministers that there was often a gap of £400 between actual cost and market value — which few prospective owners could bridge without taking out an additional loan. Houses in the Deerpark Estate, Mount Merrion, Co. Dublin, designed to cater for those earning £7-£11 per week and which were being sold for £1,985 (just within the SDAA limits), had a 'market value' of £1,600, forcing prospective purchasers to find a deposit of £250. Houses in Seafield Estate, Stillorgan, Co. Dublin, for sale at £1,900, attracted 600 inquiries but proved unsaleable when it emerged that they would attract a maximum SDAA loan of only £1,280.[105]

SDAA loans were granted by local authorities and, with the exception of those provided by Dublin and Cork Corporations, councils financed them by borrowing from the LLF. The 1948 Housing (Amendment) Act provided that the interest rate on SDAA loans should be set at a maximum of .5 per cent above the cost of money to the local authority. LLF interest rates, which stood at 3.25 per cent in 1948, rose to 5.25 per cent in October 1952. This led to a sharp fall in demand. On 28 July 1953 Bray Urban District Council reported that it had made only six SDAA loans since the rate of interest had increased, compared with 80 loans in the period January-October 1952. New borrowers were requesting £200-£300 less than the permitted maximum advance, in order to reduce the cost of repayments, and some prospective applicants had withdrawn, claiming that they could get better terms from commercial agencies.[106]

Inevitably this lead to a recession in the construction industry. By the summer of 1953 the cabinet committee on unemployment was actively exploring the possibility of providing additional grants or improving the terms on which SDAA loans were available, against the advice of Local Government, in order to encourage the construction of private housing.[107]

HOUSING AND THE SECOND INTER-PARTY GOVERNMENT: THE LOOMING CRISIS

The second inter-party government sent mixed signals to the housing sector. The proposal to establish a Capital Investment Board to advise on the government's investment programme appeared to threaten a cut in capital for housing. Against this, there was the government's pre-election commitment 'to secure the building of more houses by private and public effort, in particular by improving credit facilities and easing loan charges and the burden of deposit payments'.[108] In November 1954 the government established a cabinet committee consisting of the Tánaiste and Ministers for Finance, Local Government, Agriculture, and Social Welfare, to examine existing arrangements for financing house-building for private persons and to recommend improvements in the provision of credit facilities, including SDAA loans and possible methods of easing loan charges and the cost of deposits.[109] There is no evidence that the committee ever met.

As ever, the most immediate housing problems concerned Dublin Corporation. Although a 1953 stock issue proved relatively successful, an issue of £5m. in the summer of 1954 attracted only 513 applications, totalling £840,000. A newspaper headline described it as a 'fiasco'.[110] Since the banks refused to take up the remaining stock, Dublin Corporation was forced to survive on an increased overdraft of £3m. whose duration was limited to twelve months. Finance had watched the issue acutely: T.K. Whitaker, then a principal officer in Finance, seems to have been in regular contact with the bankers. Butler and Briscoe, the Corporation's stockbrokers, blamed its collapse on high government and municipal borrowings. The Dublin Stock Exchange listed twelve Dublin Corporation issues, with a total of £26.75m. in stock outstanding. Small investors were reluctant to subscribe because previous issues traded at low prices. The stockbrokers claimed that 'the investing public have [sic] come to regard Corporation borrowings as an annual affair without finality and is perturbed by the mounting charge for the service and redemption of municipal debt'. The fact that income tax was deducted at source from dividends, in contrast to national loans, was a further deterrent.[111] Dublin Corporation again requested permission to borrow from the Local Loans Fund, which provoked a heated correspondence between Finance Minister Gerard Sweetman and Local Government Minister Pa O' Donnell. Sweetman construed the failure of the Corporation issue as a reflection of 'diminished public confidence in the Corporation's policy and administration'. A 'critical appraisal' should be carried out in order to discover whether the Corporation's slum-clearance programme was

365

confined to genuine slum clearance. He queried the propriety of Dublin Corporation building houses for sale and providing houses for tenants who could pay higher rents. According to figures supplied by Sweetman, Dublin Corporation had employed 37 skilled and 36 unskilled workers per 100 houses built in the 1930s, against 103 skilled and 88 unskilled workers in 1953/54 — a three-fold deterioration in productivity. (The source of these figures is not stated.) O'Donnell countered with data showing that the cost per house in Dublin city, excluding site development, was lower than in other urban areas.

The views of both ministers were irreconcilable. Local Government was committed to completing a major housing programme, almost regardless of the problems which this posed for the Exchequer. As Sweetman protested to O'Donnell:

> When you speak of housing needs in Dublin being 14,000 new houses and affirm that this programme is not only desirable but essential, practicable, and in accordance with 'settled Government policy', you appear to be ignoring completely the basic problem of finance.[112]

The dispute simmered for most of 1955. In the spring Dublin Corporation sought an assurance that long-term finance would be available for its housing programme. Although Local Government regarded this as 'an old game of the Corporation', they offered 'positive assurances'. At this stage Dublin Corporation's capital needs were estimated at £6.5m., of which £5.7m. was for housing. A further £6.5m. to £7m. would be needed annually for the following four years — almost entirely for housing.

On 7 June senior officials from Finance and Local Government (including both secretaries) met to discuss the matter. Owen Redmond, secretary of the Department of Finance, stated that Finance had asked the Bank of Ireland to extend Dublin Corporation's additional overdraft facilities, which were due to expire on 30 June, until the end of the year and to increase the overdraft from £3m. to £6m., on the assumption that there would be a public issue of Corporation stock later in the year. Redmond acknowledged that, judging from the experience of the last national loan, and the recent issue for the national transport company Córas Iompair Éireann, there was 'little prospect of a successful public issue by the Corporation'. He suggested that Dublin Corporation reduce its capital expenditure and concentrate 'on really urgent rehousing'. Garvin rejected this proposal and attacked Finance's tendency to regard Dublin Corporation 'as an isolated "Robinson Crusoe"', as opposed to seeing its housing activities as 'an important part of the national programme'. He reiterated that public statements by members of the government had

> . . . clearly demanded that financial considerations should not stand in the way of housing. His Department's duty was to speed-up the housing operations and he did not see how they could depart from this because of financial anxieties unless some financial authority made a formal public statement which was accepted by the Government to the effect that the money could not be found.

Both Departments achieved some measure of accord on the question of SDAA loans. Whitaker suggested that the capital which Dublin Corporation provided for SDAA loans — £1.65m. a year — should be financed by banks, insurance companies and building societies. Garvin agreed to consider this proposal, though he opposed Whitaker's suggestion that Dublin Corporation should cease to pay supplementary housing grants (i.e. the additional grants to first-time purchasers paid by the local authority). The committee discussed the 'stream of press publicity' issued by the Corporation, giving details of expenditure costing millions of pounds on housing, expensive flats and town planning. Garvin undertook to 'impress on the Corporation officials the lack of wisdom of such publicity'.

The above comes from an unamended record of the meeting. The revised version was even more unequivocal.

> Mr Garvin said that he could not do anything that would run counter to the Ministerial statements about the Corporation's housing drive. Neither to the members nor to any official of the Corporation could any civil servant in his Department say 'try and reduce your expenditure on housing'. To do this would be tantamount to taking the place of the government, the banks and other bodies concerned. Any statements must be made openly.[113]

On 23 September 1955, during the course of a meeting with the lord mayor of Dublin and the city manager, Pa O'Donnell broached the possibility of setting up an inquiry into Dublin Corporation's finances. O'Donnell also read out a letter from the Irish Banks' Standing Committee, which warned Corporation members not to publicise their capital needs until the outcome of an ESB loan had been assured. O'Donnell next consulted Sweetman. Following this, the Dublin city manager was informed that arrangements had been made for him to meet the Corporation's bankers. The Bank of Ireland, which had previously refused to increase the Corporation's overdraft, now offered accommodation of £3.8m., much less than the £6m. sought, on condition that the Corporation took prompt action to liquidate the overdraft by means of a public stock issue.

Corporation officials felt unable to accept this offer. A report some days later in *The Irish Times* that Dublin Corporation was seeking a £6m. overdraft prompted a stern rebuke from Owen Redmond. At this stage Dublin Corporation appears to have accepted the bank's terms, though it promptly sent a deputation to the Minister for Local Government seeking funds to liquidate the overdraft. He told them in confidence that the government had succeeded in obtaining the banks' support for a £6m. Corporation issue, despite 'great difficulty'. O'Donnell referred to the fact that a motion censuring the Minister for supporting differential rents was due to be debated by Dublin Corporation. He warned that any effort to reduce rents would undermine public confidence.

When a new Dublin Corporation stock was issued in December 1955, the banks took £2m. as agreed, 2,511 members of the public subscribed £1.8m.[114] and £1m. was provided by the government, leaving the banks holding an additional £1m.. This brought only short-term relief. Dublin Corporation was in the habit of financing its SDAA loans by retrospective borrowing, contrary to the advice of its officials. On 13 December the Dublin city manager and assistant manager pointed out that the Corporation had entered into commitments to provide almost £1.5m. in SDAA loans, though it had less than half that sum available. O'Donnell had apparently given Dublin Corporation approval to borrow £2m. in November 1955 to finance SDAA loans, though there is no evidence that the Corporation made any effort to secure this money. Instead, in an apparent effort to force the government's hand, Corporation officials informed Garvin that they proposed to advertise that they were unable to accept further applications for SDAA loans and would return those received since 21 November. O'Donnell asked Dublin Corporation to defer this action because he feared that it would lead to a collapse of private house building, 'a position which would very seriously embarrass the Government in view of expressed policy to support this form of housing activity'. In a letter to Sweetman, O'Donnell argued that the extension of the city boundary had resulted in 'practically all fringe building land' being brought into the city: if this area had remained in the county, SDAA loans would have been financed by the LLF. O'Donnell informed Sweetman that it was 'imperative' that the LLF provide Dublin Corporation with £1.5m. to meet existing SDAA commitments and to keep the scheme going while future capital requirements were being examined. As a measure of his concern, O'Donnell sent a copy of the letter to the Taoiseach.

Finance's attitude towards Dublin Corporation did not relent. Sweetman pointed to the Corporation's mixed record in recent weeks. In its favour was a resolution calling on the city manager to appoint consultants to overhaul municipal organisation and administration, though this was far outweighed by a motion which seriously reduced the scope of a differential rents scheme. Sweetman noted that 'They [Dublin Corporation] had excited a spate of unfavourable comment in the press which no doubt will be used in evidence against us when the time comes again to approach the banks for overdraft accommodation or support for a further stock issue'. He also deplored as 'anything but helpful' some of the publicity surrounding the Corporation's latest issue, 'the impression being that the City Fathers were not particularly concerned whether the loans filled [sic] or not as they would get the money in any case'. Sweetman claimed that, for 'confidential' reasons, it was impossible to grant Dublin Corporation access to the LLF 'at this juncture'. The 'confidential' reasons are not documented; they presumably refer to financial difficulties which the government was facing, possibly the impending flotation of a £20m. national loan.[115]

Press headlines on 26 January 1956, reporting that Dublin Corporation had ceased to provide SDAA loans, prompted protests from trade unionists and fears of unemployment and bankruptcies in the building industry. The joint negotiating committee of the Dublin building industry recalled the 'unqualified assurance given by each successive Government that housing activities of the Corporation would not be retarded, delayed or diminished by lack of finance', though the only statement quoted had been made by the late T.J. Murphy in 1948. Finance capitulated on 17 February. As an interim measure, and 'without prejudice to the general situation', Dublin Corporation was provided with £1m. from the Local Loans Fund. Finance also promised to explore the prospect of building societies providing 95 per cent mortgages, with the excess over the normal ratio jointly guaranteed by the government and the local authority, though O' Donnell pointed out that this would require legislation. The cabinet approved these proposals informally, though it was agreed that at this stage they should not be recorded in the minutes.

The ambivalence of the government's policy emerges once more on the occasion of a meeting between John Costello, O'Donnell and a deputation from the joint negotiating committee of the Dublin building industry on 9 March 1956. The Taoiseach confirmed the government's commitment to provide housing finance, but then spoke at length about current financial difficulties: the increase in the British bank rate, which had resulted in the failure of the £20m. national loan the previous month, and the fact that the government, Dublin Corporation, the ESB and CIE were all drawing capital from a common pool. Although it was not minuted, a letter which Costello sent to the lord mayor of Dublin some weeks later suggested that he had also referred to the government's determination to estimate the capital requirements of all state bodies before determining how far it might meet specific needs.

O'Donnell gave a much more optimistic message. He assured the deputation that he would be prepared to sanction any borrowing required for the Corporation's housing programme. 'He did not think it necessary to go any further'. O'Donnell also dismissed rumours of a financial crisis; 'in his opinion, a political party and a political organ was [sic] responsible for the present scare'. However, since the Corporation housing programme for 1956/57 was projected to cost £7.7m. and it had only £190,000 to hand in January 1956, the word 'crisis' does not seem unreasonable. Dublin Corporation needed an additional £1.5m. to fund SDAA loans: the £1m. promised from the LLF would cover approvals only until the end of May 1956.[116] Dublin Corporation managed to negotiate a limited overdraft accommodation of £870,000 on its revenue account, but a request for an overdraft of £1.38m. on its capital account was refused. John P. Keane, the Dublin city manager, reported that the bankers had 'painted a lugubrious picture not alone of the Financial position of the Corporation but of the country as a whole'.

In April 1956, senior officials in Finance and Local Government met to discuss Dublin Corporation's capital needs for the coming year. T.K. Whitaker concluded that an allocation of £4m. 'would not impose any undue restrictions'. Shortly afterwards, Local Government expressed concern at what it deemed

> . . . a new development . . . a recent semi-official letter from the Minister for Finance to the Minister for Local Government that, for planning purposes, Dublin Corporation should assume that £4m. is the maximum that may be borrowed in any year as long ahead as can be foreseen. They are to be warned against entering into commitments on any other assumption. The Minister for Finance will require regular bulletins on the Corporation's capital programme.

Local Government believed that 'it would be invidious or impossible for this department to tell the Corporation which projects to drop'.[117]

Although the above suggests that steps were being taken to control capital expenditure on housing, when the cabinet considered the 1956 Housing (Amendment) Bill, it decided to increase the income limits for eligibility for supplementary housing grants. This decision, which was not recommended by Local Government, was guaranteed to undermine all estimates of the capital needs of local authorities.[118] By April 1956 the perilous state of government finances made it essential to achieve cuts in local authority borrowings and Costello asked Local Government to prepare a revised programme which would ensure that LLF issues for housing (outside Dublin city) were reduced by £3m..

The Department's reply, which was dismissed by Finance as 'a long unhelpful document, not sufficiently clear, without a single specific instance in it of a possible reduction, but full of the difficulties to be faced (which are patently exaggerated)', revealed that most LLF loans were issued *after* schemes and payments had been sanctioned. Many loans were drawn down over a period of years; money for land acquisition was generally borrowed *after* the land had been acquired, by which time local authorities had already accepted tenders; borrowings for SDAA loans covered mortgages which councils had already signed or cases where applicants had entered into commitments to build or buy a house on foot of a provisional loan approval; outstanding commitments for supplementary housing grants were believed to total up to £3m.. In order to reduce the cost of LLF loans, it would prove necessary to check on the undertakings which each housing authority had given. In the meantime, local authorities would enter into further commitments unless the government issued 'clear and detailed instructions' forbidding them from doing so. Pending completion of the necessary inquiries, the Minister for Local Government sought permission to sanction all loans which had been recommended in cases where local authorities had made binding commitments.

Finance was determined to secure the necessary cuts and this uncompromising stance forced Local Government to come up with potential savings of £1.1m. on anticipated LLF issues of £6.35m.. The Department also approved Finance's proposal to restrict eligibility for SDAA loans and gave a commitment not to approve further housing schemes in areas which had met their 1947 targets unless there was a proven need. Where the 1947 target had not been realised, further houses would be sanctioned only if they were needed to replace unfit dwellings or to rehouse serious cases of overcrowding. However, Local Government reiterated that the potential savings were limited, 'unless the Minister had the authority of the Government to refuse sanction to schemes solely on the grounds of shortage of money'.[119]

Why was the cabinet unwilling to take this step? Did it fear public protests, or the government's collapse? The alternative, cuts by subterfuge, with Local Government bearing the opprobrium, was opposed by the Custom House. On 3 May the government approved total capital expenditure of £43.65m. for the 1956/57 financial year, with a ceiling on the Local Loans Fund of £5.7m. — £4.55m. for housing. This reduction was to be achieved without a formal change of government policy and without any public announcement. To ensure that it was carried out, Finance demanded quarterly estimates of demands on the LLF and new loan sanctions, broken down under housing and other subheadings.

On 7 June 1956 Dublin Corporation announced that no further applications for SDAA loans would be accepted until further notice. The Department of Local Government was inundated with protests by groups ranging from the SDAA Applicants Association to the

Ballyfermot Newly-Weds Association and the Dublin and District House-Builders Association.[120] In July the cabinet imposed further cuts of £5m. as part of an emergency budget. On 30 August it was decided that savings of £340,000 would be effected between the vote for Local Government and the Road Fund. In addition, the Ministers for Local Government and Finance would consult about the possibility of further savings on the Local Loans Fund.[121] O'Donnell pointed out that any additional cuts in the sum available from the LLF would pose considerable difficulties for the Department, adding that his position was made more difficult by the government's decision that he should not issue instructions that important works such as housing should be delayed or abandoned for financial reasons. He made it clear that he was not prepared to issue such instructions without the government's authority. In the following months, O'Donnell repeatedly sought, but without success, government approval to take formal decisions that would make it possible to achieve cuts in local authority spending. In the meantime, to effect the necessary curbs, he was forced to rely on informal conferences with county managers — whose powers the government had been committed to restricting. However, in a confidential memorandum to the Taoiseach, following a meeting with the Dublin and District House-Builders Association on 31 October 1956, O'Donnell claimed that 'unless policy is reconsidered, there is no means by which he [as Minister for Local Government] can ensure that local authorities will not undertake further commitments on such services as supplementary housing grants and Small Dwellings Acquisition Acts advances, the administration of which are outside his control'. LLF advances and applications were running well in excess of the limit set, despite the fact that Local Government was approving only issues which were necessary 'to obviate a serious break-down of local services'.[122]

O'Donnell's firm stance seems to have been effective in winning some important concessions during the summer and autumn of 1956. Shortly after the announcement that Dublin Corporation would not accept applications for SDAA loans until further notice, O'Donnell informed an agitated deputation from the Dublin and District House-Builders Association that building societies were now prepared to consider applications for 95 per cent mortgages over 35 years, provided that they were guaranteed by the government and local authorities. This was a major achievement in the Department's long-standing efforts to place finance for private housing on a permanent footing. Local authorities in the Dublin area announced that they would adopt this scheme,[123] which would provide mortgage guarantees for families earning less than £12 per week. The financial crisis brought further long-term gains: following the Bank of Ireland's rejection of Dublin Corporation's request for a further overdraft on its capital account, Dublin Corporation was granted a loan of £400,000 from the Local Loans Fund and Cork Corporation was given permission to apply.[124]

Dublin Corporation remained free to determine the composition of its capital expenditure, subject to a ceiling of £4m.. Although it had been assumed that approximately £1m. of this sum would be dedicated to SDAA loans, the Corporation determined to devote all its resources to local authority housing. Funds for SDAA loans were also scarce in Dublin County Council, which had experienced increased demand following the cutbacks imposed by Dublin Corporation in 1955. In August 1956 the Council ceased accepting new applications and decided to restrict future applications to families with an annual income of less than £624 and to set a price ceiling of £2,000 on the houses financed.

Although three major building societies — the Irish Permanent, the Educational Building Society and the Irish Civil Service Building Society, which together accounted for over 80 per cent of all building society advances — had adopted the mortgage guarantee scheme, the Educational Building Society and the Irish Civil Service Building Society were unable to make any loans until 1957. The Irish Permanent had provisionally approved 64 applications, but would consider only applications from large urban areas. This meant that little capital was available for private housing.

A deputation from the Dublin and District House-Builders Association met O'Donnell to demand that the Department use its influence to persuade Dublin Corporation to provide SDAA loans. Since the government was now providing Dublin Corporation with capital via the LLF, the deputation believed that it should be in a position to influence its allocation, but a record of the meeting prepared for the Taoiseach minuted:

Any attempt by the Minister for Local Government to dictate to the Corporation how the money should be spent would probably lead to trouble — especially since the Corporation could argue that money was being diverted from slum clearance and other working-class housing operations for Small Dwellings purposes.

The government's hands were tied as a result of its commitment to giving greater autonomy to local authorities. Further restrictions on SDAA loans resulted from the Housing (Amendment) Act 1956, which had reinterpreted Section 32 of the 1950 Act — the clause referring to market value — in a more restrictive light; it imposed a new limit on SDAA mortgages of 95 per cent of market value exclusive of any grants. The clause, which appears to have been designed to curb house costs and to prevent builders from levying site fees or ground rents, brought a further decline in the market for private housing. The building industry demanded its repeal, claiming that it had led to higher unemployment.

Given the government's straitened financial circumstances, in November/December 1956 it appeared unlikely that these representations would prove effective. However on 11 December 1956 the government decided that, 'as matters of urgency', the Ministers for Local Government and Finance would consider amending the definition of market value 'so as to cover the proper and reasonable cost of the erection of a house by an efficient builder' and would provide for appeals against the valuations set. The government also instructed the Minister for Local Government to inform the Dublin and District House-Builders' Association of this decision. This concession was far outweighed by the imposition of further restrictions on local authority expenditure on housing.

On 27 November, having failed over several months to get government support for this action, the Minister for Local Government issued a circular directing local authorities not to enter into commitments to provide supplementary housing grants or SDAA loans until they had obtained loan sanction from the LLF or another source. A subsequent cabinet meeting agreed to instruct local authorities to suspend supplementary grants in cases where they had unallocated balances of loans in hand.

Despite the pervasive sense of crisis during 1956/57, the fall in the number of local authority houses completed was reversed and the number of private houses completed was the second-highest of the post-war years. Dublin Corporation completed a record number of houses.

TABLE 8.5

Dublin Corporation: Dwellings completed

1950/51	2,588
1951/52	1,982
1952/53	2,200
1953/54	1,353
1954/55	1,922
1955/56	1,311
1956/57	4,784

However 1956/57 marked the end of the post-war housing drive. Employment on local authority housing schemes had peaked at 12,955 in 1950. By March 1956 it stood at 6,285 and it had fallen to 4,180 by March 1957. Sixty of the 89 housing authorities had met their targets.[125] For many years the Department of Finance and the Central Bank had both questioned the relentless increase in public capital expenditure on non-productive items such as housing. In the crisis year of 1956 — a year marked by three budgets — the criticism eventually bore fruit. In October the Taoiseach announced the appointment of a small committee of experts, the capital investment advisory committee, to evaluate the existing capital structure of the economy by sector and to advise the government on the desirable volume of public investment and on appropriate priorities.[126]

CONCLUSIONS

The immediate post-war decade proved a vital period in the history of the Department of Local Government. The importance attached to housing and the somewhat erratic commitment to relieving unemployment by means of public expenditure meant that the Department's activities held a central role in government policy. Commitments respecting housing, county management and public capital expenditure featured prominently in election manifestos during these years. The housing programme can be evaluated at various levels.

Let us begin with the most important: the number and quality of local authority and private houses constructed rose dramatically and the

Department of Local Government ably carried out the task it was set. Until 1956 it was superbly successful, despite mounting financial pressures, in ensuring that capital was readily available for housing. Although Dublin Corporation's housing programme lurched from one financial crisis to another, there is no evidence that it was seriously handicapped by a shortage of funds. The expanded housing programme appears to have been well administered and the performance of local authorities was more closely scrutinised than during the 1930s. There is no evidence of serious complaints about delays imposed by the Department. John Garvin claimed that most complaints related to delays in processing SDAA loans which were handled by local authorities, and that there was considerable pressure on the Department to take over responsibility for them.[127]

More questionable is the precise shape of government assistance for housing. The fundamental redrafting of subsidies for local authority housing, promised in the early 1950s, never took place, probably because it would have entailed greater departmental intervention, notably a requirement that all local authorities charged differential rents on a similar basis. In fact, quiet pressure by the Department had ensured that differential rents had been widely adopted by the mid-1950s; Dublin Corporation remained the outstanding exception. The spiralling cost of assistance to private housing was also in need of reassessment, particularly the practice by some local authorities of paying supplementary grants which were funded by LLF borrowings. Although Finance claimed that grants for new private houses led only to higher house prices and greater profits for builders, no research was carried out to find out what effect these grants had on the supply of new houses.

Finally, there remains the question of whether or not housing absorbed too high a proportion of government capital expenditure in the immediate post-war decade. At first blush the answer appears to be an inescapable 'yes'. However it is possible that capital expenditure on housing was not too high; rather, that investment in other sectors was too low and this may reflect wider policy failings, such as the stagnation of a protected economy, which go far beyond the remit of this book.

The evidence of these years suggests that, while the Department of Finance ranted and railed, it had yet to achieve control of key elements of public capital expenditure, such as the Local Loans Fund and the investment programmes of Dublin and Cork Corporations. There is, however, evidence that Finance was making consistent efforts to achieve such control: demanding greater amounts of information from Local Government and from the local authorities, and occasionally engaging in direct negotiations with Dublin and Cork Corporations independently of the Custom House. On occasions J.J. McElligott appears to have treated Local Government as little more than a messenger boy. In turn, the high level of expenditure associated with government policies put considerable pressure on local authority finances.

The other recurrent issue of these years remains the tension between centralisation and local autonomy. Criticism was rife of departmental interference in local affairs and of the county management system. Some of this was undoubtedly justified: surcharging local councillors for the cost of bunting to celebrate An Tóstal — a cultural festival which was celebrated in many towns during the 1950s — must be deemed bureaucratic madness. In fact there was simply no provision for such expenditure. Surcharges on councillors who claimed expenses for attending anti-partition rallies proved equally unpopular, but were much more justifiable, as were the recurrent disputes over foreign trips by councillors[128] — what would now be termed 'junkets'. However, demands for greater local autonomy accord ill with demands from the same local authorities for greater central funding for roads, housing and other purposes. Local authority staff and employees sought greater uniformity in pay and working conditions; there was strong popular demand for the processing of SDAA loans to be centralised.[129] The rival pressures for centralisation and decentralisation, are more complex than they are often painted. The period of alternating governments permits some contrasts between policies and practices under Fianna Fáil and the inter-party governments. The latter appear to have been less centralist, more inclined to pander to local wishes. Labour Party presence in the Custom House brought undoubted gains for local authority road-workers and for the expansion of house construction by direct labour.

While critical comments can be made about the management of the Irish economy during these years — the excessive emphasis on social, as opposed to productive, investment, the exhaustion of post-war external reserves — these matters were not the direct responsibility of the Department of Local Government. What can be said is that the

Department successfully carried out an enormous housing programme which brought long-term advances in the quality and supply of Irish housing, and did so without evidence of major administrative difficulties. In confrontations with other government departments and in cabinet, it kept departmental policies to the fore, defending them against attack. By 1957, however, the housing programme was largely complete, and the appointment of the Capital Investment Advisory Committee appeared to signal a change in economic policy, one which seemed likely to relegate Local Government to a less prominent role.

CHAPTER NINE

BOG ROADS OR NATIONAL ROUTES?
THE FAILURE OF A NATIONAL ROADS POLICY

The saga of road development in Ireland, both before and after independence, can be summarised as a triumph of local interests over central government. It is a story which belies allegations that Irish public administration is extremely centralised and takes little heed of local demands. The second point to note is the extent to which expenditure on roads was determined, not by transport needs, but by a concern to provide a form of famine relief or social welfare. Both these issues are perhaps most clearly seen in an investigation of roads policy during the decade or so following the end of World War II.

ROAD DEVELOPMENT BEFORE 1914

There is a surprising degree of continuity between the pattern of road expenditure under the Act of Union and under an independent Irish state, and between the attitude of the grand juries and those of democratically elected county councils. Although the British government provided a substantial amount of capital for road improvements during the course of the nineteenth century, most of it was earmarked as part of various programmes of famine or poor relief. The best-known examples are the road improvements carried out by the Board of Works or its immediate antecedent in remote areas of the west and south-west of Ireland in the decades immediately before the Famine, and the notorious programme of relief works carried out during the Famine winter of 1846/47. Succeeding periods of hardship, notably in the 1880s and the 1890s, saw further increments of government expenditure on road and bridge construction in remote western areas. Some of this investment was genuinely beneficial. By the eve of the Famine there were few parts of Ireland which were not within ten miles of public roads[1] and the country was regarded as having one of the best road networks in Europe; Mokyr suggests that there may have been overinvestment in roads.[2]

Twenty or thirty years earlier, it had been impossible to transport grain to market from remote areas such as north Mayo, and farmers were forced to turn surplus crops into more portable poteen instead.[3] Similarly the causeways constructed by the Congested Districts Board between islands off the coast of Connemara, such as Carna, reduced isolation and brought remote areas into contact with the market economy, for better or worse.[4] The Board of Works was also responsible for funding most major road and bridge construction throughout Ireland, including schemes which were not initiated primarily in order to provide relief employment. Applications for Board of Works loans were subject to detailed scrutiny. By the second half of the nineteenth century, technical responsibility for all road and bridge construction rested with county surveyors, who were appointed by the lord lieutenant following competitive examinations. A select committee which inquired into the county surveyor system in 1857 believed that it had resulted in higher standards of construction and in financial savings.[5] Central scrutiny had its limits and there is substantial evidence to suggest that landlords who served on grand juries ensured that roads on or adjoining their estates were specially favoured and that contracts for road repairs were generally awarded to their tenants. Such patronage ensured that they would be in a position to pay their rents.[6]

Most of the history of nineteenth-century road development has yet to be written. The railway revolutionised travel in Ireland during the nineteenth century and it became the main form of long-distance transport. Roads catered mainly for short-distance traffic; they were therefore the concern of local, rather than national, authorities.

Matters changed dramatically around the turn of the century. After the 1898 Local Government Act, road expenditure was determined and contracts awarded by democratically elected rural district councils and, to a lesser extent, by county councils, rather than by landlords. With the invention of the motor car and the growth of motor transport, roads began to be seen once more as a means of long-distance transport and there was a corresponding need for more central regulation. By 1914, 19,554 motor vehicles were registered in Ireland. The first regulations requiring local authorities to erect signs warning of crossroads, dangerous bends and other hazards to drivers were introduced in 1903.

Although the Local Government Board followed the example of the UK authorities in issuing a circular suggesting appropriate styles for these signs, local authorities were free to design their own. In practice the majority ignored the circular and by March 1908 only nine counties had erected any signs. Speed limits were first mentioned in the Board's report for 1908/09. Limerick Corporation wished to set the maximum speed for heavy motor cars at 2.5 miles an hour in some streets, because of possible damage to houses. The Board suggested a speed limit of 5 miles per hour. Speed limits were also enforced on roads leading to Glendalough, Co. Wicklow and on vehicles travelling to Punchestown races. In 1911 the Board reported that heavy motor traffic had been banned on the road between Kenmare and Killarney, Co. Kerry, and all cars were subject to a speed limit.[7]

Such technical matters did not create much tension between the Road Traffic Board and the local authorities. The latter largely ignored the new regulations and the Board did not press particularly hard for enforcement. However the 1898 Act had also capped the amount which local authorities could spend on road works at 125 per cent of the average sum spent by grand juries in their final three years in office — a clause that had no counterpart in the British Local Government Act.[8] Councils could exceed this limit only with the Board's approval. By 1906, however, the LGB was urging local authorities to spend additional money on roads and to put greater emphasis on reconstructing main roads, rather than on routine maintenance.

The Board was intent on creating a national road network, and an order issued in May 1899 requested county councils to designate the major routes through each county as main roads. The cost of maintaining or improving main roads would be borne by the county as a whole. However district councils, which were primarily concerned with local needs, strongly objected to paying for improvements to roads which lay outside their immediate jurisdiction. For rural district councils, improvements to by-roads and lanes yielded much greater electoral dividends and several councils were surcharged for repairing private lanes leading to single farmhouses. This issue was complicated by the fact that there was no official definition of a public road; the test applied was whether or not the road had been previously repaired by a grand jury.[9] While the Board's auditors could surcharge councils which misspent money in this way, the Board lacked the power to require councils to spend money on creating a network of main roads. It could

conduct an inquiry into a council's road improvement programme only
if local ratepayers appealed against the council's decision to designate
certain roads as main roads. Many county councils reacted to the
Board's request by passing resolutions declaring that the county
contained no main roads. Opposition to main roads was common to
nationalist and unionist councils: Antrim County Council appears to
have been the first to pass such a declaration; Fermanagh soon
followed suit, as did other counties, including Wexford. In such cases
the Board could do little other than try to persuade county councils to
change their attitudes.[10]

The difficulty which the Board faced in persuading councils to
spend money constructing a national road network is an indication of
the need for a more centralised roads policy which could draw on non-
local funds. In 1910 the British government established a Road Board
which was responsible for both Britain and Ireland. The Board would
administer the Road Fund, which received the net proceeds of motor
vehicle duties collected by the county councils and the duty on motor
fuel. This money would be advanced to county councils in the form of
grants, to finance the construction and improvement of main roads.[11] By
1911/12 county councils were being offered sums, ranging from £1,000
to £4,000 annually, towards the cost of improving main roads. Some
councils refused to accept these grants, because they were required to
finance from 20 to 50 per cent of the cost of main road improvements
from local taxation.[12] This controversy would recur for many decades to
come. The bribe of Road Fund grants failed to encourage recalcitrant
county councils to designate some of their roads as main roads. In 1925
fourteen councils in the Irish Free State had yet to take this step.

Councils were also lethargic in enforcing compliance with vehicle-
licensing regulations, and threats from the Road Board that grants
would be contingent on their doing so appear to have had little effect.[13]
Councillors remained more concerned with repairing local roads and
with determining who should be employed. Thus, by 1901 many
councils were seeking to replace the contractors who had previously
carried out road repairs under the grand juries — mostly farmers —
with workers who were recruited and paid by the council, i.e. direct
labour. The LGB approved the first direct labour schemes in 1902. By
1909 they were in operation in thirteen local authorities and were
responsible for repairing one-third of the country's 7,085 miles of main
roads and 15 per cent of the 47,850 miles of district roads.[14]

This brief account of roads policy before 1914 highlights many of the issues that were to recur after Independence: the differing priorities for expenditure of the national government and the local authorities; local resentment at being asked to bear all or part of the cost of main roads; and the concept of road expenditure as a form of employment relief. Local authorities such as Clare County Council, which had introduced direct labour schemes before 1914, tended to mention a reduction in the level of local pauperism as one of the major advantages.[15]

THE MINISTRY OF TRANSPORT

Road improvements ground to a halt during World War I, because the income of the Road Fund was requisitioned for other purposes and, as chapter two shows, resumption of the work was seriously handicapped when most county councils switched their allegiance to Dáil Éireann in 1920. In January 1920 the Road Board was superseded by a fully fledged Ministry of Transport, based in London.[16] Although there was a separate office in Dublin, it appears to have had little autonomy, particularly in sanctioning expenditure. By the end of 1921 it was described as being 'in an almost expiring condition',[17] presumably owing to inactivity as a result of being boycotted by republican councils. The duties of the Ministry of Transport were initially transferred to the provisional government's Department of Economic Affairs, though in October 1922 they were reassigned to the Department of Local Government.[18] J.P.J. Butler, engineering assistant with the Ministry of Transport's Irish roads section, retained this position with the Department of Local Government until he retired in 1923. He was replaced by James Quigley, formerly Meath county surveyor, who was appointed as the Department's chief road engineer, and later its chief engineering inspector. Three of the eight other officials in the ministry's Dublin office also served with the Department.[19] As we have seen in chapter three, their knowledge of the intricacies of the Road Fund proved extremely useful to the Free State government when it attempted to reclaim monies owed.

Although it was short-lived, the Ministry of Transport had a significant influence on the roads policy pursued during the first decade after Independence. In May 1920, before the Irish county councils had broken their links with the British administration, the ministry established an Irish roads advisory subcommittee. Its membership included civil servants, a representative of the county surveyors — the afore-mentioned James Quigley — and representatives of the General Council of County Councils, the Irish Automobile Club and the Irish Farmers' Union. The committee's first task was the classification of main roads into first-class roads — main trunk roads and roads linking major towns — and second-class roads, linking lesser towns or two main trunk roads. Progress was slow because of lack of co-operation from county councils. This was less a reflection of the Dáil policy of non-recognition of British government agencies, and more a case of the traditional hostility which Irish county councils had shown towards main roads or national roads.

In November 1921 the ministry adopted a more active approach to this problem. Colonel Butler of the Ministry of Transport was dispatched to Northern Ireland to complete the process of classifying roads, and efforts were made to carry out a similar operation in the Irish Free State early in 1922.[20] The Irish roads advisory committee was reconstituted in 1923, in direct continuity with its predecessor. At the inaugural meeting, H.S. Moylan, who served as secretary, read section 22 of the 1919 (Westminster) Ministry of Transport Act, under which the committee had been constituted. The committee continued in existence until at least 1930; file survival appears to be erratic. It determined matters such as maximum lorry weights and the criteria to be adopted in allocating grants from the Road Fund.

PLANNING A NATIONAL ROAD NETWORK 1922-32

The 1919 Ministry of Transport Act had provided for a centralised roads unit, with the ministry directly responsible for carrying out improvements to the main trunk roads; it would also hire its own surveyors. The British decision to opt for a centralised unit (though many other aspects of domestic policy, such as police and education, remained decentralised, unlike in Ireland) suggests a belief that this would prove more efficient than delegating responsibility for main road improvements to local authorities. The Irish Free State government's decision to restore responsibility for roads to the Department of Local Government — a return to the pre-1910 administrative model — meant a much more decentralised system, though the abolition of the RDCs in 1925 reduced the centrifugal tendencies to a certain extent. Some of the problems were operational: county councils lacked the modern machinery and perhaps the experienced staff needed to construct modern roads. More importantly, because local authorities were responsible for both national and local roads and preferred to spend money on the latter, there was an inevitable risk that the Department of Local Government, and the government as a whole, would come under pressure to divert resources from main roads to by-roads. The roads advisory committee also feared that money for road improvements would tend to be allocated in response to reports of distress and unemployment, with an emphasis on short-term employment creation, rather than on the basis of a long-term plan for developing a national road network.[21] James Quigley concluded that the £275,000 spent on road works in the year 1922/23, which was funded by unemployment relief grants, had given 'poor value' for money.[22]

Although the emergence of a national road plan was delayed by the government's desire to cut wage levels (in this case the wages of county council labourers which were believed to determine the wages of agricultural labourers),[23] the delay was less significant than in the case of the government's housing programme. Despite the need to rebuild roads and bridges damaged during the Anglo-Irish war and the civil war, a blueprint for a trunk road network had been prepared by the mid-1920s. A comprehensive housing plan was not drawn up until the early 1930s. The greater momentum in the case of roads may be due to the existence of the Roads Advisory Council, or perhaps to the dynamism of James Quigley, the Department's chief roads engineer.

In March 1925, the roads advisory committee decided that the Road Fund grants in the coming year should be allocated on the basis of a formula which reflected each county's expenditure on roads for the years 1912-14, its population, rateable valuation, trunk road mileage and expenditure over the preceding three years. In turn, each county should use these grants to improve or reconstruct the 3,000 miles of national roads which linked Dublin and other major cities and towns such as Cork, Limerick, Waterford, Wexford, Galway, Sligo, Castlebar and Dundalk.[24]

The 1925 Local Government Act gave the Minister the power to designate main roads in the fourteen counties which had not yet done so. When the Department announced that trunk roads would be given priority in awarding Road Fund grants, councils which had hitherto been loath to designate main roads rapidly changed tack. According to the Minister for Local Government, James Burke, the Department was 'inundated with demands from people all over the country', demanding that roads in their locality be added to the list of main roads. The Minister took 'a very strong line' against such representations. Having consulted the roads advisory committee and the department engineers, he announced his intention 'not to deviate an inch' from the original list.[25]

In order to refine the priority list for road improvements, the Department carried out a national road traffic census in 1925 and again in 1928. It also began a programme of improving the alignment and gradients on major roads, and the engineering staff tested a variety of foundations and surface dressings on sections of the busy Dublin-Naas road in an effort to determine which was most suitable. These led to the conclusion that tar-spraying was 'objectionable' and that asphalt and concrete were much more expensive than using tar-bitumen macadam.[26] Many more steam-rollers were used as the decade went on.

In 1924 the government devoted £1m. towards trunk road improvements; £250,000 came from current Road Fund income and the balance was borrowed against the Road Fund's future income.[27] An additional £450,000 was provided for this purpose in April 1925. However, the amount allocated for improvements in both 1924 and 1925 was less than the government had originally promised. Although the Road Fund income showed a steady rate of increase, in line with the rising number of registered motor vehicles — from 7,286 vehicles in 1919 to 33,836 by 1925[28] — it was not sufficient to ensure that the projected trunk road improvement scheme would be completed as rapidly as the Department wished. In 1925 it proposed that an accelerated programme should be carried out over three years on 1,500 miles of major trunk roads, at an estimated cost of £3.82m., to be funded by the Exchequer. The Departments of Finance, Agriculture and Industry and Commerce all objected to this proposal. Finance protested that the Exchequer would be unable to provide the necessary funds, given the heavy demand for capital to construct the Shannon electricity scheme and the Carlow sugar factory. Agriculture preferred to divert any available funds to reducing local authority rates, and Industry and Commerce was determined to uphold the interests of the railway companies against a roads lobby. Gordon Campbell, secretary of

Industry and Commerce, was adamant that the cost of road improvements should be borne by motor taxation, not by the general taxpayer.[29] The matter was referred to an interdepartmental committee on road transport, consisting of representatives from Industry and Commerce and Local Government. It concluded in March 1926 that expenditure on road construction, maintenance and improvements had not increased in real terms since 1914. Only one-quarter of the total mileage of trunk and link roads had been improved; the remainder had not even been maintained at 1914 standards. The contribution made by local authorities towards road expenditure had fallen in real terms. Motor taxation covered only 29 per cent of the cost of road expenditure. Commercial vehicles made a proportionately lower contribution to road costs than private cars when the damage which they caused was taken into account, and the committee tentatively recommended that they should bear a higher level of tax.[30] Its recommendations were referred to a cabinet subcommittee and it in turn reconvened the interdepartmental committee, with the addition of a representative from Finance. Although this is not minuted, it appears that the cabinet subcommittee had decided the basic parameters of future road funding. Certainly the reconvened interdepartmental committee assumed from the beginning that local authority rates should contribute 50 per cent more towards road expenditure than in 1914, a sum of approximately £1m.. Motor taxation should provide £750,000, against £561,888 in 1924/25, and motor registration taxes should be revised to reduce taxes levied on Ford cars to an 'equitable figure', in order to encourage the company to manufacture cars in Cork.

The committee also concluded that the Road Fund income would be insufficient to finance a rapid modernisation of the road network and suggested that this should be financed by borrowing against future revenue. Local rates must continue to bear 'a share' of the cost of maintaining trunk and link roads in order to free Road Fund income for development purposes.[31] Eight days after this report had been completed, the Minister for Finance announced in his 1926/27 Budget speech that £2m. would be borrowed for road improvements, though he added that he hoped he was interpreting the view of the Minister for Local Government correctly in stating 'that he had no intention of announcing any grandiose proposals. Capital expenditure will be cautiously undertaken.'[32]

Officials in Finance were extremely disgruntled about this

announcement. One minuted that the decision was: 'I take it, come to by the Executive Council, with whom I understand all members of the inter-departmental committee, except myself, were in consultation'. Joseph Brennan, secretary of the Department of Finance, tried to dissuade Ernest Blythe, Minister for Finance, from proceeding with the plan to borrow £2m., but the Minister dismissed his objections.[33] The government's decision to borrow £2m. for trunk road improvements should be seen as a triumph for Local Government, given the tight controls which Finance exercised over expenditure in the 1920s. However Finance tried to reinterpret this decision in its favour by claiming that £2m. represented the cost of all road expenditure funded from central sources. Finance was horrified to discover that Local Government saw the £2m. as additional to normal Road Fund spending. In an interesting variation on the old coals in the bathtub argument (i.e. that baths would only be wasted on working-class families), one Finance official argued that so much largesse would put 'local authorities in possession of substantial funds which they would most probably be unable to expend with advantage and expedition'.[34]

The annual Report of the Department of Local Government and Public Health for 1926/27 claimed that the government decision permitting £2m. to be borrowed against the Road Fund inaugurated 'a period of unprecedented activity in road development'. By April 1927 it claimed that almost all the money had been allocated. At the same time Local Government also allocated grants to county councils towards the cost of repairing main roads, as opposed to trunk roads, for the first time since Independence. This was a concession to county councils, which previously had been wholly responsible for such repairs. In reality the situation for road improvements was much less rosy. By 31 March 1927, only £273,491 had been paid out for major road improvements.[35] An undated memorandum in the Mulcahy papers, which appears to have been drafted about 1930, suggests that the extra £2m. was a mirage. The normal block grants for major road improvements were reduced to £250,000 in 1926 and £300,000 in 1927 in order to transfer funds to the so-called 'National Scheme', i.e. the £2m. programme. Although it was claimed that £1.875m. had been spent on the National Scheme by 31 March 1929, only £750,000 of this was funded by borrowings, the balance being taken from normal Road Fund income, and it would have been available, irrespective of any so-called £2m. scheme.[36] This assertion appears to be confirmed by the following data.

TABLE 9.1

Central government expenditure on roads 1924-32

	Improvements	Maintenance	Income*
1924/25	£718,000	nil	£770,000
1925/26	£673,000	nil	£804,000
1926/27	£736,000	nil	£888,000
1927/28	£1,500,000	£86,453	£960,421
1928/29	£932,145	£261,030	£878,442
1929/30	£358,554	£290,611	£896,883
1930/31	£450,564	£347,084	£943,000
1931/32	£510,097	£348,553	£691,000

* Road fund, plus 6d rate under Compensation to Property Act. This latter source of income ended in 1929.

Between 1925 and 1932 inclusive, central government expenditure on road improvements totalled £5.878m., almost one million pounds less than the income available from the Road Fund. If the 1924/25 ratio of improvements to income, 93.25 per cent, had been maintained, expenditure on improvements in the years 1926-28 would have been £2.47m.; in fact £2.9m. was spent under this heading. Only the additional expenditure in 1927/28 can be clearly attributed to the £2m. scheme. In later years an increasing share of Road Fund income was allocated for road repairs — over £348,000 by 1931/32. Expenditure on road improvements was reduced and the Department came under pressure to share out the money between all counties, regardless of priorities. In consequence, average grants tended to be too small to fund any major improvements. In 1931/32 only Counties Cork, Dublin and Galway received grants in excess of £20,000.

It remains unclear whether the entire responsibility for the failure to realise the £2m. National Scheme rests with the Department of Finance. The DLGPH report for 1926/27 noted that the pace of road improvements had been delayed 'due mainly to attempts of councils to carry out the works by direct labour with inadequate road plant'.[37] When the memorandum in the Mulcahy papers was drafted, apparently about 1930, more than one-third of the national road mileage remained untouched and urban roads were also in very poor repair because county councils were apparently not disposed to spend money in urban areas.[38] By this stage, expenditure on road improvements was a residual item: the money left when the Road Fund had made its contribution towards the cost of maintaining trunk and main roads. In April 1929 Richard Mulcahy, then Minister for Local Government, explained that the Department found it difficult to persuade local authorities to give advance notice of their maintenance programmes. Until these were known, the Department could not allocate any money for improvements.[39] Such an attitude precluded serious long-term planning.

Local authorities repeatedly objected to the Department's policy of giving priority to improving trunk roads and to the fact that the Road Fund paid 50 per cent of the cost of maintaining main roads but made no contribution towards maintaining minor roads. This was a long-standing grievance. At the first meeting of the Irish Road Board in 1923 P.J. O'Neill, the representative of the General Council of County Councils, protested at a proposal that national trunk roads should receive four times the amount allocated to second-class roads.[40] Localism took many forms, such as a demand from Senator Thomas Toal from County Monaghan, a member of the road advisory council, that each county should receive grants from the Road Fund equal to the sum collected in the county in licence fees and fuel excise duties. When H.S. Moylan, the senior roads official in the Department of Local Government, pointed out that this would give Dublin one-quarter of the Road Fund income, Toal lost interest in the idea.

Most local authorities wanted to channel money away from main roads towards repairing and improving minor roads, presumably because a majority of ratepayers did not own cars and undertook few long-distance journeys. In 1930 P.J. Ruttledge, Fianna Fáil TD for Mayo North, and a future Minister for Local Government, protested at the Department's refusal to sanction Road Fund grants for the reconstruction of minor roads 'leading into populous districts where unemployment was rife'. Ruttledge believed that 'people living on bog roads are as entitled as the wealthy people to have proper means of reaching their homes and conveying the produce of their farms to market'.[41] Kerry TD F.H. Crowley alleged that the conflicting priorities for road expenditure gave rise to 'eternal warfare' between the county councils and the Local Government Department.[42] The most common conflicts concerned the Department's efforts to prevent councils adding

391

lanes leading to solitary farmhouses to the network of public roads; such disputes had also occurred during the era of the Local Government Board. Resolutions demanding that 'stop-end' roads be made eligible for public funds poured in from Galway, Roscommon and Carlow County Councils.[43] To some extent they reflect ratepayers' perceptions that road expenditure was a heavy burden on the rates, from which ratepayers who did not own cars derived little if any benefit.[44]

1932-39 ROAD WORKS: A FORM OF UNEMPLOYMENT RELIEF

The forward-looking road development programme drawn up by officials in the Department of Local Government was already seriously compromised by 1930, as a result both of lack of finance and the inability and unwillingness of local authorities to give priority to main roads. The policy was probably unpopular and may have cost Cumann na nGaedheal support in the 1932 general election. If the programme was largely in tatters by this stage, the Fianna Fáil government removed any remaining coherence, as road expenditure was largely subsumed into the government's employment-creation programmes. One million pounds was borrowed on the security of the Road Fund, not for long-term road development but for employment creation; and the distribution of this money was largely controlled by Hugo Flinn, the parliamentary secretary to the Minister for Finance, who was responsible for employment schemes, rather than by the Department of Local Government. Flinn was extremely sympathetic to local interests such as Mayo County Council's preference for spending money on 'stop-end roads' and bog roads, despite the fact that 350 miles of main roads in the county had yet to be steamrolled and 453 miles of main roads were in need of reconstruction.[45]

The Road Fund also suffered 'raids'[46] to the tune of £100,000; the money was used for employment schemes. When in the years after 1938 additional money was provided for road expenditure under separate employment schemes, this was mainly spent on minor roads, with an emphasis on unskilled, labour-intensive work which carried out superficial repairs and had little merit other than relieving unemployment. By 1938 the report of the Commission on Banking Currency and Credit argued that there was little point in retaining the Road Fund as a separate entity outside the Exchequer.[47]

392

The amount available for distribution from the Road Fund showed no real growth during the years 1932-39, despite a steady rise in the number of registered motor vehicles. In 1933/34 a total of £858,000 was distributed in maintenance and improvement grants, compared with £808,547 in 1938/39. The figure fell as low as £722,940 in 1937/38. Annual reports of the Department dutifully record an increase in the national mileage of dust-free roads, from 5,137 in 1932 to 9,879 by 1939, but in 1945 more than 2,000 miles of the priority national road network identified in the 1920s had yet to be improved.

There is no evidence that the Department devoted any attention to planning for road development during these years, as it had done in the 1920s. Such an exercise could have been carried out only by a masochist: the political will to create a modern road network was utterly lacking. Irish county councils preferred to spend money on minor roads; the 1932 and 1933 Road Transport Acts, which were drafted within the Department of Industry and Commerce, set out to protect the railways by restricting the development of road freight transport.[48] There is no evidence that the Department of Local Government had any influence into this legislation.[49]

THE EMERGENCY YEARS: PLANNING FOR THE 1940s

The Emergency postponed whatever meagre prospect existed of advancing road development. Although the Road Fund was not directly threatened by wartime economy measures, its income collapsed from the 1939/40 figure of £1,138,000 to £631,000 in 1941/42, as petrol rationing brought an end to motoring except for essential purposes. There were 73,813 licensed motor vehicles in August 1939, but by 1943 this had fallen to 26,188. In 1945 there were only 7,845 licensed private cars on Irish roads. Road Fund improvement grants ceased in 1940/41 and by 1942/43, when the income was at its lowest level, only £236,015 was distributed to local authorities, less than 30 per cent of the sum available in 1939/40. Road expenditure funded by the employment scheme proved to be another casualty of the Emergency, falling from £6410,000 in 1939/40 to £355,000 by 1942/43. In 1938 the Department's engineering section was reorganised and some officials were assigned to work exclusively on roads, others to public health works. In 1941, a separate roads engineering section was re-established, though most of the officials were promptly assigned to supervise local authority turf production[50] (see chapter six), and this remained their major activity during the Emergency. Access roads to bogs appear to have had first claim on the modest resources of men and materials available for road expenditure during these years.

Despite these unpromising circumstances, the later years of the Emergency gave rise to an unexpected renaissance in road planning, which could have provided the framework for a modern national network. The stimulus was a request to Local Government from the cabinet committee on economic planning (see chapter seven) to submit plans for road expenditure in the immediate post-war years. The torrent of proposals which emerged is an indication of the frustration which the Department's road engineers must have suffered over the preceding decade. By 1943 the Department had submitted proposals for road improvements costing £6.5m.. Most surveys and plans were either complete or in preparation and awaited only the resumption of supplies and the necessary finance.

The scheduled improvements were no mere job-creation schemes. By September 1943, Ted Courtney, head of the Department's engineering section, had proposed that Irish roads be reclassified into four categories, based on the anticipated volume of vehicle traffic in the 1990s. Class 1 roads, which were expected to carry the heaviest traffic, would be dual-carriageways, with two fourteen-feet verges provided with non-slippery surfaces where cars could park in an emergency and horse and animal traffic could be accommodated. These roads would also have footpaths and two cycle tracks, though the latter would not be constructed until the volume of motor traffic appeared to make them necessary for safety's sake. The design would cater for vehicles travelling at 50 to 70 miles per hour. More modest specifications were drawn up for the other three classes of road. Planners would identify the land that would be needed for road construction over the following fifty years and it would be protected against other development by planning regulations. In the immediate post-Emergency years, priority would be given to constructing roads to a standard which would make them capable of handling the growth in motor traffic over the next twenty-five years. Unfortunately this scheme does not appear to have had many supporters outside the Custom House. The experience of the 1920s had shown that the Department's priorities for road expenditure were unlikely to coincide with those of local authorities and at a time when councils were smarting at the recent appointment of county managers (see chapter seven), this could provide yet another grievance against central government.

However the decision of the cabinet committee on 29 December 1943 to request the Minister for Local Government to state what proposal, 'if any', he had in mind for taking the initiative in planning the modernisation of major arterial routes from Dublin to Cork, Galway and Sligo, plus circular roads around Dublin, suggests that some consideration was given to allowing Local Government direct control over expenditure on class 1 roads,[51] though the idea did not subsequently recur in the minutes. In May 1944 Local Government submitted a progress report to the committee, which divided post-war road expenditure into two categories: special schemes to provide short-term employment in the event of unemployment rising sharply after the coming of peace; and investment to meet road traffic needs over the next fifty years. Under the latter heading, the Department proposed to reconstruct nearly all the country's arterial highways. On 5 September 1944, Courtney briefed the committee on these proposals.

Local Government's interest in long-term road development, with an emphasis on efficiency rather than on job creation, was in direct conflict with the cabinet committee's concern with putting unemployed labourers to work. Approximately half the £13m. spent on employment schemes between 1932 and 1946 had consisted of low-grade road and footpath repairs, and from 1932 road expenditure had become little more than an appendage of the government's employment schemes. In May 1945 the cabinet committee set up an inquiry into the operation of employment schemes, with a view to recommending possible improvements. Officials in Local Government turned out to be much more critical of employment schemes than officials in other government departments, Industry and Commerce and the Office of Public Works, for instance. These Departments were primarily concerned with providing employment; Local Government was interested in the quality of the work which was carried out and in getting value for money.

According to data provided by county surveyors, the average daily output of men engaged in employment schemes was less than half that of an ordinary labourer carrying out a similar task. The additional cost of using employment scheme workers on road works or on public health schemes ranged from 'very little' in cases where few workers were employed to 60 per cent. Additional costs of the order of 40 or 50 per cent were common. The excess costs appear to have been greatest in the Dublin area. Local authority engineers were unwilling to reject workers who were obviously unsuitable for employment lest they might be disqualified from receiving Unemployment Assistance. The Office of Public Works attempted to discredit the figures provided by the county surveyors, but with little apparent effect. In 1945 Erskine Childers, parliamentary secretary to the Minister for Local Government, submitted a lengthy memorandum to the cabinet committee, which recommended that future relief works should be carried out by contractors, who would be permitted to reject unsuitable workers, and that the rotation of workers should be scaled down.[52]

A similar emphasis on efficiency, even at the expense of employment, is evident in the deliberations of an internal group within Local Government, chaired by Childers, which examined future road plans. The working group determined that all future road reconstruction should meet 1995 standards for road curvature and 1970 standards (a standard related to projected 1970 traffic flows) for road width and amenities. They were also keen to press forward with constructing modern bridges at Lifford, Co. Donegal and in Wexford and providing by-passes at major traffic bottlenecks such as Santry, Naas, Kildare and Athlone, though they recognised that local authorities might oppose the construction of by-passes because of the potential loss of business.

In another flight of fancy, the working group proposed to engage the services of a landscape expert 'to tour certain roads and make proposals where improvement must conform with the harmony and beauty of the landscape'. In a move guaranteed to arouse opposition within the cabinet, they determined that no class 1 roads should be constructed under employment schemes and that priority should be given to the quality of roads constructed, if necessary at the cost of refusing to employ workers on rotational employment schemes. The working party recognised that their proposals would require a 'readjustment' of the basis on which the Road Fund grants were allocated. 'Even allowing for unemployment relief funds, it will no longer be practicable to allow the factor of financial poverty in any county to reduce the amount of money required by that county to carry out the Road Plan.' The working party obviously believed that the Department would be given the power to determine which arterial roads should be given priority. Childers's minute to MacEntee concluded by noting that 'the proposals involve a precedent, in that the state will be initiating planning'. He added: 'While I realise how reluctant the Government may be to interfere with local authorities more than they have already done, I note that legislation recently passed and pending under the auspices of this department continues to move in this direction constantly.'

MacEntee endorsed these proposals, with some reservations. He believed that lack of finance might make it necessary to reduce the pace of road development, not necessarily a bad thing in his opinion, since it would remove the risk that the Department was proceding faster than its expertise allowed. While he supported Childers's proposal that only contractors should construct class 1 roads, he reminded him of the government's concern with unemployment and of the need to secure cabinet assent.[53] MacEntee's reservations proved prescient: there is no evidence that the working party's proposals were ever considered by the cabinet committee. (Did MacEntee block them?) Many aspects of the proposal were political minefields, such as favouring national over local roads, further loss of local initiative and the determination to have road works carried out by contractors, who would be at liberty to hire young and efficient workers rather than men from the unemployment register.

In practice, the Fianna Fáil roads programme during the immediate post-war years followed the model of the 1930s, not that proposed by Childers and officials in Local Government. Socio-economic criteria continued to determine road expenditure and the recruitment of workers. In 1945 it was announced that schemes which were partly funded by the Road Fund must give priority to employing men on Unemployment Benefit who had been demobilised from the army. Second-choice went to men in receipt of Unemployment Assistance.[54]

The ending of the Emergency threatened the loss of up to 49,000 summer jobs on wartime turf schemes. This was much higher than the level of employment which had been provided on road schemes during the 1930s; fewer than 30,000 men had been employed in the summer of 1939.[55] As a result, Local Government was under even greater pressure to use expenditure on roads to create employment, regardless of long-term investment or considerations of efficiency. Local priorities also came to loom large in determining how the money was allocated, again in direct conflict with the Department's proposals. The government was under considerable pressure from TDs and county councillors to sanction the repair from public funds of private lanes to farmhouses. Farmers living in areas of high unemployment (which generally approximated to the former congested districts) already benefited from such a scheme, which was funded by the special employment scheme.

In 1942 Hugo Flinn had suggested to de Valera that the Fianna Fáil party believed that, in fairness, at least £250,000 should be made available for village roads, bog roads and drainage schemes in non-congested rural areas. This concession was granted in 1943, in the teeth of opposition from Local Government, though the lanes in question were not to be regarded as part of the public road network, i.e. permanently entitled to repair at public expense.[56]

Despite this concession, councils remained under pressure to declare lanes and bog roads to be public roads. By 1943 there were over 700 more miles of public roads in County Galway than in 1925, and the national mileage of county roads had risen from 35,970 in 1930 to 38,363 by 1945. The Department of Local Government utterly opposed this tendency because it meant a long-term increase in the cost of road maintenance. The Department pointed out that Ireland had an extremely high mileage of public roads, relative both to population and to the yield from motor taxation. Britain had 4.5 miles of road per 1,000 inhabitants and motor taxes yielded an average of £684 per mile of main road, whereas Ireland had 15 miles of public road per 1,000 inhabitants and a motor tax income of only £109 per mile of main road. The figures for Northern Ireland — 10 miles per 1,000 inhabitants and £258 of motor taxation for every mile of main road — were perhaps a more effective testimony to the low yield from Irish motor taxation; they also showed the cumulative impact of extending the mileage of public roads.

This problem worsened during the Emergency years as many bog roads came under temporary public control. After the Emergency, county councils and local inhabitants were reluctant to see them revert to private ownership. Mayo County Council protested that 'in many instances' bog roads 'are of far more importance to the rural ratepayers than any scheduled roads'.[57] This argument had some support within cabinet. In the summer of 1945, Finance Minister Frank Aiken proposed that the post-war improvement programme should begin by concreting lanes leading to farmhouses, when this had been completed, third-class roads would be improved, leaving work on the main highways until the last. Aiken argued: 'the order in which I suggest work should be undertaken is in accordance with greater social and economic need. It is on these roads [the lanes] that people get their feet wet and that children suffer most hardship travelling to and from school.'[58]

While the cabinet did not formally endorse Aiken's proposal, it was more in keeping with Fianna Fáil wishes and a better predictor of post-war roads expenditure than the proposals which had originated in the Custom House. In 1946/47 a special scheme of restoration grants was introduced to encourage local authorities to repair neglected roads. Councils would receive 50 per cent grants towards the cost of repairs carried out on main roads, rising to 90 per cent for every pound spent in excess of their average annual expenditure for the years 1940-46. Additional expenditure above the 1940-46 average on repairing county roads would attract a grant of 75 per cent. This was the first time that Road Fund grants had been allocated for repairing county (i.e. local) roads, though county councils had repeatedly pressed for this concession. 'Restoration' grants were intended to apply in the case of roads that had been damaged by heavy trucks carrying turf during the Emergency, but this clause was not enforced and most repairs on local roads were deemed eligible for grant-assistance. Although this concession was introduced as a temporary measure to help repair wartime damage, it was extended in 1947/48, because restoration work had allegedly been delayed as a result of the continuation of local authority turf schemes. The Department of Finance tried to stop these grants because the cost was outstripping the Road Fund income, and the surplus which had accrued during the Emergency was almost exhausted. Although motor taxation charges had been increased in the 1947 budget, the additional £300,000 in tax revenue was earmarked to pay for food subsidies rather than roads.[59] On 13 February 1948, after the general election and in the dying days of the Fianna Fáil government, the cabinet approved a free grant of £2.25m. from the Exchequer towards the cost of road restoration and agreed that grants should be retained on the existing basis until the restoration of roads had been completed.[60]

The Department of Local Government's proposals to determine road expenditure with reference to traffic volume and the most efficient means of construction would have marked a complete reversal of the approach, adopted by Fianna Fáil since 1932, of using road expenditure as a form of employment relief and giving priority to local rather than

399

national needs. Main roads stood very low in the priorities of local authorities and most county councils were determined to offload the full cost of repairs on to the Road Fund or the Exchequer. In June 1938, Martin Corry, Fianna Fail TD and a member of Cork County Council, tabled such a motion in Dáil Éireann and a similar resolution was debated at the party's 1944 árd fheis. These resolutions were inextricably linked with protests over the level of local rates. By the late 1940s, rates poundages were more than double pre-war levels. In 1949/50 the national average was 23/3 (£1.16), compared with 11/7 (58p) in the pound in 1938/39. Local Government opposed these resolutions on several grounds. It would mean a duplication of road staff, with one team responsible for national roads and another for county roads. Officials feared that this would be merely the first in a series of demands on the Exchequer to foot the bill for more and more services provided by local authorities. If the Road Fund was saddled with the cost of maintaining all national roads, it would have no money left for improvements, though a more cynical official argued that the Road Fund should assume the full cost of repairs and improvements to national roads, leaving local authorities to carry all costs associated with county roads. He believed that councils would invariably manage to find money for local roads.[61]

Despite such an inauspicious political climate, Local Government endeavoured to press ahead, however unrealistically, with its proposals. In November 1946, in spite of the fact that all available funds were earmarked for road repairs, MacEntee authorised the Department's road section to issue bulletins to local authorities, outlining plans for future road development and beginning the process of surveying the line of future dual-carriageways and other modern roads. In February 1947, Courtney, the Department's chief engineering adviser, confirmed that the survey would be confined to 3,000 miles of major roads, roads which were 'being planning on a national basis — having regard more to national rather than to local requirements'. The Department hoped that this survey would form the basis for all future allocations of improvement grants from the Road Fund, and in recognition of this fact it sought to recoup the cost of the survey engineers' services from the Road Fund, rather than from local authorities.[62] However the circulars served only to draw the hostile attention of TDs and local councillors to the Department's proposals.

Opposition to main roads became linked with a certain paranoia

about local authority officialdom, which had arisen since the
appointment of county managers. Meath TD Captain Patrick Giles
complained that local authority engineers were planning 'a new secret
highway for the future. . . . We do not want any of these highways. We
want ordinary decent roads for the plain people'; 'vast highways' would
'not be much use for the men with 5-10 acres'.[63] It was alleged that the
new roads would prove dangerous to horses, and Seán MacEntee was
forced to establish a departmental committee to examine the extent to
which smooth modern road surfaces contributed to accidents involving
horse-drawn vehicles and to advise on what steps should be taken to
provide alternative surfaces or wide verges which would be suitable for
animal traffic. When the committee eventually reported in 1952,[64] Local
Government informed the cabinet that conditions had changed
considerably since it was established. 'The chief rural road problem
now is not to provide roads safe for horses but to put the large mileage
of county roads (approximately 40,000) into proper condition to take
the growing mechanised transport of the countryside.'[65]

ROAD VERSUS RAIL: THE MILNE REPORT

The Fianna Fáil government had originally intended to issue a White
Paper outlining a programme of post-war roads development, similar to
the White Papers on housing and health, but it never materialised. Its
non-appearance suggests either that opinions on future road investment
were divided within the cabinet, or that Local Government was isolated
from the government in its wish to develop a modern national road
network. Responsibility for transport policy rested with Industry and
Commerce and that Department undoubtedly favoured rail over road.
Post-war transport policy followed the recommendations of the 1949
Milne Report, *Transport in Ireland*, commissioned by the Department
of Industry and Commerce with a remit to determine the future roles of
road, rail and canal transport and to advise on the steps necessary to
co-ordinate them. Although the Milne Report offered some comfort to
Local Government by recommending the establishment of a Central
Highways Authority which would have overriding control over the
maintenance and improvement of the highway system, i.e. removing it
from local authorities, the report recommended that government policy
should aim at ensuring that railways and canals carried as much traffic

as possible and that a differential road vehicle licensing system should be introduced in order to deter goods from being carried by road over long distances.[66] Despite the recommendations of the Milne Report, the 1950s were marked by a progressive closure of rail lines and the transfer of a growing volume of long-distance freight traffic to roads, which were often utterly unsuitable for heavy goods traffic. Local Government attempted to anticipate the traffic problems that would result from rail closures by holding regular meetings with the railway companies from 1947. In 1949 T.C. Courtney, the chief engineering adviser, became full-time chairman of CIE. However, the Department was unable to require that specific improvements should be effected, such as the strengthening of road bridges to enable them to carry heavy goods traffic, in anticipation of a planned, but unannounced, closure of a railway line.[67]

Although the closure of railway lines increased the volume of freight traffic borne on roads during the 1950s, adding to the rapid post-war shift from horse to motor transport, the absence of a national roads policy meant that roads were not improved to cope with the increased volume of motor traffic. This was partly a reflection of political realities; railways apparently remained popular with the public, even though the numbers using them were declining rapidly and, although the volume of traffic on main roads was increasing, there appears to have been little support for increasing expenditure.

This lack of logic can be partly explained by examining who bore the cost: road expenditure was believed to fall on local rates, though much of it was borne by the Exchequer. Subsidies to rail transport were sustained by the Exchequer or by the consumer. In turn, the growth of heavy goods traffic, such as creamery lorries, lorries carrying sugar beet and farm tractors on minor roads (which previously had carried only bicycles or horse-drawn traffic) increased the pressure for additional expenditure on county roads. In 1946 more than 10 per cent of so-called main roads, 1,150 miles remained unrolled, as did over 35,000 of the country's 40,000 miles of county roads.[68]

The numbers of private and commercial vehicles rose sharply in the decade following the Emergency years. There were only 7,845 licensed private cars in Ireland in 1945. With the coming of peace, this rose to 44,489 in 1946 and the total number of licensed motor vehicles increased from 30,045 to 76,552.[69] In 1946, 2,848 new cars were registered; by 1950 new registrations had risen to 17,524 and by 1951 the number of motor vehicles on Irish roads stood at almost 156,000, more than double the 1939 figure. The number of driving licences had more than doubled from 100,000 in 1939 to over 223,000 in 1951.[70]

ROAD EXPENDITURE AND THE FIRST INTER-PARTY GOVERNMENT

The formation of the first inter-party government ended whatever minor hopes existed of carrying out Local Government's planned road programme. Both Ministers for Local Government in that administration, Murphy and Keyes, gave priority to housing rather than roads, a decision which undoubtedly reflected the wishes of the electorate. As Labour TDs, both appear to have given considerable attention to the views of council labourers and their trade unions.[71] Wages for local authority workers rose sharply and direct labour was preferred to contract labour, despite the criticism of direct labour voiced by many Local Government officials. Both Ministers believed that road expenditure should be targeted towards county roads rather than main roads. Under the first inter-party government, employment on roads declined, as did the proportion of costs borne by the Exchequer. County roads, which, according to Murphy, had hitherto 'been the Cinderella of road administration', were guaranteed Road Fund improvement grants on a permanent basis. In 1949/50 they were allocated £1.2m. from the Road Fund, double the sum available for improvements to main roads. In February 1949 the inter-party government suspended the survey of main roads, which was being carried out as a first step in the long-term development programme. Two-thirds of the road network had been surveyed and sketch development plans had been prepared for half the mileage. The money saved was diverted to 'actual work on roads'.[72] The redirection of Exchequer resources from national to county roads, and the burdening of local authorities with a higher share of the cost of road expenditure, were consistent with the decision of the Milne Report that railways should remain the main carrier of long-distance traffic, with roads having the complementary role of carrying local traffic.

THE DUBLIN-BRAY ROAD: 'A TOO-COSTLY SCHEME'

The changes in road financing were tantamount to abandoning the national roads development programme. The most conspicuous casualty of the new climate was the Dublin-Bray road, the busiest in the country. Throughout the Emergency years, Local Government had argued that there was a need to devote additional money to modernising main roads in the Dublin area in order to reduce accidents and relieve congestion. Peacetime traffic flows of up to 10,000 vehicles a day were common. During the late 1930s, although Dublin city contributed one-third of the Road Fund's income, the city attracted only 6.4 per cent of average annual expenditure; a further 4.7 per cent went to County Dublin. During the Emergency, Dublin city obtained no grants from the Road Fund and 'very little' by way of grants went to Dublin County Council, though this was sufficiently supplemented by employment schemes funds to construct two sections of dual-carriageway on the Dublin-Bray road — the only stretches completed before the 1970s.

Road improvements in the Dublin area were expensive — the cost of the proposed Whitehall-Santry by-pass was estimated at £80,000 per mile, excluding the cost of land acquisition.[73] Such work would give much fewer jobs for every thousand pounds spent than repairing farm lanes. The fact that Local Government argued that the work should not be carried out by recipients of unemployment assistance made the schemes even less popular with politicians.

Dublin City and County and Dun Laoghaire received almost no funds from the 1946-50 road restoration grants.[74] This was not entirely the government's fault. Road development in the Dublin area suffered from the multiplicity of local authorities. All three local authorities were responsible for part of the Dublin-Bray road. Local authorities in the Dublin area appear to have been much less interested in roads than other councils; indeed, they often failed to claim grants for which they were eligible under employment and emergency schemes votes.[75]

In November 1947, shortly before the general election, the Fianna Fáil government had approved a grant of £500,000 from the Road Fund for major road improvements on the roads to Bray, Swords and Naas. Dublin County Council was asked to give special consideration to using the money to improve sections of the Bray road which had become 'notorious' for accidents. Early in 1948, Dublin County Council, which was then being run by a commissioner, began planning the construction of two by-passes on the Dublin-Bray road where the road ran through built-up areas and could not be widened, from Mount

Merrion to Galloping Green and from Foxrock to Loughlinstown, at a cost of £398,000. A further £91,000 was earmarked for a stretch of dual-carriageway on the Dublin-Belfast road and for improvements to the Naas road at Newlands Cross.[76]

The proposals soon became a favourite target for journalists and the general public. Newspaper headlines denounced the £100,000 per mile road. A leading article in the *Irish Independent* of 13 January 1950 dubbed it 'a too-costly scheme'. Property-owners threatened by the proposed by-passes also mounted a vocal opposition campaign. Dun Laoghaire Corporation demanded that the scheme be deferred until it had carried out a main drainage scheme and 'other essential schemes', while the Dublin County Committee of Agriculture demanded that the money be diverted to improving farm lanes.

With the change of government, it was no longer clear that the money would be available from the Road Fund and in January 1950 Dublin County Council voted by ten votes to six in favour of dropping the proposed Bray road improvements. The victors dismissed the proposal as 'squandermania'. All work was suspended on 2 February 1950.[77] Michael Keyes met the three local authorities concerned to discuss this decision. A later hand-written note on a cabinet file, apparently written by Maurice Moynihan, secretary to the government, made it clear that 'the Minister does not propose to take any further steps in this matter'. Another note stated that, according to Brendan Corish, parliamentary secretary to the Minister for Local Government, the Minister was 'anxious to avoid reopening the matter' and for that reason was 'unlikely to submit a formal memo. to Government'.

In August 1952, when Fianna Fáil was again in office, Dublin County Council voted against reviving the scheme. Although the collapse of the Bray road improvement plan could perhaps be attributed to a shortage of money, the largesse directed at other spending programmes during these years suggests that lack of political will was a much more important factor. National road improvements conspicuously did not benefit from the loan-counterpart funds generated by Marshall Aid.

ROAD EXPENDITURE IN CRISIS 1948-51

The inter-party government continued the practice of diverting revenue from the Road Fund to other purposes. As a result, it became necessary to borrow money against future Road Fund income to meet commitments for road expenditure, which were projected to reach £4.7m. for the financial year 1948/49, against projected revenue of only £2.3m..[78] Although the food subsidies, introduced in 1947, which were funded from increased motor taxation, were removed in the 1952 budget,[79] Finance continued to appropriate part of the Road Fund for general expenditure. The combined effect of these borrowings, plus the commitment to provide Road Fund grants towards the cost of maintaining county roads, meant that there was simply no money to pay for major improvements to national roads. Higher material and labour costs compounded the problem.

Local Government saw higher motor taxation as the solution to its difficulties, though in the light of the Department's admission that 'there is almost an unlimited scope for useful expenditure of money on our public roads',[80] this may have been naive. However, the decision of the Milne Report that railways should remain the main carrier of long-distance freight weakened the case for heavier motor taxation. Finance fobbed off Local Government's requests for the establishment of an interdepartmental committee on motor taxation from 1948 until the spring of 1950. The committee was chaired by Local Government with members drawn from Finance, Agriculture, Justice, Industry and Commerce, and it was expected to make recommendations for tax changes which could be implemented in the 1950 budget. Opinions turned out to be divided, with Local Government alone arguing in favour of imposing an additional £1.5m. in motor taxes, an increase of 60 per cent on existing revenue. According to Local Government, which drafted the report, 'the nearest to common ground' was a recommendation that would have yielded additional revenue of £680,000 from higher taxes on commercial vehicles and from restoring the income from the extra taxes imposed on private cars in 1947, which had been used to finance food subsidies to the Road Fund. Even this compromise proved unacceptable. Representatives of Industry and Commerce and of Agriculture objected to imposing higher taxes on commercial vehicles and tractors, and Finance refused to give up its penchant for raiding the Road Fund.[81] The government sat on the fence by requesting Local Government to report on current road conditions.[82]

The report submitted by Local Government painted a bleak picture of conditions on Irish roads in 1950. It pointed out that it was essential to carry out major structural improvements to many roads and bridges if they were to bear the increased volume of motor traffic safely. Trucks carrying loads of up to 30 tons were damaging foundations on many roads. Sections of the Dublin-Naas road had collapsed as a result of heavy traffic; a truck laden with molasses sank to its axles in the middle of the main Sligo to Letterkenny road, blocking it for three days. Some roads in County Clare were so bad that creamery lorries could not travel on them. Potholes on a main road in County Mayo caused the wheels of buses to spin and the spare-wheel carrier was damaged when it struck the road surface. Traditional hog-backed bridges, common on many roads, could not be negotiated by heavy lorries or buses.

Despite this graphic evidence, Finance asserted that 'generally speaking, main roads and county roads are in reasonably good condition'. If some roads needed to be improved, Finance argued that the cost should be met by local authorities. Before 1939 local authority rates had covered approximately two-thirds of the cost of road expenditure, with the balance borne by national resources, including the Road Fund. By 1948/49 the local and national shares had been reversed and central government was meeting approximately two-thirds of road expenditure. Finance believed that rates should meet at least half the bill for road improvements and repairs.[83] This ambition was more than achieved during the term of the first inter-party government; in 1950/51 local authorities met 53.2 per cent of road expenditure.

As a consequence of pushing more of the cost of road expenditure on to local authorities, priorities became even more responsive to local wishes. Tipperary South Riding passed a resolution demanding that all proceeds from petrol and motor taxes should be allocated in full to the local authorities, to be spent at their discretion.[84] Although the first inter-party government refused to make this concession, county councils were given complete freedom to determine the amount to be spent on improving county roads and which roads should be brought up to standard, despite the fact that the improvements were subsidised from the Road Fund.[85] Such concessions reflected the inter-party government's desire to distance itself from Fianna Fáil and the county management system by adopting a more populist stance.

Although the Emergency turf campaign finally ended in 1948, bog roads continued to feature prominently in road expenditure. When Bord na Móna took responsibility for turf production, the argument developed that it was even more necessary that bogs were accessible to heavy lorries. Bord na Móna favoured highly mechanised methods of producing turf, so employment on the bogs fell considerably. This led to demands for additional jobs to be provided on roads, to compensate small farmers who had lost 'good wages during slack farming periods'. Many families had come to regard earnings from turf 'as a regular annual affair', 'adjusting their economy accordingly'. It was argued that the redundant turf workers *cum* farmers should be employed repairing roads on the bogs where they had previously cut turf because these jobs would be close to home.[86] The Federation of Rural Workers contacted the Taoiseach to press this case and John Costello in March 1948 established a committee, chaired by Ted Courtney of Local Government. It devised a series of road and drainage schemes adjacent to bogs which would be funded under the employment and emergency scheme vote. This depleted a fund which was normally used to provide winter employment on minor road works. Patrick Lynch of the Taoiseach's Department pointed out that because the men employed on summer road works and drainage schemes would take home much less than they had previously earned cutting turf, he anticipated an increase in the numbers seeking relief employment during the winter. In fact the numbers employed on winter road schemes actually fell. However, Local Government noted that the numbers employed on road works during the summer of 1949, an average of 29,000 labourers, was significantly above the pre-war figure of 19,000. The memorandum continued:

> . . . this may be attributed to a change in the psychological outlook
> of the rural population. During the Emergency large numbers of
> the farming community were called on to assist County Councils in
> the turf production campaign. In many cases, these people,
> formerly self-employed, developed the habit of compressing their
> own work into a smaller time space and of spending the remainder
> of their working hours with County Councils. With the cessation of
> turf production, they were left unemployed in a sense, and thrown
> back on their resources and they now consider that they should be
> employed on road works.[87]

At cabinet the Minister for Local Government increasingly justified expenditure on roads by referring to the potential contribution it would make towards relieving rural unemployment.[88] He was not alone in viewing road works primarily as a job-creation programme. During the course of a cabinet discussion on roads in 1950, James Dillon noted that:

> The present system of road making and maintenance is specially designed to make both operations as expensive as possible, because roadwork in rural Ireland had become indissolubly associated with relief works in the minds of all members of Local Authorities. Consequently the price of a quiet life for the County Engineer is to ensure that a given fraction of every annual appropriation for roads is spent in the residential area of each Councillor and that in its spending the maximum amount is laid out in wages payable to the County Councillor's neighbours.

During 1949/50 the inter-party government attempted to cut spending on roads by limiting borrowings from the Road Fund. However, ministerial orders specified that all approved road schemes should make less use of machinery and employ proportionately more labourers than in recent years. The government also hoped to employ unemployed road labourers on minor drainage schemes,[89] which would be carried out under the 1949 Local Authorities Works Act. This measure was designed to provide funds for 'limited improvement works' on minor rivers, with the aim of reducing flooding and landslides. Although £1.75m. was provided for local authorities under this scheme in both 1949/50 and 1950/51, there appears to have been no corresponding reduction in demand for employment on road works, though by February 1950 the numbers employed on minor drainage schemes, 13,618, were almost equal to the number of road labourers. When sufficient jobs failed to materialise under the Local Authorities Works Act, Local Government was forced to sanction supplementary estimates for road works to provide additional employment, though the Minister protested that 'it is not a function of my Department to provide employment where needed'. Still the linkage between road works and employment had been firmly established in all minds.

Fianna Fáil and the National Development Fund

When Fianna Fáil was returned to office in June 1951, some officials in

Local Government's engineering section queried whether there was any prospect of resuming work on the abandoned national highways programme. Nevertheless Ian Bloomer, chief engineering adviser, concluded that county engineers were 'too preoccupied with roads, housing, turf, drainage etc.' to complete the abandoned survey and that it would be unrealistic to waste time resuming it, given the expectation that 'very little money will be available for real improvement work on main roads for a number of years'.[90] This assessment proved only too accurate.

Paddy Smith, the Minister for Local Government, was a veteran member of Cavan County Council and both he and his fellow ministers showed greater interest in bog roads and in Gaeltacht roads than in a national highway system. County councils were again required to produce turf to alleviate a threatened fuel shortage because of the Korean War, and the annual meeting of the General Council of County Councils on 16 August 1951 passed a resolution demanding that the government provide grants to cover the entire cost of making and improving bog roads 'in view of the fact that (a) it is in the interests of the state as a whole rather than local authorities to keep money from being sent out of the country for purchases of coal and (b) expenditure on bog roads is necessary to make turf available at economic prices.'[91] In 1952 the cabinet committee that examined the budget estimates decided to discontinue the special grants for bog roads which had been paid under the employment and emergency schemes vote; this decision meant that the Road Fund had to bear the full cost of bog road improvements. In order to protect the Road Fund against this charge, Local Government attempted to have the cost of bog access roads deemed eligible for funding under the Marshall Aid Loan Counterpart Funds, but the ECA (Economic Co-operation and Administration) committee decided that the Irish ECA mission was unlikely to approve this proposal and so the Road Fund was saddled with the cost.[92]

The major initiative in road expenditure during the term of the Fianna Fáil government of 1951-54 concerned the Gaeltacht. A permanent interdepartmental organisation was established, under the direction of Jack Lynch, then parliamentary secretary at the Department of the Taoiseach, to co-ordinate a programme of social and economic development in Gaeltacht and congested areas.[93] It recommended speeding up the programme of rural electrification, the construction of yet more piers and jetties, providing more generous housing grants, plus the construction of glasshouses — a new idea this. It also proposed that additional funds should be spent on road improvements as an aid to tourist development. The eligible areas included Clare, west Cork, Kerry, north-west Cavan, Ring in County Waterford and Counties Galway, Mayo, Donegal, Roscommon, Leitrim and Sligo. The final three counties plus north-west Cavan were probably included in order to mollify protests against the imminent closure of the Sligo, Leitrim and Northern Counties Railway. Local Government drew up a list of priority road schemes in these counties, covering almost 1,200 miles of road, which would be improved over a five-year period, at an estimated cost of £3.7m..

This proposal, which had the support of Seán Lemass, marked the death-knell of the post-war road development programme. Local Government contended that the Road Fund was in no position to bear the cost of these road improvements, and the matter was referred to Finance in November 1951. Finance did not reply until October 1952, when it pointed out that £1.84m., or 56 per cent, of the £3.3m. allocated by the Road Fund for the financial year 1952/53 was already earmarked for Gaeltacht or congested district counties (the counties listed above) without taking the special Gaeltacht road programme into account. If the £660,000 proposed per annum for this additional scheme was also drawn from the Road Fund, these counties would receive well over 60 per cent of the Fund's grants. Finance argued that this figure would be 'hard to defend', given that most revenue was raised in other parts of the country. Finance was also sceptical about the economic benefits from the proposed Gaeltacht road improvements and recommended that expenditure be deferred until it could be met either from the Road Fund or from local authority rates.[94] Nevertheless the proposal appeared to have considerable support within cabinet, which decided to spread expenditure over eight years, at a maximum annual outlay of £400,000.

When the new programme was announced, areas that had been excluded from the scheme lobbied for inclusion. Longford County Council protested at the 'grievous injustice to the former congested areas in North Longford' which were excluded, despite having a lower Poor Law Valuation than many benefiting areas. Seán Lynch, a member of Longford County Council and former 'registrar of the republican courts' in the county, wrote to de Valera urging that Drumlish electoral district be included, both on grounds of poverty and because it had been the site of the battle of Ballinamuck in 1798. Others contacted de Valera to protest that Kerry County Council was not spending its *deontas* (grant) on roads which were actually located in the Gaeltacht. Irrespective of its merits, the Gaeltacht road scheme marked a further loss of control by Local Government over roads expenditure. The decisions on how this money was spent rested with Jack Lynch in the Taoiseach's Department.

In 1952 there was yet another attempt to revise the basis of motor taxation. As we have seen, the previous effort collapsed because of fundamental disagreements between the government departments concerned. In February 1952 the government established another interdepartmental committee to examine the prospect of revising motor taxation. The committee's precise purpose remains unclear. Seán MacEntee, who was once more Minister for Finance, had given a commitment to establish such a body to Senator Frederick Summerfield, a leading member of the Irish motor industry, in the course of a debate in the Seanad during the summer of 1951. The government had received representations from the Society of the Irish Motor Traders, urging a reduction in the tax levels imposed on motor vehicles, with the loss in revenue being recouped by higher petrol taxes.[95] However, the interdepartmental committee, chaired by Local Government, concentrated on proposals which would provide additional income for the Road Fund, as opposed to meeting the wishes of Irish motor traders. It set a target of increasing the income of the Road Fund by £851,000 a year. Almost half the additional revenue would come from higher taxes on commercial vehicles, including buses, with the balance accruing from higher taxes on private cars, removing the tax exemption on state-owned vehicles, and increased charges for driving licences. Industry and Commerce objected to the higher charges on the state-owned bus company, CIE, and Finance opposed the proposal to tax state-owned vehicles.

Although Local Government informed the cabinet, in March 1952, that it had given commitments to local authorities that additional money would be available for roads in the coming year, divisions on the proposed changes ran so deep that the cabinet was unable to reach an agreement.[96] Eventually it was decided to publish a White Paper.[97] This unleashed a major lobbying campaign from interested parties such as the Society of the Irish Motor Traders, the Royal Irish Automobile Club, Ford and Dunlop. It was widely believed (not without reason) that

Industry and Commerce was determined to use the changes in vehicle licenses to drive out private hauliers and to provide a 'concealed subsidy' to CIE. County councils that had called repeatedly for higher subsidies from the Road Fund threw logic to the wind and now bombarded Local Government with resolutions expressing 'alarm' at the proposal to increase vehicle licence charges.[98] After much ado, the revised vehicle licence fees became law in December 1952 and Road Fund income rose by almost £800,000, or nearly 33 per cent, in the following year. However most of the additional income was spent on road schemes that were primarily designed to provide employment.

Unemployment loomed large in Irish political life during the autumn and winter of 1952/53. The deflationary budget of 1952, which removed food subsidies and raised indirect taxes, drove a depressed economy into serious recession.[99] Economic difficulties were further increased by the ending of Marshall Aid and by a decline in the rate of construction of local authority houses as some councils met their targets. Numbers on the register were already rising in the spring of 1952 and they continued to increase. By January 1953 there were over 71,000 on the live register, against 58,000 twelve months before, though Finance blamed the rise on the changes in entitlements following the enactment of the 1952 Social Welfare Act.[100] The Department of the Taoiseach asked government departments, state companies and local authorities to submit proposals for public works which would provide employment in the next two years. This resulted, as always, in a flood of suggestions, such as repairing footpaths at St Stephens' Green, Dublin, concreting the runway at Baldonnel aerodrome, and repairing army barracks. In February 1953 the government established an interdepartmental committee to co-ordinate these proposals and to draw up a programme of public works.[101]

Roads appeared to offer the best prospect of creating additional jobs in the short term and Local Government asked county councils to draw up a five-year improvement plan for county roads (i.e. local, not main, roads). The Department was determined that the money should be spent on reconstructing a 'limited mileage of the most important county roads', as opposed to seeing it 'dissipated on a series of unrelated works',[102] which was the more common experience. Roads in County Dublin appeared to offer scope for major expenditure. By April 1953 Dublin County Council had become 'seriously concerned at the increase in the number of unemployed persons in the county' and it requested Local Government to provide 'additional funds' for major improvements on the Dublin-Drogheda road (a national route).[103] Local Government had already pointed out to the Taoiseach's Department that Dublin gained almost nothing from the grants provided for bog roads and other special road schemes[104] and this was confirmed by a report from the special employment schemes office.[105] Most of the grants which Dublin Corporation had received from the Road Fund since 1945 had been used to cover the removal of cobblestones and redundant tramlines.

On 24 June 1953, the Taoiseach received a deputation of Dublin TDs, who demanded that additional employment should be provided on road works in their constituencies. A deputation representing the Dublin unemployed subsequently met the TDs to present a similar argument.[106] In response, the government announced that special employment schemes, which had previously been limited to winter months, would now operate throughout the year. This led to a flurry of activity. Dublin Corporation held a special meeting in Leinster House to announce the establishment of a special works committee, which would draft a programme of suitable employment schemes.[107] Trade unions and the Labour Party issued a joint statement calling for increased state capital expenditure and a reduction in red-tape, particularly by the Department of Local Government. When de Valera met trade union leaders, he played down the prospect of initiating major employment schemes and suggested that there should be greater reliance on the private sector.

Local Government took advantage of this campaign to draw up a programme of major road improvements in the Dublin area. Their memorandum painted a graphic picture of city-centre traffic congestion. It emphasised the urgent need for more car parks, for additional bridges over the Liffey, and for a ring road. An outline of a Corporation road programme, which would cost an estimated £1.6m., was included, though this could not be implemented for some time. Dublin Corporation would first need to acquire large tracts of land, which would have to be financed from Corporation funds, and these were already stretched to the limit by the housing programme.

The cabinet committee on unemployment responded to the Local Government proposals by urging all local authorities in the Dublin area to put road improvements programmes into operation as soon as possible. Dublin Corporation was given a promise that £1.6m. would be provided 'on a basis to be arranged, which will be similar to the basis on which road grants are made to other local authorities'. However, Dublin Corporation would still be required to meet the substantial cost of land acquisition. Dun Laoghaire Corporation was promised the necessary funds to carry out a road improvement programme, costing £625,000, which it had first mooted in 1949, and Dublin County Council was reminded that it could call on the £500,000 which had been allocated for improvements to the Bray road. All three councils were asked to co-operate on modernising the Bray road and the cabinet committee requested that Dublin County Council draw up plans for the construction of dual carriageways on roads leading to Naas, Belfast and Navan. The Minister for Local Government was asked to investigate the possibility of constructing a new bridge over the Liffey.[108]

By August 1953, however, the interdepartmental committee was about to be superseded by a proposal from the fertile brain of Industry and Commerce Minister Seán Lemass. In a memorandum, dated 28 July 1953, he argued that the 'fundamental cause' of chronic emigration and 'abnormal' unemployment was the 'unduly low level of capital investment by private enterprise' in Ireland. This could be reversed only if emigration was checked and 'a normal population increase secured'. Current investment opportunities were limited because prospects for import substitution had been effectively exhausted and there appeared to be few opportunities for increasing exports of manufactured goods: 'Only a rising population, with rising living standards, will create a situation in which the expansion of industrial and commercial activity will require a regular expansion of private capital investment to a degree that will eliminate abnormal unemployment.' Lemass saw a major programme of state investment as the solution to this impasse. It would provide jobs, bring about a rise in population and this in turn would stimulate private investment. He argued that the anticipated surplus on the balance of payments indicated that the government could undertake additional investment of the order of £20m. or £30m. which would create up to 30-40,000 man-years of employment 'without danger to the stability of the national economy'. Road improvements appeared to provide the most 'immediately practical works' which could be implemented. His proposed scheme would be entirely financed from national resources and supervised by a new national organisation.

It is scarcely surprising that Finance was utterly opposed to Lemass's proposal, arguing that 'it is surely a fundamental responsibility to ensure that national resources are put to the most productive use and not wasted in the creation of work mainly for work's sake'; far from regenerating the economy, the proposed public investment programme would mean 'dissipating our limited resources in providing artificial and unstable employment on works which will yield no continuing increases in production' and would ultimately lead to a fall in living standards. The Department of Finance pointed out that investment had consistently outstripped savings since 1947 and it would prove difficult to raise the necessary capital to finance the programme. It also dismissed the proposal that road works 'should be the principal element in a supplementary investment programme' as 'disappointing . . . a most expensive form of social service'.

Frank Aiken, Minister for External Affairs, was extremely enthusiastic about the Lemass proposal. He argued that the government should establish a national development fund, which would provide additional grants for public investments when the number of unemployed was 'abnormally large' or the balance of payments was in a healthy state. However, Aiken suggested that investments which would increase agricultural output, such as providing farmers with subsidised lime or fertiliser, should be given preference and that expenditure on social amenities should be relegated to second place.

The cabinet committee adopted Aiken's title, National Development Fund, though it reduced the proposed sum which would be provided to £5m., a far cry from Lemass's figure of £20m. or £30m.. The committee suggested that the money be spent on roads and other 'desirable projects of a public character'. The fund would be controlled by Finance and would operate until 31 March 1957, a period of three to four years. A sum of £5m. would be provided by government borrowing and this would be replenished annually, leaving £5m. available each year. Part of the fund would be earmarked for Gaeltacht areas and the Ministers for Finance and Local Government would decide how far this would be topped up by special grants from the Road Fund. An interdepartmental committee, chaired by Finance, would determine which other projects would be assisted. The decision to establish the National Development Fund appears to have been determined as much by political need as by the level of unemployment. Within days of the Fund's establishment, de Valera was publicising its potential in a speech in Ballinasloe during the Galway South by-election campaign.[109]

Finance persisted in opposing the Fund's existence. O.J. Redmond, secretary of Finance, enlisted the aid of his predecessor, J.J. McElligott, who was now governor of the Central Bank. In late August the Central Bank had submitted to the cabinet committee a sixteen-page critique of the National Development Fund; Finance weighed in with two six-page memoranda. McElligott noted that over the period 1947-52 net domestic investment of £266.2m. had exceeded net savings of £106.3m. by a factor of more than two to one. This had caused serious damage to the country's balance of payments. On this, as on other occasions, the 'banshee of Foster Place' (the Central Bank)[110] appears to have wailed in vain. Having lost the first round, Finance shifted its attention to the National Development Fund's terms of reference, laying particular emphasis on the requirement that only investments which would otherwise not have been carried out before 1957 were eligible for subsidy. Finance wondered how this condition could be applied to road improvements. It argued that a strict reading of the terms of reference would mean that less urgent road improvements would take precedence over essential schemes.

The cabinet committee decided that the NDF should be used to accelerate the existing road programme and that all proposals where no date had been set for commencing work would be eligible for assistance. In practice, the decision to use the NDF to accelerate programmes meant that the money would be used to finance existing expenditure. On 27 November 1953 the cabinet committee allocated grants for the coming financial year. Roads in Gaeltacht areas received a further £250,000, in addition to the £400,000 that had been earmarked.[111] The Road Fund was given an additional £1m., 'it being understood that in the resulting dispensation of the programme of works financed out of the Road Fund, regard will be had, so far as possible, to the unemployment situation in various areas through the country.'[112] A sum of £500,000 was added to the vote for employment and emergency schemes to be allocated to areas with the largest numbers claiming unemployment benefit. Local Government was awarded an additional £100,000 to be spent on schemes qualifying under the Local Authorities Works Act.[113]

Given the level of concern expressed about unemployment in the Dublin area, it might have been expected that Dublin city and county would receive a large share of the NDF allocations. Dublin Corporation demanded that £1m. should be provided from the NDF to fund the proposals drawn up by a special works committee, though Dublin Fianna Fáil TD Robert Briscoe claimed that even £1m. would be utterly inadequate.

Despite negative noises from Local Government, Dublin Corporation proceeded to hire 100 temporary staff and to appoint a head for the special works organisation. John Garvin feared that this was a subtle attempt to upgrade several members of the Corporation's engineering staff and that it threatened to destabilise the salary grades of all local authority engineers. At a meeting on 2 September 1953 he warned Corporation officials that they would have to observe existing regulations concerning the appointment of permanent senior staff. A meeting between members of Dublin Corporation and the Minister resulted in a stalemate: Local Government gave an ultimatum that all schemes should be carried out by existing Corporation departments, not by a new section.

This was not the only grievance between Dublin Corporation and the government. When de Valera, Smith and MacEntee met four Fianna Fáil TDs who represented Dublin constituencies (Robert Briscoe, John McCann, Vivion de Valera and Colm Gallagher), the Taoiseach pointed out that if Dublin were promised a grant of £1m. for a special employment programme, other local authorities would expect assistance on a similar scale. This would push demands for spending on 'unproductive schemes entirely beyond the State's capacity'.[114]

It is clear that the government expected that special works in the Dublin area would concentrate on road improvements. Dublin Corporation showed little interest in roads, though Dun Laoghaire Corporation and Dublin County Council were more enthusiastic. Dun Laoghaire submitted proposals costing over half a million pounds and Dublin County Council produced a ten-year road plan costing £2.8m.. However, both councils insisted that they would proceed only if NDF grants covered the cost of purchasing the necessary land. Local Government submitted a memorandum supporting this demand to the cabinet committee in November 1953, but the matter was deferred and it had not yet been discussed when the government went out of office in May 1954.[115] The delay may reflect the fact that plans for major road improvements in the Dublin area continued to attract hostile attention. The *Irish Independent* greeted the announcement that extra government funds were being provided for the Road Fund with the headline 'The Bray Road Again', and opposition to the scheme mounted anew.

Despite the widespread concern at the high level of unemployment in the Dublin area, neither Dublin nor Dun Laoghaire Corporations received a penny from the Road Fund during the 1953/54 financial year, though Dun Laoghaire obtained a grant of £62,662 for road works from the NDF. Dublin Corporation did obtain much larger sums than previously from the employment and emergency schemes vote. Expenditure rose from an annual rate of £100,000 in the late 1940s (£70,000 from the Exchequer and £30,000 from local resources) to over £250,000 in 1953/54 and £323,000 in the following year. Employment under these schemes rose from 6,000 man-weeks to 14,348 and 16,718 man-weeks respectively. Most of the money was spent on minor repairs to footpaths and low-grade improvements to public parks.[116] To bring this about, Local Government was forced, reluctantly, to sanction the temporary establishment of a special works department.[117] In the highly politicised atmosphere of local Dublin politics, this concession gave long-term hostages to fortune.

Local Government continued to hope that the additional £1m. which the NDF had transferred to the Road Fund would be dedicated to modernising national roads. The Department's engineers complained that surfaces on many major routes were 'worn out and bumpy'; roads were threatened with subsidence because the foundations could not cope with heavy loads and it often proved necessary to divert heavy goods vehicles away from weak or badly aligned bridges. The Department's roads section recommended that a minimum of £100,000 a year should be set aside for reconstructing main roads, such as the roads from Dublin to Naas and to Belfast.[118] However the additional grant of £1m. was diverted to the Road Fund on the assumption that it would be used to provide employment as soon as possible. Ian Bloomer lamented that this meant that it had to be spent on schemes which required the minimum planning. Although main roads received an additional £1m. during 1953/54, county roads absorbed an extra £1.5m.. It is evident, therefore, that if NDF money was spent on main roads, nearly all the additional revenue accruing to the Road Fund as a result of higher licence charges went on county roads.

By the end of the 1953/54 financial year, expenditure under the NDF totalled £1.37m.. Although the government had given a commitment to top up the fund annually to a figure of £5m., no extra money was provided in the estimates for 1954/55.[119] Having failed to prevent the establishment of the NDF, Finance was determined to cut its losses by adopting a tough budgetary stance in 1954/55. The cost of the £400,000 spent annually on improving Gaeltacht roads was transferred from the Exchequer to the Road Fund.[120] Finance also transferred the cost of other schemes from the Exchequer to the NDF as a means of neutralising its impact.

THE ERA OF RETRENCHMENT: 1954-57

The election of the second inter-party government in 1954 saw Finance renew its efforts to curb public spending. Gerard Sweetman, Minister for Finance, issued instructions that every project which had not yet been approved by the national development committee should be reconsidered, as should all schemes which had been approved but could be abandoned without a significant waste of resources. He also recommended that the Exchequer grant to the Road Fund should be limited to the amount necessary to maintain spending at the level of the previous year. This item was withdrawn from the cabinet agenda on 2 July 1954 and does not appear to have been resubmitted. In practice, although the NDF was not terminated until March 1957, it became dormant from the summer of 1954. The remaining grants were spent on minor employment schemes and other insignificant items. When it was wound up in 1957, expenditure had reached £5.255m.. Almost half of this, £2.539m., went on grants to the Road Fund. Grants under special employment schemes and the Local Authorities (Works) Act, which would probably have existed irrespective of the NDF, accounted for a further £1.56m..[121]

Thus the net effect of the NDF was to inject £2.5-£3m. into the economy over two or three years. Fianna Fáil had promised to transfer an additional £1.9m. from the NDF to the Road Fund for the 1954/55 financial year; £400,000 was to compensate the Road Fund for the cost of special grants for Gaeltacht roads. Local Government was determined that half the remaining £1.5m. would be spent on major road and bridge improvements in the Dublin area and on improvements to major arterial roads in the vicinity of Cork, Limerick and Waterford. The remaining £750,000 would be spent on county roads.[122] However in 1954/55 the inter-party government reduced the sum which was transferred to the Road Fund to £1.5m., forcing the Road Fund to bear the cost of Gaeltacht roads. In 1955/56 the government decided to made the £400,000 bill for improving Gaeltacht roads a permanent charge on the Fund, to be met by further reducing grants for main roads and bridges on main roads. At the same time it transferred an extra £200,000 from the Road Fund allocation for main roads to county roads, absorbing all the projected increase in Road Fund income.

When Local Government protested about these decisions, the government agreed to increase expenditure by the Road Fund from £4.6m. to £5m. — an increase which matched the cost of the grants towards Gaeltacht roads. The additional cost would be met by borrowing against the Fund's future income.[123] Local Government was outraged at this proposal and sought to have it reversed on the grounds that the Road Fund would be 'crippled for years to come'.

Officials also pointed out that the end of the NDF grant to the Road Fund meant that total expenditure on roads was set to fall, whereas local authorities and the public appeared to believe that it was being increased. On 29 March 1955 William Davin, parliamentary secretary to the Minister for Local Government, warned his minister of this fact, noting that 'it is evident from statements made by some Ministers and also reports of statements made at Council meetings, that the government decision is not correctly understood'. Local authority engineers were planning for additional road schemes on the assumption that money would be provided. Davin feared that this misunderstanding 'could cause an explosion in the middle of a local election campaign'. The confusion stemmed from the fact that the government had not announced that NDF money would no longer be available. In previous years, local authorities had not been notified of NDF grants until the autumn, and councils assumed that the same practice would be followed in 1955.

In late September a deputation from the Parliamentary Labour Party sought an assurance that supplementary road grants would be available from the NDF to relieve rural unemployment. One Local Government official responded to these representations with the familiar statement that 'this Department is not an employment agency' and suggested that the deputation should be referred to the special employment schemes office. However, the fact that for many years government expenditure on roads had been determined with reference to employment needs, rather than traffic problems, weakened the value of this assertion. Pa O'Donnell, Minister for Local Government, promised the deputation that he would raise the question of providing for a supplementary roads estimate at cabinet. Meanwhile Local Government was coming under pressure to provide work during winter months for seasonal turf workers who had been laid off by Bord na Móna. Although Finance rejected Local Government's request for a supplementary estimate for roads, on 4 November 1955 the cabinet provided an additional £600,000; £500,000 would be raised by borrowing against the Road Fund, the remaining £100,000 would come from the almost-moribund NDF. None of this money could be spent on main roads, unless it was needed to complete a scheme which had not been finished because the funds were exhausted. O'Donnell gave a commitment that councils would be free to allocate the extra money to either road works or to minor drainage schemes carried out under the Local Authorities (Works) Act, a decision which marked a further attenuation in the rationale of the Road Fund, which would have to repay this money.

Officials in Local Government particularly resented the fact that Finance had insisted that the additional money should not be spent on main roads. They regarded this as creating 'a very undesirable precedent which would leave the way open for further interference by the Department of Finance in details of roads policy'. Local Government believed that it would be preferable to permit each council to decide how the money should be spent; this 'fits in with the Minister's policy and would be well received by county councils'.[124] Left to their own devices, there is little doubt that councils would have spent almost all the money on county roads.[125] Eventually the additional £500,000 was provided by a special Exchequer grant, rather than by borrowing against the Road Fund. Over £432,000 went on county roads.

Although councils demanded additional money for road works again in 1956, the financial screw was tightening. Grants for main road improvements were reduced by £200,000 in the 1956 estimates; the money was transferred, as before, to county roads, where expenditure had risen by £500,000 in the previous year.[126] However by the summer of 1956 the government was finding it increasingly difficult to finance its borrowings and it was also facing an acute balance of payments crisis. All public expenditure came under review following the emergency budget of 26 July 1956. Capital expenditure proved a particular target. The Road Fund was raided to the tune of £500,000. In August 1956 Local Government instructed councils not to commence work on any new main road improvements; work in progress was to cease by 25 September. Following widespread protests, this order was effectively reversed in October. Local authorities were instructed to spend on county roads the money saved from closing down main road improvements, though O'Donnell conceded that any council that wished to spend the money on main roads was free to do so. This meant that a further sum of £353,000 was transferred from main roads to county roads.

By October 1956 there were threats of petrol rationing as a result of the blockade of the Suez Canal, the main route for oil coming from the Middle East to Europe, and Road Fund income fell for the first time since the end of World War II. The government also cut the money available for road works carried out under the minor employment schemes and urban employment schemes. The brunt of these reductions was borne by the county boroughs, which received only £100,000, as against £300,000 in the previous year. The grant to Dublin Corporation fell from £258,000 in 1954/55 and £163,000 in 1955/56 to a mere £50,000 in 1956/57. Expenditure on rural employment schemes in twelve western counties fell by more than 50 per cent.[127] Smaller reductions applied to bog road development schemes and rural improvement schemes — work on rural lanes in non-western areas, which was partly funded by the benefiting farmers. Local Government had the unpalatable task of ensuring that local authorities complied with the new austere regime. Officials in the Custom House were fully aware that, in policing local authority spending, they would be accused of acting 'contrary to the publicly stated policy of the Minister for Local Government in relation to local matters': that he would reduce the extent of central interference. They evaded the issue by blaming the Department of Finance.[128]

Nothing which could be remotely identified as a national roads policy existed by 1956. The far-sighted plans of the wartime years had been eroded by a combination of lack of funds, government pandering to local political interests, and the pressure of unemployment statistics. The Road Fund, originally established to provide finance for main roads, was being used for a variety of quasi social purposes. Most 'improvement grants' were spent on low-grade maintenance, while

TABLE 9.2

Road expenditure by central and local authorities
(£m.)

	Central	Local	Total	Main Roads	County Roads	Other* Expenditure
1947/48	£2.67	£1.79	£4.46	£2.30	£1.90	£.26
per cent	59.8	40.2	100	51.6	42.6	5.8
1948/49	£4.20	£2.10	£6.30	£3.46	£2.60	£.24
	66.6	33.3	100	54.9	41.3	3.8
1949/50	£2.33	£2.65	£4.98	£2.00	£2.80	£.18
	46.8	53.2	100	40.2	56.2	3.6
1950/51	£2.38	£2.81	£5.19	£2.10	£2.80	£.29
	45.9	54.1	100	40.5	53.9	5.6
1952	£2.50	£3.30	£5.80	£2.28	£3.15	£.37
	43.1	56.9	100	39.3	54.3	6.4
1953	£3.30	£3.79	£7.09	£3.43	£3.63	£.03
	46.5	53.5	100	48.40	51.20	40
1954	£5.78	£4.25	£10.03	£4.43	£5.12	£.48
	57.6	42.4	100	44.2	51.0	4.8
1955	£5.66	£4.45	£10.11	£4.42	£5.20	£.49
	56.0	44.0	100	43.7	51.4	4.9
1956	£5.67	£4.72	£10.38	£4.07	£5.81	£.50
	54.6	45.4	100	39.2	56	4.8
1957	£4.03	£6.04	£10.08	£3.47	£6.03	£.58
	40	60	100	34.4	59.8	5.8

* Bridges and other miscellaneous items.

Source: Annual Reports of the Department of Local Government

large tracts of road along the western seaboard were wholly maintained by the state under a variety of employment schemes. One Local Government official claimed: 'It is in fact little exaggeration to say that in the whole of South Connemara from Galway to Slyne Head and North Connemara to Clifden, the Galway County Council is scarcely responsible for any road except the main trunk routes. The position is similar in the West Cork peninsulas and in most of the other Minor Employment Schemes areas.'[129] Government capital expenditure during the immediate post-war decade has often been criticised for concentrating on infrastructure at the expense of more productive investment. Kennedy and Dowling have attempted to mitigate this criticism by arguing that such investment provided Ireland with the necessary infrastructure to cope with the faster economic growth of the late 1950s and 1960s. A detailed assessment of road expenditure belies this argument, as would any cursory analysis of expenditure on water and sewerage schemes. By the late 1950s Irish roads were no more capable of meeting the needs of a modern economy than they had been ten years earlier.

If local authorities gained greater discretionary control over road expenditure, it came at a price. In 1948 central government funded 60 per cent of expenditure on roads; local authorities bore 40 per cent. By 1956/57 the figures had been reversed.

ROAD TRAFFIC LEGISLATION

Political indifference towards developing a modern road network was mirrored by the neglect of road traffic legislation. Compliance with road-licensing regulations was low before 1914 and it probably deteriorated further during the years of the Anglo-Irish war and the civil war. During the mid-1920s the Department of Local Government and Public Health attempted to tackle the high rate of evasion of motor taxation and sought to close up administrative loopholes, such as the high number of private cars which were registered as hackneys in order to qualify for lower rates of motor taxation. Almost half of all private cars outside Dublin held hackney licences in the mid-1920s. An interdepartmental committee on the control and regulation of road traffic, which sat in 1927/28, recommended that the national speed limit for private cars should be abolished and that greater controls be

425

introduced over motor buses. It also proposed that third-party insurance be made compulsory for all motorists. The cabinet endorsed these proposals, but W.T. Cosgrave denounced an additional recommendation that penalties should be introduced for drunk driving as 'mischievous' and this proposal was dropped.[139] A Road Traffic Bill to legislate on the other items did not appear until 1931 — evidence of government indifference — and it lapsed on the dissolution of the Dáil.[130] Legislation requiring compulsory third-party insurance was not introduced until the 1933 Road Traffic Act. This Act, which also brought in penalties for drunk and dangerous driving, was not seriously revised until the 1960s.

No further significant changes took place during the 1930s, but during the Emergency years some road traffic regulations were altered to take account of specific wartime difficulties. When the war ended in 1945, Local Government feared that a resumption of normal motoring would mean a rapid rise in road traffic casualties. Anticipating this, in August 1945 it was decided to print cautionary notices that warned of the dangers of drinking and driving, and plans were drawn up for a radio and film campaign to promote road safety. The Department decided that the wartime 30 mph speed limit should be retained for some time after normal traffic resumed in order to give the public time to adjust to the new conditions; an emergency powers order to this effect was passed. Yet another order was issued late in 1945 which permitted gardaí to test the brakes and steering on all motor vehicles and on bicycles.[132]

However road traffic regulations were a matter for two Departments: Local Government and Justice. Although Local Government set the regulations, it relied on the gardaí, who were controlled by the Department of Justice, for their enforcement, and both departments did not necessarily see eye to eye on road safety. MacEntee made an indirect reference to this matter in the course of the 1947 estimates debate, when he stated that 'though the matter is not strictly or mainly within the province of the Department of Local Government, problems of road safety and measures which should be taken to promote it are under active consideration'. Local Government was keen that penalties against defective brakes and unsafe vehicles would be more strictly enforced, and the Department continued its road safety publicity campaign. In 1947, for the first time, a road safety exhibition was mounted at the RDS Spring Show and plans were in hand to develop a mobile unit to bring road safety films into schools. The Department also established a road safety consultative committee.[133]

These were relatively uncontroversial matters. However other, more contentious proposals, such as the introduction of compulsory driving tests and speed limits, were not implemented, despite the fact that the General Council of County Councils passed a resolution calling for such measures in 1949 and the Department received other resolutions in support from individual local authorities and from the Safety First Association of Ireland. Although an interdepartmental committee was established in 1953 to examine the possibility of amending the Road Traffic Acts, nothing resulted from its deliberations. In July 1956, however, the Seanad passed a motion demanding that the government take steps to reduce the high incidence of fatal traffic accidents by amending road traffic legislation,[134] and in the following month the Minister for Local Government informed his ministerial colleagues that he would shortly bring proposals for new legislation to the cabinet. He also announced that he was seeking tenders for a new booklet on road safety. The memorandum to cabinet stated, in a somewhat defensive tone, that the Minister was satisfied that 'everything necessary' was being done to expedite the administrative and legislative amendments. However, the fact that the cabinet decided that the Taoiseach and the Ministers for Justice and Local Government and the parliamentary secretary to the government would present recommendations on the steps necessary to minimise traffic accidents to a future cabinet meeting, suggests that there was a perception that Local Government had been dragging its feet.

The document, which Local Government presented to cabinet on 13 October 1956, exposed the extent of the neglect. It admitted that 'except in very minor respects', road traffic legislation was still based on the 1933 Act. The Minister, Pa O'Donnell, promised that new legislation would provide for a general speed limit, the extension of compulsory insurance to cover all passengers, and for the introduction of on the spot fines for minor traffic offences. The most obvious omission was any provision for compulsory driving tests; James Everett, the Minister for Justice, was opposed to their introduction. O'Donnell saw 'little value in an actual driving test in the conditions prevailing here, especially in rural Ireland', though he acknowledged that the 'public demand for a test for drivers must be met in some way'. As a compromise, he proposed an oral test. However James Everett believed that any form of driving test would prove to be 'a fruitful source of complaints, disputes and appeals', which would incur 'public resentment and often ridicule'. (The only member of this government who appears to have openly favoured a driving test was John O'Donovan, parliamentary secretary to the Taoiseach.) In a token, if rather fatuous, gesture towards the pro-driving test lobby, the cabinet suggested that the Minister for Local Government should include a provision in the new legislation requiring all applicants for a driving licence to make a statutory declaration that they had informed themselves of all the relevant provisions of the law and that they were familiar with the rules of good behaviour. Only drivers who had been disqualified as a result of a serious traffic offence would be required to pass a driving test. The cabinet also dropped the proposal to require bicycles to carry rear red warning lights. This proposed bill is of merely academic interest because it died with the dissolution of the Dáil in 1957 and the 1933 Act continued as the basis of all traffic legislation until 1961.

There is nothing admirable in this story of neglect. Government ministers of all major parties appear to have been equally culpable. In January 1960, following the establishment of the Department of Transport and Power, the Minister, Erskine Childers, who had been actively involved in road safety issues during his term as parliamentary secretary to the Minister for Local Government and Public Health, attempted to wrest control of road traffic legislation away from Local Government. Maurice Moynihan, secretary to the government, asked John Garvin, secretary of Local Government, for his views. Garvin (a non-driver!) pointed out that the items which gave 'greatest scope for personal opinions' were driving tests, speed limits and provisions for periodically examining motor vehicles. He informed Moynihan that

. . . successive Ministers for Local Government have had different views as to what policy should be. Memoranda proposing different lines have been circulated by the Department only to be followed by a change of Minister and consequent review of policy by the incoming Minister.

According to Garvin, this accounted for the death of the abortive 1956 road traffic bill. When Fianna Fáil was returned to office in March 1957, the government decided that the heads of the 1956 bill would form the basis of legislation, subject to minor amendments. However when Neil Blaney succeeded Paddy Smith in November 1957, he decided that a much stronger bill should be introduced, providing for both driving tests and tests on the roadworthiness of vehicles. Garvin believed that if responsibility for road traffic legislation was transferred to another Department, there would be 'yet a further repetition of Ministerial consideration and reference to other Departments', and further delays. Despite, or perhaps because of, Blaney's enthusiasm for stricter road traffic legislation, the delays continued, largely because of differences of opinion between Local Government and the Department of Justice and the gardaí over who should be responsible for enforcing the new and tougher laws.

By 1960 Local Government was arguing that the complexity of road traffic legislation was 'growing from day to day with the growth of traffic'; this made it difficult to resolve the matter by using rigid statutory provisions. Officials suggested that any bill should be drafted in the widest possible terms, giving the Minister power to modify and amend measures by means of statutory regulations without recourse to detailed legislation. Local Government also insisted that the new measures would prove worthless 'unless a firm and active line is taken in the enforcement of the law by the Garda Síochána'. The proposed bill provided for the introduction of a general 30 mph speed limit in all built-up areas, though the Minister would have power to vary the actual speed limit and to alter the areas covered. All new drivers would be required to pass a driving test. All vehicles would be immediately subject to compulsory testing of brakes and steering, and in the longer term the Department intended to introduce compulsory tests for all motor vehicles. All passengers would be covered by compulsory insurance and the fines levied for various offences would be updated.

The proposals gave rise to widespread opposition from the Departments of Justice and Transport and Power; Posts and Telegraphs and Defence both expressed minor reservations. The Departments of Justice and Transport and Power were particularly exercised by the proposal to introduce speed limits in urban areas. The Minister for Justice, Oscar Traynor, repeated the views of the 1953/54 interdepartmental committee that many motorists would regard a speed limit of 30 mph as 'merely a vexatious restriction to be evaded' where possible. He also believed that it would be difficult to enforce. Erskine Childers, the Minister for Transport and Power, was concerned that the speed limit would make it difficult for CIE buses to keep to their timetables; moreover he objected to the proposal to set a maximum speed for all buses. Objections to the proposal to introduce driving tests concentrated on who would conduct them. Neil Blaney argued that if examiners were appointed by the Minister (as in Britain or Northern Ireland), it 'would leave the way open to impossible pressure on the Minister to interfere in individual cases' — an interesting insight. However the Department of Justice opposed Local Government's suggestion that the gardaí should conduct driving tests; it claimed that the individual garda 'is no more likely to make a suitable examiner than, say, an employee of the licensing authority'. The Minister also believed that since gardaí should endeavour to 'avoid friction with ordinary law-abiding persons', they should be among the last people to act as examiners. The Department of Justice also wished to give judges a greater degree of discretion in enforcing penalties for drunken driving; the 1933 Act had applied a mandatory twelve-month driving ban, though this could be appealed to the Minister for Justice.

The cabinet gave its approval for Local Government to draft a White Paper, though the proposed speed limit on buses would be omitted pending further consultation; the question of who would act as examiners for driving tests was deferred too. The cabinet also suggested that there should be further consideration of the penalties to be enforced for drunken driving.[135] On this occasion, however, Blaney appears to have ensured that the 1961 Road Traffic Act incorporated most of the provisions recommended by Local Government, though compulsory driving tests were not introduced until 1964.

CONCLUSIONS

The *autobahns* are one of the best-remembered and least controversial achievements of the German government during the 1930s; the US Federal Highway system was a major success of the Eisenhower administrations during the 1950s. By the 1960s most developed countries had embarked on some form of national road programme, designed to cope with the demands placed on the existing infrastructure by the growth of motor traffic. Both the record of road expenditure and of road traffic legislation indicate that Irish politicians lacked any vision of modern roads or motor vehicles, as possible agents which would be used to transform the Irish economy or society. The strong political commitment to protecting the railways and the high tariff protection which was accorded to motor vehicle assembly plants stunted the potential for such a vision. Several Ministers for Local Government dreamed of seeing an Irish population which was comfortably housed. Nobody dreamed of motorways, by-passes or dual-carriageways, other than perhaps some isolated engineers.

CHAPTER TEN

THE ERA OF ECONOMIC DEVELOPMENT
1957-73

The second half of the 1950s ushered in a new age in Irish political and economic life. Gone, in theory at least, was the reliance on public expenditure to stimulate economic activity — a policy in which the Department of Local Government had played a major role. Instead, *Economic Development* and the White Paper *Programme for Economic Expansion*, both published in 1958, heralded a shift from a protectionist economic policy to one oriented towards free trade, with a corresponding shift from relying on government expenditure to stimulate economic growth to a new focus on the market: a shift which, as Garret FitzGerald has pointed out, marked an attempt to reverse the economic policies followed since 1932 and a return to the policy of the years 1922-32.[1]

The reports of the Capital Investment Advisory Committee and *Economic Development* emphasised the need to reduce investment in social amenities such as housing, in favour of more productive items. This appeared to portend a lesser role for the Department of Local Government. However, after a brief eclipse, the Department found itself confronting the problems of prosperity: new houses for the increasing number of newly-weds, water and roads to cater for new industries, and running water for rural households. As the pace of economic development quickened and Irish economic planning became more complex in the *Second Programme*, Local Government assumed a more important role. A growing awareness of the relationship between economic and physical planning was signalled both by the 1963 Planning Act, which remains the landmark legislation in this field, and by the establishment of An Foras Forbartha, the national institute for physical planning and construction research, in 1964.

Economic and social change was not unrelated to political change. The 1957 general election returned a Fianna Fáil government and the party was to remain in office until 1973. In June 1959 Éamon de Valera made way as Taoiseach for Seán Lemass, whose years as Taoiseach have given rise to a level of uncritical adulation unique in the writing of modern Irish history. Little, if any, of this hagiography has been informed by access to government archives. These show a much more interventionist, quasi presidential style of Taoiseach. In contrast to de Valera, Lemass appears to have been actively involved in many aspects of government policy. Cabinet ministers seem to have responded to this by adopting a higher personal profile in determining policy. Government files from the Lemass years reveal a much higher incidence of correspondence between ministers on legislative matters than in the past and these letters often include personal touches which suggest that they were not simply drafted by civil servants.

Despite the somewhat naive opinions expressed in *Economic Development* that tax levels would fall and the role of the state would recede, the 1960s brought a new wave of government intervention in the economy. This often led to ministers and departments contending for control: there was evident rivalry between Local Government and Industry and Commerce over which should be responsible for the building industry, between Agriculture and Local Government over rural water schemes, and between Local Government and Finance on a variety of issues. During the early 1960s, the Local Government portfolio was in extremely capable hands. Although Paddy Smith, a previous Local Government Minister, was reappointed after the 1957 election, within months he was replaced by Donegal TD Neil Blaney, who held the post until November 1966. Blaney emerges as an active minister, capable of defending the Department's interests in cabinet. He had a personal commitment to improving rural water supplies and appears to have supported greater government regulation of physical planning. 'With his departure', Desmond Roche said, 'went much of the verve and force behind the physical planning movement'.[2] It will not be possible to comment with similar confidence about Blaney's successors until the relevant files become available.

By the mid-1960s the Department was confronting many problems which are familiar today, such as planning regulations, itinerancy and casual trading. Local authorities had become involved in economic development with the establishment of county development teams in some counties. The files contain numerous references to pollution, even to nuclear power. Modern Ireland had emerged.

The years of retrenchment: the capital investment advisory committee

It is impossible to exaggerate the sense of crisis which prevailed during 1956. The government introduced three deflationary budgets, designed to eliminate the balance of payments deficit by curbing imports. In the longer term, the crisis prompted a fundamental shift in economic policy. This was signalled by a speech which Taoiseach John A. Costello made to a meeting of the government parties in October when he announced his determination to encourage exports and to favour private investment in order to relieve pressure on public investment. Investment in agriculture would take priority over all other sectors.

As part of this process, the government established a Capital Investment Advisory Committee, which would, in the words of the Department of Finance, be 'small in numbers and expert in quality'.[3] The nine-man committee was asked to advise as to the appropriate level of public investment, priorities for such investment and how it should be financed, 'with full regard to the needs and interests of the national economy'.[4] These were long-term issues; more immediately, the committee was asked to suggest how the expected £12m. deficit in the 1957/58 capital budget could be met. This was the subject of its first report.

The committee recoiled from proposing that the capital budget should be cut by £12m. because this would lead to an undesirable level of unemployment. It suggested that unspecified capital projects costing over £2m. should be postponed, 'where this can be effected without unduly aggravating unemployment'. The additional £10m. needed should be provided by transferring money from the current to the capital budget, by cutting food subsidies and by discontinuing agricultural rates relief in order to transfer money to more productive uses such as subsidising the price of fertilisers.[5]

The inter-party government had already begun to cut public capital spending before the committee had reported. When Pa O'Donnell and Gerard Sweetman met the county managers on 2 January 1957, Sweetman informed them that all applications for capital expenditure would be subjected 'to the strictest screening' and that only urgent housing and sanitary schemes would be approved. Managers were warned to obtain ministerial sanction for projects before inviting tenders, and not to enter into any further commitments to pay supplementary housing grants.[6] The inter-party government gave way to Fianna Fáil in March 1957. Finance Minister James Ryan's budget speech referred to the need for a 'reshaping' of the public capital programme 'so as to make it more directly productive', phrases which suggested that he endorsed the recommendations contained in the first report of the Capital Investment Advisory Committee.

However, Fianna Fáil appeared to adopt a less draconian approach to public expenditure. Local authorities were informed that sufficient money would be provided to permit work to resume on housing and sanitary schemes which had been postponed and that arrears in Road Fund grants would be paid. However, Ryan emphasised that the government was maintaining expenditure on roads and housing only because it was hesitant to introduce economies which would lead to a significant loss of jobs until alternative employment 'of a productive character' had been provided.[7] This announcement concealed the fact that there were practically no funds available for new capital expenditure, though local authorities were permitted to borrow money from the Local Loans Fund to pay supplementary housing grants[8] and Dublin and Cork Corporations were given additional capital to finance Small Dwellings Acquisition Act loans. A press release from Local Government dated 24 May 1957 claimed that these measures were necessary 'for restoring activity in the building industry with special reference to the renewal of private housing activity'. This concession also relieved local authorities of an embarrassing position; many had continued to approve supplementary housing grants, contrary to government instructions.[9] There was no similar relaxation of curbs on local authority housing.

The second report of the capital investment advisory committee, dated 4 November 1957, dealt exclusively with housing and sounded the death-knell of the post-war housing programme. Housing accounted for one-third of public capital expenditure — the largest single item — and in the committee's opinion it gave a 'very low financial return'. The committee suggested that the onus for providing housing should be shifted from the public to the private sector. Subsidies should be reduced for private housing and for local authority housing other than slum-clearance schemes; the money saved should be invested in 'productive projects'. There should be greater emphasis on maintaining existing properties, as opposed to building new houses. Rent Restrictions Acts should be repealed in order to provide incentives for private landlords, and the scope of SDA mortgages should be reduced. All local authorities should be required to adopt differential rents. None of these recommendations was particularly original. Most had been previously proposed by officials in the Department of Finance.[10] On this occasion they had a much greater prospect of being accepted.

Two members of the committee, trade union leader Ruaidhrí Roberts and M.J. Costello, managing director of the state-owned Irish Sugar Company, dissented from the recommendations. Both men alleged that the recommendations assumed that the Irish population would continue to fall and that they ignored the fact that the proportion of the population living in overcrowded housing remained high by international standards. They argued that housing should 'be considered an important element in the preparation of a programme for expanded production'; they proposed that a revised housing programme should provide houses for workers employed in new industries, complete the slum-clearance programme and renovate substandard houses. Minority reports are not uncommon in the history of Irish committees and commissions. This one did not go unchallenged. An addendum to the majority report, written in response to a request from the Minister for Finance, dismissed any prospect of using investment in housing to stimulate economic development and concluded that 'it might be argued that social investment in the present state of our economy, can only be the consequence, and not the cause, of economic advance'.[11]

Local Government expressed qualified opposition to the proposed cut in housing subsidies and the committee's insistence that all local authorities introduce differential rents. It refuted the assertion that the growing burden of public debt service, which the committee had claimed was 'in large part a consequence of current housing policy', was 'one of the major obstacles to any worthwhile reduction in taxation'. The Department complained that the report drew attention 'only to what it describes as undesirable consequences of policy' and failed 'to weigh these consequences against the achievements of policy'. Local Government believed that the recommendation had been framed 'in the light of existing abnormal circumstances' and might prove to 'be of little purpose' if, 'in time, the national economy is in a position to support a higher level of investment'. It pleaded that 'until the supply of accommodation, including rented accommodation, is adequate, housing policy should not be required, regardless of the needs of social and economic circumstances, to restrict its scope within a rigid pattern'.[12]

Before the cabinet had debated the committee's second report, Local Government mounted a direct challenge by submitting proposals for a Housing Bill, which would extend grants for private housing for a further two years and increase the grant per house at an estimated annual cost of £500,000, 37 per cent more than in the current year. Local Government also anticipated that the more generous grants would in turn lead to demands for additional SDA loans costing £500,000 a year. Predictably, Finance was outraged, noting that even the minority report of the Capital Investment Advisory Committee 'does not go as far as advocating increased grants for private housing'. It suggested that the government defer a decision on the bill until it had considered the committee's recommendations.[13] The cabinet compromised, approving higher grants for house improvements, access to SDA loans for those on low incomes, and uncontroversial proposals to change rates remission for new houses, but it decided to freeze grants for new houses at existing levels and deferred a decision on proposals to harmonise urban and rural housing subsidies.

The government showed a similar tendency to evade harsh decisions when it considered the second report of the Capital Investment Advisory Committee shortly afterwards, and decided that, with the exception of the recommendations concerning rent control, all other matters should be considered by the Departments of Finance, Local Government and the Gaeltacht, which three ministers should submit agreed proposals to government.[14] No submission appears to have been made. The fact that the 1958 Housing (Amendment) Act increased the grants for new private houses and raised the subsidies for labourers' cottages to the figures paid for local authority housing in urban areas, suggests that Fianna Fáil was not wholly committed to implementing the recommendations of the Capital Investment Advisory Committee.

ECONOMIC DEVELOPMENT

The third report of the Capital Investment Advisory Committee, dated 6 June 1958, recommended a 'marked increase in the proportion [of state capital programme] devoted to productive purposes'. In order to

achieve this, 'Ireland must be willing to defer certain desirable forms of social investment, mainly redistributive in their effect, in order to give a fair chance to productive investment in the first and most difficult stages of new development'. The committee nevertheless added that all redistributive investment should not be terminated, though it should be scaled down; it was unwilling to see men thrown out of work.

The report listed the sectors likely to give scope for productive investment: agriculture, fisheries, industry, tourism and education. Nothing remotely within the ambit of the Department of Local Government was mentioned.[15] The arguments in this report were similar to those presented by T.K. Whitaker, who was about to become secretary of the Department of Finance, in a paper read to the Statistical and Social Inquiry Society of Ireland in May 1956. Whitaker pointed out that over the period 1949-54 investment in 'dwellings alone formed as high a proportion of gross domestic capital formation as agriculture, mining, manufacturing and other construction combined'.[16]

By 1958, as is well known, Whitaker had written *Economic Development*, which is generally regarded as the blueprint for modern Irish economic development. The background to this document does not directly concern us,[17] though its content does. It emphasised the need to adjust to a free trade environment and to devote more resources to 'productive purposes'. Whitaker envisaged a natural decline in public capital expenditure, as investment opportunities were exhausted. Private housing needs had been largely met; many local authorities had completed or exceeded their housing targets. The main exception, Dublin Corporation, was expected to complete its programme within five or six years; earlier if heavy emigration continued. An appendix to the report, containing forecasts for capital expenditure by public authorities, envisaged expenditure on housing peaking at £9.87m. in 1959/60 and falling to £8.17m. by 1962/63; capital expenditure on sanitary and miscellaneous services was expected to fall from £2.56m. in 1958/59 to £2m. by 1962/63.[18] These are among the few statistics in *Economic Development* and they were included almost unchanged in the *Programme for Economic Expansion*. It is therefore important to establish if these targets were achieved.

Public investment during the years 1959-64 was much higher than envisaged in the *Programme*. Garret FitzGerald points out that 'in 1963-64 the Capital Budget involved expenditure of £78.5m. in current money terms as against £44.5m. in 1958 money values as planned under the First Programme: an increase of about 60 per cent, even allowing for changes in money values'. Discrepancies between projected and actual capital expenditure are shown in Table 10.1.

TABLE 10.1

Projected and actual public investment during the Programme for Economic Expansion 1959-64

	Housing		Sanitary and Miscellaneous		Total of Public Investment	
	Actual	Projected	Actual	Projected	Actual	Projected
1958/59	£6.53	£9.87	£1.78	£2.30	£37.89	£41.69
1959/60	£7.79	£9.67	£1.39	£2.30	£44.09	£44.49
1960/61	£9.03	£8.67	£1.84	£2.25	£51.27	£45.81
1961/62	£9.67	£8.17	£2.29	£2.00	£58.62	£43.98
1962/63	£11.19	N.A.	£2.26	N.A.	£65.83	£44.47
1963/64	£12.21	N.A.	£4.13	N.A.	£73.50	N.A.

Source: Adapted from Garret FitzGerald, *Planning in Ireland* (Dublin, 1968), p. 46. Actual prices are in current values.

Expenditure on housing and sanitary services lagged behind projections, as did public capital expenditure as a whole in 1958/59; in the following year, while the projected and actual totals for capital expenditure were more or less identical, expenditure on housing and sanitary services was substantially below projected levels. Only in the 1960s does capital expenditure, first on housing and then on sanitary services, outstrip projections; the trend was similar for public capital expenditure as a whole. During the years 1959-64 housing accounted for one-sixth of public capital expenditure, compared with one-third between the years 1949/50 and 1957/58. FitzGerald's conclusion, that the pattern of public investment did not depart significantly from the principle laid down in the White Paper,[19] seems correct.

The Estimates for the Department of Local Government for 1957/58 provided for a reduction of 12 per cent in current expenditure, with most of the savings coming from housing and the Local Authorities (Works) Act.[20] Actual expenditure fell by £994,240, almost double the

439

projected figure. Housing grants cost £1.5m., against a Budget estimate of £1.8m.. In 1958 Neil Blaney explained that the volume of local authority housing construction had fallen because many councils had completed their housing programmes; others were delaying schemes in anticipation of higher government subsidies.[21] The report of the Department of Local Government for 1957/58 pointed out that there were numerous vacant local authority flats and houses in Dublin city as a result of emigration.

Such statements appear to have been a deliberate effort to minimise the government's role in cutting spending on housing. In fact, a substantial share of savings were achieved by scrutinising local authority spending plans. All applications to the LLF were examined by both Local Government and Finance, and Local Government was forced to apply to Finance when demands on the LLF exceeded projections by as little as £100,000. Local Government was also required to prepare detailed forward projections for capital and non-capital expenditure, which were scrutinised by Finance.[22] Such practices meant that the projected expenditure targets in *Economic Development* were reduced in the capital budget and even those sums often went unspent. In turn, a fall in capital spending on housing brought a decline in the cost of housing grants, which were paid from the current budget. With the exception of 1959/60, the number of completed local authority houses fell until 1962/63. Private housing began to recover in 1959/60, either as a result of the higher grants announced in 1958, or in response to rising confidence in the economy; the number of private houses built rose steadily during the early 1960s.

Although *Economic Development* gave an unequivocal message — that it was essential to shift resources from public to private investment, with greater emphasis on productive projects — the government adopted a slightly different stance. Shortly after he became Taoiseach in June 1959, Seán Lemass announced that the government was determined to increase employment in sectors of the building and construction industry other than housing. He requested Dublin Corporation and other public bodies to co-operate 'in putting forward, planning and carrying out development projects of economic merits'. In a draft letter to the lord mayor of Dublin, dated 9 July, Lemass noted the 'Government's stated policy that the state should in future participate to an even greater extent than heretofore in developmental activities, including activities, which, while not directly commercial, will contribute to the overall expansion of the economy and help in the achievement of increased production.' He mentioned that the newly established planning division in the Department of Finance would examine all proposals for public investment.

Lemass sent a copy of his letter to Neil Blaney and suggested that copies be sent to the lord mayors and mayors of all the county boroughs and that Blaney send a circular letter 'similarly phrased' to the chairmen of county councils and the most important urban district councils. Although the letter uses words such as 'development' and 'increased production', it was sufficiently similar to older initiatives such as the National Development Fund to prompt a resurgence of traditional job-creation proposals.

Dublin Corporation dusted off its long-standing plans to build new civic offices plus a new bridge over the Liffey and coastal development at Clontarf (shades of the Blue Lagoon: see chapter six). Galway wished to extend the promenade and build a new road and carparks at Salthill and to remove the railings and terrace the grounds in Eyre Square. A follow-up letter from the Galway county manager to the secretary of the Taoiseach's Department emphasised that the mayor was 'anxious to assist', but he and the manager 'find difficulty in envisaging what exactly the Taoiseach has in mind . . . and what type of public project would be regarded as of economic merit.' He was probably not alone: Waterford Corporation expressed 'gratification' at the Taoiseach's letter; they saw it as an indication of 'a welcome new outlook on the part of Government in encouraging local effort'. The Corporation suggested a water scheme, reclaiming a marshy area as a possible industrial site, and developing the Tramore river.

By August officials in the Taoiseach's Department feared that the Lemass initiative would place considerable strain on the public capital programme. The Waterford city manager claimed to have received a number of requests from newspapers for a copy of the corporation's reply; he was urged not to release it without consulting the Taoiseach because the revelation that Waterford was seeking a water scheme would encourage similar applications 'which would in the ordinary way be dealt with by local authorities, without state assistance'. A note on the file minuted that 'we can hardly rely on them keeping these secret but we should not encourage them to publish, otherwise they will start competing with one another'. Competition was already rife. Cork Corporation wanted funds for main drainage and water schemes and funds to prepare factory sites. Local newspapers gave the Lemass/Blaney letters considerable publicity. On 5 September 1959 the *Connacht Tribune* headline read 'Government Plans for Big Spending', though it emphasised that members of local bodies 'did not find it exactly easy to construe the terms of the rather cryptically worded document'. Many were 'curious to discover how relief schemes can be reconciled with productive work'.[23]

Ultimately the Taoiseach's Department received over 700 specific proposals from all but eleven of the 87 local authorities which been contacted.[24] By November 1959 officials in the development division of the Department of Finance had concluded that the letters 'have yielded very few worthwhile replies', adding that this was scarcely surprising, since most work carried out by local authorities dealt with social, rather than economic, matters. Few replies met the criteria set out in the Taoiseach's letter or those spelled out in paragraph 7 of the *Programme for Economic Expansion*. Most submissions were rejected under one of seven headings; several offended under more than one criterion:

1. Social infrastructure such as schools or civic amenities.
2. Projects already in the pipeline, e.g. Dun Laoghaire's tourist development resort programme.
3. The proposals were normal local authority work, e.g. roads.
4. An attempt to revive a project which had already been rejected, e.g. Wexford's harbour development scheme.
5. An attempt 'to throw the umbrella of economic development over non-economic projects', e.g. classifying a town hall as tourist development.
6/7. The projects were minuscule in scale or impracticable, e.g. the development of fishery ports which had no prospect of expansion.

Most suggested schemes would provide employment only 'of that short-term, non-self-sustaining variety characteristic of relief works'. Several councils wished to revive the 1949 Local Authorities (Works) Act; many were keen to develop airfields. Several towns in non-tourist areas argued that constructing swimming pools and playgrounds would attract tourists. Offaly County Council wanted a swimming pool in every sizeable town in the county. Tourism provided the most popular and the most promising opportunities.

Finance rejected all proposals to develop factory sites or advance factories, because it believed that the investment was unlikely to offer any net national advantage. Officials feared that if one local authority was given grants to build advance factories, others would demand similar treatment. The Industrial Development Authority claimed that there was little demand for advance factories.[25]

Local Government used these submissions from local authorities to make the case that investment in water and sanitary services was a prerequisite for economic growth. John Garvin claimed that their economic importance was recognised by the decision to include an estimate for capital expenditure on water and sanitary services in an appendix to the *Programme for Economic Expansion*. He pointed out that an adequate water supply 'is an essential factor in the economy of a town, and the existence or promise of a supply would facilitate the establishment of new industries, if such industries were, in fact seeking suitable locations'. Similar arguments applied to sewerage and drainage.

Some weeks later the cabinet agreed to increase the Exchequer subsidy for water and sanitary schemes to 60 per cent in Gaeltacht areas and 50 per cent in all areas except Dublin city where the grant was set at 40 per cent. The repayment period for loans was extended from 35 to 50 years. However, these concessions should not be seen as indicating that Local Government had gained a key role in the economic development process. The Department was excluded from the group that decided which local authority projects should be given special assistance, though the Departments of Land, Agriculture, and Industry and Commerce were consulted, as well as state agencies such as Bórd Fáilte and the Industrial Development Authority.

Local authorities reacted angrily on learning that most applications for special state funding had been rejected. The resolution passed by Longford County Council in January 1960 'earnestly request[ing] the Government to have included in the programme for economic expansion the widening of rural passways', suggests that the message of *Economic Development* had yet to reach provincial Ireland. Kilkenny Corporation was irked that its elaborate list of proposals — which included an improved water supply, a swimming pool, and the establishment and expansion of industries manufacturing bootlaces, black marble, brewing, woollens, hosiery, boots and shoes, aluminium, sugar beet, bottles and meat and vegetable canning — had all been rejected. The *Sligo Champion* wanted a Programme of Economic Expansion just for Sligo.[26]

443

HOUSING AND CONSTRUCTION: THE EMERGENCE OF NEW ISSUES

The second report of the Capital Investment Advisory Committee relegated public housing programmes to an administrative backwater. When investment in housing revived in the 1960s, the private sector accounted for a much higher share than in the past. There is no evidence to suggest that in the late 1950s Local Government disagreed with the run-down in the public housing programme. When a deputation from the building industry met the Taoiseach early in 1959 to demand additional state aid, Local Government countered that the present rate of house-building was 'more than adequate to meet the probable loss of dwellings'. When one official in the Department tried to justify the case for a new slum-clearance programme by pointing out that the Capital Investment Advisory Committee had exempted subsidies for slum-clearance from its general strictures and much remained to be done about this, he found little support from the secretary, John Garvin, who described the existing pace of slum-clearance in Dublin city as adequate.

By the early 1960s, however, the Department had begun to redefine housing needs in a manner which appeared to foreshadow a new housing programme. The vogue for economic planning resulted in greater pressure on Local Government to provide detailed data on the numbers of people who needed housing. Finance presumably thought that this would lead to a reduction in estimated demand, but it was not the case. Local Government concluded that local authorities had previously estimated housing need solely on the basis of the numbers on waiting lists, irrespective of the merits of each case. Some categories in greatest need, such as the elderly and isolated rural poor, did not feature because they were unwilling to be rehoused since they could not afford the higher rents. Local Government decided that meeting these needs would require special measures, such as higher grants.[27] In March 1960 local authorities were instructed to carry out a new housing survey. When completed in March 1963, it revealed that 60,000 occupied houses were unfit for human habitation; 32,000 of these were incapable of repair, of which 27,000 were in rural areas. Many were occupied by one or two persons. The survey revealed that the belief that housing needs had been met by the late 1950s was wide of the mark. It identified new categories of need: smallholders, old people and workers employed in new industries.

In May 1963 Blaney sent Lemass a lengthy memorandum on future housing policy; it had been drafted following discussions with the

444

Ministers for Industry and Commerce, Finance, Lands, and Health. It argued that priority should be given to

> . . . the eradication of rural slums, a recognition of housing policy for Gaeltacht areas, a recognition of housing as an integral part of a policy of economic expansion and the necessity to accord a special place in that policy to the provision of accommodation for industrial workers, and overall, to establish a rational relationship between State sponsored building programmes and the building industry as a whole.

Blaney requested that the Minister for Local Government be given responsibility for formulating a comprehensive national housing policy and for co-ordinating the housing functions of other departments. It would include determining priorities for expenditure on housing and establishing housing standards. This must be seen as an attempt to wrest control of rural housing from the Department of Lands. Although rural housing remained a contentious topic throughout the 1960s, the problems caused by urban growth proved of greater concern.

The Capital Investment Advisory Committee had recommended that the private sector should provide the majority of new houses and that these should be financed by private institutions, such as building societies. However, once the 1956/57 financial crisis eased, the government came under pressure to increase the funds available for SDAA mortgages. When Neil Blaney submitted a memorandum to cabinet in 1960, proposing to raise the income limit for SDAA mortgages from its 1958 level of £832 a year to £1,040, he pointed out that until 1957 many local authorities had applied no income limits to applicants for SDAA loans, and councils had frequently given preference to people who had 'ample credit-worthiness'. The decision to restrict loans to applicants with an income or farm valuation below a certain level was designed to channel SDAA mortgages to those in greatest need. Blaney was at pains to point out that the proposal to raise the income limit was designed to meet 'a genuine grievance for a comparatively small group of people', who were now ineligible for mortgages because of recent pay increases. It did not mark any change in policy. He added:

> It was never our intention that people such as local officials, teachers, commercial travellers, small businessmen and particularly

those living in areas where building societies and insurance companies do not operate should find themselves barred from housing finance simply because it has been recognised in other aspects of social policy that their incomes have been devalued and compensation which they obtained brought their income above £832 per annum. The proposal is nothing more than to restore the status quo of an arrangement reached in times when much stricter control was necessary.[28]

The maximum permitted income in order to qualify for SDAA mortgages was eventually raised in June 1961.

Councils were also coming under pressure to provide houses for the increasing number of newly married couples and for key workers employed in new industries. In 1959 Local Government urged the Taoiseach not to meet a deputation from Kilkenny Corporation, which wished to discuss housing for young couples, alleging that the Corporation wished to provide housing subsidies for persons who should be expected to provide their own houses.[29] In September 1961, on the eve of the general election, Paudge Brennan, Fianna Fáil TD for Wicklow, presented Lemass with a memorial from young married couples in Arklow protesting at the lack of council houses. Lemass informed Brennan that the financial restrictions on local authority housing programmes had been removed; the Minister for Local Government was urging councils to build more houses as rapidly as possible.[30]

Such representations indicated that the demographic tide was turning. Emigration was falling; marriages were on the increase, demand for housing was rising. In a speech delivered to the Master Builders' Association in November 1962, Blaney noted that current demand for housing had equalled its peak post-war level.[31] By 1962/63 Dublin Corporation's housing list contained the names of over 4,000 families that were in urgent need of rehousing; many others had yet to be assessed. In 1959/60 1,605 Corporation houses were vacated; by 1961/62 the number of houses vacated was half that figure, and families that had surrendered houses in the 1950s in order to emigrate to England were returning and seeking accommodation.

In October 1962 Lemass informed Blaney of his fears of a severe housing shortage, particularly in Dublin. He cited letters from building craftsmen who had returned to Ireland and had found it difficult to obtain a house. Lemass was concerned that this would lead to a shortage of building craftsmen, which would push up skilled wages, and he asked Blaney whether or not it was necessary to reconsider the 'present inducements to expand production' of houses. He added, 'I think it is probable that the housing shortage may soon become the subject of public controversy, but it is in any case necessary for us to satisfy ourselves that everything possible is being done.'[32] Blaney replied that it would be difficult to increase the rate of construction of Corporation houses because of a lack of tenders. The building industry was booming and costs were rising. He had considered asking Dublin Corporation to slow down its building programme because of the threat of inflation. Although he now believed that this was unnecessary, because inflation was subsiding, he was convinced that Dublin Corporation's slum-clearance programme did not require 'any artificial acceleration', although he realised that changing trends in Irish population (more marriages and higher rates of immigration) had led to longer housing lists.[33]

Blaney's apparent complacency about the pace of Dublin Corporation's slum-clearance programme appears ironic in retrospect. Over a ten-day period in June 1963 three tenement houses collapsed in Dublin's Bolton Street and Fenian Street, killing four persons. The dangerous buildings section of Dublin Corporation reacted by issuing notices for the evacuation of 367 buildings housing 1,189 families, forcing Dublin Corporation to allocate all vacant houses to displaced families.[34] Local Government approved the purchase of 100 chalet caravans as an emergency measure. Families on the regular housing list could not now be housed. In September 1963 *The Irish Press* reported that many families returning from England could not obtain Corporation houses. Declan Costello TD, then a rising star in Fine Gael, proposed a motion in Dáil Éireann calling for the establishment of a select committee to investigate the causes of the current housing shortage and to evaluate future housing needs.[35] The motion was defeated, but Local Government conducted an inquiry into Dublin Corporation's administration of the law relating to unfit dwellings and dangerous structures, and their recommendations were incorporated in the 1964 government White Paper on housing.

THE NATIONAL BUILDING AGENCY

In June 1960 Noel Griffin, managing director of the thriving Waterford

Glass Company, wrote to the Minister for Local Government pointing out that Waterford Corporation would be unable to provide houses for the estimated 150 young male Waterford Glass employees who could be expected to marry within the next five years. Griffin pointed out that the 'present industrial drive' aimed to create 'more and better employment'. If it proved effective, more houses would be needed.[36]

In December 1960 the state-owned National Building Agency was established to provide houses for key workers. The idea originated during the course of a discussion between Lemass and the Ministers for Finance, Local Government, Industry and Commerce, and Transport and Power on how best to provide housing for workers employed at Shannon airport and the adjoining industrial estate. Although houses were ultimately provided by the Shannon Free Airport Development Company, the idea of a special housing agency was born. On 14 July 1960 Neil Blaney presented a proposal to cabinet which referred to the numerous requests to Local Government to provide houses for key industrial workers. Houses had been provided in Youghal in 1951 and in Carrick-on-Shannon in 1954, on condition that the requesting industry guaranteed to pay an economic rent. In the first half of 1960, Local Government had already been requested to provide houses for industrial workers in Cobh, Callan, Mallow, Galway and Donegal. The Department preferred to encourage the companies concerned to set up public utility societies which could avail of grants and SDAA loans: both the Irish Glass Bottle Company and the Irish Sugar Company had adopted this approach. Other companies preferred to provide rented accommodation for key workers. Councils were generally unable to supply rented houses in these cases because they had a statutory obligation to give priority to slum clearance and to relieving overcrowding. When these needs had been met, they were required by law to favour residents of their area who could not reasonably be expected to provide their own housing. Workers recruited from other parts of Ireland or from Germany were unlikely to meet these criteria. Councils were also reluctant to be saddled with houses which might be vacated if the firm for which they were constructed subsequently failed.

Blaney suggested that the government establish a registered company which would be funded by means of government financial guarantees under the State Guarantees Act of 1954. In addition to housing key industrial workers, he suggested that the agency provide housing for state employees such as gardaí; this had been a controversial matter for many years. The Minister also envisaged it providing water and waste disposal services for new industries if local authorities were unable to do so. The agency would arrange that An Foras Tionscal, the agency responsible for allocating grants for industrial development, or the factory owner would guarantee the rents of these houses. (At this stage the Industrial Development Authority was involved in industrial promotion. Both agencies merged in 1969.) If an industrial company acted as guarantor, it would collect the rents and own the houses when repayments had been met.

The Department of Finance accepted Blaney's proposal on the understanding that there would be no charge on public funds other than the normal grants available for private houses, and that the agency would provide houses only where they were clearly needed and unlikely to be provided by any other means. Cabinet approved the proposal on 22 July 1960.[37] The proposal to finance the agency under the State Guarantees Act was subsequently abandoned in favour of an advance of up to £100,000 for capital expenditure from the Industrial Credit Company. Current expenses were met by temporary overdraft.[38]

Although Blaney and Lemass both believed that there was need for an agency such as the NBA, industrialists appear to have been reluctant to become involved in providing houses for their workers. In the autumn of 1961 Lemass contacted Blaney about a German firm, Steinbock, whose factory he had recently opened in Galway. Four houses were needed for key German technicians, but Galway Corporation could provide only one. Blaney reported that the firm had not followed up on its preliminary contacts with the NBA. This, he claimed, was a common experience: many firms were prepared to provide houses for managers or executives, but expected the state or the local authority to house their workers 'without obligation on the part of the industries individually or collectively'. This, Blaney argued, 'sets in focus a problem with which the Agency is not dealing and indeed with which it is not equipped either financially or administratively to deal; the provision of local rented houses aimed purely at serving particular industries or groups of industries'. Blaney believed that providing cheap housing

> . . . was such an integral part of a programme for economic development, as is the experience elsewhere, that we may not be doing justice to the possibility of accelerating that programme by

relying too much on the present housing framework. It may be that we should undertake a less limited housing 'risk' in association with the establishment of new industries, if this can be achieved in consistency with the present overall housing programme, I think that in approaching the next phase of the economic development programme, particular advertence to this point would be reasonable.

This may be read as an attempt to boost the role in industrial development of the Department of Local Government. Lemass replied that 'if present arrangements do not serve the purpose of accelerating industrial progress, to the extent that we intended, we must look at them again.' Tadhg Ó Cearbhaill, assistant secretary of the Department of the Taoiseach, sent a summary of this exchange to Charlie Murray, assistant secretary of the Department of Finance.[39]

Blaney returned to this question in December 1962, in the course of a letter to Jack Lynch, Minister for Industry and Commerce. He expressed the belief that it was essential that the economy should be in a position to meet a growing demand 'at any centre' for reasonably low rental housing, and asked if factories should be encouraged to locate in places which had sufficient houses. One proposed investment which was lying dormant pending the resolution of Ireland's application for membership of the European Economic Community would, he claimed, require 1,000 houses — equivalent to building a new town. The cost of housing would outweigh the cost of the actual plant. Blaney argued that 'if there were a more clear policy on the location of industry, the housing issues would also be more clear. At least we would avoid the situation of urgent demand for housing chasing a decision on the location of a substantial industry.' The Minister argued that industrialists should not be awarded state grants without Local Government first being consulted to check on the availability of housing in the area. He also suggested that it would be preferable to subsidise transport costs for commuters and encourage the growth of existing communities, as opposed to the 'sudden creation of an artificial neighbourhood'.[40]

Although Blaney had envisaged the NBA playing a key role in meeting such housing needs, the agency's activities were seriously handicapped in its early years. A dispute between Finance and Local Government over whether or not the former should be required to approve the names of directors before their appointment by the

Minister for Local Government (this procedure applied to Shannon Free Airport Development Company, where the appointing department was Transport and Power),[41] delayed the constitution of a board and staff appointments.

When Lemass requested a progress report in February 1962, Blaney submitted a catalogue of woes: proposals submitted to Finance concerning appointments remained unanswered seven months later, forcing the agency to survive with one full-time administrative officer and the unofficial services of an architect. Agreement had not been reached on directors' fees and the agency was still operating from one room in the Custom House. He concluded that the 'policy of restraint by Finance on the whole subject of the Agency does not show a sense of proportion'. The Minister informed Lemass that the directors 'had personally found it possible by bluffing out the financial aspect to organise the initiation of several housing projects'. By March 1962, 36 houses had been completed or were under construction; construction of a further 62 had been approved, and other projects were under discussion. Many involved only one house.

The largest scheme approved by this date was the construction of 20 houses for the Verolme Dockyard in Cork. Lemass instructed Tadhg Ó Cearbhaill to read Blaney's letter 'with a view to getting all causes of delay eliminated'; he emphasised his 'strong desire to see the Agency in full operation as soon as possible'. Nevertheless, the NBA's role remained marginal. In October 1962 Blaney informed Lemass that the practice of charging an industrialist 6.75 per cent interest on the annual outgoings of the houses made the cost of NBA houses prohibitive for ordinary workers and caused many inquiries from industrialists to lapse 'unless he has no alternative to utilisation of the Agency's services because of the urgency of housing for higher-paid executive and key-personnel.' At the same time Finance was delaying plans to use the NBA to provide housing for gardaí, civil servants and staff of state agencies. Finance eventually gave the go-ahead for the NBA to construct garda housing in small provincial towns, and in Templemore, Co. Tipperary to house staff transferred to the new Garda Training Centre, but it objected to the NBA building houses for gardaí or transferred civil servants in larger towns such as Galway. Blaney protested to Lemass that he was 'perfectly clear that while it had never been intended that the Agency should build houses for civil servants permanently stationed in Dublin or Cork, it was the Government's intention that the Agency could be called on to handle the provision of housing in association with any decision of the Government on decentralisation of services.' Lemass discussed these problems with Dr James Ryan (Minister for Finance) and informed Blaney that he had found him 'sympathetic to the need to modify the Agency's terms of reference'. Moves were also afoot to fund the NBA by direct Exchequer borrowing because existing arrangements had proved unsatisfactory.[42] The 1963 National Building Agency Bill enabled the agency to obtain up to £2m. in capital, mostly in the form of interest-bearing advances from the Central Fund, though it was hoped to raise capital on the security of house mortgages.[43]

HOUSING: PROGRESS AND PROSPECTS

The collapse of the three Dublin tenements and the closure of many more during the summer of 1963 made it imperative to increase the number of local authority houses provided within the city. During the autumn of 1963 Local Government held discussions with Dublin Corporation with a view to using new construction methods in order to increase the number of houses built, with the 'least impact on the existing structure of the building industry'. These talks led to the purchase of a 250-acre site at Ballymun, on the northern outskirts of the city, where 3,000, mostly high-rise, dwellings would be constructed under NBA supervision. The Ballymun scheme, with its emphasis on modern design and construction methods and the involvement of a government agency, reflects official thinking on housing at this time. Similar ideas are reflected in the 1964 White Paper and in legislative proposals.

In December 1963 Blaney presented cabinet with proposals for new housing legislation, which would rationalise more than fifty separate Acts and reduce the multiplicity of subsidies paid on local authority housing. This would involve consolidating the three separate legislative codes dealing with local authority housing: the Labourers' Acts (1883-1958), Housing of the Working Classes Acts (1890-1958) and the Housing (Financial and Miscellaneous Provisions) Acts (1931-58), the revision of codes setting out who should be given priority in allocating local authority housing to enable housing authorities to bear local circumstances in mind; more flexible subsidies which could be altered to take account of changing conditions and to include special subventions for groups such as old-age pensioners, the opening of housing improvement incentives to local authorities and more stringent measures to deal with dangerous buildings.[44] Because of the wide-ranging changes involved, Local Government proposed to issue a White Paper, summarising progress since 1948 and highlighting future policy.

Housing — Progress and Prospects, which was laid before the Oireachtas in November 1964, marks the formal end of the belief that housing demand had been met. The White Paper noted that population growth, a high marriage rate, the shift from agriculture to industrial and service employment, and higher living standards all meant increased demand for housing. It set an annual target of 12-13,000 houses, almost double the 1963/64 figure of 7,500 dwellings, though it emphasised that the target should be taken 'as an indication of the order of magnitude of a desirable objective, subject to a fairly wide range of variation'. There was no discussion of the relative contributions of the public and private sectors, though a subsequent estimate suggested 5,000 local authority houses and 9,000 new private dwellings. Despite the cost of rates remission and subsidies, private sector housing was less expensive for the Exchequer than local authority housing, though it is probable that some families could have provided housing without state assistance. In his 1961 estimates speech, the minister had pointed out that it was in the interests of local authorities to help individuals to build their own houses and he appealed to the small number of councils which did not provide supplementary housing grants to reconsider their attitude.[45]

The scope of the changes is best captured in a speech which Blaney made to the annual general meeting of the NBA in October 1963. The central principle in the new policy was a desire to ensure that eligibility for local authority housing was determined primarily by need: this would involve regarding small farmers, widows, the elderly and other special categories as eligible for rehousing. References to the needs of the old and the disabled suggested that efforts were being made to spread the benefits of economic growth more widely. The traditional emphasis by local authorities on relieving unfit housing conditions would be replaced by a more comprehensive outlook, which would take account of all housing needs, whether met by the public or by the private sector. Councils should consider providing serviced sites for private housing. At the same time he envisaged an end to the tradition whereby each local authority was 'either forced by law or encouraged by custom to regard its administrative district as one of a number of independent islands'. County councils should be in a position to provide houses for small urban district councils; adjoining local authorities should rehouse each other's residents. Future subsidies for local authority housing would be used to influence the types of housing and to achieve greater flexibility in rents, with local authorities offered predetermined subsidies over a fixed period which would not be reduced if they raised rents.[46]

THE DEPARTMENT AND THE BUILDING INDUSTRY

The housing targets contained in the 1964 White Paper threatened to strain the resources of a building industry which was already coping with major factory and office development. The White Paper placed considerable faith in the ability to achieve higher productivity by using new construction techniques and by relying on specialist organisations such as the National Building Agency, An Foras Forbartha, the Institute for Industrial Research and Standards, and the National Building Advisory Council. It also suggested that the NBA might assume responsibility for public housing schemes in smaller local authorities. Special subsidies were promised for high-rise buildings and for buildings requiring 'abnormal expenditure because of location, siting or form of construction'.

The question of adopting a comprehensive plan for the building and construction sectors had last surfaced at the end of the Emergency. Then Local Government had showed little interest in the idea, and control passed to Industry and Commerce. The debate over future planning for the building industry began in January 1961 as a result of overtures to Seán Lemass from Don McGreevy of the Irish Building Centre, a body which represented the industry's interests. McGreevy was interested in setting up a committee to survey the Irish building industry in order to determine future demand, with the aim of ensuring that construction would be planned to avoid extremes of boom and slump. Local Government objected to the proposed survey; it claimed that the industry could be regulated only by issuing building licences. Officials also suspected that the letter was linked to the Centre's request for a grant of £33,000 to carry out the survey which was then being considered by an interdepartmental committee. Lemass dismissed these reservations, which were shared by Finance, as 'both misinformed and short-sighted'. He believed that the survey could bring about 'a new outlook in the building industry trade unions and a much more liberal approach to apprenticeships'. It would also, in his opinion, 'give reassurance that the present level of employment is likely to persist'.

From the 1920s, Irish politicians and civil servants had regularly expressed their belief that unions in the building industry were about to abandon restrictive working practices, only to have their hopes dashed. Although Blaney also accepted the need for a more comprehensive approach towards planning the building industry, he believed that this should be given 'independent government attention', as opposed to being carried out by an industry lobby-group. In January 1962 Tadhg Ó Cearbhaill noted that

> . . . from the point of view of Departmental interest, the building industry appears to be in a no-man's-land between Industry and Commerce and Local Government. Its problems are not generally taken up by Industry and Commerce as, say, those of the cotton industry are; on the other hand, Local Government take the line that their responsibilities do not extend beyond the administration of the Housing and certain other Acts, and that they cannot be expected to seek solutions to any general problems affecting the industry.[47]

The Building Centre survey duly went ahead. In November 1962 Lemass wrote to Blaney about the problems resulting from lack of water and sewerage services at industrial sites on the outskirts of Dublin and uncertainty as to when they would be provided. He suggested that Dublin Corporation should be in a position to announce a development programme which would include providing these services. On 1 January 1963 Lemass drafted a letter to Blaney in reaction to a speech by a leading Dublin builder, Mr Crampton, in which the Taoiseach urged the establishment of a building committee. Lemass suggested that, although Local Government was primarily concerned with housing, consideration might be given to assigning responsibility for the industry *as a whole* (emphasis in original) to a particular minister, who would call on the services of officers outside his own Department as required and possibly on the services of officers designated to liaise with the industry. Lemass emphasised that he had not developed any clear ideas as to the appropriate structures; the purpose of his letter was 'to invite your reaction to introducing some arrangements of this kind'. If Blaney's reaction was favourable, the Taoiseach would pursue the matter.

This letter does not appear to have been sent, because, as an accompanying memorandum noted, it emerged that the parliamentary secretary to the Minister for Finance, Donogh O'Malley, who was responsible for the Office of Public Works, was preparing a report on the building industry for the Minister for Finance. In the circumstances it was deemed inappropriate to write to the Minister for Local Government.

O'Malley's initiative followed a meeting at the Building Centre, which he had attended at the behest of Finance Minister James Ryan. Ryan was concerned that the building boom was putting considerable pressure on the rate of inflation and on the public capital programme, leading Finance to consider the possibility of 'throwing in' or 'holding back' certain government projects in order to flatten the business cycle. O'Malley discovered that the Building Centre had made little progress with its survey, owing to lack of resources and lack of access to official data. He recommended establishing a council representing builders, trade unions, architects and engineers, plus the Departments of Industry and Commerce, Local Government, Finance, and the Office of Public Works, to carry out a survey of current and projected building work for the coming five years and assess if there were sufficient resources for this work. The committee would also examine means of improving productivity.

O'Malley circulated a brief draft on these lines to all prospective members and received a range of supportive replies, the longest from the Minister for Local Government. Blaney mentioned that he had already written to the Taoiseach several months previously, expressing the need for some co-ordination 'on the lines you mention'; he had also asked the Minister for Industry and Commerce 'to consider taking a more positive line of policy in regard to the industrial side of the building industry'. However, Blaney believed that Finance was primarily interested in freezing public expenditure on housing in order to channel resources to the commercial building sector. He objected:

I cannot accept this if it means that within the total investment in building, the level of private investment is allowed of its own volition to reach its fullest potential at the expense of the Government's programme of social building, principally local authority housing operations.

O'Malley had spoken of the need to have government projects ready to 'throw in', in the event of a building slump. Blaney pointed out that many local authorities were unable to hire building contractors because the industry was already fully employed.

To say that all previous slumps were caused mainly by the fact that the Government of the day ran out of finance is the key-stone of the line of pressure always exerted on this Department, that expenditure on local government services must be curtailed, that we are spending too much, etc., etc. I do not want to argue the point here beyond saying that social policy on housing should not again be subordinated entirely to the economic theories of current government capital investment.

Blaney objected to Finance's proposal to control housing investment by limiting capital, and suggested that building licences would be a better option. He also noted that the recent decision of the British government to intervene in the building industry via the Ministry of Public Works might constitute a model for Ireland.[48]

Lemass welcomed O'Malley's proposals and suggested that, although Industry and Commerce appeared the most appropriate Department to supervise this committee, 'there may be a stronger case now than previously for considering the elevation of the Office of Public Works to a fully-fledged Department'. Although James Ryan was initially cool on this idea, Finance subsequently submitted a memorandum to government, recommending that a building advisory council be established under the control of the OPW.

Local Government reiterated that 'the fundamental objective of the proposals of the Minister for Finance' was to secure a reduction in capital expenditure for housing. The Department argued that the aspects of the building industry most in need of review were not those concerning Government finance or capital expenditure, but 'technical and organisational aspects such as the desirability of encouraging mechanisation, the adoption of new techniques and materials, site organisation, research on standardisation of components, increased productivity, methods of tendering and contract, the closer association of engineering and architectural roles in building etc.' No Department exercised responsibility for these questions; if the government decided to establish an advisory council, Local Government believed that it would be more appropriately controlled by a Department which was closely associated with the building industry: Local Government.

Either as a result of this memorandum or for other reasons, the government shied away from making the OPW responsible for the proposed council. Control passed to Industry and Commerce, almost by default, despite the fact that Jack Lynch, Minister for Industry and Commerce, had shown little interest in the matter. Incongruously, the cabinet decided that the council should be chaired by Donogh O'Malley, rather than by an assistant secretary in Industry and Commerce. This could be read as a rebuff to Blaney. On 25 March 1963, the date before the cabinet was due to determine who should control the council, Blaney addressed a personal letter to Lemass, which was a thinly disguised plea that responsibility be given to Local Government. He emphasised that Local Government was more closely associated with all major aspects of the construction industry — housing, roads, water, sewerage, fire protection and physical planning — than any other department and that the Local Government (Planning and Development) Bill, which was going through the Dáil, recognised the Department's planning role.[49]

The government appears to have hoped that the building advisory council would help to contain costs and increase productivity. Costs had risen sharply as a result of wage increases and the introduction of a five-day week. Dublin Corporation's housing programme was threatened by a shortage of craftsmen and the overheated state of the industry, which meant that some contracts attracted no tenders. Matters came to a head when building craftsmen went on strike in 1964. However there is no evidence that the building advisory council did anything to resolve these problems.

ECONOMIC GROWTH AND PHYSICAL PLANNING

When Local Government failed to win control of the building advisory council, it sought another means of asserting its authority. Physical planning had aroused little interest during the 1950s. Perhaps it seemed irrelevant in a country preoccupied with economic and demographic decline. Myles na Gopaleen remarked that 'the whole country lacks the population that would sustain even the fraction of "planning" that is proper to the temperament and economy of this country. . . . The problem to be addressed here is simply that of the falling birth-rate.'[50] Local Government's annual report for 1957/58 noted that only one planning authority, Dublin County Borough, had submitted a planning scheme, while twelve urban districts and seven county health districts had yet to introduce planning controls. The planning section in the Department's annual reports recorded a selection of appeals to the minister which were regarded as of interest to local authorities. Most concerned minor developments such as petrol stations, flat conversions and the use of premises for industrial purposes. From 1959 the number of appeals increased rapidly — 190 in 1958/59; 314 in 1959/60; 359 for 1960/61 — perhaps reflecting economic recovery, and a backlog emerged in the appeals process. In 1956 the population of many Irish towns was below the figure for 1851 and, with the exception of ribbon-development on approach roads, their built-up area had scarcely expanded in the previous hundred years. During the early 1960s many of these towns began to grow rapidly, placing additional pressure on the planning process.

With the decline of the protectionist mentality and a new interest in encouraging foreign investment, the government welcomed urban construction projects funded by British financial interests. When T.K. Whitaker, secretary of the Department of Finance, met representatives of the Norwich Union Life Assurance Company in 1960 to discuss the possibility of that firm investing in urban property, he mentioned that there was a considerable shortage of office accommodation in Dublin. In a written follow-up to the meeting, the company emphasised that it was 'always interested in investing in good existing commercial properties or in acquiring suitable sites for building properties for letting'. Most of their developments consisted of shops and offices in central locations 'where we may be sure of a continuing demand for accommodation'. The Norwich Union emphasised that all developments were constructed for investment purposes, not for resale: buildings would be of modern design and would meet the highest standards.

Whitaker had apparently invited Norwich Union to make

suggestions on how to encourage investment in urban property. The company argued that the legal protection afforded to tenants who occupied premises for three years, under the 1946 Rent Restrictions Acts and the 1931 Landlord and Tenant Act, acted as a major disincentive for developers: 'So long as this type of legislation existed, the redevelopment of the central areas . . . cannot be expected to progress in a manner comparable with that of other capital cities in the world today.' The company claimed that there was an urgent need for legislation which would give a landlord 'reasonable rights to regain possession of property he wishes to rebuild'. Existing 'protection of the tenant by legislation so biased in his favour' would 'prevent the process of urban replacement so necessary to every virile community' and accounted for the shortage of office accommodation in Dublin.[51]

A reform of planning legislation was therefore associated with the need to facilitate large-scale urban developments. In 1962 Lemass sought Blaney's views on 'an imaginative proposal' by Lang Development to redevelop part of central Dublin. Blaney was enthusiastic, but pointed out that it would first be necessary to enact a 'Bill to facilitate urban redevelopment' which would assist the process of adapting city and town centres to the motor age. Blaney believed that comprehensive urban redevelopment suffered from the fact that city-centres contained large numbers of small property-owners. The proposed legislation would enable local authorities to acquire all property in development areas; they could either redevelop the site or sell or lease it to a developer. Blaney favoured collaboration between developers and local authorities.[52] In an effort to resolve these questions, the government had hired Charles Abrams, a planning consultant, who was funded by the United Nations to advise on urban renewal, notably

> . . . the feasibility of redeveloping cleared central areas with a view to making the process more economic and to reduce the burden on public funds such as by a mixed development of residential, commercial and industrial enterprises. This would involve examination of the possibilities of attracting such enterprises to these areas and so designing redevelopment projects as to bring about an economic and balanced use of the available land.

The government sought advice on designating areas within a city for such uses as offices, housing and light industry; the type of investment necessary to attract business; a financial plan for the proposed redevelopment; and the procedures necessary to ensure co-ordination of public and private interests and uses.[53] Abrams went far beyond his original brief and included a review of existing planning legislation. He argued that there was a need for city and regional planning and for comprehensive new planning and development legislation to facilitate economic development. According to Michael Bannon, the 1963 Local Government (Planning and Development) Act, which adopted most of Abrams's recommendations, was a direct outcome of his report,[54] though files concerning the abortive 1961 Planning and Development Bill bring this assertion into question.

The government first considered outline proposals for planning legislation at a meeting on 6 December 1960 when Blaney was given leave to introduce the Local Government (Planning and Development) Bill in Dáil Éireann. Although the Bill was introduced the following day, no text was circulated and it is uncertain whether any then existed. Blaney appears to have regarded it as a matter of some urgency and, to reduce possible delays and on the Taoiseach's instructions, 'instead of discussing your [Blaney's] proposals in detail in the normal way', ministers were encouraged to put their comments in writing.[55] On 24 May 1961 Blaney told Lemass that he had received 'disconcerting' information from the Attorney General that drafting the Bill would take a minimum of three months.

The proposed legislation was designed to give local authorities wider powers to acquire land for development purposes. The 'rigid regulatory planning schemes required by the Act of 1934' would be eliminated; compensation rights would be directly related to any controls or restrictions imposed on property-owners, and the Bill's provisions would operate throughout the country. All developments would require planning permission, including building, demolition, material changes in land or building usage, preservation of green belts, car parking spaces or external elevations, advertising hoardings or dumping waste. In contrast to the 1934 Act, there would be no provision for betterment; Local Government argued that this was impossible to assess and collect, though developers would be required to make contributions in respect of benefits derived from the provision of public services. Although land was to be subject to functional zoning, i.e. residential, agricultural or commercial, the memorandum accompanying the initial draft of the Bill circulated in May 1961 agreed that 'industrialists should have as wide a choice of sites as possible'. Changes in land use for agricultural purposes and most farm buildings would be exempt from planning requirements. Decisions of planning authorities could be appealed.

Appeals against local authority decisions would be made to the Minister; other, unspecified, categories of appeal would be made to a planning appeals officer. Legislation would also provide for measures to preserve and control natural amenities and historic buildings, and all local authorities would be required to prepare 'development objective plans', in the form of a written statement accompanied by maps, which would be updated on a regular basis. Plans would not require ministerial approval, though the Minister would retain powers to co-ordinate individual plans in the interests of regional development. Local authorities would be empowered to acquire land either by agreement or compulsorily. They would also have power to sell or lease land to facilitate redevelopment and to provide or manage factory sites, factory buildings or caravan parks.[56]

It soon became apparent that many aspects of the Bill did not meet the approval of other ministers or departments. The Department of the Taoiseach claimed that provisions for compensation were unduly restrictive and might prove to be unconstitutional. Finance feared that the proposed legislation would cost the Exchequer substantial sums in compensation. Industry and Commerce sought to minimise the planning restrictions imposed on industrialists, both respecting location and contributions towards roads and other services.

The most heated opposition concerned the proposal to make state land and properties subject to planning regulations. The Bill was intended to apply to garda stations, post offices and other government offices, though prisons, airports and all military structures were exempt. Finance wished to retain provisions in the 1934 Act which merely provided for consultation between the state's technical officers and local authority planning officers. The Department of Lands objected to the fact that it would have to seek planning permission for houses constructed as part of land resettlement schemes and that forestry and afforestation came within the term 'development'. They argued that the application of controls by local authorities to state lands and property was contrary to legal precedent. Pleading for the exemption of forestry development, the department pointed out that this was the practice under legislation in Britain, a country where 'the question of amenities is much more thorny . . . due to their vast industrial development than it is here'. The Minister for Lands, Michael Moran, condemned the bill as 'planning gone mad'; he argued that an insistence that land commission housing require planning permission would 'provide a forum and platform for the local politicians to stop migrants coming in'.

Local Government countered that restrictions would not apply to private rural dwellings or Land Commission housing and that the provision for an appeal to the Minister would remove the dangers of vexatious local objections. Blaney discussed the matter with planning experts and then informed Moran that the controls envisaged over afforestation would apply only to roads, gates, fences and buildings on forest land. However, this failed to placate the Department of Lands. On 26 May 1961, in a decision which was to assume major significance during the 1990s in the context of the controversy over interpretative centres in the Burren, the Boyne Valley, and the Wicklow mountains, the cabinet authorised the drafting of a planning bill, on the understanding that it would not apply to state afforestation, including forest roads, fence-making in forests and the erection or reconstruction of forestry buildings; nor would it apply to telegraph poles — another bone of contention. It also instructed the Minister for Local Government to consult the Attorney General in order to ensure that none of the proposed provisions were unconstitutional. A further amendment provided that, although state buildings would not be required to obtain planning permission, the body concerned should consult the relevant local authority 'to such extent as the Minister for Local Government may determine'; if this did not resolve objections raised by the local authority, the minister or state body concerned should consult the Minister for Local Government.[57]

The objections which the Minister for Social Welfare, Kevin Boland, raised were unrelated to his ministerial office. They concerned the balance of interest between private property-owners and the community. Boland invariably favoured the former. In a letter to Blaney, dated 8 June 1961, he pointed out that, while he accepted the need to impose controls on land development in order to protect individual and community interests, such controls should always bear in mind the fundamental rights of private property. The result of the proposed Bill would be 'to effectively take all initiative out of the hands of owners and transfer completely to the Planning Authority all decisions as to the use to which any property whatever may be put'. According to Boland, 'the assumption appears to be that Local Authorities can do no wrong and that all that is necessary is to give them adequate powers and everything will be satisfactory.'

He cited cases where planning authorities had exercised their powers 'in an unreasonably rigid and autocratic manner without due regard to the inherent rights of the individual' and argued that there was a need 'to provide ratepayers with protection from the consequences of neglect or mistakes on the part of the Local Authority'. He expressed concern at the 'scandal' of unfinished housing estates which were not taken in charge by local authorities and at the fact that local authorities could compel the removal of unauthorised structures, even if they had stood for many years. This gave the local authority 'power to put a man overnight out of a business he has been operating legitimately for maybe 27 years without compensation'. Boland also believed that the Bill gave local authorities 'unnecessarily wide powers' to acquire land compulsorily; this potentially could give them a monopoly in the development of land for housing and industry. He also queried the limits set on the payment of compensation, though Local Government claimed that these were more extensive than those provided in the British planning code. Although he accepted that planning controls could not be operated if local authorities were forced to pay out large sums in compensation in respect of planning decisions, he argued that this

> . . . hardly justifies settling the compensation question in a manner satisfactory to the Local Authority only. It appears to me that if independent arbitrators are likely to award large sums of money in respect of planning decisions, it is not justifiable to legislate merely for the sake of avoiding the payment of this money but that it would be better to make the planning decisions more flexible.[58]

Seán MacEntee, Minister for Health, argued that there was need to establish an independent appeals procedure:

> When I was Minister for Local Government I found it was quite impossible for me to deal expeditiously with many appeals which came before me under the Town Planning Acts. In regard to many I found that I had to withstand pressure from various interests

affected and, in addition, necessary in the interests of justice to give each appeal my close personal consideration.

MacEntee claimed to have intended introducing legislation that would provide for planning appeals to be handled by a member of the judiciary, and suggested that Blaney give the idea 'serious consideration'. Although MacEntee sent a copy of this letter to Lemass, there is no evidence that it was given serious consideration, nor are Blaney's reactions on record. However the 1963 Planning Act was subsequently repeatedly criticised for its failure to make provision for an independent appeals procedure. In 1967 opposition parties attempted to promote a Bill providing for an independent Planning Appeals Board, and clauses providing for an appeals system were included in the Local Government (Planning and Development) (no. 2) Bill which lapsed when the Dáil was dissolved in 1973. An Bord Pleanála (The Planning Board) was eventually established under the 1976 Local Government (Planning and Development) Act, which was introduced by James Tully, Minister for Local Government in the coalition government of 1973-77.[59]

The range of objections from government departments and the views expressed by Boland give some insight into the controversial nature of the proposed planning legislation. This Bill lapsed when the Dáil was dissolved on 1 September 1961, and the new Fianna Fáil government appears to given the matter a lower priority. The Local Government (Planning and Development Bill) 1962 was introduced to the Dáil on 12 July 1962, beginning a leisurely process which ended in its becoming law in August 1963. It came into operation on 1 October 1964.

When he introduced the second reading of the 1962 Planning and Development Bill in the Dáil, Blaney spoke of efficiency, the quality of life and economic growth. Planning would make Irish towns, villages and the countryside 'better places in which to live and work', avoiding the waste of resources and 'help[ing] to foster economic development, especially in locations which offer prospects of becoming centres of commercial or industrial growth'.[60] In the optimistic growth-orientated atmosphere of the 1960s, a better environment and economic prosperity were seen as synonymous. By closely resembling the 1962 Town and Country Planning Act of England and Wales, the legislation continued the time-honoured practice of Irish planning legislation. A total of 87 planning authorities were established: 27 county councils, 4 county borough corporations, 7 borough corporations and 49 urban district councils. Each was required to draw up a development plan dealing with land zoning, traffic, urban renewal and the preservation of amenities. In rural areas plans would include provisions for improved sanitary services, though most agricultural activities were exempt from planning procedures. A planning authority could develop 'obsolete' areas — a measure which was designed to facilitate urban reconstruction, as envisaged by the Abrams report.

Bannon notes that, in contrast with the apathy shown towards the 1933 Planning Bill, the 1963 legislation aroused considerable interest. The Bill's languid passage through the Dáil gave the Department time to prepare local authorities for their new duties.[61] Establishing 87 planning authorities, each required to draft a development plan, put considerable strain on the limited planning skills then available in Ireland, and during 1962 a course of lectures by British town planning experts was organised at the Custom House for local authority staff who had responsibility for planning. Blaney was confident that those who attended 'have been sold the idea of the need for planning and redevelopment'. Dublin was seen as the key to success; in 1963 Blaney informed Lemass that he had been assured of the 'sympathetic co-operation' of the Dublin city manager who had already obtained the approval of the town planning committee to appoint a consultant on urban redevelopment. A two-year postgraduate town planning course was introduced by Bolton Street College of Technology to meet the needs of engineers and architects employed by local authorities. Plans were afoot to create additional posts for planning inspectors in the Department.

Additional help was forthcoming from another quarter. In the spring of 1963, possibly in response to the impending planning legislation, Padraig Ó hUiginn, an official of the Department of Local Government on secondment to the United Nations (he was subsequently to become secretary to the Department of the Taoiseach), wrote to Blaney suggesting that the United Nations Technical Assistance Programme might aid the establishment of a national physical planning institute. Ó hUiginn explained that, although Ireland's case for assistance was weakened by its relatively high national per capita income, the UN accepted that some developed countries such as Ireland and Iceland lacked certain types of technical expertise. The

Irish case for UN assistance was enhanced by the fact that the country was carrying out a major investment programme; the high quality of public administration was another argument in Ireland's favour.

Ó hUiginn envisaged that the proposed institute would train architects and engineers in physical planning techniques and would prepare physical development plans for local authorities which were unable or unwilling to carry out this task. The institute would also undertake basic research at national and regional levels on issues such as future trends in population settlement and land use. He remarked on the references in the Abrams report, which had been funded by the UN, to the need for research into physical planning, building materials and construction costs. The Irish government would provide premises, personnel and study fellowships for local authority officials, with the UN providing five or six experts, plus books and technical equipment, for up to five years. Ó hUiginn believed that assistance would be similar to the support which the Ford Foundation had provided in establishing the Economic Research Institute.

These proposals were very much in keeping with arguments put forward by the Department of Local Government in the debate over the proposed Council for the Building Industry. The Department saw considerable scope for reducing costs by using new materials and construction methods. The institute would facilitate the implementation of planning legislation; it was also in keeping with the modernising thrust of these years. Blaney's letter to Lemass, summarising the details of Ó hUiginn's proposal, referred to the Planning and Development Bill and the need to draw up construction standards for high-rise buildings. On 4 April 1963, following a meeting between Lemass, Ryan and Blaney, formal approval was given to the establishment of a national physical planning institute under the supervision of Local Government, on lines similar to those set forth by Ó hUiginn.[62]

Opposition emerged from an unexpected quarter. In August, Frank Aiken, Minister for External Affairs, protested that he had not been present when the matter was discussed and had not been consulted. Aiken claimed that it was unlikely that the UN would provide assistance towards the establishment of the proposed institute, but withdrew his objections the following week, when the Irish mission to the United Nations confirmed that UN assistance had been offered. Aiken appears to have feared that accepting assistance would require that Ireland be reclassified as a less developed country. An Foras Forbartha, the

National Institute for Physical Planning and Construction Research, was established in 1964; its first managing director was Padraig Ó hUiginn.

Economic Development and the *Programme for Economic Expansion* (popularly known as the First Programme) both drew a clear distinction between productive and non-productive expenditure. Little of the work of the Department of Local Government was seen as productive investment. Preliminary work for the *Second Programme* did not suggest that Finance's views had altered. In November 1961, as part of a review of estimates for future expenditure, T.K.Whitaker, secretary of the Department of Finance, wrote to John Garvin expressing concern that all available information 'indicates a continuing heavy rise in capital expenditure on housing, sanitary and other services administered by the Department'. In the boom, or near-boom condition, prevailing in the building industry, Finance believed that there were 'compelling reasons' for undertaking a 'critical review of housing grants', which were regarded as only swelling builders' profits. It also believed that, with the building sector working at full capacity, water and sewerage schemes should not undergo an 'undue expansion'. Whitaker argued that in order to give priority to productive investment, it was desirable 'to keep down' the level of expenditure on capital services administered by Local Government by agreeing that annual maximum expenditure for some years ahead would be frozen at its current figure of £12m..

In response, Garvin provided estimates which envisaged future capital requirements rising from £11.5m. in 1961/62 to £14.4m. in 1962/63 and £15.6m. in 1963/64 and 1964/65 — figures which made no allowance for wage or cost increases. He added:

> I was aware that the continuing increase in capital spending on housing, water supplies and sewerage and roads was not visualised by the Programme for Economic Development. Current trends in capital expenditure on services administered by this department are the direct result of policy decisions made and directives given in recent years by the Government, who were fully advised in each case as to the probable financial implications.

Garvin argued that capital requirements for local authority housing were 'comparatively low' and showed no upward trend. There was a need for continued investment in housing to compensate for natural obsolescence in the housing stock; any reduction in subsidies for private housing would cause marginal purchasers to turn to local authorities in search of housing at an increased cost to the state, irrespective of the social implications. High spending on urban and rural sanitary schemes was 'associated to an ever-increasing degree with the spread and development of industrial projects' and with measures to increase agricultural output and tourist development. Capital expenditure on roads should be classified as economic, not social, expenditure; road improvements had become more urgent in the light of impending EEC membership.[63]

This battle continued, despite growing evidence that higher investment in housing and sanitary services was needed to facilitate economic development. In February 1963 Finance Minister James Ryan wrote to Blaney demanding a substantial cut in Local Government's capital estimates for the coming year in order 'to make ends meet'. Ryan argued that because capital services administered by Local Government had been 'faring very well', 'it should not cause you great difficulty' if levels were frozen. He proposed to cut the amount available from the Local Loans Fund by £2m..[64] In fact, the capital allocation to Local Government rose during 1963/64.

The arguments above can be read as merely another instance of the long-standing disputes between Finance and a high-spending department which had recurred since the foundation of the state. However, by the early 1960s Finance was once more in the ascendancy, its authority reinvigorated by the new gospel of economic growth and productive investment. Although it seems that by 1963 the growing pressure on water, sewerage and housing resources, and the need for physical planning to accommodate economic expansion, had demonstrated the crucial role played by the Department of Local Government in the process of economic change, Finance's memoranda appear to indicate otherwise. Blaney's response to the proposed building industry advisory council reflected his fear that housing would continue to be marginalised as non-productive investment and that resources would be directed towards private commercial buildings.

The tone of the *Second Programme for Economic Expansion*, whose first part was published in August 1963 and the second in

August 1964, suggests that unequivocal hostility towards 'social' capital expenditure had given way to a more ambiguous attitude. Part One reiterated that priority must continue to be given to productive investment, but suggested that higher economic growth would mean that extra resources would be available for social investment such as housing — a line of argument which was also used to justify the fact that the targets for public expenditure set in the *Programme for Economic Expansion* had been exceeded.

Chapter 6 of the *Second Programme*, which dealt with physical planning, building and construction, emphasised that there was a need to ensure that 'economic and physical planning are properly co-ordinated at both regional and national level and that all major developments will be executed within the framework of a comprehensive physical planning system'. Local authorities would control the planning system at local level, while the national programme of physical planning would have three main objectives: reshaping and modernising towns and cities to meet the demands of traffic and a growing economy; identifying and developing centres of economic and social growth; and preserving and improving amenities. No reference was made to the possibility that these three objectives might prove to be incompatible. This section of the *Second Programme* was extremely dependent on the 1963 Planning Act, which required each planning authority to draw up a development plan within three years.

The *Third Programme for Economic and Social Development* gave physical planning a more prominent role, in part because the population growth of the 1960s had created new problems and because there was a growing awareness of the complexities, and possibly detrimental effects, of economic development. The first chapter of the *Programme*, laid before the Oireachtas in March 1969, struck a new note when it referred to the costs of economic growth such as 'air and water pollution, traffic congestion, noise, dereliction of cities, destruction of visual amenity and natural life'. In chapter 14, entitled 'physical planning and regional development', a strong regional policy was seen as essential if the benefits of economic growth were to be spread throughout the country. Physical planning would provide 'a necessary framework for regional development'.

The role assigned to physical planning in the *Second Programme* probably underestimated the progress in this field during the 1960s.

470

Despite acute shortages of trained staff, local authorities produced provisional plans and development plans, with strong encouragement from the Minister and Department officials. An Foras Forbartha was often essential to these achievements. In the initial development plans, covering the years 1967-72, local authorities were encouraged 'to draw up simple realistic plans which will serve while staff, skill, experience and data are being accumulated'.[65] However Local Government hoped for 'plans which will reflect and further the new role of local authorities as development forces in their areas'. By 1969, 78 of the 87 local planning authorities had produced plans and eight laggards had produced draft plans. By March 1971 plans had been completed in all but four planning authorities: Dublin County Borough, County Dublin, Galway City and Killarney Urban District Council. The original draft plan for Dublin city and county, first published in 1967, led to so many representations that it required major revision; a revised draft plan for the city, published in 1969, attracted a similar response which entailed further redrafting.

Most planning authorities were too small and too poor to carry out elaborate planning functions. Under the 1963 Planning Act, the Minister for Local Government was responsible for co-ordinating individual development plans. To achieve this, in 1964 the government decided to establish nine regions for planning purposes and to commission a series of regional plans. The regions were based on the boundaries of the areas assigned to regional commissioners in the event of invasion during the Emergency. These in turn were based on regional divisions in the army![66] In 1964 the Minister for Local Government appointed planning consultants, Myles Wright and Nathaniel Lichfield, to produce development plans for the Dublin and Limerick regions respectively. In 1966 another team of consultants, Colin Buchanan and Partners, was commissioned by the Department (by arrangement with the United Nations) to provide a regional report covering the whole country. The brief included a model development plan for Galway city, which would provide guidelines for planning in other development centres. By the mid-sixties regional planning was seen as the essential link between national economic and local physical planning.

Planning consultants were given the task of identifying centres where growth would be concentrated. Several state bodies, such as the Committee on Industrial Organisation and the NIEC (the National Industrial and Economic Council), had recommended that 'growth' or 'development centres' should be designated; they saw this as the most efficient way of allocating resources. Development centres became part of government policy in August 1965. The first two reports: — *Limerick Region* by Nathaniel Lichfield, and Myles Wright's report on the Dublin region — proved relatively uncontroversial. Lichfield recommended that growth should be concentrated on the Limerick-Shannon-Ennis corridor, with Thurles as a secondary centre. Myles Wright recommended that development should be concentrated to the west of Dublin city, around Tallaght, Clondalkin, Lucan and Blanchardstown. Drogheda and Naas-Newbridge were named as other growth centres, with Navan and Arklow as secondary centres.[67] These proposals appear to have aroused little opposition, presumably because most people in the regions lived sufficiently close to centres of growth.

The Buchanan Report, *Regional Studies in Ireland*, submitted to the Minister in 1968 and published the following year, proved much more controversial. It concluded that, in order to achieve the maximum rate of economic growth, development should be concentrated in a limited number of large towns and cities. Cork and Limerick-Shannon-Ennis should be developed as counter-attractions to Dublin and the report anticipated a doubling of population in Waterford, Dundalk, Drogheda, Sligo, Galway and Athlone between 1966 and 1986. Some towns located in areas remote from these centres were selected as local growth centres.

The government appears to have been aware of the political difficulties posed by the Buchanan Report even before it was published. Its publication in May 1969 was accompanied by a government announcement that the recommendations would be further considered in the context of proposals for regional development. At the same time, nine new regional groups — based on the nine physical planning regions, with some adjustments to the boundaries of the Dublin region — were established; they would be responsible for co-ordinating regional development in each area. In July 1969 a circular letter from the Minister for Local Government, Kevin Boland, to all city and county managers began the process of establishing Regional Development Organisations, following the model developed by the pilot organisation responsible for Limerick, Clare and North Tipperary. Each RDO would assess the area's advantages and disadvantages, under headings such as roads, water and sewerage capacity, sites and other amenities, and this report would form the basis of a regional development strategy. Local Government had a representative on each RDO. In May 1972 the government decided that development should be dispersed throughout each region, a strategy which ran directly counter to the Buchanan plan. They argued that this would minimise the dislocation caused by internal migration; it was also probably the correct political response.

Yet, even at its heyday, the vogue for physical planning had at best a limited impact on the development process. Although the *Second Programme* expressed the intention of using physical and regional planning as a framework for economic development, projected estimates for public capital expenditure on housing and sanitary services were drawn up without reference to physical or regional plans.

TABLE 10.2

Public capital programme, 1964/65 to 1968/69: projected estimates (1963 prices) and outcome (current prices)

| | Housing Project | | | | Sanitary and Miscellaneous Project | | | |
		%*	Actual	%*	Project	%*	Actual	%*
1963/64	—	—	£12.12	15.4	—	—	£4.13	5.3
1964/65	£16.61	17.3	£14.89	15.8	£4.10	4.3	£3.78	4.0
1965/66	£17.42	18.2	£18.79	20.3	£4.60	4.8	£3.63	3.9
1966/67	£18.61	19.7	£21.03	23.7	£4.90	5.2	£3.00	3.4
1967/68	£19.51	20.9	£23.25	23.7	£5.12	5.5	£2.94	3.0

* As a percentage of public capital programme.

Source: *Second Programme for Economic Expansion. Review of Progress 1964-67*, tables 31 and 32.

Projected estimates for the Public Capital Programme for the years 1964/65 to 1969/70 showed a steady increase in the provision for housing and sanitary services.[68] The *Second Programme* emphasised the need for 'a substantial continuing building programme to provide for the repair or replacement of unfit dwellings, and to meet housing needs arising from new family formation and from increasing employment at industrial centres'. Most new houses would be owner-occupied, with the state providing assistance in the form of grants and rates relief. There was yet another commitment to relax rent controls 'with full regard to the need to avoid hardship to existing tenants'. A commitment to improve water supplies was linked to the twin objectives of 'social progress and economic development'. Pure water and adequate effluent treatment systems were regarded as 'important factors in the development of industry'. Road development was needed to cater for the rapid expansion in the number of motor vehicles, from 263,000 to 382,000 between 1959 and 1964. This was expected to reach 500,000 by 1970.

The *Second Programme* was unduly ambitious, both in its targets for growth and in its detailed projections. In 1968 it was abandoned and replaced by the *Third Programme for Economic and Social Development*, which was designed to cover the years 1969-72. Housing and sanitary services were among the sectors which failed to meet the targets set in the *Second Programme*. Although the volume of private capital investment in housing rose steadily during the 1960s and public capital spending exceeded the figures set in the *Second Programme* in every year except 1964/65, the number of houses completed was below the target set in the 1964 White Paper of 12-13,000 a year, or the vaguer target in the *Second Programme* of an annual construction rate of 14,000 by 1970. The shortfall was actually more serious than the figures suggest, because the population was rising during the decade. The 1964 White Paper had accepted that its target might prove too low, 'on account of inadequate provision for the relief of overcrowding, demographic factors and possibly too low a rate of depreciation'. However, as Garret FitzGerald has pointed out, the *Second Programme* failed to include any projections for population.[69]

What accounts for the failure to reach the targets set in the White Paper? According to the 1969 White Paper, the public sector (local authorities and the NBA) was expected to provide 5,000 houses annually, with the private sector building a further 9,000. Both failed to meet their targets, but the performance of public housing was worse.

Until departmental files have been examined (a thirty-year rule applies), we cannot know the full story, though the rising cost of housing appears to be the most obvious explanation. Public capital expenditure on housing more than doubled in real terms between 1958 and 1968, though the share of total investment devoted to dwellings fell from 26.5 per cent in the years 1949-59 to 20.4 per cent for the period

1960-73.[70] Although public capital expenditure on housing exceeded the targets set in the *Second Programme* in every year except 1964/65, higher construction costs meant that fewer houses were erected. The problem was most acute for local authority housing: the 1964/65 report of the Department noted that several local authorities found it difficult to get tenders for housing schemes.

The years 1965-67 proved even more difficult. An overheated economy faced a balance of payments deficit and shortages of capital reminiscent of the 1950s. Building society funds became scarce, leading to a rising number of applications for SDAA mortgages.[71] The public capital programme for 1966/67 showed a reduction on the previous year,[72] forcing Local Government to delay sanctioning local authority housing projects, though the situation eased in July 1966, when the suspended schemes were given the green light. As housing outstripped projected estimates, it absorbed a lot of the money earmarked for sanitary services, so that by 1966 expenditure under that heading was running at only 60 per cent of target.

BALLYMUN AND THE NATIONAL BUILDING AGENCY

There is a danger that devoting undue attention to the total number of houses constructed might lead us to ignore some of the most important aspects of public housing during the 1960s. By the middle of the decade, Local Government appears to have been determined to transfer part of the responsibility for providing public-sector housing, particularly in the major cities, from local authorities to the NBA. The reasons for this are not entirely clear, though it appears to reflect the Department's belief that, since Dublin and Cork Corporations had proved incapable of erecting the number of houses needed in the past, a specialist building agency might prove more efficient. In 1965 the Department estimated that 10,000 publicly provided houses were urgently needed in Dublin. Limerick, Cork and Waterford were also believed to require an accelerated public housing programmes; there was talk of a housing crisis in Limerick. In order to ease the crisis in Dublin housing, which followed the emergency closure of many city tenements in 1963, it was decided that the NBA would supervise the construction of 3,000 dwellings at Ballymun, while Dublin Corporation could continue with its 'normal' housing programme. Ballymun was a landmark in Irish public housing: the first major high-rise development, the first large scheme built by a national agency, the first to make extensive use of prefabricated materials. Although conceived in response to a housing emergency, Ballymun soon acquired the optimistic aura of the 1960s. As Neil Blaney informed the Dáil:

> In initiating this project, we set before us certain well-defined priorities. We wanted a large volume of housing constructed to acceptable standards and to acceptable costs within a relatively short period, a high standard of planning, including play spaces, car parking and landscaping, so as to achieve the optimum integration of this new residential area with the existing city. We wanted planning to have shops, schools and other amenities provided *pari passu* with the establishment of the new community. We saw that new building methods were needed so as not to interfere with the existing structure of the industry by increasing the pressure on and competition for labour otherwise engaged on the expansion of housing output.[73]

Space would be provided for small businesses and offices. Community facilities would include a hall and meeting rooms, schools, a health clinic, swimming pool, and sites for churches, plus 36 acres of open spaces, two-thirds of this in the form of parks or gardens, with the remainder devoted to playgrounds. In this brave new world, each dwelling would be 'within easy walking distance of such a park' and the entire project would be landscaped. When the plans were unveiled in January 1965, Dublin Corporation requested that the Minister ensure that the town centre and other major facilities were constructed at the same time as the houses. Construction of the houses started in 1965, but plans for the town centre were not approved until July 1967 and work did not begin until the 1970s. By 1970 a total of 3,265 dwellings had been completed.

At this stage the Department regarded Ballymun as 'successful not only in construction and finish but also in terms of cost'. Smaller schemes were carried out in other north Dublin suburbs, Coolock, Kilmore and Kilbarrack, on the lines of the Ballymun prototype. In 1965 the functions of the NBA were extended to enable the agency to undertake any housing projects assigned by the Department of Local Government. These included schemes in Tallaght, a west Dublin suburb; Togher, Mayfield and Glen in Cork; and Rathbane in Limerick. Between April 1967 and 31 March 1971, the NBA completed 4,211 dwellings — almost one-quarter of all houses provided by local authorities. Three-quarters of the houses were built in Ballymun. The agency continued to provide houses for key industrial workers; it also built low-cost houses for sale in towns where this had not been done by speculative builders.

Both the *Second Programme* and the White Paper had emphasised that the majority of new houses provided should be privately owned. Although the number of houses completed fell short of the target, this objective was met and the proportion of housing capital provided by the private sector rose during these years. The 1964 White Paper estimated that between 1948 and 1964 the state and local authorities had contributed approximately £192m., or 85.3 per cent of capital expenditure, to housing. By 1967/68 the state was providing only half the capital required for housing, and with building society assets growing at an annual rate of 17 per cent, this trend was set to continue. This meant that the private housing sector was less amenable to the crude forms of government control which had operated in the past, i.e. rationing SDAA mortgages, so Local Government was forced to negotiate with building societies in a successful effort to persuade them to give preference in allocating scarce mortgages to new non-luxury houses. By the second half of the 1960s Local Government had emerged as the department with responsibility for the building industry as a whole: the end of a long battle. In 1966 responsibility for the National Building Advisory Council was transferred from Industry and Commerce to Local Government; it merged with An Foras Forbartha in the following year. In 1969 Local Government assumed responsibility for building societies from Industry and Commerce.

Although the *Third Programme* provided considerable scope for broadening Local Government's remit, with references in the introduction to the role of the state in providing for 'environmental improvement . . . nature conservation' and its emphasis on improving the environment and preserving the national heritage, it envisaged no major change in housing policy. Public expenditure on housing and sanitary services was projected to grow at an annual rate of 3.9 per cent — the lowest figure for any public social services and much below the projected annual increase of 5.8 per cent for public social services as a whole.

477

Table 10.3

Number of local authority houses constructed and number of private
houses which were grant-aided 1957/58 to 1973/74

	Local Authority*	New	Private Sector Reconstructed	Water and Sewerage
1957/58	3,464	2,506	8,562	1,669
1958/59	1,182	2,536	9,314	1,667
1959/60	2,414	3,928	8,074	1,513
1960/61	1,463	4,685	9,429	2,516
1961/62	1,238	4,820	8,588	2,418
1962/63	1,828	5,706	9,461	2,961
1963/64	1,856	5,975	9,563	4,124
1964/65	2,307	7,372	9,057	6,180
1965/66	2,989	8,266	9,474	7,494
1966/67	4,079	6,905	8,576	6,474
1967/68	4,045	7,972	10,290	9,022
1968/69	4,613	8,451	8,649	9,424
1969/70	4,706	8,938	8,649	9,873
1970/71	3,875	9,796	8,687	11,566
1971/72	5,106	9,616	7,591	12,594
1972/73	5,784	15,863	9,645	14,650
1973/74	6,539	18,826	9,551	13,107

Figures for local authority houses are for houses completed in that year; for
private houses, figures reflect grants paid for either new, reconstructed houses,
or grants for the installation of water and sewerage.
*Includes houses constructed by the NBA.
#Figures from 1959/60 to 1965/66, which appear in the 1966/67 Annual Report
of the Department of Local Government, differ marginally from those published
at the time in successive annual reports. The figures presented here are those in
the 1966/67 Annual Report. The discrepancies are generally minor.

HOUSING IN THE 1970s

The White Paper *Housing in the Seventies*, published in 1969 in
association with the *Third Programme for Economic and Social
Development*, estimated that 59,000 dwellings were needed to replace

unfit or overcrowded houses, plus an additional 9,000 houses a year to cope with population growth, migration and future obsolescence. It set an annual target of 12,900 to 14,900 houses by 1971 — a higher target than in 1964, though the *Third Programme* added the rider that this was dependent on satisfactory economic growth: 'If the projections on which it is based do not materialise, the houses will not be needed. If the economy does not grow, they cannot be afforded.' This suggests that, despite the change in the Programme's title, social expenditure remained subservient to economic forces. This. record number of houses was to be provided, despite a parsimonious rise in the amount of public capital, so building societies and other private sources were expected to provide the lion's share of funds. The White Paper emphasised that it was important to ensure that building societies would be free to attract savings and to set interest rates. It also gave a commitment to maintain the societies' favourable tax status, though this was modified to ensure that most building society loans went to moderately priced housing. This was in keeping with a general emphasis on achieving value for money, by seeing that state funds were used to provide smaller and less expensive houses.

Grants for private houses would be restructured 'so as to concentrate help where it is most needed and encourage the use of available capital to provide the greatest possible number of houses of reasonable standard'. From October 1969, the practice of paying higher subsidies for larger houses was reversed; maximum grants would now be provided for houses with 800 to 1,050 square feet, approximately the size of local authority houses; grants would be based on square footage, rather than the number of rooms. In a further move towards social equity, similar standards would apply to both local authority and private houses. The only alteration in existing support for local authority housing was the introduction of a special subsidy towards the cost of providing houses for key industrial workers.

Like every housing policy document published since the foundation of the state, *Housing in the Seventies* hoped to reduce the cost of housing, by encouraging local authorities to provide more serviced sites for private buyers and by encouraging non-profit groups, such as the NBA and co-operative and voluntary groups, to construct houses. Further savings were expected from the mass production of standardised components and from the drafting of revised standards for houses by An Foras Forbartha. In an effort to reduce the cost of local authority housing, Local Government issued a circular letter in 1969, stating that, while the Department was reluctant to call for any general lowering of standards, it was necessary to insist for the time being that all new schemes be designed in accordance with the revised minimum standards set in 1964. Prefabricated housing proved a disappointment, accounting for only 1,292 of the 18,212 houses built between 1967 and 1971. However, in 1970, manufacturers were invited to submit proposals for low-cost dwellings and plans were afoot to build 4,000 such houses.

The contrast between housing policy in 1957 and in the early 1970s is dramatic. Far from demand being saturated, the number of houses needed in the larger cities was now regarded as beyond the capacity of the local authorities concerned, while in smaller towns the arrival of a new factory often led to a demand for housing which speculative builders or the local council could not meet. While the building societies and other private sources were providing an increasing share of the capital needed for housing, many of the other objectives set by the Capital Investment Advisory Committee or the *Programme for Economic Expansion* had not been achieved. The share of local authority housing costs covered by rents failed to rise. By 1969 rents on local authority houses accounted for only 36.5 per cent of current receipts for housing purposes, against 36.2 per cent in 1961. Differential rents were not universal. Rates continued to bear approximately 27 per cent of housing costs, with the Exchequer carrying the remaining 29 per cent. By 1969/70 rents and annuities paid by tenants or purchasers of local authority housing, net of maintenance and other charges, contributed only 19 per cent of loan charges, a drop from the 1960/61 figure of 21 per cent.

Low rents encouraged local authorities to sell houses to sitting tenants; this was also consistent with the government's policy of favouring private home ownership. Councils had been selling labourers' cottages since the late 1930s; by 1958, 84 per cent of labourers' cottages, almost 70,000, were included in purchase schemes, against less than 10,000 houses in urban areas. The 1964 White Paper promised to simplify the sale of rural cottages and to ease the obligation on councils to put cottages which were being sold into 'good repair and sanitary condition'. The Department was less interested in speeding sales of urban houses, because they believed that 'a reserve of accommodation for renting' was necessary in towns and cities. By the late 1960s, the terms on offer to sitting tenants in towns and cities remained much less attractive than those offered to tenants of labourers' cottages.

Although a succession of government documents reiterated the intention of restoring the market for private rented accommodation, and Local Government consistently argued for the abolition of rent control, progress proved extremely slow.[74] The 1960 Rent Restrictions Act, which decontrolled vacant properties with a rateable value in excess of £25 (£30 in Dublin) together with all houses built after that date and newly converted self-contained flats, marked a modest step in this direction, as did the exclusion of houses which were owner-occupied in 1960 or which subsequently became owner-occupied. Rented property coming into a landlord's vacant possession after 1967 was decontrolled some years later.[75]

'TURN ON THE TAP': WATER AND SANITARY SERVICES

During the late 1950s, when housing was out of favour, Local Government appears to have seen water and sanitary services as providing a new focus for its energies. At one stage the campaign to provide running water in all rural homes seemed to have the potential to emulate the success of the earlier ESB rural electrification programme. However, expenditure on rural water schemes fell victim both to the shortage of public capital during the mid-1960s and to interdepartmental rivalries. By the end of the decade, the money available for water and sanitary services was increasingly absorbed by rapidly growing towns and cities.

The poor standard of water and sanitary facilities, in both towns and villages and in individual houses, rarely attracted much political interest. Expenditure under this heading seems to have been mainly seen in terms of employment, with little concern shown for public health, the environment or the quality of life. Seán MacEntee's decision in 1947 to set up a committee to examine the feasibility of introducing regional water schemes to serve households that did not have access to running water, is a notable exception to the long history of neglect. His interest appears to have been prompted by a concern with rural depopulation. MacEntee told the first meeting in September 1947:

One of these problems is to make the conditions of life in the rural areas, particularly for those who work on the land, less onerous than in some respects they now are, so that our country people may enjoy as many as possible of the advantages which town dwellers expect as a matter of course.

He argued that there was 'nothing revolutionary' in the idea of financing a major rural water programme 'within reasonable limits' from a national fund, similar to the Road Fund.

The committee was disbanded early in 1948 following the change of government,[76] and Local Government showed little interest in this topic during the next ten years; all energies were devoted to the housing programme. In 1939 capital expenditure on sanitary services amounted to £510,000, as against £3.6m. for housing. By 1952, when expenditure on housing had soared to £14.96m., expenditure on sanitary services stood at £1.086m..

Poor standards were not limited to rural areas. Until the early 1950s sewerage ran in an open drain along one side of Main Street in Banagher, Co. Offaly. On the numerous occasions when the drain became choked, sewerage flowed into the gardens of adjoining houses.[77] Grants for water or sanitary schemes were allocated on the basis of local unemployment rather than need. Water attracted smaller grants than sewerage schemes, which were believed to be more labour-intensive. Towns with low unemployment and a growing population, such as Ennis, which were often in most need of better water or sewerage facilities, tended to have their applications rejected.[78]

Although data collected in the 1956 population census suggested that over 94 per cent of inhabitants of towns with a population of 200 or over had a public water supply and 93 per cent were connected to public sewerage, a committee which reported in 1958 concluded that water supplies in many towns were deficient, while sewerage provisions were even less satisfactory, because Local Government refused to approve applications for new sewerage schemes unless the town had an adequate water supply to operate it.

Most towns discharged crude sewerage into rivers and the sea. Although this was illegal under the 1876 Rivers Pollution Prevention Act, powers of enforcement rested with the sanitary authorities, which were generally the offenders. The committee concluded that 'few people are sufficiently aggrieved by water pollution to take action', despite the fact that a polio epidemic (which was often spread by polluted water) had recently swept Ireland. Many local authorities could not afford to invest in better services.[79] This problem was particularly acute where new industries placed additional demands on facilities.

The 1958 report also highlighted the appalling standards of sanitary services in rural Ireland. According to the 1956 Census, only 52.7 per cent of the Irish population had access to public water supplies. A mere 3 per cent of rural households had public water supplied to their home, though an unspecified number had installed a private supply. This was in dramatic contrast with the ESB's rural electrification programme, which connected 163,000 consumers — over half of rural households between 1947 and 1956.[80] The ESB was keen to become involved in promoting the benefits of running water, because it believed that households which had water on tap were more likely to buy electrical appliances and to use more current. A survey of seventeen representative rural localities carried out in 1957 revealed that few households owned washing machines (13 per cent), water pumps (10.4 per cent) and water boilers (7 per cent), compared with electric radios (77 per cent) or electric irons (69 per cent).[81]

Ireland lagged far behind other European countries in the provision of sanitary services: the committee which examined the state of sanitary services in 1957/58 concluded that improvements in rural water supplies in other countries were the outcome of 'vigorous policies'. 'The extension of services was strongly directed and in some cases planned in outline by central authorities.' Although government grants towards the cost of providing running water to individual houses had been available since 1950, the take-up was low, partly because the Departments of Agriculture, Local Government and Lands operated three distinct schemes. By March 1959 only 16,230 grants had been paid.[82] The committee criticised the existence of different grant schemes and the absence of an overall plan.[83] In 1959 Local Government used this report successfully as justification for increasing the level of grant assistance for water and sewerage schemes. As additional justification, the Department noted that capital expenditure by local authorities was running below the targets set in *Economic Development*, a trend that was expected to continue.

In 1959 Local Government submitted a ten-year programme to cabinet, which would cost an average of £3m. a year, more than double existing expenditure. This had the dual objectives of providing piped water to rural areas and remedying water and sewerage deficiencies in cities and towns. The proposal signalled a major change in attitude towards rural water; previously the emphasis had been on helping householders to provide their own supply. Local Government now favoured large schemes carried out by local authorities. Once again, Finance opposed the extension of rural water supplies, arguing that this was a purely social investment, which could not be justified on public health grounds. This department also argued that capital expenditure on sanitary services had fallen, owing to 'to the satisfaction in large measure of essential needs'. Nevertheless, the cabinet approved a ten-year programme, costing an estimated £35m., which was primarily directed at providing running water in rural areas. Water and sewerage schemes in rural areas and small towns, including the cost of land acquisition, would be subsidised to the tune of 60 per cent; subsidies of 50 per cent would apply everywhere else except Dublin, where a 40 per cent subsidy was set. Loans could be spread over forty years. Local Government won this argument because the Department emphasised the potential economic benefits: higher standards of dairy hygiene, which would assist in eradicating bovine TB, and the fact that running water was a precondition for tourism and industry in rural areas.[84] By 1961 several regional water schemes, each costing over £100,000, were underway in south Wexford, north Cork and both ridings of Tipperary.

Local Government began a major campaign to publicise the benefits of running water for rural communities, enlisting the assistance of rural organisations such as Muintir na Tíre and the Irish Countrywomen's Association.[85] During 1961, the 'Turn on the Tap Exhibition' toured Ireland, and the Department commissioned a documentary film, 'Water Wisdom', which showed the transformation in the life of a typical farming community when piped water was installed. The film was scripted by Richard Power, then an official of the Department and later a well-known novelist. This publicity campaign was not superfluous: the rural water scheme aroused considerable opposition from the National Farmers' Association, which objected to the additional cost imposed on rates.[86] Most larger farmers, who dominated the NFA, already had piped water in their homes and saw no benefits from the scheme.

At cabinet Local Government's most vocal opponent was Paddy Smith, Minister for Agriculture. He echoed the views of the NFA, but there was also an element of territoriality involved: the Department of

Agriculture operated its own scheme of piped water grants and the Department of Lands provided grants in the Gaeltacht. In September 1959 the government requested the three departments to examine the possibility of consolidating all water schemes in a single department. It was decided that, while a separate scheme should continue in Gaeltacht areas, the grants provided by the Department of Agriculture should end as soon as Local Government was in a position to offer equally favourable terms. Agriculture would continue to provide grants towards the cost of installing water in farm buildings. In April 1961, Local Government proposed that all grants be unified under its control. This proposal was not welcomed by local authorities, because, while the Department of Agriculture grants were met by the Exchequer, the cost of grants paid by Local Government was shared between the Exchequer and local authorities, and Local Government was determined to ensure that councils bore their share of the cost.[87] The Department of Agriculture continued to operate its own scheme. Local Government faced similar difficulties when it attempted to assume sole control for rural housing; this also encroached on the Department of Land's role in providing houses for resettled smallholders.[88]

Seán Lemass obviously believed that the rural water scheme would prove a vote-winner in the 1961 general election because he made several speeches on the topic, describing it on one occasion as 'perhaps the most significant measure ever taken to improve the conditions of people in rural areas'. He also cited a recent encyclical, *Mater et Magistra*, by Pope John XXIII which called for equality of public services in town and country.[89] However in January 1962 Smith informed Blaney that there was growing opposition among rural organisations and farming interests to any extension of regional water schemes. In a letter, which appears to have been circulated to cabinet, Smith claimed that regional water schemes cost an estimated £350 per house, compared with £130 for the Department of Agriculture grants. He argued that individual or group schemes using ground water were preferable. In what appears to have been an overt effort to gain, or retain, control of the rural water programme, Smith suggested that Local Government lacked the personnel to deal with large numbers of grant applications and that it might be 'desirable' if Agriculture continued to operate the existing scheme. He pressed home his argument, sending Lemass cuttings from the *Irish Farmers' Journal* which denounced the cost of regional water schemes. These included details of a resolution passed by Waterford County Council against proceeding with a scheme which had been recommended by the county manager; demands by Kerry NFA that a proposed regional scheme be abandoned; and comments from Cavan NFA in the course of a discussion on rates that there were 'much more satisfactory alternatives to regional schemes'.

The NFA demanded that the government sanction higher grants to enable farmers to provide their own water supplies; it also argued that farmers who would not benefit from regional water schemes should not be required to contribute to the cost in the form of higher rates. Local Government claimed that NFA opposition was almost entirely local and was not reflected in any pressure from headquarters. In a letter dated 2 February 1962, seeking to counter Smith's case, Blaney reiterated that there was no intention of extending regional water schemes throughout the country. He pointed out that the figure of £350, cited by Smith as the average cost per house, was an upper limit for the guidance of local authorities; costs averaged £165 per house, whereas the average cost of private schemes subsidised by the Department before 1960 was £93. In a further letter in March, Blaney pointed out that the principle of ratepayers paying for services from which they would not benefit personally was well established in the case of health and local authority housing. He also expressed concern that Smith was 'now apparently prepared to accept the indefinite continuance of this arrangement [two separate rural water schemes] and to defer implementation of the government's decision of April 1961.' Blaney complained about lack of balance in the propaganda campaign, which alleged that Local Government was determined to cover the country with regional schemes at enormous cost, adding, 'what worries me most in this kind of thing is the lack of balance: sectional views are pushed to extremes and the irresponsible element in any propaganda finds a ready response in questions ordinarily free from bias.' The average cost of existing regional schemes to the rates was 1/9 (about 9p) in the pound.

By March 1963 all but four county councils had adopted comprehensive water and sewerage programmes, and Agriculture relinquished control of rural water schemes to Local Government. Compromise was the order of the day: councils were compensated for the cost of grants paid to households that would previously have been eligible for the Department of Agriculture scheme, and the 1962 Local Government (Sanitary Services) Act provided a new scale of grants and

486

Table 10.4

Department of Local Government. Cost of grants awarded for water
and sewerage schemes 1957/58 to 1966/67

	Water	Sewer
1957/58	£1,271,014	£871,873
1958/59	£619,455	£341,035
1959/60	£747,992	£324,764
1960/61	£2,300,822	£801,603
1961/62	£636,598	£569,455
1962/63	£2,541,906	£806,450
1963/64	£2,988,537	£698,437
1964/65	£2,577,734	£778,730
1965/66	£885,762	£591,055
1966/67	£1,894,053	£599,145

Source: Annual Reports of the Department of Local Government. The data is
not available in this form after 1966/67.

loans for group and private schemes, in an effort to silence those who
claimed that the government was biased in favour of elaborate regional
schemes. The 1962 Act also shifted part of the cost from rates towards
water charges. A memorandum presented to cabinet in 1962
emphasised that individual contributions towards the cost of group
water schemes could be made in the form of labour, with cash outlays
reduced to a 'token payment of as low as £5'; for old-age pensioners
this might be waived altogether.[90] This new emphasis on group water
schemes continued for the remainder of the 1960s, with various
compromises being worked out between local authorities and private
groups. A pilot group project linking 90 houses in north Kerry to a
regional water scheme set the pattern for many future schemes. By
1964 promotional activities had as their 'main theme . . . the
encouragement of private enterprise, particularly by co-operative group
schemes'.

The rural water programme was a major casualty of cuts in capital
expenditure during 1965/66, when it was decided to give priority to
housing. The scheme never regained the momentum lost and capital

expenditure for sanitary services failed to meet the targets set in the *Second Programme*.[91] Yet the scheme was well behind target even before the 1965 crisis, presumably because of ratepayer/farmer resistance. In 1969 the *Third Programme* noted: 'In view of the urgent needs of expanding built-up areas to provide for industrial and commercial growth, the primary objective of these programmes will be the provision and improvement of water and sewerage facilities in built-up areas'. Rural needs would 'continue to be met as far as possible', with local authorities providing headworks and trunks mains, which would be linked to co-operative group schemes.

Despite many pitfalls, piped water made its way into rural homes, though not as fast as had been originally hoped. In 1961 almost 290,000 houses, 42.8 per cent of the housing stock, lacked piped water; by 1971 this had fallen to 154,000 or 21.2 per cent; estimates for 1975 suggested a figure of 88,000 or 11 per cent.

ROADS

The White Paper *Economic Development* does not indicate whether it regarded expenditure on roads as productive expenditure or as social expenditure. The capital investment advisory committee says nothing about roads, probably because expenditure on roads was financed by the Road Fund and not from the public capital programme. The return of a Fianna Fáil government brought no immediate change in policy on roads: the government approved the borrowing of £900,000 on the security of the Road Fund for the financial year 1957/58 in order to maintain employment, and county roads continued to obtain the lion's share of the available funds. With the closure of many railway lines in the late 1950s, goods and passenger traffic was being transferred to dangerous and inadequate roads. In 1958 the Donegal county engineer estimated that it would be necessary to spend £600,000 on major road improvements to cope with the increased traffic resulting from the closure of the Donegal-Ballyshannon line; the county's annual main road improvement grant was £65,000. If the railway closed, a bus service would be needed on the Ballyshannon-Rossnowlagh road — a winding road that was only 14-15 feet wide in places. The government authorised the closure of this railway line, despite a recommendation from Local Government that it be deferred until major improvements were carried out on two roads. The issue was decided by a report from Industry and Commerce that the railway line was unsafe.[92]

Rail closures were extremely unpopular in most communities, partly because the resulting increase in the cost of roads was believed to fall on local authority rates, whereas subsidies to unprofitable railway lines were a matter for central government. Local Government demanded that special funds be provided to meet the additional cost of road works as a result of railway closures, and in 1959 the Road Fund (Grants and Advances) Act provided for an annual Exchequer advance of £400,000 for the years 1959/60 to 1963/64, half as a repayable loan, the remainder as a free grant. The money would also be used to finance road improvements to meet the needs of new industries in an area; in the first year, one-third of the money was allocated for this purpose. Donegal County Council received £75,000; in April 1959 Local Government decided that when the current work was complete, it would be possible to run a bus service on the Ballyshannon-Rossnowlagh road, 'provided the drivers exercise extreme care'.[93]

In 1960/61, £600,000 was allocated for special road works; this was almost evenly divided between improvements to compensate for rail closures and sums paid to three local authorities on foot of major industrial projects. In April 1961 Blaney informed Ryan that the £2m. provided under the 1959 Act, which was due to last until 1963/64, was fully committed and many demands had yet to be met. He requested a minimum additional sum of £810,000 a year for three years, citing a recent Dáil statement by Lemass in the course of a debate on railway closures that all realistic proposals for road improvements which were needed as a result of rail closures would be carefully considered. Ryan suggested that the money should be provided by the Road Fund and pointed out that the Fund's income was rising steadily as a result of economic growth. Blaney countered that most of the traffic diverted to roads consisted of large commercial vehicles which could seriously damage roads with suspect foundations. He added, 'We cannot answer exaggerated criticism of the railway–roads controversy unless we are able to show that we deal reasonably with those proportions of the claims that are shown to be well founded'. He pointed out that the growth of motor traffic had created a need for 'more extensive improvement works'.

As a result of decisions taken by the previous government, county road improvements still accounted for the largest single share of the

Road Fund in the early 1960s and Neil Blaney was not prepared to reverse this pattern until the standard of county roads had improved. Although the Department had ensured in recent years that the limited money available for main road improvements was spent on the most important 1,500 miles of roads which were designated as arterial roads, in 1962/63 only 250 miles had reached a satisfactory standard. Completing this work would cost an estimated £25m.; upgrading the remaining 8,500 miles of main roads would cost a further £72m.. Funds were also needed to relieve traffic congestion in Dublin and Cork. Since existing revenue from the Road Fund was 'strictly rationed' to meet a wide variety of urgent demands, improvements to roads affected by rail closures would have to be postponed unless special assistance was provided. The cabinet accepted this argument in principle, approving a further sum of £900,000 for three years to meet the special needs resulting from rail closures: half from the Exchequer, the balance from the Road Fund. Further expenditure under this heading would be met from the Road Fund.[94]

This debate marked a resurgence of the question first raised in the 1920s: was the income of the Road Fund sufficient to fund the cost of road improvements? The arrangements that ultimately ensued, following detailed negotiations between Local Government and Finance, suggested a growing recognition that it was not. Various annuities, which previously had been raised on the security of the Road Fund, were wiped out; repayable advances from the Exchequer to the Road Fund under the 1959 Act were transformed into a non-repayable grant and the Exchequer agreed to provide a further annual grant of £150,000 until 1963/64.[95] This amounted to the Exchequer providing grants of £550,000 towards the cost of special road works.

Motor vehicle registrations rose steadily from 253,000 in 1957 to 355,000 by 1962 and to 573,000 by 1971. Over time, the proportion of road expenditure devoted to relieving urban traffic congestion or road traffic problems caused by industrial development increased gradually. This was achieved by a series of subtle shifts in priorities, rather than by a dramatic policy U-turn. The Department's annual report for 1962/63 noted that many counties had completed their programme of improvements to county roads and others were about to do so. By contrast, over 80 per cent of main roads were in need of major improvement, and arterial roads in the Dublin area were 'seriously sub-standard and inadequate for present-day requirements'. The

Department raised the Road Fund grant towards the upkeep of main roads from 40 to 50 per cent and allocated £500,000 to provide 100 per cent grants for improvements to parts of the most important arterial roads, which would be 'selected by the Minister'.

The report also noted that some county councils were transferring to main roads grants earmarked for county road improvements. In 1964/65 the Road Fund grant for county road improvements was cut by over £150,000 and the Department announced that grants would no longer be paid in counties where the improvement programme (100% dust-free roads) was complete. Grants in other counties would be reduced in proportion to the percentage of dust-free roads. The proportion of road expenditure borne by the Exchequer or the Road Fund rose from 52 per cent in 1958/59 to 60 per cent by 1963/64. At the beginning, the shift of resources from county to main roads was achieved by introducing a variety of special grants. The 1962/63 annual report listed eleven different categories and these did not include grants under employment schemes.

The omission of roads in the *Programme for Economic Expansion* was remedied in the *Second Programme*, which accurately predicted that vehicle numbers would rise by 60 per cent during the 1960s. The *Second Programme* forecast that £100m. would be spent on roads during the lifetime of the programme, with the state bearing an increasing share of total costs. Priority would be given to main roads, particularly those near major urban areas. The *Second Programme* concluded that roads of 'at least dual-carriageway standards are already required' on the major routes radiating out from Dublin. In the light of these forecasts, Local Government requested that county managers carry out a trunk road inventory which would form the basis of a five-year improvement programme. A study entitled *Sufficiency Ratings on Arterial Roads*, which examined 1,600 miles of major roads, concluded that a substantial proportion were seriously deficient and recommended a ten-year improvement programme. The *Third Programme* reiterated the need to give priority to improving arterial roads and to relieving congestion in major urban areas, citing the relationship between an efficient road system and economic progress, and the proven correlation between road accident rates and the quality of roads. It also questioned whether or not local authorities had the necessary skills or equipment to construct a modern road system.

A report by An Foras Forbartha, *Administration of the Arterial*

Roads Programme, had recommended that responsibility for arterial roads should be transferred from local authorities to the Department of Local Government. A further study carried out by consultants recommended that the road network should be reclassified, for the first time since the 1920s, and that approximately 3,200 miles of the most important roads should become a national responsibility.

TABLE 10.5

Proposed roads reclassification

System	Group	Approx. Mileage	Percentage of Total
National	Primary	1,600	2.96%
	Secondary	1,600	2.96%
Regional	Primary	3,250	6.02%
	Secondary	3,450	6.38%
County		43,900	81.48%

In July 1969, Kevin Boland, the Minister for Local Government, announced that the government had approved legislation to be prepared to effect this transfer. Local authorities would continue to carry out work on national routes for the Department on an agency basis and would remain responsible for other roads. The Department announced that urban streets would be classified in order to draw up priorities for expenditure on improvements. In 1970/71 the grant for the upkeep of the national primary roads was increased from 50 to 100 per cent. Attention then shifted to designating regional roads.

All the above suggests a new awareness of the economic importance attached to a modern road network. By the early 1970s roads were seen as the dominant mode of internal transport and funds were now allocated to relieve traffic congestion, rather than local unemployment. Arterial roads were taking precedence over county roads. Yet finance did not keep pace with aspirations. Although motor taxes were increased in 1966 and again in 1970, the additional revenue went to the Exchequer, not the Road Fund. By 1971/72 it proved necessary for the first time to cap the sum available from the Road

Fund towards the upkeep of main, trunk and link roads at the 1970/71 figure, and Local Government was convinced that the amount provided for road improvements was seriously inadequate.

TABLE 10.6

Road expenditure 1957/58 to 1966/67 (£m.)

	Main	County	Co.Borough	Total
1957/58				
Local	£1.464	£2.952	£.272	£4.689
State	£2.127	£2.464	£.235	£4.827
Total	£3.591	£5.417	£.507	£9.516
1960/61				
Local	£1.539	£3.111	£.316	£4.966
State	£2.957	£2.598	£.288	£5.843
Total	£4.496	£5.709	£.604	£10,810
1963/64				
Local	£1.537	£3.605	£.410	£5.553
State	£5.194	£2.500	£.364	£8.058
Total	£6.731	£6.105	£.774	£13.611
1966/67				
Local	£1.853	£4.340	£.719	£6.913
State	£6.937	£2.088	£.343	£9.370
Total	£8.791	£6.428	£1.063	£16,284

Source: Annual Reports, Department of Local Government

LOCAL AUTHORITY FINANCES: RATES AND VALUATION

One of the most obvious threads running through the history of the Department of Local Government from the late 1950s is the trend towards further centralisation. Thus the NBA began to supplement the housing functions of local authorities, the Department took responsibility for national roads, while the formation of regional planning units — which admittedly included representatives from existing local authorities — suggested that the historic boundaries of local government had outlived their usefulness. Centralist tendencies undoubtedly increased during the Lemass era and afterwards. Between 1948 and 1957 the first and the second inter-party governments were committed to restoring greater autonomy to local authorities. Fianna Fáil, which was in government from 1957 until 1973, showed little enthusiasm for this idea and it appears that the bitter hostility once shown towards county managers had largely disappeared. Yet while there are undoubted differences between the years 1948-57 and the succeeding decade or so, one fact is common to both: the weakness of local authority finances, which forced the Exchequer to assume a growing share of the cost of local services, regardless of demands for greater local autonomy.

By 1953, total rateable valuation was less than 12 per cent above its 1938 level, though total expenditure on local authority services had more than tripled. Between 1946/47 and 1956/57 rateable poundages more than doubled in every county except Dublin. In most counties, agriculture continued to account for a majority of the rateable valuation, and the potential rateable income from agricultural land and buildings was severely limited by partial de-rating. Rates remission on all new buildings, which had been conceded in 1954,[96] severely limited the rise in valuation in towns and cities.

For many years Local Government believed that a general revaluation offered the only solution to the financial problems facing local authorities, but responsibility for introducing a Valuation Bill rested with the Department of Finance. Local Government first broached the possibility of carrying out a general revaluation in 1938; the idea lapsed during the Emergency. In December 1945 the Minister for Local Government requested the Minister for Finance to seek government authority to reintroduce the Valuation Bill at an early stage, 'as a preliminary step to other measures necessary to put the finances of local authorities on a sound basis'.[97] James Hurson, then secretary of Local Government, claimed that increasing the rateable poundage on the existing defective valuation, would 'create a false impression in the mind of the ratepayer that we are approaching the limits of rating', whereas if valuations were adjusted to take account of current values, poundages would be substantially reduced. However, Finance's Owen Redmond was reluctant to proceed with a general revaluation until conditions had become 'more settled', and 'money values' would 'attain such a degree of stability as to permit' a general revaluation.[98]

This discussion predated the post-war escalation in rates poundages. By the early 1950s all government faced a multiplicity of demands for a reduction in the burden of local authority taxes. The Fine Gael *árd fheis* in February 1951 demanded that a commission should be established to inquire into and report on 'the alarming increase in local taxation'. The Association of Municipal Authorities in Ireland passed a resolution demanding the establishment of a government tribunal to inquire into the rating system; identical resolutions were passed by most county councils. A memorandum from Local Government to this resolution noted:

> If set up it is quite conceivable and indeed probable that it would recommend a big increase in State Grants or a transference of administrations of some of the principal local services such as Housing or Main Roads to the state. The implementation of either of these recommendations would not be welcomed.

Local Government recommended that local authorities should be relieved of the cost of various items over which it had little control, such as maintaining courthouses, animal pounds, compensation for malicious injuries, contributions for the maintenance of children in reformatories, vocational education, unemployment assistance and county committees of agriculture.[99] The Department was extremely conscious of the conflict between demands for a reduction in rates and the simultaneous campaign for less central intervention in local affairs. Higher state grants would, it pointed out, inevitably lead to

> . . . a tightening of central control over local affairs as the state could not afford to allow money which it must itself raise and for which it must account to be spent at the sole discretion of local authorities. It is rather illogical for them to ask for a bigger voice in determining their own affairs and at the same time ask for higher state grants.

Officials were unable to suggest an obvious alternative source of finance: a local income tax would drive people away from a high-taxation area. In a summary worthy of a textbook on public finance, officials concluded that 'the rating system has stood the test of time, is not costly to administer, gives stability to the receipts of local authorities and all things considered it is fairly equitable.'[100]

AGRICULTURAL RATES RELIEF IN THE POST-WAR YEARS

In the absence of a general revaluation, the rating system creaked along. The 1946 Agricultural Land (Relief) Act continued the 1935 model of allocating rates relief on the basis of three allowances — a primary allowance, a supplementary allowance and an employment allowance — though it removed the limit on the amount provided for rates relief and replaced it with allowances based on a percentage of the rate struck, which cost £1m. more than the previous limit of £1.87m.. The cost of employment relief quadrupled. The more generous grant was intended as a temporary measure which would encourage farmers to boost output in order to feed starving post-war Europe. It was extended, however, with the result that by 1949/50 the cost of rates relief was running at more than double the 1945 level. Finance argued that rates relief provided a wasteful subsidy to larger farmers, while failing to stem the decline in rural employment.[101] However, the case for retaining the new basis of relief was strengthened by the fact that the level of rates demanded was continuing to rise rapidly. If the agricultural grant was cut, Local Government feared that it would prove increasingly difficult to maintain minimum standards of local services.[102]

After 1951 the case for retaining generous rates relief was boosted by the Fianna Fáil government's strong commitment to increasing the acreage tilled. Tillage had fallen sharply since the end of World War II, though with agricultural wages averaging £3-£4 per week, the incentive provided by an employment allowance worth an average of £5.50 per worker per year appears to have been slight. In the spring of 1952, Local Government recommended doubling employment relief and abolishing the supplementary allowance paid on holdings valued in excess of £20. However when local authorities became aware of this proposal, they were not enthusiastic. Although the 280,000 farmers whose valuations were less than £20 would be unaffected by the change, a majority of the remaining 100,000 farmers with larger holdings would be net losers, as would nearly all county councils.

The revised system of allocating the agricultural grant would save the Exchequer an estimated £400,000, with the greatest reductions coming in Counties Cork, Dublin, Kildare, Meath and Westmeath. Western counties, which were dominated by small farms, would be largely unaffected. In an effort to claw back some or all of the lost grant, Waterford County Council demanded that the employment allowance be extended to farmers' wives and other full-time female employees, and Wicklow County Council demanded that women and seasonal workers be deemed eligible. Patrick Cogan, Fianna Fáil TD for Wicklow, demanded that the revised basis of calculating the grant should be scrapped: 'I can see this news coming on the eve of the election having the effect of driving a very substantial farmers' vote into the arms of Fine Gael.'

In an effort to quell opposition, the government hastily withdrew the offending bill and published a White Paper which proposed increasing the employment allowance by a further £410,000. This did not entirely silence the critics; Sir Cecil King-Harmon wrote to the Taoiseach protesting that his rates bill would increase by 33 per cent. Contacted for a response, John Garvin pointed out that the new Bill was heavily weighted in favour of large employers of labour; another official said that King-Harmon had attempted to claim rates relief in respect of his butler![103] The amended version of the Agricultural Rates Relief Bill became law in 1953.

Originally intended to apply for a three-year period, the Bill was extended for a further five years in 1956.[104] Since the Act did not limit the cost of agricultural rates relief, it rose from £4.6m. in 1952/3 to over £5.5m. by 1956/57. Such generosity failed to stem the decline in the agricultural workforce and was equally unsuccessful in placating farmers. In 1956 a deputation from the National Farmers' Association contended that most local authority expenditure was no longer local in character and should be financed by the Exchequer, either by income tax or by a sales tax.[105] In December 1957 the NFA told the Minister that it was its long-term objective to have the cost of health, mental hospitals, road expenditure, other than by-roads and housing, made a national charge. Although Local Government pointed out that this would involve 'more than a mere financial adjustment' and would mean an end to 'dual responsibility' and the 'partnership between central and local authorities', the NFA persisted in its campaign. NFA members addressed estimates meetings of several county councils and invariably accused each county council of inefficiency. The NFA campaign did not subside and in March 1959 the Minister agreed to meet a deputation. On this occasion, NFA spokesman Dr Louis Smith extended the campaign into a fundamental assault on the whole basis of local authority finances. He claimed that health expenditure bore most heavily on the poorest counties and condemned the fact that Road Fund grants to local authorities were proportionate to local expenditure on the grounds that 'County councillors seemed to regard it as a local patriotic duty to spend as much money as they could on such schemes'.[106]

Smith's critique highlighted the many anomalies in the taxation and financing of local government. Although some of these were of long-standing, the proliferation of rates remission for new houses, house extensions and new industrial and commercial buildings added to the confusion. Local Government had pressed for an end to rates remission for new houses in 1948 because officials believed that it 'has outlived its usefulness and should not be continued indefinitely', adding that local authorities needed the full immediate benefit of any increase in valuation. However, rates relief was extended in 1948, 1951 and again in 1952.[107] In 1953 Deputy Cogan tabled a Dáil motion demanding the establishment of a commission to inquire into the method by which rateable valuations were determined; pending the report, Cogan urged that no valuations should be increased as a result of improvements.[108] Finance argued that the debate revealed 'widespread dissatisfaction with the present situation', with a succession of speakers protesting that the present system discouraged people from improving property, putting a premium on 'backwardness, inactivity and inefficiency'. According to Finance, the effective remedy lay in legislation providing for a general valuation. MacEntee replied that he would recommend that the Minister for Local Government establish a commission or committee to look at the rating system.[109] Nothing further was heard about revaluation; however, rates remission was extended in 1954 to all new buildings and those which had undergone major improvement. This concession, which was allegedly introduced to revive the depressed construction sector, was subsequently extended until 1960.[110]

DE-URBANISATION

It is doubtful whether a general revaluation would have resolved the financial difficulties facing local authorities; certainly the unhappy experience of Buncrana, Co. Donegal, the only Irish town to undergo a general revaluation, must have deterred others from following suit. When the town was revalued in 1950, the total valuation rose from £7,653 to £11,445.[111] This triggered a sharp increase in the town's contribution under the county at large demand (this is the sum paid by urban district councils to county councils) from £8,697 to £12,123. This was grossly unfair because no other urban district had been revalued and Buncrana UDC refused to pay the increased demand. The problem was resolved only by adding a special amendment to the 1954 Temporary Reduction of Valuation Act and its successor in 1960.[112]

Buncrana was not the sole instance of disagreement over financial arrangements between urban district councils and county councils. In 1943 Tipperary South Riding demanded a Local Government inquiry on this question, because rural ratepayers suspected that they were being saddled with the cost of services which benefited only urban dwellers.[113] Some urban district councils attempted to escape from their financial obligations by demanding to be de-urbanised. Cootehill and Belturbet, both in County Cavan, succeeded in doing this in 1950; Cashel and Templemore, both in Tipperary South Riding, hoped to follow their example, believing that it would lead to lower rate bills.

Such demands often reflected a town's declining economic status: Templemore had apparently never recovered from the departure of the British army; Passage West in Cork, the first Irish town to be de-urbanised, blamed the closure of the dockyards and railway line for its inability to meet its bills.[114] Granard, Co. Longford first replaced its urban district council with town commissioners during the Emergency, and then in 1953 demanded that the town be taken into county council control. A Departmental inquiry condemned Granard Urban District Council and Town Commissioners for 'shirking most of the duties imposed by the Public Health Acts. Their rate collection was bad, water supply and sewerage unsatisfactory'; housing was 'perhaps the only sign that they took their duties at all seriously', though all council houses lacked sanitary facilities. Granard benefited considerably from the dissolution of its urban district council. Longford County Council carried the cost of providing a new water scheme and sewerage scheme, though it refused to assume the remaining duties of the negligent Granard Town Commissioners. Although Granard's problems reflected the low calibre of local representatives — in 1940 proceedings were pending against both the chairman and vice-chairman for non-payment of rates — poverty was also a factor. A rate of one penny in the pound yielded a little over £17 and, although much of the urban area consisted of agricultural land, the agricultural grant did not apply to land within the boundaries of an urban district council.[115] Only Trim

UDC had a lower valuation than the dissolved Belturbet and Cootehill UDCs.[116] During the 1950s Local Government received so many inquiries from urban district councils about de-urbanisation, which were mainly prompted by their inability to bear the cost of essential water and sewerage schemes, that the Department gave desultory consideration to the possibility of de-urbanising all towns with a population of under 5,000.[117]

However, financial difficulties were not exclusive to towns in decline. Prosperity also brought its difficulties, as the case of Ennis UDC showed. In 1954 Ennis, one of the most thriving towns at this period, was about to enter a commitment to erect 95 local authority houses at a cost of almost £250,000, when the council discovered that this would mean an increase of 5/6 (27.5p) in the pound on the urban rate. It voted to suspend the decision, pending an application to the Minister for additional grants. The memorandum emphasised that hitherto 'the Council has co-operated loyally by every means in its power with the desire of the Minister to abolish slums and provide new houses for those in need of such'; they had also undertaken 'comprehensive and costly schemes' to improve water supplies. However, the increase in valuation had saddled the urban district council with a much higher county at large charge, despite the fact that most of the increase in valuation was attributable to new houses which qualified for rates remission.[118]

The financial pressures on many local authorities probably increased during the 1960s, because they were confronted with new demands: providing serviced sites, adequate water supplies for new industries, or exercising their responsibilities as physical planning authorities.

Between 1938/39 and 1948/49 the proportion of local authority expenditure which was being met by rates fell from 52.3 per cent to 39.9 per cent. During the 1950s, however, the ratio of rates to expenditure remained stable at approximately 40 per cent, largely because the agricultural grant showed little increase; it fell from 64 per cent of rates collected by county councils in 1950/51 to 47 per cent by 1959/60.[119] In contrast, the proportion of local authority revenue which was provided by rates fell sharply during the 1960s and the cost of the agricultural grant more than doubled between 1960/61 and 1965/66. Rates remission on new or reconstructed houses was extended, despite a warning from a senior official in Local Government of 'the danger of

500

TABLE 10.7

Trends in the major sources of local authority finance 1938/39 to 1970/71 (£m.)

	Rates	Grants	Miscellaneous	Total
1938/39	£6.27	£4.70	£1.67	£11.64
%	52.3	39.2	13.9	100
1948/49	£10.36	£11.14	£3.59	£25.09
	39.9	42.9	13.8	100
1958/59	£20.56	£22.23	£8.75	£41.54
	40.0	43.2	17.0	100
1969/70	£42.95	£66.05	£21.69	£130.69
	32.2	49.5	16.3	100
1970/71	£49.93	£78.33	£26.64	£154.90
	32.0	50.3	17.1	100

Source: *White Paper on Local Finance and Taxation 1972* (Prl.2745), p.9.

keeping temporary legislation in being': that it 'ceases to fulfil its purposes as an accelerator,[120] or the concern expressed by the Commissioner of Valuation at the anomalous position where farmers paid rates on old buildings, whereas those with 'good new buildings' were exempt. He complained that such concessions 'undermine[s] the valuation system, making it completely obsolete'.[121]

REFORMING THE LOCAL TAX BASE

By the early 1960s it was evident that the basis of local taxation and finance needed fundamental reform. In the financial year 1959/60, rateable valuation per capita ranged from £8.81 in Meath to £3.01 in Mayo. Nor was it coincidental that Meath had the lowest rates in the country at 26 shillings (£1.30), whereas the only county council with a higher poundage than Mayo's 47 shillings (£2.35p) was Donegal, which had the second lowest valuation per capita. Local Government was aware that using *pro rata* grants to subsidise local expenditure was regressive. In 1961 when the Department of Education proposed to introduce an extended scheme of post-primary and university scholarships, with the state subsiding the cost in proportion to each county's contribution from local taxes, Local Government argued that such a scheme would confer 'a disproportionate benefit' on areas with above-average rateable valuation and would discriminate against poorer counties. It suggested that grants be weighted on the basis of valuation and population, as had already been done under the Vocational Education Act, with higher grants being paid to Counties Donegal, Galway, Kerry, Leitrim, Mayo, the County Boroughs of Limerick and Waterford and lower grants for Counties Dublin, Kilkenny, Meath, Waterford and Westmeath. Although the cabinet rejected these proposals,[122] the intervention signalled a determination to examine the basis of local taxation.

In the early 1960s opposition to rates was strongest in western counties. In April 1961 Castlebar Chamber of Commerce passed a resolution calling on the government to establish a commission to inquire into the rating system, 'with particular reference to the feasibility of establishing a Rates Equalisation Fund and transferring the cost of Health Services to Central Authority . . . in view of the stultifying effects which exorbitant rates had on economic development in the West of Ireland'. Around this time Dr Edward Moore, Church of Ireland bishop of Kilmore, Elphin and Ardagh — which comprised Counties Sligo, Roscommon, Leitrim, Longford and Cavan, all with below-average valuations — wrote to Lemass suggesting 'a new approach to the rates question'. Dr Moore believed that Ireland could not afford to de-rate agriculture. As an alternative, he suggested imposing a ceiling on rates of 30 shillings (£1.50) in the pound in counties with average agricultural land and 20 shillings (£1) in the pound in poorer counties. Such a policy would require severe rates reductions in all counties except Meath. Local Government rejected the idea because it would interfere with local authorities' discretion to set rates. Officials also pointed out that since over 80 per cent of agricultural holdings in the bishop's dioceses had rateable valuations of less than £20, they benefited from 60 per cent rates remission. Dr Moore addressed further letters to Lemass, linking rates remission to the survival of rural Ireland, which was then a hot political issue.[123] There was also a letter-writing campaign on this matter in the press.

The first indication that the government was considering a major review of local taxation came in June 1961 when a reference to this topic was included in a draft of the speech that Seán Lemass was to read at the opening of the Economic Research Institute. T.K. Whitaker suggested that an advance copy be sent to Local Government secretary, John Garvin. Finance determined that one of the first tasks of the new Institute should be a review of local taxation, and Whitaker contacted Garvin about possible terms of reference. Garvin informed Tadhg Ó Cearbhaill by phone (evidence of a new problem confronting future historians) that he was 'very strongly opposed' to any such study, on the grounds that it would be dangerous to provoke a public discussion on matters such as a general revaluation or a revision of the agricultural grant. Ó Cearbhaill dismissed these objections as being 'of a local political nature'.

Garvin believed that when the time was appropriate a more fundamental study should be carried out than was envisaged in the Taoiseach's script. He referred to the 'deep-rooted nature of Local Government and to the many firmly-established interests involved'. He had no doubt that there was considerable scope for savings if road works were carried out by contractors on foot of competitive tenders under central government authority, but such a step would lead to 'a disturbance of the first magnitude in local employment and income' because it entailed an end to direct labour. Garvin argued that ministers should explore the implications of reviewing local taxation before announcing the forthcoming study. Both he and Blaney believed that any campaign to reform local government would be a lengthy affair.

This conversation appears to have strengthened the determination within the Taoiseach's Department to carry out 'an objective study of local taxation and local finance'. Ó Cearbhaill argued that similar fears had been expressed when the government had initiated a study which would form the basis for reforming income tax. In that case fears had proved groundless. Unless Whitaker suggested dropping this section of the speech, he recommended that it be allowed to stand. The controversy reflects a demarcation dispute between Local Government and Finance over who was responsible for policy on local taxation. Blaney argued that this was the remit of the Minister for Local Government and demanded that the matter be discussed at cabinet on 7 June, two days before Lemass's proposed speech at the opening of the Economic Research Institute.

In the event Lemass's speech mentioned that the Institute would conduct a study of local taxation and local finance. He referred to a statement made by the Minister for Finance, in which Ryan questioned 'whether the present system is adequate or appropriate to deal with the increasing activities of local bodies, or whether a more rational or more effective system could be derived'. He also suggested that local authorities might be given new sources of income. Local Government's feelings may have been assuaged by Lemass's statement, limiting the study to providing 'some basic material which will be invaluable in the review of local finance which the Minister for Local Government intends to undertake'.

In response to Lemass's speech, Blaney proposed to establish a small committee, representing all interested departments and officials of local authorities, to examine the present system of financing local government and the incidence of rates. The committee would recommend changes in existing financial arrangements, including alternative or supplementary sources of revenue. The committee would liaise with the ERI and have 'the knowledge and experience necessary to guide the Institute in their investigations and to assess their findings'. Blaney reiterated that

> . . . the major questions of the re-allocation of local and central
> functions and the re-organisation of local services are not
> appropriate for investigation by the Institute and that submissions
> on such policy matters should come from me and the other
> Ministers concerned in the administration of local services.

Blaney believed that the major problem with rates stemmed from the 'out-dated and unrealistic' valuation system; the 'only complete solution' lay in a comprehensive revision, though he feared that it might be inopportune to introduce such a Bill at present. As an interim solution, he suggested that the Commission of Valuation be given power to begin the process of revising valuations. He also asked that a specific minister be given responsibility for introducing any legislation that might arise and for implementing the proposed interim revaluation.

Blaney was not alone in having reservations about Lemass's announcement. Finance Minister James Ryan also had some (unspecified) misgivings, and Health Minister Seán MacEntee proposed that an interdepartmental committee be established with a remit similar to that outlined by Blaney. This was approved by cabinet on 4 July. The next day Blaney wrote to Lemass seeking clarification of the committee's terms:

My recollection of the trend of our discussion is that the Committee would constitute the liaison between the Departments concerned and the Institute and that the latter's expert [David Walker, author of the report[124]] would be supplied by the Committee with whatever material he requested and not necessarily all the factual material which they might compile and that his views and recommendations would be made to the Committee who would report thereon as well as making their own recommendations to me and that I would then bring the whole matter before the Government.

Lemass's reply was less forthcoming than Blaney might have wished. He vetoed the appointment to the proposed committee of a county or city manager because he believed that his inclusion

. . . would make it difficult to use the Committee in the way he contemplated when the Institute's expert submits his proposals. This expert will, I expect, present his report and recommendations to the Institute of Economic Research, and it is the Institute which will convey them to the Government (or a Minister). It is the Government (or Minister) which will request the views thereon of the inter-Departmental Committee, prior to their further consideration.

While Blaney accepted Lemass's decision to confine membership to civil servants, he persisted in trying to gain control of the ERI study, emphasising that it was 'undesirable to make any person or body responsible for submitting proposals to the Government on matters of Departmental policy except the Minister in charge of the Department concerned'. Lemass's response was ambiguous. He conceded that any submission to government arising out of the inquiry would be made by the Minister for Local Government in accord with normal procedure. However, he pointed out that the Economic Research Institute was not an organ of government and that any business it conducted with government would normally be carried out via the Minister for Finance.

The proposed inquiry into the rating system and local authority finance was inextricably linked in many minds with the problems facing the west of Ireland. On 17/18 June, Tuairim, a group founded to study Irish social problems, organised a conference on local government in Castlebar, where Owen Hughes, a member of Mayo

County Council, presented a paper outlining the merits of a rates equalisation grant, similar to that introduced in Britain in 1948. Some weeks later, when Lemass was addressing Muintir na Tíre's rural week, he referred to the inquiry as evidence of the government's intent to adjust the burden of taxation on rural communities in line with their ability to pay, as urged in Pope John XXIII's encyclical *Mater et Magistra*.[125]

The interdepartmental committee on local taxation, chaired by Michael Lawless, assistant secretary of the Department of Local Government, began work in October 1961 and by the following January, Lemass was informed that the committee had recommended that all property other than land should be revalued; it was now considering who would be responsible for carrying out the revaluation. Responsibility for initiating revaluation currently rested with local authorities, but it was agreed that it would be unrealistic to expect them to undertake this task. The committee was also examining proposals to amalgamate the agricultural grant with other Exchequer subventions in a single grant, which would be distributed on a basis similar to the British exchequer equalisation grant.

This was a matter requiring urgent attention. By 1962 Irish farmers had begun to resent successive years of low prices and were now engaged in what Finance Minister James Ryan described as 'an organised campaign . . . for a huge transfer of income to farmers'.[126] Existing provisions for agricultural rates relief were due to expire on 31 March 1962, so a solution had to be found without waiting for the ERI report. On 2 March Blaney wrote to Lemass indicating his hope that the concessions could be framed in order to assist the 'national agricultural position'. Lemass requested estimates of the valuation of farms which could be completely de-rated at a cost of (a) £6m. and (b) £7m., which seems to indicate that he intended to direct all relief towards smaller holdings. Local Government calculated that it would cost £6.15m. to de-rate all holdings under £13 valuation and £7.15m. for holdings valued at less than £16. For the same sum, they could fully de-rate all holdings under £10 and provide 60 per cent remission on holdings valued from £10 to £20.

In the event, the government decided to retain a modified version of the existing scheme, with a substantial measure of additional relief going to larger holdings, a decision which may indicate some awareness of the contents of Walker's, as yet unpublished, ERI report. Rates relief on the first £20 was increased from 60 to 70 per cent, with a new supplementary allowance of 25 per cent applying on higher valuations. Many farmers had transferred ownership of part of their land to a family member in order to benefit from the higher rates relief available on smaller holdings, and local authorities were given power to counter this trend. Employment allowances, which had previously applied only to workers aged seventeen years or over, were extended to sixteen-year-olds.

The new reliefs were announced in the 1962 Budget.[127] Although the agricultural grant now met 57 per cent of all rates levied on agricultural land, at a cost to the Exchequer of £8.5m., the concession failed to stem protests. In February 1963 Offaly County Council adjourned its annual estimates meeting for twenty-one days and demanded that the Taoiseach meet a deputation to discuss the complete de-rating of agricultural land and the possibility of making health and road expenditure a national charge.[128]

The publication in May 1962 of the ERI report *Local Government in Ireland: A Preliminary Survey*[129] had given further momentum to this campaign, by providing data which showed that Exchequer grants to local authorities had failed to keep pace with the increase in local authority expenditure throughout the 1950s. The report concluded that 'a formidable case can be built up against rates on the grounds of equity'. Rates were a progressive tax on farmers which placed a heavy burden on larger farmers; the ratio of rates to farm income appeared to be roughly twice as high as the ratio to non-farm income. Walker criticised the practice of allocating Exchequer grants to local authorities on a percentage basis, because this limited their freedom to spend money on non-grant-aided items. Percentage grants were also condemned for failing to give a greater level of assistance to poorer areas. Although counties with a high proportion of small farms obtained a larger share of the agricultural grant, the major beneficiaries were counties with many small farmers, which had high levels of local taxation. Three of the five counties with the lowest per capita rateable values — Counties Donegal, Mayo and Kerry — received below average per capita grants, while the five counties with the highest per capita values, Meath, South Tipperary, Waterford, Westmeath and Kilkenny, all received above average per capita grants.

The final report, published in 1964, incorporating new data on Irish county incomes,[130] revised the conclusion that poorer counties paid a higher proportion of income in rates and determined that 'poorer counties do receive greater support from the state than the relatively well-off ones'. However, this failed to restore faith in the system of local finance. Data showing that personal income per capita ranged from £153 in Counties Mayo and Donegal to £227 in Kildare and £231 in Dublin, had, as Walker indicated, 'important implications when Local Authorities are being asked to provide certain very important services by the State'. Walker believed that Exchequer grants should be revised to provide additional funds for poorer areas, but appeared vague about how this should be done. Data on rateable valuation per capita in different counties was 'not a particularly good indicator of the relative wealth of a county'.[131]

Walker's efforts to relate local authority grants and expenditure to county incomes per capita can be seen as an effort to establish a revised basis for allocating grants to local authorities, while avoiding the politically unpalatable step of a general revaluation. Meanwhile the interdepartmental committee on local finance and taxation concentrated its energies on the question of valuation, a process which exposed the fundamental basis of local taxation to detailed scrutiny. The committee emphasised that the valuation system had become increasingly distorted because no mechanism existed for carrying out a general revaluation, which would take account of inflation, or of changes in relative values of land or property. New properties were valued on the basis of their theoretical value in 1914. A general revaluation of buildings in County Galway, carried out between 1946 and 1950, had raised valuations by an average of 30 per cent and by 52 per cent for property in Galway borough. The valuation of some properties doubled; others remained unchanged. The committee concluded that the existing system failed to ensure that occupiers of similar premises in a locality paid rates on the same valuations, and added:

> Where a system intended to distribute taxes fairly breaks down or becomes distorted public confidence in the system is lost and some degree of hardship results. The Committee is satisfied that a widespread irrelativity among valuations exists and that this defeats the objective of equitable distribution of the rates assessed on them. The lack of public confidence in the present valuation system is indicated by recurring criticisms in the press, in local authority resolutions and in questions and comments in the Dáil and Seanad.

In a memorandum to the committee, the Commissioner of Valuation stated that 'everything points to there being no real solution to the present anomalies short of general revaluation'. This was a daunting prospect; it would take at least ten years to revalue hereditaments other than land, and a further ten years to revalue land. The committee judged that the existence of the agricultural grant indicated that land was overvalued relative to buildings and decided that only land in county boroughs and the borough of Dun Laoghaire should be revalued. However, if buildings were revalued, while land values were unchanged, there would be a substantial shift in the relative incidence of rates between land and buildings, which might be regarded as 'intolerable as well as inequitable'. To meet these objections, the committee considered basing all revaluations on 1914 prices, but then rejected this option. Conscious of the political pitfalls inherent in tampering with the rating system, the committee decided that it should first conduct a series of studies into the probable effect of a revaluation on different classes of ratepayers in different areas. A majority of the committee also recommended that responsibility for the Valuations Office be transferred from Finance to Local Government.

The committee's report, together with the studies carried out by the Economic Research Institute, did much to undermine the rating system without providing an alternative. The interdepartmental committee noted that it had 'not yet investigated potential sources of local revenue as an alternative or a supplement to rates'. However, it stated that the revenue provided by rates was 'so very substantial as, in our opinion, to rule out the possibility of our being able to recommend an alternative source or sources of local taxation in substitution completely or to any great extent for this form of taxation of property'.[132]

In October 1965 Local Government released a summary of the committee's first interim report, with the intention of informing public opinion and inspiring suggestions for reforming local taxation. In September 1966, the Minister voiced his disappointment that 'no serious worthwhile suggestions had been prompted by the report'.[133] Farmers continued to protest against rates and, in an effort to placate them, the 1967 budget announced that all holdings valued at £20 or less would be de-rated, while scale relief would be extended to those valued between £20 and £33.[134] An abbreviated version of the committee's second report, which dealt with rates remissions, was published in 1967. The third report, on rates and other sources of local authority revenue, which was published in July 1968, opted to retain rates as a major source of local revenue. It also suggested that additional revenue could be raised from local authority charges. Although the report listed local sales, entertainment and income taxes as possible sources of revenue, it concluded that local authorities would continue to depend on rates, though it saw the long-term survival of the rating system as dependent on a comprehensive revaluation. It also suggested that there was scope for altering the basis of distributing grants to local authorities, in order to ensure a more generous allocation for poorer areas, but it made no firm recommendations on this matter pending a further report.[135] In the meantime the 1970 Local Government (Rates) Act gave local authorities the discretionary power to waive rates for defined categories of persons, e.g. recipients of non-contributory old-age and widows' pensions, blind pensions, disabled persons maintenance allowance and home assistance; it also gave ratepayers the statutory right to pay their rates by instalments.

By the early 1970s local authority finances had been under investigation for a decade, but the only reforms to have taken place concerned health. The White Paper on local government reorganisation, which was presented to the both Houses of the Oireachtas in February 1971,[136] contained a government commitment to issue a White Paper on Local Finance and Taxation, and this was laid before the Oireachtas in December 1972. The White Paper endorsed nearly all the decisions of the interdepartmental committee and signalled that the government favoured moderate reform, not radical change. The government was committed to ensuring that local taxes would continue to provide a substantial share of local authority revenue. Once the possibility of introducing a local sales tax was ruled out, rates were left as the only possible source of local revenue. The White Paper conceded that the rating system needed reform, but was optimistic that reforms would yield additional revenue. Above all, the White Paper made no definite statement about the appropriate share of local expenditure which should be financed by the Exchequer. With a general election imminent, this was seen as an explosive issue, though strong hints were given that the share of local expenditure borne by central funds would be reduced.

The White Paper emphasised that it was desirable to reduce local authority dependence on Exchequer grants, because these invariably resulted in greater control of local affairs by central government, and a loss of financial and administrative freedom by local authorities.[137] Any major review of local taxation raised questions about the structure and powers of local authorities. This had been emphasised by Walker in his 1962 review of local taxation:

> Regarded as agencies of Central Government, Local Authorities do not need to have independent sources of revenue. If, however, Local Authorities are to be responsible bodies with, at any rate, some power to do things which the Central Government is not too keen that they should do then it is desirable and probably necessary that they should have some financial independence; should have taxes under their control which would enable them to finance a good deal of expenditure.[138]

Financial pressures were not the only factor pointing towards a review of the structure of local government. A White Paper on the future of the health services, published in 1966, proposed transferring administrative responsibility for these services from county councils to eight regional health authorities.[139] The emergence of Regional Development Organisations also suggested that authority was shifting from the county to larger units. Given the rate of change during the 1960s, the public service as a whole was in need of review and this was carried out by the Devlin Group, which reported in 1969.[140] The 1971 White Paper on Local Government carried out a similar review of the local government service.

The Devlin Report provides a useful snapshot of the Department of Local Government at the end of a decade of considerable change. In 1968/69 there were 43 officers in general service and 79 professional (i.e. specialist) officers above higher executive officer grade in a total establishment of 610. In 1934/35 there had been 12 general service and 34 professional officers in this grade. At first glance, the structure of the Department had changed little since the foundation of the state. There were seven basic groups: housing and sanitary services; planning and general; roads; establishment and administration; technical advisory; audit; and legal advisory: Sir Henry Robinson of the LGB might have found this reassuring. (However, the Department now contains fourteen administrative sections, grouped into four divisions, each headed by an assistant secretary.) The Devlin Report called for a clear division in each Department between those responsible for determining policy and those charged with its execution. Policy formation would be carried out by a section called the *aireacht*, which would also be responsible for policy review. On several occasions the Report expressed concern at the 'drift towards regionalism'[141] and the variety and *ad hoc* nature of the emerging regional bodies. It recommended that the Department of Local Government should be transformed into a Department of Regional Development, with a wider remit which would enable it to co-ordinate all aspects of local development on a regional basis. The *aireacht* attached to the new Department would contain three sections responsible for policy on housing and sanitary services regional planning, and development and roads.

The new Department would lose responsibility for elections, rent restrictions, combined purchase, libraries and for auditing the accounts of local authorities. These would be taken over by the Departments of Justice, Public Service and National Culture, and the Comptroller and Auditor General respectively, while 'miscellaneous welfare activities, e.g. responsibility for itinerants', would pass to the Department of Social Welfare. The new Department would gain control of both the Valuation Office and the Local Loans Fund.

Although the Devlin Report was not directly concerned with the system of local government, it did consider the distribution of functions between different bodies. It quoted the conclusion of the Maud Committee on the management of local government in Britain, that in Ireland 'central control is the most stringent of all'. Devlin was particularly critical of 'a failure to think through the roles of local authorities as executive agencies within the system of government'; the overlapping work of local authorities and government departments — the National Building Agency was cited as an example of this — which resulted in 'the diffusion of responsibility and the inhibition of developmental attitudes in local authorities'. It recommended that the Department of Regional Development delegate more responsibility to local authorities, and that detailed supervision of local authorities should be reduced and replaced with a system of controls which were similar to those exercised by Departments over non-commercial state-sponsored bodies. This would enable the Department to concentrate on 'positive constructive thinking and action'.

The 1971 White Paper on local government reorganisation was the first comprehensive review of local government since the foundation of the state. It analysed the changing nature of local administration in language which was characteristic of this era: 'local authorities, therefore, must now regard themselves and be regarded as development corporations for their areas'. Like other government papers of this period, the White Paper favoured moderate reform of local government, not revolution. The county should remain the key administrative unit, though it proposed some unspecified modifications in county boundaries. However, since 'rigid demarcation between rural and urban areas' was unsatisfactory in the light of modern circumstances, it proposed that town commissioners should be abolished, while 'in appropriate cases' the functions of small urban district councils should be transferred to county councils. A single local authority would be established for the Dublin area, and new arrangements would be considered for Limerick, Cork and Galway. To compensate for the loss of local autonomy, area committees and community councils would be established to provide a voice for local communities.

The White Paper accepted the recommendation of the Devlin Report that any new regional bodies 'should not form an extra layer of government duplicating the activities of existing authorities'. Regional authorities should be non-executive bodies, primarily concerned with regional planning and development, their function limited to securing co-operation between local authorities. It also echoed the view expressed in the Devlin Report that local authorities should be given greater autonomy by extending their permissive or discretionary powers and by easing the administrative controls exercised by the Department. However, capital expenditure would be closely controlled to ensure that it conformed with national priorities and took account of the state of the economy. It emphasises that greater autonomy for local authorities was heavily dependent on their ability to generate sufficient revenue from local sources. A healthy revenue from rates, or an alternative local tax, was a precondition for devolved government. But continued pressure for a reduction, or removal of rates from farmers and urban householders alike and the electoral imperatives of party politics, as seen in both the 1973 and 1977 general election, destroyed the prospect of greater devolution of local government.

CONCLUSIONS

The Department of Local Government in January 1973 was markedly different from the Department in 1956. Economic planning and development had created a host of new challenges and responsibilities concerning planning, roads, housing and sanitary services. New issues were coming to the fore, such as accommodation for travellers, nuclear power and environmental pollution. By the early 1970s the Department's powers had been enhanced: it now controlled all aspects of the building and construction industry which, together with the growing interest in physical planning, gave it a role in economic development; this would have been scarcely credible sixteen years earlier when *Economic Development* appeared to relegate it to obscurity. The White Papers on the structure and finances of local authorities appeared to promise a revitalised system of local taxation which would enable more administrative functions to be devolved to local authorities, giving officials in the Department more time to concentrate on planning and development. However, the fact that the government had failed to either reform the rating system or to devise a viable alternative, after almost a decade of detailed investigation, was a worrying sign. It suggested that the political will to reform local taxation was lacking; this was an issue over which the Department had no control.

Nineteen seventy-three marked the beginning of a new era for the Department of Local Government. There was a change of government. Ireland joined the European Community — a move that would have major consequences for many of the Department's programmes and policies and that ultimately would provide an important source of funding. The oil crisis that autumn provided a major shock to western economies, which brought an end to the long post-war period of record economic growth. Higher energy prices forced the Department to devote much more attention to fuel conservation. These were yet further instances of the wide variety of issues which the Department of Local Government was forced to confront.

CHAPTER ELEVEN

THE CUSTOM HOUSE AND THE PARISH PUMP

J.J. Lee began the final chapter of his history of Ireland from 1912 to 1985 by posing the question, 'How well has independent Ireland performed?'. His assessment, which compared the rates of economic growth in Ireland and in other European countries, was critical in the extreme: Lee found it 'difficult to avoid the conclusion that Irish economic performance has been the least impressive in western Europe, perhaps in all Europe, in the twentieth century'.[1] The present chapter does not ask how well the Department of Local Government and Public Health and the Department of Local Government have performed, if only because there is no objective basis on which such an evaulation can be made. It concentrates on other issues: what the history of the Department reveals about state-building in independent Ireland and in particular about the relationship between central and local government; what light it sheds on matters such as the continuity between the British administration in Ireland and the public service of the independent Irish state, or the authority exercised by the Department of Finance over public expenditure; and what it reveals about the nature of Irish society.

The most important function of any government is to uphold the rule of law and the institutions of civil society. Although the Dáil Éireann Department of Local Government made considerable efforts to sustain the system of local government during the years of the Anglo-Irish war, by 1923 the collection of rates, the most extensive form of direct taxation at that time, had collapsed in many parts of Ireland. Normal communications had broken down because of the destruction of roads and bridges. For the majority of Irish citizens who lived in the countryside and in small towns, local government and the police were the institutions of state that impinged most closely on their lives.

Between 1919 and 1921 the retreat of the Royal Irish Constabulary and the collapse of the Local Government Board's authority heralded the end of British rule in Ireland. Re-establishing local government in areas where it had broken down was therefore essential to secure the legitimacy of the Irish Free State. During the 1920s the Department of Local Government and Public Health succeeded in raising the percentage of rates collected to levels similar to those that had applied before 1914. The Department also ensured that war-damaged roads and bridges were repaired.

It was also vital that local authorities met their responsibilities to ratepayers and the general community. In 1922 Thomas Gilmartin of Tubbercurry, Co. Sligo blamed his daughter's death from fever on the fact that he had been forced to empty the family privy by bringing the waste matter through the house, because his landlord had denied him rear access. Gilmartin initially sought redress for his problems from a local IRA leader, who tried to arbitrate between the parties, rather than from the Department or from the local medical officer of health,[2] which suggests that the last two agencies were either seen as ineffective, or that the public did not universally acknowledge their role.

Improvements in housing and in the standard of public health depended ultimately on central government. The majority of local authorities lacked both the financial resources and the necessary commitment. The generous provision of cottages for agricultural labourers from the 1880s was possible only because the British exchequer provided substantial subsidies for this purpose; finding a solution to the Dublin tenement problem required a similar, if not greater, level of state assistance. Most local authorities appear to have given a low priority to enforcing public health regulations. Dublin Corporation's record of neglect in this respect before 1914 is legendary, and it is not all attributable to lack of money. Abandoning sheep-dipping and the inspection of dairy yards were among the first decisions taken by several Sinn Féin local authorities in 1920, and such actions appear to have been symptomatic of the low administrative standards that prevailed within local authorities. The reports of the Dáil Department of Local Government inspectors reveal innumerable instances of drunken workhouse masters, absentee clerks and the petty pilfering of stores. If the standard of local administration improved after 1922, as appears to have been the case, this is primarily the result of the extension of central control over local affairs and the increased reliance on professional administrators, rather than on elected officials.

Giving greater autonomy to local authorities would have condemned Irish households to lower living standards, to less healthy living conditions and to a less equitable allocation of jobs, contracts and housing. The hostile reaction of county councillors to the loss of the powers of appointment, firstly to the Local Appointments Commission and secondly to county managers, is an indication of the premium placed on such privileges. Left to their own devices, there is little doubt that most local authorities would have employed only local candidates, often regardless of merit, and, as the actions of Sligo Corporation and Roscommon Town Commissioners indicate, local authority housing would frequently have been allocated to those with the appropriate connections, often irrespective of need. Many local politicians appear to have subscribed to what Thomas H. O'Connor, the historian of the Boston Irish, has described as the 'politics of help and succor',[3] but the help and succour did not necessarily reach the worst-housed and the most impoverished.

The intervention of the Local Government Department resulted in higher standards of local government and greater equality of opportunity, be it the opportunity to work for a local authority, or entitlement to a council house. The hostile attitudes displayed in many communities towards the provision of labourers' housing in the 1930s suggest that, without the Department's intervention, many councils would have been reluctant to provide sufficient cottages. There is little doubt that, as the representative of a native government, the Department of Local Government was in a position to intervene much more forcefully in the affairs of Irish local authorities than the Local Government Board, though it appears to have exercised this power selectively. For example, the Department went to considerable efforts to make sure that local authorities built sufficient houses; it was much more phlegmatic about councils that failed to implement planning legislation. By 1947 no Irish local authority had fully complied with the 1934 Planning Act.[4]

The desire to secure jobs and housing, often irrespective of the means adopted, is perhaps understandable in a country where lack of employment caused many men and women to emigrate and where low living standards often meant that it was difficult to obtain decent housing at a moderate cost. A secure job in a council office that went to an outsider meant one less job for a local man or woman. The private papers of Richard Mulcahy are filled with letters from priests, nuns, Christian Brothers and tenuous acquaintances — all seeking state jobs for deserving friends and relatives. Donnchadh Ó Briain, Fianna Fáil TD for West Limerick, was asked to use his influence to secure the appointment of a constituent as a clerical officer to Limerick County Council (Ó Briain refused); another correspondent sought temporary relief work on the river Deel drainage scheme (Ó Briain made successful representations on his behalf). Donnchadh Ó Briain was also approached by constituents for assistance in securing local authority houses and repairs to council houses.[5]

The practice of councillors awarding jobs to their political allies and co-religionists predated the foundation of the state. In the early twentieth century many local authorities in Ulster were alleged not to employ a single catholic, whereas in County Monaghan, a county with a sizeable protestant population, all thirty-seven jobs in the county council's gift went to catholics.[6] After 1922 there was greater autonomy in local government services in Northern Ireland than in the Irish Free State; indeed, responsibility for education was devolved to the local authorities. Buckland notes that 'local authorities [in Northern Ireland] were frequently party battlegrounds and sources of patronage'.[7] It may be foolhardy to assume that a more decentralised local government service in independent Ireland would have followed a similar path, yet the resentment expressed at the appointment to local government posts of 'the indirect murderers of poor Kevin O'Higgins',[8] and at the continued employment by local authorities of former unionists, suggests that we should not underestimate the extent of political divisions within the Irish Free State, and the degree to which they would have influenced local appointments.

We know little about the views of ratepayers concerning low standards in local administration. In 1921 the Dáil Department of Local Government inspector for County Clare reported that the townspeople of Kilrush, a town that was alleged to have the 'worst urban district council in Ireland', indicated 'an amount of disaffection . . . a mixture of indifference and despair amounting to the loss of citizens' honour and dignity'.[9] In 1931 Richard Mulcahy, Minister for Local Government, claimed that the commissioners who assumed responsibility for local government from dissolved local authorities were universally popular; he received many letters asking that they be retained. One came from a Mayo parish priest, who wrote that, 'it was a God sent gift to Mayo the day you superseded the late county council. That librarian appointment was unfortunate but I am told that you have retrieved the position of the Government a thousand fold.'[10] Were such attitudes commonly held, or are the complaints made by local councillors and politicians at the loss of local autonomy more representative of public opininion? Jim Kennedy, the town clerk of Thurles, who corresponded regularly with Mulcahy, claimed that local government officials welcomed the appointment of commissioners.[11]

Kevin O'Higgins claimed that 'The civic sense, the community conscience, is feeble in Ireland'.[12] Although O'Higgins was referring to Irish democracy in general, and not specifically to local government, some leading Irish politicians appear to have believed that the shortcomings of those involved in local politics were much more serious than the failings of members of the national parliament. During the years of the first and second Dála, it is clear that Cosgrave and O'Higgins saw a descending scale of probity, with the lowest standards being found among the smallest local authorities — the rural district councils and town commissioners. Kevin O'Higgins berated county councillors for their obsession with claiming Ministry of Transport grants and retaining local hospitals when the future of the Irish nation was at stake. At issue are two overlapping, and often conflicting, strands in Irish politics: one motivated by an idealistic concern with goals such as national independence, even if they involved major personal sacrifice, and another that was primarily concerned with more mundane matters such as jobs and contracts. Yet contradicting O'Higgins's belief that local authorities were concerned only with material benefits, Seán T. O'Kelly, Minister for Local Government from 1932 to 1939, proposed to dispense with county councils because he believed that councillors preferred to waste their time in 'the furtherance of national agitations', as opposed to providing local services.[13]

Both comments suggest that there was some confusion over the appropriate role of local authorities in the Irish state. English local government was originally built around the parish: an institution which had considerable historical legitimacy. In Ireland the Gaelic local units, the townlands, where justice appears to have been dispensed by a local *rí* (king) gradually disappeared under British rule.[14] Although Irish people had a strong sense of identity with their native area, this was not necessarily coterminous with a rural district, a poor law union or even a county. David Fitzpatrick claims that the 'placenames carrying

519

emotional or cultural constructions', which appear in the letters home written by Irish emigrants to Australia during the nineteenth century, 'seldom belonged to counties and never to provinces'.[15] John A. Murphy has identified the Gaelic Athletic Association as a major factor in strengthening this sense of county, which suggests that the process took place only during the twentieth century.[16] Before 1898 the size of the Irish parliamentary electorate far exceeded the numbers who were eligible to elect poor law guardians or members of municipal corporations. Irish democracy was born with a focus on Westminster, not on local politics. Political organisations, such as that created by Daniel O'Connell or the Parnellite Irish Parliamentary Party, grew from the top down, not from local roots. Dublin Corporation, the country's leading local authority, which was controlled by nationalists from the mid-nineteenth century, appears to have seen itself as a substitute for the absent national parliament, rather than as a body with primarily local responsibilities; after 1898 county councils showed a similar tendency. In 1946 Seán MacEntee dated the beginnings of 'real local democracy' in Ireland to 1935, the year when the electorate for local elections was brought into line with the parliamentary electorate.[17]

Before 1922, both the Poor Law Commission and the Local Government Board treated Irish local authorities with a degree of mistrust and condescension, which can be seen as reflecting a metropolitan, or perhaps a colonial, superiority. This attitude applied both to local authorities that were under landlord control (it was particularly strong during the Famine years), and to democratically elected councils, though it was more pronounced in the latter case. In 1900 Sir Henry Robinson noted with relief that the new councils 'are not so difficult to lead as you might think from the aggressive tone of their resolutions about us'.[18] Robinson's urge to lead rural and county councils is understandable, given his professed belief in the racial inferiority of the native Irishman. After 1898 local councils tended to contest the Local Government Board's authority by pointing out that, while they had been elected by Irish voters, the Local Government Board had no such mandate. This attitude should have ended with the passing of British rule, yet this does not appear to have been the case. In 1921 the chairman of Louth County Council boasted that he had thrown the Local Government Board inspector out of the council chamber and would treat the Dáil inspector in a similar fashion. When Dublin Corporation was dissolved in 1923, *The Freeman's Journal* accused it of 'treating the Government elected by the Irish people as a foreign Government'.[19]

During the years 1920-22 the Dáil Department of Local Government appears to have been as eager to lead Irish local authorities as Sir Henry Robinson had been; many communications from Kevin O'Higgins exude a similarly patronising air and an impatience with local concerns. In February 1922 one inspector of the Dáil Department of Local Government reported from Cork that 'the people here will not take everything lying down even from a Dáil Department. . . . They resent being told how they may insure their ambulances etc., they feel competent to do this themselves.'[20] More than forty years after Robinson, a senior official in the Department of Local Government remarked of the proposed parish councils: 'What is needed is not a unit of self-government or local government but a unit of obligation'; he would welcome an obedient body that would respond willingly when the Department asked it to carry out certain duties.[21]

During the first ten years of its existence, the DLGPH appears to have ended some of the more vexatious forms of supervision that the Local Government Board and the Dáil Éireann Department of Local Government had exercised over local authorities. The practice of requiring councils to submit their minutes to the Department ceased, and with it the tedious annotation of each decision minuted in the correct colour of ink. The team of inspectors employed by Dáil Éireann was disbanded. From the mid-1920s, inspectors tended to be used for specific functions, such as holding an inquiry into the need for a slum-clearance scheme, as opposed to acting as general intelligence officers on the doings of local authorities. The Department also claimed that the appointment of city managers made it possible to reduce the degree of scrutiny by Dublin. Reforms of this nature were primarily of benefit to officials rather than politicians and would have counted for little with most councillors in comparison with the loss of control over local appointments. However, the surviving auditors' reports show a continuing concern with red tape and detailed regulations,[22] which must have caused anger and frustration in the offices and council chambers of many local authorities. The Department consistently expressed resentment at the Department of Finance's efforts to scrutinise its operations. Did officials in the Custom House ever reflect on the parallels between their anger at the demands imposed by Merrion Street, and the disgruntlement of local authorities?

The Cumann na nGaedheal and Fianna Fáil governments displayed an apparent lack of sympathy with local democracy during the first twenty years after independence. Both postponed local elections, ostensibly because the government was in the process of reforming local government. Nevertheless, there are important differences between the attitudes of the two parties. For Cumann na nGaedheal, reform of local government was motivated primarily by the wish to save public money, and by a commitment to high standards in public life. Brian Maye claims that the party had no organisation in the countryside and that in the towns it was made up of 'influential people and their social circles'.[23] Such supporters would have given higher priority to reducing taxes than to retaining access to local patronage.

Fianna Fáil was organised on a much tighter basis; it was also less concerned with reducing public expenditure and more committed to interventionist policies. Reducing the autonomy of local authorities improved party discipline, and ministers believed that it also helped government to run more smoothly. Paul Sacks claims that in the first decades after independence the local organisations of county councillors 'were largely personal and individualistic and thus made little contribution to the growth of a powerful grass-roots party organisation'. According to Sacks, 'the growth of partisan competition occurred, ironically, only after the powers of local representatives had been curtailed with the introduction of the county-manager system in 1940'.[24]

Several Fianna Fáil ministers were of the opinion that deliberating bodies such as Dáil Éireann or local councils obstructed the government's work. This belief is best expressed in de Valera's statement, in 1933, that the Dáil should be given 'say six months holidays', so that the cabinet could get on with the urgent tasks in hand without having to waste time on parliamentary duties.[25] The wish to override local authorities was motivated by a similar impatience. In November 1932, Lemass wanted to take relief works under the direct control of central government, perhaps using 'dictatorial powers' in order to put a scheme in place as soon as possible;[26] Hugo Flinn made several attempts to have responsibility for initiating relief works given to the Office of Public Works, as opposed to waiting for local authorities to respond to government grants. Seán T. O'Kelly considered setting up a small housing board which would supplant the functions of both local authorities and the Department of Local

Government. In 1945 Erskine Childers, then parliamentary secretary in the Department of Local Government and Public Health, proposed that, in the interests of efficiency, responsibility for national roads should be taken away from local authorities.

In keeping with this functionalist approach to local government, Fianna Fáil ministers appear to have consulted local officials, rather than local politicians, about local government matters. Seán T. O'Kelly introduced the practice of holding annual meetings with county secretaries to discuss topics of immediate concern, such as the state of rate collection and how the housing programme was faring. After 1942 this annual meeting was attended by county managers. In 1940, when the government was eager to press ahead with establishing parish councils, it summoned county secretaries, not chairmen of county councils, to Dublin for a special meeting. When Ireland appeared to be threatened with a fuel famine in 1947, de Valera met the county engineers and urged them to make special efforts to harvest more turf. The files give little indication that local councillors were consulted before important changes were introduced in local government legislation, though the General Council of County Councils and the Assocation of Municipal Authorities made representations to the Minister on many occasions. The meetings that Patrick O'Donnell, Fine Gael Minister for Local Government in the second inter-party government, held with councillors to hear their views on county management, appear to have been unique.

By 1948 Irish politics seems to have been divided on party lines over the question of decentralisation. Although Cumann na nGaedheal, the antecedent of Fine Gael, had first introduced city management, by that date Fine Gael was committed to a more decentralised system of local government — one that gave greater power to elected members. In 1948 the aims of Clann na Poblachta included 'decentralisation based upon local control to secure the development of civic responsibility'.[27] The joint statement of policy objectives issued by Fine Gael and Labour during the 1954 general election campaign included a commitment to restore local democratic rights.

Yet it would be dangerous to overstate the contrast between a centralist Fianna Fáil government and the other parties. On the one hand, the second inter-party government's expressed commitment to greater local autonomy meant that it was unwilling to tell Dublin Corporation how it should allocate the capital that the government had provided from the Local Loans Fund. (Given that the sum available was insufficient to finance all the planned investment programme, the government may also have preferred to place the onus for the cutbacks on Dublin Corporation.) On the other hand, between 1948 and 1951, Labour Ministers for Local Government (who were committed to advancing local autonomy) introduced national wage rates for council road labourers and standard pay and superannuation conditions — actions which seriously undermined the autonomy of local authorities, particularly those with the lowest rateable valuation. Such contradictory positions were probably inevitable: the trade union movement was committed to ending regional wage differentials for all jobs.[28] By the 1950s, most Irish people would have assumed that they were entitled to uniform standards in public service. The inter-party government that appealed to emigrants to return home by promises of employment and good living conditions could scarcely qualify this by offering lower standards of pay or housing in County Mayo than in County Meath.

While, superficially, the story of local government since independence appears to be characterised by a single-minded push for greater centralisation, the reality is more complex. Seán MacEntee, Fianna Fail Minister for Local Government during the Emergency, argued that the system of county management had been introduced in order to save local democracy from the twin evils of inefficiency and corruption.[29] Fianna Fáil took the wishes of local councils, and of the electorate, into account when allocating public funds for local expenditure. If local authorities lost control of appointments, the losers were the councillors. Voters, particularly rural voters living in western counties, were placated by the provision of government grants for culs-de-sac and for slate roofs to replace the traditional thatch, and with state-funded seasonal employment for carrying out minor repairs on roads and drains — a frugal Irish variant of bread and circuses. Any scrutiny of how money for roads, housing and sanitary services was allocated suggests that objective national needs were rarely accorded priority; rather, expenditure was determined by a combination of factors, such as resolutions at *ard fheiseanna*, representations from Dáil deputies and local interest groups, public opinion as expressed in newspaper headlines, and ministerial intuitions about what was appropriate for an Irish state. Thus in 1932 the cabinet voted extra assistance for rural labourers' housing, though civil servants believed that clearing urban slums was much more urgent.

Successive governments extended housing grants for private owners and rates remission for new houses, often against the advice of officials in Local Government, because they proved extremely popular. When a government was committed to a programme that gave rise to opposition from some interest groups, such as the regional water schemes that were being provided in the early 1960s, it quietly modified the programme to take account of their views. This was perhaps less true of the Cumann na nGaedheal government of 1922-32: a more politically astute administration would probably have reduced the authority of the Local Appointments Commission and restored some measure of discretion in appointments to local authorities.

Many proposals for greater centralisation were rejected or substantially modified. In 1922 the Irish Free State reversed the British government's policy of giving responsibility for roads to a Ministry of Transport and restored control to the local authorities. Most of the first-generation of county managers were not, as Seán T. O'Kelly originally wished, bright young civil servants from the Custom House, but former county secretaries whose outlook would have been much closer to that of local councillors. In 1932, Fianna Fáil made a serious effort to reduce the authority of the Local Appointments Commission in favour of the local authorities, and both inter-party governments strove to replace the county managers with a system that gave greater control to elected representatives. Nevertheless, the Local Appointments Commission and the county management system survived, despite being widely criticised, because both measures had a strong administrative rationale, and it proved difficult either to reverse them or to devise practicable alternatives that would mollify objectors.

Dáil deputies assumed a critical role in the process of mediating between national and local interests. This began to emerge as early as 1920/21: Wexford deputies actively opposed the Dáil Department of Local Government's plans to rationalise the county's workhouse and hospitals; in County Mayo the Dáil inspector found that councillors gave greater credence to a local deputy than to the instructions which he transmitted from the Department. We should, however, regard with caution the attitude of TDs towards the relative responsibilities of central and local government. Although both the Cumann na nGaedheal government and successive Fianna Fáil governments faced criticism from their back-bench deputies for failing to take greater account of the wishes of local authorities, some of this may have been posturing. While the files relating to Local Government refer only in passing to representations from Dáil deputies, it is evident that they were a constant feature of life. If all decisions on housing grants, drainage schemes and road works had been devolved to local authorities, one wonders how most TDs would have spent their time. Certainly the number of parliamentary questions would have been much reduced.[30] J. J. Lee has remarked:

> Local interests therefore have to be hawked prominently around the national political arena, instead of being decided at less obtrusive local level. It is less the intensity of localism that is peculiar to Ireland than the mechanisms devised to elevate the local to the national. Indeed localism has become even more pronounced, and inevitably so, as the role of central government has grown. The prominence of the local at national level is the reverse side of the coin of administrative centralisation.[31]

In 1956, when the second inter-party government considered the possibility of devolving control over housing grants to local authorities, John Garvin, secretary of the Department, suggested that Dáil deputies would resent the change because it would place councillors on an equal, or possibly a stronger, footing than the deputies vis-à-vis voters.[32]

With the exception of the office of city manager, the primary thrust towards reforming local administration appears to have come from ministers, rather than from civil servants. In 1934 Edward McCarron, who had played an active role in introducing city management, voiced his opposition to O'Kelly's proposal to abolish county councils. During the 1960s when the Lemass government was looking at the possibility of reforming local taxation and local government administration, John Garvin pointed out that, although there would be considerable scope for savings if road construction was placed under central government control, this would entail 'a disturbance of the first magnitude in local employment and income . . . to the deep-rooted nature of Local Government and [to] the many firmly-established interests involved.'[33] Officials frequently acted to protect local authorities from being overridden by central government, emphasising that public works or housing programmes should be initiated by local authorities, rather than by central government. The Department was generally, though not universally, opposed to the granting of rates remission for new buildings, because it believed that it was essential to protect the revenue yield from local taxes as a symbol of local responsibility. For similar reasons, it consistently emphasised that if the state assumed responsibility for the cost of local services, such as housing or main roads, this would automatically mean a further loss of local control.[34] Such attitudes may stem as much from the innate conservatism of civil servants, and from self-interest, as from concern with local democracy: if responsibility for relief works, road construction and housing was transferred to the Office of Public Works, the Road Board and the Housing Board respectively, what tasks would remain for a Department of Local Government?

After 1922 there was a sustained fall in the proportion of local expenditure that was financed by rates, and an increase in the share covered by central funds. It proved easier to disband local authorities than to create new ones; it proved easier to hand power to county managers than to devise new mechanisms that would ensure that local administration was both efficient and was widely regarded as being democratic; and it proved easier to erode the income from rates by granting successive concessions to farmers and to home-owners than to devise an alternative source of local revenue.

Demands by Irish citizens for more generous state assistance for programmes such as housing, coupled with the failure to provide local authorities with an expanding source of locally generated revenue, proved to be critical factors promoting greater central control. By 1898 Irish local authorities were saddled with a taxation system that had already shown itself inadequate to meet the expenditure required of local authorities. The British government had introduced partial de-rating of agricultural land, first in Britain and then in Ireland, to placate the demands of British and Irish landlords. The concession, which took no account of the long-term financial needs of local government, had particularly serious implications for Ireland, given the country's heavy reliance on agriculture. Further reliefs were granted on several occasions after 1922, often as temporary expedients, but they tended to be retained for many decades.

Rateable values were determined by a valuation system that contained anomalies, and was known to vary in its incidence between different parts of Ireland.[35] Yet it was not until the early 1960s that a serious effort was made to reform the system of local taxation. Although the Economic Research Institute provided copious quantities of statistical data and an interdepartmental committee deliberated the matter at length, no major changes resulted. By contrast, in 1963 a minority Fianna Fáil government introduced a general sales tax — the turnover tax — despite widespread objections.[36] Turnover tax, the antecedent of the modern value-added tax, together with PAYE, which was introduced in 1960,[37] provided a growing revenue for the modern Irish state — or rather the modern centralised state. By comparison, because local authorities were forced to survive with an outmoded system of taxation, they became increasingly dependent on the Exchequer: a tribe of mendicants at the doors of Government Buildings or the Custom House. Meanwhile, Exchequer assistance was allocated to local authorities in the form of a complex mixture of pro rata grants and interest subsidies which often brought disproportionate benefits to richer areas. Similar anomalies had been highlighted in 1900 in the report and minutes of the Royal Commission on Local Taxation and in a series of studies carried out in Britain in the 1930s.[38]

If a minority government could successfully introduce the unpopular turnover tax, it should arguably have been possible to implement a new system of local taxation. However the competing responsibilities of different government departments acted to block reform. Although the Department of Local Government was primarily responsible for local affairs, the Valuation Office was under the control of the Department of Finance, which was also responsible for taxation in general. The Departments of Agriculture and Industry and Commerce intervened to protect the interests of the farming community and business, often at a cost to local revenue. Several, if not all, these departments may have had a vested interest in not reforming local taxation. Higher income from locally raised taxes would have resulted in greater resistance to increases in centrally imposed taxation. That was not in the interests of the Department of Finance. While the revenue provided by turnover tax was essential if the government was to meet its commitments, devising an alternative source of local revenue did not carry the same priority: the money for local services could, and indeed did, come from central government. This permitted successive administrations to avoid taking difficult decisions.

There is little evidence that ministers or officials in the Department of Local Government considered these broader questions, except when they sat as members of interdepartmental committees. It is interesting that the decision in 1961 to examine the basis of local taxation originated in the Taoiseach's Department and was opposed by the Department of Local Government. Most of the Department's attention was devoted to overseeing the enormous mass of local government legislation and to securing sufficient funds for its programmes. Twentieth-century Irish society has been extremely dependent on the state to meet its economic, social and even cultural needs. Since it was the Department responsible for providing services such as roads, water, sewerage, housing, libraries, parks and swimming pools, the demands on Local Government were almost infinite.

Ronan Fanning's history of the Department of Finance, the first departmental history to make use of Irish government archives, suggested that the Irish civil service continued to be dominated by the personnel and administrative practices inherited from Dublin Castle and that it was firmly under the control of the Department of Finance. According to Fanning, 'transferred civil servants numbered about 21,000, of whom eighty-eight had left or been dismissed by the British for political reasons', whereas only 131 civil servants employed by the Irish Free State had served under Dáil Éireann in the pre-Treaty period.[39] The Department of Local Government and Public Health presents a much weaker case of administrative continuity than Fanning intimates. Major administrative changes in local government were introduced during the 1920s,[40] and the argument about continuity of personnel should be seriously qualified.

As we saw in chapter three, none of the most senior administrative officials of the Local Government Board transferred to the Ministry of Local Government in 1922. Although Edward McCarron, James Hurson, Thomas McArdle and John Collins, the first four secretaries of the Department, were all former officials of the LGB, their backgrounds differed radically from the Board's leading civil servants. It would be an insult to the intelligence and the personalities of men such as Edward McCarron and John Collins, who were both educated by the Irish Christian Brothers, to assume that they followed blindly in the footsteps of Sir Henry Robinson or E. Coey Biggar, medical commissioner of the LGB, who was described by the officials of the Dáil Department of Local Government as the leader of the diehards.[41] However, the fact that John Costello emphasised McCarron's educational background and his membership of the Gaelic League in the course of a speech in Dáil Éireann (see chapter four), suggests that some Fianna Fáil deputies regarded him as an upholder of the British administrative system. In fact McCarron's formation was almost identical to that of the leaders of the Irish revolution.[42] A detailed study of the personnel of other government departments in the early years of the state probably would reveal a similar pattern. The apparent continuity in policy and procedure between the British administration in Ireland and the administration of independent Ireland may owe less to the legacy of the British administration than to the ideology of Irish nationalism (or its absence) and to the influence of the Irish educational system, in particular to the educational background of civil servants.[43]

Some qualifications should also be made concerning the ability of the Department of Finance to override the wishes of spending departments. While it would be naive to assume that Finance did not exercise considerable influence over departments such as Local Government, equally it would be ingenuous to assume that Finance was all-powerful. In particular, it is vital to distinguish between Finance's rhetoric concerning the evil of non-productive public expenditure and the burden of dead-weight debt, and the reality as indicated by trends in government expenditure. The authority of the Department of Finance appears to have been much more assured in the 1920s and again after 1958 than in the intervening period. In the 1920s this authority stemmed from the fact that the government's policy mirrored that of Finance in its opposition to increasing public expenditure; this may also explain why a major spending department, such as Local Government, did not mount a serious challenge to the restrictions that were imposed. After the publication of *Economic Development*, government policy again became almost synonymous with the views of the Department of Finance; moreover, by this stage Finance had implemented effective measures to ensure that capital expenditure by local authorities did not exceed the targets that were set. In the intervening years, the views of the Department of Finance concerning public expenditure were often in conflict with government policy; this meant that the department found it more difficult to enforce its views.

We should also distinguish between matters that were under Finance's immediate authority and those that were controlled by departments, such as Local Government, which might not share Finance's philosophy. Throughout most of the 1920s, Finance succeeded in excluding local authorities from borrowing money for housing from the Local Loans Fund, which it administered, and it succeeded in preventing Dublin and Cork Corporations from gaining access to the LLF until the mid-1950s. However, when Seán T. O'Kelly was Minister for Local Government and Public Health, that Department successfully extended housing grants on a number of occasions, in defiance of Finance, by the expedient of bringing bills to cabinet, and, on at least one occasion to the houses of the Oireachtas, without first submitting them to the Department of Finance. During the 1950s, at a time when Finance constantly reiterated the necessity of curbing government expenditure, local authorities repeatedly exceeded the limits set for local authority borrowings from the LLF, and gave commitments to pay housing grants, which they could not immediately meet.

This disregard of Finance's strictures probably happened because the governments in question had given public commitments that the housing programme would proceed, regardless of cost; it is not improbable that Local Government may have connived in these transgressions. The fact that central government expenditure rose from 11.6 per cent of Gross Domestic Product in 1938 to 35 per cent of GDP by 1955, the highest proportion among eleven western European countries,[44] is not consistent with the stereotype of an all-powerful and parsimonious Department of Finance. By the end of the 1950s, however, the emphasis which *Economic Development* had placed on productive investment and on meeting the targets set by economic planners meant that Finance was in a much better position to control expenditure by the Department of Local Government and by profligate local authorities.

The evidence presented throughout this book suggests that interdepartmental rivalries often proved more significant barriers to implementing new policies than the opposition expressed by the Department of Finance. Plans to take most adult men off the dole, in order to employ them on relief works, were not carried through, largely because of interdepartmental disagreements on how this should be done, and which government agency would be in control. In the early 1950s, differences between Local Government and Industry and Commerce concerning motor taxation resulted in a stalemate that lasted for several years; the introduction of driving tests was delayed because of a disagreement between the Departments of Justice and Local Government over who should carry out the tests.

The scope of the 1963 Planning Act was reduced in deference to the objections of other government departments. Rivalry between Local

Government and Agriculture delayed the provision of running water in rural areas. Had both departments been in agreement about how this should be carried out, or if the Department of Agriculture had remained aloof from this matter, the objections raised by farming interests would have had much less influence. Differences between the Department of Local Government and the Department of Finance should be seen as specific cases within the pattern of interdepartmental conflicts. During many such negotiations, individual government departments appear to have represented specific interest groups: thus on rates remission or running water, the Department of Agriculture acted as a spokesman for farming interests; in resisting pressure for stronger road traffic legislation, the Department of Justice appears to have represented the views of the gardaí, and Local Government often reflected the opinions of local authorities and their officials. Interdepartmental disagreements are also frequently motivated by a department's desire to increase its authority; this was perhaps most apparent during the Lemass era, when Local Government, the Office of Public Works and the Department of Industry and Commerce were all manœvering to secure control over the building industry. Such interdepartmental wrangling is an almost inevitable consequence of cabinet government. The usual solution — referring the matter in dispute either to an interdepartmental committee of civil servants, or to a committee of the interested ministers — tends to result in minor amendments to the status quo, rather than to radical change. In other cases, matters that concerned more than one department were neglected, because nobody was prepared to assume responsibility.

The development of a library service is one instance: the Department was unwilling to become involved in expanding the role of public libraries until a library policy had been determined by others; neither was the Department prepared to develop the role of local libraries as cultural centres, because this was seen as primarily a matter for the Arts Council.[45] In the 1950s the Department of Local Government and the Department of Lands were fully capable of pointing out the others' failures in the matter of protecting great houses, but neither appears to have been willing to assume responsibility: Local Government argued that this did not fall within the scope of housing policy, and suggested that an interdepartmental committee, the all-purpose procrastinating body, should be established to examine the problem. There is no evidence that this was done.[46]

Since independence, Irish society has shown a strong reliance on the state to bring about social, economic and cultural change. This reflects the widespread belief that most undesirable developments, whether it was the decline of the Irish language, or the collapse of nineteenth-century Irish industry, could be blamed on hostile actions taken by an alien state. With the notable exception of the Cumann na nGaedheal governments of 1922-32 and the cautious tone found in *Economic Development*, Irish governments and Irish electorates have shown a remarkable faith in the ability of governments to almost single-handedly transform the economy, often in defiance of the laws of economics and despite past failures. Such a mentality was most pronounced in the aftermath of the Emergency, when the inter-party government apparently believed that a large programme of public expenditure would reverse emigration and transform the Irish economy. In 1953 Seán Lemass suggested that the government should embark on a major programme of road works, particularly in western areas, with the aim of reviving private investment in manufacturing industry. The stimulus would come from the wages paid to road labourers, which Lemass hoped would be spent on goods manufactured by protected Irish industries. In both these cases, programmes controlled by the Department of Local Government were seen as holding the key to economic revival.

However Irish governments were rarely content merely with devising schemes to encourage economic expansion: they consistently attempted to direct aid to precise areas, or to specific socio-economic groups. Thus money for roads was channelled to the west of Ireland, and towards areas that had lost wartime employment on the bogs; grants for water and sewerage went to localities with large numbers on the unemployment assistance register, in the belief that this would resolve long-standing problems of unemployment and the decline of the west. Rates remission on agricultural land was adjusted in an effort to provide farmers with an incentive to hire male labourers. The manner in which various programmes of the Department of Local Government were manipulated in order to achieve these socio-economic ends is similar to the ambitious social objectives that were imposed on Irish industrial policies.[47] In both instances it appears that the outcome was a less effective allocation of money for roads and sanitary services and a less successful industrial policy. While filling in potholes on farm lanes in the west of Ireland may have provided supplementary income for impoverished smallholders in the short term, it is unlikely to have prevented emigration or to have brought long-term prosperity.

The legislative programmes of the Department of Local Government and Public Health and the Department of Local Government had other significant implications for twentieth-century Irish society. Perhaps the most important change that they brought about was the revolution in Irish housing. By 1981 less than one-quarter of Irish houses dated from before 1919, and most of these had been improved with the assistance of state grants; 54 percent of houses had been erected after the Emergency. In 1946 only 6,449 families in towns and cities were buying their homes with the aid of a mortgage, and almost three-quarters of houses in urban areas were rented. By 1981 there were over 360,000 mortgages outstanding on private houses. Although the poor performance of the Irish economy in the decade after World War II meant that fewer Irish households could afford the cars, washing machines and refrigerators which were becoming commonplace in the United States and in Britain, the policies implemented by the Department of Local Government ensured that, like their British and American counterparts, they could dream of becoming home-owners. During the early 1950s, when the housing programme was absorbing over 30 percent of the public capital programme, this aspiration stretched the state's finances almost to breaking-point. It was only when the private housing market had been established with the aid of government-funded mortgages, that building societies, insurance companies and banks assumed responsibility for providing most of the necessary capital.

No other programme associated with the Department achieved the same level of commitment. Government expenditure on housing, particularly on assisting owner-occupied housing, proved consistently popular with voters. However there appears to have been little public interest, and presumably few votes, in pressing forward with improvements in running water and sanitary services. Surviving files indicate that the seashore on the south side of Dublin Bay was heavily polluted by sewerage in the 1930s; however, public interest in water pollution is of recent origin. Similarly there was little awareness of the benefits of physical planning. In 1947 Westport Urban District Council told the Department that 'Westport was built as a planned town and the inhabitants are quite satisfied with it. The Council cannot see any worthwhile benefits from Town Planning . . . .' The only draft development plan prepared in County Mayo by the late 1940s concerned Knock shrine: the Department dismissed it as 'quite fanciful' because it provided for railway and bus stations plus an airfield, and envisaged the shrine receiving up to 250,000 pilgrims in future years.[48]

The Department's files also suggest that there was little public support for a modern road network. Until the 1960s car owners were very much a minority, and most Irish people spent their adult life in the community where they were born. While historians have recognised that the majority of citizens of the Irish Republic have had little contact with Northern Ireland, there appears to be an unstated assumption that a similar ignorance or suspicion never existed between other regions on this island. Yet in the 1920s, one mother from County Galway wrote to Richard Mulcahy, begging him to use his influence to have her son, a garda, transferred from Letterkenny, County Donegal to a location closer to his home. She claimed that her son disliked the people in that area and alleged that they were lax in their religious practices. He was so unhappy in Letterkenny that he was threatening to emigrate to America if he could not live closer to home![49] Perhaps this letter should be dismissed as a spurious argument which the writer concocted in the hope of enlisting a minister's support, but that might be incorrect.

A major cause of resentment concerning the work of the Local Appointments Commission related to the hiring of outsiders. This is not surprising: in 1926 over ninety percent of the population of rural Ireland lived in the county of their birth and most 'migrants' had merely moved a short distance from an adjacent county. While it might appear absurd that a young man would emigrate to America because he was homesick in County Donegal, the United States probably offered a community of neighbours and friends that was not available in Letterkenny. Perhaps one of the most important, and unacknowledged, tasks of the Department of Local Government was to help break down local suspicions and local divisions, gradually establishing an awareness that the official coming from Dublin no longer belonged to a different political and religious caste; ensuring equality of services and of opportunities for people, whether they lived in County Monaghan or in County Mayo.

Some of the consequences of the Department's work may appear to us to be undesirable. We may deprecate the monotonous uniformity in council housing and in the layout of private housing estates, the replacement of picturesque thatched roofs with slate, and the tendency to let old cottages and farmhouses become derelict because rural families took advantage of government grants to build modern bungalows; the lack of interest shown by the Department in preserving great houses. The abolition of rural district councils and the loss of power by surviving local authorities may also give rise to remorse in certain quarters. But we should acknowledge that these outcomes were not foisted on unwilling Irish citizens by authoritarian administrators, or by outside governments. The Ireland that the Department helped to create is an Ireland that reflected the values and the wishes of its politicians, its officials and its citizens. However imperfect, it must be seen as a monument to that society.

NOTES

INTRODUCTION

1. Sir Philip Sidney, *An Apology for Poetry or The Defence of Poesy* (1595). Edited by Geoffery Shepherd (London, 1965), p. 105.
2. University College Dublin Archives, herafter UCDA, McGilligan Papers, P 35a/94.
3. PDDE, 24 October 1945, col. 565.
4. Flann O'Brien, *The Best of Myles* (London, 1968), p. 289.
5. For an excellent discussion of health policy, see Ruth Barrington, *Health, Medicine and Politics in Ireland 1900-1970* (Dublin, 1987).
6. Joseph Robins, *Custom House People* (Dublin, 1993).

CHAPTER ONE

1. Edward McParland, 'Strategy in the planning of Dublin, 1750-1800', in P. Butel and L.M. Cullen (eds), *Cities and Merchants: French and Irish Perspectives on Urban Development 1500-1900* (Dublin, 1986), pp. 97-108.
2. J. H. Andrews, 'Road planning in Ireland before the railway age', *Irish Geography*, 5, no. 1 (1964), pp. 24-26.
3. Oliver MacDonagh, *Ireland: The Union and its Aftermath* (London, 1977), p. 34.
4. Virginia Crossman, *Local Government in Nineteenth-century Ireland* (Belfast, 1994), pp. 2,3, 7.
5. William L. Feingold, *The Revolt of the Tenantry: The Transformation of Local Government in Ireland 1872-1886* (Boston, 1984), p. 14.
6. Crossman, *Local Government*, pp. 28-29, 1, 11.
7. *Local Government and Taxation of Ireland Inquiry. Special report by W.P. O'Brien* (LGB inspector), 1878, c. 1965.
8. *Report on the Sanitary Conditions of the Labouring Population of Great Britain*. 1843 [509], xii.
9. R. B. McDowell, *The Irish Administration 1801-1914* (London, 1964), pp. 167, 173.

10. Andrews, 'Road Planning', pp. 27-29.
11. Joseph Robins, *Custom House People* (Dublin, 1993), p. 1.
12. Mary E. Daly, *The Famine in Ireland* (Dublin, 1986), p. 44.
13. *Report of Select Committee appointed to Inquire into the Duties, Functions and Mode of Remuneration of County and District Surveyors in Ireland* 1857 session 2 (270) ix.
14. Oliver MacDonagh, 'Ideas and institutions, 1830-45', in W.E. Vaughan (ed.), *A New History of Ireland. V. Ireland under the Union I. 1801-70* (Oxford, 1989), pp. 216-17.
15. Mary E. Daly, *Dublin: The Deposed Capital 1869-1914* (Cork, 1984), p. 220.
16. David Dickson, 'In search of the old Irish poor law', in R. Mitchison and P. Roebuck (eds), *Economy and Society in Scotland and Ireland 1800-1939* (Edinburgh, 1988), pp. 149-59.
17. Christine Bellamy, *Administering Central-local Relations 1871-1919. The Local Government Board in its Fiscal and Cultural Context* (Manchester, 1988), p. 8.
18. *Special report by W.P. O'Brien*, 1878, c. 1965.
19. Feingold, *The Revolt of the Tenantry*, p. 15.
20. Gerard O'Brien, 'The new Irish poor law in pre-famine Ireland; a case history', *Irish Economic and Social History*, Vol. XII (1985), p. 34.
21. *Poor Law Commission Ireland. Copy of Report of Messrs. Bromley and Stephenson to Lords of Treasury,* 4 May 1854.
22. McDowell, *Irish Administration,* pp. 176, 181.
23. Feingold, *The Revolt of the Tenantry,* pp. 19-23.
24. Josef Redlich and Francis W. Hirst, *The History of Local Government in England.* Edited and introduced by Bryan Keith-Lucas (London, 1958) pp. 111-16.
25. MacDonagh, *Ireland,* pp. 36-44.
26. Bromley and Stephenson, 1854.
27. National Archives, hereafter NA, Dáil Éireann Local Government files, hereafter DELG. For specific examples, see chapter two.
28. For a biographical profile, see Joseph Robins, *Custom House People* (Dublin, 1993), pp 82-85.
29. Sir Henry Robinson, *Memories: Wise and Otherwise* (London, 1923), p. 12.
30. *Reports of the Commissioners Appointed to Inquire into the Conditions of the Civil Service in Ireland. Report on the Local Government Board and General Registry Office and Minutes.* 1873 (c. 514-I), xxvi, para. 226.
31. Feingold, *The Revolt of the Tenantry*, p. 17.
32. *Reply of Poor Law Commission to recommendations of Bromley and Stephenson, 19 June 1854.* 1854-5 (0.28), xlvi, 213.
33. O'Brien, 'New Irish poor law', p. 35.
34. David Fitzpatrick, 'Famine, entitlements, seduction and the state', Paper read at New York University conference on Famine and Hunger, May 1995.
35. T. P. O'Neill, 'The administration of relief', in R.D. Edwards and T. D Williams (eds), *The Great Famine* (Dublin, 1956), pp. 212-32.

36. McDowell, *Irish Administration,* pp. 209-12.

37. Mary E. Daly, 'Famine relief efforts, 1846-47: A question of competence', paper read at New York University conference on Famine and Hunger, May 1995.

38. O'Neill, 'The administration of relief', p. 213.

39. Christine Kinealy, 'The poor law during the great famine: an administration in crisis', in E.Margaret Crawford (ed.), *Famine: The Irish Experience, 900-1900* (Edinburgh, 1989), p.160.

40. Daly, *The Famine in Ireland,* p. 93.

41. James S. Donnelly, 'The administration of relief 1847-51', in *New History of Ireland. V. Part I,* p. 329.

42. McDowell, *Irish Administration,* p. 168.

43. Ruth Barrington, *Health, Medicine and Politics in Ireland 1900-1970* (Dublin, 1987), p. 9.

44. *Special report by W. P. O'Brien,* 1878.

45. Crossman, *Local Government,* p. 3.

46. McDowell, *Irish Administration,* p. 202; *Special Report by W. P. O'Brien.*

47. Bromley and Stephenson.

48. *Report of Commissioners on Civil Service in Ireland. Report on Local Government Board and General Registry Office.*

49. Roy M. MacLeod, *Treasury Control and Social Administration. A Study of Establishment Growth at the Local Government Board 1871-1905* (London, 1968), p. 10.

50. R. Barry O' Brien, *Dublin Castle and the Irish People* (London, 1912), pp. 109-10; Robinson, *Memories,* pp. 97-98.

51. Eunan O'Halpin, *The Decline of the Union. British Government in Ireland 1892-1920* (Dublin, 1987), p. 9.

52. *R. C. on the Poor Laws. Report on Ireland* 1909 (cd. 4630), xxxvii, para. 82.

53. O'Brien, *Dublin Castle and the Irish People,* pp. 109-10. Robinson, *Memories,* pp. 97-98.

54. William F. Bailey, *Local and Centralised Government in Ireland. A Sketch of the Existing System* (London, 1888), p. 30.

55. *Report LGBI* 1873; John Collins, *Local Government* (second edition, Dublin, 1963), p. 134.

56. *Report LGBI, 1873, 1878.*

57. *Select Committee on Alteration in Laws on Local Government and Taxation of Towns.* 1877 (357) xii, evidence qs. 1165-90, 2819, 2872, 4030.

58. Daly, *Deposed Capital,* p. 220.

59. *Select Committee on Taxation of Towns,* q. 6371.

60. Feingold, *The Revolt of the Tenantry,* pp. 30-31, 214-15; 181.

61. O'Brien, *Dublin Castle,* p. 110.

62. *Reports LGBI* 1887, 1888 and 1889.

63. Feingold, *The Revolt of the Tenantry,* pp. 179-83.

64. Robinson, *Memories,* p. 23.

65. *R. C. on the Poor Laws. Report on Ireland,* p. 24,

66. Robinson, *Memories,* p. 23.

67. *R. C. on the Poor Laws. Report on Ireland*, p. 24.
68. Robinson, *Memories*, pp. 45-46.
69. *R. C. on the Poor Laws. Report on Ireland*, pp. 26-27.
70. Robinson, *Memories*, pp. 103, 79.
71. *Report LGBI* 1887.
72. L.P. Curtis, *Coercion and Conciliation in Ireland 1880-1892. A Study in Conservative Unionism* (Princeton, 1963), p. 263.
73. Robinson, *Memories*, p. 98.
74. Curtis, *Coercion and Conciliation*, pp. 363-65.
75. Timothy P. O'Neill, 'The food crisis of the 1890s', in E.M. Crawford (ed.), *Famine*, pp. 177-78.
76. *Report LGBI* 1891.
77. O'Neill, 'Food crisis', p. 179.
78. *Report LGBI* 1892.
79. *R. C. on the Poor Laws. Report on Ireland*, p. 28.
80. O'Neill, 'Food crisis', pp. 183-84.
81. W. L. Micks, *History of the Congested Districts Board from 1891 to 1923* (Dublin, 1925).
82. Report by W.P. O'Brien; Feingold, *The Revolt of the Tenantry*, pp. 169-71.
83. Quoted in Andrew Gailey, *Ireland and the Death of Kindness. The Experience of Constructive Unionism 1890-1905* (Cork, 1987), p. 41.
84. James Loughlin, *Gladstone, Home Rule and the Ulster Question 1882-93* (Dublin, 1986), p. 218.
85. Catherine Shannon, 'Local Government in Ireland, the politics and administration', MA, UCD 1963, p. 139.
86. *Final Report of the R.C Appointed to Inquire into the Financial Relations of Great Britain and Ireland* (c. 8262), 1896, xxxii. Pauric Travers, 'The financial relations question, 1800-1914', in F.B. Smith (ed.), *Ireland, England and Australia. Essays in Honour of Oliver MacDonagh* (Cork, 1990), pp. 50-56.
87. Gailey, *Death of Kindness*, pp. 44-45; Shannon, 'Local Government', pp. 146-50.
88. *Memories*, pp. 124-25.
89. Collins, *Local Government*, pp. 25-26.
90. Travers, 'Financial relations', p. 65.
91. Shannon, 'Local Government', pp. 146-50.
92. *R.C. Local Taxation. Minutes of Evidence*, vol. V. 1900 (cd. 383) xxxvi, para. 23396.
93. *Report LGBI* 1899; Shannon 'Local Government', pp. 142-46.
94. Shannon, 'Local Government', p. 298.
95. Robinson, *Memories*, p. 128.
96. Shannon 'Local Government', pp. 151-55.
97. They were not permitted to charge interest to the rates, but could offset it against interest earned on credit balances.
98. *Report LGBI* 1900.
99. Gailey, *Ireland and the Death of Kindness*, pp. 138-39.

100. *R.C Local Taxation, Minutes*, paras. 23409-434.
101. Quoted in Shannon, 'Local Government', p. 309.
102. Shannon, 'Local Government', p. 292.
103. Con Lehane, *Ireland's Burden under British Boards* (Dublin, 1905), p. 28.
104. The General Council of County Councils has been almost entirely ignored by historians. It was founded in 1904, and its first chairman was Sir Thomas Esmonde MP. Six northern councils seceded from the council when a political resolution was proposed and Cork County Council, which was controlled by the dissident nationalist William O' Brien MP, was also absent in 1911. (Evidence of M.A. Ennis, chairman of the General Council's standing committee on legislation to Committee on Irish Finance. Evidence, 1913 *Committee on Irish Finance.* evidence 1913 (cd. 6799), xxx qs. 3169-71.)
105. *Report LGBI* 1901.
106. Shannon 'Local Government', pp. 293-94.
107. For details, see chapter nine.
108. I am indebted to Professor Nial Osborough, Law Faculty, UCD for this information.
109. *Civil Service Commissioners Report 1873.*
110. Names of fourth-class clerks in 1854 were McDonnell, Daly, Bolger, Martin, Pelly, Rice, Beggs, McCollum, Dillon, Finch and Ewing.
111. *R.C. Civil Service, Fourth Report. Evidence* 1914 (cd. 7340), xvi, q. 27249.
112. Brendan O'Donoghue, 'The office of county surveyor. Origins and early years', paper presented to Institute of Engineers of Ireland Heritage Society, November 1992, pp. 4-5.
113. *Taxation of Towns* 1877 q. 2522.
114. Patrick Maume, *D.P. Moran* (Dublin, 1995), pp. 18-20.
115. *Report LGBI* 1902.
116. Shannon, 'Local Government', pp. 279-80.
117. *Irish Builder and Engineer,* 9 March 1907. I am indebted to Brendan O'Donoghue for this reference and for information on the wider question of county surveyors.
118. Information supplied by Brendan O'Donoghue.
119. Mary E. Daly, 'The formation of an Irish nationalist elite? Recruitment to the Irish civil service in the decades prior to independence 1870-1920', *Paedagogica Historica, International Journal of the History of Education,* Vol. XXX , no. 1 (1994), pp. 281-301.
120. *RC Civil Service, Fourth Report. Evidence*, paras. 76-78.
121. O'Halpin, *Decline of the Union*, p. 17.
122. Daly, 'Formation', pp. 298-99.
123. Robinson, *Memories*, pp. 117, 16-19, 129-30.
124. *RC. Civil Service. Fourth Report. Evidence.*
125. For a biography of Kirkwood, see Robins, *Custom House People*, pp. 75-78.
126. *Civil Service Commissioners Report* 1873, paras. 76-78 and 222.
127. Bellamy, *Administering Central-local Relations*, pp. 116, 146-47.

128. *Civil Service Commissioners. Evidence* 1873, paras. 223-26.

129. *Returns Names, etc. of Each Person Appointed Without Competitive Examination to Any Position in the Public Service During the Period 29 June 1895 to 5 December 1905 with an Annual Salary of £100 or Upward.* 1912-13 lvi, HC paper 454.

130. McDowell, *Irish Administration*, p. 35.

131. *Return of Local Government Board Inspectors now in Service 1906*, lvi.

132. Robinson, *Memories*, pp. 226-27.

133. *Report LGBI* 1902,1909.

134. Eunan O'Halpin, 'The origins of city and county management', in *City and County Management 1929-1990. A Retrospective* (Dublin, 1991), p. 2.

135. Bellamy, *Administering Central-local Relations*, pp. 100, 155.

136. *Report of the Departmental Inquiry Appointed by the Local Government Board to Inquire into the Public Health of the City of Dublin* 1900 (cd. 243) xxxix, 681; Surgeon Col. D. Egar Flinn, *Official Report on the Sanitary Circumstances and Administration of the City of Dublin with Special Reference to the Causes of the High Death-Rate* (Dublin 1906, Thom for HMSO); *Report of the Departmental Inquiry Appointed to Inquire into the Housing Conditions of the Working Class in Dublin 1914* (cd. 7269) xviii, 513.

137. Daly, *Deposed Capital*, pp. 313-18.

138. Re Britain, see Bellamy, *Administering Central-local Relations,* pp. 46-48.

139. Redlich and Hirst, *Local Government in England,* Vol. I, pp. 205-06.

140. Asa Briggs, *Victorian Cities* (London, 1968 edition), p. 40.

141. *RC Local Taxation. Final report, England and Wales,*1901 (cd. 638), xxiv, 413.

142. *RC Local Taxation, Ireland,* 1902 (cd. 1068), xxxix, 9.

143. *RC Local Taxation,* qs. 26851-3. W. L .Micks.

144. *RC Local Taxation,* qs. 24845, William Field MP; 25253-7 Hugh de Fellenberg Montgomery.

145. ibid., qs. 23388-94.

146. *RC Local Taxation. Report on Valuation in Ireland* 1902 (cd. 973), xxxix, 1.

147. ibid., minutes q. 23534.

148. *Select Committee on Irish Valuation Acts,* 1904, vol. vi.

149. Shannon, 'Local Government', pp. 283-89.

150. *Returns of Local Taxation in Ireland, 1919.*

151. *RC Local Taxation,* qs. 24845, 25253-7.

152. ibid., qs. 26545-7.

153. *Report LGBI* 1900.

154. Shannon, 'Local Government', pp. 289-91, 284, 304.

155. In 1863, 53 per cent of the £720,843 collected in rates went on indoor relief; by 1883 indoor relief absorbed only 41 per cent of the £1.147m. revenue of boards of guardians.

156. *Reports LGBI* 1886-96.

157. Shannon, 'Local government', pp. 136-37; Gailey, *Ireland and the Death of Kindness*, p. 44.

158. Gailey, *Ireland and the Death of Kindness*, pp. 222-23; O'Halpin, *Decline of the Union*, p. 74.

159. The Irish report of the *RC on the Poor Laws* claimed that the proposal for a state medical service reflected the personal views of E. Coey Bigger.

160. *Vice-Regal Commission on Poor Relief* 1906 (cd. 3203), li.

161. This had been a matter of long-standing grievance. After the Famine, landlords and some large farmers proved extremely adept at redrawing DED boundaries to minimise their rates bills. See James Donnelly Jr., 'The journals of Sir John Benn-Walsh relating to the management of his Irish estates, 1823-64', in *Cork Historical Society Journal*, Vol. LXXX (1974), pp. 106-07. The Dublin suburbs managed to offload most of the cost of poor relief on to the highly taxed and poorer city. Daly, *Deposed Capital*, pp. 226-28.

162. *RC Local Taxation*, qs. 25122, 26227.

163. O'Halpin, *Decline of the Union*, p. 97.

164. Travers, 'Financial relations question', pp. 50, 56; Patricia Jalland, 'Irish home-rule finance: a neglected dimension of the Irish question, 1910-14', *IHS*, Vol. XXIII, no. 91 (May 1983), p. 235.

165. *Report of the Committee on Irish Finance* 1912-13 (cd. 6153), xxiv, , p. 5.

166. Timothy W. Guinnane, 'Intentional age-misreporting, age-heaping, and the 1908 Old Age Pensions Act in Ireland', *Population Studies*, Vol. XLV (1991), pp. 497-518. Timothy W. Guinnane, 'The poor law and pensions in Ireland' *Journal of Interdisciplinary History*, Vol. XXIV, no. 2 (autumn 1990, pp. 271-91.

167. Tom Kettle, *Home Rule Finance* (Dublin, 1911), p. 27.

168. Erskine Childers, *The Framework of Home Rule* (London, 1911); Kettle, *Home Rule Finance*.

169. Daly, *Deposed Capital*, pp. 314-15.

170 Kettle, *Home Rule Finance*, p. 127.

171. Daly, *Deposed Capital*, p. 317.

172. Lawrence W. McBride, *The Greening of Dublin Castle. The Transformation of Bureaucratic and Judicial Personnel in Ireland 1892-1922* (Washington, 1991), pp. 179-80.

173. TCD Dillon Papers (hereafter DP), 6801/186a.

174. McBride, *Greening*, pp. 206-07.

175. Leon Ó Broin, *Dublin Castle and the 1916 Rising* (London, 1966), p. 45; NLI Brennan Papers 26155 confirms that such a review was carried out by the LGB, but gives no details.

176. DP 6801/166, meeting 5 March 1915.

177. Leon Ó Broin, *No Man's Man. A Biographical Memoir of Joseph Brennan* (Dublin, 1982), p. 35.

178. DP 6801/166.

179. DP 6801/161, first conference, 17 February 1915; 6801/163, second conference, 24 February 1915.

180. DP 6801/166, 5 March 1915.

181. DP 6801/163, 24 February 1915.

182. DP 6801/186.
183. Maurice Hayes, *Minority Verdict. Experiences of a Catholic Public Servant* (Belfast, 1995), pp. 5, 43.

CHAPTER TWO

1. Richard Davis, *Arthur Griffith and Non-violent Sinn Féin* (Dublin, 1974), pp. 132-36, 77-78.
2. J. L. McCracken, *Representative Government in Ireland. A Study of Dáil Eireann 1919-48* (Oxford, 1958) p. 31.
3. Dorothy Macardle, *The Irish Republic* (London, 1968), pp. 254-55.
4. McBride, *The Greening of Dublin Castle*, p. 244.
5. Fanning, *Finance*, pp. 59-60.
6. LGBI Minutes,
7. Murray Fraser, 'John Bull's other homes: state housing and British policy in Ireland 1883-1922'. Ph.D thesis, University College London 1993.
8. David Fitzpatrick, *Politics and Irish Life 1913-1921: Provincial Experience of War and Revolution* (Dublin, 1977), p. 187.
9. N/A Dáil Éireann, Dáil Éireann (hereafter DE), 2/372 W.T. Cosgrave, abstract of ministerial career. Originally the American term 'secretary' was used instead of 'Minister', but it never became generally accepted. Arthur Mitchell, *Revolutionary Government in Ireland. Dail Eireann 1919-22* (Dublin, 1995), p. 33.
10. Dáil Éireann, published debates of the First Dáil, hereafter PDDE, 19 June 1919, p. 130.
11. DE 2/243 July-September 1919.
12. PDDE, First Dáil, 19 August, p. 143.
13. DE 2/45.
14. PDDE, 19 June 1919.
15. DE 2/243.
16. Fitzpatrick, *Politics and Irish Life 1913-21*, p. 185; PDDE 19 August 1919, p. 143.
17. Charles Townshend, *The British Campaign in Ireland 1919-1921* (Oxford, 1975), p. 67.
18. Michael Laffan, '"Labour must wait": Ireland's conservative revolution', in Patrick J. Corish (ed.), *Radicals, Rebels and Establishments* (Historical Studies Vol. XV, Belfast, 1985), p. 215.
19. DE 2/372 and 2/388. O'Higgins was appointed on 19 April.
20. DE 2/243. Local Government Department report no 1. No date given, but probably shortly after 11 May 1920.
21. DE 2/243 Circular letter from Department of Local Government to all county councils, rural district councils and boards of guardians, 1 June 1920.
22. Macardle, *Irish Republic*, Appendix 33.
23. Fitzpatrick, *Politics and Irish Life*, p. 186.

24. PDDE, 29 June 1920, pp. 169, 185.
25. DE 2/243 Dáil Éireann Commission of Inquiry into Local Government, interim report 4 August and Appendix A.
26. CSORP 1920/20971 Local taxation returns from LGB.
27. DE 2/62 Instructions concerning severing links with the British Local Government Board and safeguarding of funds, 10 August 1920.
28. PDDE, 6 August 1920, pp. 203-05.
29. CSORP 1920/20971.
30. DE 2/243.
31. N/A Dáil Éireann Local Government Department Files (hereafter DELG) 9/17, Dublin County Borough and Corporation.
32. DELG 11/23 Galway County Council, inspector's report, 25 July 1921.
33. DELG 27/3 Tipperary South Riding County Council, 29 March 1921.
34. Fitzpatrick, *Politics and Irish Life*, p. 333.
35. DELG 3/6 Carlow County Council; Fitzpatrick, *Politics and Irish Life*, p. 190.
36. DELG 20/8 Louth County Council; DELG 30/11, 3 March 1921, minutes Westmeath County Council.
37. DELG 11/23 Galway County Council, 9 December 1920.
38. DELG 12/16 Kerry County Council.
39. DELG 3/6 Carlow County Council .
40. DELG 22/18 Meath County Council; DELG 26/9 Sligo County Council.
41. Townshend, *British Campaign*, p. 138.
42. DELG 4/13 Cavan County Council, 20 November 1920.
43. Fitzpatrick, *Politics and Irish Life*, p. 191.
44. MacArdle, *Irish Republic*, pp. 308-09, 396.
45. DELG 6/44 Cork County Council, report Liam de Roiste, 28/4/21.
46. DELG 22/18 Meath County Council, 29 April 1921.
47. DELG 31/12 Wexford County Council, public statement 31 March 1921.
48. DELG 12/16 Kerry County Council. An Seabhac, chairman of the council, raised this possibility in correspondence with Austin Stack on 21/2/21.
49. DELG 29/13 Waterford County Council minutes.
50. DELG 11/23 Galway County Council.
51. DELG 25/11 Roscommon County Council.
52. DELG 22/18 Meath County Council, 8 November 1920.
53. DE 2/155 proposals of English [*sic*] Local Government Board re collection of rates and counter-action by LGD.
54. DELG 3/6 Carlow County Council.
55. DELG 25/11 Roscommon County Council; DELG 22/18 Meath County Council.
56. Anthony Gaughan, *Austin Stack: Portrait of a Separatist* (Tralee, 1977), p. 140.
57. DELG 11/23 Galway County Council. My thanks to Dr Diane Urquhart for identifying Miss Cashel.
58. Macardle, *Irish Republic*, pp. 307-08; Mitchell, *Revolutionary Government*, p. 63.

59. DELG 11/23 Galway County Council, 30 August 1920, letter from S. MacNiocall, county solicitor.
60. DELG 3/6 Carlow County Council, letter dated 2 September 1920.
61. DELG 21/19 Mayo County Council, report 4 March 1921.
62. DELG 11/23 Galway County Council, O'Higgins to Miss Cashel, 30 December 1920.
63. Fanning, *Finance*, pp. 83-93.
64. DE 2/516 Financial crisis in Dublin Corporation, June-October 1920.
65. DELG 9/17 Dublin Corporation, Cosgrave to Murphy, 16 February 1921. The South Dublin Union's problems were caused by the fact that contributions owed it by Rathmines and Pembroke Urban Councils – neither under Sinn Féin control – had been garnisheed to meet malicious injury awards.
66. DE 2/243.
67. DELG 25/11 Roscommon County Council.
68. DELG 13/11 Kildare County Council, 6-7 October 1920.
69. CSORP 1920/24267, November 1920.
70. DELG 30/11 Westmeath County Council; DELG 16/9 Leitrim County Council; DELG 23/14 Monaghan County Council.
71. DELG 5/18 Clare County Council.
72. DELG 27/13 Tipperary North Riding County Council.
73. DELG 3/6 Department of Local Government to Carlow County Council, 20 November 1920.
74. DELG 23/14 Monaghan County Council.
75. DE 2/243 Report DELG, 20 January 1921.
76. Townshend, *British Campaign*, pp. 135, 141.
77. DELG 31/12 Wexford County Council, public statement 31 March 1921.
78. DELG 13/11, Kildare County Council, 6, 13 and 17 December 1920.
79. DELG 31/12 Wexford County Council; DELG 3/6 Carlow County Council, minutes 14 December 1920.
80. DELG 31/12 Wexford County Council; DELG 24/7 Queen's (now Laois) County Council; DELG 26/9 Sligo County Council.
81. DELG 22/18 Meath County Council, letter from O'Higgins, 15 December 1920.
82. DELG 31/12 Wexford County Council, letter dated 14 December 1920.
83. DELG 3/6 Carlow County Council, minutes 20 December 1920.
84. DE 2/243 report DELG, 20 January 1921.
85. DELG 20/8 Louth County Council, Cosgrave to Murphy, 22 January 1921.
86. PDDE 25 January 1921, p. 253.
87. DELG 9/18 Dublin County Council report, 27 January 1921.
88. DELG 32/12 Wicklow County Council.
89. DELG 2/243 Report DELG May 1921. Treasurers had been reappointed by Cavan, Cork, Donegal, Galway, Kerry, Kildare, Kilkenny, Longford, Meath, Monaghan, Offaly, Roscommon, North Tipperary, Waterford and Westmeath County Councils but not by councils in Counties Carlow, Clare, Dublin, Laois, Leitrim, Limerick, Louth, Mayo, Sligo, South Tipperary,

Wexford and Wicklow.

90. DELG 16/9 Leitrim County Council, June 1921; DELG 31/12 Wexford County Council, 24 February 1921; DELG Sligo County Council, February 1921.

91. DELG 13/11 Kildare County Council.

92. DELG 9/18 Dublin County Council, 22 August 1921.

93. DELG 23/14 Monaghan County Council, January 1921.

94. DELG 5/18 Clare County Council; DELG 2/243 Report DELG May 1921.

95. PDDE, 11 March 1921, p. 270.

96. DELG 12/16 Kerry County Council; report of chairman, An Seabhac, to Austin Stack 21/2/21.

97. PDDE 11 March 1921, pp. 269-70.

98. DELG 9/18, 22 August 1921.

99. He was among the Irish Volunteers imprisoned following the 1916 Rising; subsequently served as assistant secretary in the Irish Free State's Department of Local Government and Public Health. See Macardle, *Irish Republic*, Appendix 3.

100. DE 2/61. Department of Local Government, appointment of auditors.

101. DELG 6/18 Clare County Council; DELG 12/16 Kerry County Council.

102. PDDE, 25 January 1921, pp. 253-54.

103. DELG 13/11 Kildare County Council; DELG 6/44 Cork County Council.

104. DELG 16/9 Letrim County Council, report 16/4/21; DELG 31/12 Wexford County Council.

105. K. Theodore Hoppen, *Elections, Politics and Society in Ireland 1832-1885* (Oxford, 1984), p. 436.

106. DELG 20/8 Louth County Council, O'Higgins to Murphy (chairman), 29 September 1921.

107. DELG 6/44 Cork County Council.

108. DELG 15/11 King's (now Offaly) County Council, September 1921 and 9/2/22 O'Higgins to Tom Dunne.

109. DELG 6/44 Cork County Council, 11 October 1921.

110. DELG 24/7 Queen's (now Laois) County Council.

111. DELG 29/13 Waterford County Council, 22 February 1922.

112. DELG 13/11 Kildare County Council.

113. DELG 17/15 Limerick County Council, September/October 1921.

114. DELG 12/16 Kerry County Council, inspector's reports, 12 and 13 January 1922.

115. DELG 26/9 Sligo County Council.

116. DELG 15/11, inspector's report, 8 November 1921.

117. DELG 6/44 inspector D. O'Donovan, 18 October 1921.

118. DELG 27/30 Tipperary South Riding, inspector's report, 21 February 1922.

119. DELG 4/13 Cavan County Council.

120. DELG 21/19 Mayo County Council.

121. DELG 5/18 Clare County Council, inspector's report, 28 November 1921.

122. DELG 12/16, Kerry County Council, inspector's reports, 12 and 14 October 1921.

123. DELG 12/16 Kerry County Council, 21 February 1921.
124. DE 2/243 Local Government Commission, minority report by Denis Carolan Rushe and untitled memorandum by James McGee. Both undated.
125. DELG 22/18, Meath County Council.
126. DE 2/243, 3 May 1921.
127. PDDE, 25 January 1921, pp. 253-54.
128. Gaughan, *Austin Stack*, p. 140.
129. DE 2/243.
130. DELG 7/22 Donegal County Council, 8 September 1920; 3 June 1921. See also DELG 16/9 Leitrim County Council, and DELG 4/13 Cavan County Council report by inspector, Miss N.O'Sullivan.
131. e.g. DELG 31/12 Wexford County Council, 29 December 1920.
132. DELG 6/44 Cork County Council, inspector's report, 2 February 1922.
133. DELG 21/19 Mayo County Council.
134. DELG 6/44, Cork County Council, 2 February 1922.
135. DELG 12/16, Kerry County Council, inspector's report, 12 January 1922.
136. DELG 21/19 Mayo County Council, 24 August 1921.
137. DELG 16/9 Leitrim County Council.
138. DELG 15/11 King's (Offaly) County Council, inspector's report, 6 September 1921.
139. DE 2/468.
140. DELG 21/19, Mayo County Council, 17 December 1921.
141. DELG 13/11, Kildare County Council (this is misfiled), 28 October 1921.
142. DELG 14/15 Kilkenny County Council, report by inspector J.A. Gleeson, 6 February 1922.
143. e.g DELG 13/11 Kildare County Council, 1 February 1922.
144. e.g DELG 5/18 Clare County Council, 9 August 1921.
145. Emmet O'Connor, *Syndicalism in Ireland 1917-23* (Cork, 1988), pp. 23-26.
146. O'Connor, *Syndicalism*, p. 63; Fitzpatrick, *Politics and Irish Life*, pp. 245-46.
147. Emmet O'Connor, *A Labour History of Waterford* (Waterford, 1989), pp. 144-45.
148. DELG 21/19 Mayo County Council.
149. Laffan, '"Labour must wait"', p. 215.
150. Townshend, *British Campaign,* p. 69.
151. PDDE, 6 August 1920, p. 203.
152. DE 2/243.
153. DELG 31/12 Wexford County Council.
154. DELG 25/11 Roscommon County Council, 11 November 1920.
155. DELG 27/13 Tipperary North Riding County Council.
156. DELG 21/19, Mayo County Council.
157. DELG 17/15 Limerick County Council, 6 November 1920.
158. DELG 13/11 Kildare County Council.
159. DELG 22/18 Meath County Council, 24 November and 2 December 1921.
160. PDDE, 11 March 1921, pp. 269-70.

161. DELG 17/15 Limerick County Council.
162. DELG 12/16 Kerry County Council, DELG to county council, 4 August 1921.
163. Fitzpatrick, *Politics*, p. 253.
164. DELG Tipperary South Riding County Council.
165. PDDE, 11 March 1921, p. 274.
166. DELG 22/18, Meath County Council, April 1921.
167. PDDE, 22 August 1921, p. 35.
168. DE 2/243 10 May 1921.
169. DELG 3/6 Carlow County Council, minutes 9 August 1921.
170. DELG 17/15, Limerick County Council, 5 September 1921.
171. PDDE, 25 August 1921, p. 70.
172. DELG 31/12 Wexford County Council.
173. DELG 4/13 Cavan County Council, 15 July 1921.
174. DELG 21/19 Mayo County Council.
175. DE 2/243, July 1921.
176. DELG 19/13, Longford County Council.
177. DELG 16/9 Leitrim County Council, February 1922.
178. DELG 31/12 Wexford County Council, inspector's report, 23 August 1921.
179. DELG 15/11 King's (Offaly) County Council.
180. PDDE, 22 August 1921, p. 36; DELG 11/23, Galway County Council. Thomas Quinn, rate collector to Department of Local Government, 21 July 1921.
181. DELG 21/19 Mayo County Council.
182. DELG 32/12 Wicklow County Council, June-December 1921.
183. DELG 31/12 Wexford County Council and DELG 24/7 Queen's (Laois) County Council.
184. DELG 24/7 Queen's County Council.
185. PDDE, 17 August 1921.
186. DELG 12/16 Kerry County Council.
187. DELG 31/12, Wexford County Council, 12 December 1921.
188. DELG 13/11 Kildare County Council.
189. DELG 27/30 Tipperary South Riding County Council.
190. DELG 31/12 Wexford County Council, January 1922.
191. PDDE, 11 March 1921, pp. 269-70; Mitchell, *Revolutionary Government*, pp. 150-54.
192. PDDE, 17 August 1921.
193. DELG 5/18 Clare County Council, October 1921.
194. DELG 15/11 King's (Offaly) County Council.
195. DELG 31/12 Wexford County Council.
196. DELG 13/11 Kildare County Council, 27 September 1921.
197. DELG 21/19 Mayo County Council, October 1921.
198. DELG 15/11 King's (Offaly) County Council, July 1921.
199. DELG 31/12 Wexford County Council, 9 August 1921.
200. DE 2/466 Collection of rates in County Leitrim, October 1921.
201. DELG 7/22 Donegal County Council, December 1921.

202. DE 2/243. Report by W. T. Cosgrave.
203. DELG 11/23 Galway County Council, 29 October 1921.
204. DELG, 21/19 Mayo County Council, August 1921.
205. Mitchell, *Revolutionary Government*, p. 343.
206. DE 2/465 Administrative committees for counties and county boroughs, proposed establishment of.
207. e.g. Macardle, *Irish Republic*; Townshend, *British Campaign in Ireland*.

CHAPTER THREE

1. Robinson, *Memories*, p. 310.
2. DELG 34/1 Representations to Minister for Local Government from institutions.
3. DELG 33/1 Correspondence re sick leave.
4. NA. Department of the Environment (hereafter D/E), LG 25, also labelled LGB no. 27159/1921. Allocation of staff north and south.
5. NA Department of Finance (hereafter D/F), Fin 1/76/24 Estimates of LGB attached file. James MacMahon CSO to Treasury, 5 January 1922.
6. D/E LG 703. Ministry of Transport, otherwise labelled IR65. Government of Ireland Act. Transfer of Ministry of Transport Duties.
7. D/E LG 36 Reorganisation, November 1921.
8. DELG 33/1.
9. D/E Fin 1/76/24.
10. D/E LG 703.
11. Patrick Buckland, *The Factory of Grievances. Devolved Government in Northern Ireland 1921-39* (Dublin, 1979), pp. 18-19; McBride, *Greening*, pp. 245-47.
12. Ronan Fanning, *The Irish Department of Finance 1922-58* (Dublin, 1978), pp. 12-13.
13. D/F, Fin 1/76/24.
14. D/E LG Reorganisation.
15. D/E LG 25.
16. NA Department of Taoiseach, previously President's Department S series, S 1.
17. Robinson, *Memories*, pp. 324-25.
18. Fanning, *Finance*, p. 31.
19. D/F Fin 1/76/24.
20. William O'Brien was a former principal inspector of taxes who was appointed secretary of the Treasury, the highest position in the new Irish civil service on 28 February 1922. He served in that post until 22 February 1923 when he became head of the Irish Revenue Commissioners. Fanning, *Finance*, pp. 38-60.
21. NA G (Government), 1/1, 21 January 1922. Minutes, provisional government.
22. D/F Fin 1/76/24.

23. Fanning, *Finance*, pp. 36-37.
24. S 1, 18 January 1922.
25. D/F Fin 1/76/24.
26. PDDE 1 June 1926, col. 93.
27. Fanning, *Finance*, p. 63.
28. Department of the Environment Establishment Files 108/19/23. This series has not been transferred to the National Archives; O'Halpin, *Decline of the Union*, pp. 164-65.
29. DELG 33/1.
30. D/E General Files, G 287. Transfer Exchange between Britain and Ireland.
31. G1/1, Minutes, 21 and 27 January 1922.
32. DE 2/243 Memorial to Cabinet. No date. Unsigned.
33. DE Establishment Files. These have not been transferred to the National Archives.
34. Fanning, *Finance*, pp. 40-41.
35. PDDE, 1 March 1922.
36. S. 1.
37. D/E LG 701 Roads.
38. *First Report Department of Local Government and Public Health* (hereafter DLGPH), p. 17.
39. D/E G 36 Reorganisation. In October 1922 de Lacy was appointed assistant secretary.
40. D/E LG 25.
41. D/E Secretary's Files; no number, labelled, Finance, General File.
42. G1/2, 4 May 1922.
43. D/E Secretary's Files, Finance, General File.
44. DELG 33/1.
45. UCD Archives (hereafter UCDA) Mulcahy Papers, P7/C/86 (4). Rates of subsistence. Allowances. Department of Local Government.
46. D/E LG 36.
47. D/E Establishment Files.
48. UCDA Blythe Papers, P 24/1783, pp. 163-67.
49. D/E Sligo Box 698. Minutes Tobercurry Board of Guardians, 15 May 1922.
50. DE 2/243, Report Local Government Department, April 1922.
51. PDDE, 26 April 1922, p. 261.
52. Michael Hopkinson, *Green Against Green. The Irish Civil War* (Dublin, 1988), p. 89.
53. *First report DLGPH*, p. 21.
54. S 1602, maintenance of road communications, July 1922.
55. S 4278 Distress and unemployment in Saorstát Éireann, 20 July 1922.
56. D/E 2/243. Report DELG April 1922.
57. G1/1.
58. S 921 Provisional Government.
59. S 921; D/F Fin /1/13/3 Local taxation account.
60. D/F Fin 1/13/3.
61. S3393 Anglo-Irish War 1916-22. Local Authorities Indemnity Act 1922.

62. PDDE, 23 November 1923, col. 1212.
63. PDDE, 9 February 1923, col. 1424.
64. Brennan Papers, Ms 26201 Road Fund.
65. D/E Roads Section Box 704. Road Fund. Claims against the British government, 8 July 1919.
66. D/E General Files LG 36.
67. D.E Roads Section, Box 704, no date.
68. LG 46, DB/202 Damage to Property (Compensation) Act 1923.
69. *First report DLGPH*, Appendix G, p. 187. Report on road work by James Quigley.
70. D/F Fin 1/635/8.
71. D/E Roads Section LG 701.
72. D/Fin F 136/1/24. The Local Loans Fund in its relation to Ireland.
73. Fanning, *Finance*, pp. 170-74.
74. *Report of Commission of Inquiry into Banking, Currency and Credit.* 1938 R.38, p. 15.
75. Fanning, *Finance*, p. 139.
76. S 921 Local taxation grants withheld.
77. Fanning, *Finance*, p. 139.
78. D/E LG Box 52 G 276/7 Malicious injury decrees. Pre-special period decrees.
79. S 3796 Governor General. Officials of local authorities resigned or dismissed before the Truce, 1925.
80. D/F Fin 72/10/24 Compensation for Loss of Local Office (War Period Bill), 1924; LG 58, 27/14.
81. D/E G 506. Local Government Temporary Provisions Act Local Officers and Employees Order No. 1.
82. *Second Report DLGPH*, pp. 30-31.
83. Mervyn Miller, 'Raymond Unwin and the planning of Dublin' in Michael J. Bannon (ed.), *A Hundred Years of Irish Planning. Vol. I. The Emergence of Irish Planning 1880-1920* (Dublin, 1985), pp. 263-306.
84. Michael Bannon, 'Irish planning from 1921 to 1945: an overview', in Bannon (ed.), *A Hundred Years of Irish Planning. Vol. II* (Dublin, 1989), p. 15.
85. D/E Dublin Files, Box 207. Secretariat File no. 112.
86. D/E Dublin Files, Box 205. 13682/1926. Dublin Reconstruction Act 1924.
87. D/E Dublin Files, Box 259 123225/32 Enquiry re Municipal Art Gallery.
88. Kilkeel Board of Guardians was the first to do so on 30 June 1920; by the end of July 1920, Belleek and Downpatrick RDCs and Newry Board of Guardians had followed suit. Eamon Phoenix, *Northern Nationalism. Nationalist Politics, Partition and the Catholic Minority in Northern Ireland 1890-1940* (Belfast, 1994), p. 90.
89. Phoenix, *Northern Nationalism*, pp. 74, 85, 146, 148, 152, 153, 155, 163.
90. DELG 27/30 Tipperary South Riding County Council (Misfiled), 1 December 1921.
91. S 577 North-east Ulster memorial deputation to Collins and Griffith, February 1922.

92. Tim Pat Coogan, *Michael Collins. A Biography* (London, 1990), pp. 347, 357, 383-85. D. H. Akenson, *Education and Enmity: The Control of Schooling in Northern Ireland, 1920-50* (Newton Abbot, 1973), p. 52.
93. Phoenix, *Northern Nationalism*, pp. 203, 209-210.
94. PDDE, 10 May 1922, pp. 373-74. This is the only reference I have seen to a Board of Directors of Local Government.
95. D/E Secretary's Files, no number.
96. For a profile of Mulcahy, see Robins, *Custom House People*, pp. 98-101.
97. D/E Secretary's files no. 3.
98. e.g. Ronan Fanning, *Independent Ireland* (Dublin, 1983), pp. 60-70.
99. Fanning, *Finance*, chapter 3.
100. D/E LG 36 Reorganisation.
101. PDDE, 1 June 1926, col. 93.
102. D/E General Files, Staff returns 1927 and 1931.
103. D/F, Supplies Series, S72/1/24 Local Government Bill.
104. Information supplied by Brendan O'Donoghue.
105. UCDA P 24/616. Cumann na nGaedheal Annual Convention, 13 May 1925. Cited in Patricia Duffin, 'An examination of Local Government under the Cumann na nGaedheal administration', MA UCD 1992, p. 29.
106. It appears that before 1920 many rural district council either failed to hold their four statutory meetings or kept no minutes. I am grateful to Chris O'Mahony, Limerick archivist, for this information.
107. *First report DLGPH*, pp. 53-55.
108. PDDE, 29 May 1925, col. 1588.
109. S 3646 Local Government Ireland Act.
110. PDDE, 29 May 1924, cols. 1594-1787.
111. UCDA P24/507 W. Gilligan (DLGPH) to Ministry of Finance.
112. D/E General files LG 237 Local Government Act 1931.
113. *First report DLGPH*, pp. 22-24.
114. Augustine Birrell, *Things Past Redress* (London, 1937), p. 219.
115. R. O. Connor and C. Guiomard, 'Agricultural output in the Irish Free State area before and after independence', *Irish Economic and Social History*, Vol. XII, pp. 89-97.
116. D/F, S72/7/1926 Collection of rates through the post office.
117. D/E Offaly files, Box 656, 89143/39 Overdraft.
118. PDDE, 29 March 1927, col. 469.
119. D/E General files G 5642/39 Roscommon Town Commissioners.
120. D/E General files G 1572/43 Rathkeale Town Commissioners, abolition of.
121. S 1962 Dublin Corporation: half pay to imprisoned employees.
122. D/E Dublin files, Boxes 161 and 162.
123. D/E Dublin files, Box 167. Dissolution of Dublin Corporation.
124. D/E Dublin files, Box 239.
125. Daly, *Deposed Capital*, pp. 236-38.
126. S 6532 Greater Dublin Commission of Inquiry.
127. Eunan O'Halpin, 'The origins of city and county management', in *City and County Management, 1929-1990. A Retrospective* (Dublin, 1991), p. 8.

128. *Report of Greater Dublin Commission of Inquiry* (Dublin, 1926).
129. O'Halpin, 'Origins', p. 9.
130. John J. Horgan, *The Cork City Management Act. Origins, Provisions and Application* (Cork, 1929). Foreword. My thanks to Dr Maura Cronin for providing me with a photocopy of this pamphlet.
131. D/E Dublin files Box 167, 20 May 1924.
132. Monahan was elected as a Sinn Féin member of Drogheda Corporation, where he served as mayor and a member of Louth County Council, in 1920. Edward McCarron, then an LGB auditor, had charged the previous Drogheda Corporation with corruption. From 1920 to 1922 he corresponded regularly with W.T. Cosgrave and seems to have been the latter's main source of information on local government in County Louth. When Kerry County Council was dissolved in 1923, he became county commissioner. From there, he was transferred to Cork as city commissioner. 'Silhouette: Philip Monahan', in *City and County Management*, pp. 117-20.
133. D/E G 246/32 Cork City Borough Management Bill 1929.
134. O'Halpin, 'Origins', p. 10.
135. D/E G246/32, 10 January 1927.
136. S 5265 Cork City Management Bill.
137. Horgan, *Cork City Management Act*, pp. 7-8.
138. D/E G246/32.
139. PDDE 28 June 1928, cols. 1851-73; 30 November 1928, cols. 1153-54.
140. S 4870 Local Elections Dublin Act.
141. S 6533. Memorandum on Local Government (Dublin) Bill prepared for executive council.
142. PDDE col. 971, 26 February 1930.
143. UCDA Desmond FitzGerald Papers, P 80/1101 C.
144. UCDA Mulcahy papers, P 7/C/86 (2). Memorandum on employment of ex-servicemen (no date). Temporary clerical employment.
145. UCDA P 7/B/57.
146. DLGPH second report, p. 17.
147. S 3406 Anti-state activities, officials and members of local authorities.
148. S 4616 Local Government (Temporary Provisions) (Amendment) Act 1924.
149. S 3646 Local Government Act 1925.
150. S 6248 Local Government Act 1933.
151. UCDA P 7/C/86 (4).
152. D/E General files, LG 278 Proposal repeal of section 71 of Local Government Act 1925.
153. PDDE, 3 June 1924, col. 1773.
154. D/F 72/7/1925 Local Authoriities (Appointment of Officers) Bill.
155. S 45346 Local Authorities (Officers and Employees) Act 1926.
156. PDDE 19 May 1926, cols. 1816-20; 20 May 1926, cols. 1849-50.
157. S 2548 Local Appointments Commission procedure.
158. S 5454 Local Appointments Commission, appointment of Medical Officer for Scotstown, Co. Monaghan.
159. S 2548 Local appointments commission, procedures.

160. PDDE 1 June 1928, cols. 131-35; 1 November 1928, col. 1300. The committee consisted of eleven Dáil deputies: O.G Esmonde (chair), S. Brady, F.H. Crowley, E. Doherty, T. Hennessy, M. Jordan, T.J. Murphy, J.S. Myles, S.T. O'Kelly, D. O'Mahony and F. C. Ward. It reported in February 1930.
161. S 2359 Local Authorities (Officers and Employees) Act. Action following on report. S 9377 Select Committee Local Authorities (Officers and Employees) Act.
162. S 2548.
163. Joseph Lee, *Ireland 1912-1985* (Cambridge, 1989), pp. 161-67.
164. D/E Mayo Files, 21376/48. Appointment of Miss Dunbar-Harrison as county librarian.
165. D/F, S72/2/24.
166. S 6396 Appointment of Professor Smiddy as economic adviser.
167. DE 2/243 22 April 1922.
168. D/F, S72/2/24 W. D. to Codling, 22/3/24.
169. S 6532.
170. PDDE, 9 February 1923, col. 1435.
171. PDDE , 29 April 1931, col. 554.
172. D/E General files, LG 237 Local Government Act 1931.
173. PDDE, 24 April 1930, cols. 779-81.
174. S 3629 Relief of rates on agricultural land.
175. S 3446 Local Government (Collection of Rates) Act 1926.
176. D/F, S 72/7/1926 Collection of rates through post office.
177. S 3446; D/ F S72/5/1926. Bill to Re-enact sections 6 and 7 of the Local Government (Collection of Rates Act) 1924.
178. *Second report DLGPH,* p. 21.
179. *Report Commission of Inquiry into Derating* 1931 P. 373.
180. S 3629.
181. S 3803 Rates on Agricultural Land Act 1924.
182. *First report DLGPH,* p. 21.
183. S 3629.
184. UCDA P 6/C/86.
185. Members were Herbert Smith (Agriculture), John Leydon (Finance), Gordon Campbell (Industry and Commerce) and E.P. McCarron (Local Government).
186. UCDA P 24/126 Memorandum on rates in relation to agricultural and industrial production, interdepartmental memorandum March 1929.
187. PDDE 24 April 1930, col. 779.
188. Cab 4/98, 30 July 1929.
189. *Report of Commission of Inquiry into Derating.*
190. S 3629.
191. Philip G. Irwin, 'The economic policy of the Cumann na nGaedheal government 1929-32: the issue of agricultural de-rating', MA, UCD 1984.
192. S 7386 Relief of rates, motion by Deputy de Valera; PDDE 26 March 1931 col. 2177.
193. *Report DLGPH* 1927-28, p. 3; *Report DLGPH* 1928-29, p. 3

194. For a discussion of the Treasury view, see Peter Clarke, *The Keynesian Revolution in the Making, 1924-1936* (Oxford, 1988), chapter 3.
195. D/F Fin 1/664/17 Loans: Suspension of grants out of Local Loans Fund.
196. D/E Dublin Files Box 205 13682/1926 Dublin Reconstruction Act.
197. D/F Fin 1/664/17 Loans: suspension of grants out of local loans fund.
198. D/E Dublin files Box 205.
199. Murray Fraser, 'John Bull's other homes', 1993, chapter 5.
200. D/E Roads LG 701.
201. D/E Box 710 Roads Advisory Committee Minutes 1923.
202. PDDE 21 April 1926, col. 163.
203. *Report DLGPH* 1926, p. 61.
204. D/E Sligo Box 702. 7/50/39 Tobercurry water supply and sewerage inquiry, 1928-37.
205. D/E Waterford Box 766. 2/325/41 Kilmacthomas water supply.
206. Colm Lincoln, 'Working class housing in Dublin 1914-30', MA, UCD, 1979, pp. 65-67.
207. Fraser, 'John Bull's other homes', p. 192.
208. PDDE 20 March 1929, col. 1557.
209. Mary Casteleyn, *A History of Literacy and Libraries in Ireland. The Long Traced Pedigree* (Aldershot, 1984), pp. 170-212.
210. D/E G 286/13/11 Listowel Library.
211. Casteleyn, *Literacy and Libraries,* p. 220.
212. D/E Dublin files Box 205 13682/1926.
213. *DLGHP First Report*, pp. 141-43.
214. D/F F23/14/24.
215. S 4278 Distress and unemployment in Saorstát Eireann.
216. D/E LG 107 12037/37 Unemployment Relief Act 1931.
217. D/F F88/10/30 Relief schemes, administration of.
218. UCDA P7b/67.

CHAPTER FOUR

1. Robins, *Custom House People*, pp. 102-04.
2. Fanning, *Finance*, p. 216.
3. S 6252 Provisions of employment proposals, 1932.
4. *Irish Law Reports*, 1932, pp. 207-15. *The state at the prosecution of the Minister for Local Government and Public Health* v. *the Joint Committee of Management of the District Mental Hospital Court*. The challenge was rejected.
5. S 2548 Local Appointments Commission procedure.
6. S 8052 Local Appointments Commission: functions of President and Executive Council.
7. S 6248 Local Government Act 1933.
8. S 2548.
9. D/E LG 278 proposal to repeal of section 71 of 1925 Local Government Act.

10. S 6248.
11. S 7890 Local Government Act 1936.
12. S 6460 Sligo town clerkship, 1933.
13. D/E Sligo Boxes 691, 692.
14. PDDE 22 March 1934, cols. 1423-30.
15. D/E Secretary's files S 260 Commission of Inquiry into the Civil Service, 1934.
16. S 6744 DLGPH appointment of secretary.
17. PDDE 3 February 1937, cols. 62-65.
18. S 6744; S 9419 Portrane mental hospital appointment.
19. S 6744.
20. PDDE 3 February 1937, cols. 93-94.
21. NLI Brennan Commission, evidence Ms. 956, 8 February 1933 qs. 6570-6660.
22. *Report of Commission (on) the Gaeltacht* 1926 R 23/27.
23. PDDE 23 May 1939, cols. 86-87.
24. S 14740A Civil service and local authority appointments.
25. S 14740 A-D Civil service and local authority appointments.
26. S 14740 E.
27. S 2548 Appointments Commission procedures 1942.
28. S 6341. Reduction in salaries of employees of local authorities.
29. D/E LG 247 G33952/31 Deputation of Irish Local Government Officials Union to Department 1931.
30. D/E LG 292 Local Services (Temporary Economies) Act 1934.
31. D/E Dublin Box 186. 5848/40 Engineers file no. 1.
32. *Irish Law Reports* 1933, p. 517. Supreme Court, 8-11 May and 31 May. *The state at the prosecution of the Kerry County Council. Thomas O'Connor and others* v. *the Minister for Local Government & Public Health.*
33. D/E LG 644. Officers of Local Authorities Bill. Bill to Validate Action under Section 15 of 1923 Act.
34. Kieran A. Kennedy, Thomas Giblin and Deirdre Mc Hugh, *The Economic Development of Ireland in the Twentieth Century* (London, 1988), p. 46.
35. S 3629 Relief of rates on agricultural land.
36. S 2851 Local taxation grants.
37. S 7390 Relief of rates on agricultural land 1932.
38. S 7389 Relief of rates on agricultural land 1933/34.
39. S 6911 Rates on Agricultural Land (Relief) Act 1935.
40. S 11042. Rates on Agricultural Land (Relief) Acts 1935-c.1960.
41. D.F. S 84/46/38 Rates on Agricultural Land (Relief) Bill 1939.
42. S 11042.
43. Raymond Crotty, *Irish Agricultural Production: Its Volume and Structure,* (Cork, 1966), pp. 152-53.
44. D/E Waterford Box 776. 18558/31 (c) Dissolution of Waterford County Council, inquiry.
45. S84/39/37. DLG Local Government Bill; McElligott to DLGPH, 28 October 1938.

46. D/E LG 104 G 451/1 Conference with county secretaries, 2-3 March 1937.
47. LG Box 198. General G 468 County Limerick seizure and sale of cattle.
48. *Commission on Banking Currency and Credit,* p. 106, para. 175.
49. M. O'Donoghue and A.A. Tait, 'The growth of public revenue and expenditure in Ireland', in J. A. Bristow and A.A. Tait (eds), *Economic Policy in Ireland* (Dublin, 1968), pp. 278-93.
50. *Commission on Banking Currency and Credit,* p. 82, para. 128.
51. ibid., p. 85, para. 133; Fanning, *Finance,* p. 358.
52. D/F 599/30 Joseph Brennan, memorandum on borrowing, 1923.
53. S 4278; D/F F88/4/26.
54. *DLG and PH First Report,* pp. 141-43.
55. D/F F23/14/24.
56. Cited in Fanning, *Independent Ireland,* p. 71.
57. UCDA FitzGerald Papers, P 80/1081 DLG W.J. Gillian, statement re. conditions in Adrigole.
58. D/E Box 774 Waterford File no. 5989/31 Dungarvan UDC.
59. S 4278 Distress in Saorstát Eireann. Minutes Clifden RDC 22 January 1924.; D/F F23/14/24 Memorandum on Relief Grants.
60. D/F F88/4/26 Relief Schemes Vote 1926-27.
61. R 38/2 *Committee on Relief of Unemployment 1927. Final Report.*
62. LG 107/12037/37 Unemployment Relief Act 1931.
63. D/F F88/10/30 Relief Schemes, administration of.
64. S 6252 Provision of employment schemes 1932.
65. D/F F74/7/32 Road Fund: proposed allocation of £1m. to local authorities to carry out road works for the relief of unemployment.
66. PDDE, 11 May 1932, cols. 1513-4.
67. D/F F74/7/32. Proposed allocation of £1m. to local authorities to carry out road works for the relief of unemployment.
68. D/F F88/16/32 Vote for relief schemes.
69. D/F F74/7/32.
70. S 12072 Employment schemes vote.
71. D/F F88/8/32. Budget provisions for relief of unemployment. Allocation to DLGPH.
72. Fanning, *Finance,* pp. 247-51.
73. S 6274 Economic committee of the cabinet.
74. D/F F88/8/32 Budget provisions for relief of unemployment. Allocation to DLGPH.
75. D/E Sanitary section 208/1. Public health schemes, labour content and expenditure analysis.
76. D/F F88/12/33. Relief schemes vote 1933-34. Allocation to DLGPH.
77. D/F F88/8/34. Relief schemes vote 1934-35. Allocation to DLGPH.
78. D/F F88/12/33.
79. D/F F88/8/34.
80. D/E LG 609. Relief works vote.
81. D/E Sanitary 208/1.
82. D/E Sligo L 885/40 Coolooney sewerage scheme.

83. PDDE, 10 May 1933, cols. 736-46.
84. PDDE, 9 May 1934, cols. 633-37.
85. Collins, author the book *Local Government* (Dublin, 1953), served as secretary of the Department of Local Government from 1947 to 1948. For a profile, see D. Roche, 'A memoir of the author', in *Local Government* (second edition, 1963), pp. 7-16 and Robins, *Custom House People*, pp. 119-22.
86. S 8786. Committee on public works. First interim report.
87. D/E Sanitary 208/1 Public health schemes: précis of Garvin's evidence.
88. S 8786.
89. S 8786 OPW memo, 12 July 1935.
90. ibid. Finance memo, 15 August 1935.
91. D/E LG 145, S1689/39. Rotational system of employment.
92. LG 145, 29 October 1935.
93. Statements made in the report of the Committee on Widows and Orphans Pensions suggest that Unemployment Assistance was regarded as a demeaning payment.
94. S 8787. Committee on relief works, third interim report.
95. ibid., 18 April 1936.
96. C.S. Andrews, *Man of No Property* (Dublin, 1982), p. 172.
97. S 9600 Rotational employment schemes 1937.
98. Robins, *Custom House People*, pp. 112-14.
99. LG 145 Employment schemes conference, 6 May 1937.
100. D/E Dublin Box 222. Report of city manager on relief works, December 1938.
101. D/E Dublin Box 222. Report of city manager on relief works, December 1938.
102. D/E Secretaries Files, S 441. Emergency schemes memoranda.
103. D/E Dublin Box 191. 85180/37 Liffey water supply file.
104. D/E Dublin Box 191, 255382/36 Dun Laoghaire sewerage works at Bullock harbour.
105. D/E Offaly, L21950/41. Clara water supply inquiry.
106. D/E Dublin Box 279. Housing Board minutes, 25 April 1936.
107. D/E Dublin Box 195, 196. 3497/3/48.
108. D/T S 12072 Employment schemes.
109. D/F F61/64/48, obtained in UCDA McGilligan Papers, P35a/94.
110. Robins, *Custom House People*, pp. 169-73.
111. Mary E. Daly, *Industrial Development and Irish National Identity 1922-39* (Syracuse and Dublin, 1992).

CHAPTER FIVE

1. Joel Mokyr, *Why Ireland Starved: A Quantitative and Analytical History of the Irish Economy 1800-1850* (London,1983), p. 7.
2. Mary E. Daly, 'Working-class housing in Scottish and Irish cities on the eve

of World War I' in S. J. Connolly, R. A. Houston and R. J. Morris (eds), *Conflict, Identity and Economic Development. Ireland and Scotland 1600-1939* (Preston, 1995), pp. 222-23.

3. Mary E. Daly, *A Social and Economic History of Ireland since 1800* (Dublin, 1980), p. 98.

4. Daly, *Deposed Capital*, pp. 257-58, 281-82, 290.

5. Michael Gough, 'Socio-economic conditions and the genesis of planning in Cork', in Michael J. Bannon (ed.), *A Hundred Years of Irish Planning. Vol. I*, p. 309.

6. P.J. Meghen, *Housing in Ireland* (Dublin, 1963), pp. 6-9.

7. Jane Morton, 'The 1890 Act and its aftermath — the era of the "Model Dwellings"' in Stuart Lowe and David Hughes (eds), *A New Century of Social Housing* (Leicester, 1991), pp. 29-32; Daly, 'Working-Class Housing', p. 226.

8. Daly, *Deposed Capital*, pp. 312-14.

9. John W. Boyle, 'A marginal figure: the Irish rural labourer', in Samuel Clark and James S. Donnelly (eds), *Irish Peasants: Violence and Political Unrest 1780-1914* (Dublin, 1978), p. 327.

10. *Reports from Poor Law Inspectors on the Wages of Agricultural Labourers in Ireland* (c. 35), 1870, xiv, pp 11, 30.

11. James S. Donnelly, *The Land and the People of Nineteenth-Century Cork* (London, 1975), p. 240.

12. Boyle, 'Marginal figure', p. 327.

13. Donnelly, *Cork*, p. 241.

14. Meghen, *Housing in Ireland*, pp. 14-24.

15. Nicholas J. Synnott, 'Housing of the rural population in Ireland', *Journal of the Statistical and Social Inquiry Society of Ireland*, Vol. XI, 1903-04, pp. 226-27.

16. *Report LGBI* 1884.

17. Boyle, 'Marginal figure' p. 332; James O'Shea, *Priests, Politics and Society in Post-Famine Ireland. A Study of County Tipperary 1850-1891* (Dublin, 1983), p. 129.

18. *Report LGBI* 1884; O'Shea, *Priests*, p. 131.

19. Synnott, 'Housing of the rural population', p. 220.

20. O'Shea, *Priests*, pp. 127-32.

21. *Report LGBI* 1895.

22. Boyle, 'Marginal figure', p. 333.

23. *Report LGBI 1901*.

24. Shannon, 'Local Government', pp. 293-94.

25. Synnott, 'Housing of the rural population', p. 216; Synnott, 'Proposals for a New Labourers' Bill: an attempt to solve the rural housing question in Ireland', *Journal of the Statistical and Social Inquiry Society of Ireland*, Vol. XI, 1905-06, p. 413.

26. D/E Housing, Box 48. 217/18. Origins of the DLGPH's outline specifications.

27. Bannon, 'The genesis of Irish planning', pp. 189-260.

28. Mark Swenarton, *Homes Fit for Heroes* (London, 1981), p. 71.
29. *Report of the Proceedings of the Irish Convention,* Appendix XVI, Report of the Housing Committee, 3 April 1918.
30. Fraser, 'John Bull's other homes', pp. 182-86; 208.
31. D/F Fin 1/137 Housing grant of £1m.
32. D/E Secretary's files, unnumbered.
33. Fraser, 'John Bull's other homes', p. 245.
34. *First report DLGPH,* p. 80.
35. Mervyn Miller, 'Raymond Unwin and the planning of Dublin', in Bannon, *Emergence of Irish Planning,* pp. 263-306.
36. PDDE, 20 March 1929, cols. 1549-1766.
37. Jane Darke, 'Local political attitudes and council housing', in Lowe and Hughes (eds), *A New Century of Social Housing,* p. 162.
38. S 3366 Building Facilities Act,; Fraser 'John Bull's other homes'.
39. S 4278A Distress and unemployment in Saorstát Éireann.
40. PDDE, 25 January 1924, col. 669.
41. S 5054 Town Tenants Commission of Inquiry 1927; S13168 Rents and Mortgage Interest Restrictions Acts; D/F S032/5/29 Economic committee 1929.
42. PDDE, 29 October 1924, cols. 430-446; B.J. Graham and Susan Hood, 'Town tenant protest in late-nineteenth and early-twentieth century Ireland', *Irish Economic and Social History,* Vol. XXI, 1994, pp. 39-57.
43. D/F S 32/4/26 Housing Amendment Bill 1925; S4335 Housing and Town Planning Acts 1925.
44. PDDE, 7 November 1924, col. 1007.
45. D/F S 32/4/26; S4335.
46. S 6027 Housing Bill 1930.
47. D/F S84/10/30 Housing Bill 1930.
48. D/F S32/4/25 Housing Bill 1925.
49. D/F F136/31/26. DLGPH housing loans. Proposal to make Local Loans Fund available for local authority housing loans.
50. PDDE, 5 June 1929, col. 763.
51. PDDE, 20 March 1929, cols. 1549-1766.
52. D/F S32/1/29 Housing Bill 1929.
53. *DLGPH report,* 1930, p. 108.
54. S32/4/30 Grants to local authorities under the Housing Acts 1929 and 1930.
55. PDDE, 20 March 1929, cols. 1549-1766.
56. *Committee on the Relief of Unemployment. Final report* 1928, pp. 7-8.
57. Lincoln, 'Working-class housing', p. 55.
58. D/F F136/31/26.
59. D/F F136/31/26.
60. S32/1/29 Housing Bill 1929.
61. *Committee on the Relief of Unemployment,* Appendix B.
62. S 3642 Dublin Corporation housing programme.
63. D/E Dublin Box 167. Inquiry into Dublin Corporation.
64. D/E Dublin Box 242, H 303/330. Fairbrothers' Fields housing scheme.

65. S. J. Bradenburg, 'Housing progress in the Irish Free State', *Journal of Land and Public Utility Economics,* Vol. VIII, no. 1. Feb. 1932, p. 6, as cited in Lincoln, 'Working-class housing'.
66. This five-man committee, chaired by M.R. Heffernan, TD, parliamentary secretary to the Minister for Posts and Telegraphs, was established in 1927 to scrutinise public expenditure. The other four members were civil servants, two from Finance. It eventually issued a preliminary report in 1931. Fanning, *Finance,* pp. 192-201.
67. S32/5/29 Economy Committee 1929. Housing subsidy.
68. Lincoln, 'Working-class housing', pp. 65-67.
69. D/F S32/4/30 Grants to Local Authorities under Housing Acts 1929 and 1930.
70. D/F S84/5/31 Housing (Miscellaneous Provisions) Bill 1931.
71. S 6193. Housing (Miscellaneous Provisions) Act 1931.
72. D/F S84/5/31.
73. S 6193 DLG Memorandum on Bill, 15 September 1931.
74. *Report DLGPH* 1931, pp. 247-50.
75. S 6193.
76. D/F S84/5/31.
77. Marion Bowley, *Housing and the State 1919-44* (London, 1945), p. 129.
78. D/F F60/10/33. Rates of interest charged by LLF. McCarron, secretary of Local Government, described Seán T. O'Kelly carrying a 'fiery cross through the country', urging local authorities to expand their housing programmes.
79. e.g. Cormac Ó Gráda, *Ireland: A New Economic History 1780-1939* (Oxford, 1994), pp. 439-40.
80. S 6193.
81. S 6280 1932 Housing Miscellaneous and Financial Provisions Bill.
82. Meghen, *Housing* , p. 43.
83. *Report Commission on Banking, Currency and Credit,* para. 170.
84. D/F F60/10/33 Local loans. Revision of rates of interest.
85. *Report Commission on Banking, Currency and Credit,* para. 548.
86. D/F S84/17/34 Housing (Financial and Miscellaneous Provisions) Amendment Bill 1934.
87. D/F S84/19/36. Housing (Financial and Miscellaneous Provisions) Amendment Bill 1936.
88. S 8237 Housing (Financial and Miscellaneous Provisions) Acts 1932 and 1934, Amendments.
89. D/F S84/17/34.
90. S8832 Housing (Financial and Miscellaneous Provisions) Act 1936.
91. S 10341 Housing and Labourers' Act 1937
92. S 11081 Housing (Amendment) Act 1939.
93. D/F S84/24/37. Housing and Labourers' Bill.
94. *Report Commission on Banking Currency and Credit,* para 607.
95. D/E General files. G 273/1/1; G 273/1/2, G 273/1/3. Local Government (Remission of Rates) Bill 1940.
96. S 6034 Labourers' Act 1930.

97. D/E Dublin box 279 S 178. Minutes of Housing Board, 19 May 1936.

98. D/E Offaly, box 666. County Offaly housing inquiry June 1936.

99. D/E Dublin; Dublin labourers' housing inquiry, H 136074/1935, evidence paras. 34527 and 38893.

100. Housing Board Minutes, 23 October 1935.

101. Housing Board, 6 April 1936, letter to Sligo Board of Health.

102. ibid., November 1935.

103. S 6289 Sales of labourers' cottages. Commission of inquiry.

104. D/E Waterford Box 761 9357/35. Waterford Board of Public Health.

105. D/E Sligo Urban District Council, box 691, file 10610/36.

106. D/F F61/47/33. Tralee Urban District Council. Loan of £43,000 for erecting houses under the Housing of the Working Classes Act.

107. D/F S32/6/36. Housing schemes, necessity for obtaining provisional sanction of Minister of Finance regarding cost per house.

108. D/F F60/10/33. Rates of interest charged by LLF.

109. S 6275. Housing Board, proposals.

110. PDDE, 23 November 1932, cols. 1-3.

111. The only records which have come to my notice were misfiled in D/E Dublin box 279 S 178. These relate mostly to 1936, with some material from 1934 and 1935.

112. PDDE, 5 July 1934, col. 1554. where O'Kelly spoke of members of the Board interviewing unco-operative local authorities.

113. Housing Board Minutes, 28 February 1936, 5 June 1936.

114. Daly, *Industrial Development and Irish National Identity,* pp. 118-120.

115. S 6137A Cement industry.

116. Housing Board Minutes, 18 January 1935.

117. Housing Board Minutes 30 January 1936.

118. *Report of Inquiry into the Housing of the Working Classes of the City of Dublin,* R 75/1 1939-43, para 351.

119. *Banking Commission.* Evidence given by Dublin and District House-Builders Association, pp. 1009-1045.

120. Daly, *Industrial Development,* pp. 135-50.

121. D/E General files G 269/8/29a. Dublin C. B. stock file no. 2.

122. *Banking Commission,* para. 617. D/E H 263/4 Memo of meeting re Housing Finance between Department of Local Government and directors of Irish Civil Service Building Society, 11 March 1940.

123. D/E Dublin files, box 290 Dublin Housing Inquiry; private sitting 4 April 1940; memo. submitted on behalf of Irish Banks' Standing Committee.

124. D/E G 269/8/29a. Dublin CB stock file no. 3.

125. Dublin Files, box 290. Dublin Housing Inquiry memo. submitted on behalf of Irish Banks' Standing Committee.

126. D/E Housing box 30; D/F F40/4/38. Financing the housing programme of Dublin Corporation.

127. D/E Housing 205/5. General building aspects: finance and policy c. 1940.

128. Dublin Housing Inquiry, para. 121.

129. Mary E. Daly, 'Social structure of the Dublin working class, 1871-1911,

Irish Historical Studies, Vol. XXIII, no. 90 (November 1982), p. 131.

130. *Commission on Banking, Currency and Credit*. Evidence, pp. 852-53.

131. D/E Dublin; summary of evidence by W.C. Dwyer to Dublin Housing Inquiry.

132. Dublin Housing Inquiry, paras. 202-09.

133. ibid., DLGPH supplemental memorandum 30 March 1939.

134. Miller, 'Raymond Unwin and the planning of Dublin', pp. 263-306.

135. D/E housing, Box 30, no separate file number.

136. S 11478A.

137. D/E G269/8/28a Cork Corporation stock file.

138. *Report Commission on Banking, Currency and Credit, Reservation no. 11.*

139. *Commission on Banking, Currency and Credit*. Evidence, pp. 220-37; 583-594; 1009-45.

140. *Commission on Banking, Currency and Credit*. Evidence Dublin and District House-Builders Association, pp. 1009-45.

141. For details of the Control of Manufactures Acts, see Mary E. Daly, 'An Irish-Ireland for business? The Control of Manufactures Acts, 1932 and 1934', *Irish Historical Studies*, Vol. XXIV, no. 94 (1984), pp. 246-72.

142. S 10553 A. Building societies promoting and financing.

143. Daly, *Industrial Development and Irish National Identity 1922-39.*

CHAPTER SIX

1. F.S.L. Lyons, *Ireland since the Famine* (London, 1971), pp. 557-58.

2. D/E Roads, box 744. Turf; Seán MacEntee to secretary.

3. See Robins, *Custom House People,* pp. 152-56, 197.

4. S 11445/B Emergency powers in time of war.

5. S 11980 Measures necessary to provide in an emergency for the conduct and functions of government 1940.

6. S 12171 October 1940. Department of Local Government. Problems in event of attack on country.

7. Fanning, *Finance*, pp. 336-38.

8. D/E LG 156 Air raid precautions.

9. S 12045 Cabinet committee on emergency problems, minutes.

10. S 12161 Emergency war measures. Security and operation of industrial and public utility plants.

11. S 12164 Maintenance of essential services in emergency.

12. D/E General files LG 156 IR 142 emergency 1940, matters arising.

13. S 12278 Local authorities: powers in regard to defence in the event of emergency 1942.

14. Robert Fisk, *In Time of War* (London, 1983), p. 220.

15. D/E General files. LG 192 ED 1681/4. Boughing of trees on routes for evacuation.

16. D/F S72/9/41 Communal feeding.

17. S 11903 Minutes of Cabinet committee on emergency problems.

18. Fisk, *In Time of War*, p. 434.

19. D/E Dublin box 224, H 2708/42 Air raid damage North Strand.
20. D/E Sanitary section box 15 Fire Brigades Act 1940/ 221/8.
21. R 62-1 *Report of Tribunal of Inquiry into Pearse Street Fire.*
22. D/E Fire Brigades Act 1940.
23. *Report of Tribunal of Inquiry into Fire at St. Joseph's Orphanage, Cavan,* P 6144.
24. D/E 1940/221/8.
25. Fisk, *In Time of War*, pp. 420-21.
26. D/E 1940/221/8.
27. *Comparative tables relating to local taxation and the expenditure of local bodies in the period 1932-44.*
28. D/E G 276/1 Economy in public expenditure.
29. D/E G 285/7 Emergency powers order no. 321, 1944.
30. S 11953A Local authority employees: increase of wages, 1940-44.
31. S 11616 Dublin Corporation workers: increased wages 1940.
32. Seán Redmond, *The Irish Municipal Employees Trade Union 1883-1983* (Dublin, 1983), p. 104.
33. O'Connor, *Labour History*, p. 141.
34. S 11616.
35. Redmond, *Irish Municipal Employees*, pp. 105-07.
36. S 11648 Employment schemes in Mayo.
37. S 11953A Local authority employees; increase of wages 1940-44.
38. *DLGPH report* 1941/42 app. liii, p. 233.
39. S 11951 Local authorities cost of living bonus stabilisation.
40. *Report DLGPH* 1941/42, pp. 18-19.
41. G 322/1 Local government bill 1945.
42. D/E Secretary's files S 527. Turf production. Conference with county engineers.
43. Fisk, *In Time of War*, pp. 253-55.
44. Andrews, *Man of No Property*, pp. 118-21; 172-77.
45. D/E roads box 743. Fuel policy. Memorandum on production of emergency turf 1941-2.
46. D/E roads box 738. T 783 A. Engineering inspectors' reports 1942.
47. D/E Roads box 739. Unnumbered file. Transfer of turf functions 1943.
48. D/E box 738 T 783A.
49. D/E roads box 743 TA 161G Wages and conditions re employment on turf.
50. D/E roads box 748 TA 183. Emigration to Great Britain and Northern Ireland.
51. D/E roads box 743. TA 161.
52. D/E roads box 704 Section 411/2. Turf production by local authorities: piece rates.
53. D/E roads box 743. County surveyors' conference re turf February 1944.
54. D/E roads box 750 TA 124G. Plans for turf production 1946.
55. D/E secretary's files S 527. Turf production. Conference with county engineers.
56. D/E secretary's files S 530 Road and turf workers' wages.

57. D/E roads, box 704, 125G. Plans for turf production in 1947.
58. See Robins, *Custom House People*, pp. 133-35.
59. D/E roads, box 750. Turf Development Board proposals volume I.
60. Fanning, *Finance*, pp. 317-19.
61. S 11478 A. Building industry. Position during the European war.
62. D/F S32/1/39 State aid for houses, urban and rural.
63. Fanning, *Finance*, p. 321.
64. S 11466 European war 1939: economic policy of government.
65. M. O'Donoghue and A.A. Tait, 'The growth of public revenue and expenditure in Ireland', in J.A. Bristow and A.A. Tait (eds), *Economic Policy in Ireland* (Dublin, 1968), p. 288; J. J. Lee, *Ireland 1912-1985*, p. 226.
66. *Comparative Tables Relating to Local Taxation and the Expenditure and Receipts of Local Bodies in the Period 1932-44.*
67. Fanning, *Finance*, p. 316.
68. S 11478A. Building industry: position during the European war.
69. S 11466 European war, economic policy of government.
70. S 11478B.
71. S 11686 1940 Housing (Miscellaneous Provisions) Amendment Act.
72. S 11466.
73. S 11478B.
74. D/E Secretary's files, S 449 Economic planning 1943.
75. S 13059A. Housing, post-war development.
76. S 12280A Road tax refund to private motorists.
77. D/E LG 701 Roads: road works programme, post-war.
78. S 12763 Road Traffic Act 1933. Amendments by Emergency Powers Orders.
79. S 12828A Motor vehicles: maximum speed limits.
80. LG 701.
81. D/E roads 230/1 memo. December 1942.
82. S 11466.
83. D/E 230/1.
84. S 11227 Derelict Sites Act 1939.
85. S 11995A. Unemployment (Relief Works) Act 1940.
86. S 11227.
87. S 11916A. Dublin corporation workers, increased wages.
88. S 11227.
89. S 11916A. Relief of unemployment in Dublin and Dun Laoghaire.
90. S 11466.
91. D/E Road files Ir/163 Construction Corps. Provision of civil work for.
92. S 13101 Full employment: file includes a press-cutting of Flinn's speech from *The Irish Independent*, 6 July 1940.
93. Lee, *Ireland 1912-1985*, pp. 226-28.
94. S 12882A. Planning for post-war situation, general file.
95. Michael Bannon, 'Irish planning from 1921-45', in Bannon (ed.), *Planning: The Irish Experience 1920-1988*, pp. 43-44.

96. S 6619A. Town planning general file.
97. K.I. Nowlan, 'The evolution of Irish planning 1934-64', in Bannon (ed.), *Planning*, pp. 73-74.
98. For details, Bannon,'Irish planning', pp 49-56.
99. S 12884 Planning for the post-war situation: the Department of Finance.
100. S 13059A.
101. *Royal Commission on the Distribution of the Industrial Population*. 1939-40. Cmd. 6153, iv, 263.
102. S 6619A.
103. S 13059A Post-war housing.
104. Lee, *Ireland 1912-1985*, pp. 229-30.
105. S 11916A.
106. S 12887 Planning for the post-war situation. Minister for Local Government and Public Health.
107. S 13026 Cabinet committee on economic planning: proceedings.
108. S 11916A.
109. S 13026.
110. S 13061 Post-war planning: roads.
111. A future President of Ireland. See Robins, *Custom House People*, pp. 133-35.
112. D/E Roads section box 711; Minutes parliamentary secretary re road planning. 1944-45.
113. S 13058 Village halls; D/E G275/1 Village halls.
114. S 12882A. Planning for post-war situation. General file.
115. S 13166 Planning for post-war employment: water and sewerage schemes.
116. Lee, *Ireland 1912-85*, p. 229.

CHAPTER SEVEN

1. *Reports DLGPH*; 'A Chronology of Local Government 1918-1990', in *City and County Management 1929-90*.
2. PDDE, 3 June 1942, col. 1038.
3. UCDA P 24/616. Cumann na nGaedheal Annual Convention, 13 May 1925. Cited in Patricia Duffin, 'An examination of Local Government under the Cumann na nGaedheal administration', MA, UCD 1992, p. 29.
4. S 6466 Local government: adoption of managerial system, memo, 1 March 1934.
5. O'Halpin,'Origins of city and county management', p. 14.
6. D/E G 324/1 Local Government Bill 1953. County Management Amendment Bill 1953.
7. S 6466 Local government: adoption of managerial system, memo, 1 March 1934.
8. D/F F60/10/33. Local loans fund revision of rates of interest.
9. S 10533 Waterford City Management Act 1938.
10. S 10685A. County Management Bill 1939.

11. D/E General files. County Management Bill 1940. Memoranda: observations by sections, auditors, county secretaries.
12. S 10685B.
13. D/E General files. County Management Bill 1940.
14. S 12729 County Management Acts 1940 and 1942, Amendment.
15. Calculations based on the personnel details included in *City and County Management, 1929-90.*
16. S 10685A.
17. D/E General files. County Management Bill 1940.
18. S 10685B.
19. PDDE, 5 December 1939, cols. 191, 928.
20. S 12729.
21. Collins, *Local Government*, p. 82.
22. S 11150 Local Government Act 1941.
23. Seán Faughnan, 'The Jesuits and the drafting of the Irish Constitution of 1937', *Irish Historical Studies*, Vol. XXVI, no. 101 (May 1988), pp. 97-98.
24. S 10519A/1. Parish councils, general file.
25. PDSE, 4 October 1939, cols. 1255-58.
26. Devane had urged de Valera to provide for a family vote in the 1937 Constitution. Faughnan, p. 98.
27. D/E Secretary's files. S 556 Parishes, guilds etcetera, memorandum on structure of local government and social services.
28. S 11962 Civil defence service and parish councils: co-ordination of functions.
29. S 10519 A/2.
30. S 11962 Civil defence service and parish councils: co-ordination of functions.
31. S 10519/A/3.
32. D/E Secretary's files. S 556.
33. D/E G 322/1 Local Government Bill 1945.
34. PDDE, 3 June 1942, cols. 903, 921.
35. PDDE, 2 April 1941, col. 1306.
36. PDDE 3 June 1942, cols. 882-995; 16 June, cols. 1027-1131; 17 June, cols. 1187-1274.
37. PDDE, 28 October 1943, cols. 1350-53.
38. Collins, *Local Government*, p. 31.
39. D/E G 232/14. Association of Municipal Authorities conference.
40. PDDE, 19 September 1943, col. 1583; 20 September, col. 1746.
41. S 13671A. County management system, powers of local boards. Decision to publish memorandum as White Paper.
42. UCDA MacEntee papers, P 67/282. Memorandum from Aodh de Blacam on county management system and rural depopulation, 4 December 1946.
43. S 13678 Cabinet Committee on Economic Planning.
44. PDDE, 18 June 1946, col. 2047.
45. S 12729B County Management Acts amendments.
46. S 14442, A and B. Local government; County Administration Bill 1950.
47. D/E File marked S 704, but stamped 'General' and tied together with G 306/2 Part VI: Local Loans Fund issues.

48. Robins, *Custom House People*, pp. 149-51.
49. S 12729D.
50. PDDE, 30 June 1954 col. 807.
51. D/E G 324/1 Local Government Bill 1953. County Management (Amendment) Bill.
52. S 12729D.
53. *Report of the Commission on Vocational Organisation,* pp. 314-16.

Chapter Eight

1. Profiles of Patrick Smith, John Collins and John Garvin can be found in Robins, *Custom House People.* For Collins, see also Desmond Roche, 'A memoir of the author' in John Collins (ed.), *Local Government* (Dublin 1963, second edition), pp. 7-16.
2. UCDA P67/286. Transfer of functions from Local Government to Social Welfare, 1947.
3. D/E Sanitary files, 248/2. Borrowing for health institutions and services.
4. John O'Hagan, 'An analysis of the relative size of the government sector: Ireland 1926-52', *Economic and Social Review,* 12 no. 1 (October 1980), p. 30.
5. N.F. R Crafts, 'The golden age of economic growth in Western Europe, 1950-1973', *Economic History Review,* Vol. XLVIII, no. 3 (August 1995), p. 440.
6. Finola Kennedy, *Public Social Expenditure in Ireland* (Dublin, 1975), p. 5.
7. Kieran A. Kennedy and Brendan R. Dowling, *Economic Growth in Ireland: The Experience since 1947* (Dublin, 1975), p. 172.
8. Patrick Lynch, 'The Irish economy since the war, 1946-51', in K.B. Nowlan and T. D. Williams (eds), *Ireland in the War Years and After 1939-51* (Dublin, 1969).
9. Lee, *Ireland 1912-85,* pp. 230-32.
10. *The Post-War Building Programme.*
11. PDDE, 29 May 1945, cols 1200-01.
12. PDDE, 8 May 1946, col. 2369; 12 June 1946, col. 1717.
13. PDDE, 12 June 1946, col. 1754.
14. PDDE, 8 May 1947, col. 2253.
15. *Report DLG* 1948; *Housing White Paper,* paras. 30-32.
16. PDDE, 20 May 1947, cols. 910-16.
17. S 13597. Post-war unemployment: relief measures.
18. *The Post-War Building Programme.*
19. S 9600B rotational employment schemes.
20. Rumours of government corruption surrounding the proposed sale of Locke's distillery in Kilbeggan, Co. Westmeath led the government to establish a tribunal in 1947 to investigate the story. Although the tribunal concluded that the rumours were without foundation, there is little doubt that Fianna Fáil was damaged by the episode. For details, see Andy

Bielenberg, *Locke's Distillery, A History* (Dublin, 1993); Lee, *Ireland 1912-1985*, pp. 296-97.

21. Noel Browne, *Against the Tide* (Dublin, 1986), p. 99; Kevin Rockett, Luke Gibbons, John Hill, *Cinema in Ireland* (London, 1987), pp. 76-80.
22. O'Connor, *Labour History*, pp. 155-56.
23. S 11953 C/2. Local authorities employees increase of wages.
24. S 13578 Local Government Bill 1945.
25. *Report DLG* 1950-51, p. 14.
26. S 11953 C/1.
27. S 11953D.
28. S 11953 C/2.
29. Collins, *Local Government*, p. 66.
30. S 11953D.
31. S 84/23/1939 Superannuation of officers and employees of local bodies amendment bill 1939.
32. S 13079 A-C. Local Government Superannuation Act 1948.
33. PDDE, 9 June 1948, col. 737.
34. S 13893A Housing bill: Dáil motions and PQs.
35. PDDE, 9 June 1948, col. 736.
36. PDDE, 4 May 1948, cols. 1039, 1051.
37. S 14670 *Ireland is Building*.
38. This minority report was in stark contrast to the extremely orthodox views on financial matters which were expressed in the majority report. It argued that the state should print bank notes, which would be backed by Irish resources, e.g. land and minerals, and that the state should use the money to create employment and develop natural resources.
39. If allowance is made for inflation, this increase was much less than was generally believed.
40. Under Marshall Aid, Irish importers seeking dollars applied to the government. If their application was granted, they paid for these dollars in Irish currency. This money, the Loan Counterpart Fund, or, in the case of the small amount of Marshall Aid provided in grant rather than loan form, the Grant Special Account, was then available to the government for domestic investment. Bernadette Whelan, 'Ireland and the Marshall Plan', *Irish Economic and Social History*, Vol. XIX, 1992, pp. 49-70.
41. PDDE, 3 May 1950, cols. 1628, 1631; 4 May 1949, col. 484.
42. PDDE, 5 July 1950, col. 671.
43. S 14880. Inter-departmental emergency preparations committee; S 14882 A-C Supplies and services files.
44. Fanning, *Finance*, pp. 461-72.
45. PDDE, 2 April 1952, cols. 1134-35.
46. PDDE, 6 May 1953, cols. 1196-99.
47. D/E Housing, Box 38, H 208/1 Housing programmes, Dublin Corporation and London County Council.
48. S 15042 Statement of government policy, June 1951. S 15713, principal objects of policy of inter-party government, 1954.

49. D/T S 14105 A. Housing (Amendment) Act 1948.
50. D/E Housing Box 48, 217/15. Housing: alternative forms of construction.
51. S 13059B, Housing, post-war development, 21 October 1949.
52. D/E 217/15.
53. D/E Housing N201/3 Housing standards.
54. DLG, *Housing. A Review of Past Operations and Immediate Requirements* 1948.
55. D/E Housing Box 55, 228/1 Housing manual.
56. D/E Housing Box 72, 249/1 Westmeath County Council, resolution.
57. D/E Town and regional planning; D 85/1 Dispersal of industries.
58. N 201/3.
59. D/E Housing, box 37, 207/13. Reserved housing, general file.
60. D/E Secretary's files S 669. Fuel economy.
61. S 13059G memorandum on housing finance and related matters.
62. D/E Housing, box 40, 210/2 Dublin housing inquiry report, system of tenancy allocations.
63. D/E 207/13.
64. S 13059B.
65. D/E Housing box 35, Co-operative housing in Sweden.
66. D/E Housing Box 48, 217/16 Guild system of building.
67. D/E Housing, box 49, 281/3. Direct Labour: memorandum from Federation of Builders.
68. D/E box 49, 218/4 Direct labour: statement of parliamentary secretary at Portarlington and Builders' Federation reply.
69. D/E Housing, box 48, 218/1. Bonus scheme re direct labour.
70. D/E Housing, box 51, 281/10 Correspondence with the Department of Finance re direct labour 1948.
71. D/E Housing, box 48, 218/5/1 committee on direct labour; Box 50 218/8; Direct labour, representations to Taoiseach by builders' federation.
72. D/E 218/8.
73. G 269/8/28H. Financing Cork Corporation's capital, April 1956-61.
74. D/E General G 269/8/29 a Dublin County Borough Stock File. no. III.
75. G 269/8/28 H.
76. D/F F 61/65/48. Dublin Corporation Housing Finance. Available in UCDA P 35a/94.
77. D/E G 269/8/2c. Cuttings from *Irish Independent,* 2 February 1949; *The Irish Times,* 14 October 1949.
78. F 61/65/48.
79. S 13059C.
80. S 13059 D/1.
81. G 269/8/29B.
82. S 13059/D1.
83. G 269/8/29C.
84. S 13059D.
85. S 14478A Local Loans Fund.
86. S 13831 B State and local authorities, financial position.

87. S 13059D2. G. Meagher, memorandum on housing finance.
88. S 13831C.
89. S 13059 D2.
90. H 208/1.
91. D/E Housing, 231/7/1 Valuation of SDA houses.
92. S 5054; S 13168 Rents and Mortgage Restrictions Acts.
93. The phrase refers to first-generation Dublin residents. It comes from A.J. Humphreys, *New Dubliners. Urbanization and the Irish Family* (London, 1966).
94. S14105 A Housing (Amendment) Act 1948.
95. S 14105B.
96. S 14826 A 1950 Housing (Amendment) Act.
97. S 14682A2 and H 205/8/1.
98. S 15664 Housing (Amendment) Bill.
99. D/E H 246/1 Box 71 H246/1 Housing Bill 1954.
100. S 14862 A/2; H205/8/1.
101. D/E Housing box 44, H 212/7/2 Supplementary housing grants, County Kerry.
102. D/E Housing box 75. 261/1 Housing Bill 1956.
103. D/E General G 273/11 Local Government (Temporary Reduction of Valuation) Bill 1955.
104. D/E Secretary's files S 231/7/1 Valuation of SDA houses.
105. D/E Housing box 59, 231/4 SDA Acts.
106. D/E general files, G 306/1 Local loans fund estimates.
107. S 13059D2.
108. S 15713, principal objects of policy of inter-party government, 1954.
109. S 13059E.
110. D/E G269/8/29G. Dublin Corporation, stock issue.
111. G 269/8/29 I Dublin Corporation, stock issue 1955.
112. D/E G269/6 Marketability of government and municipal stocks.
113. G 268/8/26C Dublin Corporation capital requirements 1955.
114. G 269/8/26C.
115. S 13059E. O'Donnell to Sweetman, 17 December 1955.
116. S 13059E.
117. G 269/8/29K.
118. S 13059F.
119. S 13059E.
120. G 269/8/29K.
121. S 13059F.
122. S 13059F.
123. S 13059F.
124. G 269/8/29K.
125. S 13059F.
126. Fanning, *Finance*, p. 506.
127. D/E Housing box 75. 261/1 Housing Bill 1956.
128. D/E General files, G1-6; G 60-77; G 80-99 auditors; surcharges. Surcharges

are decided by individual auditors, who are independent both of the Minister and of the Department.

129. D/E G 267/1 Housing Bill 1956.

CHAPTER NINE

1. T. W. Freeman, *Pre-Famine Ireland* (Manchester, 1957), p. 112.
2. Joel Mokyr, *Why Ireland Starved. A Quantitative and Analytical History of the Irish Economy 1800-1850* (London, 1983), pp. 182-83.
3. Austin Bourke, 'Towards the precipice: the potato in pre-Famine Ireland", in Jacqueline Hill and Cormac Ó Gráda (eds), '*The Visitation of God'? The Potato and the Great Irish Famine* (Dublin, 1994), p. 23.
4. Charles R. Browne, 'The ethnography of Carna and Mweenish in the parish of Moyruss Connemara', *Proceedings Royal Irish Academy*, Vol. VI, 1900-02, pp. 504, 525-26.
5. *Select Committee Appointed to Inquire into the Duties, Functions and Mode of Remuneration of County and District Surveyors in Ireland* 1857 session 2 (270) ix.
6. Crossman, *Local Government*, pp. 28-29.
7. *Report LGBI,* 1904-5; 1907-8; 1908-9; 1910-11.
8. Shannon, 'Local Government', pp. 151-55.
9. *Report LGBI,* 1899-1900; 1903-04.
10. *Report LGBI,* 1905-06; 1906-07.
11. NA D/E Roads LG 701 Roads. Draft memorandum to government on post-war roads programme.
12. *Report LGBI*, 1910-11.
13. *Report LGBI*, 1911-12.
14. *Report LGBI*, 1902-03; 1910-11.
15. *Report LGBI*, 1910-11.
16. D/E LG 701.
17. D/E Roads LG 703, Ministry of Transport IR 65. This is a reference to a British Ministry of Transport File, which was subsequently refiled by the DLGPH.
18. LG 701; *First Report DLGPH*, p. 17.
19. D/F Fin 1/826/9 Ministry Local Government Roads Department. Particulars of staff transferred by virtue of Roads Powers Order 1922.
20. D/Fin 1/635/8 Road Grants: amount due out of Road Improvement Fund to local authorities.
21. D/E Roads Box 710 Minutes roads advisory committee 1923.
22. *First Report DLGPH*, Appendix G. Report on road work by James Quigley, p. 187.
23. S 3602 Inter-departmental wages advisory committee on wages of road workers.
24. Roads Advisory Committee, minutes 13 March 1925.
25. PDDE, 1 June 1926, col. 87.

26. D/F F74/5/25 Proposed road schemes: 1,500 miles of trunk roads.
27. D/F F74/7/26 Road fund advances bill 1926.
28. D/E Roads LG 701. Part of the increase may reflect better tax collection, rather than a growth in motor traffic.
29. D/F F74/5/25.
30. S 2674 Report of the interdepartmental committee on road transport. First report 1 March 1926.
31. ibid., second report 13 April 1926. David S. Jacobsen, 'The political economy of industrial location: the Ford Motor Company at Cork, 1912-26', *Irish Economic and Social History*, Vol. IV, 1977, pp. 36-55.
32. PDDE, 21 April 1926, col. 163.
33. D/F F74/7/26 Road Fund Advances Bill, 1926.
34. D/F F74/5/25.
35. *Second report, DLGPH*, 1926-27, pp. 119-21, 132.
36. UCDA Mulcahy Papers, P 7/c/86 (2). Memo. re Road Fund.
37. *Second report DLGPH,* 1926-27, p. 136.
38. UCDA, P7/c/86(2).
39. PDDE, 10 April 1929, cols. 76-77.
40. D/F Fin 1/635/8 Road Grants: amount due out of Road Improvement Fund to local authorities.
41. PDDE, 10 April 1929, col. 100.
42. PDDE, 29 April 1931, col. 550.
43. D/E G 275/1 Village Halls; G 272/1 Dáil motion that upkeep of main roads, mental hospitals and vocational education should be a national charge.
44. PDDE, 1 May 1930, col. 1317.
45. D/F. F74/7/32. Proposed allocation of £1m. to local authorities to carry out road works for the relief of unemployment.
46. When Winston Churchill was British Chancellor of the Exchequer during the years 1924-29, he diverted money from the Road Fund, which was earmarked for road improvements, and used it for other purposes. Critics accused him of 'raiding the Road Fund'.
47. *Report Commission Banking Currency and Credit,* p. 322, para. 525.
48. James Meenan, *The Irish Economy since 1922* (Liverpool, 1970), pp. 160-61.
49. S 6513 Road Transport Act 1933.
50. LG 701.
51. S 13026. Cabinet Committee on Economic Planning, proceedings 1942-45.
52. S 9600 Inter-Departmental Committee on State-aided Employment Schemes, 1945-46.
53. LG 701.
54. D/E roads IR.190 Employment schemes for demobilised defence forces.
55. S 9600 Childers Memorandum, pp. 43-44.
56. S 11638 Employment schemes, financial provisions 1940s.
57. D/E Roads Section, no date. Main roads as a national charge.
58. S 13101 Planning for full employment.
59. D/E Roads MT 221/1/B . Review of motor taxation 1950-52.
60. S 13061 Roads: post-war development.

61. D/E Roads files. Main roads as a national charge.
62. D/E Roads Section, Box 95. Main roads survey, general 1946-53.
63. PDDE, 13 June 1946, cols. 1913, 1830 1867.
64. Department of Local Government. *Report of Committee on Road Surfaces for Animals and Animal Drawn Traffic* Pr. 620.
65. S 13061/B2 Report of committee on road surfaces, 16 July 1952.
66. *Report on Transport in Ireland,* by Sir James Milne, 1949 R 70/2 P. 9201.
67. D/E roads IR/170. Conference with railway companies and Department of Industry and Commerce re standards for classification and layout of roads.
68. D/E roads IR/176.
69. LG 701.
70. MT 220 /1C.
71. S 15058 DLG progress reports, 1949- .
72. D/E roads, Box 95, main roads, general survey 1946- .
73. D/E roads, arterial roads: 24 January 1950. Memo from DLG to Government re development of Bray Road.
74. S 13061/B 1 DLG memo, 1 March 1950.
75. S 13061/B2.
76. S 13061/B2. DLG 22/7/53. Memo for cabinet committee on provision of employment. Road works in Dublin area.
77. D/E roads section. Memo on arterial roads scheme.
78. S 13061/B1 and B2.
79. Kennedy and Dowling, *Economic Growth in Ireland*, p. 215.
80. S 13061/B2. Utilisation of American grant counterpart funds, Annex L.
81. M.T 220/1C Report committee on revision of motor taxation.
82. S 13061/B1.
83. D/E Roads section MT 220/ 1C.
84. S 13061/B1.
85. S 13061/B2. Department of Finance memo for government. Utilisation of American Grant counterpart fund, 22 November 1951.
86. D/E roads, Box 754 201/2/1. Provision of employment for turf workers displaced on cessation of hand-won turf campaigns.
87. S 14286 Discontinuance of hand-won turf produced by Bórd na Móna and local authorities; provision of employment for unemployed workers.
88. S 13061/B1. DLG memorandum for Government, 23 December1948.
89. S 13061/B1.
90. D/E Roads, Box 95. Main roads survey general 1946-53.
91. D/E Secretary's files S 662. Conference with county and city managers, 1 November 1951.
92. S 13061/B2.
93. S 15042 Statement of government policy 1951.
94. S 13061/B2.
95. MT 220/5 Proposals for revision of motor taxation.
96. S 13061/B 2 Report committee on revision of motor taxation, March 1952.
97. D/E roads MT 220/1C review of motor taxation, 1950-52.
98. D/E MT 220/1D. Revision motor taxation 1952: deputations.

99. Kennedy and Dowling, *Economic Growth*, pp. 214-17.
100. S 13101 B, 2 February 1953. Prior to this legislation, some unemployment insurance claimants deliberately elected to draw unemployment assistance because they then became eligible for employment on public works. The new legislation prevented them from doing so until benefit entitlements were exhausted.
101. S 13101 B2.
102. S 13061 B2.
103. S 15551 National Development Fund.
104. S 13101 B2.
105. S 15553A, State-aided building and construction works 1953.
106. S 15551 B; S15553A; S11916 Relief of unemployment in Dublin and Dun Laoghaire.
107. S 11916.
108. S 13061/B2.
109. S 15551A. National Development Fund. Fianna Fáil retained the seat which was vacant following the death of Frank Fahy.
110. Fanning, *Finance,* p. 469, citing Maurice Moynihan, *Currency and Central Banking in Ireland 1922-60* (Dublin, 1975), p. 341.
111. S 15551B.
112. S 13061/B2.
113. S 13101/C/1.
114. S 11916 C.
115. S 13061/B2, 19 November 1953.
116. D/E roads R 201/8/4.
117. S 11916C.
118. R 201/4/1 Road Fund grants general.
119. How one reads the 1954 budget depends on how the £10m. borrowed by the ESB is treated. Capital expenditure stood at £36m. in 1954/55, against £40.6m. in 1953/54. However Kennedy and Dowling argued that to make figures comparable with previous years, when ESB borrowings were financed by central government, the £10m. should be included. This raises total capital expenditure to £46.0m.. Kennedy and Dowling, *Economic Growth,* p. 217.
120. S 13601 C1.
121. S 15551 C NDF Department of Taoiseach, 28 May 1957.
122. D/E R 201/7/2c proposals 21 August 1954 Box 720.
123. S 13061 C1 memo DLG 1955.
124. R 201/7/38 proposals for transfers to Road Fund 1955/56.
125. R 201/4/4c; R 205/3 representations from councils demanding a transfer of Road Fund grants from main to county roads, plus press-cuttings on this subject.
126. PDDE, 8 May 1956.
127. This money was provided in District Electoral Divisions containing large numbers in receipt of unemployment assistance in Counties Cavan, Clare, Cork, Donegal, Galway, Kerry, Leitrim, Limerick, Longford, Mayo, Roscommon and Sligo.

128. D/E Roads R 201/8/4 Box 727.
129. R 201/8/4, 18 June 1956.
130. S 4456 Road Traffic. Report of interdepartmental committee.
131. S 5961A Road Traffic Bill 1931.
132. S 13721A Road Traffic, general file, 1945.
133. PDDE, 29 May 1947, cols. 929-30.
134. PDSE, 18 July 1956, cols. 571-615.
135. S 13731 C.

CHAPTER TEN

1. Garret FitzGerald, 'Mr. Whitaker and industry', *Studies,* 48 (1959), pp. 138-50.
2. Desmond Roche, 'Local Government', in Frank Litton (ed.), *Unequal Achievement* (Dublin, 1982), p. 135.
3. Fanning, *Finance*, p. 506.
4. The committee's members were chairman John Leydon, representative of financial interests; General M.J. Costello, managing director of Comhlucht Siúcra Éireann (the Irish Sugar Company), and William Bland, chairman of the Agricultural Credit Corporation; C.K. Mill, a director of Arthur Guinness; Kevin McCourt, a leading member of the Federation of Irish Industry; Ruaidhrí Roberts, secretary of the Irish Trade Union Congress, and economists Charles Carter, Patrick Lynch and Louden Ryan.
5. *First Report of Capital Investment Advisory Committee*, Pr. 4041 1957.
6. D/E LG 565.
7. PDDE, 8 May 1958, cols. 937-56; 7 May (Estimates DLG) cols. 895-99.
8. DLG Circular no. H. 7/57.
9. S 13059F Housing.
10. e.g. S 13831G. State and local authorities financial position.
11. *Capital Investment Advisory Committee. Second Report. Minority Report. Addendum to Majority Report. Comments on Minority Report.* Pr. 4406, 1958.
12. S 15725C Capital investment advisory committee.
13. S 16451 Housing legislation: 1958 Housing Amendment Act.
14. S 15725C.
15. *Capital Investment Advisory Committee. Third report.* Pr.
16. T. K. Whitaker, 'Capital formation, saving and economic progress', in B. Chubb and P. Lynch (eds), *Economic Development and Planning* (Dublin, 1969), pp. 60-61.
17. Fanning, *Finance,* ch. x; Ronan Fanning, 'The genesis of *Economic Development'* in John McCarthy (ed.), *Planning Ireland's Future. The Legacy of T. K. Whitaker* (Dublin, 1990), pp. 112-27.
18. *Economic Development,* especially para. 41 and appendix 5.
19. FitzGerald, *Planning in Ireland,* p. 44.
20. PDDE, 7 May 1957, col. 893.
21. PDDE, 8 July 1958 cols. 26-29.

22. D/E G 306/2 Local Loans Fund estimates.
23. S 16666A Economic Development: discussions by Taoiseach with certain organisations.
24. S 16673A. Economic Development: proposals submitted by local authorities. Final report.
25. S 16666B.
26. S 16666B.
27. D/E H 217/24 Review of housing and sanitary schemes and prospects, 1958-60; 207/13 Houses for old people, 1959-.
28. S 13059/H/61.
29. S 13059G.
30. S 13059/H/61.
31. S 17365/A/62. Building industry.
32. S 17365/B/62.
33. S 17365/A/62.
34. PDDE, 23 October 1963, cols. 79-80.
35. S 17365/C/63.
36. D/E Housing 207/9/1, 29 June 1960.
37. S 16889A Housing and ancillary activities; National Building Agency.
38. S 16889/B/62. NBA progress report to 12 March 1962.
39. S 16889/B/61.
40. S 17365/A/62.
41. S 16889A.
42. S 16889/B/62.
43. PDDE, 4 December 1963, cols. 617-19.
44. S 17537/A/63. Building Industry.
45. PDDE, 4 July 1961, cols. 19-20.
46. S 17365/C/63.
47. S 17365A/62.
48. S 17365/A/63, 18 December 1962.
49. S 17365/B/63.
50. Flann O'Brien, *The Best of Myles*, p. 383.
51. D/E H 209/54/2. Investment in Ireland by British insurance companies.
52. S 17365/C/63.
53. Charles Abrams, *Urban Renewal Project in Ireland*.
54. Michael Bannon, 'Development planning and the neglect of the critical regional dimension', in Bannon (ed)., *Planning: The Irish Experience*, p. 129.
55. S 16968/B/61 Planning and Development Bill.
56. S 17082/A/61 Local government policy: inter-departmental committee on local taxes and finances.
57. S 16968/A/61. Planning and Development Act
58. S 16968/B/61.
59. Bannon, 'Development planning', pp. 187-88; footnote no. 79.
60. PDDE, 12 November 1962, col. 1762.
61. Bannon, ibid., p. 130.

62. S 17365/C./63.
63. D/E sanitary services, Box 25, 259/3 Five Year Programme.
64. S 17365/A/63.
65. R. Stringer, 'The urban development plan: the next steps', *Industrial Development and the Development Plan,* p. 41, cited in Bannon, 'Development plan', p. 133. This section draws heavily on Bannon.
66. Desmond Roche, 'An outline of the regional situation in Ireland, Britain, France, Italy', *Administration,* 21, no. 1 (1973), pp. 27-40.
67. Nathaniel Lichfield and Associates, *Report and Advisory Outline Plan for the Limerick Region* 1966; Myles Wright, *Final Report and Advisory Outline Plan for the Dublin Region* 1966.
68. *Second Programme,* p. 275.
69. FitzGerald, *Planning in Ireland,* p. 114.
70. Kennedy, Giblin and McHugh, *Economic Development of Ireland,* p. 168.
71. PDDE, 27 September 1966, cols. 49-55.
72. PDDE, 9 March 1966, col. 1307.
73. PDDE 27 April 1965, cols. 65-69; 27 September 1966, cols. 55-56.
74. S 13168D. Rent and Mortgage Restriction Acts.
75. *Housing in the Seventies,* p. 42.
76. D/E Sanitary Services (SS) 3, Report of committee on water and sewerage and other functions of sanitary authorities, 1958.
77. D/E Offaly, 4125/2/42; 2311/51.
78. D/E Sanitary Services, SS7.
79. D/E SS3.
80. Michael Shiel, *The Quiet Revolution. The Electrification of Rural Ireland, 1946-1976* (Dublin, 1984), p. 152.
81. D/E sanitary files box 6, 205/12. Rural water supply general file.
82. S 13166D/63 Public health works: post-war planning, water supply schemes.
83. SS3.
84. D/E SS box 10, 208/10/2. Financing.
85. D/E SS box 7, 205/12/3.
86. D/E SS box 25, 259/3. Five-year programme.
87. S 13166/D/61. Public health works, rural water supplies.
88. S 17365/B/63. Building industry.
89. S 13166C1.
90. S 13166/D/63.
91. *Public Capital Expenditure.* 1965 Pr. 8562, p.9.
92. D/E Roads, R 246/0. Termination of services on Donegal-Ballyshannon rail line.
93. D/E R246/9.
94. S 13061/C2/61. Roads: post-war development.
95. S 16589 Road Fund Grants and Advances Act 1959.
96. S 12913/C2 Rates remission.
97. S 13765 Foreign trade development file, contained a hand-written memo to this effect dated 7 December 1945.
98. S 6778 A and B. Valuation Bill.

99. D/E General G 272/2. Local services which might be a national charge.
100. G 275/16. Establishment of a tribunal to investigate high rates in Dublin, c. 1950-51.
101. UCDA P35/c/87.
102. S 11042 C1. Rates on agricultural land, relief acts.
103. S 11042/C2.
104. S 11042D.
105. D/E Secretary's files S 285/40. Relief of rates on agricultural land. Deputation from NFA.
106. D/E G 285/40. Relief of rates on agricultural land.
107. S 12913 C1/C2. Rates remission.
108. G273/g. Local government remission of rates bill 1953 and temporary reduction of Valuation Bill 1953.
109. PDDE, 4 March 1953, col. 2205.
110. S 12913/C/2.
111. G 273/14. Local government temporary reduction of Valuation Bill 1960.
112. S 12913D.
113. D/E General files G 275/33/3. Tipperary South Riding, adjustment order. Financial relations between county councils and urban district councils; G 285/33/1. Demands of county councils on urban district councils.
114. G 251/1/2 De-urbanisation: Belturbet and Cootehill; G285/32 Templemore UDC, increased rates, de-urbanisation; G 110 Passage West Inquiry.
115. G 251/1. Granard Town Commissioners, proposed dissolution. G 251/1/1 Granard Urban District. Proposal to add to Longford County Council.
116. G 251/1/2.
117. G 251/1/3. Proposed de-urbanisation of towns under 5,0000 population.
118. S 13831/F/1. State and local authorities, financial position.
119. David Walker, *Local Government Finance in Ireland. A Preliminary Survey* Research Institute Paper no. 5, 1962, p. 13.
120. D/E G 273/11 Local Government (Temporary Reduction of Valuation Bill), 1955.
121. D/E G 273/14 Local Government (Temporary Reduction of Valuation Bill), 1960.
122. S 15980/61 Establishment of an extended scheme for the provision of post-primary and university scholarships.
123. S 11042/F/61.
124. David Walker, *Local Government Finance and County Incomes.* ERI paper no. 18, March 1964.
125. S 17082/A/61. Review of finance and local taxation.
126. PDDE, 10 April 1962, col. 1584.
127. S 11042/F/62.
128. S 11042/F/63.
129. David Walker, *Local Government Finance in Ireland. A Preliminary Survey.*
130. E.A Attwood and R.C. Geary, *Irish County Incomes in 1960,* ERI report no. 16, September 1963.

131. David Walker, *Local Government Finance and County Incomes*, ERI paper no. 18, March 1964.
132. S 17082/A/63.
133. PDDE, 27 September 1966, col. 88.
134. PDDE,11 April 1967, cols. 1268-9.
135. *Inter-Departmental Committee on Local Finance and Taxation. Report on Rates and other Sources of Revenue for Local Authorities.* Prl. 89. 1968
136. *Local Government Reorganisation* Prl. 1572.
137. *White Paper on Local Finance and Taxation* Prl. 2745.
138. Walker, *Local Government Finance in Ireland. A Preliminary Survey*, p. 4.
139. *The Health Services and their Further Development* 1966.
140. *Report of Public Services Organisation Review Group*, 1966-69 Prl. 792.
141. *Report of Public Services Organisation Review Group*, 5.3.29.

CHAPTER ELEVEN

1. J.J. Lee, *Ireland 1912-1985*, pp. 511-21.
2. D/E Sligo files, Tobercurry RDC 1922.
3. Thomas H. O'Connor, *South Boston: My Home Town* (Boston, 1988), p. 84.
4. D/E Planning Box 111 PL 36/4/1.
5. Seán Fitzpatrick, 'Donnchadh Ó Briain. Requests and representations: an unsung life of fidelity to Fianna Fáil', MA, UCD 1994.
6. Paul Bew, *Ideology and the Irish Question. Ulster Unionism and Irish Nationalism 1912-1916* (Oxford, 1994), pp. 74-75.
7. Patrick Buckland, *The Factory of Grievances. Devolved Government in Northern Ireland 1921-39* (Dublin, 1979), p. 38.
8. UCDA, Mulcahy Papers, P 7/B/57.
9. DELG 5/18 Clare County Council.
10. D/E General files, LG 237 Local Government Act 1931; UCDA P 7/C/88 Rev P.E. Brett, Kilmeena, Westport, to Richard Mulcahy, 28 August 1931.
11. UCDA P7/B/67, 4 July 1927.
12. Kevin O'Higgins, *The Catholic Layman in Public Life: An Address to the Catholic Truth Society* (Dublin, 1923).
13. S 6466 Local government: adoption of managerial system, memo, 1 March 1934.
14. Desmond McCabe, 'Law, conflict and social order. County Mayo 1920-1845', UCD, Ph.D thesis, 1991.
15. David Fitzpatrick, *Oceans of Consolation. Personal Accounts of Irish Migration to Australia* (Cork 1995), p. 618.
16. John A. Murphy, 'Cork. Anatomy and essence' in Patrick O'Flanagan and Cornelius G. Buttimer (eds), *Cork. History & Society* (Dublin, 1993), pp 1,4.
17. UCDA P67/282. MacEntee to Aodh de Blacam, 1946.
18. Quoted in Shannon, 'Local Government', p. 309.
19. D/E Dublin files, Boxes 167. Dissolution of Dublin Corporation.

20. DELG 6/44.
21. D/E Secretary's files. S 556.
22. D/E G 100-199.
23. Brian Maye, *Fine Gael 1923-1987* (Dublin, 1993), pp. 22-23.
24. Paul Sacks, *The Donegal Mafia. An Irish Political Machine* (New Haven and London, 1976), p. 63.
25. Daly, *Industrial Development and Irish National Identity*, p. 104.
26. S 6274; Daly, *Industrial Development*, p. 63.
27. Quoted in Colman O'Sullivan 'The IRA takes constitutional action: a history of Clann na Poblachta 1946-65',UCD, MA 1995, p. 185.
28. Daly, *Industrial Development and Irish National Identity*, p. 121.
29. UCDA P67/282.
30. The Department of the Environment files relating to Parliamentary Questions are available in the National Archives.
31. Lee, *Ireland 1912-1985*, p. 547.
32. D/E Housing box 75. 261/1 Housing Bill 1956.
33. S 17082/A/61.Review of finance and local taxation.
34. G 275/16. Establishment of a tribunal to investigate high rates in Dublin, c. 1950-51.
35. W.E. Vaughan, 'Richard Griffith and the tenement valuation', in G.L. Herries Davies and R. Charles Mollan (eds), *Richard Griffith 1784-1878* (Dublin, 1980).
36. Fergal Tobin, *The Best of Decades. Ireland in the 1960s* (Dublin, 1984), pp. 75-76.
37. Meenan, *The Irish Economy since 1922*, p. 246.
38. J.R. and U.K. Hicks, *Standards of Local Expenditure. A Problem of the Inequality of Incomes* (Cambridge, 1943).
39. Fanning, *Finance*, p. 57.
40. Fanning acknowledges this point in *Independent Ireland,* p. 70.
41. UCDA P 24/1783, p. 164.
42. Tom Garvin, *Nationalist Revolutionaries in Ireland 1858-1928* (Oxford, 1987), pp. 33-56.
43. Daly, 'The formation of an Irish Nationalist Elite?' The unwillingness to recruit a substantial number of university graduates and the preference given to promoting men (and they were overwhelmingly men) who had been admitted as junior clerks undoubtedly increased the odds in favour of continuity in policy and administrative procedures.
44. N.F. R. Crafts, 'The golden age of economic growth in Western Europe, 1950-1973', *Economic History Review,* Vol. XLVIII, no. 3 (August 1995), p. 440.
45. D/E G 326/3 National Development Fund. Proposals for the provision of libraries, 1954.
46. D/E G 364 Preservation of Mansions and Large Houses. Submissions by the Department of Lands.
47. Daly, *Industrial Development and Irish National Identity*.
48. D/E Planning Box 111, PL 36/4/1.
49. P 7/B/74.

BIBLIOGRAPHY

MANUSCRIPT SOURCES

NATIONAL ARCHIVES

Chief Secretary's Office Registered Papers
Minutes of the Local Government Board 1900-21

Papers relating to the First and Second Dála
Cabinet Minutes,1919-21, de 1/1-1/3.
Dáil Éireann Committee Files, DE 2 Series.
Dail Eireann Local Government Department Files (DELG) Series

Minutes of Provisional Government, G Series
Minutes of the Executive Council
Department of the Taoiseach files, S series

Department of Finance files
Fin — Finance series
S — Supplies series

Department of the Environment Files
County Files
Finance
General, G
Housing
Local Government, LG
Planning
Roads
Sanitary Services, SS
Secretary's Files, S

NATIONAL LIBRARY OF IRELAND, MANUSCRIPT ROOM

Brennan Papers
Evidence to Brennan Commission on the Civil Service
Evidence presented to the Commission on Vocational Organisation

TRINITY COLLEGE DUBLIN, MANUSCRIPT ROOM

John Dillon Papers

UNIVERSITY COLLEGE DUBLIN ARCHIVES DEPARTMENT

Ernest Blythe Papers
Desmond FitzGerald Papers
Seán MacEntee Papers
Patrick McGilligan Papers
Richard Mulcahy Papers
Donncha Ó Briain Papers

PRINTED MATERIAL

Published Debates Dáil Éireann Published Debates Seanad Éireann

Irish Independent
The Irish Press
The Irish Times
Irish Law Reports

IRISH GOVERNMENT PUBLICATIONS

Reports, Department of Local Government and Public Health 1922-1947.
Reports, Department of Local Government 1947/48-1976/77.
Report of Committee of Inquiry [into the] Determination of Rent and Mortgage Interest (Restrictions) Act 1920, 1923.
Report of Commission [on] the Gaeltacht 1926 R 23/27
Report of the Greater Dublin Commission of Inquiry 1926 R. 32.
Report of the Committee on the Relief of Unemployment. Final Report. 1928 R 38/2.
Report of the Commission of Inquiry into Derating 1931 R. 43, P. 373.
Reports of Commission of Inquiry into the Civil Service 1932-35. 1936 R 54/2-5.
Report of the Tribunal of Inquiry into the Pearse Street Fire 1937 R62-1, P. 2853.

Reports and Minutes of Evidence of Commission of Inquiry into Banking, Currency and Credit, 1938 R. 38.

Report of Tribunal on Town Tenants (Occupational Tenancies) 1941 R 71/1 P. 4769.

Report of Inquiry into the Housing of the Working Classes of the City of Dublin, R. 75/1 1939-44.

Report of the Commission on Vocational Organisation 1944 R.77.

Report of the Tribunal of Inquiry into the Fire at St Joseph's Orphanage Cavan, 1943 R 74/1. P 6144.

Comparative Tables Relating to Local Taxation and the Expenditure and Receipts of Local Bodies in the Period 1932-44, K.48.

The Post-War Building Programme, I 82/1.

Housing. A Review of Past Operations and Immediate Requirements 1948. K 52, Pr. 756.

Report on Transport in Ireland by Sir James Milne, 1949 R 70/2 P. 9201.

Ireland is Building 1950 K 55.

Report of Committee on Road Surfaces for Animals and Animal Drawn Traffic 1952 K.62, Pr. 620.

First Report of Capital Investment Advisory Committee, Pr. 4041 1957.

Capital Investment Advisory Committee. Second Report. Minority Report. Addendum to Majority Report. Comments on Minority Report. Pr. 4406, 1958.

Capital Investment Advisory Committee. Third report. Pr. 4668, 1958.

Economic Development 1958 F. 58.

Programme for Economic Expansion 1958 F. 57.

Public Capital Expenditure. 1965 Pr. 8562.

Second Programme for Economic Expansion 1963 F 57/2.

Second Programme, Review of Progress 1964 F 57/4.

Second Programme, Review of Progress 1965 F 57/5.

Second Programme, Review of Progress 1966 F 57/6.

Housing: Progress and Prospects, 1964 Pr. 7981.

Third Programme: Economic and Social Development 1969 F 57/7.

Housing in the Seventies 1969 K98 Prl. 658.

Inter-Departmental Committee on Local Finance and Taxation. Report on Rates and other Sources of Revenue for Local Authorities Prl. 89. 1968

Local Government Reorganisation Prl. 1572.

White Paper on Local Finance and Taxation Prl. 2745.

Report of Public Services Organisation Review Group, 1966-69 Prl. 792.

British Government Publications

Annual Reports of the Local Government Board of Ireland, 1872/3 to 1919/20.

Report on the Sanitary Conditions of the Labouring Population of Great Britain. 1843 [509], xii.

Poor Law Commission Ireland. Copy of Report of Messrs. Bromley and

Stephenson to Lords of Treasury, 4 May 1854.

Reply of Poor Law Commission to recommendations of Bromley and Stephenson, 19 June 1854. 1854-55 (0.28), xlvi, 213.

Report of Select Committee appointed to Inquire into the Duties, Functions and Mode of Remuneration of County and District Surveyors in Ireland, 1857 session 2 (270).

Reports from Poor Law Inspectors on the Wages of Agricultural Labourers in Ireland (c. 35), 1870, xiv.

Reports of the Commissioners appointed to Inquire into the Conditions of the Civil Service in Ireland. Report on the Local Government Board and General Registry Office and Minutes, 1873 (c. 514-I), xxvi.

Select Committee on Alteration in Laws on Local Government and Taxation of Towns, 1877 (357) xii.

Local Government and Taxation of Ireland Inquiry. Special report by W.P. O'Brien (LGB inspector), 1878 c. 1965.

Final Report of the R.C. Appointed to Inquire into the Financial Relations of Great Britain and Ireland (c. 8262), 1896, xxxii.

Report of the Departmental Inquiry Appointed by the Local Government Board to Inquire into the Public Health of the City of Dublin, 1900 (cd. 243) xxxix.

Report of the RC Local Taxation. Final report, England and Wales, 1901 (cd. 638), xxiv.

Report and Evidence of the RC on Local Taxation. Report on Valuation in Ireland, 1902 (cd. 973), xxxix.

Report of the RC on Local Taxation, Ireland, 1902 (cd. 1068), xxxix.

Report and Evidence of the Vice-Regal Commission on Poor Relief, 1906 (cd. 3203), l.

Return of Local Government Board Inspectors now in Service 1906, lvi.

RC on the Poor Law. Report on Ireland, 1909 (cd. 4630), xxxvii.

Report of the Committee on Irish Finance, 1912-13, (cd. 6153), xxi.

Returns Names, etc. of Each Person Appointed Without Competitive Examination to Any Position in the Public Service during the Period 29 June 1895 to 5 December 1905 with an Annual Salary of £100 or Upward. 1912-13 lvi, HC paper 454.

Report of the Committee on Irish Finance, 1912-13 (cd. 6153), xxiv.

R.C. on the Civil Service, Fourth Report. Evidence, 1914 (cd. 7340), xvi.

Departmental Inquiry Appointed to Inquire into the Housing Conditions of the Working Class in Dublin, 1914 (cd. 7269) xviii.

Report of the Proceedings of the Irish Convention, 1918 (cd. 9019) x.

Royal Commission on the Distribution of the Industrial Population, 1939-40 Cmd. 6153, iv.

BOOKS, PAMPHLETS AND ARTICLES

'A chronology of local government 1918-1990', in *City and County Management 1929-1990. A Retrospective* (Dublin, 1991).

D. H. Akenson, *Education and Enmity: The Control of Schooling in Northern Ireland 1920-50* (Newtown Abbot, 1973).

C. S. Andrews, *Man of No Property. An Autobiography (Volume Two)* (Cork, 1982).

J. H. Andrews, 'Road planning in Ireland before the railway age', *Irish Geography*, 5, no. 1 (1964).

E. A. Attwood and R. C. Geary, *Irish County Incomes in 1960*, Economic Research Institute, report no. 16 September 1963.

Michael Bannon (ed.), *A Hundred Years of Irish Planning. Vol. I. The Emergence of Irish Planning, 1880-1920* (Dublin, 1985).

Michael Bannon, 'Irish planning from 1921-45: an overview,', in Bannon (ed)., *Planning: The Irish Experience, 1920-1988* (Dublin 1989).

——————————, 'Development planning and the neglect of the critical regional dimension', in Bannon (ed.), *Planning: The Irish Experience.*

Ruth Barrington, *Health, Medicine and Politics in Ireland, 1900-1970* (Dublin, 1987).

Christine Bellamy, *Administering Central-local Relations, 1871-1919. The Local Government Board in its Fiscal and Cultural Context* (Manchester, 1988).

Paul Bew, *Ideology and the Irish Question. Ulster Unionism and Irish Nationalism 1912-1916* (Oxford, 1994).

Andy Bielenberg, *Locke's Distillery, a History* (Dublin, 1993).

Augustine Birrell, *Things Past Redress* (London, 1937).

Austin Bourke, 'Towards the precipice: The potato in pre-famine Ireland', in *'The Visitation of God'? The Potato and the Great Irish Famine* (Dublin, 1994).

Marion Bowley, *Housing and the State, 1919-44* (London, 1945).

John W. Boyle, 'A marginal figure: the Irish rural labourer', in Samuel Clark and James S. Donnelly (eds), *Irish Peasants: Violence and Political Unrest, 1780-1914* (Dublin, 1978).

S. J. Bradenburg, 'Housing progress in the Irish Free State', *Journal of Land and Public Utility Economics,* Vol. VIII, no. 1, February 1932.

Asa Briggs, *Victorian Cities* (London, 1968 edition).

Charles R. Browne, 'The ethnography of Carna and Mweenish in the Parish of Moyruss Connemara', *Proceedings Royal Irish Academy*, Vol. VI, 1900-02.

Noel Browne, *Against the Tide* (Dublin, 1986).

Patrick Buckland, *The Factory of Grievances. Devolved Government in Northern Ireland 1921-39* (Dublin, 1979).

Erskine Childers, *The Framework of Home Rule* (London, 1911).

Peter Clarke, *The Keynesian Revolution in the Making, 1924-1936* (Oxford, 1988).

John Collins, *Local Government,* Second edition by Desmond Roche (Dublin, 1963).

Tim Pat Coogan, *Michael Collins. A Biography* (London, 1990).

N. F. R. Crafts, 'The golden age of economic growth in Western Europe, 1950-1973', *Economic History Review,* Vol. XLVIII, no. 3, August 1995.

Anthony Cronin, *No Laughing Matter. The Life and Times of Flann O'Brien* (Dublin, 1989).

Virginia Crossman, *Local Government in Nineteenth-century Ireland* (Belfast, 1994).

Raymond Crotty, *Irish Agricultural Production: Its Volume and Structure* (Cork, 1966).

Mary E. Daly, *A Social and Economic History of Ireland since 1800* (Dublin, 1980).

———, 'Social structure of the Dublin working class, 1871-1911, *Irish Historical Studies,* Vol. XXIII, no. 90, November 1982.

———, 'An Irish-Ireland for business? The Control of Manufactures Acts, 1932 and 1934', *Irish Historical Studies,* Vol. XXIV, no. 94 (1984).

———, *Dublin: The Deposed Capital. A Social and Economic History 1860-1914* (Cork, 1984).

———, *The Famine in Ireland* (Dublin, 1986)

———, *Industrial Development and Irish National Identity 1922-39* (Syracuse and Dublin, 1992).

———, 'The formation of an Irish nationalist elite? Recruitment to the Irish civil service in the decades prior to independence, 1870-1920', *Paedagogica Historica, International Journal of the History of Education,* Vol. XXX , no. 1 (1994).

———, 'Working-class housing in Scottish and Irish cities on the eve of World War I' in S. J. Connolly, R. A. Houston and R. J. Morris (eds), *Conflict, Identity and Economic Development. Ireland and Scotland, 1600-1939* (Preston, 1995).

Jane Darke, 'Local political attitudes and council housing', in Stuart Lowe and David Hughes (eds), *A New Century of Social Housing* (Leicester, 1991).

Richard Davis, *Arthur Griffith and Non-violent Sinn Féin* (Dublin, 1974).

David Dickson, 'In search of the old Irish Poor Law', in R. Mitchison and P. Roebuck (eds), *Economy and Society in Scotland and Ireland, 1800-1939* (Edinburgh, 1988).

James S. Donnelly, *The Land and the People of Nineteenth-Century Cork* (London, 1975).

———, 'The administration of relief, 1847-51', in *New History of Ireland. V. Part I.*

———, 'The journals of Sir John Benn-Walsh relating to the management of his Irish estates, 1823-64', in *Cork Historical Society Journal,* Vol. LXXX (1974).

Ronan Fanning, *The Irish Department of Finance 1922-58* (Dublin, 1978).

———, *Independent Ireland* (Dublin, 1983).

———, 'The genesis of *Economic Development*', in John McCarthy (ed.), *Planning Ireland's Future. The Legacy of T. K. Whitaker* (Dublin, 1990),

Seán Faughnan, 'The Jesuits and the drafting of the Irish Constitution of 1937', *Irish Historical Studies,* Vol. XXVI, no. 101, May 1988.

William L. Feingold, *The Revolt of the Tenantry: The Transformation of Local Government in Ireland 1872-1886* (Boston, 1984).

Robert Fisk, *In Time of War* (London, 1983).

Garret FitzGerald, 'Mr. Whitaker and industry', *Studies,* 48 (1959).

——————————, *Planning in Ireland* (Dublin, 1968).

David Fitzpatrick, *Politics and Irish Life 1913-1921: Provincial Experience of War and Revolution* (Dublin, 1977).

——————————, *Oceans of Consolation. Personal Accounts of Irish Migration to Australia* (Cork, 1995).

Surgeon Col. D. Edgar Flinn, *Official Report on the Sanitary Circumstances and Administration of the City of Dublin with Special Reference to the Causes of the High Death-Rate* (Dublin 1906, Thom for HMSO).

T. W. Freeman, *Pre-Famine Ireland* (Manchester, 1957).

Tom Garvin, *Nationalist Revolutionaries in Ireland 1858-1928* (Oxford, 1987).

Anthony Gaughan, *Austin Stack: Portrait of a Separatist* (Tralee, 1977).

Michael Gough, 'Socio-economic conditions and the genesis of planning in Cork', in Michael Bannon (ed.), *A Hundred Years of Irish Planning. Vol. I*.

B. J. Graham and Susan Hood, 'Town tenant protest in late-nineteenth and early-twentieth century Ireland', *Irish Economic and Social History,* Vol. XXI, 1994.

Timothy W. Guinnane, 'Intentional age-misreporting, age-heaping, and the 1908 Old Age Pensions Act in Ireland', *Population Studies,*Vol. XLV (1991).

——————————, 'The Poor Law and pensions in Ireland', *Journal of Interdisciplinary History,* Vol. XXIV, no. 2, Autumn 1990.

Maurice Hayes, *Minority Verdict. Experiences of a Catholic Public Servant* (Belfast, 1995).

J. R. and U. K. Hicks, *Standards of Local Expenditure. A Problem of the Inequality of Incomes* (Cambridge, 1943).

Michael Hopkinson, *Green Against Green. The Irish Civil War* (Dublin, 1988).

K. Theodore Hoppen, *Elections, Politics and Society in Ireland, 1832-1885* (Oxford, 1984).

John J. Horgan, *The Cork City Management Act. Origins, Provisions and Application* (Cork, 1929).

A. J. Humphreys, *New Dubliners, Urbanization and the Irish Family* (London, 1966).

David S. Jacobsen, 'The political economy of industrial location: the Ford Motor Company at Cork, 1912-26', *Irish Economic and Social History,* Vol. IV, 1977.

Patricia Jalland, 'Irish Home-Rule finance: a neglected dimension of the Irish question, 1910-14', *Irish Historical Studies,* Vol. XXIII, no. 91, May 1983.

Finola Kennedy, *Public Social Expenditure in Ireland* (Dublin, 1975).

Kieran A. Kennedy and Brendan R. Dowling, *Economic Growth in Ireland: The Experience since 1947* (Dublin, 1975).

Kieran A. Kennedy, Thomas Giblin and Deirdre McHugh, *The Economic Development of Ireland in the Twentieth Century* (London, 1988).

Tom Kettle, *Home Rule Finance* (Dublin,1911).

Christine Kinealy, 'The Poor Law during the Great Famine: an administration in crisis', in E. Margaret Crawford (ed.), *Famine: The Irish Experience, 900-1900* (Edinburgh, 1989).

589

F. C. King, *Public Administration in Ireland* (Dublin, 1944).

Michael Laffan, '"Labour must wait": Ireland's conservative revolution', in Patrick J. Corish (ed.), *Radicals, Rebels and Establishments* (Historical Studies Vol. XV, Belfast, 1985).

J. J. Lee, *Ireland 1912-1985* (Cambridge, 1989).

Con Lehane, *Ireland's Burden under British Boards* (Dublin, 1905), p. 28.

Nathaniel Lichfield and Associates, *Report and Advisory Outline Plan for the Limerick Region,* 1966.

Stuart Lowe and David Hughes (eds), *A New Century of Social Housing* (Leicester, 1991).

Patrick Lynch, 'The Irish economy since the war, 1946-51', in K.B. Nowlan and T. D. Williams (eds), *Ireland in the War Years and After, 1939-51* (Dublin, 1969).

F. S. L. Lyons, *Ireland since the Famine* (London, 1971).

Dorothy Macardle, *The Irish Republic* (Tralee, 1968 edition).

Oliver MacDonagh, *Ireland: The Union and its Aftermath* (London, 1977).

————————, 'Ideas and institutions, 1830-45', in W.E. Vaughan (ed.), *A New History of Ireland. V. Ireland under the Union I. 1801-70* (Oxford, 1989).

Roy M. MacLeod, *Treasury Control and Social Administration. A Study of Establishment Growth at the Local Government Board 1871-1905* (London, 1968).

Patrick Maume, *D.P. Moran* (Dublin, 1995).

Brian Maye, *Fine Gael 1923-1987* (Dublin, 1993).

Lawrence W. McBride, *The Greening of Dublin Castle. The Transformation of Bureaucratic and Judicial Personnel in Ireland, 1892-1922* (Washington, 1991).

J. L. McCracken, *Representative Government in Ireland. A Study of Dáil Éireann, 1919-48* (Oxford, 1958).

R. B. McDowell, *The Irish Administration, 1801-1914* (London, 1964).

Edward McParland, 'Strategy in the planning of Dublin, 1750-1800', in P. Butel and L.M. Cullen (eds), *Cities and Merchants: French and Irish Perspectives on Urban Development 1500-1900* (Dublin, 1986).

James Meenan, *The Irish Economy since 1922* (Liverpool, 1970).

P. J. Meghen, *Housing in Ireland* (Dublin, 1963).

Mervyn Miller, 'Raymond Unwin and the planning of Dublin', in Bannon, *Emergence of Irish Planning,* Vol. I.

Arthur Mitchell. *Revolutionary Government in Ireland. Dáil Éireann 1919-22* (Dublin, 1995).

Joel Mokyr, *Why Ireland Starved: A Quantitative and Analytical History of the Irish Economy 1800-1850* (London, 1983).

Jane Morton, 'The 1890 Act and its aftermath — the Era of the "model dwellings"', in Stuart Lowe and David Hughes (eds), *A New Century of Social Housing.*

Maurice Moynihan, *Currency and Central Banking in Ireland 1922-60* (Dublin 1975).

John A. Murphy, 'Cork. Anatomy and essence' in Patrick O'Flanagan and Cornelius G. Buttimer (eds), *Cork. History & Society* (Dublin, 1993).

K. I. Nowlan, 'The evolution of Irish planning 1934-64', in Bannon (ed.), *Planning* . Vol. II.

Flann O'Brien, *Myles na Gopaleen. The Best of Myles* (London, 1968).

Gerard O'Brien, 'The new Irish poor law in pre-famine Ireland; a case history', *Irish Economic and Social History,* Vol. XII (1985).

R. Barry O' Brien, *Dublin Castle and the Irish People* (London, 1912).

Leon Ó Broin, *Dublin Castle and the 1916 Rising* (London, 1966).

———————, *No Man's Man. A Biographical Memoir of Joseph Brennan* (Dublin, 1982).

Emmet O'Connor, *Syndicalism in Ireland, 1917-23* (Cork, 1988).

———————, *A Labour History of Waterford* (Waterford, 1989).

R. O'Connor and C. Guiomard, 'Agricultural output in the Irish Free State area before and after independence', *Irish Economic and Social History,* Vol. XII (1985).

Thomas H. O'Connor, *South Boston: My Home Town* (Boston, 1988),

M. O'Donoghue and A. A. Tait, 'The growth of public revenue and expenditure in Ireland', in J. A. Bristow and A. A. Tait (eds), *Economic Policy in Ireland* (Dublin, 1968).

Cormac Ó Gráda, *Ireland: A New Economic History, 1780-1939* (Oxford, 1994).

John O'Hagan, 'An analysis of the relative size of the government sector: Ireland 1926-52', *Economic and Social Review,* 12, no. 1, October 1980.

Eunan O'Halpin, *The Decline of the Union. British Government in Ireland, 1892-1920* (Dublin, 1987).

———————, 'Origins of city and county management' in *City and County Management, 1929-90. A Retrospective* (Dublin, 1991).

Kevin O'Higgins, *The Catholic Layman in Public Life: An Address to the Catholic Truth Society* (Dublin, 1923).

T. P. O'Neill, 'The administration of relief', in R. D. Edwards and T. D. Williams (eds), *The Great Famine* (Dublin, 1956).

James O'Shea, *Priests, Politics and Society in Post-Famine Ireland. A Study of County Tipperary 1850-1891* (Dublin, 1983).

Eamon Phoenix, *Northern Nationalism. Nationalist Politics, Partition and the Catholic Minority in Northern Ireland 1890-1940* (Belfast, 1994).

Josef Redlich and Francis W. Hirst, *The History of Local Government in England.* Edited and introduced by Bryan Keith-Lucas (London, 1958).

Seán Redmond, *The Irish Municipal Employees Trade Union 1883-1983* (Dublin, 1983).

Joseph Robins, *Custom House People* (Dublin, 1993).

Sir Henry Robinson, *Memories: Wise and Otherwise* (London, 1923)

Desmond Roche, 'A memoir of the author' in John Collins (ed.), *Local Government* (Dublin 1963, second edition).

———————, 'An outline of the regional situation in Ireland, Britain, France, Italy', *Administration,* 21, no. 1 (1973).

———————, 'Local Government', in Frank Litton (ed.), *Unequal*

Achievement (Dublin, 1982).

Kevin Rockett, Luke Gibbons, John Hill, *Cinema in Ireland* (London, 1987).

Paul Sacks, *The Donegal Mafia. An Irish Political Machine* (New Haven and London, 1976).

Michael Shiel, *The Quiet Revolution. The Electrification of Rural Ireland, 1946-1976* (Dublin, 1984).

'Silhouette: Philip Monahan', in *City and County Management. A Retrospective* (Dublin, 1991).

Mark Swenarton, *Homes Fit for Heroes* (London, 1981).

Nicholas J. Synnott, 'Housing of the rural population in Ireland', *Journal of the Statistical and Social Inquiry Society of Ireland*, part 84, 1904.

————————, 'Proposals for a new Labourers' Bill: an attempt to solve the rural housing question in Ireland', *Journal of the Statistical and Social Inquiry Society of Ireland*, Vol. XI, 1905-06.

Fergal Tobin, *The Best of Decades. Ireland in the 1960s* (Dublin, 1984).

Charles Townshend, *The British Campaign in Ireland 1919-1921* (Oxford, 1975).

Pauric Travers, 'The financial relations question, 1800-1914', in F.B. Smith (ed.), *Ireland, England and Australia. Essays in Honour of Oliver MacDonagh* (Cork, 1990).

W. E. Vaughan, 'Richard Griffith and the tenement valuation', in G.L. Herries Davies and R. Charles Mollan (eds), *Richard Griffith 1784-1878* (Dublin, 1980).

David Walker, *Local Government Finance in Ireland. A Preliminary Survey* Research Institute Paper no. 5 (1962)

————————, *Local Government Finance and County Incomes.* ERI paper no. 18, March 1964.

Bernadette Whelan, 'Ireland and the Marshall Plan', *Irish Economic and Social History*, Vol. XIX, 1992.

T. K. Whitaker, 'Capital formation, saving and economic progress', in B. Chubb and P. Lynch (eds), *Economic Development and Planning* (Dublin, 1969).

G. D. Williams, *Donegal County Council: 75 Years* (Lifford, 1974).

Myles Wright, *Final Report and Advisory Outline Plan for the Dublin Region* 1966.

UNPUBLISHED THESES

Patricia Duffin, 'An Examination of Local Government under the Cumann na nGaedheal Administration', MA thesis, UCD 1992

Seán Fitzpatrick, 'Donnchadh Ó Briain. Requests and Representations: An Unsung Life of Fidelity to Fianna Fáil', MA thesis, UCD 1994.

Murray Fraser, 'John Bull's Other Homes: State Housing and British Policy in Ireland, 1883-1922', PhD thesis, University College London, 1993.

Philip G. Irwin, 'The Economic Policy of the Cumann na nGaedheal Government 1929-32: The Issue of Agricultural De-Rating', MA thesis, UCD 1984.

Colm Lincoln, 'Working Class Housing in Dublin 1914-30', MA thesis, UCD, 1979.

Desmond McCabe, 'Law, Conflict and Social Order. County Mayo 1920-1845', PhD thesis, UCD, 1991.

Colman O'Sullivan, 'The IRA takes Constitutional Action: A History of Clann na Poblachta 1946-65, MA thesis, UCD, 1995,

Catherine Shannon, 'Local Government in Ireland, the Politics and Administration', MA thesis, UCD, 1964.

UNPUBLISHED PAPERS

Mary E. Daly, 'Famine Relief Efforts, 1846-47: A Question of Competence', paper read at New York University conference on Famine and Hunger, May 1995.

David Fitzpatrick, 'Famine, Entitlements, Seduction and the State', Paper read at New York University conference on Famine and Hunger, May 1995.

Brendan O'Donoghue, 'The Office of County Surveyor. Origins and Early Years', paper presented to Institute of Engineers of Ireland Heritage Society, November 1992.

APPENDICES

I

MINISTERS IN CHARGE OF THE DEPARTMENT SINCE 1919

Minister	Date of Appointment	Date of Termination of Appointment
L. T. MacCosgair	2 April 1919	30 August 1922
Earnán de Blaghd	30 August 1922	15 October 1923
Séamus de Búrca	15 October 1923	23 June 1927
Risteárd Ó Maolcatha	23 June 1927	9 March 1932
Seán T. Ó Ceallaigh	9 March 1932	8 September 1939
Patrick Ruttledge	8 September 1939	14 August 1941
Éamon de Valera	15 August 1941	18 August 1941
Seán MacEntee	18 August 1941	18 February 1948
Timothy J. Murphy	18 February 1948	29 April 1949
Michael Keyes	11 May 1949	14 June 1951
Patrick Smith	14 June 1951	2 June 1954
Patrick O'Donnell	2 June 1954	20 March 1957
Patrick Smith	20 March 1957	27 November 1957
Neil T. Blaney	27 November 1957	16 November 1966
Caoimhghín Ó Beoláin	16 November 1966	7 May 1970
Robert Molloy	9 May 1970	14 March 1973
James Tully	14 March 1973	5 July 1977
Sylvester Barrett	5 July 1977	15 October 1980
Raphael P. Burke	15 October 1980	30 June 1981
Peter Barry	30 June 1981	9 March 1982
Raphael P. Burke	9 March 1982	14 December 1982
Dick Spring	14 December 1982	14 December 1983
Liam Kavanagh	14 December 1983	14 February 1986
John Boland	14 February 1986	10 March 1987
Pádraig Flynn	10 March 1987	8 November 1991

John Wilson	9 November 1991	14 November 1991
Rory O'Hanlon	14 November 1991	11 February 1992
Michael Smith	11 February 1992	15 December 1994
Brendan Howlin	15 December 1994	

II

NOTES ON THE RECORDS OF THE DEPARTMENT OF LOCAL
GOVERNMENT/ENVIRONMENT IN THE NATIONAL ARCHIVES

1. The records of the Dail Eireann Ministry of Local Government for the period 1919-21 were transferred to the Public Record Office (now the National Archives) by the Department of Local Government in the early 1970s. These comprise 117 boxes, and are listed by local authority within county.

2. The Department of the Environment transferred a large quantity of records to the National Archives in 1990-93. They consist of:

    a. Registered files of the Department of Local Government 1922-1963 .

    b. Secretary's files, of the Department of Local Government 1924-1960

    c. Legal section, files and other records (including Poor Law Commissioners' Orders and Local Government Board Orders, 1838-1921) 1838-1960

    d. General files of the Department of Local Government 1922-1960

Total bulk: approximately 2,500 boxes and 350 volumes.

By far the largest series is the first, the registered files of the department. These are arranged by county, except for a small quantity arranged by subject (planning, housing, sanitary services, etc.) within county. They include personnel files for employees of the department, which are currently closed to public access unless permission is granted by the department. The files for the period 1954-63 have been listed by the department. It is intended that the records for the period 1922-53 will be listed on databases, making them accessible by subject, name if relevant, and local authority. The Secretary's Office files, Legal section files and General files are already listed. Mr Seamus O'Connor, Principal Officer (retired), oversaw the listing project, and was assisted by Mr Pat Long, Paperkeeper.

Because of acute shortage of space in the National Archives, it has been impossible to accession any further records from the Department since 1993. There are approximately 1,000 boxes of registered files awaiting transfer, as well as a large quantity of planning appeals files currently in off-site storage.

Notes on the Records and Archives of Local Authorities

Apart from the records of the Department itself, the records of the various local authorities around the country are of great potential interest to researchers.

Section 65 of the Local Government Act 1994 places an obligation on local authorities to make arrangements for the proper management, custody, care and conservation of local records and local archives and for inspection by the public of archives over 30 years old. In 1995, the Department of the Environment established a Steering Group to advise on how to proceed, and funded a nationwide survey of local authority archives by the National Archives. The survey found that the vast majority of local authorities hold archives, that these archives are of high quality, that they suffer from serious problems of disorder, dispersal and fragmentation, and that in their present condition they cannot be made available for public inspection. A great deal of work is required to place these archives in safe custody and to prepare them for public inspection.

The Report of Steering Group on Local Authority Records and Archives was published in July 1996. When launching the report, the Minister for the Environment endorsed the strategy proposed by the Steering Group and announced a funding initiative for local archives.

Catriona Crowe
Archivist
National Archives of Ireland
23 October 1996

INDEX